HISTORICAL ENCYCLOPEDIA OF
AMERICAN BUSINESS

Volume 3
Securities and Exchange Commission—
Zoning, commercial
Appendixes
Indexes

Edited by
Richard L. Wilson
University of Tennessee, Chattanooga

SALEM PRESS
Pasadena, California   Hackensack, New Jersey

Editorial Director: Christina J. Moose *Production Editor:* Joyce I. Buchea
Acquisitions Editor: Mark Rehn *Layout:* Mary Overell
Development Editor: R. Kent Rasmussen *Design and Graphics:* James Hutson
Project Editor: Rowena Wildin *Photo Editor:* Cynthia Breslin Beres
Manuscript Editor: Andy Perry *Editorial Assistant:* Dana Garey

Library of Congress Cataloging-in-Publication Data

Historical encyclopedia of American business / edited by Richard L. Wilson.
    p. cm.
Includes bibliographical references and index.
    ISBN 978-1-58765-518-0 (set : alk. paper) — ISBN 978-1-58765-519-7 (vol. 1 : alk. paper) —
ISBN 978-1-58765-520-3 (vol. 2 : alk. paper) — ISBN 978-1-58765-521-0 (vol. 3 : alk. paper) 1. United
States—Commerce—History—Encyclopedias. 2. Industries—United States—History—Encyclopedias.
3. Industrial management—United States—History—Encyclopedias. 4. Business enterprises—United
States—History—Encyclopedias. I. Wilson, Richard L., 1944-
    HF3021.H67 2009
    338.097303—dc22
                                                                                        2009002942

Table of Contents

Complete List of Contents

Volume 1

Volume 2

Volume 3

HISTORICAL ENCYCLOPEDIA OF
AMERICAN BUSINESS

Securities and Exchange Commission

IDENTIFICATION: Federal administrative agency that regulates U.S. capital markets for securities traded in interstate commerce

DATE: Established on June 6, 1934

SIGNIFICANCE: The SEC helps maintain the structural integrity of American capital markets by regulating the flow of information about public companies and by enforcing securities laws.

Public corporations are a keystone of the American economy, producing goods and services that raise living standards, providing employment, and increasing the economic welfare of the nation. To begin or to grow a business, corporations may raise capital from the public by selling shares in themselves. Investors are more likely to invest in such corporate securities if they have adequate information to make sound decisions, if the operations of capital markets are transparent, and if strong penalties minimize the impact of unscrupulous or negligent market participants. The Securities and Exchange Commission (SEC) was founded to ensure and maintain those conditions.

The American business landscape underwent a fundamental change during the last third of the nineteenth century, transforming from a predominantly agrarian to an industrial economy. The rise of big business in American history is well documented, although its causes and effects—economic, social, and political—continue to be disputed. As was the case in the railroad industry of the mid-nineteenth century, manufacturers derived significant economic benefits from using technology to expand the scale of production. These benefits were an important cause of the rise of large corporations.

Mass production results in economies of scale that reduce the cost of producing goods, allowing them to be sold at lower prices. Cheap goods increase consumption and thus the standard of living. However, businesses based on mass production require large amounts of capital to finance their plant and equipment, distribution channels, advertising budgets, and personnel. A vibrantly functioning market for corporate securities is crucial to the formation of capital in an economy.

The majority of large companies raise much of the capital they need from the public at large. Investors, of both modest and substantial means, purchase stocks and bonds in corporations for a variety of reasons. Some invest in securities to accumulate wealth over the long term. Others trade in corporate securities to make short-term profits by anticipating price movements. Yet others invest in those businesses they think are likely to be relatively more successful. Through their decisions, investors provide capital to business and allocate capital among businesses. Investment banking houses, such as that of J. P. Morgan, and stock exchanges, such as the New York Stock Exchange, serve as primary and secondary markets that help organize and direct the formation and flow of such investment capital.

UNINFORMED INVESTORS

At the turn of the twentieth century, public investors largely financed the growth in size, scale, and scope of American businesses. The implied rule governing the relation between buyers and sellers of securities seemed to be "buyer beware." Holders of stocks and bonds obtain ownership rights (either directly or as collateral) to a company's assets without possessing them. It is the corporate managers and not the owners who actually decide on the purchase, use, and disposition of corporate assets. This separation of ownership from control over assets makes it inherently difficult for the investing public to know how their money is being used.

At the beginning of the twentieth century, investors made their decisions with none of the financial and related information about companies on which investors later came to rely. Instead, rumors, tips, and guesswork shaped many investment decisions. Moreover, during this period, stock exchanges and over-the-counter markets were unregulated. The purchase and sale of securities in unregulated markets exacerbated the potential for unscrupulous and unfair business practices. These conditions limited the efficacy of American capital markets during the early twentieth century.

SPECULATION AND REGULATION

Financial history has witnessed a great many speculative bubbles and cycles of boom and bust. Usually, a boom in a given sector of the economy—such as housing, Internet stocks, or conglomerates—is triggered by some external event that causes some sectors of the economy to become more profitable than others. As more people begin to invest in these profitable sectors, they seek credit to finance further investments. Some of this credit-based investment is fueled by speculative behavior, a bet that the price of the commodity or asset being traded will increase over time. Instead of investing for the purposes of use or income, speculative investments are made solely for the purpose of realizing a profit on resale. "Flipping a house" is a telling contemporary example of this behavior.

As a boom gathers force and more and more investors are drawn into it, prices rise until they reach a fever pitch. Sooner or later, whether triggered by another external event or by some investors seeking to cash in their paper profits, a bust follows the boom. The very same investors who once sought to get into the market now want to get out. It makes sense for every individual in a theater to run to the door when someone shouts "fire." Just as a pandemonium results when all theatergoers rush for the exits, so markets collapse when all investors want to sell. Cycles of boom and bust cause enormous financial hardship and even ruin to many investors. One of the greatest such periods of hardship was the Great Depression.

Between 1899 and 1930, the number of Americans investing in securities increased twentyfold to about 10 million people. Not all were astute and informed investors; many were looking to make a quick profit. (A probably apocryphal story holds that John D. Rockefeller stopped investing in the stock market when his shoeshine boy asked him for stock tips.)

Not only were more people investing in securities during the early twentieth century, but they were also doing it with borrowed money. Rather than personally paying for an entire purchase at the time of a trade, investors would use credit to finance the bulk of their purchases, believing that stock prices would go up quickly enough to allow them to repay their debts and still realize a profit.

The extended boom of the early twentieth century ended with the stock market crash of 1929. The crash began a three-year bust phase, as the markets continued to fall, reaching their lowest value in 1932. As stock prices fell, borrowers defaulted on their repayments. Some went bankrupt. Lenders became less willing to lend money in this risky climate. The lack of available credit further diminished the demand for securities. The falling demand was responsible for the continued decrease in stock prices.

This collapse of the stock market during the Great Depression was so severe that it took until 1963 for the volume of stock traded on the New York Stock Exchange to match the volume traded in 1929 at the peak of the boom-bust cycle. It was in this context that President Franklin D. Roosevelt instituted his New Deal programs. These ambitious and far-reaching programs of government intervention and regulation were established in the belief that unregulated markets contribute to economic instability.

The SEC's Mission

In the effort to better inform investors and to regulate capital markets, the Securities Exchange Act of 1934 established the SEC as an official oversight agency for the nation's securities markets. The law not only regulated these markets but also required all publicly traded companies to disclose detailed financial information about their business activities. It expanded the requirements established by the Securities Act of 1933, which had confined the disclosure demand to only new companies seeking to issue stock for the first time.

At the end of the decade, Congress passed the Trust Indenture Act of 1939, which required all companies offering debt securities, such as bonds and notes, to conform to the standards in the law. In addition, a number of related laws were promulgated that have direct bearing on the scope and function of the SEC. For instance, the Investment Company Act of 1940 required companies whose primary business is to invest and trade in securities to disclose their financial condition and investment principles to the public. Similarly, the Investment Advisers Act of 1940 required investment advisers to register with the SEC and to act in accordance with laws that protect investors. Lastly, the Sarbanes-Oxley Act of 2002 introduced far-reaching changes to the structure and functioning of the securities markets. Some of these included requiring management to take personal responsibility for the assertions made in financial statements, creating the Public Company Accounting Oversight Board to supervise the accountants who audit such statements, and protecting whistle-blowers who inform on corporate malfeasance and fraud.

ORGANIZATIONAL STRUCTURE

The SEC is headed by five commissioners, each of whom is appointed by the president of the United States, with the advice and consent of the Senate. The president names one of these five commissioners as the chair of the SEC. To minimize the influence of partisan politics on the work of the SEC, no more than three of the five commissioners can belong to the same political party. Commissioners are appointed for a period of five years, and their appointments are staggered to ensure continuity of leadership.

The SEC is composed of four divisions, each overseeing a specific aspect of the capital markets. The Division of Corporation Finance is responsible for ensuring that companies comply with the disclosure rules that they are subject to by law. The Division of Trading and Markets is charged with monitoring the activities of all the key participants in the securities markets, including exchanges and credit-rating agencies. This division seeks to foster fair and efficient capital markets, while the Division of Investment Management aims to foster capital formation by regulating the activities of mutual funds that manage the savings of the public. Finally, the Division of Enforcement is directed when necessary to initiate investigations, bring civil action, and prosecute those companies or persons who violate securities laws. Overall, despite the inevitable pull and push of politics, and despite the continued challenges of speculative bubbles, unscrupulous traders, and fraudulent managers, the SEC has maintained its reputation as a fair and effective regulatory agency that has enabled American capital markets to be among the most efficient and effective in the world.

Sajay Samuel

FURTHER READING

Chatov, Robert. *Corporate Financial Reporting: Private or Public Control?* New York: Free Press, 1975. Exhaustive analysis of the SEC as an independent regulatory agency in the context of its relationship with the accounting profession. The central question posed by the book is: What is the proper location of regulatory authority—private bodies or public institutions?

Karmel, Roberta S. *Regulation by Prosecution: The SEC vs. Corporate America*. New York: Simon & Schuster, 1982. Impassioned critique by a former commissioner of the SEC's tendency to empha-size its prosecutorial powers. Her argument in favor of deregulating capital markets to foster capital formation was prescient.

Kindleberger, Charles, and Robert Aliber. *Manias, Panics, and Crashes: A History of Financial Crises.* 5th ed. Hoboken, N.J.: John Wiley & Sons, 2005. A classic work on herd behavior on Wall Street and Main Street by a highly respected economic historian. Describes the typical gamut of behavior—from speculative fevers to panics—that fuels boom and bust cycles.

McCraw, Thomas K. *Prophets of Regulation*. Cambridge, Mass.: Harvard University Press, 1984. Gracefully written chapter by a Pulitzer Prize-winning historian on James Landis, the founding chair of the SEC. Good synopsis of the arguments for and against regulating capital markets and persuasive description of the new style of regulation embodied by the administrative state era inaugurated by the New Deal.

Porter, Glenn. *The Rise of Big Business, 1860-1920.* 2d ed. Arlington Heights, Ill.: Harlan Davidson, 1992. A historian summarizes the causes and consequences of the rise of big business in American history. Ably covers the political, economic, technological, and social dimensions of large-scale business.

Seligman, Joel. *The Transformation of Wall Street: A History of the SEC and Modern Corporate Finance.* 3d ed. New York: Aspen, 2003. Thorough conspectus of the SEC from its inception to the passage of the Sarbanes-Oxley Act of 2002, by a noted legal scholar and securities lawyer.

Vise, David A., and Steve Coll. *Eagle on the Street.* New York: Charles Scribner's Sons, 1991. Engaging and gripping account of the SEC during the 1980's, a time of innovative financial instruments such as the junk bond and of shifts away from the ideology of regulation toward that of free-market solutions.

SEE ALSO: Bond industry; Great Depression; HealthSouth scandal; Mutual fund industry; New Deal programs; Stock market crash of 1929; Stock markets; Tyco International scandal; Wall Street.

Security industry. *See* Private security industry

Seneca Falls Convention

THE EVENT: First women's rights convention in the United States

DATE: July 19-20, 1848

PLACE: Seneca Falls, New York

SIGNIFICANCE: The Seneca Falls Convention started the struggle for woman suffrage and launched the women's rights movement, which eventually resulted in dramatic changes in women's roles in the business world.

More than three hundred men and women attended the Seneca Falls Convention and voted to approve the Declaration of Sentiments and Resolutions, which demanded that women have equal rights of citizenship, personal liberty, and property; equal wages and opportunities to be employed; guardianship of children on divorce; and the ability to participate in church and civic government.

After the initial convention, at annual meetings, attendees agreed that they needed to work for laws to allow women to obtain equal rights and suffrage, but they differed as to the priorities of these demands, and eventually the movement split into two groups. One group concentrated on obtaining suffrage and the other on gaining a wider range of women's rights. Eventually the leaders of the two groups joined together and, in 1920, were successful in passing the Nineteenth Amendment to the U.S. Constitution, which gave women the vote.

After attaining suffrage, members of the women's movement were divided on whether to support or oppose federal protective legislation for women, which limited their working hours and the kinds of jobs for which they could be hired.

The second wave of feminism during the 1960's and 1970's revived the fight for women's rights in marital matters, job opportunities, equal pay, and legal protections, and was fanned by a renewed awareness of the 1848 efforts. The women's movement, through legislative and social change, has had a profound effect on the world of business and finance.

Erika E. Pilver

SEE ALSO: Affirmative action programs; Civil Rights Act of 1964; Equal Employment Opportunity Commission; Labor history; Wages; Women in business.

September 11 terrorist attacks

THE EVENT: Three of four jumbo jets hijacked by radical Islamic fundamentalist terrorists were flown into New York City's World Trade Center and the Pentagon, while the fourth crashed during an apparent struggle between passengers and hijackers

DATE: September 11, 2001

PLACE: New York City; Arlington, Virginia; Shanksville, Pennsylvania

SIGNIFICANCE: The September 11, 2001, terrorist attacks on the United States immediately disrupted the work of businesses housed in the World Trade Center, as well as the airlines whose planes were used as weapons by the terrorists. In the long term, the attacks marked the beginning of a difficult economic period, and the resulting war did not create an economic boom.

When the first jet airliner smashed into the north tower of the World Trade Center in New York City on the morning of September 11, 2001, many observers assumed they were witnessing a horrible accident. To most Americans, it was simply inconceivable that someone could deliberately fly a plane full of people into an office building to make a political point. However, that innocence was shattered fifteen minutes later when a second airliner crashed into the Trade Center's south tower. After a few moments of confusion, it was clear that the crashes were the result of deliberate hostile acts. President George W. Bush, who was visiting a grade school in Florida as part of a program to promote educational funding, was informed by an aide that the nation was under attack. Shortly thereafter, he boarded Air Force One and was flown to a secure location.

The Federal Aviation Administration immediately ordered a halt to all commercial airline takeoffs, but two other hijacked airliners were already in the air. One, Flight 77, crashed into the Pentagon in Alexandria, Virginia, near the District of Columbia, the central headquarters of the U.S. Department of Defense and thus an actual military target. Although the airplane crash started a ferocious fire, the hardening retrofits that were in progress protected part of the affected structure. On the remaining plane, Flight 93, passengers received reports of the three earlier attacks via cellular telephones and thus realized that simply obeying the hijackers would not get them out alive. As a result, they decided to make a last-ditch attempt to fight the hijackers and regain control of the aircraft. Witnesses on the ground near Shanksville, Pennsylvania, subsequently reported seeing the plane twist and jerk in the air as though people were fighting over its controls, before it finally plowed into an empty field, killing everyone aboard. There was speculation that its target may have been the Capitol or the White House.

Within an hour after the attack, first the south tower and then the north tower of the World Trade Center collapsed, killing almost everyone who remained within. However, during the time the towers continued to stand, many thousands of people were able to escape safely.

THE NEW WORLD OF FEAR

The September 11 attacks altered not only the way people thought about war but also the way people did business. The most immediate and obvious change was in airline travel. In the first several days after the attack, while all aircraft remained grounded and people scrambled to find ground transportation to their destinations, the Federal Aviation Administration and other government bodies scrambled to determine the failures in security that had allowed so many terrorists to carry out their crimes, and to implement new security measures that would prevent a recurrence of the events. National Guard troops were stationed in airports, although they often were not issued ammunition for their weapons and their presence was primarily psychological.

Not so trivial was the revamping of the procedures for screening passengers and their luggage. Because the terrorists had hijacked the planes using box cutters, a whole list of sharp implements previously considered innocuous, including screwdrivers and nail clippers, became subject to confiscation as potential makeshift weapons. Passengers were also required to prove the harmlessness of various sub-stances they were carrying, generally by using or consuming a small portion of them. However, it was not long before complaints began to surface regarding screeners who were abusing their power. Stories of rude or unreasonable demands and seemingly mean-spirited behavior on the part of screeners began to circulate on the Internet. Many people suspected that some screeners were trying to goad people into an intemperate response that could get them posted to the infamous "no fly" list.

Some businesses had to rebuild after having lost vital personnel and files in the collapse of the Twin Towers. New awareness led to many more companies developing disaster recovery plans that included daily off-site backups of all vital digital data.

The most chilling effect on American business, however, was that of the War on Terrorism on the American economy in general. Unlike World War II, which had ended the Depression, the War on Terrorism became a continual drag on an economy already hurting as a result of the bursting of the dotcom bubble.

Leigh Husband Kimmel

FURTHER READING

Conley, Richard L., ed. *Transforming the American Polity: The Presidency of George W. Bush and the War on*

The World Trade Center towers in New York burn after being hit by passenger jets. (Courtesy: CNN)

Terrorism. Upper Saddle River, N.J.: Pearson/ Prentice Hall, 2005. A collection of essays examining President Bush's response to the September 11 attacks.

Dwyer, Jim, and Kevin Flynn. *One Hundred Two Minutes: The Untold Story of the Fight to Survive Inside the Twin Towers.* New York: Times Books, 2005. Stories of the experiences of individuals who were in the World Trade Center during the attack.

Friend, David. *Watching the World Change: The Stories Behind the Images of 9/11.* New York: Farrar, Straus and Giroux, 2006. Focuses on the process of the reporter and the historian in turning photographic and videographic evidence into coherent narrative.

Murphy, Tom. *Reclaiming the Sky: 9/11 and the Untold Story of the Men and Women Who Kept America Flying.* New York: AMACOM, 2007. Focus on aviation employees and the struggle to restore safe air travel.

Williams, Mary E., ed. *The Terrorist Attack on America.* San Diego: Thompson-Gale, 2003. A collection of documents examining various aspects of 9/11 from a variety of perspectives.

SEE ALSO: Bush tax cuts of 2001; Business cycles; Federal Emergency Management Agency; Homeland Security, U.S. Department of; Iraq wars; Nuclear power industry; Private security industry; Secret Service, U.S.; Wars.

Service industries

DEFINITION: Enterprises that provide services to customers rather than produce tangible goods

SIGNIFICANCE: Until the 1960's, the American economy was dominated by industry and manufacturing. However, as the United States increased its global trade, its economy grew, and average wages rose. This led to the development of many services industries, dedicated to providing customers with a variety of benefits. Since then, the American economy has become dominated by service industries, and it has seen a great decline in manufacturing.

A service industry can be anything from automobile repair to cosmetology, real estate agencies to restaurants. In the United States, service industries make up the majority of new jobs that have been added to the economy during the 1990's and early twenty-first century. Instead of producing physical goods, the United States economy is becoming increasingly based on producing services for consumers and businesses.

Whereas jobs involved in producing goods often require skills, in general, service industries demand far less of their employees. As a result, service industries have created a more flexible economy. Previous to the introduction of service industries, most people would stay within the same occupation for the majority of their lives, since jobs required a great deal of training. However, in an economy that is based on service industries, less training and skill are required, and people may switch occupations many times throughout their lives. This also means that each employee is more replaceable, since virtually anyone can be trained to do the same job.

ISSUES

As the United States has begun to depend more heavily on service industries, many people have stepped out to voice their concern over the ability of service industries to sustain a healthy economy over a long period of time. The increase in service industries and decrease in goods-producing industries means that the United States is more dependent on foreign countries for nearly everything but services. Since the introduction of service industries, the United States imports an increasing amount of its clothes, food, electronics, and other merchandise. This means that American consumers are at the mercy of foreign companies when it comes to price and availability.

Also, there is a fear that an economy that does not produce anything will not be able to bounce back in the event of a recession. An economy that is based on service industries depends on people buying goods and partaking in the existing services to sustain itself. If people are unable to purchase anything in a service industry, the economy will falter. Critics of service industries fear that in the event of an economic recession or depression, people will have no money to buy services, and therefore, the economy will continue to suffer. These critics would suggest an economy that incorporates a more even balance of service industries and goods-producing industries.

Despite what critics say, service industries have made a huge difference in the way that Americans live, work, and play. They are changing the way that

NUMBER OF ESTABLISHMENTS AND PAYROLL BY SERVICE INDUSTRY, 2004

Business Type	Number of Establishments (1,000's)	Annual Payroll ($ billions)
Employment services	41	106.5
Computer systems design and related services	106	77.7
Architectural, engineering, and related services	109	75.9
Offices of lawyers	173	74.1
Management, scientific, and technical consulting services	129	55.5
Accounting, tax preparation, bookkeeping, and payroll	117	46.6
Traveler accommodation	52	38.3
Personal and laundry	208	25.0
Automotive repair and maintenance	166	23.2
Investigation and security services	23	17.4
Waste management and remediation services	19	13.4
Advertising agencies	13	9.3
Veterinary services	26	6.8

Source: Data from the *Statistical Abstract of the United States, 2008* (Washington, D.C.: Department of Commerce, Economics and Statistics Administration, Bureau of the Census, Data User Services Division, 2008)

businesses compete and are forcing business owners to become more innovative in looking at how to please their customers and clients. The United States does still produce goods to a certain degree, but it is becoming increasingly obvious that service industries will continue to become a larger part of the American economy.

Jennifer L. Titanski

FURTHER READING

Albrecht, Karl, and Ron Zemke. *Service America in the New Economy.* New York: McGraw-Hill, 2001. A guidebook to how the American economy operates, and how businesses can maximize their profits through customer relations.

Daniels, Peter W. *Service Industries in the World Economy.* Hoboken, N.J.: Wiley-Blackwell, 1993. A geographer's perspective of service industries and the growth and effects of this economic sector outside of the United States and throughout the world.

Gustafsson, Anders, and Michael D. Johnson. *Competing in a Service Economy: How to Create a Competitive Advantage Through Service Development and Innovation.* San Francisco, Calif.: Jossey-Bass, 2008. A "how to" guide for businesses and business students that discusses being competitive in the service industry and can be useful in understanding the flexibility and resilience of the service economy.

Stahel, W. R. "The Service Economy: 'Wealth without Resource Consumption'?" *Philosophical Transactions: Mathematical, Physical, and Engineering Sciences* 355, no. 1728 (1997): 1309-1319. Article that presents the argument that current industrial processes are not sustainable, and moving toward a service economy is the only way that wealth can be sustained.

Young, Laurie. *From Products to Services: Insights and Experiences from Companies Which Have Embraced the Service Economy.* Hoboken, N.J.: Wiley-Blackwell, 2008. Book that attempts to give answers to some of the myths and fears surrounding service industries by telling the stories of some large companies that have attempted to create some service businesses.

SEE ALSO: Drive-through businesses; Legal services; Online marketing; Outsourcing, overseas; Rental industry; Restaurant industry; Retail trade industry; Shipping industry; Vending machines.

Servicemen's Readjustment Act.
See G.I. Bill

Sewing machines

DEFINITION: Mechanized devices using needles and thread to fasten fabric together

SIGNIFICANCE: The American sewing machine industry was one of the first industries to use nearly interchangeable parts and mass production techniques.

In early America, garments were hand-sewn in the home or in garment factories by tailors and seamstresses. From the mid-eighteenth to mid-nineteenth centuries, inventors patented various mechanical devices for stitching, but none was successful. In 1846, Elias Howe received the first of several American patents for his version of such a device. However, garment factories would not buy Howe's machine, because its needles broke easily, the $300 cost was prohibitive, and many believed the machine would lead to unemployment for tailors and seamstresses. Still, imitators copied aspects of Howe's design and tried to rectify its problems.

One inventor who succeeded was Isaac Merrit Singer, who received a patent in 1850 for an improved version of Howe's sewing machine. Singer used a straight needle instead of a curved one, and his device moved the needle vertically instead of horizontally, resulting in less needle breakage and greater operator flexibility. In 1851, Singer patented the foot-operated treadle, another improvement that substantially affected user operation. Singer simplified the production process by using nearly standardized parts, resulting in economical mass production and a more attractive price of $125.

Singer was a marketing master. He demonstrated his machine nationwide and reassured tailors and seamstresses that the new technology would enhance their output. The Singer Sewing Machine Company produced approximately 2,500 machines in 1856. Selling to Union and Confederate uniform factories, Singer boosted the number of sewing machines manufactured in 1860 to 13,000, making his company the largest sewing-machine manufacturer in the world. By 1863, Singer had tapped into the successful woodworking industry to marry the sew-

A young woman operates a treadle sewing machine in the 1920's. (Library of Congress)

ing machine to wood cabinetry and was promoting the sewing machine as an essential household product; production rose to 30,000 machines.

By 1882, Singer's company had sold approximately 800,000 sewing machines, exemplifying successful mass production techniques, use of nearly interchangeable parts, and worldwide marketing. Although the Singer Company was not the only sewing-machine manufacturer in the United States, its sales drove the American industry, and Singer's penchant for suing competitors spawned the highly publicized "sewing-machine wars." Because all sewing machines used elements originally patented by Howe, Howe successfully sued Singer and other manufacturers for patent infringement, guaranteeing him a share of every American-made sewing machine sold. The Singer Company continued to lead sales, producing 2.5 million sewing machines in 1913.

The sewing machine's mid-nineteenth century mechanics remained virtually unchanged for over a hundred years, except for electric-powered advancements that eliminated the foot-operated treadle. By the late twentieth century, sewing machines had incorporated computer technology, such as memory cards and LED advice messages. In 2001, Singer introduced digitizing software, which became an industry standard for top-of-the-line sewing machine models. Three of America's founding sewing machine companies remained in business into the early twenty-first century: Singer, White, and Wilcox and Gibbs.

Taylor Shaw

FURTHER READING

Cooper, Grace Rogers. *The Sewing Machine: Its Invention and Development.* 3d ed. Washington, D.C.: Smithsonian Institution Press, 1985.

Smithsonian Institution. *Sewing Machines: Historical Trade Literature in Smithsonian Institution Collections.* Washington, D.C.: Author, 2001.

SEE ALSO: Automation in factories; International Ladies' Garment Workers' Union; Retail trade industry; Triangle Shirtwaist Company fire; Woodworking industry.

Sharecropping

DEFINITION: Agricultural work system in which farmers worked land owned by others and shared the profits with the landowners

SIGNIFICANCE: At best, sharecropping families, often African Americans, made a few hundred dollars per year. At worst, they became stuck in never-ending debt. Sharecropping became the dominant form of labor in the South after the U.S. Civil War, and when combined with racially discriminatory laws enacted after Reconstruction, created an exploitative work situation for African Americans.

With the end of slavery, freed African Americans in the South needed to find a way to earn a living. Despite promises made during the Civil War that the federal government would give confiscated plantation land to freed people in the form of "forty acres and a mule," no such allocations were made. As a result, African Americans were economically dependent on whites. Since most southern whites had little cash at the end of the war, they could not afford to pay wages for farm labor.

Both whites and African Americans turned toward sharecropping as an alternative to rural wage labor. Because most African Americans had no access to capital, they lacked the financial wherewithal to buy their own land. Many initially viewed sharecropping as a way to build up savings and eventually enter the landowning class. In exchange for their skills and muscle, sharecroppers expected to receive tools, seed, work animals, and fertilizer, plus food, housing, supplies, and a substantial proportion of the final crop. Shares might vary from one-third to one-half for a sharecropping family, with the remainder going to the landowner to cover supplies, rent, and debts to merchants and bankers. Tenant farmers, who owned their own mules and farm implements, had rights to a larger share of the crop than did sharecroppers, who owned nothing. In practice, there was considerable overlap between the conditions of tenant farmers and sharecroppers, both of whom worked the land of others.

ADVANTAGES AND DISADVANTAGES

For African American families, sharecropping had the advantage of involving less work than farming had involved during the slave era. Families worked together on a small plot, usually growing cotton or tobacco. African American sharecroppers worked about one-third fewer hours than they had as slaves, while women and children worked less than men. Workers were no longer forced to work as hard as possible until they were exhausted, as they had been under the slave system. Sharecroppers escaped the gang system and close supervision that had characterized slave agriculture.

The disadvantages of sharecropping, however, soon became apparent. A new system of credit, the crop lien, became closely associated with sharecropping. Under this system, a planter or merchant extended a small line of credit to the sharecropper while taking the year's crop as collateral. The sharecropper could then draw food and supplies from the store of the planter or the merchant. When the crop was harvested, the planter or merchants who held the lien sold the harvest for the sharecropper and settled the debt. The system depended on the honesty of the planter.

A DISINTEGRATING SYSTEM

When Reconstruction gradually collapsed, the revived Democratic Party took steps to strengthen the hand of white landowners and weaken the bargaining position of black workers. The new racist governments in southern states instituted repressive labor legislation, such as North Carolina's Landlord and Tenant Act of 1877, which placed full authority over the crop and settlement in the hands of the planter. The law made the sharecropper into a wage earner instead of a partner in the production of a crop. Sharecropping disintegrated into an exploitative labor system that trapped black families. Planters regularly falsified accounts at the end of each year to keep their workers in perpetual debt. Some planters found excuses to dismiss tenant farmers just before their compensation was due.

When African Americans attempted to protest this injustice by quitting, the Black Codes took effect. Under these laws, African Americans who failed to enter into contracts or who broke them could be arrested for vagrancy and imprisoned. Vagrancy laws permitted the employment of convicts by private employers. The wages of such workers went into state coffers. The convict lease system rerouted black workers back into the plantation economy but on worse terms than before. The system proved especially brutal, with convicts sometimes worked to death. In 1906, the state of Georgia made $354,850 from convict leases. In essence, sharecropping became slavery. By 1900, nearly 80 percent of southern African Americans worked as sharecroppers on farms owned by whites.

The sharecropping system ended gradually during the early decades of the twentieth century. Increased mechanization reduced the need for many agricultural workers, while the New Deal during the 1930's paid landowners not to grow crops. As a result of these changes, many African American farmers were pushed off the land.

Caryn E. Neumann

A tenant farmer works in North Carolina in 1936. (Library of Congress)

Further Reading

Cohen, William. *At Freedom's Edge: Black Mobility and the Southern White Quest for Racial Control, 1861-1915*. Baton Rouge: Louisiana State University Press, 1991. Useful survey of the crucial period in African American history that spanned the Civil War, Reconstruction, and the years leading up to the Great Migration out of the South.

Foner, Eric. *Reconstruction: America's Unfinished Revolution, 1863-1877*. 1988. Reprint. New York: Vintage, 2006. This standard work on the Reconstruction era examines the struggles of former slaves to achieve economic self-sufficiency. Special attention is given to the federal government's failure to meet the economic needs of its newly freed citizens.

Gilbert, Charlene, and Quinn Eli. *Homecoming: The Story of African American Farmers*. Boston: Beacon Press, 2000. Designed as a companion to Charlene Gilbert's 1998 documentary film *Homecoming*, this volume offers a compelling introduction to the history of African American farmers and contains an excellent selection of historical photographs.

Higgs, Robert. *Competition and Coercion: Blacks in the American Economy, 1865-1914.* New York: Cambridge University Press, 2008. First published in 1976, this scholarly study offers a reinterpretation of African American economic history during the era in which sharecropping arose.

Nieman, Donald G. *From Slavery to Sharecropping: White Land and Black Labor in the Rural South, 1865-1900.* New York: Garland, 1994. Excellent history of southern agriculture that thoroughly covers the experiences of black farmworkers during their transition from slavery to sharecropping.

Royce, Edward Cary. *The Origins of Southern Sharecropping.* Philadelphia: Temple University Press, 1993. Engaging study that sees the rise of sharecropping in the South as a struggle between landowners trying to preserve the system of plantation slavery and newly freed slaves trying to acquire land and autonomy.

Tolnay, Stewart E. *The Bottom Rung: African American Family Life on Southern Farms.* Urbana: University of Illinois Press, 1999. Valuable supplement to any study of sharecropping; provides an intimate look at how African American farmers actually lived in the South.

SEE ALSO: Agriculture; Civil War, U.S.; Cotton industry; Farm labor; Indentured labor; Panic of 1873; Plantation agriculture; Slave era; Tobacco industry.

Shays's Rebellion

THE EVENT: Armed uprising by destitute farmers against the Massachusetts government
DATE: January 16, 1786-February 4, 1787
PLACE: Massachusetts
SIGNIFICANCE: Shays's Rebellion revealed the conflicting interests of farmers in rural areas and merchants along the coast of the new United States. The economic problems driving the rebellion were soon addressed, when the Articles of Confederation were replaced by the Constitution.

On January 16, 1786, sixty farmers in Greenwich, Massachusetts, signed a petition to the Massachusetts Assembly outlining their grievances against local and state enforcement of tax collection and debt assessment. The petitioners emphasized their support for the recent revolution and their willingness to pay their share of the debt that resulted from it. They expressed their concern, however, that many farmers were being imprisoned for debt. Their property was being seized and sold for less than real value, causing many farmers to flee to New York and other states.

The petitioners noted that the governor had recently sent out a proclamation urging the promotion of piety and virtue throughout the commonwealth. They felt that these values should lead the state to provide relief to those who were suffering severe economic distress. A major component of that relief would be the issuance of paper currency, making debt payment much easier.

Dissent soon spread to other states, but it was most serious in Massachusetts. When the assembly adjourned on July 8 without issuing paper currency or addressing their other demands, protesting farmers initiated an armed rebellion centered on the western town of Springfield, the location of a federal arsenal. The farmers were led by Daniel Shays, a captain in the Continental Army during the American Revolution who was now a destitute farmer. Acts of violence and intimidation continued throughout the fall and early winter.

A state militia of over four thousand men was assembled in January, 1787, in Boston and Springfield to subdue the rebels. Although Congress authorized a federal force, it never had to be used. An attack by Shays on the Springfield arsenal was quickly repulsed. When Shays was routed at Petersham on February 4, the rebellion collapsed. All involved, including Shays, were eventually pardoned.

As a result of Shays's Rebellion, the Massachusetts Assembly enacted laws to lower court foreclosure costs and to exempt clothing, tools of one's trade, and other items from debt collection. The assembly did not pass a proposed direct tax in 1787. In 1802, President John Quincy Adams observed:

The insurrection of the year 1786 forms one of the most instructive periods of the history of our country . . . [and] will give [citizens] a deeper insight into the character of this people, a more extensive view of our social organization, and its internal operations at critical times, than they could obtain by years of personal observation.

Glenn L. Swygart

FURTHER READING

McCarthy, Timothy, and John McMillian. *The Radical Reader: A Documentary History of the American Radical Tradition.* New York: New Press, 2003.

Szatmary, David P. *Shays's Rebellion: The Making of an Agrarian Insurrection.* Boston: University of Massachusetts Press, 1980.

SEE ALSO: Annapolis Convention; Articles of Confederation; Constitution, U.S.; Depression of 1784; Farm protests; Granger movement; Revolutionary War.

Sherman Antitrust Act

THE LAW: First federal law to limit cartels and monopolies from forming in restraint of trade

DATE: Signed into law on July 2, 1890

SIGNIFICANCE: The Sherman Antitrust Act was meant to protect consumers from monopolistic business practices that could drive up prices by eliminating competition. It was originally directed against the Standard Oil Company, owned by John D. Rockefeller, Sr., and provided for fines up to $10 million for corporations or $350,000 for individuals.

President Benjamin Harrison signed the Sherman Antitrust Act into law to prohibit coercive monopolies that try to control their markets by "force, fraud or theft." The act was the first federal antitrust statute in the United States, and it enshrined in American law the principle that artificial restraint of trade or commerce constitutes an illegitimate act. It prohibits not only monopolies by a single company but also agreements or conspiracies between companies to reduce competition.

In general, monopolies result in higher consumer prices due to lack of competition, but this is not always the case. Critics of the Sherman Antitrust Act argue that large companies that control their market because they achieve economies of scale in an efficient and legal manner should not be treated as coercive monopolies. Such companies may not artificially raise consumer prices but may keep prices at the levels that the market will tolerate while supplying consumer demand. As long as a large company does not artificially raise prices or arbitrarily withhold products to create shortages and drive up prices, it does not violate the Sherman Antitrust Act. Price-fixing arrangements among competing companies are a violation, as they restrain or interfere with market forces setting prices.

Interpretation of the Sherman Antitrust Act has changed over the past century. Originally, the act also prohibited many types of organized labor activities, but such actions were legalized under the Clayton Antitrust Act of 1914. Later, utility companies were granted monopolies to operate in specific areas. Their rates, however, were regulated by commissions to prevent them from artificially inflating prices.

Victoria Erhart

SEE ALSO: Antitrust legislation; Clayton Antitrust Act; Federal Trade Commission; Labor history; Northern Securities Company; Price fixing; Rockefeller, John D.; Sports franchises; Standard Oil Company; Supreme Court and commerce.

Shipping industry

DEFINITION: Enterprises that transport goods and other items for companies and individuals

SIGNIFICANCE: Virtually every business, from grocers to jewelers, depends on the shipment of materials and goods to operate. Innovations in shipping have increased profits to corporations and savings to consumers. Modern technology enables shippers to load, ship, and unload much larger quantities in a much shorter time than was previously possible, thus providing volume savings and labor cost reductions. It has also enabled the rise of new kinds of businesses, such as warehouse stores, that depend on large inventories.

Many shipping companies had been established in the United States by the mid-nineteenth century, when steamships plied inland waterways. On land, many regional and intercity horse-dependent delivery companies such as the fabled Pony Express briefly flourished. Most interstate cargo was shipped by rail, especially following the end of the U.S. Civil War. Shipping could be a very slow process, and refrigeration was unknown, placing limits on what could be shipped. Farmers and manufacturers were at the mercy of often monopolistic owners who imposed large tariffs. As the twentieth century progressed, trucks became a factor in shipping, although rail retained its dominance into the middle of the century.

By the 1930's, airlines also had become a factor, often competing with the United States Post Office (later U.S. Postal Service) in the shipping of mail and small packages. Before delivery companies bought their own fleets of planes, they had contracted with commercial airlines to carry small freight items on passenger flights. For trade from the United States to most other countries, shipping by sea was the only available method until commercial aviation became feasible.

After World War II, the shipping industry grew rapidly. Inexpensive ships that had been built for the war effort were available for purchase, and world trade was expanding significantly. Numerous new shipping companies came into being. However, loading and unloading goods from all means of transportation remained a protracted process, driven by manual labor. Loading and unloading a single multihold ship, for instance, could take many days, with shifts of men working long hours.

CONTAINERIZATION

This time-consuming, laborious process was completely transformed as a result of the development of containerization during the 1950's. Containerization is largely attributed to the efforts of one trucker, Malcolm McLean, who had about sixty rectangular metal containers loaded on a freighter. The innovative idea immediately took off. As a result, cargo could be packed into huge metal containers that then could be loaded onto ships, railroad cars, airplanes, and even semitrailer trucks.

Containerization reduces the

loading and unloading times of cargoes from several days to a matter of hours. Another advantage of the system is a reduction in theft from cargoes. It has also enabled the "big box" discount and warehouse chains to thrive. Target, Home Depot, and especially Wal-Mart are leading users of shipping containers. Refrigerated containers allow for the shipping of fresh produce from far-off locations. Special container ships were designed to take advantage of the system, and shipping costs were drastically reduced. At most ports, the use of containers accounts for almost 100 percent of cargo, except in the case of large items such as automobiles.

Ever larger ships became the norm, including huge oil tankers that were in excess of one-half million tons. These ships led to the construction of new ports and terminals to accommodate such behemoths. Ship-to-ship and ship-to-shore communication became more sophisticated with the emergence of satellites. The latter part of the twentieth century saw more innovation in shipping than any other historical period.

OVERNIGHT DELIVERY COMPANIES

The overnight delivery service is an important component of the shipping industry. Numerous companies offer this service, but several dominate the field. United Parcel Service (UPS), with its distinctively brown-clad delivery people, is a multibillion-dollar company. It arose from a bicycle

A tugboat sails past a cargo ship loading and unloading containers at the Port of Newark, New Jersey, in 2008. (AP/Wide World Photos)

messenger service founded in 1907 and eventually became a global powerhouse established in more than two hundred countries. By 1919, it was making deliveries by Ford Model T automobiles, mainly on behalf of department stores. In 1929, it began its air service on commercial airliners, but this was short-lived because of the onset of the Great Depression. At this time, UPS was established in most of the larger American cities. The air service was reestablished during the 1950's, and the company ultimately bought its own fleet of planes. During the 1980's, UPS launched its overnight delivery service. The company was by then operating some sixty-two thousand trucks around the world.

Another of the leading shipping companies is FedEx (Federal Express, originally FDX). Its commercial reach is illustrated by the fact that the company name is commonly used as a verb, as in "We'll FedEx the papers." The company was established in 1971 with the purchase of a small aircraft company to enable it to make overnight deliveries. By the late 1970's, it had developed a computer system for tracking packages. By the 1990's, it had almost a 50 percent share of the express delivery market, as compared with around a 25 percent market share for UPS, its largest competitor.

Among other major players in the express delivery field are DHL Worldwide Express (international only) and Airborne Freight Corporation. Although the leading express delivery companies account for a large share of their niche market, bulk shipping is still done via railroad, maritime vessel, and truck. Many railroad companies even have reduced or eliminated their passenger traffic to devote their resources solely to the shipment of cargo. The United States Postal Service also continues to be a major factor in the delivery of packages.

Roy Liebman

FURTHER READING

Brannigan, Martha. "Air-Freight Firms Gain Unexpectedly from an Expired Federal Excise Tax." *The Wall Street Journal*, January 3, 1996, p. A4. Describes a loophole that was created by the expiration of a tax, resulting in an increase to the profitability of air freight companies.
Frock, Roger. *Changing How the World Does Business: FedEx's Incredible Journey to Success—The Inside Story.* San Francisco: Berrett-Koehler, 2006. Well-written, but subjective, history of the founding of FedEx by Frederick Smith and of the successes and reverses it endured before becoming a mega-company. The author is a former general manager of FedEx.
Niemann, Greg. *Big Brown: The Untold Story of UPS.* San Francisco: Jossey-Bass, 2007. Insightful account of the history of UPS from its founding in 1907 by Jim Casey to the current time.
Sigafoos, Robert A. *Absolutely Positively Overnight: The Unofficial Corporate History of Federal Express.* 2d ed. Memphis, Tenn.: St. Lukes Press, 1988. Relatively objective history of FedEx that was apparently not well-received by the company as a result of its sometimes critical slant.
Trimble, Vance H. *Overnight Success: Federal Express and Frederick Smith, Its Renegade Creator.* New York: Crown, 1993. Somewhat negative portrayal of the growth of FedEx that presents a counterbalance to the generally more positive accounts that have been published.

SEE ALSO: Air transportation industry; FedEx; Postal Service, U.S.; Railroads; Transatlantic steamer service; Transcontinental railroad; Trucking industry; Vanderbilt, Cornelius.

Sit-down strike of 1936-1937

THE EVENT: Strike by General Motors employees that shut down plant operations in Flint, Michigan, and other cities
DATE: December 30, 1936-February 11, 1937
PLACE: Flint, Michigan, and Cleveland, Ohio
SIGNIFICANCE: The action against GM brought the tactic of sit-down strikes and their effectiveness to the attention of the general public. At the time of the strike, GM was a huge and powerful corporation, while the unions behind the strike were relatively weak.

A sit-down strike involves workers remaining in the workplace while on strike to prevent normal business operations from being conducted. The first such strike to become national news was conducted by the United Auto Workers (UAW), a member union of the Committee for Industrial Organization (CIO; later known as the Congress of Industrial Organizations). On December 28, 1936, a few workers

Sit-down strikers read newspapers at General Motors' Fisher Body plant in Flint, Michigan, in 1937. (AP/Wide World Photos)

in the Cleveland Fisher Body Plant of General Motors (GM) started a sit-down strike against the company. On December 30, at 7:00 A.M., fewer than fifty workers sat down on the production line in Fisher Body Plant Number 2 in Flint, Michigan. At 10:00 P.M. that night, Fisher Body Plant Number 1 was also closed by a sit-down strike. In the weeks that followed, the strike spread to other GM plants and to cities in other states.

On January 11, 1937, police stormed Fisher Body Plant Number 2 but were driven off by the strikers. This became known as the Battle of the Running Bulls, a play on words recalling the U.S. Civil War's Battles of Bull Run (1861, 1862).

Michigan governor Frank Murphy, U.S. secretary of labor Frances Perkins, and President Franklin D. Roosevelt pressured GM's management to talk with the leaders of the UAW and find a way to end the strike. Finally, after much pressure from Governor Murphy, talks did occur. As a result, GM decided to recognize the UAW as the collective bargaining agent for workers in seventeen plants and to negotiate a contract with the UAW. The workers were thus able for the first time in history to participate in the running of GM.

After the successful sit-down strike against GM, sit-down strikes became recognized as a powerful tool for workers. Such strikes occurred in many other industries, with about one-half million people participating in them.

Many labor historians call the sit-down strike against GM the most important event in labor-management relations to take place during the 1930's. As a result of the strike and its aftermath, workers became part of the decision-making apparatus in many large American corporations, including United States Steel. The UAW became a powerful union, and the CIO became a powerful organization in American labor and politics.

Richard Tuerk

FURTHER READING

Beik, Millie Allen. "The General Motors Sit-Down Strike of 1936-1937." In *Labor Relations*. Westport, Conn.: Greenwood Press, 2005.

Fine, Sidney. *Sit-Down: The General Motors Strike of 1936-1937*. Ann Arbor: University of Michigan Press, 1969.

Kuhn, Arthur J. *GM Passes Ford, 1918-1938: Designing the General Motors Performance-Control System*. University Park: Pennsylvania State University Press, 1986.

SEE ALSO: AFL-CIO; Automotive industry; General Motors; Labor history; Labor strikes.

Slave era

THE ERA: Period in United States history in which slaves, or individuals who were the property of other people, could be traded for profit and used to provide cheap, dependable labor

DATE: 1619-1865

PLACE: Primarily eastern and southern United States

SIGNIFICANCE: Slaves constituted a valuable kind of private property that could be traded or used to provide labor, usually at less cost than hiring free labor. The institution of slavery was interwoven into many aspects of law, business, and financial affairs until it ended in 1865.

When Americans during the early twenty-first century think about slavery, they usually focus on its morality, particularly the issues of exploitation, inequality, and cruelty. Slaveholders and their defenders, in contrast, tended to look on the institution primarily as a business. Most contemporary historians agree that the main reason for the existence of American slavery was the expectation that it would provide a dependable, flexible, and cheap supply of labor. Like industrial capitalists in the North, most slaveholders rationally attempted to minimize their expenses to maximize their profits. In addition to prof-

its, of course, slavery was also part of a social pattern in which the ownership of slaves was prestigious because it symbolized success.

TRANS-ATLANTIC SLAVE TRADE

From about 1502 until the mid-nineteenth century, the trans-Atlantic slave trade brought approximately 10 million African slaves to the Western Hemisphere. Approximately 50 percent of the slaves were taken to the islands in the Caribbean, some 38 percent went to Brazil, and less than 5 percent (fewer than 400,000) were brought to U.S. territory. Portuguese merchants dominated the business until the early seventeenth century, when the Dutch became a major competitor. From the early eighteenth century through the early nineteenth century, English and French merchants controlled about half the imports.

The trans-Atlantic trade was often the most profitable aspect of the slave business. When all conditions were favorable, those engaged in traffic were sometimes able to double their investments within a year. Eric Williams estimated in *Capitalism and Slavery* (1944) that the average gain was between 16 and 30 percent, and he asserted that the Industrial Revolution was largely financed from these profits. Many modern historians, however, are skeptical about the so-called "Williams thesis." Transporting slaves across the ocean was an expensive and risky enterprise that required large capital outlays. Slaves were unwilling passengers, constantly ready to revolt, and their presence required twice as many crew members as on regular commercial ships. Insurance was expensive, and special permits had to be purchased. Any number of problems, including epidemics, rebellions, and attacks by pirates, could arise on voyages, which would result in serious financial losses. Whatever the risks, however, there never seemed to be any shortage of merchants and investors ready to transport human cargo.

When historian Johannes Postama analyzed the business records of 159 Dutch slaving voyages, he found that 113 of the voyages resulted in profits on investment of at least 5 percent, which was the average return. A minority of transports were extremely profitable, one reporting a return of 88 percent. Some 14 of the voyages reported neither profit nor loss, while 32 incurred losses, with one expedition reporting a loss of 48 percent. Postama found evidence that the merchants of other countries were more successful than the Dutch. At the time, an average of 10 percent was considered a very good return on investment, and the larger British traders, with experience, organization, and stable finances, achieved profits of that scale. The many smugglers who did not pay the required fees sometimes did better financially, although they risked severe punishment and confiscation of both ships and cargo.

The transporting of enslaved Africans to America was often called the Middle Passage, because it was the second of the three states in the triangular trade among Europe, Africa, and America. It was a journey of almost five thousand miles, in which as many as 350 African captives were packed below the deck of a single ship. To prevent revolt, the captives were normally kept in chains and allowed on the deck for only a few hours of each day. According to contemporary accounts by Olaudah Equiano and others, the voyages were marked by crowding, poor ventilation, and filthy conditions. The large-scale Cambridge University Press database of the slave trade, developed by Herbert Klein and a team of historians, concluded that approximately 22 percent of the Africans did not survive the ocean crossing during the years before 1700 and that thereafter the average death rate was about 12 percent.

The trans-Atlantic slave trade gradually ended during the nineteenth century. The United States outlawed the importation of additional slaves in 1808, although smugglers continued to bring them to the South until enforcement of Abraham Lincoln's blockade in 1861. Great Britain abolished slavery throughout its empire in 1833 and established a network of treaties with other countries limiting or ending the traffic. In the famous case of the slave rebellion on the Spanish ship *La Amistad*, for example, the U.S. Supreme Court held that the slaves had been taken illegally from Africa, based on an 1817 treaty between Spain and Britain. Brazil in 1850 was the last major country to prohibit the importation of slaves from Africa. Even then, however, the illicit smuggling of slaves across the Atlantic continued until 1871, when Brazil finally adopted a gradual emancipation law.

SLAVERY IN THE ANTEBELLUM SOUTH

The use of slave labor was always most common in warm climates and in places conducive to plantation-type agriculture, with optimum-size units larger than a family farm. The first evidence of African slavery in British North America was in 1619, when about twenty Africans were purchased from a Dutch ship in colonial Virginia. It is possible that they might have initially been considered the same as indentured servants, the poor white immigrants who contracted to work four to seven years to pay for passage to the New World. By the 1660's, however, the laws of Virginia stipulated that slaves of African ancestry and their children could be held as permanent property. All thirteen colonies allowed the

An abolitionist print depicting the slave trade in the United States in 1830. (Library of Congress)

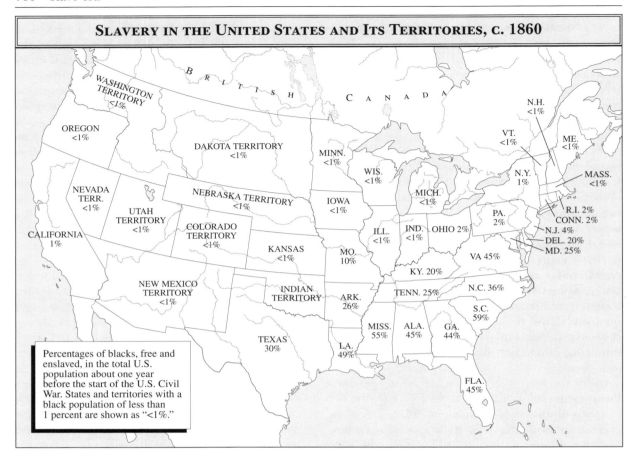

SLAVERY IN THE UNITED STATES AND ITS TERRITORIES, C. 1860

Percentages of blacks, free and enslaved, in the total U.S. population about one year before the start of the U.S. Civil War. States and territories with a black population of less than 1 percent are shown as "<1%."

ownership of slaves. The American Revolution, however, provoked a strong antislavery movement in the northern states, where there were relatively few slaves. By 1804, all the states north of the Mason-Dixon line either had emancipated slaves or were in the process of doing so.

During the first half of the nineteenth century, the Industrial Revolution and the invention of the cotton gin stimulated southerners to expand cotton production, which grew from 300,000 bales in 1830 to about 5 million bales in 1860. During these years, the U.S. produced about three-fourths of the world's supply of cotton, and it was by far the country's largest export commodity. As a consequence, the number of slaves in the South grew from fewer than 700,000 in the census of 1790, to approximately 2 million in the census of 1830, and finally to 4 million in 1860. By then, persons of African ancestry made up about one-third of the southern population. In Mississippi and South Carolina, they were

in the majority, while they represented only about 10 percent of the population in Missouri.

It is estimated that 75 percent of the labor in the cotton kingdom was performed by slaves. Although ownership varied greatly among the states in the four decades before 1860, only approximately one-fourth of white households owned any slaves at all. Slaveholders with twenty or more slaves were considered to be members of the planter class, which represented about 12 percent of slaveholders, or approximately 3 percent of total white households. Considerably less than 0.5 percent of the white population owned fifty or more slaves, which was considered the minimum necessary to belong to the planter aristocracy. However, a large percentage of slaves lived and worked in large agricultural units. More than half of them resided on plantations with thirty or more slaves, and one-fourth resided in units with fifty or more slaves. Less than 20 percent belonged to a farmer possessing a single slave family.

The states with slavery were not wealthy, and most free white persons found it difficult to make a good livelihood and stay out of debt. Contrary to the stereotype, successful planters were not genteel men of leisure; rather, they were usually skillful entrepreneurs who paid attention to efficiency and used careful financial planning. To own and operate an estate with twenty or more slaves required a large capital investment, and mistakes could easily result in financial ruin. Almost all large planters hired full-time overseers to supervise their operations, and frequently planters also hired slave drivers, who worked under the overseers. Overseers were expected to be competent managers of labor and to keep good records. Those who effectively supervised large estates were rewarded with salaries considered good for the time. Their contracts usually motivated them to be more interested in short-term results than in the long-term return on investments in slaves. Because they exacted labor from slaves who were not their property, they tended to be rather harsh and to frequently resort to corporal punishment.

PROFITABILITY

Contemporary defenders of slavery often claimed that owning slaves was a financial burden and that the institution existed for humanitarian, noneconomic reasons. Apologist James Hammond wrote in 1849 that "free labor is cheaper than slave labor," and many liberal defenders of free-market capitalism agreed with this assessment. If slave labor was unprofitable, however, historian Kenneth Stampp observes that it is difficult to explain why slaves brought such a high price and why so many southerners wanted to own them. If the employment of free workers provided an equal or greater return, one would expect that many wealthy plantation owners would have pursued this alternative strategy.

The capital investments of plantations included the cost of land, equipment, slaves, and usually an overseer. The monetary value of a slave depended on variables such as age, sex, health, and disposition. Slaveholders were willing to pay premium prices for young women of childbearing age and for healthy, strong men who did not appear prone to rebellion. Records of Georgia, collected by U. B. Phillips, indicate that the average price of a prime young male slave ranged from $700 to $1,100 from 1830 to

1850 and from $1,050 to $1,800 during the 1850's. Slaves were quite expensive in comparison to the cost of land. Although land values depended on location and quality, prime cotton-growing land usually sold for $25 to $40 per acre, and a plantation commonly used one slave for every twenty or thirty acres in production.

Journalist Frederick Law Olmstead studied slavery in several parts of the South during the years just before the U.S. Civil War. He noted that a prime field hand produced seven to ten bales of cotton a year and that the living expenses of a slave amounted to about $30 a year. Olmstead estimated an average yearly profit of about $250 per slave. This would mean that the output of a healthy field hand would pay for his purchase price in about six years, except in periods of recession. Olmstead concluded that the possibility of an attractive profit using slave labor was "moderately good, at least, compared with the profit of other investments in capital and enterprise in the North."

One of the main indications of profitability was that slaveholders often hired out their slaves at yearly rates averaging 10 to 20 percent of the slave's market value, plus maintenance. Although most slaves were rented for agricultural work, in the Chesapeake region they were often hired to work in textile factories, railroads, coal mines, and ironworks. Investigating these labor practices, historian Ronald Lewis found that industrialists reported that the renting of slaves was more profitable than the hiring of free white workers. In addition to being cheaper, slaves were not able to refuse harsh working and living conditions. By the beginning of the Civil War, according to Lewis, many business leaders of the South believed that the use of slaves provided a comparative advantage over manufacturing in the North.

On the eve of the Civil War, most slaveholders were optimistic about the future of their economic system. The typical slave field worker was not at all lazy or unproductive; on average, he worked harder and was more efficient than free white workers. According to the calculations of Robert William Fogel and Stanley L. Engerman, in *Time on the Cross: The Economics of American Negro Slavery* (1974), southern slave agriculture, because of its economy of scale and flexible use of labor, was about 35 percent more efficient than the northern system of family farming. Although many historians think that Fogel and Engerman exaggerated slavery's efficiency, the behavior of southerners before the Civil War is strong evidence that they believed "the peculiar institution" to be economically viable. Before enactment of the Thirteenth Amendment, moreover, Abraham Lincoln was unable to persuade the states of Maryland, Kentucky, Delaware, and Missouri to accept a plan for emancipation with compensation for owners of slaves.

Slaves sometimes died early or escaped, which obviously meant a large financial loss for an owner. The loss, however, was mitigated by insurance. Within a relatively large population of slaves, of course, the majority could reasonably be expected to work for an average of at least twenty years or more. Compared with free labor, slaveholders had the advantage of having firm control over how they used their labor force. They could apply harsh discipline without any concern about the worker leaving, and they did not have to be concerned about labor unions or strikes. In calculating return on investment, moreover, it is important not to overlook the potential value of babies born to slave women, who were encouraged to give birth at a young age and as frequently as possible.

CONSEQUENCES

Just as historians argue about the issue of profitability, they also disagree about whether the total effects of slavery were positive or negative on the economy. Hinton Helper, for instance, argued in *The Impending Crisis of the South* (1857) that slavery discouraged the development of resources and impoverished the majority of white southerners. Some historians have argued that the large capitalization of slave labor made it impossible for southerners to invest surplus capital in more productive sources, thereby retarding the development of manufacturing industries. Certainly it is true that the rural South was not as progressive and prosperous as the Northeast in industry and cultural achievements. It is not at all clear, however, that slavery was a significant cause. Many slaveholders, especially those in the planter class, were highly educated and competent businessmen. The relative backwardness of the South was apparently caused by a host of other reasons, including geographical features, a sparse population, and a lack of infrastructure, especially in the area of transportation. The South, moreover, enjoyed more prosperity than most foreign countries of the period.

Most historians agree that the use of slave labor exacerbated the enormous gulf that separated the slaveholding class from the nonslaveholding whites of the South. Historian Gavin Wright calculates that slaveholders owned about 93.1 percent of the region's wealth and that the average wealth of slaveholders (almost $25,000) was almost fourteen times the average wealth of nonslaveholders. It is likely that competition from slave labor tended to push down the average wages of white workers. This, of course, was beneficial to consumers, even while it marginally depressed the incomes of lower-class whites. Members of the planter class definitely possessed a disproportionate share of political power. In 1860, slaveholders occupied between 41.2 and 85.8 percent of the seats in southern legislatures, and members of the planter class occupied half of the seats in Mississippi and South Carolina legislatures.

Before the Civil War, people living in the North received a number of economic benefits, directly and indirectly, from the existence of slavery in the South. The price of cotton, so important to the textile mills, was somewhat less than it would have been without slave labor. By the 1850's, cotton represented 60 percent of the total domestic exports of the country, which helped accumulate the capital necessary for the modernization of the economy. Historian Douglas North called cotton the "proximate prime mover in quickening the pace of the country's growth." Without slavery, the South's cotton would most likely not have had as much of a competitive advantage in world trade. Income from slave labor, moreover, helped provide markets for manufactured goods from the North, thereby stimulating industrialization. Also, northern creditors and insurance companies made profits in doing business with slaveholders in the South.

Unquestionably the buying, selling, and exploitation of slaves ultimately resulted in tragic consequences for the United States. The long and bitter controversy about slavery was the major reason that the southern states seceded from the Union in 1860-1861, thereby bringing about the violence, destruction, and great expense of the Civil War. The institution of slavery was not the only cause for the development of white racism, but it was unquestionably one of the contributing factors. Even though slavery ended long ago, it continues to leave legacies of stereotypes and bitterness, and most economists acknowledge that it is one of the reasons for the economic gap between African Americans and whites. Because the past continues to have an impact on the present, many people agree with the thesis of Randall Robinson's *The Debt: What America Owes to Blacks* (2001), which insists on monetary reparations to the descendants of slaves as compensation for unpaid labor and exploitation. Similar arguments are sometimes used in defense of affirmative action programs.

Thomas Tandy Lewis

FURTHER READING

Fogel, Robert William. *Without Consent or Contract: The Rise and Fall of American Slavery.* New York: Norton, 1989. The Nobel Laureate's defense of the controversial views in the book he coauthored with Stanley L. Engerman, *Time on the Cross.*

Helper, Hinton. *The Impending Crisis of the South.* 1857. Reprint. Westport, Conn.: Negro Universities Press, 1970. A reprint of Helper's argument that slavery impoverished southerners.

Klein, Herbert. *The Atlantic Slave Trade.* New York: Cambridge University Press, 1999. An outstanding survey and analysis of the slave trade, incorporating the quantitative information in the Cambridge University Press database.

Lewis, Ronald. *Coal, Iron, and Slaves: Industrial Slavery in Maryland and Virginia, 1715-1865.* Westport, Conn.: Greenwood Press, 1979. Through an examination of the use of slave labor in ironworks and coal mines of the Chesapeake region, Lewis gives compelling evidence that the practice was more profitable than the use of free white labor.

Postama, Johannes. *The Atlantic Slave Trade.* Gainesville: University Press of Florida, 2003. A concise, readable, and scholarly work that summarizes the author's larger books and includes an up-to-date annotated bibliography.

Robinson, Randall. *The Debt: What America Owes to Blacks.* New York: Plume, 2001. Robinson calls for reparations to be made to African Americans whose ancestors were slaves.

Stampp, Kenneth. *The Peculiar Institution: Slavery in the Ante-Bellum South.* New York: Alfred A Knopf, 1975. A standard and dependable work that includes much information about the business and financial aspects of the institution.

Williams, Eric. *Capitalism and Slavery.* 1944. Reprint. Miami: Ian Randle, 2005. A new introduction by Colina Palmer graces this classic work on the economics of slavery.

Wright, Gavin. *Slavery and American Economic Development.* Baton Rouge: Louisiana State University Press, 2006. The premier scholar on the economics of slavery, Wright emphasizes the importance of slavery during the colonial period and views the antebellum period as a cold war between two systems of property ownership.

SEE ALSO: Civil War, U.S.; Cotton gin; Cotton industry; Farm labor; Indentured labor; Labor history; Northwest Ordinances; Plantation agriculture; Sharecropping; Slave trading; Texas annexation.

Slave trading

DEFINITION: Buying and selling of human beings for their labor

SIGNIFICANCE: Slave trading across the Atlantic Ocean provided revenue for northern ports in American colonies and a labor source for plantations in the American South. The slave trade supported the manufacturing and use of textiles, beverages, and other products in the North and their distribution to the Caribbean, Africa, and Europe.

The Atlantic slave trade developed in the sixteenth century as a consequence of the growth of capitalism and improved long-distance transportation. New markets in Africa and the Americas became available to European merchants and attracted those with business knowledge and the ability to accumulate capital. European goods, including wool, linen, silver, tapestries, and grain, were bartered for African slaves. Spanish and Portuguese ships acquired slaves along the central part of the western coast of Africa in return for products from the Caribbean islands, such as citrus fruits, coconuts, bananas, sweet potatoes, and maize. Among the slave traders were two explorers whose names are synonymous with the New World, Christopher Columbus and Amerigo Vespucci.

THE TRIANGULAR TRADE

The growth of sugar plantations in the Caribbean and extensive coffee production in Brazil vastly increased slave trading and attracted French, British, and Dutch merchants. What became known as "triangular trade" involved ships from European ports bringing liquor, firearms, and trinkets to Africa in return for slaves, who were brought to American sites and put to work on the plantations that no longer could attract enough indigenous workers. Slaves were valuable particularly because they could be forced to do work that immigrants of European extraction and indigenous people could not or would not do. By the 1660's, more than thirty thousand slaves were arriving each decade in Barbados, one of the chief Caribbean destinations. Later, even more slaves were brought to Jamaica. The ship captains were often paid in the form of a share in the "freight negroes" in the shipment, who became the captain's to sell. The ships returned to Europe with produce from the plantations. Sometimes the trade was not triangular; for example, Brazilian-owned ships sometimes traded Brazilian products directly to Africa in return for slaves. European colonies in the Americas soon became part of the business.

THE AMERICAN COLONIES

The occupation of the lower Hudson River Valley by the Dutch involved this area in the slave trade. By 1630, there were three hundred white settlers and about sixty black slaves in this region. Some of the slaves were owned by private settlers and some by the Dutch West India company. About twenty years later, about one quarter of the population between the settlements that later became Albany, New York, and Hoboken, New Jersey, consisted of enslaved black men, women, and children.

Slave trading did not end with the British acquisition of New Netherlands in 1664. Ships brought in slaves, ivory, ebony, gum, and beeswax in return for sugar and rum from the Caribbean. In Philadelphia, as early as 1684, slaves were being bought for cash. Quakers, who later became fierce opponents of slavery, were represented in this trading. Both in New York and Philadelphia, slaves were employed in construction or in shipbuilding. In the eighteenth century, slaves were sold in New York at auctions at wharves by commissioners and sometimes on the ships to avoid paying commissioners.

Rhode Island, a small state with limited resources other than its long coastline and good ports, depended on shipping for its economic survival. The Rhode Island city of Newport became the principal slave trading area in the American colonies, followed by Bristol and Providence. Rhode Island merchants developed excellent distilleries and therefore preferred to import molasses from the Caribbean and make their own rum. From around 1725, ships from Newport carried the liquor to colonies in the South or to Africa. The prosperity of merchants in Newport began with proceeds from the slave trade, although the greatest fortunes were not made until the early decades of the American Republic. From 1725 to 1807, a total of 934 vessels left Rhode Island to transport 106,000 slaves. The rum trade on the West African coast was monopolized by New England merchants, chiefly those with ships departing from Rhode Island. Cargo ships from Rhode Island were considerably smaller than those used by Europeans, often carrying no more than 75 to 100 slaves, as merchants found that faster loading reduced the chances of disease and death among the slaves. During the American Revolution, this trading ceased in Rhode Island.

Around 1670, slaves began arriving in significant numbers in Maryland and Virginia. British law required the American colonies to import manufactured goods, but these states had foodstuffs for export to the Caribbean. In these states, tobacco, first cultivated by Native Americans, was an important product, but by the seventeenth century, European tobacco merchants controlled more of the trade than did the middle American colonies.

The great southern port for the importation of slaves was Charleston, South Carolina, with many of its ships coming from Rhode Island. Many of the slaves brought to Charleston were destined for North Carolina, which lacked adequate ports, and Maryland, because Baltimore did not develop its harbor facilities until the American Revolution. Slavery was important in South Carolina from the first permanent English settlement in 1670. Much of the land was suitable for rice, and rice culture required workers to be able to stand knee-deep in water and stoop constantly to plant, tend, and harvest the crop. Willing workers were hard to find, so vast numbers of slaves were imported for this grueling labor. Slaves also seemed better able to withstand the yellow fever and malaria that plagued the colony. Bad as the rice fields were, they were probably less demanding than the sugar plantations in the Caribbean. Within a century of the founding of

South Carolina, the majority of its population comprised slaves and Native Americans. The profits from slave labor inevitably encouraged the purchase of even more slaves. Another product that could be profitably grown in South Carolina was indigo, valued all over the world as a source of dye. The Carolinas paid for the slaves with food, livestock, and pitch, items needed by merchants and shipbuilders.

Not all trade was barter. However, African exporters tended to refuse paper money and credit notes, although some trading was accomplished with coins from Europe and America. In the eighteenth century, gastropodic shells called cowries became an important international currency. More than 25 million shells were imported into West Africa by slave traders. Cowries had a number of advantages: They were attractive and easy to handle, did not break easily or fade with wear, and could not be counterfeited. However, although they were too cumbersome to hoard, their size made them unwieldly to transport in quantities sufficient to purchase a shipload of slaves.

Starting during the 1660's, more Africans than Europeans were entering the British colonies in America, a pattern that held into the early nineteenth century. By 1770, rum represented more than four-fifths of exports from New England. Rice and tobacco were more important than cotton, for until the invention of the cotton gin, cotton was a minor southern product. Rice exportation from the American colonies, primarily South Carolina, reached its peak in 1770, when more than 83,000 pounds left the country, but it declined thereafter.

During the last few years before the American Revolution, slave importation declined. The growing defiance against England for practices such as the taxes imposed by its Sugar Act of 1764 and its Tea Act of 1773 took the form of colonial attacks on practices regarded as essential to British economic power. Northern colonies were also finding labor by freemen more satisfactory. All but four colonies had enacted duty laws on the importation of slaves. During the conflict itself, slave trading became too dangerous and came to a halt.

THE EARLY REPUBLIC, 1776-1807

In drafting the Declaration of Independence, Thomas Jefferson charged that King George III was violating the rights of life and liberty of the people by making them a part of the "execrable commerce" of slavery. It is one of the supreme ironies of American history that Jefferson and other slaveholders were striving to find some way out of a practice that had marked commerce in the colonies for a century and a half. Most of the colonies were inclined to accept a ban on the importation of slaves, but South Carolina and Georgia would not accept a quick end to the Atlantic slave trade. As a result, the lengthy list of charges against the monarch in the declaration did not include slave trading.

Without mentioning slave trading, Article I, Section 9 of the U.S. Constitution asserted that a certain "migration or importation" of people would not be prohibited before the year 1808. As a result, United States vessels carried 180,000 slaves into the Americas between 1791 and 1810. A considerable number of these people went to various parts of Spanish America or to the French Caribbean islands of Martinique and Guadeloupe, especially after 1808, but 60 percent of them entered the United States. In 1807, Congress passed legislation banning the importation of slaves beginning on January 1 of the following year.

The records of the various states were mixed during this period. Rhode Island appears to have desisted from slave trading between 1776 and 1783, but trading resumed during the late 1780's, and in 1800, the state was represented in Congress by two slave traders, Christopher Champlin of Newport and John Brown of Providence. South Carolina barred slave trading between 1787 and 1804. From 1804 to 1808 slaves could be admitted from Africa but not from the Caribbean. During those years, two hundred ships brought more than forty thousand slaves into Charleston. Georgia restricted importation in 1793 and prohibited it after 1798.

What part humanitarian concerns played at this time is difficult to assess. The arguments against the continuation of the slave trade included the fact that slave families in the United States were increasing the black population. A higher proportion of women slaves were brought to the United States than to other places, and these women proved to be not only able workers but also the mothers of many more slaves. In some states, the growing numbers of slaves generated white fears of uprisings. Cycles of low prices for the products generated by slave labor also led to reductions of importations.

One event in 1793 altered the situation greatly: Eli Whitney's invention of the cotton gin. In 1792,

SLAVE POPULATION IN THE UNITED STATES, 1790-1860

Year	Number of Slaves
1790	697,681
1800	893,602
1810	1,191,362
1820	1,538,022
1830	2,009,043
1840	2,487,355
1850	3,204,313
1860	3,953,760

Source: Data from *Historical Statistics of the United States: Colonial Times to 1970* (Washington, D.C.: U.S. Department of Commerce, Bureau of the Census, 1975)

the United States exported 138,328 pounds of cotton. Eight years later, that figure had risen astronomically to nearly 18 million pounds. Twenty years later, two years after the federal ban on importation of slaves, that figure had nearly doubled to 35 million pounds. The mills of New England, where many citizens strongly opposed slavery, benefited enormously, as did thousands of their employees and all the buyers of cotton fabrics.

Although Congress could not ban slave trading, it could and did act against the outfitting of slave ships. A 1794 act of Congress prohibited the building, fitting, equipping, or loading of a vessel within American borders for slave trading. In 1800, Congress forbade Americans from carrying slaves from one foreign port to another. Effective enforcement of such legislation, however, was difficult.

ILLEGAL SLAVE TRADE, 1808-1865

A series of laws against slave trading did not stop the process because profits were still to be made. Many ships evaded detection, and laws were gotten around by legalistic trickery in the courts, bribery, and mild judicial interpretations of the laws. The most severe yet perhaps most futile law was passed in 1820, when Congress made slave trading by any United States citizen a capital offense. A study of American slaving and the federal law that covered the years from 1837 to 1862 found that of 125 captains and crew members prosecuted in New York, only 20 received prison sentences. No one was found guilty under the 1820 statute. Clearly, the judicial system could not bring itself to apply this harsh law. Up to the end of the U.S. Civil War, only one of the many American ship captains charged with slave trading was executed.

The application of federal laws proved difficult outside the states. Slave trading took place in Louisiana, Florida, and Texas, but Louisiana did not become a state until 1812, and Florida and Texas were not states until 1845. Slaves could be shipped to Pensacola, in west Florida, which at times was under the control of Spain or France, and then transferred to nearby Alabama, legally before 1819 and illegally afterward, or to Georgia. One piece of legislation better known for its application to boundary disputes, the Webster-Ashburton Treaty of 1842, also had the beneficial effect of forcing the United States and Great Britain to suppress the slave trade.

Cargoes remained diverse in the nineteenth century. African markets desired cotton goods, muskets, gunpowder, tobacco, rum (and sometimes other alcoholic beverages), hardware, cutlery, and trivial goods, including beads. Several developments gave rise to slave trading during the 1850's. The development of slave trading companies, particularly in New York City, created a new boom in the business. Also, an economic crisis in 1857 left many captains and crews unemployed and induced them to participate. Steam-powered ships left more space for slaves, thus enabling more profitable voyages. In Cuba, the production of sugar reached a new high during this time, inducing some southern states to seek resumption of trade.

About fifty thousand slaves were brought to the United States between the ban in 1808 and 1860, but slaves were imported even during the Civil War. The fight against slave trading involved international boarding of ships, which led to bitter conflicts among nations. As late as the 1850's, foreign ships flying American flags led to much guesswork by patrols. Inevitably, many legally operating American ships were boarded by British officials; this brought an indignant response from Washington—while other American ships were participating in the trade by carrying slaves to Cuba. The abolition of slavery in the United States by the Thirteenth Amendment on December 6, 1865, put an end to the importation of slaves.

AFTER THE CIVIL WAR

Although slave trading had virtually ceased for about a century after the Civil War, a 2003 Department of Justice report estimated that each year between eighteen thousand and twenty thousand people are brought to the United States, where they are sexually exploited or forced to work long hours under inhumane conditions for little or no pay.

Modern-day slaves people are of various races and from various countries. Some have been sold, often for as little as between forty and several hundred dollars. Others have been kidnapped or promised good jobs and a better life. They are smuggled into the country overland from Canada and Mexico, or by boat and airplane. They are forced to work as farmhands, domestics, sweatshop and factory workers, restaurant help, sex slaves, and prostitutes. Very few cases are reported. The slaves are often fearful and typically have language difficulties. Many of the slaves are subjected to violence. Although the practice of slavery is illegal and no longer morally sanctioned, some unscrupulous business executives continue to find this activity profitable.

Robert P. Ellis

FURTHER READING

Coughtry, Jay. *The Notorious Triangle: Rhode Island and the African Slave Trade, 1700-1807.* Philadelphia: Temple University Press, 1981. One of the most thorough studies of slave trading activity in a single colony, which later became a state.

Eltis, David. *The Rise of African Slavery in the Americas.* New York: Cambridge University Press, 2000. This study explains how the Caribbean slave trade spread to the colonies of Maryland and Virginia during the late sixteenth century.

Fogel, Robert W., and Stanley L. Engerman. *Time on the Cross: The Economics of American Negro Slavery.* Boston: Little, Brown, 1974. A very controversial book packed with information about slave imports, slave prices, and earnings from slavery. The controversy relates primarily to the authors' interpretations of this information, not to the data on which they are based.

Klein, Herbert S. *The Atlantic Slave Trade: New Approaches to the Americas.* New York: Cambridge University Press, 1999. A modest-sized attempt to survey the work done by mid- and late-twentieth century scholars for the benefit of the general public. Klein warns that the scholars disagree on a number of points in the history of the slave trade.

Rawley, James A. *The Transatlantic Slave Trade: A History.* New York: W. W. Norton, 1981. This book was the first detailed study of the Atlantic slave trade. The last four chapters consider the American involvement. Maps and tables are included.

Soodalter, Ron. *Hanging Captain Gordon: The Life and Trial of an American Slave Trader.* New York: Atria Books, 2006. With a strong emphasis on the impediments to effective administration of the laws against American slave trading in the nineteenth century, this books focuses on the routine of an enterprising slave trader.

Thomas, Hugh. *The Slave Trade: The Story of the Atlantic Slave Trade, 1440-1870.* New York: Simon & Schuster, 1997. Over nine hundred pages long, Thomas's book is the most detailed account of the subject. There are many references to American activity, but they are scattered under thematic topics. It is an extremely valuable history with much literary polish.

SEE ALSO: Civil War, U.S.; Cotton gin; Cotton industry; Farm labor; Indentured labor; Plantation agriculture; Slave era.

Small Business Administration

IDENTIFICATION: Independent government agency that aids, counsels, and protects the interests of owners of small businesses

DATE: Established in 1953

SIGNIFICANCE: As the largest backer of business loans in the United States, the Small Business Administration strengthens the American economy by enabling small businesses to function effectively. By providing access to credit, it stimulates growth in the small-business sector and the overall American economy.

Thomas Jefferson and Abraham Lincoln both considered small business to be the backbone of American democracy and free enterprise. The Small Business Administration (SBA) acts primarily to guarantee loans made to small businesses and thus allow them access to credit. It also provides assistance to homeowners in times of disaster. In all, the SBA has helped more than 20 million businesses and has guaranteed loans worth a total of over $45 billion. The SBA also oversees a mandate that a portion of government contracts and government surplus property go to small businesses.

The Small Business Act of 1953 was instrumental in establishing the Small Business Administration. The agency has operated effectively for more than half a century helping small-business owners start up and manage new businesses. Acting under the Department of Commerce, the SBA is headed by a presidentially appointed administrator. It is made up of separate administrative units whose responsibilities include customer service, marketing, disaster assistance, legislative affairs, equal employment opportunity, and civil rights. In addition, the SBA works to procure government contracts and to help burgeoning businesses train new employees and managers and provides information on any problems that may arise. It also sponsors business classes and counseling sessions at local community centers and schools. Any business that meets the SBA's definition of small, which is different for each industry, may qualify for a loan. SBA clients represent a cross-section of American businesses, particularly in the retail, wholesale, and manufacturing sectors, and they range in size from sole proprietorships to businesses with between fifty and one hundred employees.

SMALL BUSINESS ADMINISTRATION PROGRAMS

Listed among the types of guaranteed business loans administered through the SBA are the Loan Guarantee Program, which helps new business owners establish or expand their businesses, the Fixed Asset Financing Program, which provides funds for land or construction, and the MicroLoan Program, which deals with loans of up to $35,000. The Economic Development Program offers free counsel-

---

WHAT IS A SMALL BUSINESS?

The Small Business Administration classifies a business as small by its maximum size, measured in terms of either the number of employees or annual gross receipts.

Business Type	Maximum Size by Annual Gross Receipts ($ thousands)
Crop-producing businesses	750
Cattle-producing businesses	2,000
Household appliance dealers	9,000
Chicken-egg-producing facilities	12,500
Online retailers	25,000
Supermarkets	27,000
New car dealers	29,000
Film and video producers	29,500
Building construction businesses	33,500

Business Type	Maximum Size by Number of Employees
Apparel manufacturing	500
Furniture manufacturing	500
Logging	500
Mining and quarrying	500
Paper manufacturing	500-750
Textile mills	500-1,000
Metal manufacturing	500-1,500

Source: Data from the National Archives and Records Administration

---

ing and training, and the Business Development Program helps small businesses that are owned by disadvantaged individuals. In addition, homeowners and businesses are eligible for loans to recover from presidentially declared disasters.

The Loan Guarantee Program remains a vital source of capital for American small businesses. Although the SBA does not make loans, it guarantees loans to lender institutions such as banks and credit unions. Traditional business loans can be difficult to obtain, but the SBA ensures that small-business owners can repay loans at a slower pace, making their loans much more affordable. In addition, the SBA allows some businesses to borrow larger amounts of money, which makes working with the SBA far more viable financially for start-up businesses short on cash. SBA loans are usually intermediate in size, under $500,000. Mortgages on buildings where small businesses are located are appealing to banks and a particularly popular use of SBA loans, as are loans to finance the takeover of successful, established businesses.

CRITICISMS

In 1996, the Republican-led House of Representatives failed in its attempt to eliminate the SBA. Similarly, the George W. Bush Administration failed in its attempt to put a stop to the SBA loan program. Because of its size, impact, and longevity, the Small Business Administration has come under fire from critics calling for a full-scale evaluation. Its loan programs, critics maintain, can have a negative effect on small businesses by harming businesses that are not affiliated with the SBA. Indeed, the SBA aids only 0.4 percent of the entrepreneurs in the United States.

Some critics argue that the SBA serves political and ideological needs and that it serves the banking community—about two-thirds of all banks participate as lenders. They also insist that the SBA serves politicians, who support it merely to demonstrate their commitment to the ideal of entrepreneurship to their constituents. The SBA is also unfair because it provides services at taxpayer expense. Despite this criticism, the SBA remains the greatest guarantor of small-business credit in the country as well as a welcome source of help for those in need of counseling and training.

M. Casey Diana

FURTHER READING

Bean, Jonathan J. *Beyond the Broker State: Federal Policies Toward Small Business, 1936-1966.* Chapel Hill: University of North Carolina Press, 2002. Focuses on the impact of American politics on small businesses from the Great Depression to the creation of the Small Business Administration during the Dwight D. Eisenhower administration. Underscores the chaotic nature of small business and illustrates how Congress misinterpreted the threat to small business posed by larger corporations.

Green, Charles H. *The SBA Loan Book: Get a Small Business Loan—Even with Poor Credit, Weak Collateral, and No Experience.* Cincinnati: Adams Media, 2005. The author is a vice president of Sunrise Bank, a leading SBA lending institution. Besides being a how-to book, the volume provides a vast amount of knowledge about the workings of the Small Business Administration.

Olsen, Elizabeth. "Reports Find Errors and Fraud in Small Business Administration Contracts." *The New York Times,* July 24, 2008. Two different reports state that millions of dollars in federal contracts were awarded to unqualified companies instead of qualified small businesses; provides insights into the workings of the Small Business Administration.

Rhyne, Elisabeth Holmes. *Small Business, Banks, and SBA Loan Guarantees: Subsidizing the Weak or Bridging a Credit Gap?* Westport, Conn.: Quorum Books, 1988. Examines loan default rates, subsidies, banks' response to incentives, and ultimately the purpose of the Small Business Administration, calling for reforms. Aimed primarily at bankers, small-business owners, and legislators. Extensively researched.

Zwahlen, Cyndia. "Bill Could Open Door for Venture Capital Firms." *Los Angeles Times,* September 27, 2007. Details a controversy centering on the Small Business Administration, wealthy venture capitalists, and billion-dollar companies that could benefit from small-business programs.

SEE ALSO: Banking; Commerce, U.S. Department of; Credit unions; Export-Import Bank of the United States; Farm Credit Administration; Hurricane Katrina; Junior Achievement.

Social Security system

IDENTIFICATION: Federal government program that provides pensions, other transfer payments, and medical-expense subsidies for elderly, disabled, and unemployed persons, and for members of certain low-income groups

DATE: Authorized in 1935

SIGNIFICANCE: The Social Security system imposes a heavy wage tax on most American workers, provides cash benefits and medical-expense reimbursements for most Americans at least sixty-two years of age, and is the source of unemployment compensation and some welfare payments to low-income families. As stakeholders in the system, businesses share the costs of public retirement pension and health insurance programs with the government and their employees.

Before the Great Depression, so few companies had private pension plans for their employees that only about 5 percent of the entire American workforce was covered. Moreover, most of the private pension plans in existence provided little or no protection and unspecified benefits. The Depression of the 1930's caused many of those plans to collapse, so the New Deal administration of President Franklin D. Roosevelt created a vast system to provide pensions for the elderly, unemployment compensation for wage earners, and support for specified categories of public assistance. On August 14, 1935, President Franklin D. Roosevelt signed into law the federal Social Security Act.

The Social Security Act required employers to pay excise taxes as a percentage of employees' wages, with equal contributions paid by the employees themselves. The initial rate was 2 percent, half paid by workers and half paid by employers. Employers of eight or more employees also paid excise taxes of 1 percent in 1936 to be placed in an Unemployment Trust Fund. Workers paying the tax became eligible to receive pensions on their retirement at the age of sixty-five. Pension benefits were regarded as a right that workers earned by paying into the system. No means tests were imposed on pensioners. A separate and parallel program for railroad workers was created by the Railroad Retirement Act of 1935.

BUSINESS PARTICIPATION

The participation of business in the Social Security system and its influence on the provisions of the Social Security Act of 1935 have always been controversial. Three areas of business influence, albeit indirect and partial, on the law are notable.

First, business members of the Advisory Council to the Committee on Economic Security (CES), such as Marion Folsom of Eastman Kodak, brought with them commercial models of social welfare practices. New Dealers on the CES drew on private sector initiatives, and the work of most policy specialists spanned the public and private sectors. Even though the social insurance programs of the New Deal were government-sponsored and compulsory, they were more consistent with business thinking than they might have otherwise been. Second, concerns about business confidence during the Depression set broad constraints on the range of policy options considered, affecting the timing of initiatives,

such as phasing in payroll taxes gradually over three years. Third, the southern wing of the Democratic coalition successfully fought for considerable decentralization of the Social Security system. Provisions governing the means-tested old-age assistance program were modified to enhance local administrative control and to exclude national standards on minimum benefits. Agricultural and domestic workers were dropped from the social insurance part of the system, thereby excluding three-fifths of African American workers.

Eventually, however, employers became stakeholders in the Social Security Act. They subsidized it over the years and designed their own retirement programs around it. Business sought to stabilize welfare-state spending and prevent new incursions (such as national health care) rather than roll back established programs.

AFTER THE NEW DEAL

Business supported amendments to the Social Security Act in 1939 that added payments to spouses and minor children of retired workers and survivors' benefits paid to families in cases of premature deaths of workers. During the 1940's, business supported payroll tax freezes that kept old-age pensions small. It also supported granting old-age pensions to all elderly with work histories to prevent expansion of the means-tested old-age assistance programs.

By the 1950's, Social Security with its emphasis on Old-age and Survivors Insurance (OASI; disability was added in 1956, making it Old-Age, Survivors, and Disability Insurance, or OASDI) was a fixture in American society that garnered business support. This was the case even as payroll tax rates for OASI increased to 2.25 percent in 1959 and the rate of 0.25 percent was added for disability insurance in 1957 (a slightly higher rate was imposed on self-employed people).

Rising tax rates during the 1930's and 1940's spurred employers to create private pension plans—the second tier of the Social Security system—as tax shelters. Wage-and-price controls encouraged employers to provide benefits in lieu of additional wages. The Revenue Act of 1942 sanctioned the business practice of "integration," that is, restructuring private pension plans to take OASI into account. Increases in OASI coverage and benefits offset costs of integrated plans and spread the costs of the plan to employers who had initially been excluded from the system. In 1949, the Ford Motor Company agreed to finance pensions of $100 per month to workers retiring at the age of sixty-five who had thirty years of service with the company. However, because the company's pension was integrated with OASI, Ford only had to finance part of the $100 pensions. Ford's program set the pattern for American industry. By the late 1950's, more than half of all unionized employees in the United States were covered by integrated plans. By 1974, 46.5 percent of all persons in the private workforce participated in employer-sponsored pension plans.

EARLY RETIREMENT PROGRAMS

In 1964, the first private pension early retirement provisions appeared in the automotive industry, allowing workers to retire with reduced benefits at the age of sixty if they had at least ten years of service and at the age of fifty-five if they had at least thirty years of service. The key was "supplemental" benefits, an additional benefit paid until workers were eligible for OASDI at the age of sixty-two. During the 1973-1974 and 1981-1982 recessions, employers added "sweeteners" to the usual early retirement benefits. These early retirement incentive programs (ERIPs) extended retirement opportunities to otherwise ineligible workers when companies needed to downsize their workforces. With oil prices declining in 1986, for example, the Exxon Corporation offered immediate retirement to employees aged fifty and up who had more than fifteen years of service.

Enactment of the Employee Retirement Income Security Act (ERISA) of 1974 protected employee pension benefit rights and set standards for tax-exempt status and funding levels for pension plans. For many businesses this meant increasing their plan contributions in short order and many did. The percentage of large firms with plans having accrual values at least as great as the values of their liabilities increased from 25 percent in 1978 to 84 percent in 1987.

DEFINED CONTRIBUTION PLANS

ERISA accelerated a shift away from traditional defined benefit plans to defined contribution plans. In defined benefit pension plans, employers make pretax contributions into a pension fund for all participants. Workers are automatically enrolled, face no direct investment risk, and automatically receive payments based on wages and years of service for the rest of their lives after retirement. The Pension Benefit Guaranty Corporation (PBGC) guarantees the benefits within limits and charges insurance premiums intended to cover the plans' anticipated costs. In defined contribution plans—like the popular 401(k) authorized in 1978—workers own their own financial accounts that build value over time. Benefits are not insured, so employers do not pay insurance premiums.

Of benefit plans started before 1941, 10.4 percent were defined contribution, rising to 77.8 percent by 1987. By 1995, nearly 90 percent of all plans (623,912 of 693,404) were defined contribution plans and the number of participants in those plans was nearly double that of those in defined benefits

A 1936 poster urges Americans to apply for Social Security cards. (AP/Wide World Photos)

plans (42.7 million vs. 23.5 million). The growth of 401(k) plans was so substantial after 1984 that by the turn of the twenty-first century, they accounted for 44 percent of defined contribution plans and for about three-fourths of active participants, contributions, and assets in those plans.

Throughout the 1990's, defined contribution plans moved toward cash benefit plans, the first created by Bank of America in 1985, and to a lesser extent to pension equity plans. These hybrid plans were like traditional defined benefit plans in that the employer contributed funds into a general fund for all employees, owned the assets, made the investment choices, and bore the investment risk. Benefits were also guaranteed within PBGC limitations. Like defined contribution plans, however, cash benefit and pension annuity accruals depended on annual pay credits and annual interest credits, with employees bearing the market risk. Cash benefit plan benefits were a function of annual pay over the employee's entire career with the employer; annuity plan benefits were based on a percentage of final average earnings for each year of service under the plan. In 2005, approximately 25 percent of all workers covered by defined benefit plans had a cash balance plan, up from 4 percent in 1996-1997, and they had about 28.8 percent of all defined benefit assets.

As defined contribution plans became more popular, the idea of partially privatizing OASDI as a way to ensure the solvency of its trust fund for future generations was considered during the presidential administrations of Bill Clinton and George W. Bush. Although such plans were not adopted, the financial sector of the business community stood to gain from administering the individual accounts that would have been established. The prospect of making defined benefit payments to retired workers for the remainder of their lives was troublesome for the federal government and employers alike. Lacking the taxing power of government, many businesses took steps to minimize future obligations to retired workers.

Between 2004 and 2006, seventeen large financially healthy companies "froze" their defined benefits plans, closing them either to new employees (for example, Alcoa and Nissan N.A. in 2006, Lockheed Martin Corp. in 2005, and Motorola in 2004), new and some existing employees (for example, Verizon Communications and Sprint Nextel in 2005), or new employees and all existing employees (for ex-

ample, Coca-Cola Bottling Company Consolidated and IBM Corporation in 2006, Sears Holdings Corporation in 2005, and Circuit City Stores in 2004). More than 400,000 persons were affected by the freezes and well in excess of one million workers had 401(k) defined contribution plans instead of defined benefit plans. This shift enabled employers to reduce required contributions from 7 to 8 percent of payrolls to the 3 percent employer match. Employers were also driven to reduce total compensation burdens by rising health care costs, which had increased from 2.4 percent of total compensation in 1970 to 8.4 percent in 2006, the lion's share of which was due not to Medicare contributions but to the cost of group health care, 2 percent in 1970 and 7.2 percent in 2006. Finally, the shift to defined contributions reduced employer risks (economic, demographic, or legislative) associated with funding requirements sufficient to cover future employee benefits.

Richard K. Caputo

FURTHER READING

Berkowitz, Edward, and Kim McQuaid. *Creating the Welfare State: The Political Economy of Twentieth-Century Reform.* New York: Praeger, 1980. Argues for an enhanced role of business in passage of the Social Security Act.

Colin, Gordon. "Why No National Health Insurance in the U.S.? The Limits of Social Provision in War and Peace, 1941-1948." *Journal of Policy History* 9 (July, 1997): 277-310. Shows how business and economic interests limited further expansion of the Social Security Act of 1935 by preventing passage of national health insurance.

Derthick, Martha. *Policymaking for Social Security.* Washington, D.C.: Brookings Institution, 1979. Detailed account of factors conducive to expansion of the Social Security Act.

Gale, William G., John B. Shoven, and Mark J. Warshawsky, eds. *The Evolving Pension System: Trends, Effects, and Proposals for Reform.* Washington, D.C.: Brookings Institution, 2005. Examines trends of private retirement pensions.

Gordon, Colin. "New Deal, Old Deck: Business and the Origins of Social Security, 1920-1935." *Politics & Society* 19 (June, 1991): 165-207. Argues for a modest indirect role of business in the origins of Social Security.

Hacker, Jacob J., and Paul Pierson. "Business Power

and Social Policy: Employers and the Formation of the American Welfare State." *Politics & Society* 30 (June, 2002): 277-325. Argues for a more restricted role of business in passage of the Social Security Act.

Schieber, Sylvester J., and John B. Shoven. *The Real Deal: The History and Future of Social Security.* New Haven, Conn.: Yale University Press, 1999. Shows how business acts as stakeholders in the Social Security system.

Swenson, Peter A. *Capitalists Against Markets: The Making of Labor Markets and Welfare States in the United States and Sweden.* New York: Oxford University Press, 2002. Highlights employer support for development of the welfare state.

SEE ALSO: Ford Motor Company; Government spending; Great Depression; Income tax, personal; Medicare and Medicaid; New Deal programs; Pension and retirement plans; Presidency, U.S.; Privatization; Recession of 1937-1938; Taxation.

Space race

THE EVENT: Competition between the United States and the Soviet Union to be the first to achieve various milestones in spaceflight and exploration

DATE: Mid-1950's to mid-1970's

PLACE: United States and Soviet Union

SIGNIFICANCE: The space race was a boon to the many U.S. aerospace companies that built the necessary hardware. Technical developments and discoveries made as part of the space program led to new products and markets for American consumers. Communications and weather satellites changed the nature of television broadcasting and meteorology. Money flowed to education because of a perceived technology gap, and parts of American industry benefited from space technology spin-offs.

The launching of artificial satellites as part of a study of Earth had been planned for several years by nations participating in the International Geophysical Year, which covered eighteen months in 1957 and 1958. Citizens of the United States were unprepared, however, for the Soviet Union to put the first satellite into orbit on October 4, 1957. At that time,

the United States had launched an ambitious interstate highway transportation network, color television was in many homes, Jonas Salk had created a vaccine against polio, and it seemed that American science and industry were dominant in the world.

Americans largely assumed that their country led the Soviet Union in all fields of technology. Sputnik's launch came as a shock. It caused Americans to wonder what else the Soviets could achieve before the United States. The two nations had been locked in the Cold War since the end of World War II, as each had tried to limit the other's sphere of influence in the world. Both countries had built arsenals of nuclear weapons, and the thought was inevitable that a country that could put an object in space could also deliver a nuclear bomb across an ocean.

THE RACE IS ON

Congress reacted by passing the National Defense Education Act of 1958, authorizing more than $1 billion for a variety of educational initiatives, such as building new schools, offering financial aid for promising technology students, and supporting more classes in mathematics and physical science. Money began to flow to the educational establishment, from the childhood level through postgraduate, but mostly in the areas of science and technology.

President Dwight D. Eisenhower signed into law on July 29, 1959, an act creating the National Aeronautics and Space Administration (NASA). Its predecessor, the National Advisory Committee for Aeronautics, had been running on a $5 million annual budget; the NASA budget quickly grew to $5 billion, much of which went to private contractors and boosted the aerospace business significantly.

Not all the members of the Eisenhower administration were displeased about Sputnik. They believed that, because the satellite passed over many countries while in orbit, its launch would preclude future Soviet objections to U.S. spy satellites passing over the Soviet Union. The same logic would help clear the way for orbiting communications and weather satellites.

The Soviets launched a second Sputnik thirty days after the first, this one carrying a living animal, a dog, on a one-way trip to provide data about the effects of space travel on living creatures. The U.S.

Navy's more sophisticated Vanguard satellite was scheduled to be launched on December 4, 1957, but it exploded two seconds after launch. It was not until February 1, 1958, that the United States successfully orbited a satellite. On December 18, 1958, a U.S. satellite broadcast a Christmas greeting by the president from space. In 1959, the Soviets launched the first space probe to impact the Moon.

On July 26, 1963, the United States put Syncom-2, the first geosynchronous satellite, into orbit. A geosynchronous satellite orbits Earth at the same speed as Earth turns, remaining in a fixed orbit over a single location on the ground. This technology led to the development of satellite television, allowing home television customers to purchase dishes that could focus on "stationary" satellites to receive television transmissions.

On April 12, 1961, Soviet major Yuri Gagarin became the first man in space, when he made a single orbit of Earth and returned safely. The first American in space, Alan Shepherd, rode a spacecraft on May 5, 1961, but did not orbit. John Glenn became the first American to orbit the planet on February 20, 1962. The Shepherd and Glenn flights were among those used to develop the hardware and techniques required for a piloted Moon landing, the goal set by President John F. Kennedy, Eisenhower's successor.

Kennedy ordered his vice president, Lyndon B. Johnson, chairman of the National Aeronautics and Space Council, to come up with a way to counter the Soviet successes in space. Johnson's proposal was to put an American on the Moon before the end of the decade and return him safely to Earth. Kennedy publicly announced this goal in a speech before Congress on May 25, 1961.

Thus, the space race, which had included launches of satellites and humans into space, settled into a Moon race for the remainder of the 1960's. The U.S. Apollo program sent several astronaut teams into orbit around the Moon, and a successful landing was made on July 20, 1969, with astronauts Neil Armstrong and Buzz Aldrin stepping down from their landing craft. Five other pairs of U.S. astronauts made Moon landings after that, the last in 1972.

The program generated advances in many fields, including avionics, engineering, telecommunications, and computing. Computers went from the size of small buildings to laptops and handheld devices, thanks largely to the miniaturization necessary to limit the poundage of piloted and unpiloted space probes. Flight computers designed for the Moon landings spurred early research into integrated circuits. The fuel cell also grew out of this program, as did computer-controlled machining, later widely used in manufacturing industries. Microtechnology developed in the space program has led to business applications ranging from time-keeping to downloading music.

A dramatic moment in the space race was astronaut Buzz Aldrin's walk on the moon. (NASA)

SPIN-OFF TECHNOLOGIES

In 1962, NASA created the Technology Utilization Program, aimed at disseminating information about space technologies to the scientific community and furthering the development of commercial products in the private sector. The program was initially supported by four industrial applications centers, a number that had increased to ten by the 1980's.

After the effort to spin off space technologies for applications in a variety of businesses and industries, NASA began issuing Technology Utilization Program reports in 1973 as part of its presentations at annual congressional budget hearings. These reports proved popular enough to generate an annual book describing the space program's industrial and commercial spin-offs. The first volume was published in 1976. Copies were sent to private company executives, technology transfer professionals, economic decision makers, academics, and other groups. Since the book was first published in 1976, more than fifteen hundred NASA technologies have been listed as creating jobs, benefiting industry, and improving the quality of life in the nation.

Early U.S. Moon missions orbited the Moon to seek suitable landing sites for future missions. To help achieve this goal, NASA scientists developed computer-aided topography (CAT) and magnetic resonance imaging (MRI). Both technologies were adopted for medical applications and came to be used in hospitals throughout the world. CAT scans allow painless X-ray imaging, more clear than traditional X-ray imaging, of internal organs to diagnose problems ranging from cancer and cardiovascular diseases to muscle or bone trauma. MRIs also provide detailed internal images, using no radiation, to delineate the structure of the body. Other medical procedures growing out of the space program include needle breast biopsies and a type of kidney dialysis machine. Cardiovascular conditioners, made to keep astronauts fit in zero-gravity conditions, have led to the development of physical therapy devices used by athletes and medical rehabilitation centers.

Astronauts needed a way to keep food fresh on long flights, such as Moon orbits or landings. NASA's solution to this problem was to freeze-dry the food, using a technique similar to that employed to preserve blood plasma during World War II. Freeze-dried foods would come to be found in many homes. Conventional power tools of the 1960's were not practical for use on the Moon. There was no place to plug them in. NASA created cordless tools that relied on such power as rechargeable batteries, eventually spawning the cordless power tool industry.

Space suits had to be made of new materials to protect astronauts from the extreme hot and cold temperatures of space. These materials were later used to manufacture clothing for such groups as nuclear-reactor technicians, race car drivers, shipyard workers, and people with diseases such as multiple sclerosis.

By the early twenty-first century, more than one thousand satellites were in orbit around Earth, relaying communications, tracking vegetation, and providing climate data, among other functions. The conclusion of the space race between the two international superpowers is generally dated to July 17, 1975, when a linkup between an Apollo craft and a Soviet Soyuz craft was made as part of a joint space mission. The Soviets claimed to have won the race by placing the first man in space, and the United States made the same claim based on landing the first humans on the Moon. After the collapse of the Soviet Union in 1991, the United States and Russia joined other nations in such space ventures as the International Space Station, where scientific research is done in a space environment.

The Hubble Space Telescope, put into orbit in 1990, is mainly known for the unprecedented clarity of its images of astronomical objects. It, too, has spun off technologies used in commercial enterprises, such as digital images of breast biopsies capable of replacing surgical biopsies as a diagnostic tool to check on tumors.

Also in 1990, Japan became the third nation to launch an unmanned flyby rocket to the Moon. Thus, the space race may be continuing, as other nations develop the technology to achieve space "firsts" and spin off still more technologies as space exploration continues.

Paul Dellinger

FURTHER READING

Bizony, Piers. *Space: Fifty Years of the Space Age.* Washington, D.C.: Smithsonian, 2006. Starting with Sputnik, this book gives an overview of the first fifty years of the space age and projects what might happen in space over the next fifty years.

Cadbury, Deborah. *Space Race: The Epic Battle Between America and the Soviet Union for Dominion of Space.* New York: HarperCollins, 2006. Focuses on Wernher von Braun, arguably the best-known face of the U.S. space program, and Sergei Korolev, the Soviet rocket designer who headed his country's space program for two decades. Covers rocket research dating back to Germany's rocket weapons in World War II and how it helped pave the way for the lunar landings.

Chaikin, Andrew. *A Man on the Moon: The Voyages of the Apollo Astronauts.* New York: Penguin, 2007. Provided the basis for the twelve-part 1998 HBO miniseries *From the Earth to the Moon*, coproduced by actor Tom Hanks (who provides a foreword). Chaikin interviewed all twenty-four of the lunar astronauts and many others to compile information about the Apollo program; also touches on the earlier Mercury and Gemini programs.

Cooper, Henry S. F. *Thirteen: The Apollo Flight That Failed.* Minneapolis: Tandem Library, 1995. Shows how the people on the ground in Mission Control worked with the three Apollo 13 astronauts to bring them safely back to Earth after an accident in space that riveted world attention.

Dickson, Paul. *Sputnik: The Shock of the Century.* New York: Walker, 2007. Details the creation and launch of the Soviet Union's Sputnik and the space race that resulted, including its economic, political, and social implications; provides as background a history of all the research preceding the launch.

Moore, Sir Patrick, and H. J. P. Arnold. *Space: The First Fifty Years.* London: Mitchell Beazley, 2007. Covers the space race from the first Soviet satellite through the Apollo flights to the Moon, with additional details about space stations and unmanned probes.

Tobias, Russell R., and David G. Fisher, eds. *USA in Space.* 3d ed. Pasadena, Calif.: Salem Press, 2006. Comprehensive coverage of every major program, mission, craft, and center in the American space program.

SEE ALSO: Education; Inventions; National Science Foundation; Presidency, U.S.

Spanish-American War

THE EVENT: Conflict between the United States and Spain fought primarily over the issue of Cuban independence from the Spanish

DATE: April 25-August 12, 1898

PLACE: Cuba, Puerto Rico, the Philippines, and the Pacific Ocean

SIGNIFICANCE: Dubbed the "Splendid Little War" because of its brevity and excellent results for American interests, the Spanish-American War is often viewed as one of the key events in the American rise to international power. American participation in the war resulted, in large measure, from the activities and pressure brought to bear by business magnates and government officials who favored vast development of the U.S. military as a precursor to expanding American economic markets and political interests abroad, especially in Asia.

In the decades before the Spanish-American War, the U.S. economy was plagued by the national debt, resulting in large measure from the U.S. Civil War, a downturn in agricultural prices, high unemployment due to the failure of many railroads, the demise of those investors and banks that had paid for the railroads, the declining value of stocks, and little growth in domestic markets. Business leaders, government officials, and academics teamed together to find viable markets abroad. The ideas of one thinker in particular, Frederick Jackson Turner, caught the attention of businessmen, politicians, military leaders, and missionaries alike. Turner asserted that by the 1890's the American frontier had disappeared and that it was essential for Americans to maintain a frontier spirit, if the nation was to survive.

Soon, new views of Manifest Destiny, as well as Turner's thoughts, had been adopted by leading members of the Republican Party, among them Theodore Roosevelt, William McKinley, Henry Cabot Lodge, and John Hay. Republicans combined the concept of Manifest Destiny with Turner's theories and then added some of the opinions of Captain Alfred Mahan, who advocated that the United States construct a world-class "blue-water" navy, capable of operating effectively in international settings. In his work, *The Influence of Sea Power upon History, 1600-1783* (1890), Mahan had argued for the need to annex certain Caribbean islands, Hawaii, and the Philippines to protect U.S. commercial interests.

With McKinley as their candidate, the Republicans prepared a winning platform for the presidential election of 1896. It called for building a "steel and blue-water" navy, constructing an isthmian canal somewhere in the Western Hemisphere, obtaining access to foreign markets through reciprocal trade agreements, annexing Hawaii, and seeking new markets in Asia. McKinley easily defeated his Democratic opponent, William Jennings Bryan, and won the presidency.

THE PATH OF THE WAR

Ongoing Cuban rebellions such as the Ten Years' War and the uprising of 1895 caught the attention of American businessmen and government officials. American investments on the island had reached approximately $50 million, and import-export trade with Cuba in 1896 totaled some $100 million. The American business community feared that armed rebellion might disrupt trade and urged President McKinley to intervene in the situation. Reports of Spanish cruelty in Cuba were being funneled from the island to jingoistic American journalists, who, with their special brand of "yellow journalism," highlighted the worst of the Cuban condition.

The explosion of the U.S. battleship *Maine* on February 15, 1898, was the determining factor in pushing the nation into war. The final report of the investigatory commission of the Judge Advocate of the Navy found that the explosion had been caused by a mine. The commission found insufficient evidence to fix responsibility for the explosion on any person or entity, but U.S. public opinion had been whipped into a frenzy, as yellow journalists blamed the Spanish.

The United States declared war on Spain on April 25, 1898. Congress immediately appropriated $50 million to be used at the president's discretion and authorized the use of tariffs and a national inheritance tax to fund the war effort. A maximum rate of 15 percent was applied to estates valued over $1 million that were left to distant relatives, nonrelatives, or other entities. Military defeat of the Spaniards was quick. Spain and the United States signed a peace protocol ending the conflict on August 12, 1898.

MILITARY COST OF SPANISH-AMERICAN WAR, 1898-1899

- In current year dollars = $283 million

- In constant fiscal year (2008) dollars = $6,848 million

- War cost as percentage of gross domestic product in peak year, 1899 = 1.1%

- Total defense cost as percentage of gross domestic product in peak year, 1899 = 1.5%

Source: Data from Stephen Daggett, "CROS Report for Congress: Costs of Major U.S. Wars," Congressional Research Service, July 24, 2008

AFTERMATH

Economic and political benefits of the war were abundant for the United States. In July, McKinley had authorized the annexation of Hawaii. Under the terms of the Treaty of Paris, signed on December 10, 1898, Spain immediately ceded its colonies of Cuba, Puerto Rico, and Guam to American control and soon sold the Philippines at a cost of $20 million. As a result, the United States came to enjoy a foothold in Asia, a stronger presence in the Caribbean in Puerto Rico, and relations with a friendly power in Cuba, which was guaranteed its independence. McKinley undertook his plan to build an isthmian canal, which resulted directly in the building of the Panama Canal. The U.S. economy was now booming. The nation's international prestige grew, and the United States was on course to become a great power. The direct cost of the war was approximately $283 million.

Mark DeStephano

FURTHER READING

Cosmas, Graham A. *An Army for Empire: The United States Army in the Spanish-American War.* Columbia: University of Missouri Press, 1971. Detailed and carefully documented history and analysis of the role of the Army in every aspect of the war; an indispensable source.

McCartney, Paul T. *Power and Progress: American National Identity, the War of 1898, and the Rise of American Imperialism.* Baton Rouge: Louisiana State

University Press, 2007. This excellent work situates the war in its cultural context and considers the important role played by the search for American national identity.

Musicant, Ivan. *Empire by Default: The Spanish-American War and the Dawn of the American Century.* New York: Henry Holt, 1998. Perhaps the finest analysis to date of the causes of the war, its conduct, and its end results.

Offner, John L. *An Unwanted War: The Diplomacy of the United States and Spain over Cuba, 1895-1898.* Chapel Hill: University of North Carolina Press, 1992. Interesting comparison of the events leading up to this "unwanted" war, from both the American and the Spanish perspectives.

O'Toole, G. J. A. *The Spanish War: An American Epic, 1898.* New York: W. W. Norton, 1984. This study not only offers a clear chronology of the events leading up to and during the war but also provides significant insights into the period that are abundantly documented through personal correspondence.

SEE ALSO: Asian trade with the United States; European trade with the United States; Latin American trade with the United States; Panama Canal; Wars.

Sports, intercollegiate

DEFINITION: Sports played at the amateur level, between colleges

SIGNIFICANCE: Intercollegiate sports competitions generate considerable revenue in the United States, particularly through television revenue for basketball and football, as well as through the licensing of clothing and other promotional items. However, the businesslike aspects of college sports are at odds with their amateur status, and critics point to the costs of running these popular programs in the face of declining college budgets.

During the nineteenth century, college sports were generally informal in nature, with the students themselves organizing and running the teams. The first major scandal reported in college sports occurred in 1904, when *McClure's Magazine* printed an exposé on Yale football captain James Hogan's arrangement with the university, in which he was given free meals, a percentage of the profits from the sale of game programs, all profits from American Tobacco Company products sold on campus, and a trip to Cuba.

THE NCAA

After a series of college football deaths during the early twentieth century, President Theodore Roosevelt created the Intercollegiate Athletic Association to discuss safety in college sports. This commission grew and became the National Collegiate Athletic Association (NCAA) in 1910.

By the 1920's, college sports had increased in popularity and commercialism. They became even more of a business in the postwar era, when, thanks to the G.I. Bill, colleges had more students (and therefore more fans for their alma mater) than ever before. In response to this trend toward commercialization, the NCAA gradually shifted its focus from safety to maintaining the amateur status of college athletes by keeping college sports part of the education program and college athletes part of the student body. In 1948, the NCAA created the short-lived Sanity Code, which set academic standards for athletes and created guidelines for recruitment and compensation given to athletes. It was repealed in 1951.

With the advent of television during the 1950's, the first contracts for broadcasting games were drawn up with the NCAA. Money from early television broadcasts of games allowed the NCAA to create a headquarters and hire a full-time director. The extra revenue also allowed the NCAA to begin enforcing rules and investigating violators more easily. In the first few decades of televised college sports, the NCAA had sole authority over how many times a particular college could be showcased on television broadcasts, how much of the revenue the college would receive, and how it would be received.

During the 1970's, individual colleges and conferences wanted to begin negotiating their own television deals to make more money for themselves. In *NCAA v. Board of Regents of the University of Oklahoma et al.* (1984), the U.S. Supreme Court ruled that the NCAA had violated antitrust laws by not allowing its members to negotiate their own television contracts. With this ruling, schools and conferences began negotiating their own television deals, although the NCAA still received some of the revenue.

In 1972, Title IX required that universities receiving federal funding equally support men and women athletes. Before Title IX, few colleges had women's sports programs, but the number of female college athletes has grown steadily since its implementation. A 2007 study by the Women's Sports Foundation noted that the amount of operating expenses devoted to women's sports and the number of scholarships awarded to female athletes was not equivalent to the money and scholarships received by men's sports and male athletes at the college level. Opponents to Title IX argue that women's collegiate sports do not generate as much television revenue as men's collegiate sports do, and this inequity is justified as it support the financial health of the college. However, this argument directly conflicts with the NCAA's stated mission of stressing the amateur and educational benefit of sports for college students.

A recruiting scandal and allegations of financial mismanagement at the University of Colorado at Boulder in 2004 resulted in the resignations of football coach Gary Barnett, shown at a 2004 game; twenty-year athletic director Dick Tharp; and, the following year, UC system president Elizabeth Hoffman. (AP/Wide World Photos)

SCANDALS AND PENALTIES

After a number of scandals, including the revelations during the 1980's that Southern Methodist University was paying its players through their football boosters, the NCAA first used the Death Penalty, cancelling Southern Methodist University's entire 1987 football season. It also began setting down academic standards for student athletes, as it had with the earlier Sanity Code. These new standards required student athletes to maintain a 2.0 grade-point average.

Despite the use of the Death Penalty and the setting of academic standards, schools continued to violate NCAA rules by making payments to athletes and letting them play even if their grade-point averages were too low. It was discovered in 2002 that University of Michigan booster Ed Martin had given college basketball star (and future National Basketball Association player) Chris Webber thousands of dollars in 1994. In 1998, the Texas Tech football team was penalized for allowing a player who had a 0.0 grade-point average to remain on the team.

As college sports programs grew, so did the cost of maintaining them. Despite the money made from television and licensing, most college sports programs do not make enough from these revenues to support their programs and draw additional money from the college, including money from student fees. Smaller conferences in the NCAA, which has 1,250 member colleges, are particularly hit hard because they cannot negotiate as profitable television deals as those drawn by the larger, more high-profile conferences. This problem has continued to grow throughout the 1990's and into the early twenty-first century.

Julie Elliott

FURTHER READING

Estler, Suzanne E., and Laurie J. Nelson. *Who Calls the Shots? Sports and University Leadership, Culture, and Decision Making.* San Francisco: Wiley Subscription Services, 2005. Examines the economic and intellectual forces that act on colleges and influence decision making. Includes a discussion of gender in the formation of college athletics.

Lapchick, Richard E., ed. *New Game Plan for College*

Sports. Westport, Conn.: Praeger, 2006. Series of essays on various aspects of college sports, focusing on the economic and ethical aspects.

Sack, Allen L., and Ellen J. Staurowsky. *College Athletes for Hire*. Westport, Conn.: Praeger, 1998. Provides a strong overview of the early history of the NCAA and a two-tiered solution to problems with scandals in college sports, which includes allowing some schools to field semiprofessional teams with paid athletes.

Sperber, Murray. *Beer and Circus*. New York: Owl Books, 2000. Sperber looks at the current university situation regarding undergraduate education and college sports, arguing that the universities are spending more on athletics to the detriment of academics.

Zimbalist, Andrew. *Unpaid Professionals*. Princeton, N.J.: Princeton University Press, 1999. Looks at the history of college sports and notes how the NCAA and the increase in media attention to college sports are turning into a growing problem for colleges across the country. Includes a ten-point plan for fixing the problem.

SEE ALSO: Education; Gambling industry; Sports franchises; Television broadcasting industry.

Sports franchises

DEFINITION: Professional athletic teams playing in one of the major sports leagues governing team competition

SIGNIFICANCE: Once a secondary financial investment by wealthy fans, ownership of professional sports teams has been transformed into a major business. Moreover, the financial benefits of hosting professional teams and sporting events has led to increasing efforts by city governments to attract and keep such franchises.

Professional sports in the United States began in the last half of the nineteenth century and the early part of the twentieth century. Although many early professional sports associations failed and neither owners nor athletes tended to make much money, efforts to make such leagues successful continued. In regard to team sports, franchise owners were typically wealthy fans who also had other businesses to offset financial losses from their sports teams. As the country became richer and cities grew, interest in spectator sports increased. By the last quarter of the twentieth century, professional athletics had become a very lucrative business. Both owners and athletes frequently earned very large amounts of money.

PROFESSIONAL BASEBALL

Professional athletics were not immediately successful in the United States. Leagues often failed, and ownership of a club was a very risky business investment. In 1869, professional baseball was the first professional team sport to emerge. Two years later, the first professional baseball league, the National Association was formed, but it lasted for only a short time. In 1876, the National League replaced it. During these initial years, professional baseball struggled financially. Owners of teams suffered from bad reputations.

In 1882, a new league, first known as the American Association, formed. It challenged the National League by having lower ticket prices and locating teams in big cities. In 1903, after changing its name to the American League, it made an agreement with the National League, and together the two eventually became known as Major League Baseball (MLB). By this time, professional baseball had become quite popular. Some teams became worth large amounts of money and star players were becoming relatively wealthy.

As a result of the relative financial success of professional baseball, a significant issue arose that would later become relevant to all team sports: the regulation of player movement and compensation. All other industries were required to adhere to the Sherman Antitrust Act of 1890, which outlawed collusion between multiple companies in a given industry to set prices. In 1922, professional baseball's method of regulating players was challenged in a U.S. Supreme Court case, *Federal Baseball Club v. the National League.*

The Court upheld the heavily regulated method used by professional baseball, ruling that it was an amusement and not a traditional business, thereby meriting an exemption from the Sherman Act. As a result, the use of the reserve clause remained legal. This meant that when a player's contract expired, the team with whom the contract was signed still retained the rights to the player. The other, professional team sports in the United States would use the reserve clause as well.

Two major developments came in later decades—the construction of new stadiums and television. Beginning during the 1960's, a trend emerged in regard to the building design of stadiums. Unlike older structures that were typically constructed solely with private funds, the new stadiums were often built by cities and then rented to football and baseball teams, as they were designed to accommodate both sports. The municipalities earned revenue from advertising and the sale of concessions. This trend continued through the 1970's.

Television had a major impact on all of the four major team sports. Eventually, it became another source of revenue for all of them. Teams in larger markets, however, would develop an advantage, especially when the cable television boom emerged during the late 1970's, as those franchises could negotiate individual contracts with local cable stations.

As the bargaining power of players increased, the athletes were able to challenge owners more easily. These disagreements, however, led to multiple work stoppages in all four of the major team sports. The Major League Baseball Players Association experienced three work stoppages during the 1970's. It was the third that had the greatest impact. Though no games were canceled, the lockout of 1976 was significant because it resulted in the creation of free agency. This led to substantial increase in the salaries of good players. Though baseball experienced additional work stoppages, the popularity of the sport increased. In 1981, a strike led to the cancellation of seven weeks of games. Despite this, Major League Baseball recovered, and revenue increased nearly fourfold between 1975 and 1984, to $624 million. Furthermore, the average player's salary increased to approximately $330,000 by the mid-1980's.

Major League Baseball experienced its longest work stoppage during the mid-1990's. In August, 1994, fearing the adoption of a salary cap, players went on strike. The league failed to resolve the dispute by the end of the season, and the remaining games were canceled, including the World Series. An agreement was not reached until April, 1995, resulting in the cancellation of the first three weeks of games for the 1995 season as well. Major League Baseball survived the season-ending strike. During the early twenty-first century, although ratings and attendance declined slightly, the league still enjoyed a national broadcasting contract with the FOX network. Its players earned an average salary of $2.5 million, and the lack of a salary cap made it difficult for smaller-market teams to compete.

PROFESSIONAL HOCKEY

The first professional hockey league emerged in the United States in 1904. The International Professional Hockey League folded after just three years. In 1910, the National Hockey Association was formed. For years, it had only six teams, with four in the United States and two in Canada. Eventually the National Hockey League (NHL) came on the scene.

Owners of NHL teams were making significant profits during the late 1950's, but the players were paid low salaries. As a result, players attempted to form a union. Their efforts, however, were blocked. In 1967, the players' second effort at forming a union succeeded, as the National Hockey League Players' Association (NHLPA) came into existence. The NHL was also challenged by the formation of new professional leagues during the 1960's. In re-

A professional baseball player from the Red Sox in 1916. (Library of Congress)

sponse, the league doubled its number of franchises in 1967, with each new team paying $2 million to join.

The most significant challenge to the NHL by a competitor occurred during the 1970's. The World Hockey Association (WHA) formed in 1972. Once again, the NHL's response was expansion. In 1979, the two leagues merged, with four teams from the WHA joining the NHL.

The NHL adopted a major plan of expansion during the late 1980's. The league made this decision because of the increase in popularity of hockey during the decade. Each new franchise was required to pay $50 million. This figure far exceeded the $32 million that the National Basketball Association (NBA) was charging new clubs at the same time.

The NHL experienced a major labor-management disagreement concurrent with the one in the MLB that ended its 1994 season. The NHL owners imposed a lockout prior to the 1994-1995 season. As a result, the first half of the season was canceled, as an agreement was not reached until January 1995.

The most significant work stoppage in the history of American professional sports occurred in 2004-2005. The entire NHL season was canceled. When the strike was resolved, a salary cap was imposed, aimed at helping the small-market teams. Television exposure was reduced, however, as sports cable network ESPN no longer covered the league's games.

PROFESSIONAL FOOTBALL

The National Football League (NFL) was created in 1920. Probably more than any other sport, football was indebted to television for its rise in popularity. Television had a major impact on professional sports, as it provided another source of revenue. Related to this, the NFL implemented one of the most innovative business ideas in the history of professional sports during the early 1960's. Its teams agreed to divide the money earned from television broadcasts of their games. This became known as revenue sharing. The policy meant that teams agreed not to negotiate individual television contracts. Instead, the NFL, along with the other professional sports leagues, could negotiate television contracts as a single entity. To do so, Commissioner Pete Rozelle successfully lobbied Congress

to grant the league an exemption to the Sherman Antitrust Act.

This exemption facilitated revenue sharing, which was adopted as a way to achieve more competitive balance among the league's teams. The first television contract to broadcast NFL games following Rozelle's lobbying was given to the Columbia Broadcasting System (CBS) for $4.65 million in 1962. Just two years later, it increased to $14.1 million. Television played an important role in the rise in popularity of the league. In 1961, the NFL also acted to officially recognize the community ownership model of the Green Bay Packers, the only professional team in the four major professional sports that is operated in this manner. The NFL does not permit any other franchise to be publicly owned.

The television contract helped create a competitive and popular league. The 1980's, however, was a tumultuous decade for the sport. The league experienced two major disruptions in 1982 and 1987. In each season, the players went on strike, leading to significant work stoppages and adjustments. In 1982, seven weeks of games were canceled. At the time, the average player's salary was $120,000. In 1987, another strike occurred because of the disagreement over free agency. Only one week of games was canceled, but replacement players were used the following three weeks until the strike ended.

Regardless of the work stoppages, the league remained popular. The NFL's increase in popularity had an impact on television too. When ESPN acquired the rights to broadcast Sunday night games in 1987, it became a major success. The network would eventually create ESPN2 and other channels. The same result occurred when FOX acquired the rights to broadcast NFL games in 1994. The new network obtained several new affiliates after doing so, whereas CBS, which lost its rights to FOX, also lost affiliates.

The disagreement over free agency was finally resolved in 1993. NFL players were granted free agency in that year. Furthermore, they were guaranteed a percentage of the league's gross revenue. In return, the owners were allowed to adopt a salary cap.

The NFL has arguably been the most successful of the four major professional sports leagues. For example, the television rights for broadcasting NFL games are the largest and most expensive of any sport. According to the current contract, five networks pay a combined total of $21.4 billion over six years (2006-2011) to broadcast league games. The networks are CBS, FOX, the National Broadcasting Company (NBC), ESPN, and the NFL Network. In addition, sharing of all revenue is in place. Furthermore, the average player's salary in 2005 was nearly $1.4 million.

PROFESSIONAL BASKETBALL

The National Basketball Association (NBA) was formed in 1949. Though the league did well during its first few decades, trouble eventually developed. During the 1970's, the NBA struggled as the popularity of the league declined. Low television ratings led CBS to decline live broadcasts of the NBA finals during the week in 1980 and 1981. Instead, those games were shown on tape delay after the local news in the eastern and central time zones.

During the mid-1980's, the NBA regained popularity. Great players such as Michael Jordan, Larry Bird, and Earvin "Magic" Johnson helped attract fans, but the policies of Commissioner David Stern also played a role. After taking the position in 1984, he pursued new policies that helped boost the financial status of NBA franchises. They included the salary cap and greater marketing of the association. From 1986 to 1990, CBS paid $173 million to broadcast league games, almost twice as much as the previous four-year contract.

A major work stoppage occurred in 1998. The owners imposed a lockout, which lasted until January, 1999. The first half of the season was canceled. The league eventually recovered from the stoppage. It has the highest average player's salary of any league, at $4.9 million.

By the end of the 1990's, the popularity of professional sports also created some problems for their fans. One was the price of tickets. During the decade, ticket prices increased by three times the country's inflation rate. When concessions were added, the average cost for a family of four to attend an NBA game was $267 in 1999, a 31 percent increase since 1995.

An additional issue was the use of public money to pay for expensive new venues. Owners were using fan loyalty to request increasingly more public money to help finance the construction of arenas and stadiums, which increased dramatically. If they did not receive the money, they would threaten to move the franchise, and sometimes acted on their threats. The design of the new stadiums also became an issue. Many of them included luxurious "sky boxes." The owners were able to make more money by having fewer people in attendance but charging more for luxury seats, which were beyond the finances of average fans.

The dominance of professional leagues in the United States and Canada was also challenged. Basketball and hockey leagues in Europe are beginning to attract some of the top players in their games. Seven players from the NBA agreed to play for professional teams in Europe after the 2007-2008 season.

Despite the challenges to the NBA and the NHL by European leagues, American professional sports were generally thriving during the early twenty-first century. Between 2000 and 2004, the number of people attending sporting events rose by more than 10 percent. The NFL has increased its revenue to $7.6 billion. Furthermore, the last team to join the league paid $700 million to do so, a fivefold increase in a five-year period. As of 2008, hockey was the only major sport that lacked a lucrative television contract. Approximately one-quarter of NHL franchises were struggling financially.

Kevin L. Brennan

FURTHER READING

Conrad, Mark. *The Business of Sports: A Primer for Journalists.* Mahwah, N.J.: Lawrence Erlbaum Associates, 2006. Thorough coverage of the financial aspect of sports. Topics include the structure of the various professional sports leagues, the relationship between players and owners, and the business component of college athletics and the Olympics.

Danielson, Michael N. *Home Team: Professional Sports and the American Metropolis.* Princeton, N.J.: Princeton University Press, 2001. Examines the links between the four major professional team sports leagues and their teams' hometowns. It analyzes the role of government in attracting and keeping franchises in their respective areas.

Euchner, Charles C. *Playing the Field: Why Sports Teams Move and Cities Fight to Keep Them.* Baltimore: Johns Hopkins University Press, 1994. Focusing on three case studies, the book examines the leverage owners of professional sports teams have over local governments.

Fort, Rodney D., and James Quirk. *Pay Dirt: The Business of Professional Team Sports.* Princeton, N.J.: Princeton University Press, 1992. Historical overview of how the four major professional team sports became big businesses.

Mangan, James A., and Paul D. Staudohar, eds. *The Business of Professional Sports.* Champaign: University of Illinois Press, 1991. A collection of essays that address contemporary issues in the business aspect of professional sports.

SEE ALSO: Advertising industry; Baseball strike of 1972; Education; Sports, intercollegiate; Television broadcasting industry.

Stagecoach line, first

IDENTIFICATION: Regularly scheduled stagecoach line in New Jersey that acted as the American colonies' first public transport system

DATE: Started in 1732 or 1733

SIGNIFICANCE: The North American colonies' first regularly scheduled stagecoach line helped New Jersey residents market their products, provided a vital link on the route between New York City and Philadelphia, and encouraged the establishment of numerous subsidiary enterprises.

New Jersey's earliest European settlers used the paths created by the Lenape, the Native Americans living in the area. During the early eighteenth century, the colony began building "common highways," and by mid-century, it could boast more roads than any other colony. Among the earliest conveyances using these rudimentary roads were Jersey wagons—lumbering, long-bodied, canvas-topped vehicles with wide wheels designed to negotiate the region's soft, sandy soil. These wagons required four- and six-horse teams to pull them. Soon primitive stagecoaches, smaller versions of the Jersey wagon, were built to haul passengers as well as merchandise. They lacked windows and doors, and passengers sat on benches along the sides. Their lack of springs resulted in rides so bumpy that on occasion passengers were knocked unconscious.

In 1732 or 1733, Burlington entrepreneurs Solomon Smith and Thomas Moore (some sources name Smith and James Moon) set up a regular schedule of stagecoach runs over a northeast-southwest route known as Lawrie's Road. The service linked the New Jersey towns of Perth Amboy, a port at the mouth of the Raritan River not far from New York City, and Burlington, a port on the Delaware River upstream from Philadelphia. The line owned two coaches and seems to have made one run in each direction each week, although an advertisement in the Philadelphia *Mercury* promised more runs as needed. It is usually regarded as the first public transport system in the American colonies.

At about the same time, another line began regular service to New Brunswick, New Jersey, upriver from Perth Amboy, and by 1734, Smith and his partner, or one of their competitors, had added service to Bordentown, New Jersey, upriver from Burlington. A Trenton, New Jersey, to New Brunswick service was set up in about 1738, and a South Amboy-Bordentown service began in 1740. In each case "stage-boats" completed the connections by water to New York and Philadelphia. Much as road building had encouraged transportation, regular stagecoach runs encouraged the construction of taverns along their routes, and such establishments quickly became centers of social and business life. In fact, James Moon, presumably the same individual sometimes identified as Smith's partner, is recorded as the licensee of a tavern in Burlington in 1732. Another early source lists Smith and Moore as offering an additional service to their customers—a secure storehouse, where merchants could deposit goods awaiting transport.

Grove Koger

FURTHER READING

Fleming, Thomas J. *New Jersey: A History.* New York and Nashville: Norton and the American Association for State and Local History, 1984.

Holmes, Oliver W., and Peter Rohrbach. *Stagecoach East: Stagecoach Days in the East from the Colonial Period to the Civil War.* Washington, D.C.: Smithsonian Institution Press, 1983.

Streissguth, Thomas. *New Jersey.* San Diego, Calif.: Lucent Books, 2002.

SEE ALSO: Canals; Cumberland Road; Erie Canal; Highways; Horses; Hotel and motel industry; Pony Express; Postal Service, U.S.

Stamp Act of 1765

THE LAW: British law imposing taxes on American printed publications and documents by requiring them to bear official stamps

DATE: Went into effect on November 1, 1765

SIGNIFICANCE: The Stamp Act was effectively resisted and had little direct effect on American business. However, attempts to enforce it and the fury surrounding its adoption disrupted commerce. It provoked a series of nonimportation agreements in the colonies, temporarily halting much American trade with Great Britain.

The Stamp Act was passed by the British House of Commons on February 7, 1765, as part of British prime minister George Grenville's attempt to restore government solvency after the massive expenditures of the Seven Years' War. Lobbying against the act by colonial agents, including Benjamin Franklin, proved ineffective. There were ample precedents for stamp taxes in Britain itself, and the rates Americans would pay would be lower than those of Britons. In the American colonies themselves, the act was resisted on the grounds that the British parliament, in which colonists were not represented, had no right to tax the colonies. Resistance took the form of resolutions by colonial legislatures and the Stamp Act Congress, which met in New York City. The act was also resisted more violently by the Sons of Liberty, an underground group that attacked those designated to distribute stamps and other British government officials. Nonimportation agreements, organized boycotts of British goods, also helped persuade British merchants to lobby for repeal of the act. Organized resistance between colonies during the Stamp Act crisis helped set precedents for the American Revolution.

Grenville's government fell in July, 1764, before the Stamp Act went into effect. The new government led by the Marquis of Rockingham, a sympathizer with the colonies, repealed the act on March 18, 1766, while reserving the right to tax the colonies.

William E. Burns

SEE ALSO: Boston Tea Party; Boycotts, consumer; Navigation Acts; Parliamentary Charter of 1763; Revolutionary War; Taxation; Tea Act of 1773; Townshend Act.

Standard & Poor's

IDENTIFICATION: Financial services company that provides financial and credit information on a variety of industries and individual companies to other financial institutions, companies, and individual investors

DATE: Founded in 1941

SIGNIFICANCE: Standard & Poor's is one of the three largest financial information providers in the United States. It also provides long- and short-term credit ratings on individual companies.

The roots of Standard & Poor's trace back to 1860, when Henry Poor compiled into book format information about the economic status and range of operations of all U.S. railroads. The information was updated and published annually. Given the speed with which some railroads formed, laid track, and went bankrupt, annual updates were not sufficient to keep investors informed of the situation. In 1906, Luther Blake founded the Standard Statistics Bureau. He began publishing on five-by-seven-inch cards financial information about all types of nonrailroad companies. His information specifically covered mining and mercantile concerns both in the East and on the West Coast. These cards were updated as often as necessary.

The primary buyers of the products of both companies were banks, both public and privately held, that catered to exceptionally wealthy investors. Stock trading was largely unregulated until the early part of the twentieth century. Unscrupulous companies and individuals often manipulated the stock market and provided false and misleading information to drive the price of shares up or down. Since the two companies were selling information, not stocks themselves, information provided by them was seen by investors as more accurate and dependable. The two financial information publishers merged in 1941 to form Standard & Poor's.

In addition to providing financial information on companies and industries whose stocks are publicly traded, Standard & Poor's also evaluates the debt levels of companies and issues credit ratings quantifying the likelihood that a specific company will repay its long-term as well as short-term debt. Long-term ratings run on a scale from AAA (best quality) to D (meaning the company has defaulted on its payments). A similar scale, from A1 to D, evaluates short-term debt and the likelihood of a company paying its debts in a timely manner. This credit rating system has been widely criticized for continuing to provide favorable ratings to companies in financial distress, thus possibly misleading many investors about the financial soundness of their investments.

As a service to all types of investors, both institutional and individual, Standard & Poor's publishes a weekly newsletter that provides an overview of current activity in the U.S. economy and how that activity influences the stock market. The company's most widely known financial information product is the S&P 500, a daily snapshot of the financial health and activity of five hundred of the largest publicly traded companies. The S&P 400 covers midsized companies with market capitalization up to $10 billion. The S&P 600 covers smaller companies up to $2 billion in market capitalization.

Victoria Erhart

FURTHER READING

Cusick, Philip A. "Price Effects of Addition or Deletion from the Standard & Poor's 500 Index: Evidence of Increasing Market Efficiency." In *Selected Essays in Finance*, edited by William L. Silber. Boston: Blackwell, 2002.

Kaye, Michael. *The Standard & Poor's Guide to Selecting Stocks: Finding the Winners and Weeding Out the Losers.* New York: McGraw-Hill, 2006.

Tigue, Joseph. *The Standard & Poor's Guide to Building Wealth with Dividend Stocks.* New York: McGraw-Hill, 2006.

SEE ALSO: Banking; *Barron's*; Black Monday; Bloomberg's Business News Services; CNBC; Dow Jones Industrial Average; Pension and retirement plans; Stock markets; *The Wall Street Journal*.

Standard Oil Company

IDENTIFICATION: Powerful corporation that at one time monopolized the petroleum industry

DATE: Founded in 1870

SIGNIFICANCE: The Standard Oil Company dominated the emerging oil industry in the United States between 1870 and 1911. Ultimately incorporated as a holding company in 1899, the corporation produced, processed, marketed, and transported approximately 90 percent of American oil during the early part of the twentieth century and became the first industrial monopoly in United States history.

The origins of the Standard Oil Company date back to 1863, when John D. Rockefeller, Maurice B. Clark, and Samuel J. Andrews formed an oil refining company in Cleveland, Ohio. By 1870, Henry M. Flagler had replaced Clark in the company, and the company itself had become the largest oil refining business in Cleveland. That same year, the business was incorporated as the Standard Oil Company of Ohio. In 1882, Rockefeller and eight other trustees formed the Standard Oil Trust, which was governed by the Standard Oil Trust Agreement and enabled the group to monopolize the oil industry. The Standard Oil Company of New Jersey, also founded in 1882, was one of forty corporations owned by the trust. By 1884, the corporate headquarters had been relocated to New York City.

In 1892, the Ohio Supreme Court dissolved the trust, but because corporate headquarters had been relocated to New York City, the trust was able to continue operating until 1899. That year, the nine trustees changed the name of the Standard Oil Company of New Jersey to simply the Standard Oil Company and incorporated it as a holding company. Because a holding company's only purpose is to own other companies' stocks, the trustees transferred all the assets previously held by the trust into this new company. This arrangement allowed the Standard Oil Company to continue to monopolize the United States oil industry.

Although the Standard Oil Company succeeded in controlling the American oil industry, politicians and lawmakers continually scrutinized the company's business practices. In 1904, Ida Tarbell, a popular muckraker, published *The History of the Standard Oil Company*, in which she exposed the company's manipulative business practices to the American public. In 1906, the United States government sued the company under the Sherman Antitrust Act of 1890, claiming that the company maintained an unfair monopoly of the oil industry. In 1911, the Standard Oil Company's control of the American oil industry was

A political cartoon showing a Standard Oil tank morphed into an octopus with its tentacles wrapped around the steel, copper, and shipping industries, as well as the U.S. Capitol and a state house. One tentacle reaches for the White House. (Library of Congress)

destroyed when the United States government ordered it to divest itself of its thirty-three largest companies.

Bernadette Zbicki Heiney

FURTHER READING

Bringhurst, Bruce. *Antitrust and the Oil Monopoly: The Standard Oil Cases, 1890-1911.* Westport, Conn.: Greenwood Press, 1979.

Tarbell, Ida M. *The History of the Standard Oil Company.* Rev. ed. Mineola, N.Y.: Dover Publications, 2003.

Whitten, David O., and Whitten, Bessie E. *The Birth of Big Business in the United States, 1860-1914: Commercial, Extractive, and Industrial Enterprise.* Westport, Conn.: Praeger, 2006.

SEE ALSO: Antitrust legislation; Muckraking journalism; Multinational corporations; Organization of Petroleum Exporting Countries; Petroleum industry; Robber barons; Rockefeller, John D.; Sherman Antitrust Act.

Stanford, Leland

IDENTIFICATION: Politician, railroad president, and university founder
BORN: March 9, 1824; Watervliet, New York
DIED: June 20, 1893; Palo Alto, California
SIGNIFICANCE: Stanford was a California governor, U.S. senator, and successful businessman. As president of the Central Pacific Railroad, he was one of the "Big Four" California railroad barons who built the first transcontinental railroad. He later used his million-dollar fortune to found Stanford University.

Growing up in rural New York, Leland Stanford became a lawyer before moving to California in 1852 with his wife, Jane. He became wealthy as a merchant to the miners of California's gold rush. After a term as Republican governor of California, he was selected president of the Central Pacific Railroad. Stanford, Charles Crocker, Mark Hopkins, and Collis Huntington were the "Big Four" railroad barons, whose extensive business interests dominated California after the U.S. Civil War. Their financial and political might allowed them to complete an audacious project—the building of the transcontinental railroad—with Stanford himself driving in the Golden Spike on May 10, 1869.

After the ravages of the Civil War, the transcontinental railroad represented the figurative and actual tying together of the nation, opening the West to rapid business development. In 1885, Stanford was appointed to the U.S. Senate, where he far-sightedly favored worker-owned labor cooperatives. After the death of their only son, Leland and Jane devoted their vast estates, farms, ranches, wineries, and fortune to founding Stanford University in his honor. Stanford University opened in 1891. Attracting national attention, Stanford persuaded former President Benjamin Harrison to become the first law professor of the university in 1893. A man of many accomplishments, Stanford's greatest legacy is perhaps Stanford University, as America's outstanding universities have become central engines of American business growth.

Howard Bromberg

SEE ALSO: Education; Railroads; Robber barons; Transcontinental railroad.

Steamboats

DEFINITION: Boats that use pressurized steam to drive the mechanisms of propulsion

SIGNIFICANCE: Steamboats allowed large numbers of people and large quantities of goods to be transported by water regardless of wind conditions. Using paddles driven by an engine, steamboats were quicker than sailing ships and more comfortable for passengers than canal boats or early railroads. Steamboats operated chiefly on rivers and in the Great Lakes in the nineteenth century United States.

Inventors had begun to attempt to use steam as a means of propulsion in ancient times, but it was not until the industrial age that steam power became practical. Scottish inventor James Watt in 1769 developed a steam condenser and a system of wheels that converted up-and-down movement into rotary movement. John Fitch became the first American to apply the power of steam to water transportation in 1787, when he launched a twelve-paddle steamboat that operated like a mechanized canoe but with many more paddles. Fitch had trouble attracting financial backing, though, and he abandoned his project.

EARLY STEAMBOATS

Robert Fulton, with better financial support than Fitch could muster, created the first successful steamboat in the United States. Fulton built the *Clermont,* a boat that measured 150 feet long and 13 feet wide, with straight sides and a flat bottom that drew only 18 inches of water. It had two masts fore and aft for carrying square sails. However, it was also equipped with a low-pressure engine based on Watt's innovations. The engine sat below the deck and attached through a diamond-shaped crank to 15-foot paddle wheels on each side of the boat at the middle. In August of 1807, Fulton sailed the *Clermont* 150 miles up the Hudson River, from New York City to Albany, New York, in just thirty-two hours of travel time, plus a twenty-hour stop. Observers, frightened by "Fulton's folly," fled ashore or dropped to their knees to pray as the boat passed, emitting black smoke, showers of sparks from the pine-wood fuel, and steam from the boiler, as well as thuds from the motion of its crankshaft and piston.

The *Clermont*'s regular service took twenty-four hours to reach its destination at a speed of four to six knots, which qualified Fulton for a monopoly on steamboat operations on the Hudson River. He had passed sailing ships on the journey as if they had been anchored, underscoring the value of steam-powered boats, especially when moving upstream. Fulton extended his business to the Mississippi River in 1811, when he pioneered steamboat service on that waterway with the *New Orleans.* Fulton also designed the steamship that made the first steam-powered open-sea voyage, from New York City to Newport, Rhode Island, in 1817. However, American shipbuilders focused on the development of river and lake steamers rather than ocean liners.

Early steamboats traveled an average of fifty miles per day, while keelboats and other hand-poled and pulled vessels could do no better than twenty miles per day—less while proceeding under adverse con-

GIBBONS V. OGDEN

In Gibbons v. Ogden (1824), the U.S. Supreme Court supported the federal license of a steamboat operator over a state monopoly license holder, thus expanding federal control through the commerce clause.

Chief Justice John Marshall wrote the unanimous opinion of the Court, upholding the right of Congress to regulate interstate commerce. The issue involved competing licenses granted by New York and the federal government, to Aaron Ogden and Thomas Gibbons, respectively, to navigate steamboats on the Hudson River. New York courts had upheld the monopoly operated by Ogden, but the Supreme Court found that Gibbons's federal license nullified Ogden's state-issued license, setting a precedent of great importance both to the steamboat industry and to constitutional law.

ditions. Typically, farmers had floated their produce down to New Orleans, sold their flatboats for lumber, and then walked home along the Natchez Trace. Such a trip could take four months. In 1815, a similar trip by steamboat took about a month. Steamboats could ship freight more quickly and cheaply than the competition, while traveling easily in both directions and in all weather conditions. Equipped with more powerful engines and improved hulls, steamboats were capable of averaging one hundred miles per day by the mid-1820's.

THE PEAK AND FALL

By the 1810's, western river steamboats had developed a characteristic design: Fitted with compact high-pressure steam engines, they were built with flatter bottoms that enabled them to navigate in as little as three feet of water. By the 1820's, steamboats had become familiar sights along the rivers of the Northeast, on the Great Lakes, and on the Mississippi River. Ships, such as the 450-ton *Vesuvius*, were common. This ship could carry 280 tons of merchandise, 700 bales of cotton, and 100 passengers. Most of the Great Lakes ships carried iron ore from the upper end of Lakes Erie and Huron and returned laden with coal. At the end of the summer, much of the cargo consisted of grain. Other ships carried mail and passengers.

By 1830, there were 187 steamboats operating on the Mississippi River, the Ohio River, and their tribu-

taries. By 1850, the number of steamboats reached 536. The rivers became the capillaries of a vast system of water-based transportation. Many steamboats had all the comforts of a hotel yet traveled at a speedy twenty miles per hour. Passenger steamboats had a characteristic, wide overhang of the main deck, which covered the paddle boxes and tapered toward the bow and stern. Rising from this broad, oval platform were the double, triple, or quadruple tiers of enclosed passenger accommodations, as well as a saloon and a promenade area.

Steamboats could be dangerous. On the Mississippi River and its tributaries, large, shallow-draught steamers with immense side or stern paddle wheels were operating by the 1830's. Rival steamers would race, beam to beam, down narrow channels. Their captains could ignore safety measures and occasionally rammed their competitors to gain an advantage. Boilers, pushed beyond their limits, occasionally blew up and killed passengers.

By the 1850's, competition from railroads was beginning to eat away at the steamboat business. By this time, steamboats had made an enormous impact. They brought such vast numbers of settlers into the Indian Territory that contemporary observers attributed the colonization of the West to steamboats. Owing mostly to the construction of steamboats, the manufacture of steam engines became one of the earliest and most important industries of Pittsburgh; Wheeling, West Virginia; Cincinnati; and Louisville, Kentucky. As centers of skilled machinists, ironworkers, and carpenters, these river cities became antebellum centers of transportation and industry.

Caryn E. Neumann

FURTHER READING

Gandy, Joan W., and Thomas H. Gandy. *The Mississippi Steamboat Era in Historic Photographs, 1870-1920.* Mineola, N.Y.: Dover, 1987. Attractively illustrated history of the last years of steamboating on the Mississippi River.

Hunter, Louis C. *Steamboats on the Western Rivers: An Economic and Technological History.* Mineola, N.Y.: Dover, 1994. Interesting exploration steamboats designed to meet the challenges of navigating western rivers and their impact on western commerce and development.

Kane, Adam I. *The Western River Steamboat.* College Station: Texas A&M Press, 2004. Written by a nautical archaeologist, this volume examines how steamboats were built and how they evolved. Of special interest is Kane's discussion of modern archaeological work on steamboat remains. Richly illustrated with photographs and charts.

Ross, David. *The Willing Servant: A History of the Steam Engine.* Stroud, Gloucestershire, England: Tempus, 2004. History of the steam engine and its impact on both British and American society. Ross begins his chronicle with the invention of the first steam engine during the early nineteenth century.

Sale, Kirkpatrick. *The Fire of His Genius: Robert Fulton and the American Dream.* New York: Free Press, 2001. Well-written and balanced biography that describes how Fulton's steamboat transformed nineteenth century America.

Shagena, Jack L. *Who Really Invented the Steamboat? Fulton's Clermont Coup: A History of the Steamboat Contributions of William Henry, James Rumsey, John Fitch, Oliver Evans, Nathan Read, Samuel Morey, Robert Fulton, John Stevens, and Others.* Amherst, N.Y.: Humanity Books, 2004. Shagena, a retired aerospace engineer, traces the technological contributions of the many inventors, including Fulton, who helped create the steamboat.

Twain, Mark. *Life on the Mississippi.* 1883. Reprint. New York: Oxford University Press, 1996. Facsimile reprint of the first edition of Mark Twain's classic account of steamboating. Twain himself was a pilot on the Lower Mississippi during the late 1850's. His book includes a poignant memoir of his training during the golden age of steamboats and an account of his return to the river in 1882, by which time competition from railroads had changed steamboating almost beyond recognition.

SEE ALSO: Canals; Erie Canal; Industrial Revolution, American; Mississippi and Missouri Rivers; Postal Service, U.S.; Railroads; Shipping industry; Transatlantic steamer service; Woodworking industry.

Steel industry

DEFINITION: Enterprises that process iron ore into hardened steel; sell, distribute, and use the metal for production; and sell and distribute the resulting products

SIGNIFICANCE: Steel is fundamentally necessary for modern lifestyles, particularly in transportation and the construction of large buildings and infrastructure. Although the steel industry continues to employ thousands of American workers, the proportion of the world steel supply produced in the United States has significantly declined since the 1970's.

Many historians use the term "second industrial revolution" to describe the modernization that occurred in the years from the U.S. Civil War to World War II. The foundation for this transformation can be largely attributed to the use of Bessemer-processed steel. From the 1860's to 1945, the growth of the iron and steel industry in the United States was truly impressive. In 1860, the nation's pig iron production was only 25 percent of Britain's output; by 1895, it was 19 percent larger than Britain's, and by 1906, it was four times larger than that of Britain. In 1945, the United States produced more than half of the world's steel output. Since the 1960's, however, the relative position of the U.S. steel industry has significantly declined.

EARLY INDUSTRY

Before the mid-nineteenth century, steel was too expensive to be used on a large scale. In the cementation process of manufacturing, bars of wrought iron and charcoal were heated together for about a week. The process required three tons of expensive coke (coal with volatile material removed by heating) for each ton of steel removed. About 1850, English inventor Henry Bessemer and American inventor William Kelly discovered independently that impurities could be removed from iron by blowing air through the molten iron. Their discovery, usually called the Bessemer process, provided an inexpensive means to mass-produce steel from pig iron. Both Bessemer and Kelly obtained patents, but bankruptcy forced Kelly to sell his patent to Bessemer in 1857.

Recognizing that heavy railroad cars quickly pounded iron rails to pieces, a few British companies soon began using the Bessemer technique to make steel rails. In 1862, John Edgar Thompson, president of the Pennsylvania Railroad, purchased the expensive rails from Britain, and after a few years, he concluded that their durability justified the additional cost. In 1864, the Eureka Iron Works of Wyandotte, Michigan, became the first American company to produce Bessemer steel, and the following year the company began manufacturing steel rails on a small scale. At this time, nevertheless, many industrialists believed that the new way of making steel was only a passing fad.

A COMPARISON OF STEEL AND IRON

The American Industrial Revolution required large amounts of iron and steel products. During the first half of the nineteenth century, only cast and wrought iron could be produced commercially in the quantities needed for industrial purposes. Both materials had significant disadvantages. Cast iron (2 to 5 percent carbon) can be cast into shapes easily but is brittle. Wrought iron, which uses very little carbon, is malleable but cannot be cast into shapes. Steel, which contains up to 2 percent carbon, can be cast and is also malleable. However, until the mid-nineteenth century, it could be produced only in small and expensive batches. After Sir Henry Bessemer introduced the first commercial method of mass-producing steel, the material began replacing both cast and wrought iron for industrial and military needs.

Andrew Carnegie, who entered the iron business in 1861, became the dominant leader of the emerging steel industry. When visiting Europe in 1872, he investigated companies using the Bessemer process, and he returned to his headquarters in Pittsburgh determined to construct a huge plant able to mass-produce steel using the process. He and several associates organized Carnegie, McCardless, and Company, which between 1873 and 1875 built the Edgar Thomas Steel Works, in Braddock, a suburb of Pittsburgh. Built at a cost of about $1.1 million, the plant was able to produce 225 tons of steel rails per day. The investment was risky, but it paid huge dividends.

Carnegie became the "King of Steel" for a number of reasons, including his emphasis on efficiency, his determination to undersell his competitors, and his choice of capable associates, particularly Henry Phipps and Henry Clay Frick. Rather than stock manipulation, Carnegie concentrated on production. From his earlier experience with the Pennsylvania Railroad, he believed that the way to make money was to decrease unit costs by speeding up the flow. In addition to keeping detailed data on costs per unit of output, he pioneered the system of business organization called vertical integration, which meant eliminated middlemen, and controlled all aspects of the business, from the extracting of raw materials to the selling of finished products. He was also ruthless in firing incompetent managers and in demanding that workers endure long hours, dangerous working conditions, and low wages.

When Carnegie began manufacturing steel, other producers entered into an agreement to price rails at $70 per ton, but Carnegie sold his rails at $65 per ton. Within two decades, Carnegie had reduced the price to $25 per ton. His business methods allowed him to sell enough rails to keep his plants in continuous operation, and he used most of the resulting profits to invest in new plants and buy out many of his competitors. His growing empire included the Homestead Steel Works, the Keystone Bridge Works, the Pittsburgh Bessemer Steel Works, and the Frick Coke Company. In 1892, the same year as the controversial Homestead Strike, he and his associates consolidated their holdings into the Carnegie Steel Company, which was initially capitalized at $324 million. By 1900, the company produced one quarter of the country's output and earned a profit of $40 million a year, of which Carnegie himself received about $25 million.

FROM 1901 TO THE 1970'S

In 1898, J. P. Morgan, the preeminent finance capitalist of the age, moved into the steel industry, consolidating several small companies into Federal Steel, which challenged Carnegie's dominance. Morgan envisioned that the further integration of the steel industry into one gigantic company would eliminate much inefficiency, thereby reducing costs and increasing profits. Carnegie wanted to retire and devote his remaining years to philanthropy, as expressed in his 1889 essay, "The Gospel of Wealth."

In 1901, Morgan asked Charles M. Schwab, president of Carnegie Steel, to inquire about how much money he wanted for the company.

Carnegie gave Schwab a penciled note with the figure of $480 million (over $10 billion in 2007 dollars). Morgan accepted the offer, and he then combined Carnegie Steel Company with other companies to establish the United States Steel Corporation, which was capitalized at $1.37 billion, becoming by far the world's largest business enterprise. The new corporation employed 168,000 people and owned 213 manufacturing plants, forty-one mines, and almost one thousand miles of railroad. By 1903, it produced almost one-third of world's steel output and about half of the output in the United States.

After 1904, Bethlehem Steel became U.S. Steel's major competitor. The steel industry operated as an oligopoly, in which these two corporations and a few others set prices, and the smaller companies tended to follow their lead. Under the energetic leadership of Schwab (who had left U.S. Steel in 1903), Bethlehem Steel established an executive profit-sharing plan, applied a system of incentives to wages, and gave managers a maximum degree of discretion. During World War I, Schwab often acted as a senior spokesperson for the industry, and he was the principal factor in Bethlehem's success in obtaining war contracts.

Throughout its history, the steel industry has experienced turbulent cycles of boom and bust. From 1900 to 1940, production grew at an average annual rate of 2.9 percent, but it varied greatly from year to year. Demand for steel products fell during the Great Depression of the 1930's, but demand soared during World War II, when steel products of many kinds became crucially important in fighting the war and making the United States the "arsenal of democracy." From 1941 to 1945, the nation manufactured some 88,410 tanks, 12 million rifles, 8,812 major naval vessels, and 4,900 merchant ships. The total raw steel output reached 334.5 million metric tons, which was almost twice as much as that of Japan, Germany, and Italy combined. In 1945, the last year of the war, the United States produced about half of the world's steel output.

During the next thirty years, American production grew at a rate of 6 percent a year. To most Americans, the steel industry seemed to have a secure future, and young workers began working in the mills with expectations of stable employment until retirement age. Gradually, however, the United States found it difficult to compete with foreign producers, particularly the Japanese, who often had more modern plants and a comparative advantage in labor costs. By 1959, exports have been exceeded by imports, and the imbalance grew rapidly during the 1960's. Several countries ex-

Children walk in front of a steel mill in Homestead, Pennsylvania, in 1907. (Library of Congress)

panded production much more rapidly than the growth in demand, frequently with their governments' support. American companies frequently complained that foreign competitors were guilty of dumping, or selling their products more cheaply than production costs.

SINCE THE 1970'S

In 1971, U.S. consumption of imported steel reached a record level of 18.3 million tons, or 18 percent of the domestic market. With voluntary restraints, imports declined during the next four years, but then they grew to account for 35 percent of the market in 1998. Although U.S. production had reached a record high of 151 million tons in 1973, demand had plummeted the next year, resulting in the closing of hundreds of plants and the loss of a million jobs. In 1978, U.S. companies produced 137 million tons of steel, and four years later, production hit a low point of 73 million tons.

During the 1980's, the United States produced 15 percent of the world's output in steel. Output declined from 154 million tons in 1982 to 112 million tons in 1987 (a 25 percent drop). By then, imported steel had grown to 28 percent of consumption. The number of integrated steel companies declined from twenty companies in 1976 to fourteen in 1987. Reduced output combined with continuing modernization resulted in a significant decline in employment. Between 1973 and 1990, employment in the U.S. industry declined by 66 percent—from 500,000 steel workers to only 170,000 workers.

Steel producers managed to realize profits every year from the 1940's to 1981. Since then, however, the industry has often registered huge losses, totaling billions of dollars. During the 1980's, the industry lost about $12 billion, and twenty-five companies were forced to file for bankruptcy. The bankruptcies continued into the twenty-first century. Bethlehem Steel and seven other steel companies filed for bankruptcy in 2002 alone.

David Roderick, president of U.S. Steel (then called USX) from 1979 to 1989, was a former boxer and Marine who was determined to use tough methods to increase efficiency. He focused on the need to "direct available funds where they will provide the greatest returns." In the first six years of his presidency, the corporation closed 150 facilities and reduced capacity by almost a third, from 38 million tons to 26.2 million tons. The number of employees

fell from 166,800 to 88,753, and salaried employees declined by half. In an effort toward more efficient production, USX built a $4 billion integrated mill on Lake Erie. At the same time, Roderick was determined to diversity the corporation. In 1981, after USX purchased Marathon Oil, the corporation's revenue from steel fell from 80 percent to half of its revenue. In 1985, the purchase of Texas Oil and Gas Corporation was controversial, because it was financed by doubling the number of USX's outstanding shares. By 1999, USX produced 1.5 percent of global output and 13 percent of U.S. output.

Since the 1980's, all steel producers have experienced a severe cost-price squeeze. The industry's most dynamic sector has been the mini-mills that primarily use scrap metal. In 1977, the mini-mill sector produced about 5 percent of the nation's output. This gradually grew to 22 percent by 1991 and then exploded to almost 50 percent in 1998. In the twenty-two years to 1995, the capacity of the mini-mills grew from 5 million to 47 million tons, while the capacity of large integrated mills dropped from 154 million to 64 million tons. The leading mini-mill producer, Nucor, was profitable every year from 1966 to 2007. Nucor went from 2,300 workers in 1975 to 18,000 workers in 2007. By instituting profit sharing for workers and eliminating perks for managers, Nucor was able to avoid unionization of its plants.

In 2007, the International Iron and Steel Institute reported that the world's production of steel totaled 1,343 million metric tons. The United States, at 97 metric tons, was responsible for only 7 percent of this output, compared with 36 percent for China, 16 percent by the European Union, and 9 percent by Japan. Chinese imports to the United States quadrupled from 1998 to 1905. Despite the downsizing of U.S. firms, however, most of them were able to report good profits between 2004 and 2007, in large part because of the great demand for steel in China and other developing countries.

Thomas Tandy Lewis

FURTHER READING

Hall, Christopher. *Steel Phoenix: The Fall and Rise of the American Steel Industry.* New York: St. Martin's Press, 1997. The story of the downfall of the traditional steel industry and the emergence of the new industry dominated by mini-mills using scrap iron.

Hessen, Robert. *Steel Titan: The Life of Charles M. Schwab.* Pittsburgh: University of Pittsburgh Press, 1990. Traces the steel baron's career from day laborer to first president of U.S. Steel and founder of Bethlehem Steel, with attendant scandals and controversies.

Hillstrom, Kevin, et al., eds. *Industrial Revolution in America: Iron and Steel, Railroads, and Steam Shipping.* 3 vols. Santa Barbara: ABC-CLIO, 2005. Each of the three volumes discusses three areas of the Industrial Revolution, considering origins, innovations, entrepreneurs, labor organization, and workers' lives.

Livesay, Harold. *Andrew Carnegie and the Rise of Big Business.* New York: Longman, 2006. A relatively brief and compelling biography of the captain of industry, with analysis of background topics such as capitalism, the emergence of big business, and the Gilded Age.

Strohmeyer, John. *Crisis in Bethlehem: Big Steel's Battle to Survive.* Pittsburgh: University of Pittsburgh Press, 1994. Pulitzer Prize winner's account of how complacency and rigidity by management and labor resulted in the company's decline between 1956 and 1984.

Warren, Kenneth. *Big Steel: The First Century of the United States Steel Corporation, 1901-2001.* Pittsburgh: University of Pittsburgh Press, 2008. A comprehensive history of the behemoth organization that produced 30 percent of the world's steel output in 1901 but only 1.5 percent a century later.

SEE ALSO: AFL-CIO; Aircraft industry; Antitrust legislation; Automotive industry; Carnegie, Andrew; Gilded Age; Homestead strike; Morgan, J. P.; Railroads; Steel mill seizure of 1952; United States Steel Corporation.

Steel mill seizure of 1952

THE EVENT: Federal government's takeover of American steel mills that were about to strike during the Korean War

DATE: April-June, 1952

PLACE: Washington, D.C.

SIGNIFICANCE: The Supreme Court ruled that the U.S. president's seizure of the steel mills was unconstitutional, thus giving support to the most basic premises of a free-market economy devoid of government intrusion.

During the Korean War, the U.S. military depended on American manufacturing and technology to provide highly advanced, superior quality war materiel. A major component of many of the products used by the military—including bullets, armor plating, tanks, and airplanes—was steel, processed and sold by privately owned mills. Consequently, keeping the steel mills open and running smoothly was essential for the war effort.

During times of war, wages tend to rise, and prices often go up in a spiral of inflation caused by panic buying and resource scarcity. During World War II, President Franklin D. Roosevelt dealt with these dual economic issues by establishing central authority over both prices and wages. He did this by extending the power of his office into the marketplace.

However, the American public was not as convinced of the need for the Korean War as they had been of the importance of World War II. President Harry S. Truman was under political stress, having received a record-low public approval rating for a sitting president. His plans for central control of the economy produced no similar public support. Recognizing this, Truman began the Korean War with the clear intention of not fixing prices and wages by decree. He was a friend of labor politically and was confident that he could negotiate agreements between industry executives and labor leaders to ameliorate any economic hardships. However, he found that he was unable to solve labor and management wage disputes in the militarily essential steel industry.

When large labor unions made it clear that they were going to strike on April 9, 1952, President Truman ordered his secretary of commerce, Charles Sawyer, to both seize and operate the nation's steel mills. The president felt this action was necessary to continue the war efforts uninterrupted. It is hard to tell who was more upset at the chief executive for this heavily studied use of presidential powers. The strikers did not like being drafted to work at low wages any more than the steel giants enjoyed having their profits ruined by government intervention.

Not surprisingly, the steel industry filed suit, and

the case reached the Supreme Court. In *Youngstown Sheet and Tube Co. v. Sawyer* (1952), the justices ruled that the president may not seize private property without specific legal authority. This case is one of the most significant Supreme Court decisions defining the limits of presidential power. One result of the seizure and subsequent judgment was a clearer picture of the role of the president. After this ruling, it was clear that even in times of national emergency, the U.S. market is hardly amenable to unilateral power grabs, even by the president himself.

R. Matthew Beverlin

President Harry S. Truman announces the government seizure of the steel industry on April 8, 1952. (AP/Wide World Photos)

FURTHER READING

Dallek, Robert. *Harry S. Truman.* New York: Times Books, 2008.

Marcus, Maeva. *Truman and the Steel Seizure Case.* 1977. Reprint. Durham, N.C.: Duke University Press, 1994.

Schlesinger, Arthur M., Jr., ed. *The Election of 1948 and the Administration of Harry S. Truman.* Philadelphia: Mason Crest, 2003.

SEE ALSO: AFL-CIO; Air traffic controllers' strike; Korean War; Labor history; Labor strikes; Sit-down strike of 1936-1937; Steel industry.

Stewart, Martha

IDENTIFICATION: Media mogul and entrepreneur

BORN: August 3, 1941; Jersey City, New Jersey

SIGNIFICANCE: Martha Stewart successfully transformed her interests in cooking, home decorating, gardening, and entertaining into a multimillion dollar business. By marketing herself, she established herself as an enormously lucrative domestic arts brand name and created a profitable domestic lifestyle industry.

In 1963, Martha Stewart graduated from Barnard College in New York City with a degree in European and architectural history. From 1965 to 1973, she worked for the brokerage firm, Monness, Williams, and Sidel. In 1976, Stewart started her own catering business, and by 1986, her business had grown into Martha Stewart, Inc., a million-dollar enterprise. In 1982, she published her first lifestyle book, *Entertaining.* The success of the book, which sold more than 625,000 copies, transformed her company into an enormously popular domestic style brand.

Throughout the 1980's, the Martha Stewart name became synonymous with a particular vision of home style. Stewart showed her viewers and readers how to make their homes elegant economically, selling a version of the upper-middle-class lifestyle that was available to lower-middle-class consumers. She continued to publish domestic arts books and videotapes, host numerous television specials, and conduct lectures and seminars around the country. In 1987, the Kmart Corporation hired Stewart as a lifestyle consultant, and she started to market Martha Stewart brand-named bed and bath products for the discount store chain.

In 1999, Stewart took her company public on the New York Stock Exchange. By then known as Martha Stewart Living Omnimedia, the company saw its stock price double on its first day of trading. The initial public offering sold for $129.6 million, and as the stock's value rose, it made Stewart a billionaire on paper.

In 2004, Stewart was involved in an insider-trading scandal. She was convicted of obstruction of justice and served five months in prison. Observers noted that, because Stewart herself was synonymous with her brand, the company stood to lose far more than an average corporation whose owner was the subject of a scandal. Released from jail in 2005, Stewart returned to Martha Stewart Living Omnimedia and worked successfully to rejuvenate her brand.

Bernadette Zbicki Heiney

SEE ALSO: Book publishing; Insider trading; Magazine industry; Television broadcasting industry; Tupperware.

Stock market crash of 1929

THE EVENT: The single most dramatic decline in the the United States stock market to occur in the twentieth century
DATE: October, 1929
SIGNIFICANCE: Every sector of the American business community was affected by the stock market crash of 1929, which eliminated more than half of the value of all American assets in thirty months.

The period from the end of World War I in 1918 to the stock market crash in October, 1929, was a heady time for American investors. The *New York Times* stock index was in the 50's in 1918. By 1921, it rose to 65. It continued its steady advance until the end of August, 1929, when it peaked at 449. As the market rose, larger numbers of people, many totally inexperienced in playing the stock market, became stockholders. The advances sustained for over a decade appeared to have no end.

SOURCES OF INVESTMENT MONEY

World War I was enormously profitable for manufacturers of the materials required to wage the war. These manufacturers had large sums of money available for investment. Billions were placed in the stock market, driving stock prices up and leading to considerable speculative buying. Often, a stock bought in the morning could be sold the same afternoon at a considerable profit.

Money for investment also became plentiful during the administration of President Warren G. Harding (1921-1923). Under this administration, taxes on the wealthy were reduced substantially, making available more money to invest. Harding decided to pay off the national debt, thereby removing U.S. securities from American financial markets. Money that would normally have gone into such securities ended up in the stock market.

Excess corporate funds were used to buy large quantities of stock, and working-class Americans, most of whom had no previous experience in such financial matters, withdrew their savings from banks and put them into the rapidly expanding stock market with the expectation of reaping immediate profits. Few of these inexperienced investors had realistic notions of the hazards involved in their investments.

BUYING ON MARGIN

A pernicious aspect of the stock market speculation rampant during the 1920's was buying stocks on margin. Stock brokers encouraged their clients to buy shares by putting down anywhere from 10 to 50 percent of the purchase price. These brokers arranged for bank loans, using the shares purchased in this way as collateral. The chance to buy $1,000 worth of stock for $100 was extremely tempting, particularly if the shares purchased in this way were worth $2,000 within a few days. Inexperienced traders expected to increase their wealth dramatically through buying on margin.

Margin buying works well in markets that rise consistently, but few markets do that. If a stock bought on margin falls to the point that it is worth less than the amount borrowed on it, the lender sells it immediately for whatever price it can command, often leaving the borrower in substantial debt for the balance. Such margin calls became the bane of many stock traders' lives. For some, the only way out of debt was suicide, which some traders resorted to when the market crashed in the final months of 1929.

THE BUBBLE BURSTS

The stock market rose substantially every year from 1918 until the last quarter of 1929. Considerable money was made, but the advances were not sustainable, because, although corporate profits were up throughout the decade, they advanced only modestly. Thus, the companies' profits were insuffi-

Crowds assemble in Wall Street after the stock market crashes. (Library of Congress)

cient to justify the increase in their stocks' value over the decade. On August 31, 1929, the *New York Times* index reached its all-time high of 449. Discouraging news from the corporate world, however, soon drove the market down.

Traders who expected double-digit advances and optimistic reports from the corporations whose stock they held sensed disaster. Some bailed out as the market began to decline, and on October 23, 1929, the *New York Times* index dropped from 415 to 384. The 7.5 percent drop was a colossal one-day percentage loss. The following day, which came to be called Black Thursday, a full-fledged panic gripped Wall Street. Nearly 13 million shares were traded, a record for a single day. The index dropped another 12 points to 372.

Investors who regarded this decline as an aberration and expected a correction were mistaken. On October 28, called Black Monday, the index dropped almost 50 points on heavy volume, and the following day, Black Tuesday, it lost 43 more. The market fell more often than it advanced before it hit its bottom of 58 in June, 1932. The entire United States economy was devastated by the stock market crash and was not to recover from it until the 1940's, when World War II created an increased demand for manufactured goods and armaments.

R. Baird Shuman

FURTHER READING

Beaudreau, Bernard C. *Mass Production, the Stock Market Crash, and the Great Depression: The Macroeconomics of Electrification.* Westport, Conn.: Greenwood Press, 1996. Chapter 4 focuses on the stock market crash, and the chapters that precede it reveal how the economic expansion in the decade before 1929 led to the crash.

Galbraith, John Kenneth. *The Great Crash, 1929.* Boston: Houghton Mifflin, 1997. Thoroughly researched, well-presented account of how the stock market crash of 1929 evolved and what some of its major consequences were.

Gross, Daniel. *Pop! Why Bubbles Are Great for the Economy.* New York: Collins, 2007. Gross considers the bursting of economic bubbles to be necessary correctives for the economy.

Kindleberger, Charles, and Robert Aliber. *Manias, Panics, and Crashes: A History of Financial Crises.* 5th ed. Hoboken, N.J.: John Wiley & Sons, 2005. Assesses the psychology that fueled the worst stock market decline in United States history.

Klein, Maury. *Rainbow's End: The Crash of 1929.* New York: Oxford University Press, 2001. Well-researched account of the stock market crash of 1929. Klein examines minutely the economic policies of the two years preceding the crash.

SEE ALSO: Dow Jones Industrial Average; Financial crisis of 2008; *Fortune*; Great Depression; New Deal programs; New York Stock Exchange; Panic of 1907; Securities and Exchange Commission; Stock markets; World War II.

Stock markets

DEFINITION: Institutions that coordinate the exchange between investors of shares in publically traded businesses

SIGNIFICANCE: Stock markets facilitate buying and selling corporate stocks, provide continuous stock price quotations, and make available a way for the market to control corporations.

The first stock market in the United States was formed in Philadelphia in 1800. Speculators traded the many types of state and national government securities and stocks in banks and insurance companies. The New York Stock and Exchange Board was formed in 1817, evolving from a 1792 agreement among prominent traders. From the beginning, the stock markets were secondary markets, trading in "seasoned" securities—shares that had already been issued and purchased from the companies themselves and were now being traded among investors. The actual trading was conducted by brokers, often acting as agents for the investors and charging them a commission.

From the 1830's, railroads became the first truly big business corporations, and their stocks became a major focus of stock market trading. Exchanges were formed in other major cities; the San Francisco Stock and Exchange Board, founded 1862, specialized in gold mine shares and ranked second to New York. After the invention of the telegraph in 1844, the stock "ticker" came into wide use. Stock price quotations could be transmitted nationwide in a few seconds.

Initially, exchange trading proceeded by auction. At the same time, many trades were made directly, often outdoors in the "curb" market. By 1864, New York's Open Board of Stock Brokers had developed the "specialist" system. The specialist was a broker-dealer who specialized in a few stocks and stood ready to buy or sell at any time at a quoted price.

POST-CIVIL WAR DEVELOPMENTS

The modern New York Stock Exchange (NYSE) was formed in 1869. It incorporated the specialist system and maintained relatively strict standards regarding which companies were traded (most were not) and which individuals could become members. A major New York rival was the Consolidated Stock and Petroleum Exchange, formed in 1885.

The post-Civil War period witnessed scandals involving stock speculators such as Jay Gould, Daniel Drew, and James Fisk. Ownership of stock brought the power to control a corporation, to issue new stock for cash, and pocket the money. Defenders argued that speculation helped provide "liquidity"—that is, investors could sell their shares at any time with low transaction costs. As the new millennium dawned, stock markets had developed many modern features, such as margin trading, short selling, and options ("puts and calls").

BOOM AND BUST AFTER 1920

The twentieth century brought a long period of prosperity and rapid economic growth. Stock prices did not rise much between 1900 and 1920 but then took off. By 1929, they were worth, on average, four times what they had been in 1920. Stock ownership became widespread, partly through the creation of mutual funds and other investment companies. Speculation was extensive. The result was that stock prices rose much more than corporate profits. Yields on common stocks fell below those on high-quality bonds. When stock prices stopped rising in 1929, many investors tried to sell. From their high levels of September, 1929, stock prices lost one third of their value by November. The market decline followed the beginnings of an economic downturn, which it aggravated. By June, 1932, stock prices were on average down 85 percent from 1929. The market drop was more symptom than cause of the Great Depression, which reduced corporate profits below zero by 1933.

Stock market reform was a priority for President Franklin D. Roosevelt's New Deal. The Securities Exchange Act of 1934 established the Securities and Exchange Commission (SEC). A corporation that wished to issue securities was required to file registration documents with the SEC. These made available to the public information about the financing and management of the firm. The SEC has monitored and publicized insider trading and proxy solicitations. SEC regulation of stock markets prohibited collusive manipulations intended to drive stock prices up or down. The SEC has been credited with promoting transparency in American financial markets.

The Depression and World War II kept stock trading in the doldrums until it revived during the 1950's. The number of stock owners rose from 6.5 million in 1952 to 31 million in 1970. Trading on the NYSE grew from 200 million shares in 1940 to 1 billion shares in 1961. Stock trading continued to involve numerous regional exchanges and the American Stock Exchange (which evolved out of the curb market), as well as over-the-counter (OTC) markets. The NYSE was the dominant element. In 1971, OTC traders developed NASDAQ (the National Association of Securities Dealers Automatic Quotations).

The organization of stock markets continued to be controversial as the new millennium began. Revolutionary changes in communication and computer technology seemed to make the traditional face-to-face trading obsolete. An increasing fraction of stocks was held by institutions, particularly mutual funds. Ownership of stocks continued to expand. By 2005, about half of American households owned stocks, many through employer-sponsored 401(k) retirement plans.

FINANCIAL CRISIS OF 2008

The financial crisis of 2007-2008 led to wild fluctuations in stock prices in the United States and in

STOCK TRADING VOLUME BY MARKET, 2006

Market	Annual Trading Volume ($ billions)
New York Stock Exchange	16,311
National Association of Securities Dealers	15,436
Pacific Exchange	6,512
NASDAQ Stock Market	2,390
American Stock Exchange	721
Chicago Board Options Exchange	531
International Securities Exchange	525
National Stock Exchange	468
Chicago Stock Exchange	449
Philadelphia Stock Exchange	373

Source: Data from the *Statistical Abstract of the United States, 2008* (Washington, D.C.: Department of Commerce, Economics and Statistics Administration, Bureau of the Census, Data User Services Division, 2008)

Note: Dollar amounts as reported by the Securities and Exchange Commission.

other major countries. Stock prices initially seemed immune to distress. A price peak in October, 2007, took the widely publicized Dow Jones Industrial Average to the 14,000 level. During much of 2008, the index remained relatively steady around an average value of 11,000, ending August around 11,600. Despite wide fluctuations, the index ended September around 10,800. The Lehman Brothers bankruptcy and the need to bail out AIG (American International Group) generated huge selling of securities by financial firms both in the United States and overseas. By October 10, the index had fallen almost to 8,000, representing a decline of more than one-third since the beginning of the year. Other countries displayed similar patterns. Compared with the start of 2008, stocks had fallen 31 percent in Canada, 33 percent in Britain, and nearly 40 percent in France and Germany. Stocks of troubled financial firms declined nearly to zero. During November, 2008, stock prices experienced violent short-run movements but remained within sight of the 8,000 mark for the Dow Jones Industrial Average. The prospect of declining corporate earnings resulting from the onset of recession prevented a more vigorous recovery.

Paul B. Trescott

FURTHER READING

Bernstein, Peter L. *Capital Ideas: The Improbable Origins of Modern Wall Street.* New York: Free Press, 1992. A scholarly but entertaining review of the many systematic efforts to beat the market.

Galbraith, John Kenneth. *The Great Crash, 1929.* Boston: Houghton Mifflin, 1955. Entertaining narrative but with questionable economic analysis.

Malkiel, Burton. *A Random Walk Down Wall Street.* New York: W. W. Norton, 2007. Simple but sophisticated introduction to the world of the securities markets.

Markham, Jerry W. *A Financial History of the United States.* 3 vols. Armonk, N.Y.: M. E. Sharpe, 2002. This ambitious work is a gold mine of detail, but sometimes the big picture is hard to find.

Sobel, Robert. *Amex: A History of the American Stock Exchange, 1921-1971.* New York: Weybright and Talley, 1972. Focuses on the middle fifty years of the twentieth century on one of the nation's oldest stock markets.

_____. *N.Y.S.E.* New York: Weybright and Talley, 1975. A comprehensive history of the largest and most established of American stock markets.

SEE ALSO: American Stock Exchange; Black Monday; Bond industry; Commodity markets; Financial crisis of 2008; Mutual fund industry; NASDAQ; New York Stock Exchange; Securities and Exchange Commission; Stock market crash of 1929.

Sugar industry

DEFINITION: Enterprises that grow, market, and promote the use of sugar as an ingredient in prepared foods, a grocery item for use in cooking, and an additive to beverages and other foodstuffs

SIGNIFICANCE: The American sugar industry makes a product that nearly every American consumes—about 150 pounds annually on average. Sugar is purchased by food manufacturers as well as consumers: it is a key ingredient in many processed foods and is therefore a key component of the food industry generally.

Sugar is a product of sugarcane—a giant tropical plant of the grass family grown in the South and in Hawaii—and sugar beets, tuberous plants of the goosefoot family. Sugar's importance in world trade and politics was apparent even in the seventeenth century, when the Dutch relinquished New Amsterdam (New York) to England in return for sugar-growing Suriname (Dutch Guiana). Similarly, in 1763, France traded most of Canada to England for Guadeloupe.

Christopher Columbus introduced sugarcane plants into the New World, the Caribbean islands, where labor demands fostered the slave trade. Sugarcane, however, was not cultivated in North America until the mid- to late eighteenth century. Louisiana's sugar production started in 1751: Jesuit missionaries grew the plants in New Orleans. By the late 1750's, at least one sugar mill was operating there. In Florida, commercial production of sugarcane, begun in 1767, was disrupted by the American Revolution and did not rebound for over a century.

Early sugarcane crops mainly produced syrup and rum. A Louisiana planter, Jean Etienne Bore, began successfully making sugar around 1755, affirming the sugar industry's potential. When Louisiana joined the United States in 1803, it and Texas, with their large plantations, established what became America's sugar industry. Small farms in South Carolina, Georgia, Alabama, Mississippi, and Arkansas also raised sugarcane, mostly for syrup.

The South's weather was not as constant as was the Caribbean's, so the cane-growing season was shorter. Planters, however, had a large slave labor force and made use of innovations such as improved cold-resistant cane plants and steam-powered machines that advanced the industry. The multiple-effect evaporator machine, created in 1846 by New Orleans-born Norbert Rillieux, a biracial inventor, made sugar processing safer and more efficient. By 1850, the southern states were producing nearly half the sugar consumed in the country.

Sugar beets, popular in Europe, were not an important sugar source in America until the late nineteenth century. E. H. Dyer of Alvarado, California, built the first successful sugar-beet factory in 1870; more followed in Nebraska, Utah, and Delaware. By 1910, more beet sugar than cane sugar was being produced in the United States. Factory owners contracted with farmers to plant a certain acreage for their exclusive use, using seed the factories furnished, thus guaranteeing their beet supply.

How Sugar Is Produced

Sugarcane is harvested by hand with machetes or, since the 1940's, by machines. After rodents, snakes, leaves, and other "trash" are burned away, the cane is transported to a factory. (Environmentally concerned regions omit the burning step.) At the factory, usually located close to the cane fields, the cane is weighed, chopped or shredded, and crushed to extract the juice, which is purified using heat, lime, and flocculants, and further processed through clarification vessels and evaporators, producing syrup. The syrup is then subjected to a crystallization process that separates the remaining liquids from the crystals. The crystals are washed, dried, cooled, and bagged or stored for shipping to a refinery, where high-quality sugars, such as soft brown sugar, sugar cubes, and granulated sugar, are produced. By-products include molasses, rum, alcohol, fuel, and livestock feed.

SUGAR PRODUCTION

During the early twentieth century, 1 million tons of sugar was produced annually. By 1972, 3.5 million tons were produced each year, and about one-fourth of it was consumed by Americans. Sugar beets' labor-intensive production, which initially required considerable hand labor for cultivating the plants, was soon made easier when mechanical devices were adopted to do everything from planting to harvesting the crop.

Big corporations in large coastal cities such as New York, New Orleans, Savannah, Philadelphia, and San Francisco took over the refining arm of the industry during the 1960's. They processed raw sugar from the southern states, Hawaii, Puerto Rico, and various foreign countries. More than one hundred varieties of grades and packaging of refined sugar were marketed to meet the increasing demands of American consumers.

The sugar industry has been assisted since the nineteenth century by the federal government with several profitable benefits. It has the right to use low-paid, nonunionized, federally sponsored, immigrant "guest workers," who harvest the sugar crop. A billion-dollar-plus subsidy program provides short-term loans to growers. The industry also profits from strict federal limitations on sugar imports, which allow the industry to charge high domestic prices. For instance, when the world price of sugar was less than 3 cents per pound, Ameri-cans paid 21 cents per pound. A Commerce Department study estimated that the sugar program costs American consumers more than $3 billion per year.

OUTLOOK

Because the federal government's sugar program limits sugar imports, some American businesses profit, but others, such as candy companies, find it more profitable to close their American factories and move operations elsewhere, where sugar is cheaper. Some U.S. refineries have closed, causing job losses. Some sugar farmers have switched to other crops, leaving fewer than fourteen thousand sugar farmers in the United States at the end of the twentieth century.

By year 2000, other countries were producing annually 1.5 billion metric tons of sugar, while America was producing only 7.2 million metric tons. Sugar consumption has remained stable for more than fifty years. More processed foods contain sugar, maintaining demand. Louisiana still deals with a short growing season, and the Florida industry's invasion of the Everglades causes environmental concerns, but both states still retain their strong position in sugar production.

Jane L. Ball

FURTHER READING

Flores, Alfredo. "A Versatile New Sugarcane for Florida." *Agricultural Research* 54, no. 1 (January, 2006): 20. Recounts the Florida sugarcane industry's attempts to find a plant variety that performs well throughout the winter season.

Forbes, Steve. "Bitter Battle." *Forbes*, June 20, 2005, 30. Details the controversy between the sugar industry and Splenda, a noncaloric sweetener, precipitated by the sugar industry's intent to keep its prices high.

Mintz, Sidney W. *Sweetness and Power: The Place of Sugar in Modern History.* New York: Penguin Books, 1986. Discusses sugar's effect on human nature and culture, including its influence on world labor practices, physical relocations, and class identity formations.

Surowiecki, James. "Deal Sweeteners." *New Yorker*, November 27, 2006, 92. Examines the sugar industry's protection by the federal government, America's high sugar prices, and the nation's failure to use energy-efficient, sugar-based ethanol.

Woloson, Wendy A. *Refined Tastes: Sugar, Confectionary, and Consumers in Nineteenth Century America.* Baltimore: Johns Hopkins University Press, 2002. Analysis of sugar's role in nineteenth century American society and culture. Provides background on early foreign sugar production and consumption.

SEE ALSO: Agribusiness; Agriculture; Agriculture, U.S. Department of; Cereal crops; Cola industry; Food-processing industries; Hawaii annexation.

Supersonic jetliners

DEFINITION: Large passenger jets designed to fly safely at speeds faster than the speed of sound

SIGNIFICANCE: Supersonic jetliners seemed to represent a major advance in commercial air travel, but their costs—financial and environmental—proved to outweigh their benefits, and they never replaced slower airplanes, even for transatlantic flights.

On October 14, 1947, Chuck Yeager piloted an experimental plane, the Bell XS-1, which had been dropped from a Boeing B-29, to a speed that surpassed Mach 1 (the speed of sound). His flight proved that it was possible to "break" the sound barrier. Traveling at such high velocity was a milestone, but before reliable supersonic aircraft could be designed, a great deal of further research and development remained to be done, particularly in the areas of aerodynamics and control. Physics required different model development at such speeds, and more research was needed to provide for land takeoffs. Early supersonic research and development was generally conducted for military applications, but during the late 1950's and 1960's researchers began investigating the technology for long-distance commercial travel.

The United States government selected Boeing and General Electric to participate in a federally funded program for commercial supersonic transport (SST). Meanwhile, British Aerospace and French Aerospatiale joined forces to produce the Concorde, and the Soviet Union began developing the Tupolev, TU-144. The TU-144 flew its maiden voyage on December 31, 1968, and a few months later, in March, 1969, the Concorde prototype took to the skies. In July, the TU-144 hit Mach 2, twice the speed of sound. Nearly two years later, on March 24, 1971, amid concerns regarding supersonic jetliners' effects on the environment, high noise level, and extreme cost, the U.S. Congress rejected further funding for the Boeing supersonic model. Strong public opposition to the SST and a faltering economy effectively canceled the American program.

Two years later, at the 1973 Paris Air Show, the Concorde showed its capabilities. Tragically, at the show, the TU-144 crashed, killing everyone on board and eight people on the ground. In December, 1975, the TU-144 began limited commercial service, but the Soviet transport did not sell outside the country. Poor economic returns and a fatal accident on October 27, 1979, helped seal the TU-144's

The Concorde in 1977. (Department of Defense)

fate. The Concorde became a technical success, providing flawless international service across the Atlantic Ocean until July 25, 2000, when debris on a Paris runway caused a crash on takeoff. While the technology of the Concorde cut long-distance travel times in half, its costs in comparison to everyday flights were extravagant. In November, 2003, Concorde services were discontinued.

Once thought to be the answer to commercial travel, the supersonic jetliner proved to have economic, environmental, and political problems that limited the market for SSTs. Laws that limited supersonic commercial flight to overseas flights restricted the routes SSTs could fly. Concerns for the ozone layer and high ticket prices also limited demand for supersonic travel. Supersonic transport continues to be researched, but until the technology becomes both economically and environmentally feasible, new production is improbable.

Cynthia J. W. Svoboda

FURTHER READING

Hallion, Richard. *Supersonic Flight: Breaking the Sound Barrier and Beyond—the Story of the Bell X-1 and Douglas D-558.* Washington, D.C.: Brassey's, 1997.

Hansen, James R. *The Bird Is on the Wing: Aerodynamics and the Progress of the American Airplane.* College Station: Texas A&M University Press, 2004.

Marchman, James F., III, ed. *Encyclopedia of Flight.* Pasadena, Calif.: Salem Press, 2002.

SEE ALSO: Air transportation industry; Aircraft industry; Airships.

Supply-side economics

DEFINITION: Economic theory that proposes that greater tax cuts for those earning large incomes will improve the economy and result in increased revenue for the government by providing incentives for those with money to increase investments and produce more goods and services

SIGNIFICANCE: Supply-side economics, embraced by U.S. president Ronald Reagan during the 1980's in an attempt to boost the U.S. economy after the stagflation of the 1970's, provided the theoretical underpinnings for the large number of tax cuts that, some experts argue, led to growth in the national economy.

During the 1970's, inflation ran rampant, and as workers tried to earn enough to keep up with inflation, a large number of taxpayers were pushed into higher tax brackets. In turn, this decreased the amount of income people could spend and brought economic growth to a crawl. This negative state of financial affairs provided the opportunity for the emergence of supply-side economics, a controversial economic theory that holds that lowering the amount of tax that high-income people (who are more likely to be investors and entrepreneurs) are required to pay provides them with the incentive to produce more goods and services through investments, thus boosting the economy. In addition, because less of their earnings must go to taxes, people would feel encouraged to work more. Higher numbers of workers would enter the workforce and consequently increase the tax base. Proponents of supply-side economics argued that tax cuts would diminish tax-avoidance activity, and tax revenue would increase. Economist Arthur Laffer, who developed "the Laffer curve," is credited with illustrating how decreases in tax rates result in increases in tax revenues.

Throughout the late 1970's and early 1980's, scholars, economists, and legislators argued back and forth over the idea of supply-side economics. Lowering tax rates and increasing revenues did not go together in traditional economic theories. Keynesian theory holds that consumers and their demand for goods and services drives the economy, but supply-side economics holds that producers and their willingness to create goods and services drives economic growth.

President Ronald Reagan made supply-side economic theory the framework for his economic policies, and between 1981 and 1986, the federal income tax rate was reduced from 70 percent to approximately 33 percent. The U.S. economy experienced great increases, with the gross national product rising at a far faster pace than during the 1970's. Indeed, economic growth in the United States exceeded that of all industrial nations except Japan. Although critics pointed out that only the rich got richer, the total tax revenue collected from the wealthy also increased by 32 percent during the 1980's and seemed to support the arguments of supply-side economists. As a result, during the late 1980's, supply-side economic incentives gained prominence in the United States and throughout the world, with many countries similarly reducing their tax rates.

Controversy surrounding the effects of supply-side economics continues unabated, with critics arguing that lowering tax rates beyond a certain level will have destructive effects in the long run. Nevertheless, tax incentives for people to increase work and invest more deeply have affected U.S. financial history and remain an important economic legacy of the 1980's.

M. Casey Diana

FURTHER READING

Atkinson, Victor A. *Supply-Side Follies: Why Conservative Economics Fails, Liberal Economics Falters, and Innovation Economics Is the Answer.* Lanham, Md.: Rowman & Littlefield, 2008.

Bartlett, Bruce. *Reaganomics: Supply-Side Economics in Action.* New York: Arlington House, 1981.

Canto, Victor A., Douglas H. Joines, and Arthur B. Laffer. *Foundations of Supply-Side Economics.* Burlington, Mass.: Academic Press, 1983.

SEE ALSO: Income tax, corporate; Income tax, personal; Monetary policy, federal; Taxation; Trickle-down theory.

Supreme Court and banking law

DEFINITION: Decisions by the nation's highest court regarding the constitutionality and interpretation of banking laws

SIGNIFICANCE: American ambivalence toward banks and central bankers has never been shared by the U.S. Supreme Court, whose decisions in banking law have supported both a national bank and a national banking system, thus contributing to the growth of American industry and business.

During the early nineteenth century, Supreme Court decisions regarding banking were at the center of the first national debates over the powers of the federal government and its role in the expansion of American business. Federalists such as Alexander Hamilton believed that a chief role of the new federal government created by the 1787 Constitution was to further American manufacturing, indus-

try, and business. He believed a central national bank was necessary to accomplish that purpose.

Reflecting perhaps a suspicion of central bankers, however, the Constitution did not explicitly authorize the creation of such a bank. Thus, when Hamilton's First Bank of the United States was created by Congress on February 25, 1791, as a federal depository and guarantor of bank notes, it was destined to be at the center of a nationwide controversy about the interpretation of the Constitution, the role of the federal government in the economy, and whether the United States should be oriented in its policies toward becoming an agrarian nation of farmers or an industrial nation of trade and business.

BATTLE OVER THE U.S. BANK

The first political parties took sides in the controversy over the proper economic role of the federal government. The Democratic-Republicans, led by Thomas Jefferson, were agrarian, suspicious of government, and strict constructionists of the Constitution. The Federalists, led by Alexander Hamilton, were mercantile, supporters of a strong central government to promote business, and broad constructionists of the Constitution. In 1805, Georgia, reflecting state hostility to the Bank of the United States, enacted a tax on that bank's local Georgia branch. When the bank refused to pay the tax, Georgia seized its deposits in satisfaction of the tax debt. The Supreme Court ruled in *Bank of the United States v. Deveaux* (1809) that depositors who were citizens of Pennsylvania were entitled to sue in federal court to recover their deposits from the state of Georgia. The ruling had the effect of supporting the national bank.

After a protracted struggle, the U.S. Bank was not rechartered in 1811. In 1816, however, Congress chartered the larger and more powerful Second Bank of the United States. The famous case of *McCulloch v. Maryland* (1819) resulted. This case took on a greater constitutional significance than just the struggle over the bank. Again, a hostile state taxed the U.S. Bank, and when the federal government opposed this taxation, the constitutionality of the bank's charter was placed at issue. In upholding the power of Congress to charter the bank, Chief Justice John Marshall relied on the necessary and proper clause of the Constitution. He ruled that all powers necessary to carry out powers explicitly enumerated in the Constitution were themselves authorized by the document. Thus, the federal government was widely vested with powers to institute a central bank and to take measures that would advance the course of American business.

The state of Ohio, which also taxed the U.S. Bank, tried to evade the ruling of *McCulloch v. Maryland* by testing the legitimacy of its tax on the bank in the Ohio state courts. However, in *Osborn v. Bank of the United States* (1824), the Supreme Court proclaimed federal jurisdiction over every case involving the U.S. Bank, even if the issues at stake were questions of state law. Once again, Chief Justice Marshall had used the controversy over the U.S. Bank to assert the widest scope of federal power over the states.

In *McCulloch* and *Osborn*, the Court established that no state could tax a federal entity and that no state court could preempt federal courts from adjudicating any issues that involved federal institutions. The eastern business interests, which saw a strong federal government as essential to their financial plans, rejoiced; President Andrew Jackson did not. He vowed to destroy the Second Bank of the United States and humble its supporters. In 1832, Jackson vetoed the bill rechartering the bank. In 1835, he appointed Roger Taney, an opponent of the bank, to succeed Marshall as chief justice of the United States. These acts were essential elements in a new wave of Jacksonian democracy. Another element of Jacksonian populism was hostility to the federal courts and the U.S. Supreme Court, which Jackson blamed for favoritism toward eastern banking interests.

Dual Banking System

With the demise of the Second Bank of the United States, the U.S. banking system became characterized by a proliferation of state banks operating under state laws. This situation provided little scope for the nation's highest federal court. However, with the National Currency Act of 1863 and the National Bank Act of 1864, federal chartering of banks was reinstated and a role for the Supreme Court restored. This overlapping of state and federal chartering became known as a dual banking system. Under this system, the Supreme Court was often called on to adjudicate the competition between state- and federally chartered banks.

In *Veazie Bank v. Fenno* (1869), the Court upheld the constitutionality of federal taxes on state banks,

again asserting federal supremacy. Banks had become pivotal players in American business. They were not only depositories for savers but also loaned money and minted currency, as the Court recognized in *Oulton v. German Savings and Loan Society* (1872). The Court in *First National Bank v. Missouri* (1924) limited the powers of the national banks to those enumerated in federal statutes. For example, the Court in *First National Bank v. Lanier* (1870) found that, as federal law forbade banks from owning their own shares, they were also prohibited from loaning money on those shares.

Despite these limitations, the Court found numerous bank powers that were authorized in federal law. These included the powers to certify checks (*Merchants Bank v. State Bank*, 1870); acquire stock (*First National Bank v. National Exchange Bank*, 1875); borrow money (*Auten v. United States National Bank*, 1899, and *Wyman v. Wallace*, 1906); collect judgments and pay taxes on behalf of depositors (*Miller v. King*, 1912, and *Clement National Bank v. Vermont*, 1913); sell mortgages (*First National Bank v. City of Hartford*, 1927); operate a safe deposit business (*Colorado National Bank v. Bedford*, 1940); and advertise the word "savings" (*Franklin National Bank v. New York*, 1954). As the Supreme Court recognized in *National Bank v. Commonwealth* (1869), banks were governed much more by state financial laws than by sporadic federal legislation. However much the stage was left to the states, though, the Supreme Court continued to insist that national oversight of banks was in the end a legitimate task of the federal government, holding in *Tiffany v. National Bank of Missouri* (1874) and *Davis v. Elmira Savings Bank* (1896) that federal law overrode state law in regulating national banks.

The *Tiffany v. National Bank of Missouri* decision also established that federally chartered banks are allowed to charge the highest loan rates permitted under state law, even if state banks are restricted to lower rates. Likewise, in *Farmers' and Mechanics' National Bank v. Dearing* (1875), the Court decided that a state law forfeiting a bank debt in which excessive (usurious) interest had been charged was preempted by federal laws that allowed the bank in error to forfeit only the interest due and not the entire loan. These cases illustrate the principle, manifested repeatedly in Supreme Court decisions, that federal laws are often more favorable to banks than are state laws.

After the passage of the Glass-Steagall Act in 1933, which President Franklin D. Roosevelt is shown signing, the Supreme Court dominated banking. (AP/Wide World Photos)

FEDERAL REGULATION

Although the Federal Reserve Act of 1913 reorganized the banking system, it was only with the New Deal's Banking Act of 1933 that the Supreme Court re-emerged as a dominant force in banking law. The 1933 law, commonly known as the Glass-Steagall Act, firmly separated commercial and investment banking, expanded the branching power of national banks (previously confined to single unit locations), and created the Federal Deposit Insurance Corporation. As federal laws and regulations concerning banks proliferated, the Supreme Court would decide such issues as limitations on bank mergers (*United States v. Phillipsburg National Bank and Trust Co.*, 1970, and *United States v. Marine Bancorporation*, 1974), bank holding companies gaining ownership of investment advisory and trust services (*Lewis v. BT Investment Managers*, 1980), and the constitutionality of regional bank arrangements (*Northeast Bancorp v. Board of Governors*, 1985).

Perhaps the most controversial banking law issue to face the Supreme Court was whether banks could engage in profitable businesses that were outside the scope of traditional banking, such as insurance underwriting, securities and mutual fund investing,

international financing, and providing venture capital. In cases such as *First National Bank of Logan v. Walker Bank and Trust Co.* (1966), *Investment Company Institute v. Camp* (1971), and other cases decided during the 1960's and 1970's, the Supreme Court was reluctant to permit national banks to expand their geographical reach or to engage in such newly lucrative businesses as operating mutual investment funds. That reluctance would diminish as a result of both congressional legislation and changes in the Court's own internal composition and direction.

During the 1980's, President Ronald Reagan inaugurated a new era of federal deregulation of banking. Deposit interest rates were deregulated. Geographic and state barriers to bank growth were removed, permitting interstate banking. Banks were allowed to compete in numerous investment enterprises, such as underwriting and marketing stock and mortgage-backed securities, managing mutual funds, and selling whole-life and permanent life insurance. In cases such as *Securities Industry Association v. Board of Governors of the Federal Reserve System* (1984), *Clarke v. Securities Industry Association* (1987), *NationsBank of North Carolina v. Variable Annuity Life Insurance Co.* (1995), and *Barnett Bank of Marion County v. Nelson* (1996), the Court took the broadest view of banks' ability to engage in a wide range of practices in the new economy.

The Reagan and post-Reagan era Supreme Court, with its traditional view of the centrality of banks in the American financial system, has been supportive of the entry of banks into the fields of insurance, marketing of securities and mutual funds, and venture capital. In addition, the Court has supported the efforts of banks to extend their operations in local branches and across state lines. However, partly in reaction to the savings and loan debacle of the 1980's, the Court has also extended the legal liabilities that could be placed on banks, in cases such as *Federal Deposit Insurance Corp. v. Meyer* (1994) and *O'Melveny and Myers v. Federal Deposit Insurance Corp.* (1994). In *Atherton v. Federal Deposit Insurance Corp.* (1997), the court overruled a long-standing holding in *Briggs v. Spaulding* (1891). The *Atherton v. Federal Deposit Insurance Corp.* decision allowed states to impose stricter standards of conduct on banks, their officers, and directors than those imposed by federal statutes.

In the battles over the First and Second Banks of the United States in the beginning of the nineteenth century, the Supreme Court forcefully asserted the power of the federal government over the nation's banking and financial systems. The decisions of the Marshall Court regarding these banks also helped establish for the Supreme Court powers more extensive than those originally envisioned by the Founders. Throughout the nineteenth century, the Court upheld the powers of the federal government over banking and sided with federally chartered banks over state-chartered banks at every opportunity. At the end of the twentieth century, the Court in numerous cases upheld and advanced federal legislation that firmly asserted congressional control over most aspects of the banking system. Supreme Court decisions were an important factor in enabling banks to participate fully in the financial boom of the 1980's and 1990's, as banks became central players in highly profitable areas of an increasingly securitized, monetized, and mobile global economy.

Howard Bromberg

FURTHER READING

Horwitz, Morton. *The Transformation of American Law, 1780-1860.* New ed. Cambridge, Mass.: Harvard University Press, 2006. Explains American legal history in terms of class economic interest.

Hughes, Jonathan, and Louis Cain. *American Economic History.* Reading, Mass.: Addison-Wesley, 1998. Readable textbook with chapters on banking and business law.

Macey, Jonathan, Geoffrey Miller, and Richard Carnell. *Banking Law and Regulation.* Rev. 3d ed. Gaithersberg, N.Y.: Aspen Law and Business, 2001. Collection of Supreme Court and other court cases on banking law, with a helpful historical introduction.

Newmyer, R. Kent. *John Marshall and the Heroic Age of the Supreme Court.* Baton Rouge: Louisiana State University Press, 2001. Working directly from Marshall's papers, Newmyer emphasizes Marshall's federalist convictions.

Remini, Robert. *Andrew Jackson and the Bank War: A Study in the Growth of Presidential Power.* New York: W. W. Norton, 1967. Demonstrates how Jackson skillfully used the political and legal controversy over the U.S. Bank to shape the presidency.

Schwartz, Bernard. *A History of the Supreme Court.* New York: Oxford University Press, 1995. Compact history of the Supreme Court emphasizing Marshall's far-reaching jurisprudence.

SEE ALSO: Bank of the United States, First; Bank of the United States, Second; Banking; Congress, U.S.; Constitution, U.S.; New Deal programs; Presidency, U.S.; Supreme Court and commerce; Supreme Court and contract law; Supreme Court and labor law; Supreme Court and land law.

Supreme Court and commerce

DEFINITION: Decisions by the nation's highest court regarding the constitutionality and interpretation of laws governing commercial transactions

SIGNIFICANCE: The Supreme Court may be called on to determine the scope of federal authority to regulate interstate commerce, as well as to adjudicate commercial disputes between state governments or disputes that pit the laws of one state against the laws of another. All such decisions have profound effects on the particular businesses involved, as well as on the business climate in the nation.

One of the fundamental principles of American governance is federalism—the separation of powers between the federal and state governments. Some powers are assigned by Article I, section 8 of the U.S. Constitution to the federal government. The Tenth Amendment reserves the powers not granted to Congress to the states. Thus, when the federal government acts, it must be able to point to some power enumerated in the Constitution as authority for its action.

The Constitution grants Congress the power "to regulate commerce with foreign nations, and among the several states, and with the Indian tribes." Of the three, the power to regulate commerce "among the several states," that is, the interstate commerce power, is the most problematic. The commerce clause creates two challenges for the Supreme Court. One is to define the limits of federal power, so that Congress does not usurp the states' authority to regulate purely intrastate matters such as the health, safety, welfare, and morals of its citizens, authority that the Constitution does not explicitly allocate to the federal government. The second challenge is to ensure that states do not place substantial barriers to or burdens on interstate commerce, or discriminate against out-of-state commerce in ways that might interfere with national interests.

EARLY HISTORY

Before the adoption of the Constitution in 1789, the newly independent United States was governed under the Articles of Confederation. Congress had no power over commerce. States created barriers, such as tariffs, to interstate trade, leading to economic chaos threatening the nation's survival. In 1786, the Constitutional Convention was called to revise the articles, but instead drafted an entirely new constitution, granting to Congress greatly expanded powers, including the power to regulate interstate commerce.

The next century saw little federal legislation regarding commerce. In those cases questioning the scope of federal power that came before the Supreme Court, the Court deferred to Congress's authority. The reach of both federal and state power over commerce was considered by the Court in *Gibbons v. Ogden* (1824). A state-granted monopoly on steamboat navigation was invalidated, because it conflicted with a federal boat-licensing statute.

In *Cooley v. Board of Wardens* (1851), Pennsylvania required riverboats to take on local pilots. There was no federal rule at issue. The Court held that subjects requiring uniform national regulation could be regulated only by Congress, but subjects of local concern could be regulated by the states. This was a subject of the latter category. The states' authority to regulate when Congress might have done so but has not became known as the "dormant" commerce clause.

The Supreme Court's first effort to place limitations on the exercise of the federal commerce power came in *United States v. Dewitt* (1870). The Court invalidated a federal statute that prohibited the sale of naphtha and oil that was inflammable at less than 110 degrees as an infringement by Congress of the states' "police powers," that is, their power to regulate the health, safety, welfare, and morals of their citizens, and not a regulation of commerce.

FROM 1888 TO 1933

In the last decades of the nineteenth century, Congress became interested in regulating the economic and social order, and the Supreme Court became interested in preventing it from doing so. The Court believed the Tenth Amendment barred Congress from regulating purely intrastate commerce and from impinging on the states' police powers.

The Court adopted, temporarily, a narrow definition of commerce. It held in *Leisy v. Hardin* (1890) that the importation of intoxicating beverages is "commerce" and cannot be banned by a state. In *Kidd v. Pearson* (1888), though, the Court determined that the manufacturing of such beverages was not commerce and could be prohibited within a state. In a case involving the reach of the federal commerce power, *United States v. E. C. Knight* (1895), the Court held that the Sherman Antitrust Act of 1890 did not apply to the manufacturing of sugar.

In *Swift and Company v. United States* (1905), the Court held that stockyard bidding practices were subject to federal regulation, even though the activities took place within a single state, because they were part of the "stream of commerce." Similarly, federal regulation of the railroads was upheld, and the ability of states to set local fares was commensurately limited because such fares had an effect on interstate commerce.

As the twentieth century dawned, the Supreme Court was willing to uphold some of Congress's tinkering with the social order, including prohibiting the interstate transportation of women for immoral purposes, of lottery tickets, and of unsafe food and drugs. In 1905, however, the Court embarked on three decades of rejectionism of both federal and state forays into social and economic engineering. In *Lochner v. New York* (1905), the Court struck down the state's maximum-labor-hours legislation. The problem was not that the law interfered with interstate commerce but that it interfered with the right of the employer and employee to contract. Rather than being a valid exercise of the state's police powers, the law offended the Fourteenth Amendment's due process clause.

The Court continued to strike down state and federal laws that interfered with free markets. In some of these cases the law was held to be an improper extension of the commerce power, and in some a violation of the due process clauses of the Fifth and Fourteenth Amendments. In *Hammer v. Dagenhart* (1918), the Court struck down a federal statute prohibiting child labor, because it viewed the law as an attempt to regulate the conditions of production, not of commerce. In *Adkins v. Children's Hospital* (1923), the Court invalidated federal minimum-wage legislation for women as an infringement of liberty of contract, as protected by the Fifth Amendment's due process clause.

THE DEPRESSION AND THE NEW DEAL

In 1932, Franklin D. Roosevelt was elected president on a promise of acting immediately to repair the battered economy. Although Congress was willing to adopt virtually all of Roosevelt's legislative program, the Supreme Court would not go along. The National Industrial Recovery Act (NRA) of 1933 was overturned in *Schechter Poultry Corp. v. United States* (1935). The act allowed the president to establish codes for operating trades or industries, in this case the poultry business. The Court held that the employment practices of the poultry business did not have a direct connection to interstate commerce. In *United States v. Butler* (1936), the Court invalidated the Agricultural Adjustment Act of 1933, which empowered the federal government to pay farmers who reduced acreage under cultivation, holding that the Tenth Amendment reserved to the states the power to regulate agricultural production.

In 1937, weary of the Court's obstructionism, Roosevelt asked Congress for authority to appoint an additional six Supreme Court justices, positions undoubtedly to be filled by justices more amenable to New Deal legislation. Though not enacted, the threat to pack the Court may have had the desired effect, as the Court suddenly changed course. In *West Coast Hotel v. Parish* (1937), Justice Owen Roberts joined a new majority willing to uphold the constitutionality of state minimum-wage legislation, overruling *Adkins v. Children's Hospital* (1923).

This marked the end of the *Lochner* era. The Court did not thereafter overturn economic legislation on the basis of the due process clause. Roosevelt appointed seven justices in the next four years who

were inclined to defer to Congress's exercise of the commerce power. The extent of that deference was made clear in *Wickard v. Filburn* (1942). Congress intended to control the quantity—and thereby the price—of wheat on the interstate market by restricting the acreage that farmers could plant. Roscoe C. Filburn, authorized to plant eleven acres, grew twenty-three, harvesting 239 excess bushels. He argued that the federal commerce power did not extend to his planting, because he intended to consume the wheat on his farm and therefore was not engaging in interstate commerce. The Court held that, although the amount in question was trivial, the commerce power did apply, because in the aggregate uncontrolled cultivation by farmers small and large would have an effect on interstate commerce.

THE MODERN ERA

The aggregate theory espoused in *Wickard* was a significant expansion of the reach of the federal commerce power. This theory underpinned the Court's upholding of the Civil Rights Act of 1964 in two landmark cases, *Heart of Atlanta Motel Inc. v. United States* (1964) and *Katzenbach v. McClung* (1964). These cases involved the refusal of a hotel and a restaurant, respectively, to serve African Americans in contravention of the act's prohibition against racial discrimination in public accommodations. The Court reasoned that such discrimination in the aggregate made interstate travel burdensome, and therefore Congress had the authority to prohibit it.

The question remained as to how far this extension of the commerce power went. Had it morphed into a federal police power over health, safety, welfare, and morals? For the first fifty years after *Wickard*, no limit to the commerce power was identified. Then, in *United States v. Lopez* (1995), the Court considered a federal prohibition of the possession of firearms near schools. The effect that gun possession, a noncommercial activity, might have on the quality of education and thus the quality of the workforce was too theoretical to support a connection to interstate commerce.

As a result of the Court's decisions, it established the principle that Congress can regulate the channels and instrumentalities of interstate commerce. It may regulate persons or things moving in interstate commerce, activities that substantially affect interstate commerce, and—if they are commercial in nature—activities that in the aggregate substantially affect interstate commerce.

The power of the states to regulate commerce is limited in two ways. A state cannot discriminate against out-of-state commerce, unless it has a legitimate health or safety reason. A state cannot place a burden on interstate commerce unless justified by a countervailing benefit. The Court held in *Hunt v. Washington State Apple Advertising Commission* (1977), for example, that North Carolina could not require a particular grading system for apples, because the requirement discriminated against Washington State, whose apples were graded differently,

Martin Luther King, Jr. (right, wearing hat) and Ralph Abernathy (also wearing hat) try to check into the Hotel Albert in Selma, Alabama, in 1965. The Supreme Court used the commerce clause to rule against segregation. (AP/Wide World Photos)

and no health or safety benefit was identified. In *Raymond Motor Transportation v. Rice* (1978), the Court invalidated Wisconsin's prohibition on trailers longer than fifty-five feet, ostensibly for safety reasons. The substantial burden on interstate trucking was not justified by any benefit, as the evidence indicated that sixty-five-foot tandem trailers were just as safe. In *Maine v. Taylor* (1986), the Court upheld Maine's prohibition of the importation of live bait fish, which was intended to protect the local environment from parasites, because it supported a legitimate health and safety purpose.

Howard C. Ellis

FURTHER READING

Amar, Akhil Reed. *America's Constitution: A Biography.* New York: Random House, 2005. Studies the Constitution one provision at a time. Amar incorporates the historical events and political issues that shaped each provision, as well as the Supreme Court's interpretations in landmark cases.

Hall, Kermit L., et al., eds. *The Oxford Companion to the Supreme Court of the United States.* New York: Oxford University Press, 1992. Alphabetically arranged compendium of more than one thousand entries covering the history of the Supreme Court, biographies of the justices, and four hun-

dred of the Court's most important decisions. Recommended for high school reference collections.

Hoffer, Peter Charles, William Hoffer, James Hull, and N. E. H. Hull. *The Supreme Court: An Essential History.* Lawrence: University Press of Kansas, 2007. This survey of the history of the Supreme Court, with a chapter devoted to each chief justice's tenure, considers the role of the Court as the arbiter of the Constitution, focusing on the personalities and perspectives of the justices themselves.

Lively, Donald E. *Landmark Supreme Court Cases: A Reference Guide.* Westport, Conn.: Greenwood Press, 1999. Compendium of the entries on seventy-four of the Supreme Court's most important cases, arranged thematically, with a detailed discussion of each case, targeted at a high school level audience.

May, Christopher N., and Allan Ides. *Constitutional Law—National Power and Federalism: Examples and Explanations.* 3d ed. New York: Aspen, 2004. An overview of federalism that provides analysis of the federal interstate commerce power and the limitations of state authority to regulate commerce.

Schwartz, Bernard. *A History of the Supreme Court.*

New York: Oxford University Press, 1995. A chronological history including major chapters on the most significant cases, such as *Lochner v. New York*, as well as biographical sketches of important justices.

SEE ALSO: Commerce, U.S. Department of; Congress, U.S.; Constitution, U.S.; Presidency, U.S.; Supreme Court and banking law; Supreme Court and contract law; Supreme Court and labor law; Supreme Court and land law.

Supreme Court and contract law

DEFINITION: Decisions by the nation's highest court regarding the constitutionality and interpretation of the laws governing legally binding agreements between individuals or corporations

SIGNIFICANCE: Contract law lies at the heart of business and financial dealings among private entities. For more than a century, the U.S. Supreme Court had a significant impact on the nation's contract laws, but since the 1930's, the Court's impact on that branch of the law has been limited.

Contact law in the United States is primarily made by state legislatures and adjudicated in state courts. Because most aspects of contract law do not have a direct relationship to the U.S. Constitution or to federal legislation, the state courts are usually the final arbiters of the law in each state. The U.S. Supreme Court, nevertheless, has played a significant role in shaping four major aspects of contract law: It has interpreted the contract clause of the Constitution, determined the proper application of the freedom of contract doctrine from 1897 to 1937, recognized a relevant national general common law from 1842 to 1938, and adjudicated questions of federal contract law relating to purchases by the federal government.

CONTRACT CLAUSE

The Constitution, in Article I, section 10, prohibits states from passing "any law impairing the Obligation of Contracts." The framers apparently drafted the clause out of concern that state legislatures might help the debtor class at the expense of property interests. In *Fletcher v. Peck* (1810), the Supreme Court held that the Constitution prohibited Georgia's legislature from revoking land contracts, even though the contracts had their origins in a public land grant tainted by bribery and fraud. In *Sturges v. Crowninshield* (1819), the Court held that the contract clause prohibited state legislatures from passing bankruptcy laws that relieved insolvent debtors of their contractual obligations. In *Ogden v. Saunders* (1827), however, the justices voted 4 to 3 to uphold a New York state bankruptcy law that applied only to contracts made subsequent to the passage of the law.

Beginning during the late nineteenth century, the Supreme Court gradually allowed the states to exercise greater flexibility in regulating contracts. In the case of *Stone v. Mississippi* (1880), the Court held that the contract clause could not be used to limit a state's police power in protecting the public's health, safety, and morality. During the Great Depression, in *Home Building and Loan Association v. Blaisdell* (1934), the justices by a 4 to 3 vote upheld a Minnesota statute that attempted to limit farm and home foreclosures by temporarily extending the period for repaying loans. In addition to accepting the pragmatic justification for the law, the Court's majority reasoned that the legislature had not altered the basic integrity of the contractual obligation.

The Court appeared to return to favoring stricter enforcement of the contract clause in *United States Trust v. New Jersey* (1977): It invalidated a state law that abrogated a public bond covenant on the use of revenues. Writing for the majority, however, Associate Justice Harry A. Blackmun wrote that contractual impairments might not be unconstitutional if they were "reasonable and necessary to serve an important public purpose." In subsequent decisions, the Court tended to subordinate the contract clause to economic judgments of state legislatures. In *Keystone Bituminous Coal Association v. DeBenedictis* (1987), Associate Justice John Paul Stevens wrote, "It is well settled that the prohibition against impairing the obligation of contracts is not to be read literally."

FREEDOM OF CONTRACT DOCTRINE

From 1897 until 1937, the Supreme Court held that the due process clauses provided substantive protection for the right of employers and employees freely to negotiate employment agreements and placed strict limits on governmental interference. The Court's best-known application of the doctrine was in *Lochner v. New York* (1905), which overturned a state law limiting the number of hours that bakery employees might work. In other applications of the freedom of contract doctrine, the Court struck down a federal minimum wage law as well as a federal law prohibiting employers from firing employees who engaged in union activities.

The Court, however, upheld restrictions on contracts that could clearly be justified by the states' interest in protecting public safety and health. In 1937, it reversed the *Lochner v. New York* line of cases with *West Coast Hotel v. Parrish*, which upheld Washington State's minimum wage law. The Court's decision in *West Coast Hotel v. Parrish* terminated its tradition of applying special scrutiny to governmental regulation of employment agreements. Encouraged by this landmark decision, Congress enacted the Fair Labor Standards Act of 1938, which established a national minimum wage.

NATIONAL COMMON LAW AND CONTRACTS

The Judiciary Act of 1789 required the federal courts to follow applicable state laws. In *Swift v. Tyson* (1842), however, the Supreme Court held that this requirement did not extend to state courts' decisions on "contracts and other instruments of a commercial nature." The *Swift v. Tyson* decision initiated the establishment of a national general common law in commercial transactions, although the Supreme Court only rarely chose to review contract cases. After almost a century of controversy, in *Erie Railroad v. Tompkins* (1938), the Court reversed *Swift v. Tyson* and repudiated the doctrine of a national common law. Subsequent to the *Erie Railroad v. Tompkins* ruling, the Court has almost always declined to hear cases dealing with contract law, unless the federal government is a party to a dispute.

FEDERAL CONTRACT LAW

As the world's largest purchaser of goods and services, the U.S. government annually awards billions of dollars in contracts for the procurement of everything from office supplies to complex weapons systems. These government expenditures are governed by a body of federal contract law that is based on the Constitution, federal statutes, regulations of the Office of Federal Procurement Policy, federal court decisions, and executive orders. Although the government's right to make procurement contracts is not expressly authorized in the Constitution, the Supreme Court in *United States v. Tingey* (1831) acknowledged that it is an inherent aspect of national sovereignty.

Other noteworthy decisions of the Court include *Cooke v. United States* (1875), recognizing that when the federal government is a party to a commercial transaction, it incurs all the responsibilities of a private person in the same circumstances. A federal statute of 1917 empowers the president to modify or cancel contracts for ships or materials, while requiring just compensation for such canceled contracts as determined by the president. In *DeLaval Steam Turbine Co. v. United States* (1931), the Court held that a company was entitled to compensation for the value of the contract at the date of cancellation, but not for anticipated profits. If contracting officers exceed the authority conferred on them by statute or regulation, the Court held in *Federal Crop Insurance Corp. v. Merrill* (1947), the government has no obligation to honor the resulting contracts.

Thomas Tandy Lewis

FURTHER READING

Ely, James W. *Contract Clause in American History.* New York: Taylor & Francis, 1997. Scholarly examination of the creation, interpretation, and enforcement of the U.S. Constitution's contract clause.

_____. *The Guardian of Every Other Right: A Constitutional History of Property Rights.* New York: Oxford University Press, 2007. Includes a good introductory treatment of the contract clause and the freedom of contract doctrine; favorable toward the laissez-faire tradition.

Epstein, Lee, and Thomas Walker. *Constitutional Law for a Changing America: Institutional Powers and Constraints.* Washington, D.C.: CQ Press, 2007. Includes clear treatments of Supreme Court's decisions on the contract clause and the freedom of contracts doctrine.

Massengale, Eugene. *Fundamentals of Federal Contract Law.* New York: Quorum Books, 1991. The standard work on the complex body of laws relating to federal purchases of goods and services, with summaries of hundreds of court decisions.

Wilmott, Lindy, and Des Butler. *Contract Law.* New York: Oxford University Press, 2005. A standard textbook providing a good summary of most aspects of the topic.

SEE ALSO: Congress, U.S.; Contract law; Government spending; Presidency, U.S.; Supreme Court and banking law; Supreme Court and commerce; Supreme Court and labor law.

Supreme Court and labor law

DEFINITION: Decisions by the nation's highest court regarding the constitutionality and interpretation of legislation regulating labor unions, collective bargaining, and the rights of workers and employers

SIGNIFICANCE: Since the late nineteenth century, the precedents established by the Supreme Court have had a profound impact on the complex field of labor law, and the Court has been the final arbiter in legal disputes between organized labor and management.

Until the late nineteenth century, judicial rulings concerning labor law were the purview almost entirely of state courts. After the U.S. Supreme Court asserted its authority in the field, it went through distinct phases in its interpretation and adjudication of labor law. From the 1880's until the 1930's, the Court's majority tended to be hostile toward unions and to defend an ideology of laissez-faire constitutionalism, opposing many governmental regulations of the private sector. Then, from the late 1930's through the end of World War II, the majority was generally sympathetic toward unions, upholding legislation that protected the rights of workers to engage in collective bargaining. The Court's decisions since the war have generally been less favorable toward organized labor, based on postwar legislation that curbed some of the privileges that unions had earlier acquired. Finally, since the 1960's, the Court has made many important interpretations of antidiscrimination laws.

HOSTILITY TOWARD UNIONS

During the 1880's, the federal courts increasingly became involved in settling conflicts between private businesses and labor unions. For the next half century, the decisions of both the Supreme Court and the lower courts tended to favor business interests at the expense of organized labor. During this period, lower federal and state courts issued about three thousand injunctions requiring labor unions to terminate strikes and boycotts, and the Court generally approved of such injunctions. In a major precedent, *In re Debs* (1895), the Court upheld a federal court order that unions end the Pullman Strike and its accompanying boycotts. The Court endorsed a broad use of equity jurisdiction, treating strikes and boycotts as public nuisances, and it further recognized the federal government's constitutional authority to remove obstacles to commerce and to ensure delivery of the mails.

The Supreme Court's bias was reflected in its approach to the Sherman Antitrust Act of 1890, which broadly outlawed monopolistic practices and combinations in restraint of trade. In the famous Danbury Hatters' case, *Loewe v. Lawlor* (1908), the Court held that the statute prohibited labor unions from organizing or publicizing consumer boycotts of particular companies. Although the Clayton Antitrust Act of 1914 appeared to prohibit application of antitrust legislation against labor unions, the Court in *Duplex Printing Co. v. Deering* (1921) narrowly interpreted the act as not applying to secondary boycotts or coercive acts. Injunctions against union activities continued to be common for another decade.

From 1897 until 1938, the Court interpreted the due process clauses of the Fifth and Fourteenth Amendments to provide substantive protection for a freedom of contracts, often overturning legislation designed to improve working conditions. In *Lochner v. New York* (1905), the Court voided a statute establishing maximum work hours for employees in bakeries. In *Adair v. United States* (1908), the Court overturned the Erdman Act of 1898, a federal law that had prohibited so-called yellow-dog contracts and the punishment of workers for engaging in union activities. In this and other decisions, the justices posited that employers and employees possessed equal bargaining power. The majority of justices, however, believed that the Constitution allowed state laws specifically designed to protect the health or safety of workers. Thus, the court upheld maximum-hour laws for underground miners and women.

The Supreme Court, however, was not ready to allow Congress to regulate manufacturing under its constitutional power to regulate interstate commerce. After the Child Labor Act of 1916 (also known as the Keating-Owen Act) proscribed goods made by children from interstate commerce, the justices in *Hammer v. Dagenhart* (1918) held by a 5 to 4 vote that the law violated the states' powers under the Tenth Amendment. Congress responded with a second federal child labor law, which used the government's power of taxation rather than prohibition to achieve the same result. In *Bailey v. Drexel Fur-*

niture Co. (1922), however, the Court again ruled that Congress had exceeded its constitutional authority.

NEW DEAL-ERA DECISIONS

During the first five years of President Franklin D. Roosevelt's administration, five conservative justices (called the "five horsemen") were firmly committed to the laissez-faire perspective and opposed many New Deal reforms. In *Schechter Poultry Corp. v. United States* (1935), the conservative majority overturned the cornerstone of the New Deal's labor-relations policy, the National Industrial Recovery Act of 1933, reiterating a narrow construction of congressional power under the commerce clause. In *Morehead v. New York ex rel. Tipaldo* (1936), moreover, the justices voted 5 to 4 to strike down a minimum wage law, reiterating their support for the freedom of contracts doctrine.

The next year, however, the Court issued two monumental, landmark reversals—often referred to as constituting the "judicial revolution of 1937." In *West Coast Hotel v. Parrish*, the justices voted 5 to 4 to uphold a state minimum wage law, thereby overturning *Morehead v. New York ex rel. Tipaldo*. In *National Labor Relations Board v. Jones & Laughlin Steel Corp.*, the Court upheld the prolabor National Labor Relations Act of 1935, which guaranteed the right of employees of private businesses to organize labor unions and engage in collective bargaining. Not long after these two decisions, the retirement of conservative justices allowed President Roosevelt to appoint justices sympathetic to New Deal reforms.

The Supreme Court's change in direction reflected public opinion, which was becoming more sympathetic toward organized labor. Even before Roosevelt's election, Congress had enacted the Norris-LaGuardia Act of 1932, which unambiguously prohibited federal courts from issuing injunctions to prevent nonviolent strikes, picketing, or boycotts. In 1938, the Court upheld the statute when it overruled a lower court's antiunion injunction in *Lauf v. E. G. Shinner.*

In *Hague v. Congress of Industrial Organizations* (1939), the Court for the first time declared that the First Amendment protected the right of labor organizations to hold peaceful meetings and distribute literature without government interference. First Amendment protection was further extended in *Thornhill v. Alabama* (1940), which struck down an

antipicketing ordinance and emphasized the importance of free discussion of labor issues. In another landmark ruling, *United States v. Darby Lumber Co.* (1941), the Court interpreted the commerce clause broadly to uphold the Fair Labor Standards Act of 1938, which provided maximum hours and minimum wages for all employees who manufactured goods shipped in interstate commerce.

In interpreting the National Labor Relations Act, however, the Court did not always support the interests of organized labor. In *National Labor Relations Board v. Fansteel Metallurgical Corp.* (1939), the Court recognized the discretion of an employer to discharge workers who had participated in a sit-down strike. Although workers had the right to engage in lawful strikes, the seizure of an employer's plant was deemed a form of illegal violence. Likewise, in *Milk Wagon Drivers Union v. Meadowmoor Dairies* (1941), the Court recognized that state courts may issue injunctions to stop picketing whenever violence erupts.

COLLECTIVE BARGAINING SINCE 1945

During the years following World War II, there was a reaction against the power that organized labor had gained during the New Deal period. After the government seized coal mines in 1946, the president of the miners' union refused to obey an injunction to end the strike. The Supreme Court held in *United States v. United Mine Workers* (1947) that the union privilege against injunctions did not apply when government was the employer. Public reaction to the controversy encouraged passage of the Taft-Hartley Act of 1947, also called the Labor Management Relations Act, which placed a significant number of limitations on unions' powers and activities.

To the dismay of labor unions, the Supreme Court firmly endorsed all the provisions of the Taft-Hartley Act. In *American Communications Association v. Dowds* (1950), the Court upheld the requirement that union officers swear that they were not members of the Communist Party, based on the public interest in "the free flow of commerce." In a series of complex cases, particularly *National Labor Relations Board v. Denver Building and Construction Council* (1951), the Court upheld and broadly interpreted the act's ban on secondary boycotts, that is, on unions pressuring neutral parties to stop doing business with companies involved in labor disputes. The Court also sustained state right-to-work laws, which prohibited employees from being forced to pay union dues as a condition of employment. In *Boys Market, Inc. v. Retail Clerks' Local 770* (1970), unions were again disappointed when the Court, in spite of the Norris-LaGuardia Act, allowed a federal court to issue an injunction against a peaceful strike conducted in violation of a no-strike pledge.

The Court has continued to decide many complex National Labor Relations Act-related questions, including the question of which workers are covered under the act. In *Beasley v. Food Fair* (1974), the Court ruled that managers of a grocery store chain were supervisors rather than employees, and they therefore were not guaranteed the rights of collective bargaining. Likewise, teachers in private schools, if allowed sufficient independence in their teaching, were classified as supervisors in *National Labor Relations Board v. Yeshiva University* (1980). The Court in *Sure-Tan v. National Labor Relations Board* (1984) ruled that provisions of the National Labor Relations Act prohibiting unfair labor practices applied to undocumented workers, although in *Hoffman Plastic Compounds v. National Labor Relations Board* (2002), it found that such workers were not entitled to recover back pay.

Another long-standing National Labor Relations Act issue has been the right of collective bargaining in the public sector. In *AFSCME v. Woodward* (1969), the Eight Circuit Court of Appeals recognized that public employees had a right to unionize under the First and Fourteenth Amendments. Although the U.S. Supreme Court ruled in 1976 that the National Labor Relations Act did not apply to state and local governments, it reversed that ruling in *Garcia v. San Antonio Transit Authority* (1985). The Court held that the First Amendment protected nonpolicymaking government employees from dismissals for partisan reasons in *Elrod v. Burns* (1976). This principle was extended to promotions, transfers, and hiring of low-level employees in *Rutan v. Republican Party of Illinois* (1990).

WORKPLACE DISCRIMINATION

Before the Civil Rights movement, the Supreme Court in *Steele v. Louisville & Nashville Railroad Co.* (1944) established the doctrine of "fair representation," requiring that a labor union fairly represent all workers in a bargaining unit, regardless of race. The decision was based on a very broad interpretation of the Railroad Labor Act. Two decades later, Congress enacted an explicit antidiscrimination mandate in Title VII of the Civil Rights Act of 1964, which provided remedies for discrimination in employment based on race, sex, religion, or national origin.

The Court has interpreted Title VII to prohibit not only intentional discrimination but also employment practices that have an indirect discriminatory

Supreme Court rulings helped many win lawsuits alleging job discrimination. Nancy Wheelock Mayfield won reinstatement to her flight attendant job with American Airlines after she was forced to leave when the company learned she was married. (AP/Wide World Photos)

impact on particular groups. In the landmark case *Griggs v. Duke Power Co.* (1971), the Court ruled that hiring and promotion policies that result in a "racially disparate impact" must be clearly job related to be lawful. In *United Steelworkers v. Weber* (1979), the Court allowed employers voluntarily to grant preferences (even quotas) for members of racial minorities that are underrepresented in a particular employment category of the company. In cases such as *United States v. Paradise* (1987), the Court approved of judicially imposed quotas as remedies to overcome the present consequences of an employer's past racial discrimination.

The Court's broad interpretations of Title VII also allowed preferences for women in affirmative action programs designed to counter gender imbalance, as in *Johnson v. Santa Clara County* (1987). In *Automobile Workers v. Johnson Controls* (1991), moreover, the Court unanimously rejected a company's fetal protection rules, which had required women to be sterilized as a condition of holding positions that exposed them to high levels of lead. In 1986, the Court endorsed an Equal Employment Opportunity Commission (EEOC) regulation that interpreted sexual harassment as a form of illegal discrimination. The ruling was expanded in *Teresa Harris v. Forklift Systems* (1993).

Another labor statute requiring judicial interpretation is the Americans with Disabilities Act (ADA) of 1990, which prohibits unjustified discrimination against persons with substantial impairments and requires employers to provide "reasonable accommodations" that do not cause "undue hardship." The courts must decide the meaning of "reasonable" and "undue." Although the statute requires significant changes in the workplace, ADA plaintiffs have generally not prevailed in court, in part because of relevant Supreme Court decisions. In *Sutton v. United States* (1999), for instance, the Court held that a correctable impairment (myopia correctable by eyeglasses in this case) cannot be classified as a disability under the ADA.

Thomas Tandy Lewis

FURTHER READING

Center for Education and Employment Law. *U.S. Supreme Court Employment Cases.* 11th ed. Malvern: Author, 2005. Standard reference source providing summaries of some seven hundred significant decisions relating to labor law.

Forbath, William E. *Law and the Shaping of the American Labor Movement.* Cambridge, Mass.: Harvard University Press, 1991. Interesting scholarly account arguing that law more than culture explains the differences between the American and European labor movements.

Gorman, Robert. *Basic Text on Labor Law, Unionization, and Collective Bargaining.* St. Paul, Minn.: Pearson West, 2004. Highly respected textbook; particularly good on issues of discrimination law.

Leslie, Douglas. *Labor Law in a Nutshell.* St. Paul, Minn.: Thornton West, 2008. This succinct handbook provides useful summaries of legislation and hundreds of major court cases—an excellent introduction to the field.

Taylor, Albion G. *Labor and the Supreme Court.* Ann Arbor, Mich.: Braun-Brumfield, 1961. The standard historical work on the Court's decisions through the late 1950's.

Tomlins, Christopher, and Andrew King, eds. *Labor Law in America: Historical and Critical Essays.* Baltimore: Johns Hopkins University Press, 1992. Includes several essays devoted to important Supreme Court decisions.

Twoney, David P. *Labor and Employment Law.* 12th ed. Cincinnati: South-Western, 2003. Provides introductory definitions of legal terms and concepts and includes a great deal of historical background.

SEE ALSO: Clayton Antitrust Act; Congress, U.S.; Labor history; Labor strikes; Presidency, U.S.; Pullman Strike; Sherman Antitrust Act; Supreme Court and banking law; Supreme Court and commerce; Supreme Court and contract law; Supreme Court and land law.

Supreme Court and land law

DEFINITION: Decisions by the nation's highest court regarding the interpretation and constitutionality of laws regarding public lands and private ownership of real estate

SIGNIFICANCE: The Supreme Court, in upholding the U.S. Constitution's strong protections for the rights of private property and ownership of land, contributed to a stable economic environment that has allowed for the flourishing of American business.

The early rise to prominence of the U.S. Supreme Court was in part prompted by its concern for creating a stable business environment as expressed in its early property and land law decisions. After a relatively quiet first decade of the Supreme Court, John Marshall became chief justice of the United States in 1801. Marshall led the Court to become a strong branch of the federal government, equal in stature to the executive and legislative branches.

MARSHALL AND PROPERTY RIGHTS

Chief Justice Marshall believed in a strong federal government, able to maintain order and security and to take an active hand in developing the American continent. He believed the rule of law to be a necessary precondition for exploiting America's vast natural resources, expanding the country's manufacturing sector, and developing American business. Central to Marshall's conception of the rule of law was the security and protection of private property and the ownership of land.

In *Ogden v. Saunders* (1827), Marshall wrote in his dissenting opinion of the right of every man "to acquire property, to dispose of that property according to his own judgment, and to pledge himself for a future act." In other words, Marshall held that property, even property in land, could be a commercial instrument in a dynamic economy. This view of property and land law was at odds with that of traditional English jurisprudence, in which the courts were inclined to safeguard the great landed estates that had been handed down from the days of William the Conqueror. These estates represented the bedrock and strength of the English aristocracy. English land law, through such devices as primogeniture (inheritance by the oldest son) and the fee tail (restricting conveyances of land), did not allow for the estates to be divided or disturbed.

Marshall and his Supreme Court, in contrast, espoused a philosophy of property law that saw land as unrestricted, freely alienable, freely divisible, and freely mortgageable. Without legal restrictions, land could be treated as another commodity to be bargained for, exchanged, speculated on, and collaterized. Above all, the justices saw land as a flexible instrument in the cultivation of the great American expanse and the prospering of the American economy. Rather than being preserved immobile through centuries, American land was divided by all the sons of each generation, contributing to an egalitarian sense of land ownership.

Marshall's colleague on the bench, the scholarly Joseph Story, shared the chief justice's conception of a vigorous national government oriented toward property rights and the rapid development of the nation's farming and business potential. Like Marshall, Story helped oversee the transformation of American land law from an agrarian to a business basis. Bernard Schwartz in *A History of the Supreme Court* (1995) finds Story's opinion in *Van Ness v. Pacard* (1829) to be a dramatic example "where the traditional land law was adapted to meet the needs of the new mobile business economy rather than a static agricultural one." Under English common law, landlords owned all fixtures and permanent improvements that tenants made to their property. Story's decision in *Van Ness* greatly modified this rule, thereby encouraging tenants to make profitable improvements to land and property, as they could retain a larger share of the increased value.

Crucial to the opening of the great American

Tuscarora tribe members show their opposition to having a power plant located on their reservation in Niagara County, New York. Although their case went to the Supreme Court, the tribe lost. (AP/Wide World Photos)

land frontiers for economic development and business growth was the question of Native American lands. American law had been wrestling with conflicting claims between American Indians and European settlers from its colonial beginnings—almost always to the settlers' advantage. The issue was definitively raised before the Supreme Court for the first time in the historic case of *Johnson v. M'Intosh* (1823).

Johnson v. M'Intosh was a dispute over a vast tract of land in Illinois. The plaintiff had purchased the land from the Piankashaw during the 1770's. The defendant had purchased the same land from the U.S. government in 1818. In holding for the defendant, despite the fact that he made his purchase subsequent to the plaintiff's, Marshall declared that the sale from the Piankashaw had no legal force. Ultimate title to lands occupied by Indians was vested in the U.S. government, which alone had dominion over them. Thus the Court put into jurisprudence the reality of land competition between settlers and Native Americans.

As a result of the *Johnson* decision, the vast frontiers stretching before America's settlers were laid open to be cultivated, farmed, and developed as federal law allowed; Native Americans were unable to assert any legal claim. This was a principle of land law that the Court would continue to uphold over the next two centuries in such cases as *Cherokee Nation v. Georgia* (1831), *Worcester v. Georgia* (1832), *Lone Wolf v. Hitchcock* (1903), *Tee-Hit-Ton Indians v. United States* (1955), and *United States v. Sioux Nation of Indians* (1980).

By the completion of Marshall's tenure as chief justice in 1835, the Supreme Court had already put a decisive stamp on its jurisprudence of land law and its relation to American business. The Supreme Court gave the greatest respect to rights in private property and land and thus helped create a stable financial regime that allowed business ventures to flourish. Property rights were conceived in their most fluid form, by a Court that saw land as essentially no different from money, commodities, natural resources, and other items freely exchanged, bartered, and negotiated in a contractual economy. Neither English notions of primogeniture nor the claims of the Native Americans as prior occupants of the land could be allowed to stand in the way of the rapid amalgamation of American land and business.

The remainder of the nineteenth century saw much quieter developments in Supreme Court land jurisprudence. Beginning with *Daly's Lessee v. James* (1823), the Court adjudicated numerous cases involving the inheritance of landed estates. In *Walker v. Parker* (1839), *Daniel v. Whartenby* (1873), and *Hardenbergh v. Ray* (1894), the Court interpreted the terms of the inherited estates in a most flexible manner, despite the traditional English emphasis on the rigidity of common law estates. In *Jenkins v. Collard* (1892), the Court allowed for the conveyance of real estate that had been forfeited by a Confederate soldier, who had since received a general pardon. In *Ely v. New Mexico and A. R. Co.* (1889) and *Sharon v. Tucker* (1892), the Supreme Court upheld the doctrine of adverse possession. This doctrine, which allows for an occupier of neglected land eventually to assert legal title to that land, supports a dynamic, business-oriented view of land law. It punishes landowners who leave their lands fallow and unproductive and rewards intruders who make profitable, cultivated use of the land.

THE LAW OF ZONING AND TAKINGS

At the beginning of the twentieth century, the Supreme Court found itself once more in the thick of vital questions concerning land that carried implications for the development of American business. Zoning law (which segregates land according to its permissible uses) began in New York City in 1916, with government ordinances establishing restrictions and controls on the development and use of land. Real estate developers and boards of real estate agents saw zoning as a threat to their business and attacked its constitutionality. In *Village of Euclid v. Ambler Realty Co.* (1926), the Supreme Court upheld the constitutionality of zoning ordinances against the claim that such regulations deprived property owners of the economic value of their property without due process of law or just compensation.

The Supreme Court upheld zoning as a legitimate exercise of the state's power to enact legislation to promote the public welfare. Subsequently, the Court upheld land controls and zoning legislation that were aimed at urban redevelopment (*Berman v. Parker*, 1954) and at ensuring family and urban amenities (*Village of Belle Terre v. Boraas*, 1974, and *Ward v. Rock Against Racism*, 1989). It invalidated zoning ordinances that were found to be arbitrary and unreasonable (*Nectow v. City of Cambridge*, 1928), violated homeowners' rights to free speech by prohibiting lawn signs (*Linmark Associates Inc. v. Willingboro*, 1977, and *City Ladue v. Gilleo*, 1994), or discriminated against racial or other minorities (*Buchanan v. Warley*, 1917, and *City of Edmonds v. Oxford House*, 1995). Probably no other development in land law has done more to shape American residential and commercial patterns—and hence American business—than the law of zoning, a development encouraged by the Supreme Court with its doctrine of extreme deference to the legislative process in this area of law.

Closely related to the question of zoning is that of the takings clause of the Fifth Amendment, prohibiting government from taking private property for "public use," except in return for "just compensation" (a process known as eminent domain). The Court held that zoning did not violate this clause, even if it aggressively aimed at the prohibition of health nuisances (*Hadacheck v. Sebastian*, 1915), preservation of historic landmarks (*Penn Central Transportation Co. v. City of New York*, 1978), or a reduction in the concentration of large landed estates (*Hawaii Housing Authority v. Midkiff*, 1984). In *Loretto v. Teleprompter Manhattan CATV Corp.* (1982), however, the Court found that installation of cable facilities was a permanent occupation of property and therefore was a regulatory taking, regardless of whether the action achieved a public benefit or had minimal effect on the landowner. If land regulations went too far in diminishing the value of the property of a landowner, however, the Court ruled that they would constitute a taking for which the government had to provide just compensation.

In cases such as *Pennsylvania Coal Co. v. Mahon* (1922), *Nollan v. California Coastal Commission* (1987), *Lucas v. South Carolina Coastal Council* (1992), and *Palazzolo v. Rhode Island* (2001), the Court has been careful to protect the rights of property owners to just compensation when government legislation reduced the ability of landowners to derive economic or other value from their property. Nevertheless, in the much-controverted case of *Kelo v. City of New London* (2005), the Supreme Court continued to uphold the broadest possible power of the government to exercise eminent domain. Reaffirming its jurisprudence over the preceding fifty years, the Court held in *Kelo* that any rational government plan for land use constitutes a legitimate "public use." Although some critics have claimed that this decision represents an assault on the rights of private property, others have applauded the *Kelo* decision, claiming that a broad reading of the "public use" requirement allows flexibility for governments to promote business and economic redevelopment in their land policies.

FAIR HOUSING

With the rise of the Civil Rights movement, the Supreme Court became active in trying to eliminate discrimination in American housing and land use. In *Shelley v. Kraemer* (1948), the Court refused to enforce restrictive covenants that had been placed on properties so that they could not be sold to nonwhites. Such restrictive covenants, as acts of private discrimination, were directly banned in the Federal Fair Housing Act of 1968, which prohibits discrimination in housing on the basis of race, religion, sex, family status, or disability. In cases such as *Trafficante v. Metropolitan Life Insurance* (1972), *Shaare Tefila Congregation v. Cobb* (1987), *United States v. Starrett City Associates* (1988), and *Meyer v. Holley* (2003), the Court has tended to a broad reading of the Fair Housing Act. These decisions have been lauded by some scholars, who claim they have assisted in the integration of all segments of American society into the residential and business life of the nation.

Howard Bromberg

FURTHER READING

Ely, James W., Jr. *The Guardian of Every Other Right: A Constitutional History of Property Rights.* 3d ed. New York: Oxford University Press, 2008. Scholarly history of property rights under the Constitution and their interpretation by the Supreme Court.

Friedman, Lawrence. *A History of American Law.* 3d ed. New York: Touchstone, 2005. Emphasizes social aspects of American legal history; incisively written, with penetrating insights.

Johnson, Herbert. *The Chief Justiceship of John Marshall, 1801-1835.* Columbia: University of South Carolina Press, 1997. Leading Marshall scholar surveys his life and tenure on the Court.

Klarman, Michael J. *From Jim Crow to Civil Rights: The Supreme Court and the Struggle for Racial Equality.* New York: Oxford University Press, 2006. History of Supreme Court decisions on race relations, many of which related to land law.

Schwartz, Bernard. *A History of the Supreme Court.* New York: Oxford University Press, 1995. Concise, balanced history of the Supreme Court from its creation, with an emphasis on its four most historic decisions.

Urofsky, Melvin I., and Paul Finkelman. *A March of Liberty: A Constitutional History of the United States.* 2d ed. 2 vols. New York: Oxford University Press, 2004. Comprehensive textbook on the history of the Constitution and leading Supreme Court cases.

SEE ALSO: Congress, U.S.; Land laws; Presidency, U.S.; Supreme Court and banking law; Supreme Court and commerce; Supreme Court and contract law; Supreme Court and labor law; Zoning, commercial.

T

Taft-Hartley Act

THE LAW: Federal legislation that restricted labor unions' activities

DATE: Enacted on June 23, 1947

SIGNIFICANCE: The Taft-Hartley Act amended the prolabor National Labor Relations Act of 1935. It defined unfair labor practices and prohibited labor unions from engaging in such practices.

U.S. senator Robert A. Taft and U.S. representative Fred A. Hartley, Jr., sponsored the legislation officially known as the Labor Management Relations Act of 1947 and commonly known as the Taft-Hartley Act. A Republican-controlled Congress passed the legislation over the veto of President Harry S. Truman on June 23, 1947. The act restricted labor unions from engaging in a number of activities it defined as "unfair labor practices," including jurisdictional strikes, wildcat strikes, political strikes, and secondary boycotts.

The closed shop, or a company that only hired union members, was made illegal. Conversely, the union shop was still permitted. This meant that a union could be formed in a given business only after a majority of employees voted for its creation. Newly hired employees of union shops would be required to join the union as part of a collective bargaining agreement but were to be given a minimum of thirty days in which to do so.

The Taft-Hartley Act made it illegal for unions to contribute to political campaigns and required employers and unions to give each other sixty days' notice before striking. The act also authorized the use of federal injunctions to end strikes after eighty days if the government determined that the strike threatened the health or safety of the nation's citizens. Finally, the act required union leaders to take an oath and sign an affidavit affirming that they did not support communism.

Bernadette Zbicki Heiney

SEE ALSO: AFL-CIO; Contract law; Labor history; Labor strikes; Lewis, John L.; National Labor Relations Board; National Labor Union; Racketeer Influenced and Corrupt Organizations Act; Supreme Court and labor law.

Taiwanese trade with the United States

SIGNIFICANCE: Taiwan's economy flourished after the Nationalists fled to the island and the United States provided economic and political support. The United States was the largest trading partner of Taiwan until 2003, when that status went to mainland China.

Until it became a part of the Japanese empire in 1895, the island of Taiwan played an insignificant role in the economic history of Asia. As a limited source of natural resources but, more important, as a way station for Japanese troops en route to other parts of Asia, Taiwan experienced little economic development under Japanese hegemony. It was only after Generalissimo Chiang Kai-shek fled the Communist takeover of the mainland in 1945, bringing with him some 600,000 Nationalist troops, that Taiwan suddenly assumed enormous significance, both politically and economically. Although constituting only 15 percent of the population of the island, the rest being native Taiwanese, Chiang and his mainland followers quickly took control of both the Taiwanese government and the island's industrial complex. Chiang declared that Taiwan would be the new seat of the "Republic of China" in exile and awaited the day when what he regarded as the only legitimate government of China could return to the mainland. Almost overnight, United States aid poured into the Taiwanese treasury, and Chiang received an unconditional political and military guarantee that the United States would not allow the mainland to conquer the island under any circumstances. This guarantee remains in effect in the twenty-first century, and has served as one of the primary sources of Taiwanese economic success.

American bombing during World War II destroyed most of the island's industrial base, and it was not until the mid-1950's that Taiwan's economy showed signs of reviving its prewar production output. Since 1950, the United States has been one of Taiwan's principal trading partners. As a result of the Korean War, the presence of the American Seventh Fleet became common in the Taiwan Straits, and, as of the first decade of the twenty-first century, still represented the military commitment of the United States not only to the Republic of China but also to all American allies in Asia. Security and economic prosperity have always been linked in post-1950 Taiwan. Throughout the 1950's, the Republic of China received massive amounts of American aid, which was increased during the 1960's. Some 80 percent of this aid was in the form of grants. Slowly, but steadily, trade between the United States and Taiwan grew: The percentage of Taiwan's market exported to the United States increased from 6 percent in 1958 to 37 percent in 1973, and to 49 percent in 1984.

During the 1970's and 1980's, the Republic of China's economy grew on an average of 10 percent annually. The United States had maintained full diplomatic ties with Chiang's Kuomintang government from 1950 to 1978. In 1978, Congress passed the Taiwan Relations Act, which formally recognized the People's Republic of China as the only legitimate government of China. Despite the change of official recognition, American trade with Taiwan remained robust. From 1979 to 1987, trade between the two nations almost tripled, with Taiwan becoming the United States' fifth-largest trading partner.

Having been transformed from being primarily agricultural during the 1950's, by the 1970's, Taiwan's economy was overwhelmingly based on foreign exports. This so-called Taiwan miracle led to conflict between the United States and the Republic of China, in that, by the mid-1980's, the U.S. market accounted for 85 percent of Taiwan's foreign trade. American protests caused a strain in relations, forcing Taiwan to diversify its markets and ultimately bringing the nation even greater economic stability. Home to industries such as information and technology equipment, textiles, footwear, toys, and electronic products, Taiwan has become both a major trading power and an important creditor nation.

As a result of U.S. protests, the percentage of Taiwan's exports that were sold to the United States fell from 49 percent in 1984 to 15 percent in 2005 and 14 percent in 2006. In 2002, U.S.-Taiwan trade exceeded $50 billion, and the United States was Taiwan's largest trading partner. That same year, Taiwan joined the World Trade Organization. In 2003, the People's Republic of China replaced the United States as Taiwan's major trading partner.

Mark DeStephano

FURTHER READING

Aspalter, Christian, ed. *Understanding Modern Taiwan: Essays in Economics, Politics, and Social Policy.* Burlington, Vt.: Ashgate, 2001.

Yap, O. Fiona. *Citizen Power, Politics, and the "Asian Miracle": Reassessing the Dynamics.* Boulder, Colo.: Rienner Publishers, 2005.

Yu, Fu Lai Tony, ed. *Taiwan's Economic Transformation in Evolutionary Perspective: Entrepreneurship, Innovation Systems, and Government.* New York: Nova Science, 2007.

SEE ALSO: Asian financial crisis of 1997; Chinese trade with the United States; International economics and trade; Japanese trade with the United States; Nixon's China visit.

Tariff of Abominations

THE LAW: Protectionist U.S. import tax on manufactured goods instituted to safeguard nascent industrial and manufacturing centers in New England, Ohio, and Pennsylvania

DATE: Passed on May 19, 1828

PLACE: United States

SIGNIFICANCE: While protecting northern industrial interests, the tariff caused widespread economic hardship in the agricultural South: It led to higher prices on manufactured goods and the loss of valuable European markets for southern agricultural exports, primarily cotton.

Also known as the Tariff of 1828, the Tariff of Abominations was passed in May of 1828 to protect the northern states' new industrial centers from competition from the more established manufacturing sectors of Europe. The tariff, however, ended up increasing prices on manufactured goods in the South, and southerners were unwilling to suffer for the benefit of the North.

In 1832, the legislature of South Carolina voted to "veto" the Tariff of Abominations, declaring it unconstitutional. In doing so, the legislators were following a doctrine previously advocated by Vice President John C. Calhoun of South Carolina. Calhoun had argued that every state in the Union was a sovereign entity that had the power to decide the validity of federal legislation within its own borders, particularly if such legislation was harmful to a state's interests.

This political cartoon criticizes major figures, depicting each riding a favorite "hobbyhorse." Third from the right is John C. Calhoun, who is the driver of southern nullification of the Tariff of Abominations. (Library of Congress)

Congress and President Andrew Jackson disagreed with Calhoun and South Carolina. Congress authorized the use of force to compel states to abide by federal laws. South Carolina responded by threatening to secede from the Union. The resulting standoff became known as the Nullification Crisis. Calhoun, his presidential ambitions damaged by his advocacy of states' rights to nullify federal laws, ran for U.S. Senate and was elected at the end of the year.

Tensions eased the following year. Many of the high tariffs on imported industrial goods were reduced by the Compromise Tariff Act of 1833. Nonetheless, many historians believe the Tariff of Abominations set the stage for the U.S. Civil War thirty years later: The Compromise Tariff Act of 1833 mitigated the worst of the economic hardship on the South but did little to clarify the question of states' rights against the federal government. As a result of the Tariff of Abominations, regional differences began to harden between the protectionist industrial North and the free-trade agricultural South.

Victoria Erhart

SEE ALSO: Civil War, U.S.; Constitution, U.S.; Cotton industry; European trade with the United States; International economics and trade; Tariffs; Taxation; Underwood Tariff Act.

Tariff of 1828. *See* Tariff of Abominations

Tariffs

DEFINITION: Taxes on foreign imports and exports levied by national governments

SIGNIFICANCE: During the formative years of the United States, tariffs were very important to the growth of the economy. By imposing tariffs on imports, the United States was able to protect its fledgling manufacturing industry and encourage expansion in various sectors. The tariffs raised the price of cheaper foreign goods, especially those manufactured in England, and encouraged consumers to purchase domestic goods. This protectionist policy was instrumental in the development of the United States as an industrial country. Until the beginning of the twentieth century, tariffs were an important means of raising government revenue.

The United States government collects tariffs on imports; however, it does not collect tariffs on exports, as this practice is prohibited by the U.S. Constitution. Tariffs usually have both a revenue effect and a protective effect, but some tariffs are for revenue only. These are tariffs that are collected on imported products that are not produced in the importing country. Tariffs whose primary function is to protect one or more domestic industries in the importing country by raising the price of imported products that are the same as those produced domestically produce government revenue as well as having a protective effect. If tariffs become excessively high, they can curtail all importation of a product and thus lose their revenue-raising effect.

Tariffs are computed in three different ways. A tariff may be ad valorem, specific, or a combination of ad valorem and specific. An ad valorem tariff imposes a tax equal to a percentage of the selling price of the import. A tariff that is specific imposes a fixed or set amount of tax on each unit of the imported product sold without regard to the selling price. A tariff may also be a combination tariff that imposes both an ad valorem tax and a specific tax on an imported product.

The tariffs charged on imports from various countries with which one country trades are not the same. A country often grants the status of most-favored nation to certain of its trading partners. After entering into such an agreement, the country pledges not to charge the most-favored nation tariffs on any goods that are higher than those charged on any similar goods imported from any other country.

Developing countries at times receive special tariff rates on certain products. Certain other countries may also receive special tariff rates through special negotiations. These rates can be lower than most-favored-nation rates. They apply to products not imported from most-favored nations. A general system of preference also at times provides preferential lower tariff rates. Industrialized countries often use these preferential rates to assist developing countries to build a healthy, stable economy.

ADVANTAGES AND DISADVANTAGES

Tariffs are advantageous to a country in that they provide revenue and protect and encourage domestic production. The increase in production provides more jobs for the country's workers and contributes to a higher standard of living. Tariff rates do not always have to be high to be beneficial to a country. Preferential lower tariffs under the general system

of preference not only are beneficial to a developing country but also have an advantage for the industrialized nation granting them. By granting lower rates, the industrialized country becomes a trading partner of the developing country. Encouraged to produce and export more goods, the developing country ameliorates its economy, with the result that it is able to import more goods from its trading partner, the industrialized nation. The increased trade has a positive effect on the economies of both countries.

However, tariffs are not without disadvantages. Tariffs that increase the cost of lower-priced similar imported goods and thus protect domestic producers, encourage more production, and create jobs, would appear to be totally advantageous. However, this is not the case. Such tariffs cause the consumer to pay higher prices for the particular product protected by the tariff. Thus, the cost of the additional jobs created may be very high per job.

High tariffs can also instigate retaliatory measures by trading partners. If a country imposes high tariffs on goods imported from its trading partners, they will probably impose similar high tariffs on the goods they import from the high-tariff country. This reciprocal imposition of high tariffs then severely limits trade between the countries and may bring it to a standstill.

In general, those who produce goods for the domestic market benefit from tariffs. Those involved in producing goods include manufacturers, entrepreneurs, workers in various industries, and agricultural producers. As long as the domestic market provides a level of consumerism adequate to use the amount produced and maintain prices, these individuals are going to support tariffs and encourage the passage of high tariffs to eliminate foreign competition. However, if the domestic market is unable to consume the production and a surplus results, these same commercial entities or groups may not benefit from high tariffs. With a surplus of goods, there is a need for a larger market than that provided within the country. High tariffs on imports into one country tend to create high tariffs on that country's exports to other countries. Thus the greater world market does not readily open to the producers who are seeking new markets.

TARIFFS IN THE UNITED STATES

Tariffs have played an important role in the history and the economic development of the United

States. In the seventeenth century when America was still a colonial possession, England, in an effort to protect British commercial interests, imposed high tariffs on the major exports of the northern colonies, fish and grain in particular. These tariffs forced the colonists to find new markets in the West Indies and in southern Europe.

After the colonies became an independent nation, tariffs were used to raise revenue and pay the debt incurred during the Revolutionary War. In 1789, under the leadership of Alexander Hamilton, the country imposed an ad valorem tariff of 8 percent on thirty different commodities and of 5 percent on all other goods.

The first protective tariff was passed by Congress in 1816. Henry Clay convinced the members of Congress that true economic independence from Europe depended on increasing American manufacturing. Persuaded that prohibiting or substantially reducing the import of cheaper European goods, especially from England, would aid in developing manufacturing, Congress passed a tariff to create a protected domestic market.

By the mid-nineteenth century, tariffs had become a divisive issue between the northern and southern states. The North, interested in developing a large manufacturing industry, favored high tariffs, while the South, whose farmers and plantation owners needed to export large crops of cotton and tobacco, were in favor of lower tariffs that would encourage trade and lower tariffs on their crops to other countries.

HIGHER AND HIGHER TARIFFS

In 1828, Congress passed the Tariff of Abominations, also known as the Tariff of 1828. With the implementation of this new tariff, United States tariffs became the highest in the world. The tariff exasperated the southern states. It caused severe problems for southern exporters who relied on England as their primary trading partner. All English exports to the United States were subject to excessively high tariffs.

The Tariff Act of 1832 made some reductions in the tariff. Then on March 1, 1833, the Compromise Tariff Act provided for the tariff to be reduced gradually to 20 percent by 1842. With the secession of the South from the Union, high tariffs once again became the rule. In 1861, northern manufacturers were favored with passage of the Morrill Act. This tariff legislation set the policy that continued into the mid-1930's. High taxes on imports protected the nation's manufacturers and entrepreneurs as it built itself into the major industrial nation of the world. With free passage of goods in interstate commerce, an abundance of natural resources, an effective railroad system, and freedom from foreign competition, the nation's economy thrived. By 1900, the domestic market was purchasing 97 percent of its manufactured goods from domestic producers. The high tariffs on imports were not only protecting the domestic market but also providing half of the federal revenue as late as 1910.

Congressmen continued to be influenced by isolationist and protectionist groups through the first third of the twentieth century. During President Herbert Hoover's administration, several factions were demanding higher tariffs on imports. The farmers and agricultural interests who were suffering from low farm prices were calling for high tariffs on agricultural products. They were soon followed by manufacturing interests in demands for tariffs. Soon, protective tariffs were the main issue in all political discussion. On June 17, 1930, with the enactment into law of the Smoot-Hawley Tariff

Political cartoon taking the view that the Tariff of 1846 means the death of free trade. (Library of Congress)

Act, the obsession with excessive tariffs reached its apex. This was the last general tariff passed by Congress and also the highest in the nation's history. It raised tariffs to 60 percent of the selling price of imports. This tariff brought about the collapse of American exports, as foreign governments retaliated with high tariffs on American imports. Eventually forty countries raised their tariffs.

A Major Change in Policy

The Great Depression and World War II caused a serious interruption to world trade. This interruption to trade brought about a rethinking of trade policy and of the role the United States was to play in relation to trade with other countries. President Franklin D. Roosevelt began negotiation talks with the major trading partners of the United States. The purpose of the negotiations was to bilaterally lower trade barriers, including tariffs. In 1934, the Reciprocal Trade Agreements Act was passed. The United States had a new attitude toward trade and a new trade policy. During the 1940's, the General Agreement on Tariffs and Trade (GATT) provided rules of conduct for trading, set the stage for the lowering of trade barriers, especially tariffs, and provided an arena for resolving trade disputes between countries. Under the GATT, a series of rounds of negotiation talks to lower trade barriers began in 1947 and have continued to effectively lower tariffs. In addition, the United States has entered into free trade agreements such as the North American Free Trade Agreement (NAFTA). The heavy reliance on excessively high protective tariffs that dominated U.S. trade with other countries is no longer a part of American trade policy.

Shawncey Webb

Further Reading

Destler, I. M. *American Politics*. 4th ed. Washington, D.C.: Institute for International Economics, 2005. This comprehensive revision of a work recognized as the best book on national policy by the American Political Science Association discusses the shift from protective tariffs to labor and environmental concerns. Also proposes ways that the United States can maximize the benefits of globalization.

Eckes, Alfred E., Jr. *Opening America's Market: U.S. Foreign Trade Policy Since 1776.* Chapel Hill: University of North Carolina Press, 1995. Good over-

---

UNITED STATES TOTAL MERCHANDISE TRADE WITH FREE TRADE NATIONS, 2005-2007, IN MILLIONS OF DOLLARS

Year	Import	Export	Balance
2005	505,886	329,992	−175,894
2006	567,598	377,471	−190,127
2007	593,374	405,532	−187,842

Source: Data from United States International Trade Commission, *The Year in Trade 2007* (Washington, D.C.: Author, 2008)

Note: Free trade nations are Australia, Bahrain, Chile, DR-CAFTA, Israel, Jordan, Morocco, NAFTA, and Singapore. Trade data are from the U.S. perspective.

---

view of history of American trade and trade policies from the country's inception as a nation. Gives special attention to the Underwood Tariff Act of 1913 and the Federal Tariff Commission.

Ekelund, Robert B., Jr. *Tariffs, Blockades, and Inflation: The Economics of the Civil War.* Lanham, Md.: Rowman & Littlefield, 2004. Provides a sharp contrast between the trading situations in a single-nation-oriented atmosphere of trade and a global trading community. Explains how the United States used tariffs and other barriers to trade during a war and the resulting effects on the economy.

Northrup, Cynthia Clark, and Elaine C. Prange Turney, eds. *Encyclopedia of Tariffs and Trade in U.S. History.* Westport, Conn.: Greenwood Press, 2003. An informative collection of more than four hundred entries on the tariff acts passed by Congress between 1789 and 1930. Includes primary sources and the texts of the tariffs themselves.

Schott, Jeffrey J., ed. *Free Trade Agreements: U.S. Strategies and Priorities.* Washington, D.C.: Institute for International Economics, 2004. Edited by a member of the U.S. delegation to the Tokyo Round of the GATT agreements, this study is one of the most thorough presentations of the United States' participation in free trade agreements. It deals extensively with NAFTA and elucidates why free trade agreements are replacing tariffs.

Taussig, Frank W. *The Tariff History of the United States.* New York: Augustus M. Kelley, 1967. This classic by a Harvard economics professor and the foremost authority on tariffs until 1935 discusses the highly protective Dingley Tariff and tariffs of the early twentieth century. Taussig, a reluctant supporter of free trade but an opponent of unions, is credited as the founder of international trade theory. Also addresses the danger of retaliation by trading partners when excessively high tariffs are enacted.

SEE ALSO: Commerce, U.S. Department of; Congress, U.S.; Constitution, U.S.; Export-Import Bank of the United States; International economics and trade; Tariff of Abominations; Taxation; Underwood Tariff Act.

Taxation

DEFINITION: The imposition of charges on the property, income, or activities or citizens or corporations by a government to generate revenue

SIGNIFICANCE: Throughout American history, taxation, either through tariffs, excise taxes, property taxes, sales taxes, or income taxes, has taken a large portion of business earnings. Corporations have lobbied legislatures for relief and hired experts to reduce those taxes.

The American colonists rebelled in 1776 because of taxation without representation. Following the rebellion, Americans discovered that even with representation, they did not much like taxes. The Whiskey Act of 1791 assessed an excise tax on the distilling of whiskey; this was the United States' first internal tax at the federal level. It was promoted as a sin tax and served as the precedent for similar taxes. The objection to the tax, particularly in western Pennsylvania, was so great that a rebellion ensued and President George Washington led troops into the area to quash the insurgents. A 1794 law extended the excise tax to carriages, snuff, sugar, and salt. However, Thomas Jefferson formed a campaign around abolishing internal taxes during his successful presidential run in 1800. By 1802, all but the salt tax had been abolished. Nevertheless, the precedent had been established, and throughout the next two hundred years, Congress periodically introduced other types of luxury or sin taxes. Despite the nuisance excise taxes, the federal government acquired most of its financing during the nineteenth century from tariffs. At the state level, property taxes were the preferred form of raising government funds, although at one time or another almost every form of taxation was used at the state or colony level.

FIRST NATIONAL TAXES

The U.S. Congress passed the first national tariff law in 1789. From that date until passage of the Underwood Tariff Act of 1913, there were fifty-eight tariff laws. Tariffs provided revenues and protection for domestic companies. The 1789 Tariff Act created the first national tariff, but several states, including Massachusetts and Pennsylvania, had imposed tariffs before that date to protect industries in those states. The 1789 tariff imposed duties on imports such as tea and coffee. The tariff was intended as a revenue-raising measure, and tariff rates ran about 5 percent, with higher rates on luxury items.

The first attempt at a national income tax came in 1813, to fund the War of 1812. This tax was never instituted because the government paid the war debt with high tariffs after the war. This income tax measure did serve as a model for later income tax proposals, particularly the U.S. Civil War and 1894 income taxes. After 1812, tariffs helped the nation begin a transition from agriculture to industry. Although both the Union and the Confederacy had income taxes during the Civil War, these assessments did not apply to a large percentage of the populace. During the 1870's, congressmen from agricultural states introduced fourteen bills proposing income tax legislation. Capitalists from northeastern states did not allow any congressional votes on these bills. Therefore, the modern era of taxation began in 1909 with the passage of the corporate excise tax and in 1913 with the passage of the Sixteenth Amendment to the U.S. Constitution.

A large body of research exists concerning the development of twentieth century American tax laws. These studies have explained the forces for and against income taxes as partly based on regional, occupational, and class differences. Congressmen from the northeastern section of the country opposed income taxes because their constituents were, on average, the wealthiest in the nation. Congressmen from the South and West preferred the income tax over tariffs because of the undue burden the tariffs placed on their constituents. For example, farmers opposed tariffs as economically detrimental to agriculture because tariffs forced up prices of farm inputs, such as machinery, without protecting farm crops. Farmers complained that prices for their crops fluctuated according to the world market, while input costs were set artificially high to put money in the hands of northeastern manufacturers. The objection to the tariff was based on the feeling that it was class legislation—that it taxed the farmer for the benefit of the manufacturer.

THE SIXTEENTH AMENDMENT

From 1900 to 1909, Congress debated the questions of tariffs and taxes. Federal income tax proposals abounded. Congressmen debated how to frame these proposals in accordance with the U.S. Constitution. Nelson Aldrich, of Rhode Island, chairman of the Senate Finance Committee, was strongly opposed to any income tax provision. Instead he designed a tariff bill that dramatically increased tariff rates. This move caused a severe backlash from Democrats and moderate Republicans. These congressmen lobbied heavily for an income tax. William Howard Taft, the Republican president, and Aldrich proposed submitting a constitutional amendment to the states that would provide Congress the power to levy income taxes. Aldrich did this as a compromise measure and in the hope that the move would ultimately fail, resulting in no income tax law. The Supreme Court had previously ruled that only states had the power to tax individual incomes, but few states had effectively imposed income taxes. Therefore, Republicans did not believe that the states would ratify a constitutional amendment allowing the federal government to tax individual incomes.

Congressmen from agricultural states continued to make income tax proposals in the years leading up to 1909, but all were blocked by Republicans. A division in the power of the Republican Party in 1909, however, provided an opportunity for passage of income tax legislation. Because of a compelling speech by Senator Elihu Root, Congress passed a corporate tax bill, but not an individual income tax bill.

After the elections of 1912, the Democrats held control of both houses of Congress. With this power and subsequent ratification of the Sixteenth Amendment by the needed majority of states in 1913, Democrats quickly submitted a federal income tax law. The first income tax was part of the Underwood Tariff Act of 1913. This income tax law also incorporated the corporate excise tax of 1909. From a American population of 100 million, only 368,000 filed tax returns for 1913. Exemptions were $3,000 for individuals and $4,000 for couples. The tax rates ranged from 1 to 6 percent for income over $500,000. The less affluent did not have to file returns or pay income taxes. In total, the federal government collected about $35 million from the income tax in 1913. The number who were subject to taxation increased quickly, particularly as the nation entered World War I. The need for war financing

TAXES COLLECTED BY THE FEDERAL GOVERNMENT, 1990-2005, IN BILLIONS OF DOLLARS

Source	1990	1995	2000	2005
Individual income tax	466.9	590.2	1,004.5	927.2
Social insurance and retirement receipts	380.0	484.5	652.9	794.1
Corporate income tax	93.5	157.0	207.3	278.3
Excise taxes	35.3	57.5	68.9	73.1
Other	56.3	62.7	92.0	81.1
Total	1,032.0	1,351.9	2,025.6	2,153.8

Source: Data from the *Statistical Abstract of the United States, 2008* (Washington, D.C.: Department of Commerce, Economics and Statistics Administration, Bureau of the Census, Data User Services Division, 2008)

lowered the exemption level and subjected a larger percentage of the population to the filing requirements. Income tax collections in 1918 were seven times greater than in the preceding year and increased more in 1919 and 1920, with the latter year's collections being more than a hundred times greater than in 1913. Nevertheless, the percentage who had to pay taxes was still minimal until the outbreak of World War II.

With the entry into World War II, the U.S. government became desperate for financing. The defense expenditures alone for 1942 were double the level of federal revenues. To pay for these costs, Congress passed the Victory Tax, which made all income in excess of $624 annually subject to taxation. Moreover, with the passage of the Current Tax Payment Act of 1943, the Victory Tax was withheld from taxpayer wages, rather than letting taxpayers have until the end of the year to pay their taxes. This pay-as-you-go basis was passed for two reasons. First, it was designed to meet the needs of wage earners who were accustomed to budgeting on a weekly or monthly basis. With more low-income wage earners on the tax rolls, a budgeting mechanism for taxpayers became important. Second, it allowed the Treasury Department to collect tax revenues at a time when the taxpayers had money. This is known as the wherewithal-to-pay concept of taxation. The greatest impact of World War II on taxation was to broaden the base of taxpayers. Before the war, only 4 million taxpayers filed returns. Almost overnight, that number increased tenfold. The new regime of mass taxation succeeded primarily because of the war effort. Taxpayers on the home front felt they were doing their part in winning the war.

Congressman Wilbur Mills, who played an important role in determining tax law. (AP/Wide World Photos)

THE HOUSE WAYS AND MEANS COMMITTEE

Federal tax laws must originate in the House Ways and Means Committee. Therefore, that committee's chair is a powerful figure in Congress, and no one was ever more powerful and more effective in that role than was Wilbur Mills of Arkansas, who served in Congress from 1938 to 1977. As chairman of the House Ways and Means Committee, Mills was extremely influential. The general view among congressmen was that Mills was a despot who ruled Congress by giving out favors to those who voted with him and dealing out punishments to those who voted against his views. Given this viewpoint, he was usually able to get tax bills passed without any amendments being added. The addition of floor amendments is often what turns general tax bills into loopholes for special-interest groups. Mills would not give special-interest groups an opportunity to get an amendment added to a bill. Alternatively, another view was that Mills developed a consensus before he would let a bill come to a vote. For example, former Congressman Barber B. Conable, Jr., stated that Mills would not let a bill out of his twenty-five-person committee unless he had at least twenty-three supporting votes. Following the demise of Mills, tax bills that passed did so because they offered tax benefits to everybody—not because they represented sound legislation. The result has been a complex mass of tax laws and a system lacking internal stability.

The greatest impact of Mills's retirement was the effect that his absence from the House Ways and Means Committee had on U.S. income tax laws. Mills was known for carefully editing every tax bill to be sure that it meshed with existing tax laws. Basically, because of Mills, the Internal Revenue Code was well organized and internally consistent throughout his eighteen-year tenure as chair. Mills's leadership provided a stabilizing influence on tax laws. However, once he left the chairmanship, his successors lacked either the ability or the motivation to monitor the tax laws. The retirement of Mills led to a loss of a clear source of order and constraint, which had the effect of opening up the tax agenda to special-interest groups. As a result, the tax laws soon became a hodgepodge of miscellaneous provisions that complicated life for taxpayers and tax preparers.

Dale L. Flesher

FURTHER READING

Brownlee, W. Elliot. *Federal Taxation in America: A Short History*. New York: Woodrow Wilson Center Press, 1996. An excellent history of American taxation with explanations of why the tax laws were passed and who influenced them.

Conable, Barber B. *Congress and the Income Tax*. Norman: University of Oklahoma Press, 1989. This book covers the detailed aspects of how Congress passed tax laws in the twentieth century.

Manley, John F. *The Politics of Finance: The House Committee on Ways and Means*. Boston: Little, Brown, 1970. This is an excellent history of how Congress works on tax legislation. An entire chapter is devoted to Wilbur Mills, whom the author called one of the "most influential committee chairmen in recent years, if not in history."

Pechman, Joseph A. *Federal Tax Policy*. Washington, D.C.: Brookings Institution, 1987. A book widely used in college tax policy classes. Explains why tax bills were passed in the manner that they were.

Ratner, Sidney. *American Taxation: Its History as a Social Force in Democracy*. New York: W. W. Norton, 1942. An excellent history of the class struggles in taxation politics.

Seligman, Edwin R. A. *The Income Tax: A Study of the History, Theory, and Practice of Income Taxation at Home and Abroad*. New York: Macmillan, 1914. A classic work on income taxation before the passage of the Sixteenth Amendment.

Zelizer, Julian E. *Taxing America: Wilbur D. Mills, Congress, and the State, 1945-1975*. New York: Cambridge University Press, 2000. This volume analyzes the work of Mills and provides insights into the evolution of income taxation, Social Security, and Medicare during Mills's tenure as chairman.

SEE ALSO: Bush tax cuts of 2001; Government spending; Income tax, corporate; Income tax, personal; Internal Revenue Code; Monetary policy, federal; Sales taxes; Stamp Act of 1765; Tariffs; Tea Act of 1773; Whiskey tax of 1791.

Tea Act of 1773

THE LAW: British law granting the East India Company a monopoly over the selling of tea in the North American colonies

DATE: Act passed on May 10, 1773

SIGNIFICANCE: The passing of the act, coupled with the maintenance of the three-pence American tea tax, suggested that Great Britain felt it had a right to tax the colonists and control the North American market. This early example of trade friction led to greater political and economic discord between the colonies and Britain.

The combination of a tea boycott, competition, and extensive tea smuggling in the American colonies brought the East India Company to the verge of bankruptcy. To rescue the firm, Parliament passed the Tea Act. The law permitted the East India Company to ship tea directly to the colonies without paying duties in England and sell directly to colonial merchants, leaving out the middlemen. This cut the price of tea in America by half. The tax of three pence per pound of tea set by the Townshend Acts of 1767 remained in place.

Many colonists initially thought the duties were eliminated altogether, and the merchants consigned to sell the tea did not enlighten the public. During the summer of 1773, however, as newspapers and pamphlets revealed the true purpose of the Tea Act, public outrage grew. Smugglers of cheaper Dutch tea, such as Boston merchant John Hancock, were particularly angered by the competition. Colonists from the Carolinas to Massachusetts became convinced that the purchase of cheaper, legally imported tea would give sanction to the British government's right to tax the colonies. The Sons of Liberty in Philadelphia, New York, and Charleston intimidated American merchants into giving up their licenses to sell the tea. Only in Boston did the consignees refuse, thus setting the stage for the Boston Tea Party on December 16, 1773.

M. Philip Lucas

SEE ALSO: Boston Tea Party; Colonial economic systems; Parliamentary Charter of 1763; Revolutionary War; Taxation; Townshend Act.

Teamsters. *See* International Brotherhood of Teamsters

Teapot Dome scandal

THE EVENT: Taking of bribes by high government officials in return for leasing federal oil fields to private interests

DATE: 1921-1924

PLACE: Washington, D.C.

SIGNIFICANCE: The Teapot Dome scandal was a defining moment in American history that helped fuel the public's general distrust of government and fears of corporate-governmental collusion.

Teapot Dome was the name of an oil field in Wyoming that was classified as an emergency-only reserve field and held under the control of the Department of the Navy. Many presidents, including conservationist Theodore Roosevelt, held such reserve fields in various parts of the United States. Critics opposed placing these fields off-limits to normal drilling. They felt emergency-only reserves were unnecessary, and the secretary of the interior, Albert Fall, was one of those who shared this view.

Secretary Fall first made it possible for the secretary of the Navy to assign several emergency reserve oil fields to the Department of the Interior. He then leased the fields to the private Mammoth Oil Company, realizing a personal profit of approximately $400,000 in the process. Many civil and criminal charges were brought against Fall and others, and the case made its way to the Supreme Court after a Senate investigation. Fall was convicted of bribery and sentenced to a year in prison. The incident was another black eye on the already scandal-ridden administration of President Warren G. Harding. It took a Supreme Court decision in 1927 to render

Albert Fall. (Library of Congress)

the oil leases invalid and return the reserve fields to the Navy.

The scandal revealed the extent to which the nation's resources were in the hands of a powerful few. It thus exposed a growing need for stronger governmental protection of those resources. Subsequent administrations would take more seriously the public interest preserving the United States' natural resources. The Senate investigation into the scandal also marked the first time that Congress compelled witnesses to testify before its committees. Many observers at the time questioned Congress's authority to compel such testimony.

Fall's defenders point out that oil was relatively scarce in the United States during the early 1920's, and he may have perceived a legitimate need for American companies to gain access to the federal reserves. It was the secretive nature of his actions and the fact that he profited from them that created the public outcry. With his conviction, Fall became the first member of a presidential cabinet to be sentenced to prison for his actions in that position. The Teapot Dome scandal marked the beginning of an era when the American ideal of a government by and for the people would come to include a government that protects the interests of the people from what would come to be known as "special interests," such as the oil lobby.

Karel S. Sovak

FURTHER READING

Bates, J. Leonard. *The Origins of Teapot Dome: Progressives, Parties, and Petroleum, 1909-1921.* Urbana: University of Illinois Press, 1963.

Noggle, Burl. *Teapot Dome: Oil and Politics in the 1920's.* 1962. Reprint. Westport, Conn.: Greenwood Press, 1980.

Stratton, David H. *Tempest over Teapot Dome: The Story of Albert B. Fall.* Norman: University of Oklahoma Press, 1998.

SEE ALSO: Interior, U.S. Department of the; Military-industrial complex; Petroleum industry; Secret Service, U.S.

Telecommunications industry

DEFINITION: Enterprises involved in the two-way transmission of voices and data over long distances employing devices that use electrical currents, radio waves, or light beams as the means of transmission

SIGNIFICANCE: American business and finance have always depended on rapid and reliable communication. Telecommunications began with the telegraph, expanded with the telephone, and has become a major factor in globalization as the result of the combination of fiber-optic cable, computers, and the Internet. By the twenty-first century, revenues of telecommunications industries were estimated at $1.2 trillion, and the impact of telecommunications on other industries in the global economy was many times higher than that.

Native American communication consisted of face-to-face contact, signal fires, smoke signals, and occasionally drums. Because early European colonists in North America could read and write, they could transmit written messages by foot, horse, carriage, and ship. Such methods of communication were so slow that letters and messages took weeks to get from one place to another in North America and often months to connect North Americans with their European correspondents. The only exception to these slow forms of communications were homing pigeons, which carried written messages tied to their legs. Pigeons were faster than other forms of communications but could carry only lightweight messages for short distances. Nevertheless, American armed forces continued to use pigeons as late as World War I to transmit messages when other means were not available. Meanwhile, the first telecommunication systems were being developed.

TELEGRAPHY

The first true telecommunications device was the telegraph. In 1837, the American inventor Samuel F. B. Morse developed the first electrical telegraph that could send simple binary signals (dots and dashes) over great distances by wire. Equally important, Morse also developed a code using dots and dashes that gave his device quick acceptance. From the early 1840's through the 1860's, wires were strung between American cities to make telegraphic communication possible.

The need for rapid communications during the American Civil War substantially increased the application of telegraphy for both military and civilian purposes. Coupled with the development of railroads, an industry with which the telegraph was closely entwined, communication times across the North American continent soon dropped from weeks to mere minutes. By the end of the Civil War, the first transatlantic telegraph cable had been laid and the start of global telecommunications had begun. Over the ensuing century, the telegraph would successfully compete with telephones but would eventually give way to competition from wireless and fiber-optic communications.

TELEPHONES

Both Alexander Graham Bell and Elisha Gray are credited with independently inventing the telephone in 1876. The advantages of transmitting human voices across wires was so attractive that commercial telephone systems began forming in New Haven, Connecticut, in 1878 and in London, England, the following year. From these early beginnings, the telephone lines necessary for telephone

A telegraph operator prints a telegram in the early 1900's. (Library of Congress)

communication spread quickly within and among cities, wherever the costs of building the necessary equipment could be justified by demand.

By the end of World War II, telephones reached almost every home in the United States. In fact, because telephones were becoming an integral part of American life, they were regarded as a utility and regulated as a natural monopoly through American Telephone and Telegraph (AT&T). Later, however, changing attitudes gave rise to a movement for deregulation of utilities. By the early 1980's, this movement had become so widespread that AT&T was broken up into a series of smaller corporations. Deregulation was less of a threat to the fixed-line telephone systems than was the development of mobile telephone technology in the closing years of the twentieth century.

WIRELESS TELECOMMUNICATIONS

Small-scale wireless radio communication was first demonstrated to the National Electric Light Association by Nicolas Tesla in 1893. However, the first significant wireless radio communication was

achieved in 1901, when Guglielmo Marconi sent a message from St. John's, Newfoundland, to Poldhu, Cornwall, in England. Eight years later, Marconi received the Nobel Prize in Physics for this achievement. Wireless radio communication quickly became vital to communications between places that could not be connected by wires, such as land-to-sea, sea-to-sea, land-to-air, and air-to-air communications. Meanwhile, telephones would remain the dominant form of land-to-land communications until the development of microwave technology and satellite communications during the late twentieth century.

Mobile telephones—also known as cell phones—using microwave technology, became so cost-effective and popular by the early twenty-first century that mobile phone subscriptions would outnumber fixed-line telephone units by 2005. In less-developed countries around the world, the use of mobile telephone technology became even more popular than in the United States because it made possible the proliferation of telephones in places where it was not economical to built expensive fixed-line systems. In many countries, mobile telephone technology simply leaped over the fixed-line service stage. This, in turn, opened the possibility that importers and exporters could expand trade significantly through instant mobile phone technology.

FIBER OPTICS, COMPUTERS, AND THE INTERNET

The most primitive computers were invented during the 1930's, and large mainframe computers were used in cracking secret codes in World War II. In the fall of 1940, George Stibitz used a teletype to transmit and receive data each way between New York and Dartmouth, New Hampshire. This system used a mainframe or centralized computer and remote dumb terminals. This was the best that could be done during the 1950's, because it was only during the 1960's that researchers began to develop a technology that would allow packets of data to be sent to different computers without first traveling through a centralized mainframe. By the end of 1969, ARPANET (Advanced Research Projects Agency Network), with 4 nodes, was developed and enlarged to 213 nodes by 1981. ARPANET was a precursor to the Internet. In September, 1981, the TCP/IP (Transmission Control Protocol/Internet Protocol, or Internet protocol suite) was created;

TELECOMMUNICATIONS INDUSTRY REVENUE, 1995-2004, IN MILLIONS OF DOLLARS

Carrier	1995	2000	2002	2003	2004
Local service providers	103,792	128,075	130,941	126,860	123,067
Wireless service providers	18,627	63,280	80,467	89,342	99,465
Toll service providers	76,447	101,407	80,934	74,920	69,204
Total	198,866	292,762	292,342	291,122	291,736

Source: Data from the *Statistical Abstract of the United States, 2008* (Washington, D.C.: Department of Commerce, Economics and Statistics Administration, Bureau of the Census, Data User Services Division, 2008)

Note: Toll service providers include interexchange carriers, providers of operator and prepaid services, satellite service carriers, and toll resellers.

this protocol would serve as the basis for most of the Internet during the early twenty-first century.

Data transmission over copper lines continued to be the norm until fiber-optic technology was developed. During the 1960's, it was discovered that data could be sent through glass with a proper light source. The next step, which required using the laser as that light source, was accomplished in 1966. A kind of glass fiber with suitable communication characteristics was developed in 1970 by the Corning Glass Corporation. Matching the laser with the glass fiber, now called fiber-optic cable, occurred in 1980. Over the next decade, fiber-optic cable was laid across the globe even though the capital costs were high. Between 1990 and 2000, widespread belief that consumer demand for rapid transmission of video and other data would be sufficient to cover the costs led to the dot-com bubble, which burst in about 2000.

Although the early investors in fiber optics lost money, others bought up the fiber-optic infrastructure for pennies on the dollar and were able to offer fiber-optic services at competitive rates in underdeveloped countries. The simultaneous development of new computer software to connect computers and appropriate training linked a large number of underdeveloped countries to the developed world and had a significant impact on the globalization of technically trained people.

By 2008, almost 22 percent of the world's people were believed to have access to the Internet. This percentage climbed to more than 75 percent in North America, 60 percent in Australia and the South Pacific, and almost 50 percent in Europe. Iceland, South Korea, and the Netherlands led the world in broadband access, with about one-quarter of the population in each country being so equipped. Fiber-optic cable, computers, and the Internet provide such powerful tools for the transmission of data that usage is likely to increase in the future. Progress in this area should involve not only trillions of dollars of profit to the telecommunications industry, but also even more trillions of dollars in a wide variety of business applications.

Richard L. Wilson

FURTHER READING

Agrawal, Govind P. *Fiber Optic Communication Systems.* New York: John Wiley & Sons, 2002. Comprehensive description of the fiber-optic communications industry.

Burns, R. W. *Communications: An International History of the Formative Years.* Stevenage, Hertfordshire, England: Institution of Electrical Engineers, 2004. Broad study of all forms of communications, from prehistoric times to the eve of World War II. Devotes a great deal of space to the development of telegraphy and telephones.

Friedman, Thomas L. *The World Is Flat: A Brief History of the Twenty-first Century.* New York: Farrar, Straus and Giroux, 2006. National best-selling book setting forth Friedman's view that communications interconnections in the twenty-first century are making the world "flat" in terms of the new opportunities that have opened up around the world.

Gray, Charlotte. *Reluctant Genius: Alexander Graham Bell and the Passion for Invention.* New York: Arcade, 2006. Lively biography of the primary inventor of the telephone.

Smith, George David. *The Anatomy of a Business Strategy: Bell, Western Electric, and the Origins of the American Telephone Industry.* Baltimore: Johns Hopkins University Press, 1985. The well-known economic historian contributed this important volume to the AT&T history of the telephone series published by Johns Hopkins University Press.

Temin, Peter, with Louis Galambo. *The Fall of the Bell System: A Study of Prices and Politics.* New York: Cambridge University Press, 1987. Definitive historical study of the deregulation of the telephone system that uses original documentary materials and interviews from Bell executives.

Thompson, R. L. *Wiring a Continent: The History of the Telegraph Industry in the United States, 1832-1866.* Princeton, N.J.: Princeton University Press, 1947. Reprint. New York: Arno Press, 1972. Detailed history of the early development of telegraphy and its impact on the United States during the nineteenth century.

SEE ALSO: Bell, Alexander Graham; Bell Labs; Computer industry; Electronics industry; Federal Communications Commission; Internet; Radio broadcasting industry; Television broadcasting industry; Western Union; WorldCom bankruptcy.

Television broadcasting industry

DEFINITION: Branch of the entertainment industry that consists of organizations primarily engaged in broadcasting video signals that transmit programs to audiences

SIGNIFICANCE: During its relatively brief history, the television broadcasting industry has grown from a few experimental networks to become one of the most profitable industries in the United States, producing annual gross revenues of $160 billion during the early twenty-first century. The industry's versatility and capability to adapt to new technologies has become its greatest growth factor.

The origins of the television broadcast industry are linked to the history of television itself. In 1925, Scottish inventor John Logie Baird broadcast a moving silhouette image. Just two years later, Baird's company, the Baird Television Development Company, broadcast the first transatlantic television signal, between London and New York.

FIRST BROADCASTS

Bell Laboratories dramatically demonstrated the possibilities of television in 1927, when it transmitted pictures of U.S. Secretary of Commerce Herbert Hoover giving a speech from Washington, D.C., to New York. Bell's experiment was the first long-distance television transmission. That same year, the Columbia Phonographic Broadcasting System (later the Columbia Broadcasting System, or CBS) was founded. One year later, its first television station, W2XBS, was established in New York City, creating television's first star, Felix the Cat.

In July, 1931, CBS station W2XAB in New York City first began broadcasting regular scheduled programming seven days a week. Don Lee Broadcasting's station W6XAO in Los Angeles went on the air in December, 1931, with a regular schedule of filmed images every day except Sundays and holidays. The National Broadcasting Company (NBC) began regularly scheduled broadcasts in New York City in April, 1939, with a program dedicated to the opening of the New York World's Fair.

The Federal Communications Commission (FCC) granted the first commercial television licenses to NBC- and CBS-owned stations in New York in 1941, followed by Philco's station in Philadelphia, then licensed as WPTZ and later known as KYW-TV. After the U.S. entry into World War II, television stations joined the war effort and included illustrated war news as well as training for air-raid wardens and first-aid providers in their programming. In April of 1942, production of new televisions and other broadcasting equipment for civilian purposes was suspended and did not resume until August of 1945. By 1946, NBC, ABC, and CBS had restored their regular television broadcasts.

After years of experimentation, in 1940, the Radio Corporation of America (RCA) gave the first color television demonstration to members of the FCC board. The first demonstration of color television to the general public was made by CBS in 1950. A musical variety special, shown over a network of five East Coast CBS affiliates, became the world's first network color broadcast in 1951. However, the number of viewers was extremely limited because few possessed the color receivers necessary to watch the programs.

INFLUENCE

Since its inception, the television broadcasting industry has had a great influence on politics. During the 1952 U.S. presidential election, the Democratic Party candidate, Adlai Stevenson, bought a half-hour slot, which preempted the broadcast of the popular series *I Love Lucy* (1951-1957)—a fact that was not well received by the public. By contrast, the Republican candidate, Dwight D. Eisenhower, who used only twenty-second commercial spots, won the election.

Television has also reflected society's controversies through the decades. For example, in 1956, several Louisiana congressmen promoted a bill to ban all television programs that portray African Americans and whites interacting with one another in a sympathetic manner.

During the 1960's, when more than 90 percent of American homes had television sets, television became a powerful political tool. During the 1960 presidential election, the debates between candidates John F. Kennedy and Richard M. Nixon were televised. Kennedy appeared to perform much better on television than Nixon, and many believe that the televised debates played a role in Kennedy's electoral victory.

The 1960's also were a time when the television broadcasting industry set many new records. Following the news of the assassination of President Kennedy on November 22, 1963, regular television programming was suspended. On the following day, for the first time ever, 96 percent of all American televisions were set on the same program, Kennedy's funeral. Six years later, on July 20, 1969, the first television transmission from the Moon was seen by 600 million viewers around the world.

SOME CHANGES

The world of television was changed forever with the advent of videocassette recorders (VCRs) during the 1970's. The first videocassette recorders for home use were launched in 1971, but it was not until Sony's Betamax (1975) and JVC's VHS (1976) were launched that videocassette recorders moved into the mass market. Television had been the one medium that forced everybody to watch the same thing

at exactly the same moment, but after the arrival of VCRs, viewers could watch whatever they wanted whenever they wanted.

The 1980's saw the creation of a number of cable networks. The Cable News Network (CNN) was founded by Ted Turner as television's first twenty-four-hour news network in 1980; Music Television (MTV) was launched in 1981; the Weather Channel premiered in 1982; and Rupert Murdoch launched the Fox Network in 1986 as a challenge to the three major networks—NBC, CBS, and ABC.

The 1990's saw the rise of fast technological developments, including digital technologies such as high-definition television (HDTV), flat panel displays, home theater, and video on demand. Moreover, the rapid growth of the Internet, fast broadband access, and higher powered computers with larger storage capacity have turned Internet television into a reality. Internet television allows content delivery to a huge population with virtually no geographical limitations. Its primary models are streaming Internet television or a choice of videos featured on a Web site.

PROGRAMMING

Television broadcasting is programmed, in that a time and order are assigned to each show to be broadcast. Original or first run describes a program of one or multiple episodes created by a production company and shown for the first time on a station or network that has either paid for the production itself or for a license to broadcast the program. Syndication is the terminology used to describe the sale of the right to broadcast a television show to multiple individual stations. This includes secondary runs in the country of origin, called off-network programming, and international usage. Although it is hard to compete against first-run network programming, it is estimated that stations often capture at least 3 percent of the available audience (a critical figure when it comes to getting advertising) if they run syndicated shows.

Television scheduling strategies are employed to give programs the best possible chance of attracting and retaining an audience. In a strategy called dayparting, different types of programming are assigned to different parts of the day. In the strategy called stripping, episodes of the same syndicated series are scheduled Monday through Friday at the same time. Not having to wait an entire week to see the next episode of a series is an attractive option to many viewers. Marathons, in which episodes of a series are run one after the other, are popular on some local stations and on cable and satellite channels. Theming occurs when a station features programs with a specific theme on a particular day or week.

When a station or network schedules a number of programs that have similar demographic appeal to run consecutively, the practice is called stacking. By putting a new or weak show between two popular shows, the number of viewers of the new or weak show is generally increased through what is called the hammock effect. When the weak or new program becomes popular in its own right, it is said to have caught on. Somewhat related is the concept of tentpoling, or using popular, well-established television shows scheduled in pivotal time periods to boost the ratings of the shows around them.

Another kind of programming strategy is counterprogramming, or the practice of offering programs to attract a specific audience when another station is airing a major event. For example, if a program appeals to an older audience, a network might want to counterprogram with something that appeals to a younger audience.

FUNDING

Broadcast television is financed by advertising, television licencing, subscription, or any combination of these methods. A television advertisement or commercial is a span of television programming that conveys a message and is produced and paid for by an organization. The first television advertisement was broadcast in the United States in July, 1941, when the Bulova Watch Company paid $9 to NBC affiliate WNBT (later WNBC) in New York City for a twenty-second spot aired before a baseball game between the Brooklyn Dodgers and Philadelphia Phillies.

In the United States, television advertisements are the most effective method of selling products, especially consumer goods. This is reflected by the high prices television networks charge for commercial airtime during popular television events. A thirty-second commercial spot during the 2008 Super Bowl, an event watched by more than 90 million viewers, cost $2.7 million. Television advertising is also such a pervasive vehicle that it is considered impossible for an American politician to wage a suc-

cessful election campaign without use of television advertising.

Television advertisements are regulated by state and national laws designed to protect viewers. For example, since the 1970's, advertisements featuring cigarettes have been banned from American television. Advertisements for alcoholic beverages are allowed, but these commercials must not show the consumption of any alcoholic beverage.

Advertisement revenue provides a significant portion of the funding for most television networks. In 1977, gross television advertising revenues rose to $7.5 billion, 20 percent of all U.S. advertising. In 2006, net advertising revenues reached $26.5 billion in the United States and $123 billion worldwide. In comparison, the industry's gross revenues in the United States in 2007 were $160 billion. Television advertising is usually categorized into two levels: local and national. Local advertising makes up roughly 55 percent of all advertising revenue. In 2003, gross local advertising revenue amounted to $13.6 billion and reached $22 billion in 2007. National advertising accounts for approximately 45 percent of advertising revenue. Gross national advertising revenue came to $10.6 billion in 2003 and was estimated at $15 billion in 2007.

Political advertising accounts for more than 6 percent of total gross advertising revenue. In 2004, advertising for congressional, gubernatorial, and local races reached an estimated $1.6 billion. However, automobile makers and dealers provide the

---

ESTIMATED REVENUE AND EXPENSES FOR TELEVISION BROADCASTING, 2004-2005, IN MILLIONS OF DOLLARS

Year	Operating Revenue	Operating Expenses
2004	35,599	27,965
2005	36,297	28,776

Source: Data from the Statistical Abstract of the United States, 2008 (Washington, D.C.: Department of Commerce, Economics and Statistics Administration, Bureau of the Census, Data User Services Division, 2008)

largest share of revenue from television advertising, accounting for more than a fourth of all advertising revenue.

Another source of income for the television broadcasting industry is product placement. Product placement occurs when a brand logo is plainly visible or a character makes a favorable mention of a product in a program. It has become more prominent since the mid-1980's, but this practice can be traced to the 1940's. In 2007, revenues from product placement were estimated at $300 million.

In some countries, such as Great Britain, Australia, and South Africa, the television broadcasting industry gets most its funding from licenses, which are a form of taxation for television reception. This allows public broadcasting stations to transmit programs without, or with only supplemental, funding from advertisements.

Another method of financing for the television broadcast industry is subscription. Subscription channels are usually encrypted to ensure that only those who pay the subscription can view the channel.

Rikard Bandebo

FURTHER READING

Blumenthal, Howard J., and Oliver R. Goodenough. *This Business of Television.* New York: Billboard Books, 2006. This guide analyzes the legal, economic, and production aspects of the television industry. It includes directories of associations, governmental agencies, and production and distribution companies.

Hoskins, Colin, and Stuart McFadyen. *Global Television and Film: An Introduction to the Economics of the Business.* New York: Oxford University Press, 1998. Structured introduction to the economics of the contemporary film and television business.

Lotz, Amanda. *The Television Will Be Revolutionized.* New York: New York University Press, 2007. Accessible analysis of the technological innovations that are transforming the medium. Includes interviews, surveys, and other firsthand research.

McDowell, Walter S. *Broadcast Television: A Complete Guide to the Industry.* New York: Peter Lang, 2006. Concise in-depth look at the business of commercial television, explained here as a dynamic and interdependent system of technology, economics, and regulation.

Trost, Scott, and Gail Resnik. *All You Need to Know About the Movie and TV Business.* New York: Simon & Schuster, 1996. Reference book on practicalities of the film and television industry, but it is for the most part centered on Los Angeles.

SEE ALSO: Advertising industry; Disney, Walt; Electronics industry; Federal Communications Commission; Motion-picture industry; National Broadcasting Company; Radio broadcasting industry; Sports, intercollegiate; Sports franchises; Stewart, Martha; Telecommunications industry; Television programming with business themes.

Television programming with business themes

SIGNIFICANCE: From the beginning, narrative fiction television tended to portray and reinforce the division between the private domestic sphere and the public workplace. Most fiction programming either deals with a specific workplace or occupation or deploys the workplace as the "other" space defining the limits of home and family. Television has thus had a significant influence on the understanding of the relationship between family and work in American culture.

Although there are antecedents, one of the trends in television programming during the early twenty-first century has been the proliferation of "reality" shows. Actually, they are highly competitive game shows with winners and losers. Before their broadcast, the shows are thoroughly edited, musically scored, and often have voiceover commentary by the participants after the fact. One of the most successful is *The Apprentice.* The scenario of this show, which began airing in 2004, is that a group of sixteen young men and women perform a series of business-related challenges conceived by celebrity entrepreneur Donald Trump and his associates. Every week, at least one of the competitors is eliminated, and Trump tells the person, "You're fired!" The winner receives a six-figure job with one of Trump's companies. However, *The Apprentice* is atypical of television programming with business themes, which generally falls into three broad categories.

THE WORKPLACE

Domestic comedies such as *Father Knows Best* (1954-1963) and *Leave It to Beaver* (1957-1963) featured nuclear families in which the father had a steady job and the mother stayed at home. Rarely, if ever, did the father's job have a connection with the story. One of those rarities was the episode of *All in the Family* (1971-1983) "The Insurance Is Canceled," in which the father, Archie Bunker (Carroll O'Connor), worked as the foreman of a factory's loading dock. In a cost-cutting move, Archie's bosses ordered him to select one of his subordinates to be laid off. A bigot, Archie made his decision based on race rather than merit. He chose to lay off a highly productive Puerto Rican rather than a lazy white man.

In *The Dick Van Dyke Show* (1961-1966), Van Dyke's character, Rob Petrie, had a wife and son and worked as head writer of a popular television variety show. The creator, Carl Reiner, based the show on his own life as a writer for the famous comedian Sid Caesar. The story lines were split between conflicts involving Petrie's office and his family.

Petrie's wife, Laura, was portrayed by Mary Tyler Moore, who went on to star in her own show, *The Mary Tyler Moore Show* (1970-1977), which was mostly set in the newsroom of WJM, a Minneapolis television station. Mary Richards, Moore's character, was hired as associate producer (later producer) of the Six O'Clock News, although one of the jokes in the first episode was that the position initially paid slightly less than a secretary and considerably less than when a man held the job. However, as the character grew, she took on more and more responsibility. In the final episode, "The Last Show," the entire news staff was laid off, with the exception of one person, because of poor ratings. The joke was that management kept the incompetent news anchor, Ted Baxter (portrayed by Ted Knight).

WKRP in Cincinnati (1978-1982) was critically acclaimed for its accurate portrayal of life at a radio station. One of its best-known and most acclaimed episodes, "Turkeys Away," concerned a promotion that became a public relations disaster. Based on an actual incident at an Atlanta radio station, the station dropped live turkeys out of a helicopter over a shopping center as a Thanksgiving Day giveaway, unaware that turkeys cannot fly. The turkeys were killed, and the shoppers were endangered. In some episodes, the characters faced issues that real businesspeople face, including the need for profits in "Mama's Review," market share in "Baby, If You've Ever Wondered," and unions in "The Union."

Cheers (1982-1993) was set in a Boston bar based on the Bull and Finch Pub in that city. It portrayed the relationship between a business and its customers. Sam Malone (portrayed by Ted Danson) was the owner during the first five seasons. Between the fifth and sixth seasons, the bar was acquired by a large corporation, Malone was demoted to bartender (although he was eventually promoted to manager), and the plots of several shows were driven by the culture shock of the transition from a small business to a corporate environment. Tom Skerritt had a recurring role in the sixth season as Evan Drake, CEO of the corporation. In the eighth and ninth seasons, Roger Rees had a recurring role as Robin Colcord, a millionaire who was eventually arrested for insider trading. During those seasons, Rebecca Howe

Steve Carell (center), Jenna Fischer (left), and the rest of the cast of The Office *celebrate their nomination for a Screen Actors Guild award in 2007. (AP/Wide World Photos)*

(played by Kirstie Alley) was an ambitious business-woman who dated only men who could advance her career. After losing her job as the bar's manager, she became a cocktail waitress and in the last season married a plumber.

Two twenty-first century incarnations of the workplace theme are *The Office* and *Mad Men*. Based on a British sitcom of the same name, *The Office* is set in the Scranton, Pennsylvania, office of a paper company named Dunder Mifflin. Michael Scott (played by Steve Carell) is the clueless manager. Story lines have included the issues of downsizing, health insurance, sexual harassment, performance reviews, e-mail monitoring, drug testing, and safety training. Set during the 1960's, *Mad Men* takes place in the fictional Sterling Cooper advertising agency on Madison Avenue in New York. Don Draper (played by Jon Hamm) is the agency's creative director with a secret past. Several of the episodes involve dealing with the agency's clients, especially Richard M. Nixon's 1960 presidential campaign. Another recurring theme is the status of women in the workplace in that period.

BUSINESSPEOPLE AS HEROES AND VILLAINS

In many crime dramas, businesspeople, especially men, appear as the villains. In addition to the usual murders, rapes, assaults, and robberies, they are often shown to be guilty of rent gouging, toxic waste dumping, union busting, and manufacturing shoddy or even dangerous products. In the *Lou Grant* (1977-1982) episode "Goop," for instance, a reporter goes undercover to investigate a company suspected of the illegal dumping of chemicals. In *The Dukes of Hazzard* (1979-1985), the recurring villain was Jefferson Davis "Boss" Hogg, owner of the local bank.

The United States endured two energy crises during the 1970's, so the oil industry was much in the news at the time. On *Dallas* (1978-1991), the villain that the viewers loved to hate was J. R. Ewing (played by Larry Hagman), a Texas oilman. He sought power, acted without scruples, and manipulated other people into doing his will. He was more a caricature than a true character. One of the story lines during the show's early years concerned offshore oil leases in Southeast Asia. Another ongoing story line throughout the show's entire run was the struggle to control the family company, Ewing Oil, and battles with another company called Westar were featured

during the middle and late seasons. A merger with another oil company was the subject of the episode "Royal Marriage," and purchasing a refinery was the subject of "Taste of Success."

On *Dynasty* (1981-1989), Blake Carrington (portrayed by John Forsythe) was also an oilman, but he lived in Denver. Whereas J. R. did business in Southeast Asia, Blake did business in the Middle East and China. In the early episodes, he was just as ruthless and unscrupulous as J. R., but he softened as the years went by. The role of the villain was filled by his former wife, Alexis (played by Joan Collins), who was introduced in the second season. However, the soap opera aspects of both shows overwhelmed their business aspects. *Dynasty* in particular was known for its high campiness. The message, if there was one, was that while greed was not necessarily good, it was definitely glamorous.

One of the most sympathetic portrayals of a fictional businessperson on television took place on *Rich Man, Poor Man* (1976-1977), a miniseries based on the 1970 novel by Irwin Shaw. The parents of Rudy Jordache (played by Peter Strauss) owned a bakery, where Rudy worked after school and on weekends. He went to college and became a multimillionaire by the age of thirty-five by capitalizing on the middle-class flight to the suburbs during the 1950's.

DOCUDRAMAS

Events in business history have been dramatized in television movies and miniseries. The anthology series *The Great Adventure* (1963-1965), for instance, consisted entirely of docudramas from American history. The episodes "Six Wagons to the Sea" concerned a railroad and financial scandal in the nineteenth century and "The Colonel from Connecticut" was about the drilling of the first oil well in 1854.

Many docudramas feature people suffering disasters. In *Bitter Harvest* (1981), Ron Howard played a farmer who discovered that his animal feed was contaminated by a chemical. Based on the 1978 book by Frederick Halbert and Sandra Halbert, the show was more critical of government health officials and regulators than of the manufacturer of the feed, although there was enough blame to go around. *Lois Gibbs and the Love Canal* (1982) had a similar theme. Marsha Mason played the title character, a housewife who discovered that her house and those of seven hundred other people were built on a chemical waste disposal site.

In *Damaged Care* (2002), the target was the insurance industry, especially health maintenance organizations (HMOs). Dr. Linda Peeno (Laura Dern) was a medical reviewer for an HMO who was under pressure from her superiors to deny legitimate claims, but she eventually became a whistle-blower.

One of the best docudramas about business was *Barbarians at the Gate* (1993), based on the 1990 book by Bryan Burrough and John Helyar. Written by Larry Gelbart, it concerned the leveraged buyout of RJR Nabisco in 1988, which was the largest in history up until that time. Chief executive officer F. Ross Johnson (played by James Garner) wanted to take the company private and enlisted Shearson Lehman Hutton, then a division of American Express. However, Henry Kravis (played by Jonathan Pryce) of Kohlberg, Kravis, and Roberts also wanted a piece of the action, and their power struggle drove much of the plot.

The origin of the personal computer industry was shown in *The Pirates of Silicon Valley* (1999). It starred Noah Wylie as Steve Jobs, Joey Slotnick as Steve Wozniak, Anthony Michael Hall as Bill Gates, and Josh Hopkins as Paul Allen. None of the principals cooperated, and the show was based on the book *Fire in the Valley: The Making of the Personal Computer* (1984) by Paul Freiberger and Michael Swaine. It was set beginning during the early 1970's and concluded with a birthday party for Jobs in 1985, just before he lost control of Apple for several years.

Shows that realistically and fairly treat businesspeople have been few and far between, in part because a well-run business is probably not interesting enough to make good series television. Unlike a police station or hospital, mundane businesses rarely deal in life-and-death situations. Television writers spice up the story lines by inserting conflicts that rarely happen in a normal business.

Thomas R. Feller

FURTHER READING

Bauer, Douglas, ed. *Prime Times: Writers on Their Favorite TV Shows.* New York: Crown, 2004. This collection includes essays on *The Dick Van Dyke Show* and *The Mary Tyler Moore Show.*

Bianculli, David. *Teleliteracy: Taking Television Seriously.* New York: Simon & Schuster, 1992. Critical defense of television with comments on several shows portraying business themes.

Gitlin, Todd. *Inside Prime Time.* New York: Pantheon Books, 1983. Discusses the treatment of businesspeople in the chapter "The Temple Stands."

Medved, Michael. *Hollywood vs. America.* New York: HarperCollins, 1992. The subchapter "Evil Industrialists" argues that a disproportionate number of the villains on television are businesspeople.

Siegel, Lee. *Not Remotely Controlled: Notes on Television.* Philadelphia: Perseus Books Group, 2007. This collection of essays includes a review of *The Apprentice.*

Thompson, Robert L. *Television's Second Golden Age: From "Hill Street Blues" to "ER."* New York: Continuum, 1996. Discusses many of the major shows of the 1980's and 1990's that portray workplaces and business themes.

SEE ALSO: Bloomberg's Business News Services; Cable News Network; CNBC; Federal Communications Commission; Home Shopping Network; Motion-picture industry; National Broadcasting Company; Radio broadcasting industry; Television broadcasting industry; Trump, Donald; Video rental industry.

Tennessee Valley Authority

IDENTIFICATION: Government-owned corporation established to provide electricity and economic development to the Tennessee Valley region

DATE: Founded on May 18, 1933

SIGNIFICANCE: Through electric power production, agricultural advances, river improvements, land management, and social and recreational programs, the TVA has revitalized much of the Tennessee Valley. The agency remains an important example of how public ownership and private interests can intersect to create economic development.

In April, 1933, one month after taking office as president of the United States, Franklin D. Roosevelt recommended the Tennessee Valley Authority (TVA) Act to Congress' consideration. Roosevelt championed the plan of Senator George Norris of Nebraska to build a series of dams to control flooding, provide navigation, generate electric power, and stimulate industrial development on the Tennessee River. On May 18, 1933, Congress passed the TVA Act by a wide margin, and later that same day Roosevelt signed the measure into law. Congress appropriated $50 million for the TVA and gave it comprehensive powers for owning, developing, and operating hydroelectric resources in the economically depressed Tennessee Valley. The authority's operating region included parts of Tennessee, Alabama, Kentucky, Virginia, Georgia, North Carolina, and Mississippi.

During the 1930's, the TVA embarked on a massive engineering effort to harness the power of the Tennessee River and its tributaries. Natural resource development and regional planning were crucial to the TVA's approach to rebuilding the region. The giant turbines in the powerhouses of the TVA's dams quickly electrified rural areas. A stable power supply and a 650-mile navigable waterway attracted new industry to the poverty-stricken Southeast. Existing businesses in the region, such as the Aluminum Company of America (ALCOA), benefited greatly from the TVA's work. The TVA also brought hundreds of new jobs to the region.

Initially, a three-member board of directors managed the agency. Arthur Morgan, David Lilienthal, and Harcourt Morgan served on the first board and together led the agency through the tumultuous 1930's. Each member focused on a particular area of the TVA's work: Board chair Arthur Morgan led the engineering effort and resettlement programs for those directly affected by the projects; Lilienthal directed the electric power program and drafted power policy; and Harcourt Morgan managed an agricultural division focused on fertilizer production and educational programs for farmers.

Electric power production remains the most important facet of the TVA's operations and its history. By the mid-1930's, Arthur Morgan, who fa-vored cooperation with private power companies, clashed with Lilienthal, who encouraged expansion and competition. At the same time as these early board disagreements, the Supreme Court ruled several other New Deal agencies unconstitutional. Two legal challenges, led by George Ashwander and the Tennessee Electric Power Company, brought the TVA before the Supreme Court. In both cases, the Supreme Court upheld the constitutionality of the authority. Early board struggles resulted in Arthur Morgan's removal from the board and Lilienthal's ascendancy to the chairmanship. Lilienthal led the agency during World War II and into the early years of the Cold War.

POSTWAR DEVELOPMENT

By the 1950's, the TVA had completed more than twenty dams and largely accomplished its goal scientifically to control the Tennessee River. On the whole, subsequent TVA leaders attempted to keep electric power rates low, expand their services, develop community-based programs, encourage economic and industrial growth, and manage natural resources.

During the last half of the twentieth century the TVA found itself in the middle of several controver-

Pickwick Dam, pictured in the late 1930's, was one of the TVA projects. (Library of Congress)

sies. Its efforts to complete the Tellico Dam during the 1970's brought considerable public outcry. The Tellico project, completed in 1979, inundated several important Native American sites, further threatened the endangered snail darter, displaced local residents to make way for upscale lakefront residential communities, and flooded many acres of quality farmland. The authority also built over a dozen coal-fired power plants and began construction of nuclear power plants to keep up with increased electric demands. These projects drew fire from environmentalists, politicians, and residents. As a result, the TVA made efforts to reduce air pollution and halted construction of many planned nuclear plants.

The TVA is the nation's largest public power company. With the help of 159 locally owned distributors, the TVA serves power to about 8.8 million people in the Tennessee Valley. The authority is an international example of regional development and government regulation. Its multiple missions have resulted in untold benefits and spurred enormous economic growth in the Tennessee Valley for over seventy-five years.

Aaron D. Purcell

FURTHER READING

Chandler, William U. *The Myth of TVA: Conservation and Development in the Tennessee Valley, 1933-1983.* Cambridge, Mass.: Ballinger, 1984. In this critical assessment of the agency, Chandler questions the TVA's economic benefits and charges that the authority may have impeded growth in the region that it was intended to improve.

Hargrove, Erwin C. *Prisoners of Myth: The Leadership of the Tennessee Valley Authority, 1933-1990.* 2d ed. Knoxville: University of Tennessee Press, 2001. While reviewing the TVA's leadership, Hargrove explains how the agency remained relevant long after its dam projects had concluded.

Hubbard, Preston J. *Origins of the TVA: The Muscle Shoals Controversy, 1920-1932.* Nashville, Tenn.: Vanderbilt University Press, 1961. This survey chronicles the events leading up to and the reasons behind the creation of the Tennessee Valley Authority.

Lilienthal, David E. *TVA: Democracy On the March.* New York: Harper & Brothers, 1944. In masterful fashion, Lilienthal connects public ownership to democracy and free enterprise, arguing that the TVA represented a model of decentralization that gave economic power back to the people.

Owen, Marguerite. *The Tennessee Valley Authority.* New York: Praeger, 1973. Written by a TVA employee, this excellent introduction to the history and purpose of the authority remains a relevant work.

Purcell, Aaron D. "Struggle Within, Struggle Without: The *TEPCO* Case and the Tennessee Valley Authority, 1936-1939." *The Tennessee Historical Quarterly* 61, no. 3 (2002): 194-210. Reviews the early history behind the TVA's commitment to public power production and its relationship with preexisting private power companies in the Tennessee Valley.

SEE ALSO: Colorado River water; Dams and aqueducts; New Deal programs; Nuclear power industry; Public utilities; Water resources.

Terrorist attacks of September 11. *See* September 11 terrorist attacks

Texas annexation

THE EVENT: Annexation of the Texas Lone Star Republic by the United States
DATE: 1845
PLACE: Texas
SIGNIFICANCE: The annexation of Texas started a war with Mexico that resulted in the United States gaining a large piece of territory that extended the country to the Pacific coast. These lands provided numerous economic benefits and access to the ocean. However, the controversy over the annexation of Texas led to sectionalism that may have contributed to the starting of the U.S. Civil War.

On March 6, 1836, Texans were fighting Antonio López de Santa Anna and his troops at the Alamo, in San Antonio. The Texans sought secession from Mexican rule. Although Santa Anna won at the Alamo, he lost just weeks later at San Jacinto to Sam Houston, commander of the Texas military. As a result, Texas, no longer under Mexican rule, became its own nation, and Sam Houston its first president.

This pro-Democratic cartoon predicts the demise of Whig opposition to the annexation of Texas. James Polk (right) holds an American flag and hails Stephen Austin and Samuel Houston (holding Texas flags) in a boat. (Library of Congress)

Andrew Jackson was the president of the United States when Texas won its independence, and he pushed for the annexation of Texas. However, annexation did not happen under him, nor under his successor, Martin Van Buren. The issue of slavery was simply too dominant in the minds of American politicians, who feared that the admission of Texas as a slave state would throw the legislative balance of Congress too strongly toward a proslavery position. Therefore, Texas remained an independent nation with a population that almost quadrupled by the time Democrat James Polk ran for president in 1844.

Polk ran on a platform of expansionism, wanting to secure the annexation not only of Texas but also of Oregon. Polk handily defeated Whig Party candidate Henry Clay, causing the theretofore hesitant U.S. Congress to adopt a measure approving the annexation of Texas on March 1, 1845. Congress had taken Polk's election as a mandate for annexation.

The Mexican government was angered by what seemed to be the certain annexation of Texas by the United States, and hostilities between the two nations appeared imminent. Although the Mexican government had a number of concerns stemming from the statehood of Texas, a central concern was the location of the southern border of Texas, a border that would also be the southern border of the United States. The U.S. government held that the southern border was the Rio Grande, while Mexico protested that the border was farther north. U.S. general Zachary Taylor, attacked by Mexican troops while patrolling the southern border in May, 1945, responded by firing back, and the Mexican War ensued.

Texas was officially annexed on December 29, 1845, although the Mexican War continued until the United States gained a victory in 1848. In the ensuing treaty, Mexico ceded an area from Texas to California to the United States. By extending to the Pacific coast, the United States vastly increased its economic potential, especially in the gold, silver, iron, copper, cattle, farming, banking, real estate, railroad, and telegraph industries. However, Texas's status as a slave state is believed by some to have created sectionalism—a divide between the North and South—that may have been a step toward the start of the U.S. Civil War.

A. W. R. Hawkins

FURTHER READING

Groneman, Bill. *Battlefields of Texas.* Plano, Texas: Republic of Texas Press, 1998.

Richardson, Rupert N. *Texas, the Lone Star State.* 9th ed. Upper Saddle River, N.J.: Prentice Hall, 2005.

Silbey, Joel H. *Storm over Texas: The Annexation Controversy and the Road to Civil War.* New York: Oxford University Press, 2005.

SEE ALSO: Civil War, U.S.; Gadsden Purchase; Hawaii annexation; Mexican trade with the United States; Mexican War; Petroleum industry; Slave era.

Three Mile Island accident

THE EVENT: Nuclear power plant accident
DATE: March 28, 1979
PLACE: Three Mile Island, in the Susquehanna River, near Harrisburg, Pennsylvania
SIGNIFICANCE: The nation's worst commercial nuclear accident, the core meltdown at Three Mile Island led first to a complete halt in the construction of nuclear power plants, then to serious economic and public-relations consequences for the United States' nuclear power industry.

At 4:00 A.M., a stuck valve in the cooling system of unit 2 of the Three Mile Island Nuclear Generating Station set off a chain of reactor malfunctions that resulted in pandemonium and nearly a total meltdown. The incident began when one of the plant's main feed-water pumps failed; because water was no longer flowing, the steam generators were not removing heat from the reactor. Pressure began to increase, and a valve that should have closed after the excessive pressure was released did not do so. Plant operators assumed the valve had closed, so they were unaware that pressure was continuing to rise. Cooling water poured through the stuck valve, causing the core of the reactor to overheat. Since no instrument measured the water level in the core, operators did not realize the water level had fallen, uncovering the reactor core.

Radiation alarms, activated by contaminated water, sounded, but they were initially ignored. Not realizing the plant was experiencing a loss of coolant, operators initiated a series of actions that made conditions worse by further reducing the coolant through the core. Consequently, the nuclear fuel overheated to a point at which the zirconium cladding (tubes holding the nuclear fuel pellets) ruptured and began to melt. It was later determined that about one-half the core melted during the early stages of the accident. Radiation levels were around three hundred times expected levels, and the plant was seriously contaminated. Although the plant suffered a severe core meltdown, the building's containment wall was not breached. Such a breach could have caused a massive release of radiation into the environment.

The incident at Three Mile Island caught federal and state authorities unprepared for such an emergency. Plant personnel initially had difficulty establishing communication with the Nuclear Regula-

The Three Mile Island nuclear plant in 1999, with the damaged unit at left. (AP/Wide World Photos)

tory Commission's regional office, and there was no planned evacuation route. Governor of Pennsylvania Richard Thornburg advised that pregnant women and young children within a five-mile radius of the plant be evacuated, but no general evacuation was ordered. The crisis continued through April 1. Although the damage to the reactor was serious, the radiation was contained, and the amount released had a negligible effect on the physical health of people in the area or on the environment. The reactor was permanently shut down, and the damage caused by the meltdown was estimated at $500 million. Cleanup of the site continued through 1993.

Despite the relatively benign outcome of the accident, the fear it generated continued to haunt the nuclear power industry. Immediately after March, 1979, public approval of nuclear power fell, as did construction orders for nuclear reactors. Three Mile Island became an iconic symbol of the dangers of nuclear power, later joined by Chernobyl. The disasters in these two locations are often invoked by opponents of nuclear power seeking to build public distrust and defeat proposals for new nuclear power facilities.

Marcia B. Dinneen

A man stands outside a Goodwill thrift store and Mission church in Minneapolis in 1937. (Library of Congress)

FURTHER READING

Stephens, Mark. *Three Mile Island.* New York: Random House, 1980.

Walker, Samuel. *Three Mile Island: A Nuclear Crisis in Historical Perspective.* Berkeley: University of California Press, 2004.

Whitford, David. "Going Nuclear." *Fortune* 6 (August, 2007): 42-54.

SEE ALSO: Energy, U.S. Department of; Energy crisis of 1979; Environmental movement; Nuclear power industry; Occupational Safety and Health Act; Public utilities; Tennessee Valley Authority.

Thrift stores

DEFINITION: Enterprises that generate revenue by selling donated, mostly secondhand goods

SIGNIFICANCE: Thrift stores require minimal start-up financing while serving as fund-raising vessels for charitable organizations, low-cost retail options for consumers, and steady sources of income for ownership.

Historically, the concept of thrift arose alongside the founding of religious and private philanthropy. Organizations such as the Salvation Army (founded in 1865), American Red Cross (1881), and Goodwill Industries (1902) recognized the necessity of providing services catering to the physical and emotional needs of underserved populations. Specifically, the Salvation Army and Goodwill Industries sought to bring the Christian faith to groups marginalized by the Industrial Revolution by combining scripture with charitable works.

Although these charitable organizations began with limited resources, the revenues eventually generated by their thrift stores rivaled those of traditional retail businesses. In the 2006 fiscal year, for example, Goodwill Industries reported revenues in excess of $2.9 billion with $1.8 billion (62 percent) generated in retail sales from its global network of 2,100 thrift stores. Similarly, the Salvation Army of the United States reported $3 billion in revenues, with approximately 15 percent of its revenue generated from its nearly 1,500 thrift shops.

According to the National Association of Resale and Thrift Shops, resale is one of the fastest-growing retail segments, with an annual growth of 5 percent. Furthermore, during any given year, 16 to 18 percent of all Americans shop at thrift stores, and 12 to 15 percent shop at consignment stores. By contrast, 11.4 percent of Americans shop in factory outlet malls, 19.6 percent in apparel stores, and 21.3 percent in major department stores.

Aside from online storefronts similar to eBay and Amazon.com, thrift stores offer a low-cost and easy-to-replicate business model, while providing inexpensive retail options for customers. Additionally, secondhand shopping is no longer a passé exercise of individuals with limited incomes. Discount retailers, such as Target and Wal-Mart, have contributed to consumer acceptance of cheaper goods. Whether motivated by the desire to save the environment, to access inexpensive haute couture, or to stretch budgets during economic downturns, thrift stores have redefined secondhand retail shopping while blossoming into multibillion-dollar industries. Within the retail industry, thrift stores are viewed as ideal, in that they are associated with minimal start-up costs and the profit margins depend on donated merchandise. As such, if properly managed, a thrift store could have a revolving door of profit.

Brandy M. Brooks

FURTHER READING

Horne, Suzanne. *Charity Shops: Retailing, Consumption, and Society.* New York: Routledge, 2002.
Larned, Emily. *Thrift Store: The Past and Future of Secret Things.* New York: Ig Publishing, 2005.
Reeger, Jennifer. "Thrift Stores Are a Growing Presence." *Pittsburgh Tribune-Review,* November 26, 2005.

SEE ALSO: eBay; Online marketing; Retail trade industry; Warehouse and discount stores.

Time zones

DEFINITION: Geographic areas within which time is standardized

SIGNIFICANCE: The development of standard time and the division of the continental United States into four time zones allowed work and transportation schedules to be rationalized, helping drive the development of the United States as an industrialized society.

Time zones are industrial humanity's method of dealing with the Sun's illuminating a round, rotating Earth. While a person in Chicago observes high noon, a person in London is observing sunset, a person in Honolulu is observing sunrise, and a person in Mumbai, India, is using artificial light to illuminate the night. So long as travel and communications were slow and primitive timekeeping devices were inaccurate, this phenomenon remained of academic interest. Its first practical use was in open-ocean navigation, to solve the problem of determining longitude.

In the nineteenth century, the telegraph and the railroad enabled messages and people to travel at previously unimaginable speeds. European countries gradually instituted standardized time, placing the entire country on the solar time of the capital. However, such a solution would not have been practical for a nation as large as the United States. San Francisco's observed time would lag three hours behind official time from Washington, D.C. American railroads developed systems of time zones that allowed each region's standard time to remain reasonably close to observed solar time. However, this "railroad time" was not coordinated among the various railroad companies, leading to incompatible schedules: Major railroad stations had to display a different clock, indicating a different time, for each railroad company using that station.

In 1882, the heads of the various railroads met in St. Louis, Missouri, and worked out a system to divide the United States into four standard time zones. Each zone would be centered on a meridian of longitude 15° apart, because 15° represents one-twenty-fourth of the full 360° circle of Earth. Thus, each zone would be one hour wide. This system went into effect the following year. However, Americans resisted the institution of standardized time zones for years before they became widely accepted throughout American culture. In one town, a man who persisted in using local solar time in defiance of standard time protested being fined for contempt of court when he failed to appear at the "correct" time for a noon court date.

In 1884, Congress passed a resolution authorizing President Chester A. Arthur to call the International Meridian Conference. Although the meeting was held in Washington, D.C., the Greenwich, England, meridian was chosen as the zero point for the international time system. It was established practice in the English-speaking world to use that meridian as the zero meridian of longitude. This time zone was termed Greenwich mean time (GMT), or universal time. The conference then established twelve time zones on each side of the prime meridian, as well as the international date line in the Pacific Ocean. In actual practice, the system of time zones has become an odd patchwork, as various polities have pushed and pulled the boundaries of the time zones away from the ideal arrangement to avoid cutting communities in half.

Leigh Husband Kimmel

FURTHER READING

Barnett, Jo Ellen. *Time's Pendulum: From Sundials to Atomic Clocks—The Fascinating History of Timekeeping and How Our Discoveries Changed the World.* San Diego: Harcourt Brace, 1999.

Dolan, Graham. *The Greenwich Guide to Measuring Time.* Chicago: Heinemann Library, 2001.

Kern, Stephen. *The Culture of Time and Space, 1880-1918.* Cambridge, Mass.: Harvard University Press, 2003.

SEE ALSO: Daylight saving time; Metric system; Railroads.

Tobacco industry

DEFINITION: Enterprises involved in the growing, processing, marketing, and distribution of tobacco products

SIGNIFICANCE: The industry that evolved around leafy tobacco, more than any other cash crop indigenous to the Americas, provides a study in the dynamics of successful capitalism. The industry's historic record of phenomenal international economic success, however, must be measured against the nearly century-long process of government investigations, scientific research, and extensive litigation designed to make consumers aware of the substantive health risks from tobacco products.

Cultural anthropologists suggest that tobacco was grown by indigenous Americans as a cure-all and painkiller and to be used as part of religious rituals more than six thousand years before the arrival of Europeans on the continent. Although Spanish explorers during the sixteenth century introduced tobacco to Europe as a medicine (smoking was initially a way to administer daily dosages), settlers in the Virginia Tidewater region during the early seventeenth century realized the potential of tobacco crops for popular consumption—making tobacco the first cash crop grown in the New World.

EARLY GROWTH

The industry quickly grew in the colonies (particularly into Maryland and the Carolinas), as upper-class British developed a taste for snuff and pipe tobacco and rural and working classes for chewing tobacco. Although religious groups in England and in the colonies maintained moral objections against its use, tobacco dominated southern economic development. By the time of the American Revolution, the tobacco industry accounted for more than 100 million pounds of exported leaf annually (the colonial government used the tobacco export revenue as collateral with the French to finance the independence effort). After the Revolution, because tobacco required backbreaking labor and meticulous care from planting to curing, the southern economy came to rely on the slave trade to maintain what had become its dominant cash crop.

U.S. Civil War soldiers introduced widespread interest in cigarettes over chewing tobacco—rolling cigarettes was cheap and simple. When, after the war, communities began to legislate against public spitting, industry interest in producing rolled cigarettes grew. From an industry standpoint, rolled cigarettes promised much revenue: The process used cut bits of the plants that were usually discarded. The rolling process was painfully slow at first, but in 1881, James Bonsack revolutionized the industry by introducing a cigarette-rolling machine that enabled factory workers to produce tens of thousands of cigarettes per day. In turn, the tobacco industry began an aggressive (and in many ways innovative) campaign to market cigarettes to the growing northeastern urban centers and to markets in Europe. Economists estimate that more than one-third of the internal revenues collected by the American government during the Gilded Age came from the excise taxes from the tobacco industry alone.

A BOOST IN POPULARITY

Despite zealous reformers who sought to curb smoking, by the early twentieth century more than 3 billion cigarettes were being consumed worldwide. Companies such as Phillip Morris, R. J. Reynolds, and the American Tobacco Company thrived. Their market reach was greatly enhanced by World War I, as battle-weary soldiers were drawn to the simplicity of a smoke and to the calming effect of nicotine. The resulting cultural cachet was in turn enhanced during the Jazz Age, when smoking (especially cigars) became a significant element of chic American culture. By then, the industry was targeting women; Marlboro and Lucky Strikes were among the first so-called gentler cigarettes aimed at that demographic.

The tobacco industry reached its greatest success after World War II, when millions of soldiers, whose C-rations had routinely included cigarettes donated to the war effort by the tobacco industry, returned home addicted to the product. In the postwar economic boom, tobacco companies launched an unprecedented advertising campaign, employing clever sloganeering, captivating jingles, and celebrity spokespeople, and using the power and reach of the new media, television and radio.

Cigarettes seemed to be everywhere—television and motion picture stars, politicians, entertainers, and athletes smoked. By the mid-1960's, cigarettes were the most advertised American consumer product in the world; soft drinks were a distant second. Remarkably, during the 1950's, cigarettes became an integral part of two apparently opposing demographics—the conservative suburban lifestyle and the burgeoning counterculture movement, which regarded smoking as part of being cool and rebellious. As the production process became nearly entirely automated, moreover, the industry maximized production levels with a minimum workforce.

HEALTH RISKS

In 1826, nicotine was first isolated and defined as a poison. A substantive element of the medical community had investigated the health risks of smoking ever since, but the tobacco industry had successfully outmaneuvered the attempts by the Food and Drug Administration to enact sumptuary regulations against cigarettes by promoting smoking as a kind of wide-ranging therapy, able to both soothe and energize its consumers. As smoking became a national phenomena (during the mid-1950's, nearly 60 percent of American men and nearly 30 percent of women smoked), scientists, tracking the health of veterans from both world wars, raised increasingly strident cautions about the links between smoking and a variety of respiratory conditions, most prominently lung cancer. The tobacco industry, however, maintained that nicotine was neither addictive nor carcinogenic.

It was the bombshell report made public on January 11, 1964, by the Office of the Surgeon General (the first of a decade's worth of increasingly alarming reports) that first brought national attention to the risks smoking presented, including cancer, emphysema, heart disease, and chronic bronchitis. Indeed, within two years, tobacco companies were required to add a printed health warning on every cigarette pack—but

A tobacco market in Louisville, Kentucky, in the early 1900's. (Library of Congress)

THE BIG FIVE TRANSNATIONAL TOBACCO COMPANIES, 1999

Company	Revenue (US$ billions)	Global Market Share (%)
Philip Morris	47.1	16.4
British American Tobacco	31.3	15.4
Japan Tobacco International	21.6	7.2
Reemsta	6.1	2.6
Altadis	2.3	1.9

Source: Judith Mackay and Michael Eriksen, The Tobacco Atlas (Brighton, U.K.: Myriad Editions, 2002)

because of high pressure from the tobacco industry, the warning was kept vague and would not state explicitly that smoking endangered health until 1970. The industry, in turn, responded with much-publicized alterations to their products, most notably lower-tar and filter-tipped cigarettes that were said to lower health risks.

Increasingly scrutinized by investigative reporters, crusading lawyers, and consumer advocate groups, the tobacco industry followed a clear and consistent line of response. It questioned the validity of any medical data that suggested definitive causal links between smoking and health risks, insisted on the intrinsic economic value of the tobacco industry to the American economy, and maintained a vocal lobby that mitigated any proposed legislation geared at prohibiting the sale and distribution of the industry's products. After the Federal Communications Commission (FCC) ruled that promoting smoking without adequate indications of the risks was misleading and irresponsible—and despite enormous pressure from the tobacco lobby and stubborn resistance by the southern bloc in both the Senate and the House—a sweeping legislative package in 1970 effectively prohibited advertising cigarettes on television and radio. Print media would follow. Celebrities now appeared in public service advertisements, sponsored by the American Cancer Society, encouraging smokers to kick the habit.

As early as 1974, nonsmokers' rights groups campaigned to restrict smoking in public areas, becoming more aggressive after several landmark 1980's studies detailed the effects of secondhand smoke. In 1979, the Office of the Surgeon General made public disturbing data that suggested the deleterious effects of smoking on pregnancies, most notably a rise in stillbirths and premature births. New alarms were raised about the health risks of smokeless tobacco. In 1993, the Environmental Protection Agency (EPA) classified cigarette smoke as a Class-A carcinogen. An increased effort was made to restrict marketing strategies by the tobacco industry in print media that targeted teenagers (most notably the long legal campaign during the late 1990's directed against R. J. Reynolds' cartoon advertising mascot Joe Camel). Although the tobacco industry countered with their own data that suggested quite opposite conclusions, by the early 1990's, the big tobacco companies and their representatives were widely demonized as duplicitous, ruthless, and mercenary.

By the mid-1990's, although less than 30 percent of Americans now smoked, smoking-related diseases had become the leading preventable cause of death; state governments assessed progressively higher taxes on cigarettes to deal with the mounting catastrophic health care costs. The most prominent tobacco companies began to diversify their product lines to adjust to what was becoming an increasingly strained economic environment. Philip Morris and R. J. Reynolds, for instance, acquired dozens of food product lines during the 1990's; Liggett & Myers expanded into computers and the lucrative trading card industry; American Tobacco acquired numerous prestige liquors; and Lorillard Tobacco branched into international shipping and resort hotel management.

LITIGATION AND ITS AFTERMATH

It was in this charged atmosphere that the tobacco industry began to face a wave of litigation from states that accused it of withholding internal studies that suggested long before the 1964 report that their product was both addictive and carcinogenic. Although the industry had fended off such litigation for decades, revelations from leaked internal memos and a succession of industry whistle-blowers indicated that the industry executives had been aware for decades of nicotine's harmful effects. In 1994, enormous pressure from such revelations led Liggett & Myers to settle a lawsuit filed by twenty-two states, effectively admitting that cigarette smoking caused health problems and, far more problematic, that their marketing strategies had targeted teenagers.

The impact of that settlement was an unprecedented number of legal actions brought against the tobacco industry by nearly all the states. The result was the landmark 1998 settlement known as the Tobacco Master Settlement Agreement. At the petition of forty-six state attorneys general, the four major tobacco companies—R. J. Reynolds, Brown & Williamson, Lorillard Tobacco, and Philip Morris USA (later joined by close to forty other tobacco companies)—agreed to pay an estimated $206 billion over twenty-five years to those forty-six states to help meet skyrocketing smoking-related Medicaid costs. Florida, Minnesota, Texas, and Mississippi had previously reached separate agreements with the industry.

An additional $6 billion was set aside to support tobacco growers put at economic risk by the settlement. In addition, the tobacco companies agreed to restrict advertising and marketing of all tobacco products. Lastly, monies collected from the settlement would be used to establish the American Legacy Foundation, an advocacy group that would maintain high-profile advertising campaigns targeted at discouraging teenagers from starting to smoke.

That such a settlement—the largest civil settlement in the history of American jurisprudence—did not effectively cripple the industry points to its resourcefulness. That an industry that kills one-fourth of the consumers who use its products continues to thrive and does so without sustained advertising or deep marketing is one of the most persistent paradoxes in American business. There were immediate ramifications to the settlement: massive layoffs, a precipitous price increase, and the relocation of processing plants to developing nations, where production costs would be considerably cheaper.

As opponents of the tobacco industry quickly pointed out, however, the settlement missed the opportunity to end tobacco product manufacturing once and for all. Further, the settlement did not reflect the urgency of substantive medical data and the long-term possibilities of additional health risks from continued consumption of such products. Indeed, even as tobacco consumption declined in developed Western countries, long before the 1998 landmark settlement, the tobacco industry had already turned its attention overseas to less restricted markets in nonindustrial countries. It had particularly explored newly opened markets in the former Soviet Union, Asia (most prominently the massive markets of rural China), and the underdeveloped interior of Africa. These markets promised billions of dollars in unregulated sales.

Indeed, industry data during the early twenty-first century indicated that more than 5.5 trillion cigarettes were still being smoked worldwide annually by upward of 700 million smokers; thus, the diversified American tobacco companies still compose one of the most profitable and recession-proof industries, although courts are still assessing dozens of civil suits brought by individuals in the wake of the Master Settlement. Despite the steady decline in the number of smokers in the United States and despite overseas growers, most notably China and Brazil, that have eclipsed the United States in leaf tobacco production, the American tobacco industry has survived. In the wake of the full disclosure of the health risks of its products, it offers those same tobacco products to domestic consumers as lifestyle choices and an assertion of individual rights.

Joseph Dewey

FURTHER READING

Gately, Iain. *Tobacco: A Cultural History of How an Exotic Plant Seduced Civilization.* New York: Grove, 2002. Definitive account of the evolution of the tobacco industry that suggests how cultures shift between attraction and repulsion. Includes the economic impact as well as the influence of tobacco on American politics, culture, and religion.

Kluger, Richard. *Ashes to Ashes: America's Hundred-Year Cigarette War, the Public Health, and the Unabashed Triumph of Philip Morris.* New York: Knopf, 1997. Pulitzer Prize-winning study of the industry from its roots, particularly focused on its long campaign to subvert public investigations into the health risks of tobacco. A strong anti-industry bias.

Mollenkamp, Carrick, Joseph Karl Menn, Joseph

Menn, and Adam Levy. *The People vs. Big Tobacco: How the States Took on the Cigarette Giants.* New York: Bloomberg, 1998. Essential reading on the 1998 settlement and the long investigation leading up to the suit, provides clear account of the rise of the tobacco industry after World War Two.

Parker-Pope, Tara. *Cigarettes: Anatomy of an Industry from Seed to Smoke.* New York: Norton, 2001. Historical (and generally unbiased) account of the rise of the tobacco industry and its impact on the economic evelopment of the South.

Zegart, Dan. *Civil Warriors: The Legal Siege on the Tobacco Industry.* New York: Delacorte Press, 2001. Behind-the-scenes look at the legal challenge to the industry during the 1990's leading up to the landmark settlement case. Effective look at the psychology of whistle-blowing.

SEE ALSO: Advertising industry; Agribusiness; Agriculture; Agriculture, U.S. Department of; Colonial economic systems; Farm labor; Food and Drug Administration; Plantation agriculture; Sharecropping; Slave era; Treasury, U.S. Department of the.

Tourism industry

DEFINITION: Service enterprises that cater largely or primarily to tourists, including those providing transportation, lodging, food, entertainment, and souvenirs

SIGNIFICANCE: In the United States, tourism is an enormous industry, serving millions of international and domestic tourists yearly. The industry is a major portion of America's service sector and one of the nation's largest employers.

The tourism industry centers on the simple premise that travel for recreation and leisure is pleasurable. Tourists—who are defined as people who travel outside their homes for not more than a year and who do not earn money in the location visited—are the industry's clientele. The United Nations has designated that domestic tourism involves residents traveling within one's own country. For instance, Americans traveling throughout the United States fall into this category. Inbound tourism is the name given to tourists entering a country. Tourists from other countries visiting the United States fall into this category. Outbound tourism involves tourists traveling in another country. This would apply to Americans who visit other countries. In addition, internal tourism involves both domestic tourism and inbound tourism. The number of Americans touring the United States in addition to tourists from other countries visiting the United States would be counted for this category.

NATIONAL TOURISM

National tourism involves domestic tourism and outbound tourism. Americans touring the United States and traveling overseas would fit in here. Inbound tourism and outbound tourism together constitute international tourism. The tourism industry ranks countries in terms of number of tourists admitted and the amount of money they spend. For instance, in 2006, the World Tourism Organization ranked France as the number-one tourist destination (with 79 million tourists); Spain (58 million) was second, and the United States (51 million) was third. However, that same year, the United States ranked number one in tourism revenues, with $85 billion earned, while France earned half that amount. Shopping is the primary activity of tourists, followed by outdoor recreation and visits to historical sites and museums. Tourists from abroad and Americans visit natural wonders, large cities, historic landmarks, and gambling venues—particularly Las Vegas.

Some countries, for instance, Thailand and Egypt, strongly depend on tourism to provide hotel, transportation, and restaurant service jobs for their inhabitants. Although the United States is not dependent on tourism, the tourism industry nevertheless provides necessary jobs for Americans and contributes greatly to the U.S. economy. Indeed, tourism is either the first-, second-, or third-largest employer in twenty-nine U.S. states. In the United States, the tourist industry directly employs 7.9 million people, and an additional 18 million are employed indirectly, producing annual payrolls of $174 billion. Tourism is America's third-largest retail sales industry and contributes $98.7 billion in tax revenue. Americans traveling within the United States spend $1.5 billion per day, and international travelers, who spend an average of 15.6 nights in the country, spend $91.1 billion yearly in the United States. By 2007, the number of international tourists climbed to more than 56 million people who spent $122.7 billion dollars.

The United States benefits from varied climates that attract tourists from around the world to such holiday spots as Florida, California, and Arizona for the temperate weather. Tourists also flock to such states as Colorado and Utah in winter for their ski resorts.

HISTORY OF THE INDUSTRY

Before the nineteenth century, only the very wealthy traveled. Early travel generally involved pilgrimages to sacred locations, and the actual process was often arduous. Traveling for leisure or recreation was practically unheard of. Indeed, it was not until 1811 that the term "tourism" first came into vogue and not until 1840 that the word "tourist" was first used.

With the onset of the American Industrial Revolution and the subsequent upward mobility of the middle class, the idea of travel for leisure took hold, and the cultural concept that people were actually entitled to vacations became firmly rooted in the American mind. At first, people were drawn to beaches. Atlantic City, New Jersey, which drew tourists from New York City, became the first seaside resort in the United States. By the 1850's, tourism in the United States was well-established as an industry, especially within the major cities of New York, Chicago, San Francisco, and Washington, D.C.. In addition, the development of photography in this era enhanced the appeal of travel, especially to the West.

During the nineteenth century, steam-powered locomotives revolutionized travel simply by making the process easier and quicker. The first transcontinental railroad was completed in the United States in 1869. Similarly, during the early twentieth century, the invention of the automobile yet again revolutionized travel. By 1915, tour-guide agencies and guidebook publishers were firmly established American businesses. Traveling was once again sped up with the advance of air travel after World War II. During the 1960's, the explosive expansion of the airline industry set in place a global transportation network of airports, air traffic controllers, and the development of the U.S. Federal Aviation Administration and other regulatory agencies that allowed for the movement of large numbers of people to various locales around the world and encouraged the idea of mass travel. Mass travel made tourism Florida's largest source of income. Theme parks

This 1939 poster from the United States Travel Bureau promoted tourism in the American Southwest. (Library of Congress)

were built across the state, and in 1971, the twenty-eight-thousand-acre Disney World in Orlando added $14 billion to that area's economy. By the end of the twentieth century, tourism had significantly grown throughout the world.

VARIOUS FORMS OF TOURISM

As the idea of travel for pleasure and recreation grew in popularity, various forms of tourism emerged. Health tourism, in which ill patients traveled to milder climates to regain their health, gained in popularity in the United States during the nineteenth century after beginning in England, where inhabitants gathered at spas such as Bath to imbibe the local mineral water for their health. This form of travel has continued to grow and has become especially popular with the United States' aging population in the form of health spas. It has come to account for a large part of the revenue generated on cruises and stays at end-destination luxury hotels.

Retiree tourism has also made a large impact in

the tourism industry. Because many retirees have for years dreamt of traveling during their "golden years," they are eager customers, and because they are able to travel year-round, they can take advantage of off-season pricing. Companies specializing in retiree tourism often own their own ships and employ their own guides, offering supervised visits to such destinations as India, China, Thailand, and Egypt.

Some countries that are already tourist destinations, such as India and Eastern Europe, have burgeoning business catering to what has been termed "medical tourism." Because of the high cost of medical insurance in the United States, Americans often cannot afford prohibitively expensive medical procedures such as heart surgery, and they travel outside the country to have the necessary work done by qualified physicians. Before or after their surgeries, patients can take advantage of the host countries' tourist offerings.

Americans are also interested in expanding their tourist experiences by participating on a more active level as adventurers, becoming more immersed in local life instead of passively observing. This form of tourism has been designated "adventure travel." Traveling for educational purposes has also increased dramatically, as has geotourism, another form of tourism that attracts socially aware, environmentally concerned older travelers who seek to emerge themselves in various cultures to gain an understanding of the society.

Before travel by air became popular during the 1960's, ocean liners transported transatlantic travelers. However, the expansion of the airline industry saw a correlating deflation of the cruise industry. Travel by air was far more expedient and less expensive, and the cruise industry seemed to be on the way out. However, in 1974, Cunard began hiring entertainers to boost sales and increased luxurious services to all classes of passenger. Thus began the modern cruising industry, in which the ships themselves have, in part, become destinations.

By the 1980's, enormous floating hotels carrying more than two thousand passengers transported tourists all over the world. The desire for exotic cruises continued to grow, and the 1990's saw an increase in Americans cruising to the Amazon, Africa, and Asia. Since 2000, major cruise lines have launched sixty-four new cruise ships, some termed "megaships," capable of carrying three thousand passengers and featuring such lavish amenities as ice-skating rinks and multistory shopping centers. Smaller ships, by contrast, attract wealthier passengers with promises of exclusivity. Plans for even larger ships, featuring Broadway-style theaters, museums, and planetariums are on the drawing board.

THE TWENTY-FIRST CENTURY

During the early twenty-first century, a trend grew toward more specialized vacations. Also, the advance of the Internet greatly increased competition and lowered prices on common carriers, hotels, and rental cars. During the 1980's, the tourism industry relied on local travel agents who sought out vacation packages and made travel purchases for their clients. Contemporary tourists, however, can use the Internet to find the same deals that travel agents would find for them. They are able to take advantage of good pricing by comparing sites and by buying tickets and accommodations either early or at the last minute.

TEN CITIES OF THE UNITED STATES MOST VISITED BY OVERSEAS TRAVELERS IN 2006

Rank	City	Overseas Travelers (1,000's)
1	New York City	6,219
2	Los Angeles	2,514
3	Orlando, Florida	1,993
4	San Francisco	1,993
5	Miami	1,972
6	Oahu/Honolulu	1,733
7	Las Vegas	1,647
8	Chicago	1,062
9	Washington, D.C.	1,062
10	Boston	997

Source: Data from the *Statistical Abstract of the United States, 2008* (Washington, D.C.: Department of Commerce, Economics and Statistics Administration, Bureau of the Census, Data User Services Division, 2008)

Note: Total overseas travelers was 21,668,000. Includes travel for business or pleasure, students, and passengers in transit.

The tourism industry in the United States was severely disrupted after the terrorist attacks of September 11, 2001, when airline passenger numbers fell by nearly 45 percent, from 9 million the week before September 11 to 5 million the week after. However, the industry began to recover over the following months, thanks to grants from the Federal Reserve and the U.S. Congress.

In response to economic, social, and political factors, some American travelers have adopted the tendency to travel to more rural destinations, take trips closer to home, and shorten the length of their trips. The U.S. economy began to slow significantly in 2007, primarily because of a decline in the real-estate market and an increase in gas prices. In 2008, the World Tourism Organization estimated that Europeans would be the biggest tourist spenders because of the strength of the euro against the dollar. By the year 2020, tourism was predicted to be the world's largest industry.

M. Casey Diana

Further Reading

Belasco, Warren James. *Americans on the Road: From Autocamp to Motel, 1910-1945.* Baltimore: Johns Hopkins University Press, 1997. Documents the changing travel habits of Americans and the supportive infrastructure: motels, gas stations, souvenirs, and such.

Biederman, Paul S. *Travel and Tourism: An Industry Primer.* New York: Prentice Hall, 2007. Educational volume for both students interested in careers in the tourist industry and for travel professionals but accessible enough for the layperson merely interested in the industry. Contains contributions from academic and professional experts.

Goeldner, Charles, and J. R. Brent Ritchie. *Tourism: Principles, Practices, Philosophies.* Hoboken, N.J.: John Wiley & Sons, 2005. In addition to an analysis of the tourist industry's major concepts, this book explores new trends in travel and demonstrates how tourism can become a factor in the wealth of any nation by explaining the social, cultural, economic and psychological aspects of travel and tourism. Contains appendixes with information about key travel industry contacts and additional information sources.

Ioannides, Dimitri. *The Economic Geography of the Tourist Industry: A Supply-Side Analysis.* London: Routledge, 1998. Bridges the gap between tourism research and economic geography by providing analyses of tour operators, airlines and the hotel industry from an international perspective. Covers business cycles, labor dynamics, entrepreneurship and various governmental roles in tourism.

Ramos, Alejandro D., and Pablo S. Jiménez. *Tourism Development: Economics, Management, and Strategy.* New York: Nova Science, 2008. A global look at tourism that focuses on its economic side and discusses the use of public lands.

See also: American Automobile Association; Automotive industry; Hotel and motel industry; Hurricane Katrina; Mexican trade with the United States; Transatlantic steamer service; Transcontinental railroad; Wilderness Road.

Townshend Act

The Law: British law that placed import duties on certain goods coming into the American colonies

Dates: Passed on June 29, 1767; partially repealed on March 5, 1770

Significance: The Townshend Act interfered with colonial commerce and led to a change in colonists' consumption habits and colonial merchants' purchasing. It significantly contributed to the debate over indirect taxation that eventually led to the outbreak of the American Revolution.

Often called the Townshend Duties, the Townshend Act of 1767 was part of a series of acts sponsored by Chancellor of the Exchequer Charles Townshend designed to raise revenue of £40,000 for the British treasury for the administration of the colonies. It placed direct revenue duties on glass, paper, lead, paint, and tea imported into the colonies. The result of the Townshend Act was a resurrection of the colonial hostilities that had been created by the earlier Stamp Act of 1765. The act was tremendously unpopular in the colonies and viewed as an immediate threat to the right of colonial self-government. Some merchants forged nonimportation agreements to fight the importation duties, and colonists used local products such as homespun clothing, homemade paper, and local substitutes for British tea.

This Townshend crisis, as it was commonly called, continued, and in 1768, the Massachusetts Assembly asked Samuel Adams to draft a circular letter to the other colonial legislatures denouncing the Townshend Acts as a whole. In response to this rebellious act and to pressure from British merchants who were losing money, the British government dispatched more customs agents to the colonies to enforce the acts. Tensions increased on both sides until violence erupted in the Boston Massacre of 1770. After this incident, Parliament retreated from its position by repealing all of the Townshend duties except that on tea.

During the time the Townshend Act of 1767 was in effect, colonial imports from Britain decreased by 40 percent. As a result, the duty raised only £20,000, rather than the anticipated £40,000, for the British coffers.

Amanda J. Bahr-Evola

SEE ALSO: Colonial economic systems; Revolutionary War; Stamp Act of 1765; Tariffs; Taxation; Tea Act of 1773.

Trade. *See* International economics and trade

Trade unions. *See* Labor history

Trading stamps

DEFINITION: Stickers awarded to shoppers that can be redeemed for merchandise
SIGNIFICANCE: Trading stamps were one of the first forms of coupons issued to reward customers for repeat business. Their popularity led to the creation of other incentive programs.

Developed during the late nineteenth century, trading stamps are a form of coupons that can be collected and glued into small books. The process is simple. A trading stamp company makes money by selling the stamps to retailers. The retailers distribute the trading stamps to customers as rewards for purchases. The customer collects the stamps, then uses them as currency with the trading stamp company to purchase a variety of items. The stamps create customer loyalty and increased sales for the retailer.

In 1890, Schuster's Department Store, located in Milwaukee, Wisconsin, was the first retailer to use trading stamps in the United States. This store awarded trading stamps as an incentive to customers who paid for their purchases in cash rather than using store credit. In 1896, Sperry & Hutchinson (S&H) Green Stamps Company opened, eventually becoming one of the most profitable trading stamp companies. The use of trading stamps was not without controversy, and in 1897, a number of merchants who were not using the stamps issued a legal challenge. Trading stamps were deemed illegal by the Court of Appeals of the District of Columbia; however, this ruling was soon overturned.

The early twentieth century brought new opportunities for trading stamp companies to expand their customer base. Grocery retailers had been the primary distributors of the stamps, but as more retailers began to offer stamps, grocers began to give the stamps to all customers, not just those paying cash, in order to compete. Gas stations, a new form of retailer, became another popular outlet for trading stamps.

The trading stamp companies were the most profitable from the Depression through the 1960's. During the later part of this period, the S&H Green Stamps Company claimed that it was printing more stamps than the postal system. By the mid-1960's, almost 50 million American homes were saving trading stamps. The number of trading stamp companies skyrocketed to approximately three hundred, creating at least 17,000 jobs and payrolls of more than $500 million per year.

Trading stamps began to decrease in popularity during the 1970's, as inflation made them too costly for businesses. Large companies began to replace them with preferred customer cards and other rewards programs. In 1988, a study cited lower profits for stores using trading stamps. In 2000, the S&H Green Stamps were converted to S&H Greenpoints, digital points gained by purchases at participating online retailers and grocers, which can be redeemed for rewards. In 2008, Eagle Stamps, one of the last existing trading stamp companies, went out of business.

Theresa L. Stowell

FURTHER READING

Boone, Louis E., James C. Johnson, and George P. Ferry. "Trading Stamps: Their Role in Today's Marketplace." *Journal of the Academy of Marketing Science* 61, no. 1-2 (1978): 70-76.

LaForge, Ann E. "What's New in Trading Stamps." *New York Times*, August 16, 1987, A19.

Stankevich, Debby Garbato. "Establishing Fidelity in Loyalty Programs." *Retail Merchandiser* 41, no. 8 (August, 2001): 4.

SEE ALSO: Retail trade industry.

Transatlantic cable

THE EVENT: The laying of a telegraph cable across the Atlantic Ocean, linking Europe and North America

DATE: 1857-July 28, 1866

PLACE: Foilhommerum, Valentia Island, Ireland to Heart's Content, Newfoundland, Canada

SIGNIFICANCE: The cable reduced communication time between North America and Europe, two of the most important regions in the global economy, from days to mere seconds.

Cyrus Field, an American financier, promoted the laying of a telegraph cable across the Atlantic Ocean to connect Europe and North America. The telegraph was a remarkable invention, capable of sending information almost instantaneously to anywhere wired to receive a signal. The great limitation of the telegraph, however, was its inability to send messages across oceans. Connecting Europe and North America, the leading political and economic regions of the world during the mid-nineteenth century, presented obvious benefits, but because of the necessity to string a wire such a great distance in difficult conditions and at great expense, no one had attempted such a connection. That changed during the 1850's, when advances in metal-

lurgy and insulators led to the creation of a cable capable of surviving the harsh conditions on the ocean floor.

Under the leadership of Field, an investment company received monetary support from the British and American governments to attempt to lay the first transatlantic cable in 1857. Two warships, HMS *Agamemnon* and USS *Niagara*, converted to temporary cable-layers, rendezvoused in the middle of the Atlantic, connected their cables, and headed toward their homelands, rolling out the cable behind them. The line soon split, and the ships abandoned the project for the year. The next year, the ships tried again, and this time succeeded in laying the cable. On August 16, 1858, Queen Victoria sent the first message over a transatlantic cable to President James Buchanan.

The success was short-lived, however, as the cable failed within a month. Investors were hesitant to spend money on another attempt, and the U.S. Civil War disrupted plans to try to lay another cable. Field was ready to try again, however, in 1865. The new cable would use a better, more water-resistant insulation. Field leased the mammoth RMS *Great Eastern* to lay the cable. At 32,000 tons and nearly 700 feet long, it was by far the largest ship in the world at the time. More important, it could carry the three thousand miles of cable needed by itself, making a mid-ocean rendezvous and the splicing of two cables unnecessary. Its first attempt ended in failure, however,

An 1858 woodcut celebrating the laying of the transatlantic telegraph cable. (Library of Congress)

when the cable snapped in mid-ocean. In 1866, Field tried one last time. This time, cable was laid without a flaw, and it proved to be much more durable than the earlier line. The cable became a financial success, justifying Field's confidence in the new technology.

Steven J. Ramold

FURTHER READING

Gordon, John S. *A Thread Across the Ocean: The Heroic Story of the Transatlantic Cable.* New York: Walker, 2002.

Hearn, Chester. *Circuits in the Sea: The Men, the Ships, and the Atlantic Cable.* Westport, Conn.: Praeger, 2004.

McDonald, Philip Bayaud. *A Saga of the Seas: The Story of Cyrus W. Field and the Laying of the First Atlantic Cable.* New York: Wilson-Erickson, 1937.

SEE ALSO: Bell, Alexander Graham; Bell Labs; Fiberoptic industry; Industrial Revolution, American; Telecommunications industry; Transatlantic steamer service.

Transatlantic steamer service

IDENTIFICATION: Steam-powered maritime transportation between Europe and America

DATE: 1819-1950's

SIGNIFICANCE: The advent of steam engines greatly increased the speed by which ships could travel between North America and Europe, thus increasing the speed by which passenger traffic and trade could be moved. This technology was part of the United States' Industrial Revolution and greatly expanded the nation's access to global markets and culture. Steamers also significantly increased the opportunities for luxury passenger travel, tourism, and immigration to the United States.

Although engineers had experimented with steamships since the late eighteenth century, the first steam engine that was officially used for business was created by Robert Fulton and used to power a river steamboat in the United States in 1807. In 1819, the *Savannah* became the first steamer to cross the Atlantic Ocean, taking a month to complete its trip. The British began regular transatlantic steam passenger service in 1838. By then, advances in navigation and technology reduced the length of the crossing to half that of *Savannah*'s first journey. Advances in technology continued throughout the nineteenth century: During the middle of the century, steamers shifted from paddles to propellers, further increasing their speed and maneuverability. Although transatlantic sailing ships were being phased out by the 1880's, most steamers still had sails built on them until the late nineteenth century, because their steam engines were not sufficiently reliable.

The British dominated transatlantic steamer passenger service through the end of the nineteenth century, with the Cunard and White Star Lines competing against each another. This competition continued during the early twentieth century, as steamers began to replace steel with iron and the ships grew even larger. The rapid change caused by transatlantic travel and the sheer power of the engineering models behind it encouraged an arrogant belief that the new technology was infallible. This arrogance is believed to have contributed to the sinking of the *Titanic* in 1912. The vast loss of life caused by this tragedy led to increased regulation of steamers, particularly regarding passenger travel.

The transatlantic steamer Liverpool. (Library of Congress)

Although advances in technology led to the creation of great steamships, they also led to their demise. By the early twentieth century, some ships were beginning to burn oil for fuel. These oil-powered ships signaled the movement toward more efficient travel, as they did not require the immense manpower necessary to shovel coal to keep a steamer moving. Eventually, oil turbines were replaced by diesel engines, and transatlantic steamers were phased out by the mid-twentieth century, after one hundred years of dominating the Atlantic.

Brion Sever

FURTHER READING

Adams, John. *Ocean Steamers: A History of Ocean-Going Passenger Steamships, 1820-1970.* London: New Cavendish Books, 1993.

Baker, Rodney, and Leonard Baker. *Great Steamers White and Gold: A History of Royal Mail Ships and Services.* Glendale, Calif.: Ensign, 1993.

Garzke, William, and John Woodward. *Titanic Ships, Titanic Disasters: An Analysis of Early Cunard and White Star Superliners.* Jersey City, N.J.: Society of Naval Architects, 2004.

SEE ALSO: European trade with the United States; Immigration; Steamboats; Transatlantic cable.

Transcontinental railroad

IDENTIFICATION: Railroad spanning the United States from its eastern to western coasts, consisting of the Union Pacific and Central Pacific lines

DATE: Completed on May 10, 1869

SIGNIFICANCE: The transcontinental railroad facilitated U.S. trade with Asia and allowed for the development of the resources of the West and movement of settlers to its land.

Although interest in a transcontinental railroad existed before the U.S. Civil War, the choice of a route was complicated by the sectional debate, as the North and the South each wanted the first line to be in their own region. However, during the U.S. Civil War, Congress did not have to consult with southern wishes, and the Pacific Railroad Bill was passed in the summer of 1862. The law created a new federally chartered corporation, the Union Pacific Railroad, to build a railroad west from Nebraska. It also granted a charter to an existing California railroad, the Central Pacific, to build eastward from Sacramento, California.

The government gave massive quantities of aid to these two corporations. The railroads were given not only the right-of-way on the land where the track would be laid but also millions of acres of public land, which the railroads could sell to help pay construction costs. The initial legislation gave the two railroads 10 square miles (later increased to 20) of public land for each mile of track built. Altogether, the Union Pacific and Central Pacific received about 45 million acres. The government also loaned the companies $16,000 per mile for tracks laid across level land and up to $48,000 per mile for tracks laid across mountainous terrain. When the two lines met at Promontory Summit in the Utah Territory on May 10, 1869, the Union Pacific had

Railroad officials and employees celebrate the completion of the first transcontinental railroad in Promontory Summit, Utah Territory, on May 10, 1869. (AP/Wide World Photos)

built about 1,080 miles of track and the Central Pacific approximately 690 miles.

Economists have noted that the western railroads were built ahead of demand, meaning that there was no customer base to serve in much of the area the railroads crossed. However, the railroads promoted the creation of towns and cities as well as the development of land along the route for agriculture, mining, and logging. The railroads, along with improvements in communications such as the telegraph and the telephone, made it possible for American businesses to operate efficiently on a nationwide scale for the first time.

Mark S. Joy

FURTHER READING

Ambrose, Stephen E. *Nothing Like It in the World: The Men Who Built the Transcontinental Railroad, 1863-1869.* New York: Simon & Schuster, 2000.

Bain, David Hayward. *Empire Express: Building the First Transcontinental Railroad.* New York: Penguin Books, 1999.

Renehan, Edward J., Jr. *The Transcontinental Railroad: The Gateway to the West.* New York: Chelsea House, 2007.

SEE ALSO: Amtrak; Forestry industry; Gadsden Purchase; Mexican War; Panama Canal; Railroads; Stanford, Leland; Time zones; Vanderbilt, Cornelius.

Transportation, U.S. Department of

IDENTIFICATION: Federal cabinet-level department designed to coordinate and develop national transportation policy on land, sea, and air

DATE: Established in 1966

SIGNIFICANCE: Because the Department of Transportation oversees all forms of transportation in the United States, on land, water, and air, a wide range of businesses from airlines to railroads to shipping to automobile manufacturers are affected by its polices. DOT took over thirty different transportation agencies and programs from other departments of the federal government when it was created. Most of these had significant connections to businesses.

The U.S. Department of Transportation (DOT) was created in the flurry of legislative activity initiated by Lyndon B. Johnson in the greatest set of bureaucratic changes since the Great Depression. The act creating DOT was signed into law on October 15, 1966, and the agency began operating on April 1, 1967. The newly created department gathered together some thirty different agencies and programs that had been scattered throughout the federal government. Many of these came from the Department of Commerce, which highlighted the business connections that would be one of the most prominent characteristics of DOT. Other programs that became part of DOT were programs previously under the Department of Defense that had commercial rather than military applications.

Only a few programs have ever been removed from the department. The National Transportation Safety Board, part of the original DOT, became a separate regulatory body in 1975 because it was inappropriate for an accident-investigating body to be subject to the control of DOT because of its strong links with transportation businesses. Similarly, the U.S. Coast Guard and the Transportation Safety Administration were added to Department of Homeland Security in the belief that such defense-oriented departments should not be subject to excessive commercial pressure.

DIVISIONS OF DOT

The Office of the Secretary is the policy-level office coordinating all the divisions in the Department of Transportation. There are eleven individual operating administrations within the department, each of which has important business constituencies. The Office of the Inspector General—a division in all cabinet-level agencies—was created as a staff agency to maintain the integrity of the department.

The Federal Aviation Administration oversees U.S. airlines and airports, including the air traffic control system. Accidents causing loss of life are investigated by the National Transportation Safety Board, an independent agency since 1975.

The Federal Highway Administration is responsible for administering the Federal-Aid Highway Construction Program, which provides federal funds for constructing and maintaining the federal highway system, including interstates, U.S. highways, and many state highways. This program is funded through the gasoline tax. The Federal Highway Administration also manages the Federal Lands Highway Program, which provides for the construction of roads within federal lands not subject to any state jurisdiction, such as those in the Forest Service and the National Park Service. This division is in very close contact with any businesses involved in the planning and construction of U.S. highways.

The National Highway Traffic Safety Administration is one of the most significant agencies within DOT because it provides a key regulatory function in setting standards regarding automobile safety and fuel economy that automobile manufacturers must follow.

The Federal Motor Carrier Safety Administration was created on January 1, 2000, to reduce crashes, injuries, and fatalities involving large trucks and buses. This agency has a direct effect on businesses transporting goods and people across the country. It also has a hazardous materials regulatory function.

The Federal Railroad Administration oversees the railroad industry. It promulgates and enforces rail safety regulations, conducts research on rail safety, manages railroad assistance programs, and is responsible for trying to rebuild Northeast Corridor rail passenger service.

The Federal Transit Administration conducts technical research and provides funding for local public transit systems in the United States. Local public transit systems include buses, subways, commuter rail, light rail, monorail, streetcars, passenger ferryboats, trolleys, inclined railways, and other people carriers, including commuter vans.

The Maritime Administration maintains the National Defense Reserve Fleet, which makes ships available in national emergencies. The shipping industry provides all the ships that make up the National Defense Reserve Fleet, so it has a direct connection with the Maritime Administration. Other programs in the administration provide subsidies for shipping and operate the U.S. Merchant Marine Academy.

The St. Lawrence Seaway Development Corporation is a not-for-profit corporation responsible for the safety and efficiency of shipping through the St. Lawrence Seaway. It coordinates its activity with a comparable not-for-profit corporation in Canada.

The Research and Innovative Technologies Administration (RITA) is one of the divisions added to DOT. It gathers important data, research findings, and technology within the department. In addition to promoting safety and efficiency, RITA is also charged with attempting to reduce costs within the department. The administration supervises DOT's five-year research-and-development plan.

The Pipeline and Hazardous Materials Safety Administration was brought into being by legislation on November 30, 2004. The sharp increase in the number of shipments of hazardous materials to about one million per day led to the creation of this new program. As oil and natural gas pipelines are in essence a form of shipment of hazardous materials, this agency is in charge of both hazardous-materials shipment and pipelines.

The Surface Transportation Board was created in 1995 to take the place of the Interstate Commerce Commission, which was abolished after more than a century of service. The Surface Transportation Board is a quasi-judicial regulatory body that has jurisdiction over railroad rates and services; trucking, moving van, and noncontiguous ocean-shipping company rate matters; certain intercity passenger bus matters; and pipelines rates and services not covered by the Federal Energy Regulatory Commission.

The Homeland Security Act of 2002 authorized the establishment of the Department of Homeland Security, which, on March 1, 2003, assumed management of the U.S. Coast Guard and the Transportation Security Administration, formerly part of DOT.

SUCCESSES AND CHALLENGES

There can be little doubt that the Department of Transportation has played a very constructive role in developing award-winning transportation policy among its various business constituencies. However, the cost of the wars in Iraq and Afghanistan has deprived DOT of badly needed funds. The chief challenge facing DOT is the lack of funding for transportation infrastructure in the United States. The collapse of the I-35 Interstate highway bridge in Minneapolis in 2007 highlighted the problem of the relative age of parts of the American infrastructure, including railways and airports. For example, the airline industry needs significant new sources of funds to implement an air traffic control system using global positioning satellites as its primary source of locating aircraft, but DOT is unable to help the industry.

Richard L. Wilson

FURTHER READING

Arnold, Peri E. *Making the Managerial Presidency: Comprehensive Reorganization Planning, 1905-1996.* 2d ed. Lawrence: University Press of Kansas, 1998. Serious academic examination of the efforts to reform the bureaucracy of the national government to improve managerial innovation.

Bourne, Russell. *Americans on the Move: A History of Waterways, Railways, and Highways.* Golden, Colo.: Fulcrum, 1995. A broad overview of U.S. transportation policy from early in American history to the book's writing.

Davidson, Janet F., and Michael S. Sweeney. *On the Move: Transportation and the American Story.* Washington, D.C.: Smithsonian National Museum of American History/ National Geographic, 2003. A solid, if popular, look at transportation policy throughout American history.

Dilger, Robert Jay. *American Transportation Policy.* Westport, Conn.: Praeger, 2003. Thorough academic examination of transportation policy.

Larson, John Lauritz. *Internal Improvement: National Public Works and the Promise of Popular Government in the Early United States.* Chapel Hill: University of North Carolina Press, 2001. A history of transportation policy from early in U.S. history that sheds light on the federal policy situation at the end of the twentieth century.

SEE ALSO: Air traffic controllers' strike; Air transportation industry; Bridges; Highways; Public transportation, local; Railroads; Shipping industry; Trucking industry.

Treasury, U.S. Department of the

IDENTIFICATION: Cabinet-level department of the federal government responsible for promoting the prosperity and stability of the nation's economy by assisting in regulating and enforcing laws dealing with money, taxes, and other financial matters

DATE: Established in 1789

SIGNIFICANCE: The Treasury Department has a far-reaching effect on the U.S. economy and all its private and public financial institutions through the department's responsibility for managing the federal government's finances and enforcing laws that ensure the safety and soundness of American and international financial institutions.

In 1789, the U.S. Congress passed an act that created the U.S. Department of the Treasury. This act outlined and prescribed all the department's duties, functions, and responsibilities for maintaining, protecting, and assisting in the growth of the nation's economy. The Treasury Department is the main federal agency charged with maintaining and securing the economic safety of the United States. Its duties include a wide range of activities, from advising the president on various economic issues, enhancing and creating corporate governance in financial institutions, assisting other countries with building a stable world economy, predicting and preventing all global economic disasters or crises, and regulating and protecting the economy of the United States by enforcing the economic and tax laws needed to maintain appropriate growth and stability of the nation's economy.

TWO MAJOR DIVISIONS

The Treasury Department is organized into two major components: the departmental offices and the operating bureaus. The departmental offices are responsible for the formulation of policy and management for the entire department. The operating bureaus carry out the specific tasks assigned to them by the department. Of the two branches, the operating bureaus make up 98 percent of the department's workforce. Twelve bureaus are charged with numerous responsibilities; however, their main missions are the same, to protect and maintain the United States economy.

The basic functions of the Department of the Treasury include producing postage stamps, currency, and coinage; managing all federal finances; collecting taxes, duties, and all other monies owed to the government; paying all bills that the United States owes other nations; supervising national banks and credit institutions; advising the president and other governmental officials on financial and tax-related policies and issues; enforcing federal finance and tax laws; and investigating and prosecuting those individuals who engage in counterfeiting, forgery, or tax evasion.

THE BUREAUS

Of the twelve bureaus of the Treasury Department, only four are responsible for enforcing and investigating the numerous and intricate laws regarding the economic well-being of the United States. The four bureaus that protect and enforce the various financial and tax laws of the United States are the Alcohol and Tobacco Tax and Trade Bureau (TTB), the Internal Revenue Service (IRS), the Financial Crimes Enforcement Network (FinCEN), and the Office of the Inspector General (OIG). Until 2003, there were three other bureaus involved in law enforcement and investigative functions that operated under the auspices of the Treasury Department. However, these bureaus were reassigned and given new investigative and protective missions within the newly created Department of Homeland Security. These bureaus were the Federal Law Enforcement Training Center (FLETC), the U.S. Secret Service, and U.S. Customs (which became the U.S. Customs and Border Protection Bureau, or CBP).

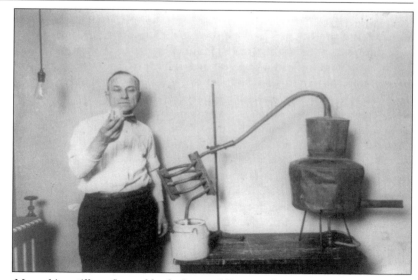

Moonshine still confiscated by the Internal Revenue Bureau, part of the Treasury Department, between 1921 and 1932. (Library of Congress)

THE ALCOHOL AND TOBACCO TAX AND TRADE BUREAU

In 2003, the Bureau of Alcohol, Tobacco, and Firearms (ATF) was split into the Alcohol and Tobacco Tax and Trade Bureau, which remained with the Treasury Department, and the Bureau of Alcohol, Tobacco, Firearms, and Explosives, which was placed under the Department of Justice. The purpose of the TTB is to collect excise taxes on alcohol, tobacco, firearms, and ammunition that are owed to the federal government and to guarantee that alcoholic beverages, tobacco products, and firearms are produced, labeled, distributed, and marketed in agreement with federal law. The TTB employs more than six hundred people, many of whom are analysts, chemists, investigators, and auditors. Tax collection as a function of the TTB originated with the original Bureau of Alcohol, Tobacco, and Firearms, created more than two hundred years ago. The ATF

was one of the earliest law-enforcement and tax-collecting Treasury agencies.

INTERNAL REVENUE SERVICE

The Internal Revenue Service is the largest of the twelve Treasury bureaus. It is responsible for determining, assessing, and gathering tax revenue in the United States. The IRS deals directly with more Americans than any other institution, public or private, in the continental United States. It also is one of the world's most efficient tax administrators, collecting more than $2 trillion in taxes per year. One of the major goals of the IRS is to ensure that all Americans understand and carry out their tax obligations to the federal government. To make sure that all federal tax laws are carried out and administered fairly and justly, the IRS maintains both a collections division and a criminal investigation branch, known as the Criminal Investigation Unit (CI).

The Criminal Investigation Unit consists of nearly three thousand special agents. These agents investigate suspected cases of money laundering and violations of tax and Bank Secrecy Act of 1970 laws. Although the IRS shares jurisdictions over money laundering cases and Bank Secrecy Act violations with various other federal agencies, the IRS is the only agency that has sole investigative jurisdiction over criminal violations of the Internal Revenue Code.

The special agents who make up the law-enforcement arm of the IRS are some of the most elite financial investigators in the world. Financial investigations take hundreds of hours and, in some cases, involve thousands of financial records and tax statements. These Criminal Investigation agents focus their efforts on three distinct areas: legal-source tax crimes, illegal-source financial crimes, and narcotics- and terrorist-related financial crimes. Specifically, these agents look into such crimes as public and governmental corruption, tax evasion, health care fraud, telemarketing fraud, money laundering, and various other forms of finance-related frauds. Overall, the Criminal Investigation Unit has one of the highest conviction rates in federal law enforcement. Those who are prosecuted by the IRS usually pay severe fines and may be sent to federal prison.

FINANCIAL CRIMES ENFORCEMENT NETWORK

The Financial Crimes Enforcement Network, established by the Treasury Department in 1990, is charged with establishing, overseeing, and implementing policies to detect and prevent money laundering, terrorist financing, and financial crimes perpetrated by international organized crime.

It has worked to maximize information sharing and gathering among all branches of law enforcement and agencies in the regulatory and financial sectors to fight the complex crime of money laundering, which is thought to be the third-largest business in the world. FinCEN's approach, using network systems, employs cost-effective yet meaningful methods to combat money laundering both domestically and globally.

FinCEN's main goal is to support law-enforcement investigative efforts, foster interagency and global cooperation against domestic and international financial crimes, and provide U.S. policy makers with strategic analyses of domestic and worldwide money-laundering developments, trends, and patterns. FinCEN maintains and operates one of the largest repositories of information on money-laundering activities available to law enforcement nationally and internationally. Overall, FinCEN has been a leader in the global fight against money laundering.

FinCEN's staff includes approximately two hundred employees, many of whom are intelligence research specialists from both law-enforcement and financial communities, law-enforcement support staff, and law-enforcement and legal analysts. In addition, there are approximately forty long-term detailees from twenty different law-enforcement and regulatory agencies from around the United States. As part of a collective bureau, these individuals are charged with finding the links between the individuals and financial institutions engaging in money laundering.

OFFICE OF INSPECTOR GENERAL

The Office of Inspector General (OIG) was established in 1989 by the secretary of the Treasury. The OIG is led by an inspector general appointed by the president of the United States with the consent of the Senate. The inspector general reports to the secretary of the Treasury through the deputy secretary. The inspector general provides the secretary with independent and unbiased reviews of all department operations. The inspector general is also required to keep the secretary and the entire Congress up to date regarding all problems, concerns, and deficiencies relating to the administration of department programs and operations. Serving with the inspector general is a deputy inspector general, who is responsible for assimilating all bureau reports and investigations. Aside from the inspector and the deputy, the OIG has a staff of one hundred full-time civil servants who are responsible for record keeping, external auditing, report writing, and internal investigations. In regard to investigations, it is vital that all erroneous or criminal behavior be dealt with at once. Audits and investigations that indicate any form of specious or suspected criminal activity are usually passed on to the Department of Justice for further investigation and appropriate action. It is the main goal of the OIG to act as an internal investigation mechanism for the Department of the Treasury, so that a fiduciary environment in which the United States economy can grow and prosper can be achieved and maintained.

One of the main tasks of the OIG staff is to create and submit semiannual reports regarding the activities and investigations of the office. Disclosures of problems, abuses, and deficiencies in the Treasury department are highlighted and brought to the attention of Congress and to the secretary of the treasury. The reports also offer recommendations of what the department should do to correct particular abuses and deviancies. Overall, the OIG plays an integral role for the Department of the Treasury by making sure that all operations by the twelve bureaus are carried out efficiently and without corruption and deceit.

Paul M. Klenowski

FURTHER READING

Kaufman, Judith, ed. *United States Department of Treasury: Current Issues and Background.* New York: Nova Science Publishers, 2003. Provides both a historical overview and an in-depth understanding of prominent issues facing the Treasury.

Kinsey, J. C. *Working for the IRS.* Cutten, Calif.: Iris Books, 1997. A former IRS auditor shares some important facts about the workings of the Treasury.

Terrell, John. *The United States Department of Treasury: A Story of Dollars, Customs, and Secret Agents.* New York: Duell, Sloan, and Pearce, 1966. Offers a great historical look at the Treasury, from its inception through the early 1960's.

Walston, Mark. *The Department of the Treasury.* New York: Chelsea House, 1989. A basic explanation of what the department is and does.

Yancey, Richard. *Confessions of a Tax Collector: One Man's Tour of Duty Inside the IRS.* New York: HarperCollins, 2004. This text offers a personal look of one man's experience as an employee of the Internal Revenue Service.

SEE ALSO: Alcoholic beverage industry; Currency; Drug trafficking; Hamilton, Alexander; Internal Revenue Code; Justice, U.S. Department of; Mint, U.S.; Monetary policy, federal; Organized crime; Prohibition; Taxation; Tobacco industry.

Triangle Shirtwaist Company fire

THE EVENT: Deadly fire in a clothing factory
DATE: March 25, 1911
PLACE: New York City
SIGNIFICANCE: In the aftermath of the horrible Triangle Shirtwaist Company fire, in which 146 people—mostly women immigrants—died, major reforms in labor and fire-safety laws were passed, and women workers and immigrants worked together to improve their working conditions and treatment.

The Triangle Shirtwaist Company manufactured shirtwaists, that is, very popular cotton blouses. The building in which the factory was housed was ten stories high and supposedly fireproof. Like many sweatshops, it was overcrowded, and conditions were unsafe. Some of the fire doors were locked, and one of the fire escapes collapsed in the fire.

On March 25, 1911, a fire began in the factory, as the workers were about to leave for the day. People jumped out of the building to their deaths, falling right through the safety nets firefighters held for them. Frances Perkins saw part of the fire and served on the commission that later investigated it. She vowed that she would prevent anything of the sort from happening again. In 1933, she became secretary of labor under President Franklin D. Roosevelt. Perkins was America's first female cabinet member. Partly as a result of her experiences connected with the Triangle fire, she fought to improve working conditions and labor laws, especially for women, often siding with labor against management.

Most of the workers who died were female Jewish and Italian immigrants. The fire galvanized the immigrant communities to work for better conditions for workers, especially through the International Ladies' Garment Workers Union (ILGWU), which greatly helped improve conditions, especially safety conditions.

In October, 1911, in the aftermath of the fire, New York State passed the Sullivan-Hoey Fire Prevention Law, requiring that factory owners install sprinkler systems and creating a single fire commission with powers previously divided among six agencies. New York also set up the Factory Investigating Commission, chaired by U.S. Senator Robert Wagner, and overhauled or enacted around three dozen laws dealing with factory safety.

The outrage that accompanied the Triangle Fire was soon forgotten, but the event itself pointed to the many terrible problems that workers faced. The fire helped prepare for a series of laws that greatly improved conditions for workers. It also helped lead to the founding of the American Society of Safety Engineers in October, 1911. The society was dedicated to improve occupational safety, health, and environmental conditions in industry, education, and government.

The main thing the fire led to was a change in the relation between government and business. Before the fire, government largely left business alone. Af-

People demonstrate to protest the deaths in the Triangle Shirtwaist Company fire on March 25, 1911. (National Archives)

ter the fire, government felt compelled to pass and enforce laws to protect workers. Although other serious fires occurred in various industries, many historians argue that the Triangle Shirtwaist Company fire represents the beginning of local, state, and national governments' attempts to achieve better working conditions. The fire could therefore be seen as an early impetus for the passage of the National Labor Relations Act of 1935, often called the Wagner Act after the man who earlier chaired the Factory Investigating Committee.

Richard Tuerk

FURTHER READING

Babson, Steve. *The Unfinished Struggle: Turning Points in American Labor, 1877-Present.* Lanham, Md.: Rowman & Littlefield, 1999.

Orleck, Annelise. *Common Sense and a Little Fire: Women and Working-Class Politics in the United States, 1900-1965.* Chapel Hill: University of North Carolina Press, 1995.

Von Drehle, David. *Triangle: The Fire That Changed America.* New York: Atlantic Monthly Press, 2003.

SEE ALSO: International Ladies' Garment Workers' Union; Labor, U.S. Department of; Occupational Safety and Health Act.

Trickle-down theory

DEFINITION: Economic theory holding that if a government provides benefits to big business and tax breaks to the wealthy and investors, those benefits eventually filter down to the lower classes

SIGNIFICANCE: Proponents of the trickle-down theory contend that economic gains by the wealthy (such as tax cuts) result in investment or purchases that ultimately result in more jobs for the middle and lower classes by creating economic growth that increases demand for goods and stimulates production. In contrast, they contend, increases in tax rates initially produce more revenue, encourage savings, and stimulate investments but ultimately hinder production and decrease revenues in business.

The phrase "trickle-down theory," coined by Will Rogers, gained fame during the 1932 election and was used to describe President Herbert Hoover's economic policy in failing to deal with the Great Depression. With the advent of President Franklin D. Roosevelt's New Deal programs, the theories of the British economist John Maynard Keynes began to take hold during the 1940's and 1950's. Keynesian economics espoused that the federal government must take an active role in creating jobs and stimulating the economy through aggressive tax cuts, government regulation of business, social programs for the poor, and increases in spending. Keynes argued that low interest rates stimulated borrowing and helped increase the money supply, which in turn encouraged consumers to spend.

The administration of President John F. Kennedy began to implement Keynesian policy, passing major tax cuts during the early 1960's. However, with the presidency of Lyndon B. Johnson came an escalation of the Vietnam War, and the Johnsonian Great Society's War on Poverty caused government spending on programs to skyrocket and inflation rates to rise rapidly. During the 1970's, it became increasingly difficult for monetary and fiscal authorities to deal effectively with the problem of increasing inflation, burgeoning government, unemployment, and falling productivity levels in labor. Personal savings went down, an energy crisis ensued, and rising interest rates caused an adverse effect on business investment.

The federal budget increased dramatically, from $94 billion in 1960 to $577 billion by 1980. During the 1980 presidential election, Ronald Reagan began campaigning on a Republican platform of economic recovery that closely resembled trickle-down economic theories. Reagan's economic policies countered Keynesian philosophy and were often called "Reaganomics" or supply-side economics. When Reagan was elected, his administration implemented a strategy of limited government regulation and an expanded private sector to control inflation. These tactics included tax breaks for companies, reductions in social welfare programs, increases in defense spending, and decreasing government regulation in certain industries.

The 1980's represented a good time to invest money and delve heavily into the stock market, but throughout the decade, income distribution worsened between the social classes. Lower taxes on businesses allowed for real estate opportunities and the development of new factories throughout the United States. The subsequent deregulation of savings and loans, communications, and transportation industries brought forth streamlined operations and new technologies that made business transactions more efficient. However, mergers, consolidations, and takeovers became commonplace, because smaller enterprises were not able to compete. By the end of the twentieth century, the losers of Reagan's trickle-down legacy were middle managers, who found their positions displaced by either emerging computer systems or restructuring and downsizing that occurred in companies. The power of labor unions was also disrupted, and wages fell for unskilled and semiskilled industrial workers.

Gayla Koerting

FURTHER READING

Fink, Richard H, ed. *Supply-Side Economics: A Critical Approach.* Frederick, Md.: Altheia Books, 1982.

Kimzey, Bruce W. *Reaganomics.* New York: West, 1983.

Schiller, Bradley R. *The Economics of Poverty and Discrimination.* 10th ed. Upper Saddle River, N.J.: Pearson/Prentice Hall, 2008.

SEE ALSO: Great Depression; New Deal programs; Supply-side economics; Taxation.

Trucking industry

DEFINITION: Enterprises that transport and distribute raw materials, works in progress, and finished goods using vehicles such as semitrailers, box trucks, or dump trucks

SIGNIFICANCE: The trucking industry has a saying, "If you bought it, a truck brought it." There is scarcely a business or industry in the United

States that does not rely on the trucking industry as an essential part of its operations. In 2006, 70 percent of the total volume of freight in United States was moved in more than 25 million trucks carrying up to 10 billion tons of materials.

Native American transport was on foot, horseback, or by canoe. The earliest European settlers used ships and boats for transportation by water whenever possible but expanded the range of land travel to a variety of carts and wagons. In the nineteenth century, railroads were introduced and carried an increasing percentage of the heaviest freight over long distances. Railroads were limited by the availability of the track that had been laid and could transport goods only from one fixed site to another. Beyond railroad depots, carts and wagons pulled by oxen or horses were still required for final delivery to the end user.

Although trucks were invented during the late nineteenth century, it was only shortly before World War II that a combination of gasoline-powered internal combustion engines and the replacement of chain drives by gear drives enabled the development of the tractor-trailer rig. Although the trucking industry grew during World War I, trucks were still limited to very low speeds because they used iron and solid rubber wheels on primitive roads, except in cities where pavement existed. With the development of inflatable tires and the proliferation of paved roads, truck speeds and differences increased. After 1920, the development of diesel engines, power-assisted brakes and steering, fifth wheel coupling, and standardized trailer sizes made truck transportation an attractive shipping option.

LEGISLATION AND REGULATION

By 1933, all forty-eight states had enacted some type of weight legislation, but the standards varied so much that eight years later, the Interstate Commerce Commission informed Congress that the highly variable truck weight limitations were an impediment to interstate truck transport. The state-based truck weight limits continued until 1956, when the federal government first established a maximum gross vehicle weight of just over 73,000 pounds. In 1974, the Federal-Aid Highway Act Amendments set a maximum gross vehicle weight of 80,000 pounds but failed to establish a federal minimum weight. In response, six neighboring states

along the Mississippi River did not increase their truck weight limits to 80,000 pounds and created a barrier to interstate commerce. This problem was not corrected until the passage of the Surface Transportation Assistance Act of 1982.

Another significant issue in the trucking industry concerns the rules governing the number of hours that truck and bus drivers are allowed to drive at a single stretch, the total number of hours in a twenty-four-hour period, and the number of hours of rest mandated between driving stretches. Called service regulations, the first rules of this type were enacted in 1938, and the rules have grown significantly stricter as time has passed.

The 1980's brought a nationwide movement in the direction of deregulation, which was applied to the trucking industry by the Motor Carrier Act of 1980. At the same time, the International Brotherhood of Teamsters union, which had previously been a major force for workers in the trucking industry, lost a series of legal and economic battles. The truckers effectively lost much of their union representation, and lower pay became standard for drivers. Truckers began to face increased pressure to drive longer hours with fewer breaks to maintain a satisfactory paycheck.

As a federal regulation of truck weights stabilized, the trucking industry became increasingly important to the movement of goods over long distances. Railroads continued to be the most efficient movers of very bulky solid cargoes such as coal, and pipelines were used for liquids such as petroleum products. Still most manufactured goods were increasingly carried by trucks. The extensive highway network meant that trucks could travel virtually anywhere.

In 1956, Malcolm McLean developed the concept of containerized intermodal shipping. Modern containerized intermodal shipping meant that a single container, once loaded, could be transported by ships, trains, and trucks without needing to be reloaded. All forms of transportation benefited by this new system, but trucks seemed to have the most to gain. The total number of trucks increased from 1 million in 1920 to over 18 million trucks by 1970.

Along with these economic and technological developments, there were certain societal changes. As citizens' band (CB) radios became commonplace in trucks (and later cars), people began to form an image of long-distance truck drivers as

REVENUE GENERATED BY TRUCKING, 2000-2005, IN MILLIONS OF DOLLARS				
Type of Trucking	2000	2003	2004	2005
Local trucking	48,837	52,409	56,657	63,214
Long-distance trucking	103,973	104,224	116,570	128,679

Source: Data from the *Statistical Abstract of the United States, 2008* (Washington, D.C.: Department of Commerce, Economics and Statistics Administration, Bureau of the Census, Data User Services Division, 2008)
Note: Local trucking is within and around a metro area, long-distance trucking is between metro areas.

modern-day cowboys and even outlaws. The use of CB radios to inform other truck drivers of the presence of law-enforcement officials who could ticket them for speeding or other violations gave long-distance truckers their outlaw image. Gradually plaid shirts, trucker hats, and CB slang became popular with the general public, and motion pictures, country music songs, and even television shows about truckers were created. By the 1980's, the trucker mania had subsided somewhat. CB radios continued to be used by truckers, but cell phones replaced CB radios for most automobile drivers.

PROGRESS AND POLLUTION

There are certain inherent limits to truck weight and size that affect productivity. Twenty-first century gains in productivity in the trucking industry have come through improved communications and certain transformations in the way that business is conducted. One key issue was to diminish the number of empty loads, which was reduced through modern communications. The development of wireless computers and the Internet has allowed freight brokers to serve as intermediaries and to coordinate freight. Improved communications and global positioning satellites have also improved coordination and productivity.

This has allowed many businesses to improve their productivity by adopting just-in-time strategies for the delivery of supplies. Under this concept, businesses reduce costs associated with excessive inventory and larger warehouses by scheduling more frequent deliveries. Grocery stores have always required frequent deliveries every two or three days for perishable food items, and their costs have dropped as more efficient communication becomes possible. Hospitals have also improved their patient services and decreased their warehousing costs with just-in-time strategies. Retail stores, particularly Wal-Mart, have benefited from this strategy. Adoption of this strategy enabled Wal-Mart supercenters to add groceries to the range of products they offer.

Diesel exhaust fumes have always been unpleasant, especially in an urban environment or a concentration of trucks and buses, and the slowness with which the fumes dissipate has long been a concern. The carcinogenicity of diesel exhaust fumes was suspected in 1988 and conclusively established in 2002. In addition to aggravating a number of breathing disorders, diesel fumes emit greenhouse gases and contribute to global warming. This has led to a concerted effort to find alternative fuels. Biodiesel, a nontoxic biodegradable form of diesel fuel in its pure form, has become increasingly popular. New environmental standards limit the amount of sulfur that can be included in diesel fuel. Many cities have begun experimenting with either compressed natural gas or battery-operated electric buses to avoid the noxious fumes from buses powered by diesel fuel. Although the trucking industry is expected to continue to grow, pressures to find alternatives to using diesel and other petroleum fuels will increase.

Richard L. Wilson

FURTHER READING

Baiman, Ron, Heather Boushey, and Dawn Saunders. *Political Economy and Contemporary Capitalism: Radical Perspectives on Economic Theory and Policy.* Armonk, N.Y.: M. E. Sharpe, 2000. This collection of essays examines the trucking industry from a perspective sympathetic to planning and socialism.

Dow, Louis A., and Fred Hendon. *Economics and Soci-*

ety. Englewood Cliffs, N.J.: Prentice Hall, 1991. These co-authors, though strongly influenced by the free-market economics of Adam Smith, look at economics in a social context.

Drew, Shirley K. *Dirty Work: The Social Construction of Taint.* Waco, Tex.: Baylor University Press, 2007. A sociological study of the perception of various blue-collar trades, including trucking.

Stern, Jane. *Trucker: A Portrait of the Last American Cowboy.* New York: McGraw-Hill, 1975. A popular, somewhat nostalgic look at truckers and trucking.

Stern, Jane, and Michael Stern. *Way Out West.* N.Y.: Harper Collins, 1993. Another popular examination of truckers and trucking.

Willis, James. *Explorations in Macroeconomics.* 5th ed. Redding, Calif.: North West, 2002. This mainstream text examines trucking from a macroeconomic perspective, explaining the impact of trucking on society.

SEE ALSO: Highways; Hoffa, Jimmy; International Brotherhood of Teamsters; Railroads; Shipping industry; Transportation, U.S. Department of.

Donald Trump. (AP/Wide World Photos)

Trump, Donald

IDENTIFICATION: American real estate tycoon and businessman

BORN: June 14, 1946; New York, New York

SIGNIFICANCE: Trump became an iconic figure, helping define a new generation of celebrity tycoons whose success was built as much on maintaining an image of success as on financial savvy. He set out to own as much New York City real estate as possible and to redesign the New York skyline.

Donald Trump graduated from the Wharton School of Finance in 1968 and began working alongside his father, a millionaire property developer in Queens, New York. After revitalizing an Ohio apartment complex and realizing a $6 million profit, Trump moved to Manhattan to begin building his real estate empire.

Trump's first major deal was optioning the Penn Central Railroad yard as a building site for the Jacob K. Javits Convention Center (1979-1986). Trump was disappointed that he was not allowed to name the center after himself. In 1979, he leased a site next to Tiffany's and erected a $200 million apartment-retail complex, Trump Tower. This signature building was the first Trump-branded property in New York.

During the 1980's, Trump branched out into casino ownership and continued developing the Trump brand. By 1986, he owned three of the world's largest casinos: Trump's Taj Mahal, Trump's Marina, and Trump Plaza.

In 1990, Trump's personal fortune dropped from $1.7 billion to $500 million, with $900 million of debt. His business debt reached nearly $3.5 billion, and Trump's Taj Mahal and Trump Plaza were both forced to file for bankruptcy. However, by 1997, Trump had recovered and was worth more than $2 billion. In 2008, Trump owned more than 18 million square feet of Manhattan real estate as well as golf clubs, resorts, casinos, and other properties throughout the United States. He continues to develop the Trump brand throughout the world.

A very public and charismatic personality, Trump

became a best-selling author, producer and host of the television show *The Apprentice*, co-owner with the National Broadcasting Company of the Miss Universe Organization, and chief executive officer of many consumer product lines, including men's clothing. Like his buildings, Trump's products are emblazoned with the Trump name and benefit from his brand recognition.

Leslie Neilan

See also: Construction industry; Hughes, Howard; Real estate industry, commercial; Real estate industry, residential; Television programming with business themes.

Truth-in-advertising codes

Definition: Industry standards designed to guide advertisers

Significance: Truth-in-advertising codes provide guides for voluntary regulation within the advertising industry that serve the public interest and help raise public trust in advertising.

As the United States prospered during its early years, businesses promoted themselves through advertising. Exaggeration of product merits were commonplace, and untruths were rampant and unchecked. Although not all advertising claims were false or misleading, the early caveat, "Let the buyer beware," seemed an accepted standard for most advertising claims. Over time, however, dubious advertising claims increasingly harmed businesses that practiced truthful advertising.

Laws against fraud and deception stopped some false-advertising practices, but it was often impossible to prove the truth or untruth of many advertising claims or to prove consumers had suffered damages, even in cases when advertising claims were fraudulent or deceptive. In 1872, the U.S. Congress authorized the U.S. postmaster general to forbid the use of the mail system to "persons operating fraudulent schemes." This was the first attempt to use federal law to regulate misleading advertising. However, the postmaster's authority did not extend to many advertising practices that varied in degree from exaggeration to outright deception.

The emerging advertising industry sought a remedy through public education and advocacy of voluntary advertising changes. In 1904, various organizations were consolidated to form the National Federation of Advertising Clubs of America (late renamed the Associated Advertising Clubs of America). Through this organization, highly successful "vigilance committees" policed members' advertisements. In 1911, the organization adopted what it called "Ten Commandments of Advertising." This was the first formalized code of advertising in the United States. The first commandment was: "Thou shalt have no other gods in advertising but Truth." During that same year, *Printers' Ink*, the leading magazine of the advertising industry, published a "Model Statute" for advertising based on existing statutes in several states, and encouraged all states to adopt the statute as law.

Through the National Vigilance Committee's educational efforts, truth-in-advertising codes, based on the Model Statute, were adopted in 1914. The committee's name changed, and it eventually became the National Better Business Bureau. Bureau members drove the truth-in-advertising movement regionally and then nationally. By 1922, twenty-three states had enacted the Model Statute into law, and the bureau's practice of counseling and educating advertisers was well established.

From the 1920's to 1960, truth-in-advertising remained a significant issue. Modifications to acceptable standards of advertising, including special rules for new media such as radio and television, were implemented. Under joint sponsorship by the bureaus and the Advertising Federation of America, the advertising industry adopted the "Advertising Code of American Business" in 1964. By 1970, the bureaus were consolidated with other organizations into the Council of Better Business Bureaus, which has continued operating in to the twenty-first century. Its educational and counseling efforts now include Internet advertising, and the organization publishes a code that includes basic advertising principles, which are as follows:

- The primary responsibility for truthful and nondeceptive advertising rests with the advertiser. Advertisers should be prepared to substantiate any claims or offers made before publication or broadcast and, upon request, present such substantiation promptly to the advertising medium or the Better Business Bureau.

Truth-in-advertising codes were partly the result of claims like those made in this 1840's advertisement for an Egyptian life elixir. (Library of Congress)

- Advertisements which are untrue, misleading, deceptive, fraudulent, falsely disparaging of competitors, or insincere offers to sell, shall not be used.
- An advertisement as a whole may be misleading although every sentence separately considered is literally true. Misrepresentation may result not only from direct statements but by omitting or obscuring a material fact.

Taylor Shaw

FURTHER READING

Lears, Jackson. *Fables of Abundance: A Cultural History of Advertising in America.* New York: Basic Books, 1994.

Tungate, Mark. *Adland: A Global History of Advertising.* Philadelphia: Kogan Page, 2007.

SEE ALSO: Advertising industry; Congress, U.S.; Truth-in-lending laws.

Truth-in-lending laws

DEFINITION: Federal and state laws regulating consumer credit, designed to ensure that individuals are given accurate information concerning the cost and terms of loans, emphasizing real estate but including credit cards and other forms of consumer credit

SIGNIFICANCE: Truth-in-lending (TIL) laws are a cornerstone of consumer credit legislation. They promote the growth of the consumer credit industry by making the terms of credit easier to understand. In theory, this allows people to compare loans offered by different lenders, encouraging competition. In general, federal statutes do not regulate the actual terms of a loan, but only the form in which it is presented.

Truth-in-lending laws are a response to the explosion in consumer credit transactions during the late twentieth century. Lenders offered what appeared to be low interest rates, but added fees or calculated interest according to formulae that increased the actual percentage considerably. This made it difficult for even a financially sophisticated person to compare loans and left many people paying far more than they had anticipated.

In 1968, under President Lyndon B. Johnson, Congress enacted the first comprehensive truth-in-lending statute, the Consumer Credit Protection Act. The law required clear and conspicuous disclosure of loan terms, in a prescribed format, and provided legal remedies for consumers for lender noncompliance. A key feature of TIL disclosures is the annual percentage rate (APR), expressing, on an annual basis, the actual cost of borrowing money, including any fees charged by the lender. A powerful legal remedy in home refinancing and home equity loans is rescission, which allows a borrower to cancel a loan secured by his or her principal residence for up to three years if the proper disclosures were not made at the time.

The 1968 act spawned a great many lawsuits. Lenders complained of difficulty with complying with its complex provisions, and consumers complained of information overload. In 1980, under President Jimmy Carter, Congress added TIL simplification provisions to the Depository Institutions Deregulation and Monetary Control Act.

Other additions to TIL laws include the Fair

Credit and Charge Card Disclosure Act of 1988 and the Home Ownership and Equity Protection Act of 1994. Some states have their own TIL laws, which may be more favorable to consumers than the federal statute.

Proliferation of home loans with unaffordable terms despite TIL reveals some of the limitations of these acts. Borrowers often receive disclosures too late in the process to make comparisons, or are victims of bait-and-switch tactics by unscrupulous loan brokers. Disclosure requirements on variable-rate mortgages have proven inadequate, and penalties—for example increases in interest rates on a credit card if a payment is late—can be hidden in the fine print. Consumer confusion about loan terms, resulting in poor credit decisions, is still very much a part of the American business scene.

Martha Sherwood

FURTHER READING

Renard, Elizabeth, and Kathleen Keest. *Truth in Lending.* Boston: National Consumer Law Center, 1999.

Simmons, Pamela. "The Federal Truth in Lending Act: What You Don't Know Can Hurt You." *Real Property Law Reporter* 27, no. 6 (2004).

SEE ALSO: Advertising industry; Contract law; Credit card buying; Mortgage industry; Truth-in-advertising codes.

Tupperware

IDENTIFICATION: Plastic kitchenware that used an innovative marketing and distribution model

DATE: Founded in 1939 as the Earl S. Tupper Company

SIGNIFICANCE: Tupperware became an American icon by pioneering the party-plan, direct-sales system. Tupperware has been sold chiefly by women (a majority of whom have no professional sales qualifications), who demonstrate the products to gatherings of friends in their

homes. Although Tupperware products are not sold through stores, annual sales volumes exceeded $1 billion by the beginning of the twenty-first century.

Tupperware began when Earl Silas Tupper, an amateur inventor and designer, invented a new plastic material from a refined version of polyethylene. Throughout the 1930's, Tupper had striven to become rich by improving women's lives. The plastic designs that he created would allow him to achieve his goal by producing labor-saving, flexible, lightweight containers that prevented spills, blocked odors, and stopped spoilage. Despite acclaim from home magazines, however, initial sales of Tupperware remained low. American women had no idea how to use Tupper's products.

Brownie Wise, a single mother and Tupperware dealer, began holding Tupperware parties in private homes to demonstrate the products to women in their own neighborhoods. This approach proved to be a great success, and in 1951, Tupper withdrew Tupperware from all retail outlets to focus exclusively on direct sales. Wise became the face of Tupperware as vice president of Tupperware home parties. By the mid-1950's, the Tupperware party had become symbolic of suburban postwar America. Tupper focused on design, while Wise focused

At a home party in the 1950's, company dealer Brownie Wise throws a piece of Tupperware into the air to demonstrate its strength. (Smithsonian Institution, National Museum of American History, Behring Center)

on sales to the nation's huge pool of stay-at-home mothers. Tupper terminated Wise in 1958, but her sales strategies cemented the success of the company.

Since the mid-1990's, about 85 percent of Tupperware sales have been generated outside of the United States. By 2000, a Tupperware party took place somewhere in the world every 2.5 seconds, and an estimated 90 percent of American homes owned at least one piece of Tupperware.

Caryn E. Neumann

SEE ALSO: Catalog shopping; Chemical industries; Fuller Brush Company; Home Shopping Network; Stewart, Martha; Women in business.

Turnpikes

DEFINITION: Toll roads, usually main roads
SIGNIFICANCE: Turnpikes, combined with other types of roads, provide a reliable, networked way to move goods from one location to another, contributing to the growth of the economy as towns and cities grow up around major road junctions and increased markets for goods and services are created. Private turnpikes are also business ventures designed to make a profit for their owners.

Following the American Revolution, state and local governments became responsible for the creation and maintenance of public roads. Some elected to charge tolls for the use of these roads. The first such public toll road, from Alexandria, Virginia, to Snickers Gap in the Shenandoah Mountains, opened in 1785. The condition of the roads, the need to link various towns and cities, and problems related to predictability of revenue generation and the enforcement of fees caused states to reach out to the private sector for a more workable solution to public transportation needs. Precedent for this overture had been set by the success of private toll bridge companies that were chartered in the northeast, beginning in 1786 with the Charles River Bridge in Boston. These toll bridges brought their investors a healthy annual rate of return.

The Commonwealth of Pennsylvania granted the first charter for a private turnpike to merchants in Lancaster, Pennsylvania, in 1792. Constructed over a two-year period, the sixty-two-mile Lancaster Turnpike opened in 1794 and quickly became the principal means by which goods were shipped between points throughout the route and on the smaller non-toll roads that connected to it at principal junctions. Many other jurisdictions followed suit, such that by 1800, there were sixty-nine chartered turnpike companies and six times as many just ten years later, accounting for about one-third of all business incorporations for the period. By the mid-1840's, well over a thousand such enterprises had been chartered, although due to various regulatory and economic conditions, a large percentage of these companies failed. In some states, governments insisted on exempting large numbers from having to pay a toll. The cost of building these turnpikes varied considerably according to whether they were using already existing road surfaces or had to build a road from scratch. States such as Pennsylvania, Virginia, and Ohio subsidized private turnpike companies, but other states refused. The bulk of these

Toll booths at the Pennsylvania Turnpike in 1942. (Library of Congress)

turnpikes did not become profitable, although many managed to cover annual operating expenses.

The huge benefit of turnpikes was the manner in which they opened up large parts of the growing nation to commercial activities. Merchants, farmers, land owners, and residents in the vicinity of such roads benefited from lower costs of obtaining raw and finished materials and of transporting goods to markets even in faraway places. Over time, towns emerged at important junctions, and some of them grew into cities. The network of roads formed by turnpikes and other roads greatly enabled the push westward of the young nation.

Dennis W. Cheek

FURTHER READING

Baum-Snow, Nathaniel. "Did Highways Cause Suburbanization?" *The Quarterly Journal of Economics* 122, no. 2 (2007): 775-805.

Fein, Michael R. *New York Road Building and the American State, 1880-1956.* Lawrence: University Press of Kansas, 2008.

Wood, Frederic J., and Ronald Dale Karr. *The Turnpikes of New England.* Pepperell, Mass.: Branch Line Press, 1997.

SEE ALSO: Automotive industry; Cumberland Road; Highways; Transportation, U.S. Department of; Wilderness Road.

TVA. *See* Tennessee Valley Authority

Tyco International scandal

THE EVENT: Looting of Tyco International by its chair to fund his lavish lifestyle

DATE: 2002

PLACE: United States

SIGNIFICANCE: With revenues in 2001 of $38 billion and 240,000 employees worldwide, Tyco was one of America's largest conglomerates, but a 2002 corporate fraud case nearly destroyed the firm. By the time the dust of the scandal had settled, the company stood $28 billion in debt, and its shareholders had lost over $90 billion, more than 80 percent of Tyco's peak market value.

Former Tyco CEO Dennis Kozlowski enters Manhattan State Supreme Court in 2005. (AP/Wide World Photos)

Tyco Laboratories began operations in 1960, performing experimental work for the U.S. government. The firm went public in 1964 and quickly expanded, mostly by acquisition, to exploit the commercial applications of its work. Dennis Kozlowski joined the company in 1975 as an assistant controller. The company subsequently shifted its focus from growth to profits within its three primary divisions: fire protection, electronics, and packaging. Kozlowski joined Tyco's board in 1987 and became president and chief operating officer two years later. Kozlowski engineered a coup to become Tyco's chief executive officer (CEO) in 1992 and the chair of the board in 1993. He diversified the company, branching into health care. Tyco eventually became the second largest producer of medical devices in the United States.

Kozlowski's business practices raised some eyebrows. In 1999, the Securities and Exchange Commission (SEC) initiated an inquiry into Tyco's practices that resulted in a restatement of the company's earnings. In January, 2002, questionable accounting practices came to light. Tyco had forgiven a $19 million, no-interest loan to Kozlowski in 1998 and had paid the CEO's income taxes on the loan.

Kozlowski enjoyed an extravagant lifestyle, with multiple homes, lavish parties, a racing yacht, and numerous charitable donations. His most notorious expenditure was $2.1 million on a party celebrating his wife's fortieth birthday in Sardinia, Italy, that featured a life-sized ice sculpture of Michelangelo's David with vodka flowing from its penis. To pay for these and other expenses, Kozlowski used over $75 million of Tyco funds. None of these expenditures was publicly revealed to the company's shareholders.

Kozlowski resigned on June 2, 2002, just before being charged with evading more than $1 million in New York State sales taxes on art purchases. In September, 2002, the SEC filed a civil enforcement action against Kozlowski and two other top executives, charging that they had failed to disclose Kozlowski's forgiven loans. In 2005, Kozlowski and Mark Swartz, Tyco's chief financial officer, were convicted of twenty-two counts of fraud and received prison sentences of eight to twenty-five years as well as fines and compensation orders that totaled $240 million.

Kozlowski's successor at Tyco replaced 220 of the firm's 250 top managers. All board members who had served under Kozlowski had resigned by 2003. The corporate governance consultant Institutional Shareholder Services (ISS) had classified only four of Tyco's eleven directors as completely independent, and most of the board's nonexecutives were long-serving members. The firm survived the scandal, albeit in a shrunken state.

Caryn E. Neumann

FURTHER READING

Farrell, Greg. *Corporate Crooks: How Rogue Executives Ripped Off Americans . . . and Congress Helped Them Do It!* Amherst, N.Y.: Prometheus Books, 2006.

Hamilton, Stewart, and Alicia Micklethwait. *Greed and Corporate Failure: The Lessons from Recent Disasters.* New York: Palgrave Macmillan, 2006.

SEE ALSO: Business crimes; Justice, U.S. Department of; Securities and Exchange Commission.

U

UFW. *See* United Farm Workers of America

UMWA. *See* United Mine Workers of America

Underwood Tariff Act

THE LAW: Federal legislation that reduced import tariffs and created the federal income tax
DATE: Signed into law on October 3, 1913
SIGNIFICANCE: Initially touted as an act to lower tariffs, the longer term significance was the manner in which the act attempted to offset the loss of tariff revenue—namely by creating the federal income tax on individuals. Consumers were provided with competitively priced products, and manufacturers were encouraged to be more efficient in their production processes.

Also known as the Revenue Act of 1913, the Underwood Tariff Act was called for by President Woodrow Wilson in a special session of Congress in April, 1913. Wilson's call for a reduction in tariffs marked the first time that a president had spoken to a joint session of Congress in more than one hundred years. As a result, there was heavy media coverage of Wilson's move to lower the average citizen's cost of living. Congressman Oscar Underwood of Alabama shepherded the bill through the House, and it passed easily in May, 1913. The Senate, however, was influenced by lobbyists. It was not until September that the bill passed. The law reduced tariffs to the lowest that they had been in more than fifty years. The average rate went from 41 to 27 percent.

To compensate for the lost revenue, the act created a federal income tax. The Sixteenth Amendment to the Constitution had been ratified on February 3, 1913, allowing for an income tax. Initially, the income tax applied to few individuals, and this aspect of the act was not considered significant.

Also included in the act was a provision to allow the establishment of an independent study commission to provide the president and Congress with ad-

vice on the proper rates for tariffs. The Federal Tariff Commission was created in 1916 to collect expert information on the fiscal and industrial effects of customs duties. The commission still exists in the twenty-first century under the name of the International Trade Commission.

Dale L. Flesher

SEE ALSO: Income tax, personal; Tariff of Abominations; Tariffs; Taxation.

Unions. *See* Labor history

United Farm Workers of America

IDENTIFICATION: Labor union for agricultural workers
DATE: Founded in 1966
SIGNIFICANCE: The United Farm Workers organizes for the rights of agricultural workers and has been instrumental in changing labor laws and securing more equitable contracts.

The United Farm Workers of America (UFW) occupies a unique place in the history of American agribusiness and labor relations. Formed as an activist union for agricultural workers during the mid-1960's, it has conducted consumer boycotts and engaged in direct action to pressure growers, food industries, and government to confront the often miserable working conditions in agricultural labor. Emerging from Chicano activism and multiracial labor organizing in food industries, the UFW has always combined labor organizing with campaigns for economic justice and civil rights.

The UFW is part of a long and complex history in agricultural labor relations. Most histories of the UFW emphasize its genesis in the government-sponsored bracero program (1942-1964), which was aimed at recruiting Mexican workers for American agriculture. Agricultural workers in general faced dismal working conditions, in part because none of the labor protections of the 1935 National Labor Relations Act (NLRA) applied to agriculture. Work

César Chávez takes the California lettuce strike issue to Chicago and the Midwest in 1979. (AP/Wide World Photos)

and housing conditions could be extremely poor, and education was inadequate for workers' children who moved frequently. Pesticide poisoning plagued the health of adult and child laborers, and racial prejudice in the American Southwest and California added to the stress for agricultural workers and their families.

Labor activists César Chávez and Dolores Huerta helped organize the National Farm Workers Association (NFWA) in 1962 to address some of the critical problems facing agricultural workers. In 1966, Chávez and other activists who were organizing a grape boycott aimed at California producers linked the NFWA with the Agricultural Workers Organizing Committee (AWOC), a group working on the Delano grape strike with the AFL-CIO. These two groups next merged to form the UFW. The UFW continued the fight for protective measures in health, housing, education, and for equitable con-

tracts with growers and across agribusiness. In 1975, the UFW was instrumental in California's adoption of the Agricultural Labor Relations Act (ALRA), which finally secured the right to collective bargaining for agricultural workers, and the union has since prioritized immigrant labor rights.

The UFW broke important ground in American business history by using nonviolent tactics drawn from the Civil Rights movement, such as boycotts and mass marches. Chávez, for many years the public face for the UFW, also adopted the strategy of political fasting, a tactic he shared with the Indian international human rights leader Mahatma Gandhi. This creative fusion of human rights philosophy with labor organizing has allowed the UFW to bring to the forefront the moral dimension of American economic and labor relations.

Sharon Carson

FURTHER READING

Ferris, Susan, Ricardo Sandoval, and Diana Hembree. *The Fight in the Fields: César Chávez and the Farm Workers Movement.* New York: Harvest/Harcourt, 1998.

Shaw, Randy. *Beyond the Fields: César Chávez, the UFW, and the Struggle for Justice in the Twenty-first Century.* Berkeley: University of California Press, 2009.

Soto, Gary. *Jessie de la Cruz: A Profile of a United Farm Worker.* New York: Persea Books, 2002.

SEE ALSO: Agribusiness; Agriculture; Bracero program; Chávez, César; Farm labor; Immigration; Internal migration; Labor history; Latin American trade with the United States; Mexican trade with the United States.

United Food and Commercial Workers

IDENTIFICATION: Labor union representing American and Canadian workers in the retail food, meatpacking, food processing, poultry, and related industries

DATE: Founded in 1979

SIGNIFICANCE: The United Food and Commercial Workers International Union strives to improve and protect the rights of workers by fighting for competitive wages, health care reform, retirement security, safe working conditions, and the right to unionize.

The Amalgamated Meat Cutters Union and the Retail Clerks International Union merged in 1979 to form the United Food and Commercial Workers International Union (UFCW). By merging with several smaller unions between 1980 and 1998, the UFCW expanded its membership to represent over one million workers, becoming the second-largest union by membership affiliated with the AFL-CIO until 2005. On July 29 of that year, the UFCW disaffiliated with the AFL-CIO to help form the Change to Win coalition with six other unions. As a member of this coalition, the UFCW provides a powerful voice in the effort to rebuild the American labor movement and restore the proper balance between working America and corporate America.

The UFCW works in a wide range of industries that include the health care, poultry, food processing, meatpacking, manufacturing, retail food, textile, and chemical trades. The UFCW's membership has grown to over 1.4 million. It is the largest union of young workers in America, with more than 40 percent of its workers under the age of thirty. The UFCW works to improve the lives and livelihoods of workers, their families, and their communities. Specific goals of the UFCW are to achieve better wages, affordable health care, retirement security, and safer working conditions and to provide an independent voice in the workplace. On average, the added pay and benefits received by UFCW members are eighteen times more than the cost of their union dues. UFCW members in the retail food industry earn over 30 percent more in wages than their nonunion counterparts.

Since September 19, 2007, the UFCW has been involved in food security issues in New York, organizing grocery store workers and assisting in the development of new food policies that help ensure the availability of safe, fresh, nutritious, and affordable food for all people in the state. To ensure food access, the UFCW has encouraged the preservation and development of supermarkets in low-income communities and partnerships between supermarkets, local food manufacturers, regional farms, and urban agriculture to create more local jobs and increase the sale of locally produced foods in New York.

The UFCW is actively involved in reforming Wal-Mart's business practices throughout the United States and Canada to provide competitive wages, better working conditions, and affordable health care for Wal-Mart workers. At the heart of these battles is UFCW's commitment to preserve the values and standard of living for hardworking, middle-class workers and to preserve a land where hard work is respected and those who do the work are protected.

Alvin K. Benson

FURTHER READING

Chaison, Gary N. *Unions in America.* London: Sage, 2005.

Dannin, Ellen. *Taking Back the Workers' Law: How to Fight the Assault on Labor Rights.* Ithaca, N.Y.: ILR Press, 2006.

Midkiff, Ken. *The Meat You Eat: How Corporate Farming Has Endangered America's Food Supply.* New York: St. Martin's Press, 2004.

SEE ALSO: Fast-food restaurants; Food-processing industries; Great Atlantic and Pacific Tea Company; Labor history; Labor strikes; Meatpacking industry; Poultry industry; Restaurant industry; Wal-Mart.

United Mine Workers of America

IDENTIFICATION: Labor union primarily for mine workers

DATE: Founded on January 22, 1890

SIGNIFICANCE: The United Mine Workers of America has been instrumental in changing the way in which companies and workers regard each other and in improving labor relations between the groups.

By organizing the workers in the coal mines, the United Mine Workers of America (UMWA) changed the way in which coal-producing companies operated their mines. By establishing standardized wages, workdays, and coal-weighing procedures, the UMWA benefited both miners and coal companies by eliminating much of the price-fluctuation in the coal market and producing greater stability of coal supply and demand. The union improved working conditions for miners through collective bargaining and made health and safety a significant concern.

On January 22, 1890, in Columbus Ohio, the Trades Assembly Number 135, the miners' branch

UMWA president John L. Lewis (right) discusses the coal situation with Representative John Nolan, chair of the Labor Committee of the House of Representatives, in 1922. (Library of Congress)

of the Knights of Labor, and the National Progressive Union of Miners and Mine Laborers merged to form the United Mine Workers of America. The membership consisted of bituminous coal miners and other workers in and around mines in the United States and Canada. The group took the American Federation of Labor (AFL) as its model and affiliated with it. The UMWA was one of the first AFL affiliates to accept all ethnic groups. The union concentrated on building its strength and gaining recognition. Its goals included an eight-hour workday, increased wages for miners, standardized weighing of coal, and the right to collective bargaining.

WORKING CONDITIONS AND STRIKES

The miners' working conditions were anything but desirable. They worked long hours for pay as low as 80 cents an hour, with no health or safety provisions. They were at the mining company's mercy financially as they lived in company housing and bought items only at the company store. Buying anywhere other than the company store could result in their being fired.

When non-English speaking immigrants—Italians, Poles, and others—arrived in the United States, the mine owners began replacing their Irish, Welsh, and other English-speaking workers. The mine owners reasoned that these workers would understand less about what was happening and be easier to control. The scheme failed as the new workers, unhappy with the harsh conditions of their work, joined the Irish, the Welsh, and the others in protest.

The strongest means of protest for the miners was striking, which the UMWA used repeatedly. However, the strikes took a heavy toll on the miners because they were usually violent and resulted in death or serious injury for many participants. The miners struck in 1894 and in 1897. On September 10, 1897, in Lattimer, Pennsylvania, nineteen miners were killed by police and many others injured in what became known as the Lattimer massacre. On April 20, 1914, the Ludlow massacre in Colorado resulted in the deaths of both miners and members of their families. On May 19, 1920, at Matewan, West Virginia, twelve men were killed during a strike. The strikes continued throughout the century. In Harlan County, Kentucky, in 1973, the miners struck, and again there was bloodshed. The following year, on November 12, after the national UMWA contract expired, 120,000 miners struck. This time, negotiation replaced violence, and in three weeks, a tentative agreement reopened the mines. In 1989-1990, miners, with the active participation of their wives, held a nonviolent strike against Pittston Coal in Virginia.

GAINS MADE

The strikes brought about significant improvement in company-miner relations. With John Mitchell as UMWA president and chief negotiator, the strike of 1897 resulted in the first agreement between the union and mine operators in the Central Competitive Field (Pennsylvania, Ohio, Illinois, and Indiana). The union received recognition, wages were increased, union dues were deducted from miners' paychecks, and an eight-hour workday and uniform standards for weighing coal were implemented. However, none of these gains applied to mines outside of the Central Competitive Field.

Mitchell spent the rest of his presidency working to extend the union's influence into other mining regions of the country.

John L. Lewis, president of the UMWA from 1920 to 1960 and an autocratic leader, was devoted to increasing wages and safety for miners. An impressive speaker, he often played on his listeners' sympathy for miners' families to gain higher wages. During World War II, Lewis's concern for the miners caused him to break the no-strike pledge to gain wage increases. In 1943, 400,000 miners struck under his authority. He was instrumental in gaining passage of the Federal Coal Mine Safety Act of 1952. Lewis continued to fight for good working conditions for miners until his retirement.

THE UMWA AFTER LEWIS

In 1960, Thomas Kennedy became the union president but died in 1963. Under the next president. W. A. "Tony" Boyle (1963-1972), the union suffered from internal corruption, culminating in the 1974 conviction of Boyle for the murder of his rival Joseph "Jock" Yablonski. Union membership declined because of the corruption and also because of mechanization of the mines. In 1969, the union obtained passage of the Federal Coal Mine Health and Safety Act, providing compensation for victims of black lung disease. In 1972, the Miners for Democracy took control of the union and implemented reforms. By 2002, the union, which continued to concern itself with fair treatment of workers and health concerns, had about one half the members it had in 1950.

Shawncey Webb

FURTHER READING

Brisbin, Richard A., Jr. *A Strike Like No Other Strike, 1989-1990.* Baltimore: Johns Hopkins University Press, 2002. This discussion of UMWA's strike against Pittston Coal Group looks at miners' strategies, the corporation's strategies, corporate power, and the role of the judicial system.

Dubofsky, Melwyn, and Warren Van Tine. *John L. Lewis: A Biography.* Champaign: University of Illinois Press, 1986. This biography describes Lewis's life and contains information on his role in the UMWA.

Martelle, Scott. *Blood Passion: The Ludlow Massacre and Class War in the American West.* Piscataway, N.J.: Rutgers University Press, 2007. An unbiased account of the chasm between mine operators and miners, the strategies of each, and life in an early twentieth century company town. Selected bibliography, appendixes, and index.

Mother Jones. *Autobiography of Mother Jones.* Edited by Mary Field Parton. White Fish, Mont.: Kessinger, 2007. Contains Mother Jones's account of miners' working conditions, strikes, and efforts to organize labor. Introduction by Clarence Darrow.

Shogan, Robert. *The Battle of Blair Mountain: The Story of America's Largest Labor Uprising.* Boulder, Colo.: Westview Press, 2004. A detailed account of a conflict between West Virginia miners and mine owners. Bibliography, photographs.

SEE ALSO: AFL-CIO; Coal industry; Coal strike of 1902; Labor history; Labor strikes; Lewis, John L.; Mineral resources.

United Nations Monetary and Financial Conference. *See* Bretton Woods Agreement

United States Steel Corporation

IDENTIFICATION: Major steel producer that was the largest corporation in the world during the early twentieth century

DATE: Founded on February 25, 1901

SIGNIFICANCE: The United States Steel Corporation was perhaps the most heralded American company throughout much of the twentieth century and had a major impact on the world's economy. The sheer size of the organization led to innovations in accountancy because the merged entity was simply too big to be understood with conventional financial statements.

Under the leadership of J. P. Morgan, the steel holdings of Andrew Carnegie, located primarily in Pittsburgh, Pennsylvania, were merged in 1901 with those of Elbert H. Gary, located primarily in northern Indiana, to form the United States Steel Corporation (U.S. Steel). Six smaller companies were also a part of the merger, and four others joined later in 1901. The total capitalization was over $1.4 billion, which made it the first billion-dollar corporation and the largest company in the world. At its start, the company produced two-thirds of the nation's steel. By 1911, the share of the nation's steel produced by the company had decreased to about 50 percent, and by the twenty-first century, that share has declined to around 10 percent. Nevertheless, in 2008, the company had nearly 50,000 employees, down from its peak of 340,000 in 1943.

Because the total entity was a conglomeration of a dozen formerly independent companies, the accountants, Price Waterhouse, had to figure out how to report the corporation's results in a manner that would be understandable to stock market investors. The solution was the invention of consolidated financial statements. The first full-year annual report for U.S. Steel was a classic of industrial reporting. Detailed data were provided for production levels, inventories, debt, acquisitions, employees, and stockholders. Photos of factories were provided, which was a first for annual company reports. In later years, particularly the 1940's and 1950's, the company remained innovative in its financial reporting, but the focus changed to emphasize methods that would enhance reported income, whereas during the early years, the accounting methods were innovative in that they produced conservative income numbers.

U.S. Steel's business dominance began to decline after 1950, partially because of the actions of the U.S. government, but it remained a venerable institution. In 1952, during the Korean War, President Harry S. Truman tried to take over the company's production facilities to resolve a labor union crisis, but the U.S. Supreme Court blocked the takeover. A later president, John F. Kennedy, was slightly more successful in 1962, when he got the company to reverse a price increase that the president thought would be harmful to the nation's economy. The government intervened again in 1984, when a takeover of National Steel Company was prevented. Despite setbacks, U.S. Steel has remained the largest steel company in the United States, although it is far from being the largest corporation.

Dale L. Flesher

FURTHER READING

Cotter, Arundel. *The Authentic History of the United States Steel Corporation.* New York: Moody Magazine and Book Company, 1916.

Vangermeersch, Richard G. *Financial Accounting Milestones in the Annual Reports of United States Steel Corporation: The First Seven Decades.* New York: Garland Publishing, 1986.

Warren, Kenneth. *Big Steel: The First Century of the United States Steel Corporation, 1901-2001.* Pittsburgh: University of Pittsburgh Press, 2001.

SEE ALSO: Accounting industry; Carnegie, Andrew; Gilded Age; Homestead strike; Labor strikes; Mineral resources; Morgan, J. P.; Steel industry; Steel mill seizure of 1952.

USA Today

IDENTIFICATION: Daily national newspaper
DATE: Founded on September 15, 1982
SIGNIFICANCE: *USA Today,* targeted at a general, less sophisticated audience than other national newspapers, was credited with an innovative strategy for successful journalism, even as it was criticized for lowering the standards of the journalistic profession.

In 1981, Allen Neuharth, chief executive officer of the Gannett Company, announced plans to produce a new national newspaper that would target a general audience. In an era when many newspapers had decreasing circulations, this plan to print another paper caused many people in the industry to doubt its business practicality. Despite this cynicism, Neuharth's innovative paper *USA Today* rapidly gained a following and soon influenced other editors to adopt some of its features.

The original premise of the paper was not to replace local or national newspapers but to provide travelers, businesspeople, and the general public with a weekday paper that had an attractive, easy-to-read format. *USA Today* was to have deeper coverage of news, money, sports, and life than local papers generally provided, but it would feature more succinct articles than the *New York Times* and its competitors, as well as colored pictures and graphics and simple information boxes. Special features also were to include a front-page index and a color weather map. The paper was designed to be a commuter's paper, featuring top news and sports stories.

The first edition of *USA Today* was launched in the Washington-Baltimore area. Soon thereafter,

Allen Neuharth, the CEO of Gannett Newspapers, examines the first issue of USA Today *on September 12, 1983.* (AP/Wide World Photos)

editions were available in Atlanta, Minneapolis, Pittsburgh, Chicago, and Denver. Over the next few months, the paper spread to other large cities, including Detroit, Houston, Los Angeles, Miami, New York, Philadelphia, San Francisco, and Seattle. Although not greeted equally well in each city, circulation grew substantially as distribution increased.

Although the popularity of *USA Today* was quickly assured, many media reports continued to describe the paper with disfavor. They likened its format and content to the food served at fast-food chains, sometimes referring to *USA Today* as "McPaper." During the first decade, readership increased, finally making it the most widely read newspaper in the United States, but advertising sales did not increase proportionally. In 1993, *USA Today* finally reported a profitable year. As the paper found its niche, increasing the depth of some of its news coverage and evaluating and analyzing new marketing opportunities, other newspapers followed its lead by adding color and increasing their leisure and travel sections.

USA Today grew to achieve a readership of 5 million people. Bed and breakfasts, hotels, airports, and other travel centers have come to rely on it as a standard media offering that is available both in print and online. Offshoots of the paper include *Sports Weekly, USA International,* and book and video projects. *USA Today* has become one of the most influential newspapers in the United States.

Cynthia J. W. Svoboda

FURTHER READING

Prichard, Peter. *The Making of McPaper: The Inside Story of "USA Today."* Kansas City: Andrews, McMeel & Parker, 1987.

Rider, Rem. "Against All Odds: Left for Dead by the Pundits, *USA Today* Celebrates Its Twenty-Fifth Birthday." *American Journalism Review* 29, no. 5 (October-November, 2007): 4.

SEE ALSO: Book publishing; Cable News Network; Magazine industry; Newspaper industry.

Utilities. *See* Public utilities

V

Vanderbilt, Cornelius

IDENTIFICATION: American businessman who built empires in shipping and railroads
BORN: May 27, 1794; Port Richmond, Staten Island, New York
DIED: January 4, 1877; New York, New York
SIGNIFICANCE: Vanderbilt amassed his shipping and railroad fortunes by using ruthless business practices against his competitors and selected family members. On his death, he left the first fortune created by an industrial empire.

In the United States, the name Vanderbilt is synonymous with wealth and luxurious living. Cornelius Vanderbilt, from a large but unsuccessful farming family of Dutch and English descent, built the industrial fortune behind the name. Semiliterate, but canny and shrewd, Vanderbilt displayed at an early age the characteristics that would enable him to build an industrial empire. In dealing with his family, business rivals, and potential partners, he was abrupt, harsh, unceremonious, sarcastic, and uncivil.

Cornelius Vanderbilt. (Library of Congress)

It was Vanderbilt's hard work and great physical strength that distinguished him when he plied the waterways around New York City, ferrying both passengers and freight. By undercutting his rival's prices and challenging the Fulton and Livingston monopolies on the Hudson River, Vanderbilt amassed profits that helped him build and sail more steamboats. A combination of good luck and an exceptionally well-run company enabled him to accumulate his first fortune and the honorary title of "commodore" while in his forties. Parsimonious by nature, Commodore Vanderbilt used his wealth to invest in the development of a short sea route to the Pacific, hoping to gain a financial advantage shipping to California during the gold rush. His vessels sailed to Nicaragua and navigated a series of rivers and lakes to transport goods and people to California rather than taking the lengthier route around South America.

Vanderbilt keenly knew when to both invest in and exit from a company. Accepting that steam locomotives would replace steamships, he shifted his investment strategy to railroads. Investing in the New York and Harlem Railroad, Vanderbilt successfully manipulated company stock shares, creating revenue that enabled him to purchase a dozen railroad lines, including the New York Central, and to create a second fortune in his seventies. Carefully acquiring stock, underpricing his competitors, strategically increasing a company's public shares for sale, manipulating legislatures, and challenging laws and monopolies always worked for Vanderbilt until he met Jay Gould and lost millions in watered-down Erie Railroad stock. After his death, his fortune was lavishly spent by his descendants.

William A. Paquette

SEE ALSO: Gilded Age; Railroads; Robber barons; Shipping industry; Steamboats.

Vending machines

DEFINITION: Mechanical devices that dispense commodities (often food, beverages, or cigarettes) in return for money
SIGNIFICANCE: The popularization of vending machines as a means of selling a variety of products

revolutionized American marketing in the twentieth century. As vending machines, and the security surrounding them, evolved, the variety of products distributed increased manifold.

The first vending machine in recorded history was invented in 215 B.C.E. by the ancient Greek mathematician Hero. That first machine was a coin-activated device that dispensed sacrificial water in an Egyptian temple. It was eighteen hundred years later that the next recorded vending machines were made. In 1615, snuff and tobacco vending boxes appeared in English taverns. These tobacco machines were less sophisticated than was Hero's, since they left much to the honesty of the customer. All an inserted coin did was open the box. Once the box was open, customers could take out as much tobacco as they wanted. One of the first U.S. patents on a vending machine, used to sell postcards, was issued in 1886 to Frederick C. Lynde.

If any one person can be considered the father of vending machines in the United States, it would be Thomas Adams, the founder of the Adams Gum Company. Adams began the first successful vending operation in America in 1888, when he placed gum machines on the elevated railroad platforms in New York City. Other early vending machines included scales (which vended a service), strength testers, and hot water vendors (which served people who had no other source of hot water). These were followed around 1900 by cigar vending machines in Chicago and an automatic divorce machine in Utah.

Gumball vending machines were introduced in 1907, at the same time that the round gumball was invented. Vending machines soon offered everything: In Philadelphia, a completely coin-operated restaurant called Horn & Hardart Automat was opened in 1902 and stayed open until 1962. In 1926, the American inventor William Rowe in-

vented the cigarette vending machine. Cigarette vending machines remained popular until the 1980's, when state laws began restricting the sales of cigarettes to minors. The machines fell out of use, because there was no way to keep children from purchasing cigarettes from them. One of the major early manufacturers of vending machines was the Vendorlator Manufacturing Company of Fresno, California. The company's machines of the 1940's and 1950's primarily sold bottled soft drinks, and they later came to be considered classics.

GAMBLING AND CHANGE MACHINES

During the late nineteenth century, coin-operated gambling machines (slot machines) became popular. The vending machine industry does not consider gambling machines to be a part of the vending industry, because they do not vend merchandise. They are also much more heavily regulated than are vending machines, so the logistics of placing them are considerably different. The machines nevertheless affected the industry, inducing it to research the dangers of fraud. During the early

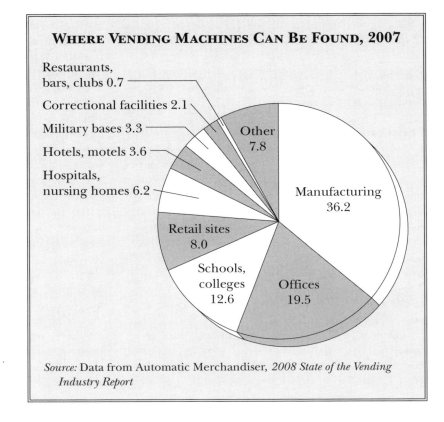

WHERE VENDING MACHINES CAN BE FOUND, 2007

Restaurants, bars, clubs 0.7
Correctional facilities 2.1
Military bases 3.3
Hotels, motels 3.6
Hospitals, nursing homes 6.2
Other 7.8
Retail sites 8.0
Schools, colleges 12.6
Offices 19.5
Manufacturing 36.2

Source: Data from Automatic Merchandiser, *2008 State of the Vending Industry Report*

twentieth century, a nickel with a string tied to it or a lead slug could be used fraudulently to trigger a slot machine or a vending machine. It was not until the 1930's that the slug rejector was perfected.

The invention of the slug rejection device led to growth in the vending machine industry during the 1930's and 1940's. In addition to boosting the slot machine industry, slug rejectors prevented children from stealing gum or candy from machines. As a result, gum and candy vending machines became commonplace. By the 1960's, soft drink and coffee machines were equally ubiquitous, as were newspaper machines and even stamp machines at post offices. Occasionally, fishing enthusiasts could find vending machines next to their favorite fishing holes that dispensed cans of worms on the deposit of a coin.

The main advantage offered by vending machines is their convenience. Machines are not restricted to an eight-hour workday; they can provide goods and services around the clock. Moreover, they are much cheaper than paid labor. Machine owners must still pay employees to restock and maintain machines (or do it themselves), but they do not need to pay an hourly wage to a salesperson.

Change machines are also not considered a part of the vending machine industry, although they are often found next to machines that take only coins. Change machines thus contribute to vending machine sales, but like gambling machines, they form a separate if related category.

PRODUCTS AND SERVICES SOLD

Soft drink machines were introduced just before the turn of the twentieth century. By 1906, the improved models would dispense up to ten different flavors of soda. The drinks were dispensed into a drinking glass or tin cup that was placed near the machine (there was usually only one glass or cup to a machine because paper cups had not yet been invented). Health officials were concerned that everyone using the machine drank from the same cup. Then, vendors began setting buckets of water next to the machines, so each customer could rinse the cup before drinking from it.

The year 1909 witnessed the invention of the pay toilet. Although pay toilets remain popular in other countries, they have largely disappeared from the United States because of arguments that they discriminate against women.

The 1930's witnessed improved machines. In addition to slug rejectors, change machines were perfected during the decade. These improvements led marketers to experiment with vending machines. Coin-operated washing machines were introduced during the 1930's: During the Great Depression, some appliance dealers attached coin-metering devices to washing machines that they sold. People who bought the machines on credit were thus able to accumulate money to make their monthly payments by using their appliances. Soon, enterprising appliance dealers placed such coin-operated washing machines in apartment-house basements. Eventually, dedicated coin-operated laundries appeared.

Following World War II, there was a surge of innovation in the vending machine industry. Much of that surge was due to the discovery of vending machines by industrial management. Before the war, the management of most factories had been merely tolerant of vending machines, but they soon discovered that the machines could be a low-cost means of keeping workers happy. They kept workers on the premises during breaks, and the easy availability of candy bars and soft drinks increased productivity. As a result, the demand for vending machines exceeded the supply during the late 1940's.

Despite advances made by the vending machine industry during the 1950's, one major limitation to the industry's growth remained until the early 1960's: Vending machines could sell only low-priced items, because machines could accept only coins. The early 1960's witnessed the invention of vending machines that would accept and make change for paper currency, paving the way for the industry's expansion into more expensive grocery items, as well as various kinds of tickets.

The first use of vending machines to issue tickets was at an Illinois racetrack, where pari-mutuel tickets were dispensed on deposit of $2. Penn Central Railroad became one of the first transportation companies to sell tickets by means of vending machines. These machines, used in high-traffic areas, permitted passengers to buy train tickets without the need to interact with a person. They accepted one-dollar bills and five-dollar bills as well as coins.

There are problems involved with the use of vending machines. Primary among these are mechanical failure and vandalism of the machines. Moreover, not every product can be successfully sold by machine. Several requirements make some goods more suitable to machine vending than others. First, the most successful products will generally be those that consumers are predisposed to purchase, such as those already supported by national advertising campaigns. Second, products must enjoy a high turnover to justify the costs of purchasing, deploying, and servicing machines. A third factor is the relationship between the location of machines and the location at which products will be consumed or used. Usually, products must be usable within a short distance of the machine; otherwise, consumers might prefer buying them at dedicated stores.

Although tangible merchandise is the most commonly sold category of vending machine commodity, services are also offered. Coin-operated laundries are among most common service vendors. Other machines that sell services include scales, parcel lockers, and pay toilets. Some motel beds include a coin-operated massage feature, and coin-operated telescopes and binoculars are located in national parks, on the roofs of major skyscrapers, and at other tourist locations. Coin- and card-operated copying machines have experienced a large boom, particularly in libraries and at twenty-four-hour copy stores. Perhaps the most ubiquitous single service-vending device, however, is the parking meter.

Advances in telecommunications have made possible the use of credit cards to operate vending machines. Such devices are most common in locations that also have human cashiers with credit card machines. Thus, one can use a credit card at a machine to purchase transportation tickets, motion-picture tickets, or copies at a copy center. Even soft drink machines may occasionally accept credit cards, however. The technology behind these machines is related to that behind automatic teller machines (ATMs). The latter devices are not considered to be part of the vending machine industry proper, but swift, secure verification of financial information is necessary for both devices to operate. Similarly, while not technically vending machines, credit-

This vending machine at the Dallas Stars Center ice rink in Frisco, Texas, in 2007 takes credit cards. (AP/Wide World Photos)

card-operated gasoline pumps have increased the number of twenty-four-hour service stations and changed the way people buy gas. The influence of credit cards on the vending machine industry will most likely grow in the future.

The United States is not alone in the development of vending machines. In fact, the United States is not as advanced as some other nations of the world. For example, in Japan, credit-card-operated machines have been used widely since the 1960's. The future will see a broadening of product lines offered in vending machines, as marketers recognize the opportunities that exist in automatic retailing.

Dale L. Flesher

FURTHER READING

Amann, Fred. "Automated Cashless Services: A Trilogy." *Vend*, March 15, 1970, 19-20. This article from the leading journal for vending machine operators discusses the role of vending machines that accepted credit cards in 1967.

"From Peanuts to Panties." *Sales Management*, June 3, 1960, 38-42 and 116-118. Provides highlights from the history of vending machines and includes an extensive discussion of the variety of products being sold via vending machines during the late 1950's.

Hanna, Charles. *The Vending Industry: History, Trends, Secrets, Opportunities, Scams.* Kearney, Nebr.: Morris, 2001. The sections on history and scams are particularly useful.

Manning, W. J., Jr. "Automatic Selling: A Business in Billions." *The Management Review,* October, 1960, 15-21. A history of the vending machine industry that emphasizes technological breakthroughs.

Schreiber, G. R. *A Concise History of Vending in the U.S.A.* Chicago: Vend, 1961. Short history of vending machines published by the leading journal in the industry.

Segrave, Kerry. *Vending Machines: An American Social History.* Jefferson, N.C.: McFarland, 2002. Traces the influence of the vending machine in American culture from its beginnings through the end of the twentieth century; includes an extensive bibliography and index.

SEE ALSO: Cola industry; Credit card buying; Currency; Drive-through businesses; Fast-food restaurants; Motion-picture industry; Retail trade industry; Tobacco industry.

Video rental industry

DEFINITION: Branch of the entertainment industry that engages in renting prerecorded video material for home and personal viewing

SIGNIFICANCE: After starting in 1979 with a single retail outlet in Los Angeles, the video rental industry boomed during the 1980's and became a fixture in consumers' spending during the 1990's, grossing an average of $1 billion yearly. With the arrival of digital versatile discs (DVDs) and the Internet during the 1990's, the industry experienced a period of increasing technological sophistication that has led to the creation and reinvention of new business models.

The history of the video rental industry is linked to the introduction of videocassette recorders in the consumer market. In 1977, Andre Blay established the Video Club of America to sell the first prerecorded motion picture videocassettes. Blay's success inspired George Atkinson, a small-store owner in Los Angeles, to create the first video rental outlet, the Video Station, in 1979. Most analysts predicted that Americans would prefer to buy rather than rent videocassettes, but Atkinson's great insight was that videocassette recorders (VCRs) would decline in price and become a mass-market item. In December, 1979, competition between the Radio Corporation of America (RCA) and Sony pushed prices of VCRs below $1,000 for the first time. Atkinson's idea was so successful that many followed in his footsteps.

As VCRs proliferated, film studios tried to diminish the rental industry by adding surcharges of up to $10 for each videocassette sold to rental stores; However, by 1983, most studios had revoked these charges and welcomed the rental industry. By 1990, the market had changed from one of small independently owned stores to one dominated by a few large firms. The biggest, Blockbuster, had more than two thousand outlets and controlled 15 percent of the rental market. By 1996, 85 percent of all American households owned at least one VCR, and videocassette rentals exceeded $1 billion per year.

Toward the end of the 1990's, the rental industry underwent another change with the advent of digital versatile discs (DVDs). Film studios then began releasing DVDs at lower prices than those for videocassettes. Moreover, retailers could begin selling DVD versions of films on the same days that the videocassette versions were available only for rental. By 2003, DVD rentals were outnumbering videocassette rentals.

Only two decades after the first video rental store had appeared, an entirely new business model revolutionized the industry. In 1999, Netflix began renting DVDs through the mail for flat monthly fees to subscribers who used the Internet to place their orders. Within two years, Netflix claimed to have enrolled more than 3.5 million subscribers in the United States alone. This model was soon copied by other companies, including Blockbuster, some of which also rented other video-based materials, such as video games. By 2007, more than 9 million households had online subscriptions to video rental services, which were generating more than one billion dollars in annual revenues. Meanwhile, the annual revenues of traditional video stores declined to about $60 million.

In 2007, with the rapid increases in the number of online video downloads and new interactive services such as video on demand, many analysts predicted the imminent end of the video rental industry. However, 2008 witnessed a new reinvention of this always evolving industry, when Steve Jobs, chief executive officer of Apple, announced the addition of a movie-rental feature to iTunes. In February, Apple added 1,000 films to its library.

Rikard Bandebo

FURTHER READING

Dana, J. D., and K. E. Spier. "Revenue Sharing and Vertical Control in the Video Rental Industry." *Journal of Industrial Economics* 49, no. 3 (2001): 223-246.

Narayanan, V. G., and Lisa Bren. *That's a Wrap: The Dynamics of the Video Rental Industry.* Cambridge, Mass.: Harvard Business Publishing, 2002.

SEE ALSO: Copyright law; Fiber-optic industry; Films with business themes; Fishing industry; Music industry; Rental industry; Telecommunications industry; Television broadcasting industry; Television programming with business themes.

Vietnam War

THE EVENT: Conflict between North and South Vietnam in which the United States first supported French efforts, then provided aid and U.S. troops to South Vietnam

DATE: 1959-1975

PLACE: Southeast Asia

SIGNIFICANCE: When the United States began sending combat forces to Vietnam in 1965, the American economy became overstimulated by the war expenses, resulting in higher wages, higher prices, and significant inflation. Government spending on the war and tax increases burdened American businesses despite war-related contracts. At the end of the war, the U.S. economy suffered from stagflation and no peace dividend materialized.

At the end of World War II in 1945, the American business community worried that countries that became communist would separate themselves from the capitalist system that drove the American economy. The decision by President Harry S. Truman to contain communism globally was cheered by U.S. businesses. In Vietnam, the nationalist movement fighting against French attempts to reestablish colonial power was led by Ho Chi Minh, an avowed communist. Ho's allegiance to the Communist Party persuaded the United States to place its support behind France.

For the American business community, Vietnam was essentially economically irrelevant. Pre-World War II U.S. trade with colonial French Indochina—Vietnam, Cambodia, and Laos—was very light. In 1939, U.S. exports to Indochina were worth just $2.5 million and U.S. imports, primarily rubber, added up to $10.7 million. After World War II, American businesses were interested in strengthening the Japanese and West European economies so that these countries could withstand the surge of communism. However, Japan and France viewed Vietnam as a vital potential market with important natural resources.

FRANCE GOES TO WAR

The United States grudgingly sided with France when war broke out in Vietnam. After Ho Chi Minh rejected a French proposal for limited Vietnamese autonomy, French warships bombed the Vietnamese-held harbor of Haiphong on November 23, 1946. While France sought U.S. aid for its war in Vietnam, it also jealously guarded its colonial economic privileges. It objected, for example, to oil exploration in Vietnam by Texaco.

On May 8, 1950, Truman agreed to provide aid for the French war effort, officially funneled through the semi-independent state of Vietnam founded that year. From 1950 to mid-1954, the United States supported the French war in Vietnam with some $3.6 billion, paying 75 to 80 percent of the French war expenses with U.S. taxpayer money.

U.S. AIDS SOUTH VIETNAM

The Geneva Accords of July 21, 1954, temporarily halted the Vietnam War. Cambodia and Laos became independent. Vietnam was temporarily partitioned into the communist North Vietnam and the noncommunist South Vietnam. U.S. support of South Vietnam enabled Ngo Dinh Diem to stabilize the Republic of Vietnam (RVN) in South Vietnam after the October 23, 1955, referendum. From 1955 to 1959, the United States provided Diem with $1.7 billion in military and $1.2 billion in economic aid.

U.S. representatives in Saigon were unhappy with Diem's unwillingness to use U.S. economic aid to promote Vietnamese economic development and his spending up to two-thirds of the aid on consumer goods, often imported from France. Diem's distrust of private versus state-owned enterprises exasperated American businessmen in South Vietnam. They also fought against Vietnamese restrictions on direct foreign investment and wanted some guarantees against nationalization of American-owned businesses in Vietnam.

Beginning in late 1950, the United States sent U.S. soldiers to act as military advisers to Diem. When war in South Vietnam flared up again in 1957, the number of soldiers grew from the initial 77 to more than 1,000 in 1961. At a rough annual cost of $25,000 per soldier, this cost the United States an additional $25 million.

By late 1963, Diem was losing the fight against the communists. The United States acquiesced to a coup that killed and replaced him with a military junta. However, even ever-increasing American aid could not win the junta's war against the communists. Year after year, the war in South Vietnam cost the U.S. economy more money, with few positive results.

Determined to keep South Vietnam from becoming communist, President Lyndon B. Johnson authorized the landing of U.S. Marines in Da Nang on March 8, 1965. In April, 1965, Johnson offered North Vietnam a billion-dollar economic aid program if the North stopped its aggression in South Vietnam, but Hanoi declined. By May, 1965, Johnson was forced to ask for the first supplemental budget increase of $700 million to finance the war in Vietnam for the remainder of fiscal year 1965. By

August, the U.S. economists began warning that the costs of the Vietnam War could cause economic trouble. However, President Johnson still believed the U.S. economy was strong enough to pay both for the Vietnam War and his Great Society social projects without a tax increase.

FROM BOOM TO INFLATION

The United States' full-scale engagement in the Vietnam War increased government spending for military operations, equipment, and aid to Vietnam. Low unemployment dropped further as young men were drafted for temporary military service, leading to a significant rise in labor costs. Prices rose as U.S. companies passed on these higher costs to their customers. In December, 1965, the Federal Reserve raised the discount rate from 4 to 4.5 percent to fight inflation.

In early 1966, the U.S. economy boomed. Americans bought new cars, fearing that the government might restrict domestic car production as was done in the Korean War. This fear proved groundless, but consumer spending increased, as did wages and prices. The consumer price index, which had been increasing annually at a rate of 1.2 percent from 1960 to 1964, rose at the rate of 3.5 percent in 1966. The wholesale price index rose, climbing from an annual rate of 0.0 percent to 2.2 percent in 1966. This increase was driven by direct and indirect government expenses for the Vietnam War and the Great Society programs. A tightening of the money supply by the Federal Reserve led to the credit crunch of 1966.

For the 1966 U.S. budget, the $4.4 billion for direct war expenses had to be supplemented by an additional $1.4 billion, and the war continued to rage with no end in sight. A proposed 1967 tax increase to cover the cost of the Vietnam War failed, and the government resorted to deficit spending.

OPPOSITION TO THE WAR

By 1968, the majority of U.S. businesses turned against the war in Vietnam. Together with many other segments of American society, the business community was disillusioned by the communists' surprise Tet offensive in February. By the end of fiscal year 1967, the original budget for direct military expenditures to fight the war in Vietnam nearly dou-

MILITARY COSTS OF MAJOR TWENTIETH CENTURY WARS

War	Years of War Spending	Military Cost ($ billions)
World War I	1917-1921	253
World War II	1941-1945	4,114
Korea	1950-1953	320
Vietnam	1965-1975	686
Persian Gulf War	1990-1991	96

Source: Data from Stephen Daggett, "CROS Report for Congress: Costs of Major U.S. Wars," Congressional Research Service, July 24, 2008.

Note: Cost is in constant fiscal year 2008 dollars.

bled from $10.2 billion to $19.4 billion, and $21.4 billion was projected for fiscal year 1968. Indirect costs of the war, such as those incurred by keeping draftees out of the civilian economy and providing for future veterans' benefits and pensions, were not included in these budgets.

The American business community was deeply concerned about the cost of the war in Vietnam, viewing the conflict as predominantly a drain on the domestic economy and the trigger for unhealthy inflation. Businessmen blamed the March 14, 1968, run on the dollar and the ensuing gold crisis on the Vietnam War and disliked the increase in domestic unrest caused by antiwar demonstrations. U.S. business leaders felt that the United States could not continue to pay for both the Vietnam War and the Great Society, stabilize the dollar, and avoid new taxes. The business community was also aware that what people perceived as the government's misconduct in handling the war was creating massive distrust of big business. America's New Left combined opposition to the Vietnam War with popularization of its anticapitalist agenda.

Government spending for the Vietnam War also affected the U.S. trade balance, diminishing the surplus from about $4.7 billion in 1967 to a mere $1.4 billion in 1968. American businesses complained that the leaders of South Vietnam spent much of American economic aid on French consumer goods.

Given the U.S. business community's dissatisfaction with Johnson's conduct of the war in Vietnam, it is not surprising that stocks jumped on March 31, 1968, when Johnson announced that he would not seek reelection and would try to negotiate peace with North Vietnam. In June, 1968, Congress finally enacted a 10 percent tax surcharge to help pay the cost of the Vietnam War.

END OF U.S. INVOLVEMENT

When Richard M. Nixon became president in January, 1969, he did so with a promise to end the war. Unemployment was still at a low 3.6 percent, because the draft had removed many young men from the labor pool. The consumer price index rose 4.9 percent annually, the growth of the gross national product slowed, corporate profits declined, and utilization of production capacity fell.

The business community was pleased with the prospect of reducing U.S. troops in Vietnam and ne-

gotiating with the North to end the war. However, when Nixon instead announced on April 30, 1970, that American troops had entered Cambodia, the U.S. stock market plunged by 15 percent. As the draft slowed down, the unemployment rate began to rise. The Federal Reserve's decision to increase the money supply during the 1970 fiscal crisis further heated up inflation.

As Nixon tried to wind down the Vietnam War, its cumulative effects hit the U.S. economy. The country slid into a recession from 1970 to 1972. In 1971, the trade balance turned negative. The dollar was devalued in 1971 and 1973. Then, the United States suffered stagflation, or economic stagnation coupled with high inflation.

Nixon finally negotiated a peace deal with North Vietnam on January 27, 1973. As the U.S. economy entered a severe recession from November, 1973, to March, 1975, there was little U.S. business support for aid to South Vietnam, and Congress cut aid from $1 billion to $700 million in 1974. Although American companies still did business in South Vietnam in 1974 and about ten thousand Americans were employed by the South Vietnamese government in military and economic advisory positions, the deterioration of the military situation after January, 1975, led to the U.S. economic disengagement from South Vietnam. Saigon fell on April 30, 1975, ending the war with a communist victory.

AFTERSHOCKS IN U.S. BUSINESS

Engagement in the Vietnam War from 1965 to 1975 cost the United States about $111 billion, worth about $686 billion in 2008 fiscal year constant dollars. Some 58,000 U.S. soldiers were killed. The cost of the economic reintegration of about 7.9 million U.S. soldiers who served in Vietnam, most of them draftees, and their claims to veterans' benefits (education, medical expenses, and pensions) is very difficult to calculate. Estimates vary widely and are billions apart. In 1987, the unemployment rate of Vietnam War veterans was 5.2 percent, higher than the 4.3 percent rate for the general population.

After the Vietnam War ended, there was no peace dividend because the Department of Defense easily swallowed the roughly $22 billion budgeted annually for the war until 1973. The money saved was spent on other defense projects and used to offset rising costs due to inflation.

In May, 1975, President Gerald R. Ford imposed

a U.S. trade embargo on Vietnam. It was lifted in February, 1994, only because U.S. businesses complained that the embargo deprived U.S. companies of opportunities enjoyed by European and Asian competitors. After lifting the embargo, U.S. exports to Vietnam rose from $7 million in 1993 to $173 million in 1994, and imports from zero to $50 million. After the United States recognized the Socialist Republic of Vietnam in 1997, Vietnam joined the World Trade Organization in 2007. That year, the United States imported $10.6 billion worth of Vietnamese goods and exported nearly $2 billion worth, signs of an unbalanced, but vigorous, trade relationship.

R. C. Lutz

FURTHER READING

Campagna, Anthony S. *The Economic Consequences of the Vietnam War.* New York: Praeger, 1991. Discusses the economic impact of the Vietnam War on the United States during the conflict. Pays close attention to all aspects of the economy, including the reintegration of Vietnam veterans. Tables, bibliography, index.

Herring, George C. *America's Longest War.* New York: McGraw-Hill, 1996. Covers economic issues within a general history of the Vietnam War. Informative and well written. Illustrated, notes, bibliography, index.

Karnow, Stanley. *Vietnam: A History.* 2d ed. New York: Viking Press, 1997. Standard history of the Vietnam War that pays attention to the effect of the war on American businesses as it discusses the conflict. Although it does not contain a separate chapter on economic issues, reading this widely available book gives useful insight into this aspect of the war. Illustrated.

LaFeber, Walter. *The Deadly Bet: LBJ, Vietnam, and the 1968 Election.* Lanham, Md.: Rowman & Littlefield, 2005. Comprehensive review of how the negative economic impact of the Vietnam War affected the 1968 U.S. presidential elections. Author writes accessibly and with interest in economic issues. Illustrated, notes, bibliography, index.

Lawrence, Mark Atwood. *Assuming the Burden: Europe and the American Commitment to War in Vietnam.* Berkeley: University of California Press, 2005. Excellent study of how the United States came to support France's retaking of its Indochinese colony for a variety of economic and political reasons. Scholarly but accessible work. Notes, bibliography, index.

Schulzinger, Robert. *A Time for War.* New York: Oxford University Press, 1997. Section "Economic Effects of the War" summarizes the late 1960's. Illustrated, notes, index, bibliography.

SEE ALSO: Asian trade with the United States; Drug trafficking; Immigration; Iraq wars; Korean War; Military-industrial complex; Wars.

W

Wages

DEFINITION: Compensation in money paid to hired labor

SIGNIFICANCE: Wages are a major component of business costs, and wage policy is an important tool for management. Wage income is the principal source of consumption spending.

Firms employ labor to produce and earn profits. In a competitive free-market economy, wages are determined by the supply of and demand for labor of various descriptions. Real wages measure the amount of goods and services represented by the money wage. The supply of labor reflects the size, composition, skill, education, and attitudes of the population. Demand for labor reflects labor productivity and demand for the firm's product.

Although colonial North America was sparsely populated, it possessed a vast amount of fertile land and other natural resources. Consequently, labor productivity and real wages were high relative to their counterparts in European countries. Many Americans were self-employed as farmers, craftspeople, or owners of small businesses. Because land was cheap and fertile, workers always had the option of becoming independent farmers, and employers had to pay a sufficient wage to compete with this opportunity. The exception was the South, where slavery was a response to the labor shortage and less hospitable climate.

Throughout its history, the United States has been a high-wage country. Labor productivity and demand for labor grew steadily, reflecting the upgrading of labor education and skills, growth of productive capital, and improvements in technology and organization. High wages and a freely competitive labor market attracted millions of immigrants, but over the long run, demand for labor outran supply. Researcher Donald Adams estimated that real wages during the 1960's were about thirteen times as large as those in the first decade of the nineteenth century. Considering the radical change in the items of consumption, these comparisons cannot be very precise. However, it is clear that both the number of hours worked per person and the physical demands of work declined substantially over the same period.

THE NINETEENTH CENTURY

In 1800, only about 10 percent of the labor force were employees, and that proportion rose only to 30 percent by 1850. At that time, the principal form of wage labor was on farms. Around that time, male farmworkers received about $8 a month plus meals and sleeping accommodations worth another $6 a month. To the modern reader, these seem absurdly low, but prices were correspondingly low. Numerous observers indicated that in 1820-1840, a hired farmworker could earn and save enough in a year or two to purchase a farm productive enough to support a family. Such wage rates were well above the minimum needed for survival.

The earliest major manufacturing industry was textile production, which began in New England. Around 1820, nearly half of the employees of water-powered textile mills were children, who were paid on the order of 18 to 25 cents a day. Most of the other textile workers were adult women, who were paid around 40 cents a day. As late as 1910, children constituted as much as one-sixth of the labor force.

For men, construction became a major form of wage employment. There was always a need for houses, barns, and shops, but from the 1820's, major construction operations extended the nation's transport systems—first canals, then railways. A dollar a day was a common wage for arduous manual labor. Heavy industry became a major employer, with iron and steel significant industries by 1860. Transport innovation raised the productivity of labor in most sectors. Researchers Adam and Stanley Lebergott estimated real wages rose from 1800 to 1860 by anywhere from 50 to 100 percent.

The U.S. Civil War generated severe inflation, destroyed human and material resources, and disorganized production in the South. Not surprisingly, real wages were lower in 1861-1879, on average, than before the war. From that point, real wages showed steady improvement, rising about 50 percent between 1860 and 1910. This was quite a remarkable achievement. Immigration was high over that entire period, adding to labor supply. Labor unions played only an inconsequential role. The rise in real wages was a testimonial to the effect of competition among employers in a period of rapid technological and organizational improvement.

THE TWENTIETH CENTURY

The powerful and unmistakable improvement in real wages continued into the 1970's, after which the evidence becomes harder to interpret. Child labor faded away, while female labor-force participation expanded greatly. Henry Ford created a sensation in 1914, when he set wages at $5 a day for his automobile workers. Government became a major employer, leading to the creation of a substantial segment of non-market-determined wages. The number of workers engaged in farming reached a peak in 1920, then declined. Wage and salary employees, who constituted only 46 percent of employment in 1900, accounted for 89 percent in 2005.

The labor market was severely shocked by the major economic depression of 1929-1940. The decrease in aggregate demand led to massive unemployment, reaching a peak level of 25 percent in 1933. Money wage rates fell—but apparently no more than prices, so real wage rates (per hour) hardly declined. Various government interventions attempted to prevent wage declines. Wage policy was an important part of the National Industrial Recovery Act of 1933 and the National Labor Relations (Wagner) Act of 1935. The Davis-Bacon Act of 1931 required firms supplying construction services to the federal government to pay the equivalent of union scale. The Fair Labor Standards Act of 1938 established the federal minimum wage, which began at 25 cents an hour. Creation of the overtime penalty wage helped reduce the average workweek.

World War II restored full employment, attracted many more women into the labor force, and increased the scope and power of labor unions. Wages came under the same control programs as prices. Income-tax withholding was introduced, and employers were also obligated to deduct wage taxes for Social Security, unemployment compensation, and (after 1965) Medicare. An important response to high income-tax rates and wage controls was the spread of fringe benefits—wage supplements such as paid vacations and sick leave, retirement benefits, and medical insurance.

MODERN WAGE ISSUES

One issue commonly discussed is whether real wages continued to rise after 1970. By 2006, money wages were vastly higher than in 1970—hourly earnings rose from $3.40 in 1970 to $16.76 in 2006. However, consumer prices increased as much or more. So estimated real wage rates in 1982 prices actually declined from $8.46 in 1970 to $8.24 in 2006. Real earnings per week show an even larger decline. However, these results, estimated by the Department of Labor, conflict with other data in the national income accounts. Total compensation of employees, divided by total employment and adjusted to remove inflation, virtually doubled between 1970 and 2006. Real personal disposable income per capita and real consumption per capita both more than doubled between 1970 and 2006. Part of the discrepancy arises because the Labor Department wage series does not allow for fringe benefits. The cost of some benefits, such as medical insurance, increased greatly after 1970.

Another way of comparing 1970 with later years is provided by researchers W. Michael Cox and Richard Alm, who estimated the number of hours of work it would take to buy various consumer products in their book, *Myths of Rich and Poor: Why We're Better Off than We Think* (1999). Most products required fewer hours of work to purchase, suggesting rising real wages.

The safest conclusion is that real wages after 1976 did not show the same clear-cut increase as in earlier years. Estimated labor productivity roughly doubled between 1970 and 2006, however, many people felt their real wages did not increase.

WORK TIME IN MINUTES REQUIRED TO BUY VARIOUS PRODUCTS

Product	1920	1950	1970	Late 1990's
Milk, half-gallon	13	16	10	7
Bread, half-pound loaf	37	6	4	3.5
Oranges, dozen	69	21	15	9
Gasoline, gallon	32	11	6.4	5.7
Chicken, 3 pounds	147	71	22	14
Big Mac	—	—	10	8

Source: Data from W. Michael Cox and Richard Alm, *Myths of Rich and Poor: Why We're Better Off than We Think* (New York: Basic Books, 1999)

EMPLOYEE COMPENSATION AND PRINCIPAL COMPONENTS, 1970 AND 2006, IN BILLIONS OF DOLLARS

Type of Compensation	1970	2006
Wage and salary		
Government	117	1,021
Other	434	5,005
Employer contributions		
Pension and insurance	42	971
Government social insurance	24	452
Total	617	7,448

Source: Data from *Economic Report of the President Transmitted to the Congress February 2008 Together with the Annual Report of the Council of Economic Advisers* (Washington, D.C.: Executive Office of the President, Council of Economic Advisers, 2008)

Between 1970 and 2006, the two employer components of fringe costs rose from about 11 percent of total compensation to 19 percent.

Another frequently discussed issue is whether there was significant discrimination in the wages of women and ethnic minorities. Certainly there were significant differences in pay among these groups. According to the *Statistical Abstract of the United States* (2008), median weekly earnings in 2006 were $671 for all ethnicities and both genders. For men, the median weekly earnings were $743, with whites drawing $761, blacks $591, and Hispanics $505. For women, the median weekly earnings were $600, with whites drawing $609, blacks $519, and Hispanics $440.

A large part of the observed pay differences can be explained by differences in age, education, experience, and types of work. In earlier times, employment discrimination based on race and gender was widespread. However, economists have long contended that a profit-seeking market economy overrides prejudice because greedy entrepreneurs will be quick to hire undervalued workers, eroding discriminatory pay. Some recent statistical studies (trying to compare workers from the different groups with the same qualifications and job specifications) continue to find discrimination. Others do not. What is evident is that the more clear-cut differences in pay have gradually been reduced by a combination of market competition and government anti-discrimination policies.

INFLUENCE OF LABOR UNIONS

The relative importance of unions grew after the National Labor Relations Act of 1935, reaching a maximum during the 1950's, when about one-third of private-sector employees were union members. Since then, the proportion has declined; in 2006, it was only 7 percent. Union strongholds such as the steel and automotive industries have declined in relative importance. Researcher Barry Hirsch provides estimates of the extent to which union wages have exceeded nonunion wages in major sectors. For the private sector as a whole, the union premium was about 40 percent in 1973 and declined only slightly, to about 35 percent, by 2006. Most economists believe these gains come at the expense of consumers and nonunion workers, because unions do not in general raise worker productivity very much. Evidence of the continuing importance of unions was observed in the hardships of unionized Michigan-based automobile manufacturers versus the thriving condition of newly established (nonunionized) automobile factories in other areas, particularly in southern states.

Paul B. Trescott

FURTHER READING

Atack, Jeremy, and Peter Passell. *A New Economic View of American History.* New York: W. W. Norton, 1994. Chapter 19 gives an excellent overview of the market for labor from a historical perspective.

Ehrenberg, Ronald G., and Robert S. Smith. *Modern Labor Economics.* 6th ed. New York: Pearson/Addison Wesley, 1996. This college-level text puts wages into historical and analytical perspective. There are chapters on pay and productivity, discrimination, and the influence of unions.

Hirsch, Barry T. "Sluggish Institutions in a Dynamic World: Can Unions and Industrial Competition Coexist?" *Journal of Economic Perspectives* 22, no. 1 (Winter, 2008): 153-176. His short answer is "not very well." Good historical review of the extent and influence of unionization.

Lebergott, Stanley. *Manpower in Economic Growth: The American Record Since 1800.* New York: McGraw Hill, 1964. Historical development of wages (there are lots of examples) is integrated with all elements of labor supply and demand.

"Symposium on Discrimination in Product, Credit, and Labor Markets." *Journal of Economic Perspectives* 12, no. 2 (Spring, 1998): 63-126. William Darity and Patrick Mason present evidence of persisting discrimination, while James Heckman takes a skeptical view.

SEE ALSO: Business cycles; Child labor; Farm labor; Immigration; Inflation; Labor history; Labor strikes; Minimum wage laws; National Labor Relations Board; Women in business.

Walker, Madam C. J.

IDENTIFICATION: African American entrepreneur and philanthropist
BORN: December 23, 1867; Delta, Louisiana
DIED: May 25, 1919; Irvington-on-Hudson, New York
SIGNIFICANCE: The daughter of former slaves, Walker became the first female millionaire in the United States by developing and marketing hair-care products for African American women.

Madam C. J. Walker was born Sarah Breedlove. She was orphaned when she was ten years old and widowed with a young daughter when she was only twenty years old. In 1889, she moved to St. Louis, Missouri, where she often earned only $1.50 per week as a washerwoman. Determined to create a better life for her family, in 1903, Breedlove began selling Wonderful Hair Grower for the Poro Company. A firm believer in self-improvement, she also took night-school classes. In 1905, she joined family in Denver and continued to sell hair-care products. In 1906, she married C. J. Walker, a newspaper sales agent whose name she later used to represent her company.

Shortly thereafter, Walker developed her own line of hair-care products for African American women. She claimed that her "secret formula" came to her in a dream. Others have speculated that the ingredients were based on the Poro products. She adopted the title of "Madam" and traveled extensively selling products and training women in the "Walker Method" of hair care.

In 1910, Walker relocated her company from Pittsburgh to Indianapolis, building offices and a manufacturing plant. The Madam C. J. Walker

A 1920 advertisement for Madam C. J. Walker's preparations, including cold cream and hair and complexion products. (Library of Congress)

Manufacturing Company provided work for approximately three thousand African American women. An additional twenty thousand agents sold Walker products throughout the United States, the Caribbean, and Central America. Her financial success allowed her to contribute generously to numerous organizations devoted to enhancing the status of African Americans. At the time of her death, Walker's estimated worth was $700,000.

Beth A. Messner

SEE ALSO: Seneca Falls Convention; Women in business.

Wall Street

IDENTIFICATION: New York neighborhood that is home to the major U.S. stock markets and is the traditional center of American securities trading
DATE: First housed financial trading during the late eighteenth century
SIGNIFICANCE: Wall Street is considered by many to be the financial center of the world. It is both an actual center of financial activity and a symbol of that activity. Wall Street has come to stand for America's economic power and pride and for the capitalist system itself.

Wall Street is the financial area surrounding a road of the same name in lower Manhattan. An actual wall was built in this area by the Dutch to protect against potential British attack during the middle of the seventeenth century, and the name remained after the wall was taken down. The term refers to more than just physical location, however, as a corporation is considered to be a "Wall Street company" based on its involvement in financial services, rather than its actual location on Wall Street.

The Wall Street area contains some of the oldest sky-scrapers in the world, and it is the location of the former World Trade Center that was destroyed on September 11, 2001. It houses a number of important United States stock exchanges, including the New York Stock Exchange (NYSE) and NASDAQ (National Association of Securities Dealers Automated Quotients). The place where U.S. monetary policy is executed, the Federal Reserve Bank of New York, is also located on Wall Street.

Wall Street is often used to stand for both the financial industry and those who work in that industry. Politicians and other social commentators routinely oppose Wall Street to Main Street to suggest the divergent experiences and interests of working- and middle-class people on one hand and wealthy investors and brokers on the other hand. This divergence has been complicated, however, by a trend during the late twentieth and early twenty-first centuries toward many middle-class persons investing in the stock market through their retirement plans.

Brion Sever

SEE ALSO: American Stock Exchange; Financial crisis of 2008; NASDAQ; New York Stock Exchange; Securities and Exchange Commission; Stock markets; *The Wall Street Journal.*

A view of Wall Street east from Nassau Street around 1911. (Library of Congress)

The Wall Street Journal

IDENTIFICATION: Daily international business newspaper published by Dow Jones & Company
DATE: Launched on July 8, 1889
SIGNIFICANCE: From its inception, *The Wall Street Journal* has provided reliable information for investors. It has become the quintessential source for specific facts as well as detailed studies of companies and industries. The newspaper also reaches beyond the marketplace, covering other areas of concern to its readers.

In November, 1882, two employees of the Keirnan News Agency decided to start their own financial news company. However, to create a successful business, Charles Henry Dow and Edward Davis Jones realized that they needed the abilities and financial contribution of Charles Milford Berstresser, another Keirnan employee. The three decided on the name Dow Jones & Company and set up shop at 15 Wall Street, close to the New York Stock Exchange. Initially, they called on banks, brokerage houses, and the various exchanges to get news tidbits, published as bulletins on flimsies.

In November, 1883, the firm added the *Customers' Afternoon Letter,* a summary of the day's market developments that sometimes contained a hint of financial things to come. Soon the publication had a circulation of more than one thousand and was regarded as an important source of financial news. In May, 1884, the firm purchased a printing press. It was small and cranked by hand, but the printed product was a vast improvement over the handwritten bulletins. By 1889, Dow Jones & Company employed fifty people, including Clarence W. Barron, its first out-of-town reporter, based in Boston.

The two-page *Customers' Afternoon Letter* was insufficient for publishing all the financial news the firm was gathering. A Campbell flatbed press was purchased, and on July 8, 1889, *The Wall Street Journal* was born. It was printed daily, except Sundays and stock exchange holidays, during the late afternoon, to include the day's financial activities. It cost 2 cents per issue, had four pages, and was hand-delivered to a few hundred subscribers. Policies of the newspaper were clearly stated, including its aim to be a paper of news, not opinion, and to provide a "faithful picture" of financial news on Wall Street.

The newspaper was unique in that it printed statistical and financial information not available in other daily publications. Its motto, "The truth in its proper use," reflected the newspaper's credo not to be influenced by advertisers or speculative interests. Reporters were warned against trading slanted stories for inside tips on stocks. On April 18, 1893, the paper moved to larger quarters to accommodate its growing circulation. By 1898, the first morning edition was published, and *The Wall Street Journal* was printing more than financial news. If something had the slightest impact on the economy, it was included. In 1902, Barron purchased Dow Jones & Company for $130,000. Within eight years, the circulation of the newspaper more than doubled from 7,000 to 18,750. Barron broadened *The Wall Street Journal*'s geographic presence by linking it with newspapers he owned in Boston and Philadelphia.

A NATIONAL NEWSPAPER

In the summer of 1929, *The Wall Street Journal*'s circulation had risen to nearly 50,000, and the financial future of both the newspaper and the country looked good. It appeared that each crisis in the stock market benefited circulation because people needed to know what was happening, and in October, the paper launched its Pacific coast edition, becoming the first daily to be published on both the East and West coasts. Although circulation increased in 1930 to 52,000, with another 3,000 subscribers to the Pacific coast edition, the impact of the Depression was soon felt. By 1933, the circulation of the combined editions was 28,000 subscribers; publisher Kenneth "Casey" Hogate decided the paper could no longer support two editions and, in September, 1934, dropped the evening edition. Other changes instituted by Hogate both rescued the paper from bankruptcy and paved the way for its transition from a financial to a business daily. New features included stock market quotes and columns, such as "Heard on the Street," "Mirror on Washington," and "What's News."

Under Bernard Kilgore, Hogate's successor, the paper was revitalized and became the nation's first national daily. Kilgore knew that to increase circulation, the paper had to change from a financial trade publication to a general newspaper, specializing in business and financial news. The December 8, 1941, issue, with its feature article on the implications of war for business, proved the newspaper was more than a stock-market-oriented publication; it was a national newspaper. The newspaper broadened its news coverage, included a wider range of subjects, and introduced new columns. A key feature on the front page explained the "whys" behind selected news events and how they affected business. In 1947, the paper won its first Pulitzer Prize.

A GLOBAL NEWSPAPER

In the summer of 1970, a Harris Poll proclaimed *The Wall Street Journal* America's "most trusted" newspaper, and by November, 1975, the paper was the first to use satellite technology, simultaneously printing the paper in eighteen plants throughout the country. Because of its increased coverage of news beyond the financial, the newspaper continued to grow in circulation and size. The *Asian Wall Street Journal* was launched in 1976 in Hong Kong, and *The Wall Street Journal*'s European edition began publication in 1983.

Over the years *The Wall Street Journal* has continued to evolve. It has redesigned its front page, added color and photographs, and established an online presence. With its reputation for independence and integrity, *The Wall Street Journal* is the authoritative resource for business, local and global, and its excellence in both financial and general news coverage has earned more than thirty Pulitzer

Prizes. The purchase of the newspaper by international media mogul Rupert Murdoch in 2007, for $5 billion, began another era for an American icon of publishing.

Marcia B. Dinneen

FURTHER READING

Crossen, Cynthia. "It All Began in the Basement of a Candy Store." *The Wall Street Journal*, August 1, 2007, p. B1+. A lengthy article, detailing the history of the newspaper, from the founders to Rupert Murdoch.

Crovitz, L. Gordon. "Publisher's Letter: Embracing Change to Build on a Tradition of Excellence." *Wall Street Journal*, January 2, 2007, p. G1. Discusses changes in the paper and its basic credo.

Dealy, Francis X., Jr. *The Power and the Money.* New York: Carol, 1993. A history of the newspaper, its successes, and its failures.

Rosenberg, Jerry M. *Inside The Wall Street Journal.* New York: Macmillan, 1982. Focuses on individuals who developed the newspaper, editors, and their accomplishments.

Wendt, Lloyd. *The Wall Street Journal.* Chicago: Rand McNally, 1982. Detailed history of the newspaper, centering on people who shaped it.

SEE ALSO: Advertising industry; *Barron's*; Bloomberg's Business News Services; *The Economist*; *Forbes*; *Fortune*; Newspaper industry; Stock markets; *USA Today*; Wall Street.

Wal-Mart

IDENTIFICATION: Chain of discount stores
DATE: Founded on July 2, 1962; incorporated on October 31, 1969
SIGNIFICANCE: Wal-Mart's rise to become one of the most successful business franchises in American history can be seen as either a Cinderella story, wherein a humble clerk from a small southern town built a mighty corporation through pluck and perseverance, or the sad saga of how aggressive merchandising and ruthless expansion led to the downfall of small businesses and the homogenization of the American marketplace.

Sam Walton opened the first Wal-Mart store in Bentonville in his home state of Arkansas in 1962.

His business approach was a simple one and continued to be company policy for decades: cut prices as low as feasibly possible and make up for lower profit margins on individual items with sheer volume of sales. By the end of the 1970's, Walton had created a chain of dozens of stores throughout much of the South and Midwest. In its first two decades, the chain tended to feature very inexpensive merchandise, some of which was often assumed to be shoddy and inferior. This aspect of the store was very much in keeping with the sort of traditional American shop of the early twentieth century that it originally exemplified: the five-and-dime store, so called because the items sold were inexpensive.

However, by the time that Walton stepped down as chief executive officer (CEO) in 1988, the corporation had begun to offer not only better merchandise but also a greater selection of wares, including furniture, clothing, and toys, especially in the labyrinthine Wal-Mart Supercenters first opened that year, called "super-Wal-Marts" by consumers. By 1998, Wal-Mart had begun to sell drugs, gardening and automotive supplies, and groceries. These and further additions made Wal-Mart an economical one-stop shopping center for many of America's working-class and middle-class families. For much of the first decade of the twenty-first century, the corporation was the largest in United States, bringing in annual revenues of $1.5 billion to $3 billion.

Although the chain was phenomenally successful, Wal-Mart's detractors complained that the corporation underpays workers and unfairly discourages labor unions. On a broader level, social critics have seen Wal-Mart's ascendency as the beginning of the end of small, independent American businesses and therefore as a major cause of lack of diversity in the marketplace and of the loss of community identity. During the early twenty-first century, tourists began to note how, in small towns in some parts of the United States, strangers were often

World's Five Largest Companies, 2008, by Revenue, in Millions of Dollars, Ranked by *Forbes*				
Rank	Company	Revenue	Profit	Assets
1	Wal-Mart	378,799	12,731	163,514
2	Exxon Mobil	372,824	40,610	242,082
3	Royal Dutch Shell	355,782	31,331	269,470
4	BP	291,438	20,845	236,076
5	Toyota	230,201	15,043	326,099

Source: Data from *Forbes*

given directions to local sites according to where the local Wal-Mart was situated, whereas in the past the point of orientation might have been a church, a school, or a natural feature of the landscape. Misgivings about the chain entered pop culture in caricatures, such as Megalo-Mart in the satiric FOX cartoon series, *King of the Hill* (started in 1997), and inspired numerous watchdog Web sites, such as WakeUpWalMart.com and WalMartWatch.com. In 2008, this backlash against Wal-Mart inspired H. Lee Scott, Jr., the corporation's CEO, to launch a campaign to rehabilitate the chain's image through attention to health care issues and the environment.

Thomas Du Bose

Further Reading

Bianco, Anthony. *Wal-Mart: The Bully of Bentonville— How the High Cost of Everyday Low Prices Is Hurting America.* 2006. Reprint. New York: Currency Doubleday, 2007.

Fishman, Charles. *The Wal-Mart Effect: How the World's Most Powerful Company Really Works—and How It's Transforming the American Economy.* New York: Penguin Press, 2006.

Norman, Al. *The Case Against Wal-Mart.* Atlantic City, N.J.: Raphel Marketing, 2004.

See also: Boycotts, consumer; Retail trade industry; Shipping industry; Thrift stores; United Food and Commercial Workers; Warehouse and discount stores.

War of 1812

THE EVENT: Military conflict between the United States and Great Britain

DATE: June 18, 1812-February 16, 1815

PLACE: The Atlantic Ocean, the American western territories, Canada, upstate New York, the Gulf Coast, and New Orleans

SIGNIFICANCE: The United States declared war on Great Britain partly in response to British interference with American maritime commerce and partly out of a desire to gain territory to the north and west. The Americans failed in their attempt to gain Canadian territory, but after the war's end, international commerce was able to resume unhindered.

By 1812, many sailors in Great Britain's Royal Navy had deserted to sign on with American naval and merchant ships, where pay and conditions were better. Constantly needing sailors, British naval vessels frequently stopped American ships to take, or "impress," sailors, whether they were British deserters or not. This practice was supported by the Orders in Council issued by the British cabinet, and it formed a major American grievance against the British. A particularly egregious incident in 1807 involved the British warship *Leopard*, which stopped the American ship *Chesapeake* and impressed four sailors, hanging one before sailing off. In an attempt to halt such outrages, the Americans resorted to economic measures: The Embargo Act of 1807 banned American trade with foreign ports, and the Non-Intercourse Act of 1809 banned trade with France and England.

THE WAR

Although the British government repealed the onerous Orders in Council in June, 1812, President James Madison requested and Congress granted a declaration of war against Britain on June 18, 1812, before the news of the repeal reached the United States. The initial actions of the war were naval engagements in the Atlantic Ocean connected with the British blockade of the American coast. The American navy was small but boasted several impressive ships, especially the *Constitution*, which bested the British ship *Guerrière* on August 19, 1812, in a three-hour battle and earned the

nickname "Old Ironsides," because British cannonballs could not penetrate its hull. Campaigns in the West did not go well for the Americans, as Fort Mackinac in Michigan, Fort Dearborn (Chicago), and Fort Detroit fell during July and August of 1812, and the American invasion of Canada was unsuccessful.

The most significant action in the Great Lakes was the Battle of Lake Erie (September 10, 1813), as Oliver Hazard Perry transferred from his disabled flagship *Lawrence* to the *Niagara*, from which he continued the battle and forced a British surrender. Throughout 1813 and 1814, British raiding parties devastated coastal towns along the Chesapeake Bay, causing fear and disrupting commerce, but the most humiliating episode of the war for the Americans was the British burning of Washington, D.C., on August 24 and 25, 1814, in retaliation for the American burning of the Parliament building in York, Canada. Such a blow was difficult to recover from, as most of the government buildings and some private residences were destroyed.

The British targeted Baltimore, Maryland, because it was a center for American privateers who preyed on British shipping. A two-pronged British attack by land and sea in September, 1814, failed, inspiring Francis Scott Key to write the poem that became known as *The Star Spangled Banner* and later became the national anthem. The British fleet sailed off, ending the threat in the Chesapeake. As part of their tactics, the British had offered slaves their free-

---

MILITARY COST OF THE WAR OF 1812, 1812-1815

- In current year dollars = $90 million

- In constant fiscal year (2008) dollars = $1,177 million

- War cost as percentage of gross domestic product in peak year, 1813 = 2.2%

- Total defense cost as percentage of gross domestic product in peak year, 1813 = 2.7%

Source: Data from Stephen Daggett, "CROS Report for Congress: Costs of Major U.S. Wars," Congressional Research Service, July 24, 2008

dom and transported several thousand slaves to British possessions. This was done both for humanitarian reasons and to disrupt the economic life of the region. During September, 1814, the British attempted to split New England states from New York by moving south from Canada through Lake Champlain. After this thrust was thwarted, the British withdrew.

THE TREATY

Although the United States had beaten back British military efforts on land and sea, the Americans had not conquered Canada and had acquired a huge debt, and the economy was in serious decline. Meanwhile, Britain's debt was increasing and it faced economic problems of its own. Both sides therefore agreed to peace talks in Ghent, the Netherlands. Britain desired to end the war to reach closure in Europe after Napoleon's first defeat and exile. The United States was troubled when members of the Federalist Party in New England met at the Hartford Convention (December, 1814-January, 1815) to consider succession from the nation because the war had seriously damaged the New England economy.

The Treaty of Ghent was signed on December 26, 1814, before Andrew Jackson's defense of New Orleans, (December, 1814-January, 1815) prevented Britain from choking off American trade to the interior of North America. A British victory at New Orleans might have altered the provisions of the Treaty of Ghent, which was ratified by the United States on February 16, 1815. The main provisions of the treaty were a return of territories to their prewar status and recognition of the prewar border between Canada and the United States. In 1827, Britain agreed to pay £250,000 compensation for slaves carried away during the war. With the final defeat of Napoleon in June, 1815, impressments of sailors by the British ceased to be an issue.

Mark C. Herman

FURTHER READING

Benn, Carl. *The War of 1812.* Osceola, Wis.: Osprey, 2002. Short treatment with excellent maps and illustrations; useful coverage of the war's military engagements.

Borneman, Walter R. *1812: The War That Forged a Nation.* New York: Harper Collins, 2004. Focuses on the war's importance for securing American independence and providing a basis for additional territorial expansion.

Langguth, A. J. *Union, 1812: The Americans Who Fought the Second War of Independence.* New York: Simon & Schuster, 2006. This narrative focuses on the key personalities of the conflict and the role that individual effort played in the major battles.

Latimer, Jon. *1812: War with America.* Cambridge, Mass.: Belknap Press, 2007. Written from a British perspective, this scholarly work views the war as part of the much larger conflict with Napoleon.

Mahon, John K. *The War of 1812.* Gainesville: University Presses of Florida, 1972. Reprint. New York: Da Capo Press, 1991. Detailed, scholarly, analytical study that covers the background, events, and ending of the war.

SEE ALSO: Bank of the United States, Second; Depression of 1808-1809; Embargo Acts; European trade with the United States; Inflation; Panic of 1819; Piracy, maritime; Revolutionary War; Wars.

War surplus

DEFINITION: Real property and materials produced for military operations that are no longer needed by the federal government and are offered for public sale

SIGNIFICANCE: The availability of supplies and equipment initially manufactured for armed conflict, and the designation of industrial facilities and military installations as no longer required by the government, has resulted in the development of a number of business opportunities for entrepreneurs and large corporations. Practices for disposal of surplus property have generated significant controversy after every major conflict.

Most Americans associate the term "military surplus" with items of personal clothing and equipment made for use by soldiers during wartime that have been obtained and sold to the public by retailers operating small specialty stores set up for that purpose. Personal gear actually makes up only a small portion of the military surplus that, for more than two hundred years, has been made available by the government as a means of disposing of unnecessary or outmoded assets. Included in the list of surplus items have been various forms of weaponry, industrial properties, and real estate, including entire military installations deemed no longer necessary. Although the federal government has passed along some of its military surplus to its allies, either as outright grants or through discount purchases, it has also made billions of dollars of surplus materials available to individuals and corporations, allowing for the establishment or enhancement of businesses that have been instrumental in the growth of the American economy.

Surplus materials were available after the Revolutionary War, the War of 1812, and the Mexican War. During the early years of the republic, the sale of war surplus materials provided much needed revenue to the national treasury. Because military clothing and personal equipment was not then radically different from items produced for use by the general populace, it was often easy for the government to obtain what it needed from civilian sources and to find buyers for surplus. After the U.S. Civil War, the government found it had large amounts of personal and organizational gear on hand when the massive Union and Confederate armies were demobilized. Various military bureaus within the uniformed services, as well as the secretaries of war, the Navy, and the Treasury, all had a hand in managing the sale or transfer of surplus materials. Both the government and the business community suffered from the absence of a coordinated system for disposing of surplus from the various branches of the armed forces.

SALES OF SURPLUSES

As warfare became increasingly more complex, industrial mobilization and the consequent problems of disposing of surplus became more challenging. For example, during World War I, the United States undertook a hitherto unprecedented effort to place the nation's economy on a wartime footing to supply its allies and mount its own expeditionary force to fight in Europe. When that conflict ended in November, 1918,

the government found itself with some $4 billion in surplus equipment and supplies.

A concerted effort was made to coordinate sales of much of this material to the public, and as a consequence a new form of business sprang up across the country: the Army-Navy store. Entrepreneurs bought clothing and other personal gear from the government at bargain prices and then sold it to the general public, many of whom were already familiar with the quality of this merchandise. Stockpiles of materials such as copper, leather, and steel were sold off gradually, so as not to cause severe economic harm to businesses trading in those commodities. Sales of more expensive assets, such as plants built with government support to produce munitions, chemicals, and other materials for the war effort, were often sold off at a fraction of the cost of construction. Government officials were accused of giving preferential treatment to large corporations, which were able to obtain high-value assets with relatively minimal investment. There were thousands of complaints that the Woodrow Wilson administration mishandled sales of surplus property.

When European nations went to war in 1939, the administration of President Franklin D. Roosevelt realized it would be only a matter of time before the United States would be required to join in the hostilities. Determined to avoid some of the mistakes that

This military surplus store in Miami sold out its gas masks after the terrorist attacks on September 11, 2001. (AP/Wide World Photos)

had plagued the Wilson administration in disposing of surplus after World War I, Roosevelt's advisers as early as 1940 began drafting plans for a postwar industrial buildup. These plans incorporated a scheme for managing military surplus, including industrial plants built or modified for production of war materiel.

PROFITING FROM SURPLUS

Principles for using the war surplus as a means of rejuvenating the peacetime economy were incorporated into the Surplus Property Act of 1944, which specifically stated that small businesses were to be the chief beneficiaries of government efforts to return surplus property and equipment to the general economy. The War Assets Administration was established to handle sales of nearly $40 billion in surplus materiel. The rush to demobilize and the ability of larger corporations to outbid small enterprises for the most lucrative real estate, buildings, and expensive equipment left many small-business owners—including thousands of returning veterans—at a disadvantage.

One group that did manage to profit from the availability of surplus equipment being sold at pennies on the dollar was the owners of Army-Navy stores, who soon found themselves in possession of items such as clothing, bedding, dining ware, tools, and outdoor equipment that had proven useful during the war. A ready group of consumers was happy to purchase these items, and for nearly half a century, stores featuring military surplus did a booming business in virtually every region of the country. As materials became available after the Vietnam War during the 1970's and the Persian Gulf War during the 1990's, dealers were able to update their stock. During the 1990's, however, it became increasingly more difficult for them to obtain surplus items from the government. Undaunted, these entrepreneurs began contracting with firms that made equipment for military use, obtaining directly from manufacturers items that had the look and feel of the gear being issued to soldiers, sailors, airmen, and marines.

In addition to these individual store owners, other groups of businesspeople have benefited greatly from the government's efforts to dispose of unneeded equipment and real estate. At the end of both World War I and World War II, aircraft, vehicles, and heavy equipment were returned to manufacturers for a fraction of their original cost, or auctioned to firms who wished to convert them for civilian use or simply turn them into scrap metal, a commodity with substantial commercial value. Additionally, beginning in 1945, the government sold off more than a thousand industrial facilities to businesses wishing to continue manufacturing products for which these plants had been designed, or to companies wishing to convert them to produce other goods. Large corporations involved in chemical, textile, aviation, or automotive manufacturing were able to increase their assets by purchasing specialized facilities for a fraction of what it had cost the government to construct them. At the same time, the government benefited by seeing some return on its investment, and millions of individuals, especially veterans, benefited because jobs were created in these facilities.

THE DLA SUPERVISES

When the Defense Logistics Agency (DLA) was created in 1961 to bring better organization to all military supply operations, the new agency was assigned as one of its missions the sale of surplus property. Initially, the agency worked closely with businesses and individuals to conduct auctions at which surplus items not designated for use by other government agencies or U.S. allies were offered to the public. What the government and the business community soon learned was that it was not necessary for there to be a war to have a surplus of war products available. The constant changes in the size and composition of the fighting force and its support services, and the rapid pace of technological advances, made much military gear—personal items, transportation and engineering equipment, and weapons systems—obsolete much more quickly than in the past.

To manage disposal of surplus property, the Defense Logistics Agency established the Defense Reutilization and Management Service (DRMS), which in turn opened offices at various locations throughout the country to manage the cataloging, storage, and sale of millions of items valued at billions of dollars. The advent of the Internet as a tool of commerce also had an impact on the ability of the public to obtain surplus military equipment and supplies. In 2001, the Defense Reutilization and Management Service entered into a partnership with a private firm that took over responsibility for storage and sales of surplus. That firm established a Web site and began conducting online auctions.

Under Defense Logistic Agency supervision, detailed procedures were established for determining not only which items might be sold but also the condition in which they would be released from the government to private buyers. Because many items declared surplus by the military still had potential for use as weaponry or for intelligence purposes, the services were directed to develop a process to identify sensitive items so that these could be "demilitarized" before sale. Despite these precautions, poor supervision and a confusing bureaucracy often resulted in private citizens and businesses being able to purchase high-dollar, militarily sensitive equipment such as radar systems, weapons, and delivery systems. As a result, a lucrative business in arms trading sprang up during the 1970's and extended well beyond the close of the twentieth century.

From time to time, businesses and local communities have benefited from the government's decision to cease operating an entire military installation. A number of forts, air bases, and naval stations passed to states, counties, or private organizations in this fashion. Beginning in 1989, under the terms of a law passed by Congress to assure fair assessment of an installation's value for continuing use, the Base Realignment and Closure (BRAC) Commission conducted hearings and designated installations to be closed, with real estate assets being transferred to other entities. Some were sold to commercial developers, who in turn have converted existing facilities or demolished them to transform these sites for private or community use. Thriving business parks and new residential communities were created on sites of former military installations in nearly every region of the country, often providing handsome profits for those willing to invest in these redevelopment efforts.

Laurence W. Mazzeno

FURTHER READING

Brandes, Stuart D. *Warhogs: A History of War Profits in America.* Lexington: University Press of Kentucky, 1997. Briefly describes government efforts to dispose of surplus property after the world wars. Also examines the larger issue of the government's relationship with the business community from the eighteenth through the twentieth centuries.

Cain, Louis, and George Neumann. "Planning for Peace: The Surplus Property Act of 1944." *Journal of Economic History* 41, no. 1 (March, 1981): 129-135. Examines the federal government's efforts to maximize benefits and limit ill effects caused by the disposal of war surplus after World War II. Outlines objectives of the law passed to control production and eventual disposal of property.

Cary, Peter, et al. "Weapons Bazaar." *U.S. News and World Report* 121, no. 23 (December 9, 1996): 26-37. Describes problems of controlling sales of weapons to U.S. citizens, foreign nationals, and foreign governments. Outlines the elaborate process the Defense Logistics Agency established to classify and dispose of surplus arms, missiles, aircraft, and ammunition.

Chiles, James R. "How the Great War on War Surplus Got Won—or Lost." *Smithsonian* 26, no. 9 (December, 1995): 52-61. Details the quantities and varieties of war surplus that the government needed to dispose of at the end of World War II, methods used to transfer usable property to various businesses and individuals, and the ill-feeling caused by what the public perceived as haphazard and unfair allocation of resources.

Koistinen, Paul. *Planning War, Pursuing Peace: The Political Economy of American Warfare, 1920-1939.* Lawrence: University Press of Kansas, 1998. Includes a discussion of efforts of the Wilson Administration to dispose of surplus materiel after World War I; reports on results of federal commissions charged with overseeing government operations during and after hostilities.

Wyld, David C. "Government Liquidation: How Online Auctions Will Replace Bob's Army-Navy Store." *Journal of Internet Commerce* 4, no. 4 (March, 2006): 41-58. Describes efforts at the Department of Defense to take advantage of electronic methods of advertising and selling surplus materials, and explains officials' efforts to subcontract the process to a private firm to manage online sales and store surplus equipment and supplies for the government.

SEE ALSO: Government spending; Iraq wars; Military-industrial complex; Vietnam War; Wars; World War I; World War II.

Warehouse and discount stores

DEFINITION: Retail stores that stock wide varieties of goods, some at unusually low prices

SIGNIFICANCE: The rise of discount and warehouse stores fundamentally changed the economic landscape for American consumers by offering a large variety of products in a single location at relatively low price markups. These stores used bulk purchasing to undersell mom-and-pop neighborhood stores and drive them out of business.

Discount stores differ from traditional department stores by stocking a large selection of self-service goods, often including food, and containing checkout stands at a single place rather than having service counters in each department. They also may include such convenient features as photo-processing centers and pharmacies. They represent their prices as lower than those of more conventional retailers. Often, they will sell an extremely popular item at a loss to bring customers into the stores, but other items may be sold at the same prices as at traditional stores.

Warehouse stores are an evolution from discount stores. They usually stock goods in massive, floor-to-ceiling displays and have roving employees rather than clerks stationed at any one service point. They require the consumer to purchase most products in bulk, at presumably commensurate savings. They may also require payment of an annual membership fee.

AN EVOLUTIONARY PROCESS

These discount and warehouse chains gradually evolved from the department stores that arose in the latter part of the nineteenth century, their growth being facilitated by the development of mass-marketing techniques. Macy's; Sears, Roebuck; and Montgomery Ward were among the earliest and best-known department stores, and the Sears mail-order catalog, a fixture in almost every rural home, became legendary. From these roots, so-called variety stores also arose and became popular.

Smaller versions of full-service department stores, sometimes known as five-and-tens or five-and-dimes, sprang up. The most famous was the Woolworth chain found in almost every small town; its discount subsidiary was Woolco. Another popular and ubiquitous chain store was Kresge, which ul-

timately begat Kmart. Unable to compete with larger-scale operations, the last remaining Woolworth stores finally went out of business during the late 1990's. Their modern-day successors are low-price chains such as the 99 Cent Stores.

With the spread of the Great Depression during the 1930's, discount pricing grew more prevalent. Grocery supermarkets became an increasing factor, often replacing small mom-and-pop businesses entirely or causing them to combine into supermarkets. One of the very first discount stores was a radio and appliance store opened in Manhattan around 1937.

The further burgeoning of discount stores as a major factor in the economic lives of ordinary American families came during the late 1940's. It coincided with the return of millions of veterans who had served during World War II and with the baby boom that followed. In general, the late 1940's and the 1950's were a time of strong economic growth and high demand for goods and services. Growing families came to rely on the competitive pricing that discount stores could offer as a result of their bulk purchasing power and streamlined distribution networks. For the chance to buy more cheaply priced goods, customers were willing to give up some of the personal attention they had perhaps been accustomed to from small, individually owned businesses.

By the mid-1960's, an estimated 60 percent of consumers were shopping at discount stores. The Consumer Goods Pricing Act of 1975 also affected the ability of individually owned businesses to compete with the big chains. It effectively reversed the fair trade legislation of the 1930's that was meant to protect small businesses by regulating pricing.

One of the earliest successful discount chains is considered to have been Two Guys, originally known as Two Guys From Harrison, named after the New Jersey town where it was established. It eventually grew to include hundreds of stores. E. J. Korvette's was another discount pioneer that began during the early 1950's. Other major discount chains included Adray's, Zayre's, White Front, and T G & Y, as well as GEM and Fedco, which were both established to serve government employees and those in the military.

Many of these smaller chains expanded too quickly and began going out of business a scant dozen years later when the major discount chains began to undercut them. Kmart, Target (established by the Dayton Corporation that operated department stores), and Wal-Mart all were founded in 1962. They soon began their dominance of the discount market. Volume sales enabled these chains to make money while operating on low profit margins per item. By 1974, Kmart was the first of the major chains to have expanded into all forty-eight contiguous American states.

WAL-MART AND WAREHOUSES

Of the discount powerhouses, the only one that was not the product of an already existing chain was Wal-Mart. Sam Walton founded the first Wal-Mart in Arkansas, and the company gradually expanded into a giant, sometimes controversial behemoth. A later arrival, resembling the more traditional department store but offering almost continuous price-saving "sales," was Kohl's. Factory-outlet stores, mainly operated by companies to divest their retail stores of discontinued items, were another price-saving innovation. Mail-order houses such as L. L. Bean also became popular for certain types of specialty goods such as clothing.

About twenty years after the major successful discount chains were established, huge warehouse stores began to appear. Founded in 1983, Costco, one of the major warehouse chains, has a presence in hundreds of locations. It carries a wide variety of mostly brand-name products and often purveys food, prescription drugs, and gasoline as well. It caters somewhat to the slightly more well-off consumer and has expanded its reach into Europe and Asia. Sam's Club, the warehouse spinoff of Wal-Mart, is also found in numerous cities. Such warehouse chains as Home Depot, aimed at the do-it-yourself trade, are more limited in product scope.

Roy Liebman

FURTHER READING

Bosworth, Brandon. "Making Paradise Affordable: Life Would Be Harder for Many Americans Without Discount Stores." *The American Enterprise* 17,

Shoppers wend their way through a Costco in Chicago in 2008. Warehouse stores tend to do well during downturns in the economy. (AP/Wide World Photos)

no. 5 (2006): 34-37. Examines the effect that the growth of discount stores has had on the average American family and finds them to be a positive development.

Johnson, Walter E. "Warehouse Chains Roll into Secondary Markets: Are You Ready for Them?" *Do-It-Yourself Retailing* 160, no. 4 (1991): 47-54. Looks at how the expansion of warehouse chains into smaller communities will affect the economies of those areas.

Parker, Philip M. *2007-2012 World Outlook for Discount Stores.* San Diego, Calif.: Icon Group International, 2006. Assesses the outlook over a five-year period for discount stores in about two hundred countries, including their prospects for profitability. Enables quick comparisons among countries.

Van Housen, Caty. "The 'Big Box' War to Begin with Mom 'n' Pops in the Middle." *San Diego Business Journal* 14, no. 31 (1993): 6-7. Argues that the inevitable result of the arrival of warehouse stores is that small stores cannot compete on price and range of products and are forced out of business.

Vedder, Richard K., and Wendell Cox. *The Wal-Mart Revolution: How Big-Box Stores Benefit Consumers, Workers, and the Economy.* Washington, D.C.: AEI Press, 2006. Although Wal-Mart has often been demonized for ruthless business practices, the authors have looked at communities before and after its stores are established. They maintain that, overall, the company has been a force for good.

SEE ALSO: Catalog shopping; Montgomery Ward; Retail trade industry; Sears, Roebuck and Company; Shipping industry; Thrift stores; Wal-Mart.

Wars

DEFINITION: Armed conflicts between the United States and other sovereign nations or entities

SIGNIFICANCE: Throughout history, both declared and undeclared wars have caused the U.S. government to work closely with the business community in mobilizing the nation's economy to support military operations. Wars often determined the use of natural resources, the production of goods, the availability of labor, and the opportunity for businesses to generate profits from their efforts to support the country in a time of crisis.

Viewed from an economic standpoint, American engagement in warfare from the eighteenth into the twenty-first century has always had a significant impact on the nation's business community. Although some wars have been initiated in part to either protect or enhance the country's economic interests, all have led to shifts in the relationships between government and private commercial enterprises, often changing radically the fortunes of individuals, companies, and even entire industries. Private industry has played a key role in times of war, because the United States has always operated from the premise that when the government needed resources for military operations, private enterprise could and would supply what the military required. As a result, armed conflicts have given business leaders opportunities to demonstrate patriotism but have simultaneously provided them a chance to improve their companies' bottom lines.

BOOM AND BUST

From the establishment of the republic until the end of World War II in 1945, the United States resisted the establishment of a large standing army and the creation of government-controlled facilities to manufacture weapons and equipment needed for warfare. Hence, wars tended to create what can

best be described as a boom-and-bust economy during the period from the initial decision to prepare for war through the months (sometimes years) after hostilities ceased. When conflicts arose, the country was forced to mobilize rapidly, requiring many businesses to ramp up production or switch from manufacturing items for civilian use to ones required by the armed forces. At the same time, industries were stepping up production cycles, often taking on additional workers, and the government was increasing the number of people in uniform. This situation led to a favorable environment for labor, most notably during World War II when the vestiges of unemployment caused by the Great Depression were eliminated, and women were hired in great numbers to take the place of men drafted into the military services.

At these times, certain materials were needed in greater quantities to produce weapons and ammunition, manufacture the gear for military personnel, or build vehicles needed to transport fighting forces. Prices for commodities in high demand such as steel, copper, chemicals, and even textiles rose dramatically. During such times, businesses that expanded to meet demands for war materiel saw income and profits rise. To finance wars, the federal government was often forced to issue bonds to generate the substantial capital needed to pay business owners for goods and services. This decision provided investors with opportunities to purchase government securities at good rates of interest with minimal risk. After hostilities ceased, many companies found it necessary to downsize. That action, coupled with the arrival of returning veterans, often led to massive unemployment. The situation was particularly critical after World War I, when more than one million veterans joined thousands of others looking for work in a country that could not employ them all.

THE RESPONSE OF BUSINESS

Historically, the response of the business community in supporting wars has been mixed. Many executives have complied readily with government requests. At other times, however, the president and senior members of his staff have found it necessary to impose regulations on business to ensure that the nation had sufficient resources to equip its fighting force while controlling as best as possible the inevitable inflationary pressures resulting from increased demand for limited resources. Action was also necessary to guard against unscrupulous suppliers, who saw war as a means of generating substantial payments for their goods.

Profiteering began as early as the Revolutionary War and was a problem during every conflict that followed. Practices included hoarding scarce commodities to drive up prices, conducting black-market operations, substituting poorer quality goods for those ordered, shortchanging the government on deliveries, and bribing public officials to obtain lucrative contracts. During both World War I and World War II, the government created elaborate systems for reviewing production and delivery of goods to cut down on profiteering, but the practice continued. Despite knowing that some businesses were unfairly profiting from the work they performed for the military, the administrations of both Woodrow Wilson and Franklin D. Roosevelt showed great reluctance to exercise the one tactic they had at their disposal to curtail such activity: government takeover of private industry for the duration of the conflict. Although that happened in a few cases, it was more generally left to businesses to behave ethically in supporting the war effort. Periodically, Congress addressed problems of profiteering, passing laws to penalize profiteers in 1944, 1985, and 2007.

GOVERNMENT CONTROLS

In the twentieth century, the need for total mobilization before both world wars caused major changes in the way the federal government dealt with the business community. At the outset of World War I, the cumbersome methods used by the military to contract for materiel proved woefully inadequate as a means of mobilizing for a large-scale modern conflict. At this time, war plans took no account of the nation's economic capacity, and bureaus in the Army and Navy were often competing with each other to contract with businesses for the same items. To correct the problem, the Wilson administration made a concerted effort to enlist the services of industry executives as advisers in placing the nation to a wartime footing.

Hundreds of committees and commissions, such as the War Industries Board in World War I and the War Production Board during World War II, set priorities for production and allocation of key resources. These advisory groups, dominated by se-

This World War II poster encouraged Americans to buy war stamps and bonds to help pay for the war effort. (Library of Congress)

nior executives from America's most important industries, also assisted in handling labor relations, which often became testy in industries in which unions were strong. Union leaders felt it important to assure members that management would not take undue advantage of labor during national emergencies.

The Wilson administration had significant problems managing labor relations, and a number of work stoppages occurred as the country prepared to mount its expeditionary force. Roosevelt was more successful than his predecessor in convincing private industry to support the war, partly because the policies developed by his administration minimized the negative impact of shortages, so inflation was—by contrast with the World War I—relatively mild. Roosevelt's advisers, many of them industry executives, worked hard to develop methods for determining the fair prices of needed goods. The practices allowed businesses to profit—but not

PRESENCE OF CONTRACTOR PERSONNEL DURING U.S. WARS OR CONFLICTS

Military Operation	Estimated Personnel (1,000's)		Estimated Ratio of Contractors to Military Personnel
	Contractor	Military	
Revolutionary War	2	9	1 to 6
Mexican War	6	33	1 to 6
U.S. Civil War	200	1,000	1 to 5
World War I	85	2,000	1 to 24
World War II	734	5,400	1 to 7
Korea	156	393	1 to 2.5
Vietnam	70	359	1 to 5
Gulf War	9 [a]	500	1 to 55 [a]
Balkans	20	20	1 to 1
Iraq theater as of early 2008	190	200	1 to 1

Source: Data from Congress of United States, Congressional Budget Office, "Contractors' Support of U.S. Operations in Iraq," August, 2008

[a] The Saudi Arabian government supplied significant amounts of products and services during Operations Desert Shield and Desert Storm; these personnel are not included in the data.

[b] Iraq theater equals Iraq, Bahrain, Jordan, Kuwait, Oman, Qatar, Saudi Arabia, Turkey and the United Arab Emirates.

excessively—from their government work, while not bankrupting the U.S. treasury. Nevertheless, during the war, salaries of executives at many companies rose dramatically, while those of workers were adjusted modestly to account for inflation.

Partly as a result of careful planning by the Roosevelt administration, the boom economy created by the nation's buildup for World War II did not collapse when hostilities ceased in 1945. A greater factor, however, was actions by communist-ruled nations, including the Soviet Union and China. In the eyes of most Americans, these nations suddenly seemed to pose a new threat to world peace. The government therefore found it expedient to maintain a fairly large force under arms and continue purchasing items for national defense. Military and civilian leaders in the newly established Department of Defense made a convincing case to the American populace that the country was still engaged in warfare—the Cold War. Further, they argued that the United States would not have the luxury of a long lead time to mobilize if new enemies initiated nuclear warfare.

Those in industries such as aviation, weapons production, and hi-tech security systems, which had grown exponentially during the war years, found a continuing and ready market for their wares, and leaders in what became known as "the defense industry" developed close working relationships with senior Defense Department officials. This alliance between the military establishment and contractors was dubbed "the military-industrial complex" by President Dwight D. Eisenhower in 1961. It led to many tacit arrangements that would keep businesses in the defense industry operating (often at high rates of production) for the next half-century.

LATER WARS

In times of limited war such as the Vietnam conflict, the Persian Gulf War, and especially the war in Iraq, the nation's economy as a whole was not adjusted to support military operations. Manufacturers in defense industries saw some increased profits and concurrently required additional labor to meet the military's demands, but in general these wars had fewer repercussions on the national economy than had the global conflicts of the first half of the twentieth century. One industry, however, was notably affected by U.S. military involvement in the Middle East. America's demand for oil had risen sharply by the 1990's; therefore, threats to supplies anywhere in the world influenced the bottom line of global energy companies headquartered in the United States—and these firms ultimately passed along increased costs to American consumers.

Since the 1990's, several changes in the government's management of military operations have had notable effects on American business. For example, one group that saw significant increases in government work were those willing to provide services in the combat zone. Firms specializing in food service, construction, and security were granted sizable contracts to perform functions formerly managed by the military, thus freeing up soldiers to carry out their principal combat functions. Accusations that these firms charged excessive rates or were awarded highly profitable no-bid contracts led to political scandal and created a sense of distrust toward big business in many Americans.

At the same time, virtually every business in the country felt the effect of the Department of Defense's policy to rely more extensively on National Guard and Reserve troops to augment active-duty units in time of conflict. For both the Persian Gulf War and the Iraq War, thousands of citizen-soldiers were called to active duty, forcing employers to either find temporary replacements or manage without them. While the impact of this policy was fairly mild during the Persian Gulf War, the extended need for combat and support troops in Iraq and Afghanistan after 2003 resulted in multiple call-ups for many reservists, often for as much as a year at a time. Their employers were left in the unenviable position of having to make other arrangements to ensure that business operations continued smoothly. Industries relying on skilled workers such as computer technicians, law-enforcement professionals, and medical and legal personnel were especially hard hit.

Laurence W. Mazzeno

FURTHER READING

Brandes, Stuart D. *Warhogs: A History of War Profits in America.* Lexington: University Press of Kentucky, 1997. Analyzes the involvement of various businesses in wartime, concentrating on tendencies of business leaders to generate income from sup-

porting mobilization and efforts of government officials to control both production and profits.

Conner, Valerie Jean. *The National War Labor Board: Stability, Justice, and the Voluntary State in World War I.* Chapel Hill: University of North Carolina Press, 1983. Detailed study of the relationship between the federal government and the business community during World War I. Explains how the government controlled a number of industries vital to the war effort and redirected production to support the armed forces.

Gropman, Alan L. *Mobilizing U.S. Industry in World War II: Myth and Reality.* Washington, D.C.: National Defense University Press, 1996. Examines the federal government's efforts to mobilize for war, focusing on activities to direct businesses to produce materials needed for military operations. Includes appendixes detailing production of war-related items and a list of government agencies involved in managing resource acquisition and allocation during the war.

Koistinen, Paul. *Arsenal of Democracy: The Political Economy of American Warfare, 1940-1945.* Lawrence: University Press of Kansas, 2004. Discusses efforts to mobilize the United States for war against the Axis powers. Includes a discussion of the government's interactions with and control of key industries capable of producing weapons and supplies essential to the war effort for the United States and its allies.

_____. *Beating Plowshares into Swords: The Political Economy of American Warfare, 1680-1865.* Lawrence: University Press of Kansas, 1996. Explores the relationship between the government and business during the colonial period, the American Revolution, the War of 1812, the Mexican War, and the American Civil War.

_____. *The Military-Industrial Complex: A Historical Perspective.* New York: Praeger, 1980. Explains the emergence of the military-industrial complex during and after World War II; traces its roots to America's earliest national conflicts. Provides a brief summary of government-business relationships during periods of conflict from the American Revolution to the Cold War.

_____. *Mobilizing for Modern War: The Political Economy of American Warfare, 1865-1919.* Lawrence: University Press of Kansas, 1997. Traces the growing interdependence of the federal government's military branches and certain businesses from the Civil War through the Spanish-American War and World War I. Explains how the government organized to fight overseas.

SEE ALSO: Arms industry; Civil War, U.S.; French and Indian War; Iraq wars; Korean War; Mexican War; Military-industrial complex; Revolutionary War; Spanish-American War; Vietnam War; War of 1812; War surplus; World War I; World War II.

Washington, Booker T.

IDENTIFICATION: Educator and advocate of African American business
BORN: April 5, 1856; near Hale's Ford, Virginia
DIED: November 14, 1915; Tuskegee, Alabama
SIGNIFICANCE: Using his educational and political influence, Washington spearheaded African American entrepreneurship during the early twentieth century by advocating the process of gradual economic and social advancement that could eventually lead to economic independence and self-reliance for African Americans.

Booker T. Washington. (Library of Congress)

After working in salt furnaces and coal mines as a young man, Booker T. Washington attended Hampton Institute in Virginia. In 1881, he organized the Tuskegee Institute in Alabama as a normal and industrial school for African Americans. The school focused on industrial training that would develop self-respect and economic independence for African Americans. In 1895, he expressed his belief that African Americans must attain a level of economic equality with whites before they pushed for social equality.

In 1900, Washington organized the National Negro Business League (NNBL), with the goal of establishing economic independence for African Americans. Graduates from Tuskegee began spreading out into positions of influence, many as entrepreneurs. Washington motivated African Americans to become indispensable, successful businesspeople, no matter how small their business might be. He encouraged them to emulate others who were successful so that they could generate the financial resources necessary to continue their upward climb. Washington believed that businesspeople were the ultimate role models.

Washington taught African Americans the importance of work, no matter how modest the labor. He emphasized the connection between business and real estate ownership and the ability to have greater control over what happened in the lives of African Americans. He taught that the cornerstone of economic independence was saving and investing money. After his death in 1915, black entrepreneurship began fading back into the shadows of the past.

Alvin K. Benson

SEE ALSO: Carver, George Washington; Civil Rights Act of 1964; Civil Rights movement; Education; Garvey, Marcus.

Washington, George

IDENTIFICATION: President of the United States, 1789-1797
BORN: February 22, 1732; Bridges Creek (later Wakefield), Westmoreland County, Virginia
DIED: December 14, 1799; Mount Vernon, Virginia
SIGNIFICANCE: In addition to being the first U.S. president and commanding general of the Revo-

lutionary War, Washington was one of the richest men in the American colonies on the eve of the American Revolution.

Although better remembered for his political and military career, George Washington had a critical role in the business and financial life of the early United States. Born into Virginia plantation gentry (but not the highest rank), Washington was educated by tutors and early learned to be a surveyor, a skill that not only assisted his early military career but also helped develop his lifelong interest in land speculation. Although his father and older half brother both died before he was twenty, Washington began a successful agricultural career at Mount Vernon. He did not inherit his land until he was thirty, but his marriage to the wealthy widow Martha Custis when she was twenty-seven provided him with great wealth early in life.

A successful manager of land and slaves, Washington was also a tireless entrepreneur of agricultural industries. Washington manufactured a wide range of farm equipment and was the largest brewer in America. Of necessity, he was heavily involved in the import-export business.

As one of the wealthiest men in America, Washington had a fundamental understanding of what government had to do to create an environment conducive to business and finance. His distress at Great Britain's failed colonial economic policy was partly what led to him to join the revolutionary cause. The failure of the Articles of Confederation led him to preside over the drafting of the U.S. Constitution, which was critical to the early economic success of the nation.

Washington agreed to serve as the first U.S. president to further secure America's business development and to ensure that its new government would be established successfully. He chose Alexander Hamilton, the brightest economic mind in the country at the time, as the first secretary of the Treasury. Hamilton's plans were contained in a series of major reports: the *Report on the Public Credit, January, 1790, Second Report on the Public Credit, December, 1790,* and the *Report on Manufactures* (1791).

In his reports, Hamilton made his case for fully funding all Revolutionary War debt, creating the First National Bank, founding the Merchant Marine,

George Washington. (White House Historical Society)

and imposing the first internal tax. These measures laid the foundation for America's early economic progress. The U.S. public credit moved from near bankruptcy to enjoying the highest international credit rating in a dozen short years. Washington's recognition that the United States could not afford to fight a war with either Britain or France led him to hold fast to a foreign policy of peace despite numerous insults from America's foreign competitors.

Richard L. Wilson

SEE ALSO: Bank of the United States, First; Colonial economic systems; Constitution, U.S.; Franklin, Benjamin; Government spending; Hamilton, Alexander; Presidency, U.S.; Revolutionary War; Taxation.

Water resources

DEFINITION: Totality of the water available nationally for drinking, irrigation, power generation, and all other practical uses

SIGNIFICANCE: The exploitation of natural resources, including water resources, has driven the economic development of the United States since its inception and reaches back to the founding of the European colonies during the late sixteenth and early seventeenth centuries. Given water's essential role in Earth's biosphere, there is virtually no aspect of business that has not been dependent, directly or indirectly, on regular access to it.

Although the water resources of the United States include precipitation and surface water (lakes, rivers, and so on), most of the nation's water is found in the soil and in aquifers. As the demand for water has increased, seawater has become increasingly important in coastal areas. English colonists on the eastern shores of North America relied primarily on small-scale farming to sustain themselves, although in the southern colonies, the use of slave labor encouraged a plantation system of agriculture. In both North and South, the growth of crops was generally assured by abundant rainfall.

From the earliest days, the colonies' numerous watercourses were harnessed by mills equipped with a variety of waterwheels, allowing their owners to supplement manual labor with water-powered machines. Acting under the terms of a 1620 charter, English colonizer Sir Ferdinando Gorges built a gristmill (for grinding grain into meal) on the Newichewannick River in Maine. Rapidly flowing water was necessary to the functioning of mills, but where a suitable stream was lacking, one could be provided. Two decades after Gorges built his mill, English colonists dug a canal near Dedham, Massachusetts, to carry water from the Charles River into the Neponset River. They then harnessed the flow of water to run their own mill. Delaware inventor Oliver Evans built a fully automated gristmill on Red Clay Creek in Delaware in 1782 and subsequently patented the design.

The first sawmills in North America appear to have been built in Jamestown, Virginia, in the very early seventeenth century, but numerous others followed in short order. Besides running the saws themselves, water could also be used to power the carriages moving the logs through the sawing process. Depending on the terrain, timber workers floated cut logs down existing streams to the mill or built long wooden flumes down which logs could be carried by flowing water. Watercourses were essential in early years for transporting cut lumber to market as well.

At first, mills might employ only one or two workers on a part-time basis, but as the century progressed, industrial development and manufacturing became increasingly important. In 1790, three entrepreneurs built the country's first mechanized textile mill on the Blackstone River in Pawtucket, Rhode Island. Such developments led to the creation of numerous subsidiary activities and enterprises, creating communities and spurring the growth of their economies.

Whereas farmers had relied on surface water or dug shallow wells for their drinking water, towns and cities came to require centralized systems to provide adequate supplies of household water. As early as 1652, the Water Works Company of Boston, Massachusetts, put together a system of wooden pipes to carry water from nearby springs to a small central reservoir. This system proved inadequate, and in 1795, the Aqueduct Corporation began supplying the city with water from Roxbury's Jamaica Pond. Meanwhile a water pumping plant built by Hans Christopher Christiansen in 1755 began carrying water to a seventy-foot tower in Bethlehem, Pennsylvania. By the end of the eighteenth century, there were sixteen waterworks in the country, all but one of them privately owned.

THE NINETEENTH CENTURY

At the beginning of the nineteenth century, the area of the United States had grown to 888,811 square miles, of which 24,065 square miles were inland water. The country remained predominantly agricultural for the early decades of the century, but while rainfall provided water for crops in the East, watering by irrigation proved necessary west of the one-hundredth meridian of longitude. In 1847, members of the Church of Jesus Christ of Latter-Day Saints set an example by creating a large-scale canal system in Utah.

Thanks to its water resources, the United States could boast more than ten thousand mills at the beginning of the nineteenth century. The country's first integrated cotton textile mill, the Boston Manufacturing Company, was built in 1814 on the Charles River in Waltham, Massachusetts, by Francis Cabot Lowell and several fellow entrepreneurs. Selling stock, Lowell and his partners chose a location on the Merrimack River to build an industrial center that would become known as Lowell. Recognizing that the river's waters would be an ideal source of power, the company dug an extensive system of canals and built textile mills on their banks. By mid-century, Lowell's ten major mill complexes employed some ten thousand workers,

The Croton Reservoir at 5th Avenue and 42nd Street in New York City in 1850. (New York Historical Society)

many of them immigrants from Ireland, and the city had become the largest manufacturing site in the country.

Lowell's growth led to the creation of similar complexes, and by 1840, there were over sixty-six thousand mills in the United States. Nearly one-half were sawmills and nearly one-third gristmills, with the remainder involved in producing textiles and tanning hides.

The development of the turbine revolutionized industry during the 1840's. Although they are essentially waterwheels, hydraulic turbines take advantage of the pressure and velocity of water in an enclosed casing to produce increased power in a smaller space. American engineer James B. Francis developed an efficient "reaction turbine" in 1849, and within two decades, the turbine had become the principal source of power in New England's mills.

Despite waterpower's role in the industrial growth of the country, the use of the steam turbine and steam power in the second half of the century quickly eclipsed it in importance, and by 1889 some 80 percent of the power produced in the country was steam. However, the development of hydroelectricity—in which turbines harnessed waterpower to create electricity—altered the geography of the country's economic development once again. Power could be transmitted on overhead lines, making it unnecessary to site plants near rivers. The first such transmission appears to have taken place in Or-

egon in 1889, when electricity was transmitted thirteen miles from a power station at Willamette Falls, near Oregon City, to Portland. In 1896, a line twenty-two miles long was built to transmit alternating current from a power station on the Niagara River to Buffalo, New York.

Throughout the century, outbreaks of disease encouraged the creation of hygienic municipal water systems. Such a system went into operation in Philadelphia, Pennsylvania, in 1801, spurred by an epidemic of yellow fever. Designed by Benjamin Latrobe, the system used steam engines to pump water from the Schuylkill River. An outbreak of cholera prompted New York to create its own system for fresh water. The Croton Aqueduct project—which involved a dam, four reservoirs, and a fifty-mile aqueduct—opened in 1842 and cost over $10 million. Thirty years later, Poughkeepsie, New York, which drew water from the Hudson River, became the first city in the country to filter its water supply. In 1896, there were 3,196 waterworks in operation, 47 percent of which were privately owned.

THE TWENTIETH CENTURY AND AFTER

By the beginning of the twentieth century, the area of the United States had grown to 3,022,387 square miles, of which 52,553 square miles were inland water. The Great Lakes, lying between the United States and Canada, accounted for another 60,052 square miles. Water use would rise steadily for most of the century, reaching 180 billion gallons per day in 1950 and 440 billion gallons per day in 1980. By 1985, use had dropped about 10 percent as a result of economic, technological, and legal factors. In 2000, use totaled 408 billion gallons per day, nearly 80 percent of it drawn from surface sources.

The passage of the Newlands Reclamation Act of 1902 led to federal financing of irrigation projects in the West, although water users were expected to pay back the costs over time. Among many such projects, the Colorado River Project and the Columbia River Basin Project were the largest. At the turn of the twentieth century the amount of water used for irrigation had been just over 20 billion gallons per day—half of the country's total water use. The figure for irrigation rose to 150 billion gallons per day in 1980, although it fell somewhat in the remaining years of the century, accounting for one-third of the country's water use at the beginning of the twenty-first century.

Hydroelectricity remained important, with its generation concentrated in mountainous regions with heavy precipitation. Here, too, the federal government played an important role, funding major projects such as the Tennessee Valley Authority (TVA). Created in 1933, the TVA eventually generated power to more than 8.3 million people in seven southern states. By the end of the twentieth century, hydroelectricity accounted for about 10 percent of the country's electrical power production.

Thermoelectric-power water use—that is, its utilization in generating electricity in steam turbines and in cooling equipment involved in generating electricity by other means—accounted for a growing percentage of the nation's water use in the second half of the twentieth century. Such use was estimated to be 40 billion gallons per day in 1950, less than one-quarter of the total, but it rose to 210 billion gallons per day in 1980. Like other uses, thermoelectric-power use dropped in subsequent years, but it totaled 195 billion gallons per day in 2000—nearly half of the nation's total. Depending on their location, thermoelectric power plants were able to draw on the nation's increasingly important coastal waters, which totaled 42,528 square miles at the end of the twentieth century. Other industrial use of water rose to 47 billion gallons per day in 1970 but fell afterward.

The twentieth century saw an improvement in municipal water supply systems. In 1908, Jersey City, New Jersey, began treating its water supply with chlo-

rine, becoming the first American city to do so on a wide scale. In 1945, Grand Rapids, Michigan, began fluoridating its water supply to fight tooth decay. The post-World War II population boom led to the expansion of water systems, and by the beginning of the twenty-first century, it was estimated that the annual cost of operating the nation's water systems was more than $3.5 billion. The average American residence used more than 100,000 gallons of water per year at a cost of about $200.

In the second half of the twentieth century, water became a matter of growing concern, with federal legislation such as the Safe Drinking Water Act of 1974 (amended in 1986 and 1996) setting higher standards for water drawn from all sources. As demand for water grew and the extent of pollution became evident, desalination became economically viable. The nation's first fully operational seawater desalination plant was opened in 1961 at Freeport Texas. Initially, the plant produced some one million gallons of useable water per day, with costs running between $1 and $1.25 per thousand gallons.

Grove Koger

FURTHER READING

Holmes, Beatrice Hort. *A History of Federal Water Resources Program, 1800-1960.* Washington, D.C.: U.S. Department of Agriculture, Economic Research Service, 1972. Succinct chronological account of the U.S. government's role in managing water resources.

Hunter, Louis C. *Waterpower in the Century of the Steam Engine.* Vol. 1 in *A History of Industrial Power in the United States, 1780-1930.* Charlottesville: University Press of Virginia, 1979. Authoritative and exhaustive analysis of waterpower in the development of the nation. Numerous illustrations, tables, appendixes, and bibliographical notes.

Milazzo, Paul Charles. *Unlikely Environmentalists: Congress and Clean Water, 1945-1972.* Lawrence: University Press of Kansas, 2006. Examines pioneering efforts by federal legislators to ensure the quality of the nation's water supply. Illustrations, bibliography.

Outwater, Alice B. *Water: A Natural History.* New York: Basic Books, 1996. Overview by an environmental engineer of the nation's water resources and historical survey of their development, management, and mismanagement.

Rowley, William D. *Reclamation: Managing Water in*

the West. Vol. 1 in *The Bureau of Reclamation: Origins and Growth to 1945*. Denver: Bureau of Reclamation, U.S. Department of the Interior, 2006. Comprehensive history of the bureau's operations in providing irrigation water to the arid west. Illustrations, maps, bibliography.

SEE ALSO: Agribusiness; Agriculture; Canals; Colorado River water; Dams and aqueducts; Erie Canal; Fishing industry; Irrigated farming; Mineral resources; Mississippi and Missouri Rivers; Public utilities.

Western Union

IDENTIFICATION: Initially the major company in the telegraph industry; later a worldwide provider of financial and communications services

DATE: Founded in 1851

SIGNIFICANCE: The telegraph, invented in 1837, provided the first technology for rapid communications and gave businesses the ability virtually instantaneously to contact their own branches, other companies, or consumers. Through a series of mergers, Western Union became the major company in the telegraph industry, driving its development and expansion.

The New York and Mississippi Valley Printing Telegraph Company was created in 1851. Hiram Sibley and Ezra Cornell were principal figures in this firm. In 1856, after a series of mergers united numerous companies in the Midwest, the resulting corporation adopted the name Western Union. In 1861, Western Union completed the first transcontinental telegraph line. In 1884, the company was one of the original eleven stocks listed in the Dow Jones Industrial Averages. By 1900, Western Union had acquired more than five hundred telegraph companies and was operating in several countries around the world.

By the mid-twentieth century, new developments in communications were making the telegraph less significant, and Western Union moved into a variety of other communication and financial services. It had long been involved in some aspects of these businesses, however—introducing the first successful stock ticker in 1869, money transfer services in 1871, and the first consumer credit card in 1914. In 1980, for the first time, the company's revenue from money transfer fees exceeded its revenues from telegraph services.

As did many other American businesses, during the late twentieth century Western Union went through a series of mergers, changes in corporate

The general operating department at the Western Union Telegraph Building, New York, in the 1870's. (Library of Congress)

structure, and attempts at diversification. In 1993, the company was facing bankruptcy and, in an effort to protect the historic Western Union name, changed its name to New Valley Corporation. In 1994, the most profitable operations of New Valley were sold to First Financial Management Corporation and operated as Western Union Financial Services. In 1995, First Financial Management Corporation merged with the First Data Corporation. First Data spun Western Union off in 2006 by selling it to investors as an independent, publicly traded corporation. A symbolic milestone in the company's history occurred in January, 2006, when the last telegraph message was delivered.

Although no longer in the telegraph business, Western Union remains a worldwide financial services and communications giant. An important part of its business is money transfers by immigrant workers around the world, who send funds to their families in their home countries. In 2007, Western Union, operating in more than two hundred countries, reported making more than 167 million consumer-to-consumer money transfers and more than 400 million consumer-to-business transactions.

Mark S. Joy

FURTHER READING

Burns, R. W. *Communications: An International History of the Formative Years.* Stevenage, Hertfordshire, England: Institution of Electrical Engineers, 2004.

Thompson, R. L. *Wiring a Continent: The History of the Telegraph Industry in the United States, 1832-1866.* Princeton, N.J.: Princeton University Press, 1947. Reprint. New York: Arno Press, 1972.

SEE ALSO: Bell, Alexander Graham; Telecommunications industry; Transatlantic cable; Transcontinental railroad.

Whaling industry

DEFINITION: Commercial hunting and processing of whales to harvest their meat, blubber, oil, and other raw materials

SIGNIFICANCE: From the mid-eighteenth century to the early nineteenth century, American whalers dominated the seas. Whaling not only generated saleable products but also offered careers to numerous men of little means, including escaped slaves. However, as the industry hunted whales to the brink of extinction and as other, less expensive, products took the place of those supplied by whales, the industry eventually collapsed.

In the United States, commercial whaling was connected with the Quaker colony of Nantucket for much of its early history. As members of a religious minority, the Massachusetts colony's Quakers had been forced to live on Nantucket Island, where farming was impossible and the only way to make a living was by fishing. Initially, colony members only towed whales to shore for butchering and processing. In this period, the Nantucketers hunted "right whales," so called because they were the "right" whales to be hunting.

EARLY COMMERCIAL WHALING

In 1712, a whaler captained by Christopher Hussey, after being blown out to sea, brought in a new kind of whale, a sperm whale, named for the clear fluid, or spermaceti, that filled its enormous head cavity. Larger than right whales and carrying less blubber, sperm whales held enormous value for the colonists. Spermaceti candles, for instance, burned clear, unlike those made from animal tallow, which smoked. Sperm whale oil, when burned in oil lamps, did not give off the bad smell produced by right whale oil.

During the 1750's, Nantucket Islanders began building brick furnaces onboard their ships and fortifying the ships for long sea voyages. These treks, stretching literally around the world, would surge in popularity as whaling became increasingly profitable over the next forty years. Whale oil and parts could be used for any number of products. All whales produced lamp oil. Baleen whales, including right whales and Bowhead whales, produced baleen plates that were used in umbrella ribs and corsets. Spermaceti candles and ambergris perfume (made from a particular part of the sperm whale's intestine) were popular sperm whale products, and sailors carved scrimshaw on sperm whale teeth.

A ship's crew earned a portion of the vessel's profits from selling whales, theoretically motivating them to stay at sea until the ship's hold was full of oil. However, as the men had to buy almost all their supplies from the ship's owners while at sea, they often spent their profits before returning to shore. They

THE FAMOUS WHALE HUNTER, CAPTAIN AHAB, AND MOBY DICK

His three boats stove around him, and oars and men both whirling in the eddies; one captain, seizing the line-knife from his broken prow, had dashed at the whale, as an Arkansas duellist at his foe, blindly seeking with a six inch blade to reach the fathom-deep life of the whale. That captain was Ahab. And then it was, that suddenly sweeping his sickle-shaped lower jaw beneath him, Moby Dick had reaped away Ahab's leg, as a mower a blade of grass in the field. No turbaned Turk, no hired Venetian or Malay, could have smote him with more seeming malice. Small reason was there to doubt, then, that ever since that almost fatal encounter, Ahab had cherished a wild vindictiveness against the whale, all the more fell for that in his frantic morbidness he at last came to identify with him, not only all his bodily woes, but all his intellectual and spiritual exasperations. The White Whale swam before him as the monomaniac incarnation of all those malicious agencies which some deep men feel eating in them, till they are left living on with half a heart and half a lung. That intangible malignity which has been from the beginning; to whose dominion even the modern Christians ascribe one-half of the worlds; which the ancient Ophites of the east reverenced in their statue devil; — Ahab did not fall down and worship it like them; but deliriously transferring its idea to the abhorred White Whale, he pitted himself, all mutilated, against it. All that most maddens and torments; all that stirs up the lees of things; all truth with malice in it; all that cracks the sinews and cakes the brain; all the subtle demonisms of life and thought; all evil, to crazy Ahab, were visibly personified, and made practically assailable in Moby Dick. He piled upon the whale's white hump the sum of all the general rage and hate felt by his whole race from Adam down; and then, as if his chest had been a mortar, he burst his hot heart's shell upon it.

Source: Herman Melville, *Moby Dick: Or, The Whale* (1851)

were then indentured to take another cruise with the ship to discharge their debts. By far, the majority of the working hands on American whaling ships were African Americans, as a whaling career offered them the same essential opportunities as it did to whites, while many whites spurned whaling as ordinary hands. Whaling ships also provided runaway slaves with places to hide from their former masters.

Whaling's center shifted from Nantucket to Hudson Bay after the latter location proved to have a better harbor for fortified whale ships, which were built to last for years at sea. Occasionally, a whale ship would be lost to the seas or, very rarely, to whale attack. Such losses cost the landside ship owners heavily, as, after outfitting a ship, they already had to wait years to see a profit from it. Such stories as that of Mocha Dick, a white whale said to have attacked numerous ships and been harpooned on nineteen different occasions before finally being killed off the coast of Switzerland, and the tragedy of the whale ship *Essex*, sunk by an angry sperm whale, spurred Herman Melville to write *Moby Dick: Or, The Whale* (1851).

WHALING'S DECLINE

Whaling began experiencing a decline in popularity as early as the 1860's. Two factors led to its decline. First, fossil fuels offered a cheaper source of lighting fuel than did whale oil, reducing the demand for sperm whales. Second, right whales and Bowhead whales had been hunted to the brink of extinction. Whalers temporarily boosted the industry through the use of steam-powered harpoon cannons, making captures easier, safer, and less expensive, and allowing them to capture faster and larger rorqual whales, such as the enormous blue whale.

During the early twentieth century, whale oil

could be made into products ranging from medicines to margarine, and whale meat enjoyed brief popularity during World War II, when other meat products were scarce. However, the central fact remained: Whale populations worldwide were declining. After World War II, whaling nations formed the International Whaling Commission (IWC) to regulate and set quotas on whaling. However, whalers could not agree on low enough quotas, and quotas proved hard to enforce, leading to an upsurge in whaling during the 1950's and 1960's.

Whale populations continued to decline. Moreover, human perceptions of whales and whaling began to shift during the 1970's, and whaling was perceived as both unnecessary and unnecessarily cruel. Finally, in 1982, the IWC declared a moratorium on all whaling, with only minor loopholes, to give whale populations a chance to recover. The moratorium has not been lifted, as populations continue to struggle, and many former whaling companies have turned to offering whale tours, eschewing hunting altogether.

Jessie Bishop Powell

FURTHER READING

Chrisp, Peter. *The Whalers.* New York: Thomson Learning, 1995. Aimed at junior high school students, this work is nonetheless fully applicable to high school and college audiences. Includes discussions of commercial whaling and the downfall of modern whaling beginning during the 1860's.

Dolin, Eric Jay. *Leviathan: The History of Whaling in America.* New York: Norton, 2007. History of whaling including its rapid growth in the American colonies to its heyday in the nineteenth century and its ultimate demise. Several chapters focus on the products and business of whaling.

Ellis, Richard. *Men and Whales.* New York: Knopf, 1991. Examines whaling from colonial days until the 1986 moratorium. Includes inland whaling, as well as the more well-known business of whaling at sea.

McKissack, Pat, and Fred McKissack. *Black Hands, White Sails: The History of African-American Whalers.* New York: Scholastic, 1999. Details the lives of African American whalers. Discusses the reasons such jobs were readily available to them, including white distaste for rough professions.

Philbrick, Nathaniel. *Into the Heart of the Sea: The Tragedy of the Whaleship Essex.* New York: Viking, 2000. Examines the whale attack that sank the *Essex,* leading its crew to set forth for land in whale boats, where most perished at sea. Includes thorough discussion of whaling as a Quaker business and its Nantucket Island origins.

SEE ALSO: Alaska purchase; Beef industry; Fishing industry; Fur trapping and trading; Horses; Pork industry; Poultry industry.

Whiskey tax of 1791

IDENTIFICATION: Excise tax assessed on the distilling of whiskey
DATE: Enacted on March 3, 1791
SIGNIFICANCE: The whiskey tax was the United States' first internal federal tax, and it was promoted to Congress as a "sin" tax; it thus served as the precedent for similar taxes in future years.

In the wake of the Revolutionary War, the United States needed to pay its war-related debts. Secretary of the Treasury Alexander Hamilton proposed a tax on distilled spirits as a way simultaneously to raise money to repay debts and to impose moral discipline on the American people. Hamilton thought the consumption of whiskey represented a threat to the country's virtue. The law levied a tax of 7 cents per gallon on spirits produced in the United States (mostly whiskey) and 10 cents per gallon on products distilled from foreign materials (mostly rum). The tax was 28 percent of the 25-cent selling price for a gallon of whiskey.

Distillers in the Northeast were able to shift the tax burden to consumers, but distillers in the underdeveloped areas had to absorb the burden themselves. As a result, farmers in Washington Country, Pennsylvania, led by a county prosecutor named David Bradford, began assaulting tax collectors. Often, these assaults took the form of "tar and feathering." That is, tax collectors were coated in hot tar and then had feathers dumped on their bodies.

In 1794, President George Washington called out 12,950 militiamen to enforce the tax. Washington, along with Virginia governor Harry Lee, led the militia into Western Pennsylvania. The rebel farmers quickly surrendered. A treaty of sorts was signed by an antitax committee that agreed to submit to U.S. laws in exchange for a pardon on previous offenses.

The whiskey tax opened the door for additional excise taxes on so-called luxury items. A 1794 law extended the excise tax to carriages, snuff, sugar, and salt. However, Thomas Jefferson promised to abolish internal taxes during his presidential campaign in 1800. By 1802, all but the salt tax had been repealed. Nevertheless, the precedent had been established, and throughout the next two hundred years, Congress periodically introduced other types of luxury or sin taxes.

Dale L. Flesher

SEE ALSO: Alcoholic beverage industry; Hamilton, Alexander; Revolutionary War; Taxation; Tobacco industry; Whiskey Trust.

Whiskey Trust

IDENTIFICATION: Monopoly led by a whiskey distiller in Colorado

DATE: Founded in May, 1887

SIGNIFICANCE: The Whiskey Trust was an oddity during the late nineteenth century in that it was one of the few failed monopolies of the era. Although most monopolies prospered by dominating their industries, the Whiskey Trust could not control the whiskey business and ultimately failed.

During the late nineteenth century, many industries evolved into monopolies as one producer dominated an industry and either organized its competitors within its monopoly or drove them out of business. The distilling industry was no different. A variety of distillers vied for control of the industry, but Julius Kessler, an Austrian immigrant who manufactured his self-named whiskey in Leadville, Colorado, came to dominate them. Kessler outmaneuvered distillers in the West by selling his whiskey directly to saloon owners throughout the region instead of marketing it through a regional distributor. This allowed Kessler to bypass the middleman and sell his whiskey at a lower price than his competitors could. Instead of competing with Kessler, in 1887 other distributors joined Kessler in the Whiskey Trust, formally known as the Distiller's Securities Corporation. This Kessler-led monopoly dominated the spirits industry throughout the country. Kessler limited the number of major producers, closed more than half of the large distilleries controlled by the trust, and artificially created a whiskey shortage that drove up prices. The trust defended its actions by claiming that its products were purer and of higher quality than the locally produced moonshine.

The trust ran into some opposition, however. The distillers of the Whiskey Trust produced blended whiskeys of neutral spirits with artificial flavoring, a technique that clashed with those of traditional bourbon producers in Kentucky, Tennessee, and other states. The bourbon producers refused to join the Whiskey Trust, and the trust was not powerful enough to drive the bourbon producers out of business. The trust also could not control all the numerous independent and small-scale producers. Distilling was a relatively simple process, and the trust could not drive all competitors out of the market. Intense competition actually caused the trust to temporarily enter receivership in 1895. The trust was also the target of government investigations for charges of tax evasion and bribery of public officials.

The death blow to the trust, however, was the advent of Prohibition in 1920. When alcohol production became illegal, most distillers either went out of business or used their machinery for other purposes. Kessler sold his business and retired in 1921, returning to his native Austria. When Prohibition ended in 1933, strong federal antitrust laws and stringent alcohol regulations prevented the recreation of the Whiskey Trust.

Steven J. Ramold

FURTHER READING

Clay, Karen, and Werner Troesken. "Strategic Behavior in Whiskey Distilling, 1887-1895." *The Journal of Economic History* 62, no. 4 (December, 2002): 999-1023.

Troesken, Werner. "Exclusive Dealing and the Whiskey Trust, 1890-1895." *The Journal of Economic History* 58, no. 3 (September, 1998): 755-778.

Waymack, Mark, and James Harris. *The Book of Classic American Whiskeys.* New York: Open Court, 1995.

SEE ALSO: Alcoholic beverage industry; Antitrust legislation; Prohibition; Restaurant industry; Whiskey tax of 1791.

White-collar crime. *See* Business crimes

Wilderness Road

IDENTIFICATION: Key route for immigrants and settlers moving west past the Appalachian Mountains to open new communities in undeveloped parts of the nation

DATE: In operation from 1775 to around 1840

SIGNIFICANCE: The Wilderness Road was the major route for more than 200,000 people migrating west, at about the time the United States was coming into being. It provided a path for commerce in goods, livestock, and mail. In later years, some portions of the original Wilderness Road became paved routes for transportation arteries.

No less a figure than the legendary frontiersman Daniel Boone was among some thirty-five men who were hired to clear a trail into Kentucky for the Transylvania Company in 1775. The company had obtained title to the route from the Cherokee and Iroquois, though not from the Shawnee, who at-tacked the party on March 24, 1775, killing some of its members. The rest regrouped and completed the trail.

The trail looped for more than two hundred miles through Virginia, south into Tennessee, then north into Kentucky. Originally limited to foot or horseback traffic, it was further developed in 1792, when the Kentucky legislature funded improvements. Within four years, wagons began to carry families west to open up homes and businesses. Cabins built along the way served as the basis for future settlements.

Richard Henderson, of the Transylvania Company, hired Joseph Martin to open a land office in what is now Lee County, Kentucky, to help prospective settlers find land to settle. Martin's Fort, built in this area of the Cumberland Gap, boosted Kentucky settlements by providing a connection back to Virginia and North Carolina. Business lifelines were strengthened in 1792, when part of the Wilderness Road stretching from Bean Station, Tennessee, through the Cumberland Gap in Virginia, to Danville, Kentucky, was designated as a postal route.

The road was abandoned around 1840, as other means of access were developed. Much of it was later incorporated into the routes of modern highways, linking the historical road that opened up much of the nation to commerce to the busy transportation arteries of the twentieth and twenty-first centuries.

The Wilderness Road continues to be an economic asset. In Virginia, the state tourism corporation has established a network of museums and other points of interest to visitors. In doing so, programmers have linked the historic Wilderness Road with other eighteenth century migratory paths, such as Great Road and Valley Pike. Virginia advertises the Wilderness Road as stretching from the city of Winchester, near the state's border with West Virginia and Maryland, southward through Shenandoah, Rockbridge, and Botetourt counties, through the Roanoke and New

Old Wilderness Road, High Bridge, Kentucky, in about 1907. (Library of Congress)

River Valleys, and into the tip of western Virginia. Historians have disputed the accuracy of claiming all this as the Wilderness Road, but it remains an effective tourism marketing strategy. In any case, some 43 million Americans may claim descent from families that migrated along the road.

Paul Dellinger

FURTHER READING

Green, Fess. *Wilderness Road Odyssey: A Cyclist's Journey Through Present and Past.* Blacksburg, Va.: Pocahontas Press, 2003.

Kincaid, Robert L. *The Wilderness Road.* Whitefish, Mont.: Kessinger, 2007.

Williams, John Alexander. *Appalachia: A History.* Chapel Hill: University of North Carolina Press, 2002.

SEE ALSO: Canals; Cumberland Road; Homestead Act of 1862; Land laws; Mississippi and Missouri Rivers; Railroads; Stagecoach line, first; Tennessee Valley Authority.

Wobblies. *See* Industrial Workers of the World

Women in business

SIGNIFICANCE: Despite the steady rise in the percentage of women in the corporate workforce since World War II, women have faced a number of challenges, legal and social, in achieving equality in the business world.

Women have always worked, but society has not always equally valued their work and that of men. The advent of the American Industrial Revolution brought an ever-increasing compartmentalization of social life. Women and men who worked side by side on the farm in an agrarian culture became separated in a manufacturing-oriented society. Women stayed home and tended to child rearing and domestic responsibilities while men went to the city or factory to seek wage labor. The gender separation of the private sphere, or home life, from the public sphere, or working world, was not an equal division of labor. Male wage labor and public work was accorded greater value and direct compensation. In economic terms, men's work had exchange value because the money earned could be used to purchase goods. Away from public view, child care and housework became devalued and were not financially compensated. In economic terms, this work had use value but not exchange value. These economic realities were rooted in lingering beliefs about the proper roles for men and women in Western culture. The Cult of True Womanhood, a social belief that dominated the nineteenth century, regarded women as too moral and pure to participate in the harsh, competitive realities of the business world.

IMPACT OF WORLD WAR II

World War II ruptured historical ideas about women working. While men participated in the armed services, women replaced them in factories that supported the war effort and maintained domestic goods. The role reversal altered women's consciousness about paid labor. Although most working women were laid off after the war, opinion polls indicated that the majority of women enjoyed the experience of working and wanted to continue. Since the large but brief drop-off following the war, the annual percentage of women participating in the labor force has increased steadily. Women, however, have not been universally accepted into the workplace.

At first, women were segregated into positions in which it was deemed fitting for them to work. These positions, such as clerical or nursing, were often in the service of more prestigious male positions and entitled women to lower compensation. A gender-based division of labor was thus created. Even when women managed to enter a male-dominated position, they often found that the job was transformed into a less prestigious one, for which they received lower pay. An example from the corporate world is the position of clerk. An office clerk was a highly regarded, responsible employee at the beginning of the twentieth century. As women entered the profession, it became a more routinized, subservient, and lower-compensated position. Nevertheless, the latter part of the twentieth century saw business demographics change dramatically from the almost exclusively white male appearance of the 1950's. The prevalence of businesswomen during the 1980's was attested to by the proliferation of magazines targeted to women such as *Working Woman* and *Working Mother*, the emergence of support organizations for working women, and the greater use of inclusive language to describe jobs.

CHALLENGES AT THE OFFICE

Numerous obstacles have prevented or discouraged women from participating in corporate life in North America. The most obvious obstacle has been sexism. Before 1967, when an executive order added sex discrimination to the areas covered by Title VII of the Civil Rights Act of 1964, there was no federal law to prevent employers from refusing to hire women because of their gender. The pervasive belief was that women should not participate in paid labor; if they did, it was only for extra money (referred to as "pin" money) beyond what their husbands brought home. This belief assumed a middle-class, married existence that did not apply in the case of single women and poor families. Given these beliefs, women's average wages have been low, representing only a fraction of men's wages. This pay difference is often referred to as the wage gap. The Equal Pay Act of 1963 ended wage discrimination in jobs in which the qualifications and responsibilities are equal; however, proving wage discrimination is often difficult because seldom do two individuals possess exactly the same qualifications and responsibilities. Although the wage gap improved somewhat during the twentieth century, women's wages still hovered at approximately two-thirds to three-fourths of men's wages during the 1990's.

Another challenge facing women who wish to enter the corporate world has been sexual harassment. Although it exists at all levels within corporations, sexual harassment has been a particularly vexing problem for women seeking to advance in leadership positions, because sexual harassment is an issue of power. Statistics are difficult to obtain, but evidence indicates that sexual harassment is pervasive and that the remedies may be as bad as the harassment itself. The majority of women who are harassed eventually leave their positions.

Another obstacle for corporate career women is

WORKER GENDER, 1975-2007				
	Men		Women	
Year	Number of Workers (1,000's)	Percentage of Men Working	Number of Workers (1,000's)	Percentage of Women Working
1975	51,857	71.7	33,715	42.0
1980	57,186	72.0	42,117	47.7
1985	59,891	70.9	47,359	50.4
1990	65,104	72.0	53,689	54.3
1995	67,377	70.8	57,523	55.6
2000	73,305	71.9	63,586	57.5
2005	75,973	69.6	65,757	56.2
2007	78,254	69.8	67,792	56.6

Source: Data from Bureau of Labor Statistics, Current Population Survey, 2008

childbearing. Taking time off to give birth and rear children can severely hurt a woman's career advancement; a similarly qualified male who does not take such time off faces no such obstacle. Before the Pregnancy Discrimination Act of 1978, no federal law protected women against discrimination leading to hiring, firing, or promotion related to pregnancy. Not until 1993 did the United States enact a federal family leave law, though it is weak compared with its European counterparts. The Family and Medical Leave Act of 1993 provides for twelve weeks of unpaid, job-protected leave for the care of a new child or sick family member; European versions of the law provide for paid leave. The unpaid aspect of the law has caused many to speculate that only the wealthy are likely to take advantage of it.

The combination of these challenges has resulted in slowing the climb of women up the corporate ladder. Despite these obstacles, however, women continue to be hired at corporations in record numbers. The 1980's and 1990's found more women in middle management, though few have broken through the "glass ceiling" to achieve top management positions. Even during the 1990's, the number of women who were chief executive officers (CEOs) of *Fortune* 500 companies could be counted on one hand.

CHALLENGES AT HOME

Women who work have often faced special challenges at home as well as at their workplaces. The legacy of associating domestic labor with women remained strong at the turn of the twenty-first century. Statistics reveal that although women have entered the workforce in record numbers, those living with husbands or boyfriends have not significantly decreased their domestic labor. On average, marriage brings with it seven to ten hours of additional housework for women. This leaves them with a double duty of paid labor and housework. The extra work asked of women is sometimes referred to as the second shift. The stress associated with this double duty was the source of much discussion during the 1990's. The superwoman syndrome is a term coined to describe efforts by women to be successful at the workplace and at home. The standards for domestic success were established by the previous generation of mothers who, by and large, stayed home and were able to maintain high norms of cleanliness and order around the house.

In addition to primary responsibility for housework, women are still generally regarded as the primary parental caretaker. The pressure to provide significant time for the needs of children is another source of stress for women in the workforce. The availability of affordable, quality child care is a major issue for working women. Many corporations recognize the need to offer affordable child care; a 1990 survey indicated that 64 percent of the companies surveyed offered some type of child care assistance, and only 9 percent offered in-house child care. Large corporations have the resources to offer such benefits, but small businesses, which employ the majority of all workers in North America, are less likely to provide child care.

ECONOMIC CHALLENGES

Lower corporate profits during the 1980's and 1990's caused many companies to seek innovative methods for trimming costs. One method was the increased use of what is known as contingency labor. Contingent labor is a catch-all category that includes temporary employees, contract employees, job sharing, and part-time work. Corporations view contingent labor as positive because they are seldom obligated to provide such employees with benefits or make long-term commitments to them. Contingent employees can usually be laid off with little notice. Contingent employment has become a gender issue in North America and Europe because the vast majority of contingent employees are women. Socially, contingent employees are not considered part of the company and usually do not forge the same kind of relationships as permanent employees. The work is often routine, and little effort is given to explaining the context for it. Because they lack a strong relationship to the company, contingent employees are also subject to a higher frequency of sexual harassment. The increasing trend toward contingent employment is likely to receive continued feminist and legislative attention.

OVERCOMING THE CORPORATE ENVIRONMENT

Despite the challenges that confront women, they are still entering the workforce in record num-

---

THE STRUGGLE FOR EQUALITY IN THE WORKPLACE

Women took to the workplace largely during World War II, when the nation called its men to take on the war efforts and left the running of the country to women. After the war ended, it took nearly twenty years for civil rights to be brought to the nation in the form of equal pay and laws against discrimination in the workplace. That fight by women led to the formation of the Equal Employment Opportunity Commission, the National Organization for Women advocacy group, and even the Equal Rights Amendment, which sought to bring equal rights as a constitutional amendment. The act, passed by Congress, failed to be ratified by the necessary states. However, more laws came on the scene to help protect females in the workplace, including adding pregnancy as a protected "disability" in the Americans with Disabilities Act (ADA) of 1990. Another measure taken to help ease the transition of women into the workplace is the Family and Medical Leave Act (FMLA) of 1993, which provides time off from work to care for a family member or nurture a child.

Karel S. Sovak

bers and working their way through the corporate environment. One issue surrounding the greater presence of women is whether the corporation will change them or if they will change the corporation. Corporations in North America were established by men with male standards and expectations for communication, socialization, motivation, and so on. Women are attempting to succeed in a male environment, but do they have to adopt stereotypical male behavior? The answer is yes and no. Some women have succeeded by emulating male behavior, whereas others have found that their own skills have brought them success. One key method for women's success during the 1980's and 1990's has been effective mentoring. As women break into managerial positions, they act as mentors to women who have managerial potential, although good mentors can be male or female.

Some feminists advocate affirmative action as a method for overcoming sexism in hiring practices. Although equal opportunity (or nondiscrimination) is mandated by federal law, affirmative action is the voluntary response of corporations to actively hire women, members of ethnic groups, and people with disabilities. Such hiring practices are intended to improve corporate performance through greater diversity and to provide opportunities for people who have faced discrimination.

Another response advocated by some feminists is the notion of comparable worth, which is intended to help overcome the wage gap. Many male-dominated sectors of the economy offer higher wages than sectors dominated by women. This is true even when the skill level for the female-dominated position is equal to or greater than that of the male-dominated position. For example, in the same corporation, a truck driver is often compensated at a higher wage than an executive secretary, who typically possesses computer knowledge, managerial responsibility, and time management and writing skills. Some argue that the reason for the pay differential is historical gender discrimination. One method to overcome such discrimination is to have a compensation system that attempts to measure skills and abilities objectively and to determine comparable worth and pay accordingly. Many companies have adopted objective compensation systems, though market forces are still the major determinant of pay level.

The Body Shop, Mrs. Fields Cookies, and Mary Kay Cosmetics are examples of businesses started by women. A number of women who have been frustrated by the male-dominated corporate environment have started their own companies. In many parts of North America, the number of women applying for business licenses surpassed those sought by men during the 1990's. Some theorize that women possess skills that represent a good fit for business ownership, including the ability to handle a number of varied tasks, good communication skills, and flexibility. The availability of numerous support organizations and financial assistance have led women to open their own businesses in record numbers.

Twenty-first Century Trends

Despite the advances in the workplace made by women during the late twentieth century, a significant gap in pay continued to exist into the twenty-first century. Although women can and do obtain the position and responsibility within companies at a much higher pay rates than in years past, those roles do not always provide a pay scale equivalent to that of their male counterparts. One argument that has been made in regard to pay is that women do not ask for what they feel they are worth. Many women, despite their ability to master their assigned duties, apparently do not wish to risk not obtaining their positions by asking for their full value. Instead, they hope that by proving themselves on the job they will be rewarded. Through the first decade of the twenty-first century, the gender gap in pay continued to hold steady, with women earning about seventy-five cents for each dollar men earn doing similar work. This corporate bias is trending downward, and should lessen as more and more baby boomer executives, many of them men, retire and pass those roles onto successors.

In some large corporations, such as PepsiCo, Xerox, Kraft Foods, and Avon, women have made great strides, with women rising to chief executive officer and chair of the board levels. Other companies, such as Morgan-Stanley, Procter & Gamble, and DuPont, appeared ready to move women into top positions. Even with these advances, women still trailed the top male executives when it comes to income, with men making four times what women do. However, the gap has been closing.

Maurice Hamington
Karel S. Sovak

FURTHER READING

Amott, Teresa L., and Julie A. Matthaei. *Race, Gender, and Work: A Multicultural Economic History of Women in the United States.* Boston: South End Press, 1991. Detailed account and analysis of North American women's work histories for various cultural groups, including the experiences of American Indians, Chicanas, European Americans, African Americans, Asian Americans, and Puerto Ricans.

Anderson, Terry H. *The Pursuit of Fairness: A History of Affirmative Action.* New York: Oxford University Press, 2004. Addresses all aspects of the history of affirmative action and equal employment opportunity law and practice in the United States, with special attention to the rights of women workers.

Fagenson, Ellen A. *Women in Management: Trends, Issues, and Challenges in Managerial Diversity.* Newbury Park, Calif.: Sage Publications, 1993. Collection of essays by economists, female managers, and business scholars focusing on the issues facing female managers in a diverse corporate environment.

Godfrey, Joline. *Our Wildest Dreams: Women Entrepreneurs Making Money, Having Fun, Doing Good.* New York: Harper Business, 1992. Describes the growing phenomenon of female entrepreneurs and how these women redefine success beyond simply the bottom line.

Gregory, Raymond F. *Women and Workplace Discrimination: Overcoming Barriers to Gender Equality.* New Brunswick, N.J.: Rutgers University Press, 2005. Traces the history of federal measures enacted to prevent employers from discriminating against women in the workplace. Uses court cases to illustrate points.

Iannello, Kathleen P. *Decisions Without Hierarchy: Feminist Interventions in Organization Theory and Practice.* New York: Routledge, 1992. Brings feminism and organizational theory together in an analysis of three feminist organizations and a proposition for a modified consensus model as a nonsexist approach to structuring organizations and businesses.

Nicarthy, Ginny, Naomi Gottlieb, and Sandra Coffman. *You Don't Have to Take It! A Woman's Guide to Confronting Emotional Abuse at Work.* Seattle: Seal Press, 1993. Discusses the variety of emotional challenges that women face at work; explains legal remedies and strategies to overcome discrimination.

SEE ALSO: Affirmative action programs; Civil Rights Act of 1964; Equal Employment Opportunity Commission; International Ladies' Garment Workers' Union; Nooyi, Indra K.; Seneca Falls Convention; Stewart, Martha; Tupperware; Walker, Madam C. J.

Woodworking industry

DEFINITION: Enterprise that encompasses timber felling, lumber dressing and milling, and the manufacture of goods made from wood

SIGNIFICANCE: The American woodworking industry was one of the most successful large-scale production industries in the world, maximizing the use of a natural resource and driving improvements in machinery and manufacturing technology that led to interchangeable parts and mass production. The industry was successful because of its ability to meet consumer demand, to redirect itself during wartime, and to adapt to changing needs.

From America's establishment, the country's vast forested acreage provided valuable wood products. Eighteenth century soldiers and former soldiers, experienced in the mobilization of large armies, were ideally suited to manage woodworking enterprises that encompassed immense operations from forest to delivery of finished goods. With plentiful resources, available laborers, and unique operational expertise, the woodworking industry thrived. By 1800, the industry's most profitable enterprise was large-scale shipbuilding. Other woodworking enterprises included the manufacturing of carriages, wagons, furniture, and clocks.

The Industrial Revolution of the nineteenth century significantly affected the woodworking industry, resulting in a profusion of patents for machines to make woodworking production more efficient, less costly, and more profitable. The industry benefited from improved designs for such machinery as band saws and conveyor belts, the advent of electric-powered machines in 1873, rearrangements of factory floor machinery, and resequencing of processes to render them more efficient. These early innovations contributed to the mass production of wood products.

During World War I, many woodworking machines were adapted to fashion metal parts, and woodworking factories were repurposed to produce artillery components, especially replacement parts for small firearms. War efforts produced innovations, such as metal ball bearings and self-feed ripsaws, that contributed to faster and more easily adjustable woodworking machines. Both the redirecting of existing technologies and the adaptation of new technologies contributed to industry's prosperity during the war and enabled it to recover quickly afterward. Ships were eclipsed by other woodworking products, including solid and veneer furniture, wooden automobile interiors, railroad cars, and domestic construction materials.

Following U.S. entry into World War II, the government took control of the woodworking industry. Indigenous lumber was transported worldwide to build American strongholds in foreign countries. Woodworking machines were redesigned to produce war products, and factories were once again reconfigured for more efficient production. Woodworking factories appropriated for wartime production also benefited from government-sponsored machine upgrades and increased volume capabilities, boosting the postwar industries in home construction, furniture making, and wood by-products such as rayon and plastics.

During the Korean War, government takeover of the woodworking machinery resulted in the development of high-precision machine tools that again aided the postwar woodworking industry. Hardened steel gears became the standard, machined jigs produced interchangeable parts, and gang ripsaws and wide-belt sanders spurred the particleboard industry. In the latter part of the twentieth century, the lumber industry faced new challenges brought on by the environmental movement and a call to fell timber, as nearly as possible, in a sustainable fashion.

Taylor Shaw

FURTHER READING

Kinney, Thomas A. *The Carriage Trade: Making Horse-Drawn Vehicles in America.* Baltimore: Johns Hopkins University Press, 2004.

McGaw, Judith, ed. *Early American Technology: Making and Doing Things from the Colonial Era to 1850.* Chapel Hill: University of North Carolina Press, 1994.

SEE ALSO: Construction industry; Environmental movement; Forestry industry; Papermaking industry; Steel industry.

World Trade Organization

IDENTIFICATION: International organization designed to monitor, negotiate, and facilitate worldwide trade

DATE: Founded on January 1, 1995

SIGNIFICANCE: The World Trade Organization's purpose is to improve the economic standing of its members. The United States and other member states have seen increased global trade, greater access to cheaper goods, and better international relations with one another. However, the WTO is somewhat controversial, because many nations see the organization as catering to the interests of large countries, such as the United States, while ignoring others.

After World War II, many questions arose about what sorts of global institutions could be created to facilitate better economic and political cooperation in the international community. The founding of the United Nations created some assurance that political disputes could be settled through peaceful means, instead of through war. The General Agreement on Tariffs and Trade (GATT) was established in 1947 to remove trade barriers, lower tariffs, and create the free movement of goods between nations that signed the treaty, including the United States. The agreement was relatively successful in accomplishing some of its aims, but it was limited in its abilities, because members sometimes chose not to follow its mandates.

The GATT remained a force in the global economy up until 1995, when trade negotiations resulted in the creation of the World Trade Organization (WTO). The WTO had the same purpose as the GATT, to create the free movement of goods between its member states, but it sought to hold its members more accountable to lower their tariffs than could a treaty alone. The WTO also included in its aims the improvement of national service sectors rather than just industries. The United States and the other members of GATT were the first members of the WTO when it was created on January 1, 1995.

As an international body, the WTO has been extremely successful in liberalizing trade among its member states. Those states have enjoyed great economic benefits resulting from the removal of tariffs. The ability to trade freely with other nations has led to huge economic growth for the United States, and the country has experienced an increase in the amount of choices in goods that its consumers may purchase, as well as a reduction in prices for items such as food and clothing. By all accounts, the WTO has made positive developments in global trade. However, some critics would say that not all countries have experienced the economic growth or have benefited from liberalized trade to the extent that the United States has. Some smaller member countries have yet to see the economic benefits associated with free trade. The WTO has therefore been criticized as being one-sided, benefiting trade giants such as the United States at the expense of smaller nations.

Jennifer L. Titanski

FURTHER READING

Matsushita, Mitsuo, Petros Mavroidis, and Thomas Schoenbaum. *The World Trade Organization: Law, Practice, and Policy.* New York: Oxford University Press, 2006.

Narlikar, Amrita. *The World Trade Organization: A Very Short Introduction.* New York: Oxford University Press, 2005.

SEE ALSO: Agriculture, U.S. Department of; Asian trade with the United States; Canadian trade with the United States; Chinese trade with the United States; European trade with the United States; Gadsden Purchase; International economics and trade; Japanese trade with the United States; Latin American trade with the United States; Mexican trade with the United States.

World War I

THE EVENT: Large-scale European conflict between the Allies and the Central Powers in which the United States became a reluctant participant

DATES: July 28, 1914-November 11, 1918, in Europe; April 6, 1917-November 11, 1918, for the United States

PLACE: United States, Europe, and Asia

SIGNIFICANCE: During the war, the United States government dramatically increased taxes and expanded economic controls over business and industry. Despite its great expense, the war spurred American economic growth and enhanced the country's financial status in the world.

When World War I began, President Woodrow Wilson officially declared neutrality, but he was determined to assert the rights of the United States to conduct commercial relations with belligerent countries to the maximum extent possible. The resulting maritime conflict with Germany finally persuaded Wilson to ask Congress for a declaration of war. If the United States had not intervened in the war, it appears likely that the Central Powers would have prevailed.

The nineteen months of American participation in the conflict were extremely costly, in terms of both military personnel and war materials. In 1914, the armed forces of the United States included only about 200,000 men, but by the war's end, about 4 million men had served in the army, and about 2 million had served overseas. The total deaths for the armed forces were 12,432, with more half caused by disease—a large percentage from the influenza pandemic. Battle casualties included 48,909 deaths and 230,074 seriously wounded. U.S. government expenditures for the war totaled approximately $35.5 billion, which included almost $10 billion in loans to the Allies. The public debt reached more than $26 billion in August, 1919, or about $242 per person.

EARLY EFFECTS OF THE EUROPEAN WAR

In June and July of 1914, as the European countries were in the process of going to war, the initial impact on the United States was a financial crisis. Numerous European investors sold their American securities, causing a rapid drop in the price. Responding to the panic, the New York Stock Exchange (NYSE) closed its doors on July 31 and did not fully reopen for four and a half months, the longest shutdown in the exchange's history. Most Europeans were anxious to convert their American investments into gold, but a scarcity of ships put a limit on gold exports, resulting in a drastic decline in the dollar's exchange value. The financial panic produced a short but rather severe recession, in which the number of unemployed Americans more than doubled—from about 1 million in 1913 to 2.2 million in 1914.

The economic crisis, however, continued only for a few months. By early 1915, the recession had been replaced by a business boom, generated by the growth in European demand for all kinds of goods and products. American annual exports to Europe grew from about $1.5 billion in 1913 to $3.8 billion in 1916. During these same years, annual imports from Europe declined from $900 million to approximately $633 million. The decline in European exports expanded the demand for American products in many parts of the world. Total exports, therefore, more than doubled between 1913 and 1916, from about $2.5 billion to about $5.5 billion.

The increased demand for American goods had a beneficial effect on almost all segments of the economy. In 1916, the index of manufacturing production was 30 percent higher than in 1913. During this period, bank deposits also grew 30 percent, and bank loans increased from $14.6 million to $17.9 million. The nation's annual steel production grew from 31.3 million tons to 42.8 million tons. Opportunities for workers expanded greatly, primarily in northern factories. Many southerners, especially

This poster announced the launching of ninety-five ships by the Shipping Board Emergency Fleet Corporation on July 4, 1918. (Library of Congress)

African Americans, moved from the rural South to the urban North in search of jobs. The numbers of unemployed Americans declined to about 200,000 in 1916 from the 2.2 million who were unemployed in 1914.

During the three years before the United States entered the war, the economic boom resulted in an increase in prices. The index of wholesale prices increased almost 24 percent, and consumer prices went up about 11 percent. Hourly wages of manufacturing workers rose from 29 cents in 1913 to 31 cents three years later, and their annual wages went from about $578 to $651, which was very similar to the increase in the prices of consumer goods. Gross farm income grew from about $7.6 billion to $9.5 billion. At least half of this increase, however, was offset by inflation, and the parity ratio of farm prices actually declined from 100 to 94.

U.S. INTERVENTION

Early in the war, the British severely restricted the right of neutral countries to trade with Germany. When Secretary of State William Jennings Bryan called on belligerents to accept the liberal principles in the Declaration of London of 1906, the British government insisted on an expanded list of contraband goods. The U.S. State Department issued a mild protest on September 28, 1914, but to no avail. Later that year, the British added to the number of contraband items and revived the doctrine of continuous voyage, which authorized the seizure of neutral ships going to the Baltic area under control of the German navy. On November 3, 1914, the British government announced the mining of the North Sea. On March 11, it proclaimed a blockade of all German ports and authorized the seizure and confiscation of all merchant vessels entering or coming from a German port. U.S. exports to Germany dropped from $169.3 million in 1914 to less than $1.2 million in 1916. During the same period, trade with the Allies exploded from $800 million to $3 billion.

From the war's outbreak in July, 1914, until April, 1917, the European nations ran a balance-of-payments deficit of about $5.5 billion, creating substantial financial strains. The British and French governments met part of this deficit with gold shipments, of which about $1 billion came to the United States. They also financed the deficits by borrowing from private creditors. In August, 1914, the U.S. government announced that bank loans to countries at war were "inconsistent with the true spirit of neutrality." Three months later, however, the policy was modified, and the National City Bank was allowed to loan $10 million to the French government. In September, 1915, the Wilson administration reluctantly approved the floating of a loan of $500 million to France and Great Britain. By April, 1917, American investors had purchased almost $2.5 billion in bonds from the Allies, in contrast to only $20 million in German bonds.

By early 1917, American prosperity had become somewhat dependent on a continuation of export markets. Many financial experts feared that the defeat of England and France would have grave consequences for the U.S. economy. Unquestionably, the United States' close financial relationship with the Allies predisposed the country to favor the Allies and to oppose German policies. The majority of historians, however, agree that an even more important reason for U.S. hostility to Germany was its use of submarines to sink merchant ships. Two days after Germany resumed its policy of unrestricted U-boat warfare on February 1, 1917, President Wilson broke off diplomatic relations. The sinking of five American ships, combined with the Zimmermann note, in which the German foreign minister proposed an anti-U.S. alliance with Mexico and Japan, brought about a declaration of war on April 6, 1917.

FINANCING THE WAR

Even before the United States entered the war, Congress, in September, 1916, doubled the lowest personal income tax rate from 1 to 2 percent, increasing the maximum tax to 15 percent on incomes of more than $1.5 million. The minimum corporate income tax was increased from 1 to 2 percent, with a special 12.5 percent tax on profits from munitions manufacturing. In March, 1917, a second revenue act required businesses to pay an 8 percent tax on excess profits, which was defined as more than 8 percent return on invested capital.

After entering the war, Congress in 1918 raised the lowest personal income tax rate to 6 percent and raised the maximum to 77 percent on taxable income. The minimum corporate income tax was increased from 2 to 6 percent, with an increase in the excess profits tax from 20 to 60 percent. The law also increased the estate tax rate to a maximum of 25

percent and increased excise taxes on alcoholic beverages, transportation, and many other items. Based on these changes, tax revenues grew from $716 million in 1916 to about $3.6 billion in 1918, which constituted some 25 percent of the gross domestic product.

The government financed about one-third of the war by taxation and two-thirds by selling bonds and Treasury notes, paying interest rates of between 3.5 and 4.5 percent. Emphasis was on the sale of Liberty and Victory bonds, sold in small denominations to citizens. To encourage sales, the government sponsored five Liberty Loan Campaigns, which brought celebrities such as Charlie Chaplin, Babe Ruth, and Enrico Caruso to appear before huge and enthusiastic crowds, resulting in sales of about $19 billion. The total public debt of the country grew from $1.3 billion in April, 1917, to $25.5 billion in January, 1919.

During the war, the Federal Reserve focused on the credit demands of government and business rather than attempting to check inflation. The general reserve requirements for member banks were reduced by 50 percent, and the banks were permitted to increase their reserves by borrowing from the Federal Reserve Banks at low interest rates. The exportation of gold was prohibited except by a special license, so as to protect the credit base by conserving gold. The Federal Reserve note circulation, moreover, increased from $150 million to approximately $2.5 billion. The expansion in credit and currency resulted in a 25 percent increase in total deposits. Not surprisingly, the inflation rate soared; from 1915 to 1918 the consumer price index rose about 50 percent and consumer prices more than doubled.

WARTIME ECONOMIC REGULATIONS

Because of the great costs of the newer military technologies, victory to a large extent depended on the efficient management of the economy. In August, 1916, Congress began the process of developing controls with the Council of National Defense, which was charged with investigating the nation's defense and preparing for the possibility of war. The council was made up of six cabinet members and an advisory commission of seven people appointed by the president. In early 1917, the council established the Munitions Standards Board, soon replaced by the General Munitions Board, which attempted to coordinate the purchases of the Army, Navy, and Allies. Because the two agencies lacked enforcement powers, however, their recommendations were frequently ignored.

After the United States entered the war in April, 1917, the existing agencies and departments were unable to effectively deal with the growing shortages. President Wilson responded in July with an executive order creating the War Industries Board (WIB), which was reorganized with greater powers under the leadership of Bernard Mannes Baruch in March, 1918. The WIB set production quotas, allocated raw resources, and encouraged businesses to increase production though standardization. Whenever possible, the WIB tried to obtain cooperation through persuasion, but when necessary, it possessed the power to set priorities for the purchase of scarce materials, so that failure to comply with a WIB directive could result in the inability to obtain materials. No steel, copper, cement, or other important materials could be used without WIB approval. In his autobiography, Baruch relates how he coerced Henry Ford, John Dodge, and other executives at automakers to curtail the production of automobiles in favor of tanks and military trucks. In extreme cases, the WIB even had the power to seize property.

The WIB's price-fixing committee attempted to stabilize prices by negotiating three-month agreements for maximum prices that companies might charge the government. It preferred to obtain "agreed rather than decreed prices." The committee concentrated on prices for the government, and it gave relatively little attention to the prices charged to civilian consumers. The committee had no power to restrain labor costs. Although the committee promoted stable prices for short-term periods, it was unable to effectively control inflation during the last year of the war.

The war created critical shortages in many consumer areas but especially in food. In August, 1917, Congress passed the Lever Food and Fuel Control Act, which gave President Wilson broad regulatory powers. Wilson then created the Food Administration (FA) and appointed Herbert Hoover as its head. Hoover conducted an educational program to urge citizens to reduce their consumption, calling for meatless Mondays and wheatless Wednesdays. The program resulted in a 15 percent reduction in consumption without rationing. In addition to persuasion, the FA had the power to license producers, distributors, and retailers of food products. Failure to follow an FA regulation could result in the cancellation of a company's license, thus forcing it to discontinue operations. The FA's specialized agencies set the "fair prices" the government would pay for various foods, and because the government was the largest single purchaser, food prices remained relatively stable. Food exports increased from 7 million tons per year before the war to 19 million tons in 1919.

Railroad transportation was a special problem. The three thousand private railroad companies were unable to cope with the unprecedented growth in passengers and materials transported. On January 26, 1918, President Wilson ordered the temporary nationalization of the railroads as an emergency measure. The U.S. Railroad Administration, headed by Secretary of the Treasury William Gibbs McAdoo, was in charge of the operation. Congress enacted the Railroad Control Act in March, 1918, which fixed the compensation for each company and specified that government control would end twenty-one months following ratification of a peace treaty. Experts disagree about whether government operations were efficient.

During the war, organized labor, for the first time, was given equal recognition with industry. Labor representatives were represented in most of the powerful regulatory agencies. In April, 1918, President Wilson created the War Labor Board (WLB), which had the purpose of arbitrating disputes between employers and workers. After the American Federation of Labor, led by Samuel Gompers, pledged to support the war and avoid strikes, the WLB upheld the right of workers to join unions and bargain collectively and encouraged contracts based on a living wage, which helped workers but worsened the problem of inflation. Union membership almost doubled during the course of the war.

A number of other agencies were created during the war. The War Trade Board had almost complete control over trade and commercial relations with other counties. The Bureau of War Risk Insurance provided marine insurance because the risks of oceanic transportation were too great to be handled by private companies. The War Finance Corporation provided for businesses that were considered vitally necessary for the progress of the war.

During the war, the federal government established agencies for the regulation of all major sectors of the economy, and the imposition of so many regulations was a new experience for American businesses. By 1918, it is estimated that between 20 and 25 percent of the nation's output in goods and services was devoted to the war. When the war ended, the government generally yielded to pressure and quickly terminated the regulatory agencies. As a result, the country faced severe problems of inflation, reconversion, and labor-management conflict. These experiences motivated the government to seek a more gradual termination of wartime programs following World War II.

ECONOMIC CONSEQUENCES

The majority of American businesses became more prosperous during the war. Companies selling munitions to the government did particularly well. The American International Shipbuilding Corporation, for instance, organized the largest shipyard in the world at Hog Island near Philadelphia, where it built 122 large ships. The assets of the DuPont Company increased fourfold. The index of manufacturing production showed that most of the growth occurred from 1913 to 1916, and there was almost no growth in production from 1916 to 1918. Much of the increased profits in the latter years resulted from higher prices. The index of wholesale prices grew from 85.5 in 1916 to 131.3 in 1918, reflecting the problem of inflation. Although many companies reported large increases in before-tax profits, sharp increases in corporate income taxes substantially limited their after-tax profits. The United States Steel Corporation reported sales of $561 million and after-tax profits of $81 million in 1913, compared with sales of $1.3 billion and after-tax profits of $125 million in 1918. The after-tax earnings of Swift and Company, which were $9.25 million in 1913, rose to about $35 million in 1917. They declined, however, to $28 million in 1918, even though sales that year grew by almost 40 percent.

Most workers benefited moderately from the war. Unemployment almost disappeared, and the number of employed workers expanded from 38 million in 1914 to 44 million in 1918. The average annual wage in manufacturing, which was about $580 in 1914, grew to about $950 in 1918. A substantial part of the increase, however, was offset by the growth in the cost of living. For many workers outside manufacturing, wages just barely kept up with inflation.

The average number of hours worked per week decreased from 55 hours to about 52 hours. Union membership grew from 2.5 million in 1914 to about 3.4 million by late 1918. Because of the no-strike pledge, not many labor strikes occurred before armistice.

The war years did not see much change in the number of farms or in agricultural output, except for substantial increases in hogs and wheat. Because of the increased demand, gross farm income grew from $7.6 billion in 1914 to $17.7 billion in 1917. The parity ratio (ratio of prices received index to the prices paid index, based on the years 1910-1914) rose from 94 in 1916 to a peak of 118 in 1918, although nonfarm prices began to outstrip farm prices the next year.

One of the significant long-term changes from the war was the shift from an economy with relatively few governmental regulations to an economy almost entirely planned and controlled by the government. Although the majority of these controls ended with the return of peace, they provided a repertoire of precedents that would later be drawn on in designing the programs of the New Deal and World War II.

From the perspective of international history, probably the most significant change from the war was the shift in the economic balance of power. The war accentuated the favorable balance of trade in the United States, with exports growing twice as

CONSUMER PRICE INDEX, 1914-1921 (1967 = 100)

Year	All Items	Food, at Home	Rent
1914	30.1	29.8	49.6
1915	30.4	29.4	49.9
1916	32.7	33.1	50.5
1917	38.4	42.6	50.1
1918	45.1	49.0	51.0
1919	51.8	54.6	55.2
1920	60.0	61.5	64.9
1921	53.6	46.7	74.5

Source: Data from *Historical Statistics of the United States: Colonial Times to 1970* (Washington, D.C.: U.S. Department of Commerce, Bureau of the Census, 1975)

large as imports. As a result, the United States shifted from a debtor status to the world's greatest creditor. Investments in other countries doubled from $3.5 billion to about $7 billion, whereas foreign investments in the United States decreased from $7.2 billion to $3.3 billion.

Thomas Tandy Lewis

FURTHER READING

Baruch, Bernard. *American Industry in the War: A Report of the War Industries Board.* New York: Prentice-Hall, 1941. Detailed information about the WIB's regulations and relations with businesses. Not for beginners.

_____. *Baruch: The Public Years.* New York: Holt, Rinehart and Winston, 1960. A personal and interesting summary of Baruch's career, including his direction of the WIB.

Cuff, Robert. *The War Industries Board: Business-Government Relations During World War I.* Baltimore: Johns Hopkins University Press, 1973. A scholarly work emphasizing that the WIB "never overcame its diversity to win centralized, autonomous power."

Hawley, Ellis. *The Great War and the Search for a Modern Order: A History of the American People and Their Institutions, 1917-1933.* 2d ed. Long Grove, Ill.: Waveland Press, 1992. Argues that the country instituted a modern managerial order and the world's first mass consumption society after World War I.

Hughes, Jonathan, and Louis Cain. *American Economic History.* 6th ed. Reading, Pa.: Addison-Wesley, 2006. A clearly written, standard textbook that includes an excellent chapter on how World War I affected business and industry.

Kennedy, David. *Over Here: The First World War and American Society.* 2d ed. New York: Oxford University Press, 2004. A comprehensive, highly acclaimed book that includes an excellent chapter on political economics.

Schaffer, Ronald. *America in the Great War: The Rise of the War Welfare State.* New York: Oxford University Press, 1994. Describes how the demands of the war resulted in an unprecedented extension of governmental controls over the economy.

SEE ALSO: Arms industry; Great Migration; Inflation; Military-industrial complex; Taxation; War surplus; Wars; World War II.

World War II

THE EVENT: Global war fought by most of the economic and political powers of the day, who divided into two groups, the Axis and the Allies

DATE: December 8, 1941-September 2, 1945

PLACE: Europe, Asia, North America, South America, Africa, Australia

SIGNIFICANCE: World War II played a major role in the recovery of the American economy from the Great Depression, in making the United States the leading economic power in the world, stimulating consumer production, and incurring national debt.

After World War II began in Europe with Germany's occupation of Poland in September, 1939, the U.S. government declared its neutrality, but President Franklin D. Roosevelt stated that while the United States could be neutral in deed, it could not be neutral in thought. Washington was clearly on the side of the Allies—England and France—and opposed to Nazi Germany. The country was even more concerned with Japan, which had been at war in China since 1937. The war had a major impact on the American economy. Secretary of Agriculture Henry A. Wallace believed that American farmers would suffer, but profits from business began to increase almost immediately.

Before the war, hostility between labor and capital flared because of the Great Depression and business opposition to the New Deal. However, the boom stemming from Roosevelt's commitment to making the United States the arsenal of democracy to aid the Allies in the war effort led to a new spirit of cooperation between economic rivals, much of it mandated by the government. The confrontation between the U.S. government and business and industry that had dominated the 1930's ended, as both sides realized that they needed each other. Although isolationism had been popular before the war, businessmen realized that they were losing world markets and turned to Washington for help, readily supporting Roosevelt's commitment to the Allies. The government, for its part, recognized that it needed the manufacturers to supply the war material necessary to aid the Allies and prepare the American defense. Instead of nationalizing industries, Washington worked with the private sector, providing lucrative contracts guaranteeing cost of

FEDERAL GOVERNMENT SPENDING, 1939-1950, IN MILLIONS OF DOLLARS

Year	Department of the Army	Department of the Navy	Department of the Air Force	Interest on the Public Debt	Veterans Compensation and Pensions	Other	Total
1939	695	673		941	417	6,116	8,842
1940	907	891		1,041	429	5,787	9,055
1941	3,939	2,313		1,111	433	5,459	13,255
1942	14,326	8,580		1,260	431	9,441	34,038
1943	42,526	20,888		1,808	442	13,704	79,368
1944	49,438	26,538		2,609	495	15,906	94,986
1945	50,490	30,047		3,617	772	13,377	98,303
1946	27,987	15,164		4,722	1,261	11,192	60,326
1947	9,172	5,597		4,958	1,929	17,267	38,923
1948	7,699	4,285		5,211	2,080	13,681	32,956
1949	7,862	4,435	1,690	5,339	2,154	17,993	39,473
1950	5,789	4,130	3,521	5,750	2,223	18,131	39,544

Source: Data from *Historical Statistics of the United States: Colonial Times to 1970* (Washington, D.C.: U.S. Department of Commerce, Bureau of the Census, 1975)

production plus substantial profits, called a cost-plus policy, heartily endorsed by Secretary of War Henry L. Stimson, a Republican.

Speed and quantity of production took priority over questionable tactics. For example, Standard Oil received a light fine for an antitrust bargain it made in 1941 (before the United States was in the war) with the German company I. G. Farben, agreeing not to manufacture synthetic rubber. Meanwhile, natural rubber had become difficult to obtain because Japan had invaded Southeast Asia, and the U.S. government had to subsidize the manufacture of synthetic rubber in a crash program during the war, turning the patents and factories over to private companies after the war ended.

Roosevelt created oversight agencies to ensure production and labor peace, including the Office of Production Management (OPM), the War Production Board (WPB), and the Office of Price Administration and Civilian Supply (OPACS), and he adapted other New Deal agencies, such as the National Labor Relations Board (NLRB), for the war economy. The Reconstruction Finance Corporation (RFC), originally created for small businesses and home owners in the Depression, now gave loans on favorable terms to expand industry for wartime production, and as defense jobs increased employment, the government canceled the Works Progress Administration (WPA), which had provided jobs during the Depression.

INDUSTRY

Early in 1941, with war on the horizon, the U.S. government called for the construction of two hundred merchant ships. Roosevelt also created the Office of Production Management under William S. Knudsen, president of General Motors, to coordinate defense construction. Knudsen immediately announced that the production of aluminum and the manufacture of machine tools were the country's most important needs. After the United States entered the war, the president replaced the OPM with the War Production Board, under Donald M. Nelson, former president of Sears, Roebuck and Company and an assistant to Knudsen. In April, 1942, the government established the War Manpower Commission under Paul V. McNutt, a former governor of Indiana and head of the Federal Security Agency. In May, 1943, Roosevelt established the Office of War Mobilization (OWM), under former senator James F. Byrnes, to coordinate domestic activity on behalf of the war effort. Chester C. Davis, a former head of the American Agricultural Administration (AAA) in the New Deal, became the government food administrator charged with improving farm production, which had slumped after a boom year in 1942. The government also established the Office of War Information (OWI) under newspaper reporter and radio commentator Elmer Davis to supervise war news and propaganda.

The automotive industry agreed to cut production of civilian cars to concentrate on building vehicles for the military. When the United States entered the war in December, 1941, more drastic steps were taken, and all production of new cars and trucks ceased. During the war, Ford Motor Company alone made 8,600 bombers, 278,000 jeeps, and 57,000 airplane engines.

Labor

American workers benefited from plentiful jobs during World War II, although government controls over unions and workers were strengthened. In 1940, the Supreme Court ruled that decisions of the National Labor Relations Board could not be appealed. In another labor decision, the court ruled that Inland Steel of Chicago did not have to recognize the Congress of Industrial Organizations (CIO) as the company's sole bargaining unit. The forty-hour workweek had begun as a result of the Fair Labor Standards Act of 1938, although in February, 1943, the president issued an executive order calling for a forty-eight-hour workweek as a minimum in defense plants, and also in 1943, the WPB forbade 27 million workers from leaving essential defense jobs.

There had been considerable friction between the two largest labor groups in America, the craft-oriented American Federation of Labor (AFL) and the Congress of Industrial Organizations, but, in 1940, William Green, the president of the AFL, called for talks with the rival organization. The fiery president of the CIO and leader of the coal miners, John L. Lewis, resigned in November, 1940, in protest of Roosevelt's unprecedented election for a third term, and Philip Murray of the United Steelworkers succeeded him.

Strikes and labor disputes continued to trouble the defense industry. In January, 1941, the workers at the Allis-Chalmers Manufacturing Company, an agricultural machinery maker, went out on strike. Within two months, the government had established a National Defense Mediation Board under Clarence A. Dykstra, a university president and director of the selective service system, to deal with disputes, and shortly thereafter, Ford settled a strike with CIO autoworkers.

President Roosevelt, in June, 1941, sent in troops to take over North American Aviation in Los Angeles and replace the striking workers there. Meanwhile, A. Philip Randolph, leader of the Brotherhood of Sleeping Car Porters, was planning a march on Washington to demand racial justice in the American workplace. To prevent this strike, the president issued Executive Order 8802 on June 25, 1941, establishing the Committee on Fair Employment Practices and ending racial discrimination in government agencies, job-training programs, and industries and companies with defense contracts. The committee was ordered to investigate violations of the executive order. More African American workers entered in the workforce in the defense plants, and in June, 1943, a large race riot erupted in Detroit. Thirty-five people, mainly African Americans, were killed in two days.

On December 8, 1941, the day after the Japanese attack on Pearl Harbor and the day the United States entered the war, labor and industry leaders agreed to have no strikes or lockouts and settle all disputes peaceably. Both Green and Murray signed no-strike pledges, but Lewis's United Mine Workers of America (UMWA) withdrew from the CIO. In the spirit of the agreement, General Motors agreed to a 10-cent-an-hour raise and the autoworkers union ended its demand for a closed shop (one that excluded nonunion employees).

Nevertheless, in May, 1943, Lewis called a strike of coal miners. When the National War Labor Board, established in 1942, ordered them back to work, the coal miners refused. The government seized the coal mines, and Congress passed a law authorizing fuel administrator Harold Ickes, former secretary of the interior, to seize coal for industry and private use. Lewis then sought admission of the UMWA into the AFL. Later in the year, Roosevelt ordered the seizure of railroads to prevent a railroad strike but returned them to the private sector after the owners and the unions agreed to settle their dispute. In another case, the National War Labor Board judged that the CIO's demands for a contract extension with Montgomery Ward was justified, and it ordered the company to comply. However, Seward Avery, the company chair, refused, and federal troops seized the plant.

In March, 1945, strikes at the Chrysler Corporation and Briggs Manufacturing closed ten factories.

LEND-LEASE

In March, 1940, Roosevelt prepared to sell war material to England. Because this was technically a violation of American neutrality, the measure was hotly debated. Furthermore, Great Britain could not pay for the material, and it was to be provided on the basis of exchange for the lease of bases for U.S. troops in British colonies and later payment, a policy called lend-lease. The Lend-Lease bill was sent to Congress after Roosevelt's controversial third-term election victory in November. Congress passed the act in March, 1941, and extended it to France, China, the Soviet Union, and other opponents of the Axis. Initially, it was to end in 1943, but it was continued for the whole war. The Axis powers regarded this as an act of war, and several American ships carrying war material were attacked and sunk by German submarines. Furthermore, Roosevelt and Winston Churchill had met in August, 1940, in Newfoundland and signed the Atlantic Charter, outlining the goals of the war, before the United States had even entered the conflict.

PRICE CONTROLS AND RATIONING

The Office of Price Administration (OPA; independent agency since 1942) and War Production Board established price controls and rationing on all manner of goods, starting with gasoline and rubber. The OPA froze the price of steel, but the industry gave the workers a small (10 cents per hour) wage increase as a hedge by the industry against future strikes. In April, 1942, the OPA established rent controls, and in May, sugar was rationed. Soon ration books and coupons appeared. By the end of 1942, coffee was put on the list of rationed items. Different items were added as the war progressed. In 1943, shoes were limited to three pairs a year per person; the agency also ra-

tioned canned goods, meat, fish, and cheese. With rationing, a black market flourished, and Americans spent well over a billion dollars in illegal purchasing.

Toward the end of the war, rationing eased. In May, 1944, the agencies cut back on meat, with the exception of some cuts of beef. In August the WPB permitted the resumption of production of some consumer goods, increasing the number in succeeding months, but in March, 1945, the OPA froze the price on clothing until the end of the war, and from January 15 to May 8, 1945, the government ordered a reduction of the use of energy (a dimout) to save on fuel. In April, sugar rations were reduced by a quarter. In June, Congress extended the authority of the OPA for another year, but soon rationing of gasoline and automotive engine oil ended. The War Manpower Commission ended wage controls. As soon as the war was over, President Harry S. Truman ended restrictions on consumer production and collective bargaining, restoring the free market system. The WPB lifted the controls on more than two hundred products. However, rationing of a number of items, such as shoes, tires, butter, and meat, continued for a number of weeks. In August, New York State laid off 100,000 wartime workers. The second half of 1945 saw a number of labor strikes and slow-

An Office of Price Administration official guides a woman and her daughter as they use war ration book two for the first time. (Library of Congress)

downs, for example in coal mines, automakers, and the telephone company.

Several financial measures taken during the war included the sale of defense savings bonds, begun in May, 1941. The Revenue Act of 1942 increased those subject to income tax from 39 million to 42 million people, and the Current Tax Payment Act of 1943 started the withholding of income taxes from salaries throughout the year.

Bretton Woods Conference

Even before the United States entered into the war, Secretary of State Cordell Hull proposed a postwar policy for the end of trade barriers and equal access of all nations for raw materials. However, only in July, 1944, did the Allies meet to discuss and plan financial affairs for the postwar world at a conference held at the Mount Washington Hotel in Bretton Woods, New Hampshire. Representatives from forty-five Allied nations attended. Germany had been already defeated, and the war with Japan concluded the following month. The conference discussed the financial needs of the postwar world, the measures to be taken, and what organizations and institutions would have to be formed. One of the effects of the conference, along with other economic conferences of the war era and the war itself, was to shift the world economic center to the United States and make the dollar rather than the British pound and the French franc the standard for international currency.

The delegates agreed that freedom of trade among all nations was a necessary condition of healthy international commerce and that a universal agreement on international exchange was needed to prevent single nations or small groups of nations from disrupting trade, which would lead to war. For this purpose, the conference promoted the International Monetary Fund and the International Bank for Reconstruction and Development to aid in postwar reconstruction.

Impact

The war effort proved to be an unprecedented success in providing the armament for the Allied victory. Geographically distant from Axis bombing, the United States could build the weapons needed for its own armies and those of its Allies. The war materials produced included almost 300,000 planes, 400,000 pieces of artillery, 44 billion rounds of am-munition, and an additional 47 million tons of artillery ammunition. The United States also turned out more than 93,000 ships and 86,000 tanks.

World War II created a boom in the American economy. The need for war production lifted the United States out of the Depression by providing full employment, record profits for business, and high wages for workers. New areas of production were introduced, and despite the wartime rationing, manufacture of consumer goods also received an impetus, which took off after the war was over.

The wartime prosperity increased corporate and business profits at an astounding rate. The one hundred largest U.S. corporations received more than 70 percent of the contracts, and hundreds of thousands of smaller companies closed. Farm income increased two and half times, despite the loss of 800,000 hands, as agriculture benefited mainly from the creation of larger farms. Workers' wages doubled during the war years (from $25 to $50 a week), in part because of overtime. The labor force increased by more than 20 percent, with 60 percent of American women entering the workforce. African Americans found opportunities earlier denied them, and 1.2 million of them entered the workforce. Tens of thousands migrated from the South to the North for industrial jobs. Labor unions increased their membership by almost 50 percent, from 10.5 million to almost 15 million. However, one of the costs of this production was the indebtedness that it brought about.

After the war, the industrial force was converted to peacetime use by an increase of production of consumer goods. The Truman administration tried to keep production in bounds by maintaining the wartime commissions, but pressure from business and the public forced Congress to relax the restrictions. Another consequence was the postwar baby boom, which produced an exceptional spike in the American birthrate after a decade and a half of the Depression and war. The effects of this phenomenon on the economy and society endured throughout the rest of the century and beyond.

Frederick B. Chary

Further Reading

Bondi, Victor, ed. *American Decades, 1940-1949.* Detroit: Gale Research, 1995. Examines all aspects of American life during the 1940's. Chapter 3 deals specifically with business and the economy.

Includes a time line of significant events. Contains a bibliography.

Boughton, James M., and K. Sarwar Lateef, eds. *Fifty Years After Bretton Woods: The Future of the IMF and the World Bank—Proceedings of a Conference Held in Madrid, Spain, September 29-30, 1994*. Washington, D.C.: IMF, 1995. A detailed examination of the historic conference.

Brandes, Stuart D. *Warhogs: A History of War Profits in America*. Lexington: University Press of Kentucky, 1997. A scholarly monograph examining profiteering in American wars and the attempts to control it. Covers the whole history of the United States. Contains tables, notes, and a bibliography.

Davis, Kenneth S. *FDR: The War Years 1940-1943—A History*. New York: Random House, 2000. A scholarly but readable biography of the president by a respected professor.

Koistinen, Paul A. C. *Arsenal of World War II: The Political Economy of American Warfare, 1940-1945*. Lawrence: University Press of Kansas, 2004. The most important monograph dealing with the subject. Contains notes, bibliography, and figures.

_____. *The Hammer and the Sword*. New York: Arno Press, 1979. Examines the role of labor in World War II.

Lee, Susan, and Peter Passell. *A New Economic View of American History*. New York: Norton, 1979. A standard economic history of the United States covering the whole scope of American history, including the World War II era.

SEE ALSO: Automotive industry; Bretton Woods Agreement; Great Depression; Korean War; Labor strikes; Lend-Lease Act; Military-industrial complex; National Labor Relations Board; Steel industry; War surplus; Wars; World War I.

WorldCom bankruptcy

THE EVENT: Financial failure of WorldCom, a major telecommunications company, after an internal auditor discovered large-scale fraud by management

DATE: Filed for bankruptcy on July 21, 2002

PLACE: Clinton, Mississippi

SIGNIFICANCE: The publicity surrounding the uncovering of the WorldCom fraud resulted in greater auditor oversight over American corporations and greater government oversight over auditors. In 2002, Congress passed the Sarbanes-Oxley Act, which held senior executives responsible for the accuracy and completeness of corporate financial reports.

In 2002, WorldCom was the second-largest long-distance phone company in the United States. It had achieved this size largely by acquisitions, such as that of MCI Communications in 1998. However, the telecommunications industry had begun a downturn in 1999. WorldCom's stock had begun falling from its high of more than $64 in June of 1999, and its attempt to acquire Sprint in 2000 failed, largely because of government pressure.

Eugene Morse, an auditor working under Cynthia Cooper, discovered irregularities that suggested fraud in 2002. Cooper, Morse, and others in the Internal Audit department began an investigation of the fraud, despite being ordered to stop their work by Scott Sullivan, WorldCom's chief financial officer. Cooper learned that the company had misallocated nearly $4 billion of expenses. She became fearful of retribution from those who had perpetrated the fraud and worried about all the WorldCom employees who might lose their jobs if the fraud were revealed. Nevertheless, she refused to be intimidated and alerted the company's outside auditing firm.

On July 21, 2002, WorldCom filed for Chapter 11 bankruptcy, with $107 billion in assets, making it the largest bankruptcy in U.S. history at the time (exceeded by the bankruptcy of Lehman Brothers, with assets of $639 billion, in 2008). After WorldCom entered into bankruptcy, additional audits found other schemes that brought the total fraud to more than $11 billion.

In 2005, Sullivan was convicted of securities fraud, conspiracy, and seven counts of filing false reports with regulators, and Chief Executive Officer Bernard Ebbers was convicted of securities fraud and conspiracy charges. One of the motivations for creating the fraudulent financial statements was that Ebbers and Sullivan received sizeable bonuses and stock options when the company was profitable. Thus, the company was made to look more profitable than it really was. Ebbers was sentenced to twenty-five years in federal prison for his part in the fraud, and Sullivan was sentenced to five years as part of a plea agreement in which he agreed to testify against Ebbers.

The bankruptcy of World-Com has often been attributed to its fraudulent accounting. However, most likely neither the fraud nor its discovery are responsible for the downfall. The company's stock was already falling. Corporate decisions, such as loading the company with debt and making inappropriate acquisitions; the Internet mania that swept the country at the time; and the implosion of the telecommunications industry all played a role in reducing the company's value. It seems likely that the company was going to go bankrupt because of poor management and that the fraudulent accounting acted primarily to hide the depth of WorldCom's financial troubles from the world for a while.

Dale L. Flesher

Bernard Ebbers, former WorldCom CEO, leaves Manhattan federal court in 2006. (AP/Wide World Photos)

FURTHER READING

Colvin, Geoffrey. "The Other Victims of Bernie Ebbers' Fraud." *Money,* August 8, 2005.

Cooper, Cynthia. *Extraordinary Circumstances: Journey of a Corporate Whistleblower.* New York: John Wiley & Sons, 2008.

Jeter, L. W. *Disconnected: Deceit and Betrayal at World-Com.* New York: John Wiley & Sons, 2003.

SEE ALSO: Accounting industry; Antitrust legislation; Business crimes; Enron bankruptcy; Incorporation laws; Justice, U.S. Department of; Telecommunications industry; Tyco International scandal.

WTO. *See* World Trade Organization

Z

Zoning, commercial

DEFINITION: Land-use laws regulating the permissible locations and activities of businesses

SIGNIFICANCE: Commercial zoning, nonexistent in early American history, has come to play a crucial role in the land-use patterns of American business over the last century. Businesses are confined to certain locations, commercial operations are regulated, and residential subdivisions are developed in accord with zoning ordinances.

During the early years of the United States, property rights in land were considered nearly absolute. The law allowed commercial property owners the untrammeled acquisition, use, and disposal of their land. Thus, commercial enterprises of every kind—stores, factories, offices, hotels, and restaurants—were free to locate in any population center, even among residences, churches, schools, and parks. Commercial usage of property was largely unrestrained except for inherently dangerous industrial processes, which might be subject to nuisance laws.

Occasional controls on height, size, and noxious uses of commercial buildings were enacted around the turn of the twentieth century. In 1916, New York City enacted the first comprehensive zoning plan that divided the city into "business," "residential," and unrestricted districts. By 1925, over five hundred cities had implemented zoning plans classifying land by the permitted use, bulk, and shape of any commercial buildings located on it. Some property owners, especially those in the real estate industry, were alarmed by what they claimed to be an intrusion into the constitutional right of landowners to hold and utilize property wherever and however they saw fit. In *Euclid v. Ambler Realty* (1926), the U.S. Supreme Court rejected a challenge by a real estate firm to the constitutionality of zoning. Within five years, thirty-five states, supported by the federal government, had passed zoning laws that regulated the geography and patterns of commerce.

The authority for commercial zoning derived from state legislation under the inherent power of governments to regulate the use of property for the health, safety, morals, and welfare of their citizens. Zoning codes were usually the work of local city councils and commissions, assisted by professional land-planning experts. Over the years, numerous administrative procedures were created to allow for individual variations from zoning plans. Businesses could follow these procedures for obtaining individual relief from zoning regulations by seeking an amendment, variance, conditional use, special exception, or rezoning from the municipal board authorized to make adjustments. Such a process only emphasizes, however, how much zoning mechanisms defer market forces and business decisions—for better or worse—to the deliberations and politics of local planners and citizen groups.

POSTWAR COMMERCIAL ZONING

Since World War II, almost all urban areas in the United States have employed commercial zoning plans. In addition, the extensive postwar creation of suburbs and housing developments throughout the United States has followed the pattern of commercial zoning, regulating the number of residences, family composition, acreage, building size, lot size, aesthetic considerations, historic preservation, and recreational usage of residential life. Perhaps the central characteristic of zoning is that it excludes industry, commerce, temporary housing, and even apartment buildings from bedroom communities and single-family neighborhoods. Industrial performance standards are a form of commercial zoning that seek more specific regulations of industrial uses. Industrial performance standards mandate explicit requirements in controlling such industrial by-products as noise, smoke, smell, vibration, dust, glare, heat, radioactivity, and emissions.

Communities have used commercial zoning to preserve or change their economic demographics. Zoning has long been used to attract industrial uses so as to increase the municipal tax base. Some zoning plans provide for total exclusion of commercial enterprises from residential zones. Municipalities have made use of both cumulative zoning and exclusive zoning. Cumulative zoning, also known as "Euclidean" zoning, allows "higher" uses in lower-rated zones, such as permitting residential uses in commercial and industrial zones. Exclusive zoning permits only the designated use, for example, allowing only factories to locate in industrial zones. Cumulative zoning was the norm in early zoning plans; exclusive zoning has been the modern trend. Related to commercial zoning are the creation of "enterprise" zones, which are economically disadvantaged and blighted areas. Businesses are eligible to receive commercial and tax incentives if they remain in or relocate to enterprise zones.

CONTROVERSY

Neighborhood homogenization, suburban sprawl, overheated housing development, and environmental degradation have been blamed on rigid, or misguided, or self-interested zoning laws. Commercial zoning raises both economic and legal issues of its own. From an economic perspective, commercial zoning has its critics who claim that segregating commercial uses benefits neither business nor residential districts. It has been claimed that forcing residents into their cars for a drive to a supermarket or to a doctor's office saps towns and villages of the diverse commercial and housing patterns that make for charming and habitable cities. Likewise, restrictive commercial zoning may give rise to legal challenges for anticompetitiveness, infringement of commercial free speech, and racial and economic discrimination.

In response, some states have required municipalities to allow their fair share of commercial usage as well as low-income housing. Planned unit developments (PUDs), beginning to appear in the United States during the 1960's, benefit from relaxed zoning requirements in exchange for keeping open space in air or on land. During the 1970's, municipalities began to compensate businesses for the restrictions imposed on them with transfer development rights (TDRs), which grant development rights in other parcels of land. The use of TDRs as compensation found support in the landmark historic-preservation case *Penn Central Transportation Co. v. New York City* (1978).

In the last twenty years, many municipalities have strictly regulated the kinds of businesses that can locate in certain commercial zones. For example, they have sought to confine adult entertainment businesses to red-light zones, if not to ban them entirely. Some of these zoning ordinances have been chal-

lenged on First Amendment grounds. Likewise, zoning that seeks to reduce commercial competition by restricting new or competing businesses from locating in certain areas has been found to violate federal antitrust laws. Although commercial zoning began in urban areas, one of the most heated areas of contention in contemporary zoning is in agricultural districts. Much of the land outside urban areas has been zoned for agricultural and rural use. With the extension of residential development into these rural areas, land developers and subdividers have clamored for rezoning to accommodate new housing; land conservationists have fought to maintain and often strengthen zoning regulations to preserve farmland and rural areas.

Howard Bromberg

FURTHER READING

Ellickson, Robert, and Vicki Breen. *Land Use Controls: Cases and Materials.* 3d ed. New York: Aspen, 2005. Collection of judicial cases and notes regarding commercial zoning and other issues of land use.

Elliot, Donald L. *A Better Way to Zone: Ten Principles to Create More Livable Cities.* Washington, D.C.: Island Press, 2008. Identifies what the author regards as problems with zoning that interfere with urban development and suggests solutions.

Fischel, William. *The Economics of Zoning Laws: A Property Rights Approach to American Land Use Controls.* Baltimore: Johns Hopkins University Press, 1987. Economic analysis of commercial zoning.

Platt, Rutherford. *Land Use and Society: Geography, Law, and Public Policy.* Rev. ed. Washington, D.C.: Island Press, 2004. Comprehensive survey of the legal, cultural, and geographical issues facing land use and zoning planners.

Wolf, Michael Allan. *The Zoning of America: Euclid v. Ambler.* Lawrence: University Press of Kansas, 2008. History of the landmark U.S. Supreme Court case brought by an Ohio real estate company challenging the constitutionality of zoning.

SEE ALSO: Construction industry; Land laws; Real estate industry, commercial; Real estate industry, residential; Supreme Court and land law.

APPENDIXES

Glossary

abatement: Reduction of the amount of tax levied on an entity

abolitionist movement: Nineteenth century movement to do away with slavery

accounting: Systematic recording, analyzing, and reporting the financial data of a business or corporation

accounts payable: Balance due to a creditor in a current account

accounts receivable: Balance due from a debtor on a current account

affirmative action: Positive steps taken to increase representation of women and minorities in areas of employment, education, and business

agency shop: In labor law, a unionized workplace where employees who are nonunion workers must pay fees to the union; illegal in states with right-to-work laws

agency theory: Theory explaining the relationship between the principals (shareholders) and agents (company managers); an issue is ensuring that their goals are compatible

aggregate demand: Total amount of goods and services demanded in an economy in a given time period

agribusiness: Industry engaged in the production and sale of crops and livestock on a large scale

agricultural revolution: Period during which farmers began to produce crops using different, more efficient methods

agriculture: Sector of the economy encompassing the production of food crops and livestock

American Dream: Belief or hope that an energetic, hardworking person can become prosperous

amortization: Gradual reduction of book value of an asset

annual report: Yearly financial report of a corporation, used to assess performance by stockholders, investors, and analysts

annuity: Type of insurance that provides the insured a regular income after reaching a specific age in return for paying a set premium

antitrust laws: Laws to protect trade and commerce from unlawful restraints and monopolies or unfair business practices

appreciation: Increase in value of currency or other assets; the opposite of depreciation

apprenticeship: Practice of learning a trade through practical experience under skilled workers

arbitrage: Almost simultaneous purchase and sale of securities in different markets so as to profit from price discrepancies

arbitration: Means of settling disputes so as to avoid or resolve strike issues

artificial seniority: In discrimination law, granting minority or female workers extra years of work credit to make up for past acts of discrimination

artisans: Workers who make products in limited quantities, often using traditional methods

assembly line: Physical arrangement whereby partially finished goods move from worker to worker

asset: Something of value that a person or business owns

asset, intangible: *See* intangible asset

associationalism: Government-business cooperation to boost speed of output

associative state: Process by which government facilitates private interactions without having a source of power itself

assumption-of-risk doctrine: Principle that holds that when workers take a job, they are aware of and accept any risks involved

audit: Official examination of a company's financial accounts and records for the purpose of verification

augmented product: Core product plus any additional services and benefits supplied. *See also* core product

automated teller machine (ATM): Computerized device that provides customers of a financial institution access to funds or account balances

automation: Technique of making an apparatus, process, or system operate by mechanical or electronic means

baby boom: Marked rise in birthrate between 1946 and 1964

back pay: Compensation for past economic loss caused by an employer's discriminatory employment practices or other failure to pay wages due an employee

backward integration: Obtaining ownership or increased control of an organization's supply systems. *See also* forward integration, vertical integration

bailout: Government intervention, through loans or other means, to save failing institutions or corporations considered vital to the economy

balance of trade, favorable: Situation in which a country's exports exceed its imports for a given time period

balance of trade, unfavorable: Situation in which a country's imports exceed its exports for a given time period

bank failure: Inability of a bank to meet credit obligations; closing of insolvent banks

bankruptcy laws: Laws that allow businesses or individuals with more debts than assets to liquidate their assets to relieve their debts; businesses and individuals may also receive partial relief for their debts and reorganize or create a repayment plan, respectively

bartering: Trading by exchanging commodities rather than cash

bear market: Market in which the main trend in security or commodity prices is downward and each high and low is lower than the previous. *See also* bull market

benefit segmentation: Dividing the population into different groups according to the benefits wanted or needed and the costs to be avoided

bimetallism: Use of two metals jointly as a monetary standard

Black Friday: September 24, 1869, the date on which a financial panic began on Wall Street

Black Monday: October 19, 1987, when the Down Jones Industrial Average of stocks fell by more than 500 points.

Black Tuesday: October 29, 1929, when the stock prices on the New York Stock Exchange collapsed, leading to the Great Depression

blacklisting: Figuratively or actually listing persons or companies to stop doing business with

block trades: Large amounts of securities being traded, usually by institutional investors

blue-sky laws: Laws that regulate the offering and sale of securities

board of trade: Association of bankers and businesspeople to promote common commercial interests

bond: Interest-bearing certificate sold by corporations and governments to raise money for expansion or capital

bottom-up planning: Management system in which programs are developed by middle- and lower-level managers plus other employees or volunteers, who work out the details and follow through on them. *See also* top-down planning

boycott: Cessation of dealings with a business to show disapproval or force acceptance of some condition

bracket creep: Movement into a higher tax bracket resulting from income increases intended to offset inflation

brand equity manager: Person who monitors brand management to prevent dissipating brand value through short-term profit maximization

breach of contract: Failure, lacking legal excuse, of a promisor to perform according to contract terms

breakeven: Point at which the revenues from sales equal the financial costs of a product

bull market: Market in which the main trend in security or commodity prices is upward, and each high and low is higher than the previous. *See also* bear market

business cycles: Repetitive cycles of economic expansion and recession within an industry

business school: Institution that offers courses in aspects of business such as marketing, finance, and law

capital: Collective term for a body of goods and monies from which future income can be derived

capital market: Market for securities in which companies and governments can raise long-term funds

capitalism: Economic system based on private ownership and control of the means of production

capital-intensive business: Business that requires large amounts of financial resources to produce goods or services

cartel: Combination of independent companies designed to limit competition or fix prices

cash flow: Cash money flowing into and out of a business

catalog shopping: Purchasing items after viewing descriptions and often a photograph of the items in a publication from a mail-order company. *See also* mail order

catchment area: Geographic region from which the bulk of an organization's customers are drawn

category killers: Giant cut-rate retailers that threaten small stores in the categories of products sold by the big stores

caveat emptor: Principle in commerce by which the buyer alone is responsible for determining a product's quality before purchasing it

center firm: Big, capital-intensive business; the opposite of a peripheral firm

certificate of deposit: Time deposit that cannot be withdrawn until its maturity date, at which time it can be renewed or withdrawn

chain store: Store that is part of a group of stores that share the same ownership and name and sell the same line of goods

charter: Document conferring rights on an individual or group of people

chattel: Movable article of personal property not attached to a building

checks and balances: Practice of dispensing political power and creating mutual accountability among political entities

chief executive officer (CEO): Top-level officer in a corporation, often chair of the board of directors or president

chief financial officer (CFO): Top-level financial officer in a corporation

chief operating officer (COO): Corporation officer who manages day-to-day operations

child labor: Employment of children under the legally determined age in factories, stores, and other locations

civil rights: Rights of personal liberty guaranteed to citizens

Civil Rights movement: Large-scale social movement during the 1950's and 1960's that fought racial discrimination in employment, housing, travel, and public accommodations

closed shop: Establishment that hires only union members in good standing

cluster sampling: Sampling of a population by dividing it into heterogeneous groups (clusters), each of which is representative of the total population

codes of fair competition: Plans intended to standardize prices for the same products made by different companies

COLA: *See* cost-of-living adjustment

collective bargaining: Process in which union representatives negotiate with management over the terms of agreements dictating the conditions of employment

commodity: Any item that can be bought or sold and delivered, and is indistinguishable among producers

communism: Economic system characterized by the collective ownership of property and the organization of labor to benefit all workers

community property: Property owned in common by husband and wife

Confederate currency: Paper money that lacked gold or silver backing but was used by Southerners during the U.S. Civil War as a medium of exchange

conglomerate: Corporation that is made up of companies operating in diverse, unrelated fields

conglomerate merger: Merger between two noncompetitive companies

consignment shop: Store that sells goods and pays a percentage of the sales price of any particular item to the person who brought it in

consumer price index (CPI): Economic indicator published monthly by the U.S. Bureau of Labor Statistics that measures changes in the average cost of goods and services bought by consumers

contingency budget: Funds set aside in advance to finance a response to an unexpected event

contract: *See* specific type of contract

contract laws: Laws pertaining to an agreement between or among parties in which each party has obligations and consequences for breach of those obligations

contributing negligence doctrine: Principle under which, if an accident occurs at work, the employee is at least partially responsible

convenience goods: Products that consumers purchase frequently, immediately, and with a minimum of effort in comparison and shopping. *See also* shopping goods, specialty goods

"coolie" labor: Derogatory term applied to the unskilled workers from China and other parts of Asia who supplied manual labor after the abolition of slavery

cooperative: Business owned and controlled by those who use its services or are employed by it

coordinated decentralization: Concept whereby local entities are held accountable to state or federal standards while adapting methods to local conditions

copyright: Document granting exclusive right to publish and sell literary, musical, or artistic work

corporation: Organization created by a government charter that allows people to associate for a common purpose under a common name

core product: Central elements of a product that serve basic consumer or societal needs. *See also* augmented product

cost-of-living adjustment (COLA): Adjustment made to a source of income to counteract effects of inflation

cotton gin: Machine that mechanically removes the seeds from cotton fibers

counterfeiting: Production of imitations with the intent to present them as the real, original item

counting house: Originally, the site at which a business operated; later, the accounting operations of a firm

coupon: Certificate entitling its owner to something of value, such as interest in the case of a bond or a price discount from a retail store

covenant: In property law, a written agreement that places restrictions on use of property; normally passes from owner to owner over time

CPI: *See* consumer price index

craft union: Union organized on the basis of a specified set of skills or occupations

creative destruction: Technology that replaces outmoded technologies

credit card: Card allowing its owner to buy goods and services by charging them to an account and paying for them later

credit unions: Cooperative financial institutions that are privately owned and controlled by their members

currency: Unit of exchange that facilitates the transfer of goods and services; one form of money

customer service: All the supplementary services provided to satisfy consumers and outdo competitors

dairy industry: Sector of the agricultural industry that produces milk, butter, and cheese, mainly from cattle

daylight saving time (DST): Practice of advancing or turning back clocks for purposes such as extending daylight, safety, and utility savings

debit card: Card that allows its user to deduct money from a bank account after entering a personal identification number (PIN) either to obtain cash or to pay a retailer

deficit financing: Borrowing by a government agency to make up for a revenue shortfall

deficit spending: Spending of public funds raised by borrowing rather than by taxation

deflation: Falling prices. *See also* inflation, stagflation

demand, elasticity of: *See* elasticity of demand

demand, pent-up: *See* pent-up demand

demand-side economics: Theory that advocates the use of government spending and growth in the money supply to stimulate demand for goods and thus economic expansion

demographic segmentation: Differentiating people according to variables such as age, sex, religion, and income

department store: Store selling a wide variety of goods that is divided into separate sections featuring different types of products

depletion allowances: In tax law, deductions from gross income allowed for use of exhaustible commodities

depreciation: Noncash expense that reduces the value of an asset as a result of wear, age, or obsolescence, or loss of value of a country's currency relative to that of other countries; the opposite of appreciation

depression: Severe or long recession; often an economic downturn in which the real gross domestic product declines by more than 10 percent. *See also* Great Depression, recession

deregulation: Process by which governments remove, reduce, or simplify restrictions on businesses

discount store: Store that sells products at prices below those of traditional retailers

diversification: Process of entering new markets with products that were not previously offered by the organization

dividend: Portion of profit or earnings distributed by a corporation to its stockholders

dot-com bubble: Period, roughly 1995-2001, during which stock market values in Western countries rose rapidly in the Internet sector before declining

Dow Jones Industrial Average (DJIA): One of several stock market indices that gauge the performance of American stock markets

downsizing: Decrease in employees to enhance continued company profitability

drug trafficking: Criminal trade in illegal or controlled substances

dry county/town: County or town whose government prohibits the sale of alcoholic beverages. *See also* wet county/town

DST: *See* daylight saving time

dual economy: Existence of two separate economic systems in a nation or area

due process: Constitutional limitation providing for a person's right not to be deprived of life, liberty, or property without a fair and just hearing

dumping: Trade practice of selling products in foreign countries at artificially low prices

Dust Bowl: Period during the 1930's of severe dust storms, causing major ecological and agricultural damage to American prairie lands

duty: Tax imposed on the exportation or importation of goods

e-commerce: Purchasing or selling goods on the Internet. *See also* online marketing

economies of scale: Lower per-unit costs that result from production facilities with greater capacity

elasticity of demand: Responsiveness of the demand for a good or service to an increase or decrease in its price

e-mail: Sending and receiving messages through a computer or other electronic device

embargo: Legal prohibition of commerce and trade

emigration: Outflow of nationals from a country; the opposite of immigration

empowerment: Increasing capacity of employees to make choices that may result in their desired actions and outcomes

energy crisis: Steep decrease in the supply of energy resources in a community, leading to higher prices

entrepreneur: Person organizing, managing, and assuming the risk of a new business

environmental movement: Scientific, social, and political movement for addressing environmental concerns

e-payments: Electronic transfer of funds to make payments to creditors

equal opportunity employer: Employer who agrees not to discriminate against any employee or job applicant because of race, color, religion, national origin, sex, physical or mental disability, or age

equity: In security law, an ownership claim on a business interest, usually a security with no repayment terms such as a share of stock

excise tax: Tax on the sale of goods

exculpatory contract: Contract that releases one party from liability for wrongdoing

exports: Goods conveyed from one country or region to another for purposes of trade; the opposite of imports

farm subsidies: Government programs to support prices of agricultural products and stabilize farm income

fast food: Food, usually of lower quality and price, that can be prepared and served quickly

fellow-servant doctrine: Principle that holds that an employer is not responsible for an employee's injury if it is caused by a coworker's negligence

feminist movement: Social and political movement to advance women's rights

financing, deficit: *See* deficit financing

fixed cost: Cost that remains unchanged for a given time period despite changes in the number of items produced or services performed. *See also* variable cost

flat tax: Tax, usually based on income, that has the same tax rate for each taxable unit

food stamps: Government-issued coupons redeemable for food that are sold or given to low-income persons

foreclosure: Termination of a mortgage, in which after the borrower defaults, the mortgage holder takes possession of the property by court order

formalization: Process in which management establishes structures and procedures to determine priorities among competing management objectives

forward integration: Obtaining ownership or increased control of a company's distribution chain. *See also* backward integration, vertical integration

401(k) retirement plan: Retirement savings account funded through pretax payroll deductions

four P's: Product, price, place, and promotion, the basic ingredients in marketing that influence a consumer's decision to buy

franchise: License granted to individuals or businesses to market a company's goods or services in a given area

free silver movement: Nineteenth century movement advocating unlimited coinage of silver

free trade: Trading of goods among countries without tariffs or other governmental interference

frequent-flyer program: Service offered by airlines to reward customer loyalty

futures: Agreements to deliver a commodity at a future date at a specific price

garnishment: Legal process by which a creditor appropriates a debtor's wages

gas wars: Competition, by lowering prices, between or among service station owners to stay competitive

GDP: *See* gross domestic product

generic competitor: Competitor offering a product that, while different, satisfies the same general consumer need

genetic engineering: Direct manipulation of an organism's genes to enhance or impart a desired characteristic

Gilded Age: Period during the late nineteenth century of major American population growth and extravagant display of wealth

glass ceiling: Figurative barrier that keeps women from advancing into management positions

globalization: Integration of national economies into international ones

GNP: *See* gross national product

gold rush: Period of feverish migration into an area where gold has been discovered, in search of wealth

gold standard: Commitment among countries to fix prices of domestic currencies in terms of a specified amount of gold

golden parachute: Generous severance agreement that a corporation manager negotiates

gospel of wealth: View associated with Andrew Carnegie that large sums of money should not be in the hands of those ill-equipped to handle them

Granger movement: Nineteenth century American agrarian movement centered on advocacy groups known as the Grange

Great Depression: Worldwide economic depression brought on in part by the collapse of the U.S. stock market in 1929. *See also* depression

Great Migration: Migration of about 7 million African Americans out of the southern states to other areas of the United States

Great Society: Set of domestic programs involving social reforms that were proposed or enacted on the initiative of President Lyndon B. Johnson

greed decade: 1980's, when financial innovators received outrageously high earnings relative to their responsibilities

greenback: U.S. Treasury note printed with green ink, which replaced gold and silver as legal tender for most public and private debts

gross domestic product (GDP): Total market value of the goods and services produced in a given year; investment, government, and consumer spending plus the value of exports, minus the value of imports; includes only goods and services produced in the United States, regardless of the nationality of the producer

gross national product (GNP): Value of all the goods and services produced in a given year plus the value of the goods and services imported, minus the value of the goods and services exported; includes goods and services produced by U.S. firms operating overseas but does not include goods and services produced by foreign firms in the United States

handshake agreement: Business transaction carried out without a contract

hedge fund: Fund that invests in almost any opportunity in any market in which impressive gain at reduced risk seems possible

holding company: Corporation that owns enough voting stock in one or more companies to exercise control over them

homestead exemption laws: Laws that protect home values from property taxes, creditors, and circumstances arising from death of a homeowner's spouse

homesteading: Acquisition of U.S. public land by filing an application, living on and cultivating the tract, and filing for a deed

horizontal price fixing: Agreement among competitors to charge noncompetitive prices

hostile takeover: Attempt to gain control of a company that is strongly resisted by the target firm

hunter-gatherer society: Society whose primary means of subsistence is direct procurement of edible plants and animals from the wild

identity theft: Fraud that involves getting benefits by pretending to be someone else

immigration: Inflow of foreign nationals into a country; the opposite of emigration

imports: Goods brought in from another country or area for purposes of trade; the opposite of exports

income tax: Tax on a corporation or person's income; may be local, state, or federal

indentured labor: Work done for a prespecified period of time to pay off a debt, or workers under such contracts

Indian removal: Federal policy that sought to relocate Native American tribes east of the Mississippi River to lands west of the river during the 1830's

individual retirement account (IRA): Retirement savings account that offers tax advantages for the depositor

Industrial Revolution, American: Period between 1790 and 1914, when the United States changed from an agrarian to an industrialized economy

industrialization: Social and economic change from an agrarian society to one that relies on mechanized production

inequality of wealth: Disparity in the distribution of economic assets

inflation: Rise in price levels over time. *See also* deflation, stagflation

infrastructure: Public and quasi-public facilities and utilities, such as transportation and communications systems, water and power lines, and schools, that are necessary for the functioning of an economy

insider trading: Trading of a corporation's securities by people with access to nonpublic information

installment buying: System of paying for goods or services with payments over time

intangible asset: Something of value that has no physical substance, such as goodwill in a firm, a brand, or patent

interest rate: Percentage of the principal paid as a fee on borrowed capital

interlocking directorate: Practice of corporate board directors serving on boards of multiple corporations

internal migration: Movement of groups of people from one area of a country to another

IRA: *See* individual retirement account

jobber: Person who buys buy merchandise from manufacturers and sells it to retailers

joint-stock company: Company in which only the amount invested can be lost, unlike in a partnership

junk bond: High-risk bond that offers high yields; a speculative bond

just-in-time manufacturing: A management technique in which raw materials and parts are not stored in inventory but bought and delivered as needed

Keynesian economics: Theory of economics that holds that active governmental intervention in the marketplace and monetary policy is the best way to ensure economic growth and stability

labor union: Organization of workers formed to advance the interests of its members

laissez-faire: Theory or system of government that holds that governments should not intervene in the economy

lend-lease: Program during World War II in which the president of the United States supplied Allied nations with war materiel in return for payments made directly or indirectly

leveraged buyout: Use of a target company's asset value to finance acquisition debt

loan, nonperforming: *See* nonperforming loan

lottery: Form of gambling in which the winner is selected by the drawing of lots from people who have paid to participate

Louisiana Purchase: Acquisition of the vast Louisiana Territory from France in 1803

machine boss: Person at the head of a political group that controls enough votes to ensure political and administrative dominance in a community

macroeconomics: Study of broad, aggregate variable and how they affect the economy as a whole

mail order: Order for goods, online, by telephone, or through the mail, to be delivered by conventional or express mail. *See also* catalog shopping

market niche: Segment of a market that can be distinguished from the rest of the market by specific characteristics

market penetration: Percentage of a market captured by a specific product

market segmentation: Identification of homogeneous submarkets or segments within the target market

marketing, online: *See* online marketing

Marshall Plan: Four-year program begun in 1947 to provide reconstruction assistance to seventeen European nations following World War II

mass production: Large-scale production of goods with interchangeable, standardized parts, typically to reduce per-unit costs and thereby increase sales

Medicaid: U.S. government-administered health program for low-income individuals

Medicare: U.S. government-administered health insurance program for people aged sixty-five or over or who meet other special criteria

merchant marine: Fleet of U.S.-owned ships engaged in transportation of goods in and out of the United States in peacetime that, in wartime, serves as an auxiliary to the Navy to deliver troops and military supplies

merger: Combination of two or more companies to form a single one

microeconomics: Study of economics that analyzes the market behavior of individual companies, households, or specific industries

migration: Movement from one locality to another. *See also* Great Migration, internal migration

minority: Portion of the population that differs from the majority population in some respect

mint: Place where coins, medals, or tokens are made

mixed economy: Capitalist economy in which part of the production is owned by the government

mom-and-pop store: Small business establishment owned and run primarily by members of a family

mommy track: Career path for female employees who reduce their work commitment in an implicit or explicit reduction in opportunities for advancement

monetarism: Theory that stable economic growth can be ensured only when the rate of increase in the money supply matches the capacity for productivity growth

money supply: Total amount of money available in an economy

monopoly: Situation in which a single company owns all or most of the means of producing or selling a service or commodity

moonlighting: Working at more than one job

mortgage: Loan document creating a lien against property that becomes void on payment

muckraking: Searching out and publicly exposing real or apparent misconduct of prominent people or businesses

mugwumps: Republican political activists who supported the Democratic candidate Grover Cleveland in the 1884 presidential election because they rejected the corruption associated with the Republican candidate

multinational corporation: Corporation that manages production or delivers services in at least two countries

mutual fund: Investment company that combines the money of its shareholders and invests the funds in a wide variety of securities

natural disaster: Emergency situation that poses a threat to human life or property and has a natural cause

net income: All revenues and gains minus all costs and expenses; also called net profit

net worth: Total assets minus total liabilities

New Deal: Set of domestic programs proposed or enacted on the initiative of President Franklin D. Roosevelt to combat the Great Depression

nonperforming loan: Loan on which interest is overdue and the principal is not likely to be paid back because its value is greater than the asset, such as real estate, against which the loan was made

nonprobability sampling: Sampling technique that does not employ techniques that enable inference from information obtained from samples to the general population

obsolescence, planned or built-in: Making an item in such a way as to ensure the likelihood of its wearing out or becoming outdated

oligopoly: Market in which an industry is dominated by a small number of sellers

online marketing: Shopping on the Internet. *See also* e-commerce

opinion leader: Individual who influences other people's buying and consumption behavior

opportunity cost: Possible benefits from an alternative that must be given up to pursue a certain course of action

option: Right to buy or sell a particular asset at a specified price

organized crime: Operation of illegal businesses by groups formed and bound together by the pursuit of monetary profit

outsourcing: Use of workers from outside companies (often at lower pay) to perform duties previously done by workers within the core firm

over-the-counter market: Stock market for securities not sold in large volumes and therefore not listed on a stock exchange

panic: Sudden, widespread fright concerning financial affairs

patent: Grant made by a government that gives the creator of a particular invention the sole right to control the manufacture, use, and sale of that invention

pay television: Subscription-based television services

peddler: Traveling trader who played a significant role in supplying isolated populations with basic and diverse goods, particularly during the U.S. Civil War era

pension: Sum of money paid regularly, usually as a retirement benefit

pent-up demand: Strong consumer demand resulting from the unavailability of a product

peripheral firm: Small, labor-intensive business; the opposite of a center firm

physiocrat: Member of a group of economists who held that government should not interfere with the operation of natural laws and that land is the source of all wealth

piracy: Unauthorized use of another's product, invention, or concept

plantation agriculture: System of agriculture based on large-scale land ownership and exploitation of labor and the environment

Ponzi scheme: Investment swindle that appears to be paying high returns by paying off early investors with money put up by later investors; typically the only source of revenue is through new investors

Populist movement: Movement critical of big business in the 1870's that started with farmers and became a national political party; favored agrarian interests, free silver coinage, and government control of monopolies

portfolio: Collection of security holdings of an individual or company

price elasticity: Extent to which an increase or decrease in the price of a product results in a corresponding fall or rise in demand for the product

prime rate: Interest rate announced by a bank to be the lowest available at a particular time to its most creditworthy customers

principal: Face value of a note on which interest is calculated

privatization: Conversion from public to private control or ownership

proactive selling: Seller's actively seeking out prospective consumers. *See also* reactive selling

progressive tax: Tax structure in which those who have higher income levels pay a higher percentage of their incomes. *See also* regressive tax

Progressive movement: Movement in the first two decades of the twentieth century characterized by reformers touting social justice, general equality, and public safety

Prohibition: Ban on the sale, manufacture, and consumption of alcohol from 1920 to 1933 in the United States

psychographic segmentation: Division of the market according to people's lifestyles, values, attitudes, and personality

property tax: Tax levied on real or personal property

public utilities: Public or quasi-public businesses, subject to government regulation, that provide essential commodities or services such as water and electric power

quality circle technique: Technique in which small groups regularly meet to address work-related problems, especially those involving quality of a product or service

quality control: Process used to ensure a desired level of quality in a product or service

quota sample: Sample group chosen to reflect the makeup of the group from which it was selected

rational expectations theory: Theory of economist John Muth that proposes that people in the economy make choices based on their rational outlook, past experiences, and the available information; thus economic expectations predict the future state of the economy

reactive selling: Seller's responding to consumers seeking a product. *See also* proactive selling

real income: Income measured by how much the money will buy rather than the amount received

rebate: Return of a portion of the cost of an item, either immediate or by mail

recession: Period lasting longer than a few months of significant reduced economic activity across the economy; technically two consecutive quarters of negative economic growth measured by a country's gross domestic product. *See also* depression

red herring: In securities law, a prospectus not yet approved by the Securities Exchange Commission

regressive tax: Tax that is applied so that those with lower incomes spend a larger portion of their income on taxes than those with higher incomes. *See also* progressive tax

rescission: Cancellation of a contract

retirement plan: Plan for setting aside money to be used in retirement

return on investment (ROI): Ratio of net profit to total investment (total debt plus total equity)

revolving charge account: Credit account in which the borrow pays no interest or fees if the full balance is paid within a set time, usually thirty days after the transaction

sales tax: Tax levied on the sale of goods and services, usually calculated on a percentage of purchase price

sampling, nonprobability: *See* nonprobability sampling

savings bond: Debt security issued by the U.S. Department of the Treasury to pay for the government's borrowing needs

scab: Nonunion worker who replaces a striking worker, or a union member who refuses to strike or returns to work before the strike is over

segmentation: *See* specific type of segmentation

selling, proactive: *See* proactive selling

selling, reactive: *See* reactive selling

seniority, artificial: *See* artificial seniority

sharecropping: System of agriculture in which a person uses someone else's land in return for a share of the crop

shopping goods: Goods that are purchased by consumers only after they have comparison shopped. *See also* convenience goods, specialty goods

sit-down strike: Strike in which groups of workers take possession of a workplace by "sitting down" at their workstations

sit-in strike: Strike in which protesters occupy a place in which they are unwanted and refuse to leave voluntarily

smuggling: To import or export goods without paying customs or other taxes

Social Security: Government program designed to provide for basic economic welfare of individuals and their dependents

socialism: Economic system in which the means of production, distribution, and exchange are owned collectively or by a centralized government

soil bank: Program under which the U.S. government pays farmers to take cropland out of production

space race: Competition between the Soviet and U.S. governments to be the first to accomplish landmarks in space exploration

specialty goods: Items that are unique or unusual enough for consumers to seek them. *See also* convenience goods, shopping goods

spending, deficit: *See* deficit spending

stagflation: Period of sluggish economic growth accompanied by inflation and high unemployment. *See also* deflation, inflation

Standard & Poor's: Company that publicizes financial research and analyses on stocks and bonds

stock: Share of ownership in a corporation

stock exchange: Organized market for buying and selling securities

stock market crash: Sudden, dramatic decline of stock prices across a significant cross-section of a stock market

stockout: When demand for an item cannot be fulfilled from on-hand inventory

stockpiling: Gradual accumulation of a reserve of some item

stratified sampling: Process of grouping members of a population into homogeneous subgroups before doing random sampling within each group

strike: Collective, organized cessation or slowdown of work. *See also* sit-down strike, sit-in strike

strikebreaking: Actions taken to end strikes, including hiring of workers to replace striking workers

subsidies, farm: *See* farm subsidies

sunbelt migration: Movement of populations into the southern United States

supply-side economics: Theory that holds that greater tax cuts for those earning large incomes will improve the economy and result in increased revenue for the government by providing incentives for those with money to increase investments and produce more goods and services

surety: Agreement to fulfill an obligation if a principal fails to pay or act as promised

surtax: Graduated tax in addition to the normal tax on an amount by which income exceeds a specified sum

sweepstake: Marketing promotion that entices consumers to enter a drawing of chance

synergy: Phenomenon in which two or more agents get together to create an effect greater than could be gained from the separate entities

takeover, hostile: *See* hostile takeover

target market: That portion of the total market that a company selects to serve

tariff: Tax imposed on products imported into a country

tax: *See* specific type of tax

telemarketing: Telephone solicitation of sales of products or services

temperance movement: Movement in the late nineteenth century that pushed for laws to prohibit consumption of alcoholic beverages

third-party payer: Person or organization that provides funding for projects, products, or services that benefit the user or consumer

thrift store: Store that sells used items, often for charity

time zones: Geographic regions within which the same standard time is used

top-down planning: Management system in which programs are implemented by top-level management, with little or no input from lower-level employees. *See also* bottom-up planning

trade show: Large exposition designed to promote awareness and sales of products, especially new ones within an industry

trademark: Brand or part of a brand given legal protection by restricting its use to owners

trading post: Shop or store where trade is conducted, usually in sparsely settled regions

trading stamp: Stamp, given to retail customers for purchasing a certain amount of goods, that can be redeemed for selected merchandise

trafficking: Illegal or improper exchange of goods

transatlantic steamer service: Ocean crossing by steamboat, beginning in the early nineteenth century

transcontinental railroad: Railroad line over the Rocky Mountains that connected a Midwest terminal and the Pacific Ocean, thus enabling travel by railroad across the United States

travelers' check: Internationally redeemable draft payable on purchaser's endorsement against the original signature on the draft

trickle-down theory: Economic theory that holds that investing money in companies and giving tax breaks to the wealthy is the best way to stimulate the economy and that the benefits will trickle down to the lower classes

trust: Property interest administered, invested, or held by one person for the benefit of another

turnpike: Expressway that charges a toll for its use

undifferentiated marketing strategy: Strategy in which the market is viewed as an aggregate and products and promotions are designed to appeal to the greatest number of consumers possible

unenforceable contract: Agreement that is otherwise valid, but when breached, cannot be enforced by a court of law

union: *See* labor union

unit contribution margin: Difference between a product's selling price and the costs associated with producing and selling it

usury laws: Statutes that prohibit finance charges above a certain level

value-added tax: Tax in which a tax is levied on a product's value at each stage of production, thus becoming a cumulative tax paid by the consumer

variable cost: Cost that changes as the number of items produced or services performed changes. *See also* fixed cost

vending machines: Coin-operated machines that dispense merchandise, often food items

venture capital: Money invested, often at sizable risk, in a new business or new product

vertical integration: Obtaining control of all or most of the progressive stages between raw material and finished product. *See also* backward integration, forward integration

voodoo economics: Term used by President George H. W. Bush during the 1970's to describe supply-side economics

Wall Street: Name of the financial district in lower Manhattan in New York where major stock exchanges, brokerages, and banks are located

war surplus materials: Wide variety of merchandise no longer needed by the military and sold to the public

wealth, inequality of: *See* inequality of wealth

wet county/town: County or town whose government allows sale and consumption of alcoholic beverages. *See also* dry county/town

whistle-blower: Employee who, against the will or knowledge of an employer, informs the public about a harmful or illegal activity undertaken by the company

white-collar crime: Crimes committed by individuals or corporations during the course of business, usually for economic reasons

withholding tax: Tax deducted from wages and forwarded to the Internal Revenue Service by a person's employer

working capital: Assets of a business that can be applied to its operation

yellow-dog contract: Agreement in which employees understand that they will be dismissed if they join a union

zoning: Division of a jurisdiction by ordinance into sections reserved for different uses

Victoria Price

Bibliography

GENERAL WORKS

Blackford, Mansel G., and K. Austin Kerr. *Business Enterprise in American History.* Boston: Houghton Mifflin, 1986. Discusses the successes and failures of major corporations, along with the development of government regulations. Also examines how business history has changed and progressed.

Blaszczyk, Regina Lee, and Philip B. Scranton, eds. *Major Problems in American Business History: Documents and Essays.* Boston: Houghton Mifflin, 2005. Provides a good background in business history. Combines period documents with essays by leading scholars and industrialists.

Boyce, Gordon, and Simon Ville. *The Development of Modern Business.* New York: Palgrave, 2002. Looks at how corporations have grown historically, arguing that modern businesspeople can learn from the past. Focuses on a wide variety of business issues.

Chandler, Alfred Dupont. *The Visible Hand: The Managerial Revolution in American Business.* Cambridge, Mass.: Belknap Press, 1977. Timeless work arguing that managers play a direct and vital role in business. Holds that the visible hand of management is more important than the invisible hand of the market. One of the first important histories of business managers.

DiBacco, Thomas V. *Made in the U.S.A.: The History of American Business.* New York: Harper & Row, 1987. This narrative study discusses American businesspeople over the years. Generally treats the individuals mentioned in a positive way.

Lamoreaux, Naomi R., and Daniel M. G. Raff, eds. *Coordination and Information: Historical Perspectives on the Organization of Enterprise.* Chicago: University of Chicago Press, 1995. Examines how information is controlled and how it in turn controls businesses. Discusses historical cases in which information was not available to all competitors and the effects of regulation.

Nace, Ted. *Gangs of America: The Rise of Corporate Power and the Disabling of Democracy.* San Francisco: Berrett-Koehler, 2003. Examines the changes in corporation law between the founding of the United States and the present. Argues that the U.S. Constitution and the Founders were not as probusiness as the government is now and that corporations prevent adequate regulation.

Polanyi, Karl. *The Great Transformation.* New York: Beacon Press, 2001. Looks at the effects of modern corporations and capitalism on the marketplace and society. It also argues for the need for government intervention and regulation, pointing out the dangers of the unregulated corporate system.

Prechel, Harland N. *Big Business and the State: Historical Transitions and Corporate Transformation, 1880's-1990's.* Albany: State University of New York Press, 2000. Examines how corporations have changed over the past century, arguing for three waves of development. Also analyzes property rights and how corporations have pressured states into creating favorable environments for them.

Sobel, Robert. *The Age of Giant Corporations: A Microeconomic History of American Business, 1914-1992.* 3d ed. Westport, Conn.: Greenwood Press, 1993. Details the changes in business, arguing that corporations have played a large role in economic growth. Studies management, marketing, and finance largely, as well as the relationship between politics and business.

Truitt, Wesley B. *The Corporation.* Westport, Conn.: Greenwood Press, 2006. Examines how corporations have evolved over time. Discusses both practical modern-day concerns about creating and managing a corporation and historical developments. Also suggests some factors that divide long-term corporations from fleeting ones.

Zunz, Oliver. *Making America Corporate: 1870-1920.* Chicago: University of Chicago Press, 1990. Written by a history professor, it focuses on work culture and the rise of business managers rather than high-level executives. Includes a discussion of the role of women in early corporations and stresses the role of opportunity.

BUSINESS LEADERS

Baida, Peter. *Poor Richard's Legacy: American Business Values from Benjamin Franklin to Donald Trump.* New York: W. Morrow, 1990. Mixes a study of leading businessmen with the critics of the day. Includes a discussion of each era's various how-to and self-help business literature. Overall negative view of modern businesspeople.

Klein, Maury. *The Change Makers from Carnegie to Gates: How the Great Entrepreneurs Transformed Ideas into Industries.* New York: Times Books, 2003. Klein argues that successful (defined here as those who create industries) entrepreneurs have specific skills that most businesspeople lack. Among those are a superb level of dedication to their businesses and a commitment to creating something new.

Leibovich, Mark. *The New Imperialists: How Five Restless Kids Grew Up to Virtually Rule Your World.* Paramus, N.J.: Prentice Hall, 2002. Analyzes the leaders of the technological age, suggesting that their childhoods played a large role in making them the successes that they are. Looks at what drove them to succeed. Includes portraits of Jeff Bezos, Bill Gates, and Larry Ellison.

Lowenstein, Roger. *Buffett: The Making of an American Capitalist.* New York: Main Street Books, 1996. Examines what made Warren Buffett such a successful capitalist investor. Unlike many major figures, Buffett did not build but rather invested. Details Buffett's success rather than pretending to tell how to invest as successfully as Buffett.

Tedlow, Richard S. *The Watson Dynasty: The Fiery Reign and Troubled Legacy of IBM's Founding Father and Son.* New York: HarperBusiness, 2003. Examines the personalities that led International Business Machines (IBM) for more than fifty years. Reveals the flawed tycoons who founded and directed IBM. Discusses how IBM created a cult of its leaders and the company.

Warren, Kenneth. *Triumphant Capitalism: Henry Clay Frick and the Industrial Transformation of America.* Pittsburgh: University of Pittsburgh Press, 1996. Combines a traditional biography with an examination of the steel industry of the late nineteenth century. It includes Frick's interactions with Carnegie.

Watts, Steven. *The People's Tycoon: Henry Ford and the American Century.* New York: A. A. Knopf, 2005. Examines the man and the myth that were and are Henry Ford. Includes a discussion of his huge successes but also delves into his less known anti-Semitism, controlling tendencies, racism, and antimodernity.

Young, Jeffrey S., and William L. Simon. *iCon: Steve Jobs, the Greatest Second Act in the History of Business.* Hoboken, N.J.: Wiley, 2005. This work examines the rise, fall, and subsequent rise of Jobs. Discusses his success with the iMac and iPod.

CORPORATIONS

Bain, David H. *Empire Express: Building the First Transcontinental Railroad.* New York: Viking, 1999. Covers the ordinary workers, well-known titans, and overlooked power brokers who brought about the first railroad. Examines the backroom deals, scandals, and intrigue, as well as the effects on the Native Americans and the workers who built the railroad.

Billstein, Reinhold, et al. *Working for the Enemy: Ford, General Motors, and Forced Labor in Germany During the Second World War.* New York: Berghahn Books, 2000. Examines the interaction between American corporations and the German government in the World War II era. Also discusses and interviews some of the slave laborers who worked in the plants these corporations built.

Black, Edwin. *IBM and the Holocaust: The Strategic Alliance Between Nazi Germany and America's Most Powerful Corporation.* New York: Crown Publishers, 2001. Controversially argues that IBM directly gained from the Holocaust in terms of sales and profit, while still keeping its distance legally, and that the Nazis used IBM technology to be efficient in their genocide.

Carlson, W. Bernard. *Innovation as a Social Process: Elihu Thomson and the Rise of General Electric, 1870-1900.* New York: Cambridge University Press, 1991. Combines a study of Thomson with a look at the modern corporation's use of research and development, and the success of General Electric. Argues that business, innovation, and marketing are all needed for success.

Cleveland, Harold van B., and Thomas F. Huertas. *Citibank, 1812-1970.* Cambridge, Mass.: Harvard University Press, 1985. Outlines the founding and rise of Citibank, one of the largest banks in the United States. Explains Citibank's relationship to the Great Depression and its effect on the economy since.

Kirsch, Max H. *In the Wake of the Giant: Multinational Restructuring and Uneven Development in a New England Community.* Albany: State University of New York Press, 1998. Looks at the effect of large corporations' restructuring and plant movement on communities. Argues that these small communities are like small countries in their development.

Lane, Bill. *Jacked Up: The Inside Story of How Jack Welch Talked GE into Becoming the World's Greatest Company.* New York: McGraw-Hill, 2008. Favorable look at Welch and how he ran General Electric. Written by his speechwriter, it suggests that Welch was a master communicator and that is one reason for his success.

Meyer, Stephen. *The Five Dollar Day: Labor, Management, and Social Control in the Ford Motor Company, 1908-1921.* Albany: State University of New York Press, 1981. Examines the early days of the Ford Motor Company and discusses Ford's desire to control his workforce. Also discusses the rise of business managers and how technology changed throughout the period.

Ortega, Bob. *In Sam We Trust: The Untold Story of Sam Walton and How Wal-Mart Is Devouring America.* New York: Times Business, 1998. Discusses Walton's and Wal-Mart's rise to dominance and the firm's retailing innovations. Emphasizes Wal-Mart's destructive practices and ruthless behavior. Should be read with the Slater book.

Slater, Robert. *The Wal-Mart Decade: How a New Generation of Leaders Turned Sam Walton's Legacy into the World's Number-One Company.* New York: Portfolio, 2003. Favorable view of Wal-Mart, written with the help of inside executives. Argues that good leadership turned Walton's vision into a modern company. Should be read with the Ortega book.

ETHICS AND CRIME

Eichenwald, Kurt. *The Informant: A True Story.* New York: Broadway Books, 2000. Examines the story of Archer Daniels Midland (ADM) and the 1990's price-fixing case that the U.S. government brought against it. Discusses ADM's tactics, the role of the whistle-blower (an ADM vice president), why the case developed as it did, and the corruption throughout.

First, Harry. *Business Crime: Cases and Materials.* Westbury, N.Y.: Foundation Press, 2002. Lists many cases of business crime and discusses how the crimes have changed over time.

McLean, Bethany, and Peter Elkind. *The Smartest Guys in the Room: The Amazing Rise and Scandalous Fall of Enron.* New York: Portfolio, 2003. Examines the reasons for the failure and its resulting effects. Notes the management failures that allowed the disaster.

Markham, Jerry W. *A Financial History of Modern U.S. Corporate Scandals: From Enron to Reform.* Armonk, N.Y.: M. E. Sharpe, 2005. Looks at a modern period in America's financial history. Discusses the scandal, the resulting reforms, and some of the market changes that have come about as a result.

Martin, Michael T., and Marilyn Yaquinto. *Redress for Historical Injustices in the United States: On Reparations for Slavery, Jim Crow, and Their Legacies.* Durham, N.C.: Duke University Press, 2007. Wide-ranging book examining the issue of reparations. Discusses some of the companies that benefited from slave labor.

Mills, Daniel Quinn. *Wheel, Deal, and Steal: Deceptive Accounting, Deceitful CEOs, and Ineffective Reforms.* Upper Saddle River, N.J.: FT/Prentice Hall, 2003. Discusses how deceitful accounting is done, and why the reforms, in the wake of Enron and other scandals, did not create real change.

Rapoport, Nancy B., and Bala G. Dharan. *Enron: Corporate Fiascos and Their Implications.* New York: Foundation Press, 2004. Lengthy work looks at what went wrong at Enron. Includes contributions from a variety of academics and discussions of ethical and legal issues as well as the obvious financial ones.

Terris, Daniel. *Ethics at Work: Creating Virtue in an American Corporation.* Waltham, Mass.: Brandeis University Press, 2005. Discusses how ethics has developed over the past decades, and the problems that lax ethics have caused. Surveys the ethics program at Lockheed Martin and outlines its successes and failures.

Weisman, Stewart L. *Need and Greed: The Story of the Largest Ponzi Scheme in American History.* Syracuse, N.Y.: Syracuse University Press, 1999. Looks at how a small company managed to run a pyramid scheme for a decade without getting caught. A micro-history of an unethical corporation.

FINANCIAL HISTORY

Baxter, Maurice G. *Henry Clay and the American System.* Lexington: University Press of Kentucky, 1995. Henry Clay's American System was the first protective system of the nineteenth century. Details its progress, weaknesses, strengths, and legacy. Also discusses Clay's political career.

Bruner, Robert F., and Sean D. Carr. *The Panic of 1907: Lessons Learned from the Market's Perfect Storm.* Hoboken, N.J.: John Wiley & Sons, 2007.

Examines the banking crisis that was partly behind the creation of the Federal Reserve system. Discusses the role of J. P. Morgan in ending the crisis.

Eisner, Marc Allen. *From Warfare State to Welfare State: World War I, Compensatory State-Building, and the Limits of the Modern Order.* University Park: Pennsylvania State University Press, 2000. Argues that World War I was what created the modern state. Suggests that the associational model adopted during that conflict has limited the government.

Fuhrer, Jeffrey C., and Scott Schuh. *Beyond Shocks: What Causes Business Cycles?* Boston: Federal Reserve Bank of Boston, 1998. Examines the general phenomena of business crises. Looks at modern-day factors, historical factors, and how things have changed over time. Also discusses the roles of technology and the government.

Gosling, James J. *Economics, Politics, and American Public Policy.* Armonk, N.Y.: M. E. Sharpe, 2007. Discusses the historical and present relationship between government policy and economics. Highlights the modern-day debates over economic policy in areas such as inflation, the national debt, and trade policy.

Hartcher, Peter. *Bubble Man: Alan Greenspan and the Missing Seven Trillion Dollars.* New York: W. W. Norton, 2006. Argues that Greenspan knew about the overvalued stock market and did nothing. Blames Greenspan for the dot-com crash and the resulting stock market problems of the early twenty-first century. Should be read with the Woodward book.

Klein, Maury. *Rainbow's End: The Crash of 1929.* New York: Oxford University Press, 2001. Argues that a change in the national psyche played a large role in the 1929 crash and resulting Depression. Examines many individuals and the national mood at the time.

Matson, Cathy, ed. *The Economy of Early America: Historical Perspectives and New Directions.* University Park: Pennsylvania State University Press, 2006. Combines efforts by several different historians who focus on the early American economy. Discusses a wide variety of issues, from slavery to corporations to agriculture.

Morris, Charles R. *Money, Greed, and Risk: Why Financial Crises and Crashes Happen.* New York: Times Business, 1999. Examines many of the various financial crises in American history. Argues that overvalued prices are the central issue, not why the crashes happened or why things got so bad.

Richardson, Heather Cox. *The Greatest Nation of the Earth: Republican Economic Policies During the Civil War.* Cambridge, Mass.: Harvard University Press, 1997. Looks at the economic efforts undertaken in the U.S. Civil War and details their long-lasting effects. Also discusses the origins of the associated legislation.

Shull, Bernard. *The Fourth Branch: The Federal Reserve's Unlikely Rise to Power and Influence.* Westport, Conn.: Praeger, 2005. Discusses the Federal Reserve's efforts in past crises and the increasing amount of power held by that body. Relates how the Federal Reserve changed over the years in a symbiotic relationship with politics.

Sinclair, Timothy J. *The New Masters of Capital: American Bond Rating Agencies and the Politics of Creditworthiness.* Ithaca, N.Y.: Cornell University Press, 2005. Details the power that bond rating agencies have and their interaction with the growing global credit market. Discusses historical trends and the modern-day situation.

Wicker, Elmus. *Banking Panics of the Gilded Age.* New York: Cambridge University Press, 2000. Examines the 1893 and 1907 crises and their solutions, along with their relationship to the Federal Reserve. Discusses the causes and the role of the national government in these panics.

_____. *The Banking Panics of the Great Depression.* New York: Cambridge University Press, 1996. Examines the banking crisis of the Great Depression and its relationship to the overall economic woes of the time. Discusses the performance of the Federal Reserve as well.

_____. *The Great Debate on Banking Reform: Nelson Aldrich and the Origins of the Fed.* Columbus: Ohio State University Press, 2005. Discusses the late nineteenth century banking crises and the rise of the Federal Reserve Board. Argues that Nelson Aldrich played a larger role than previous historians have acknowledged.

Woodward, Bob. *Maestro: Greenspan's Fed and the American Boom.* New York: Simon and Schuster, 2000. Proposes that Alan Greenspan, through his leadership of the Federal Reserve Board, played a critical role in leading the economy to a great boom during the 1980's and 1990's. Discusses how Greenspan came to make his decisions. Should be read with the Hartcher book.

FOREIGN TRADE

Aaronson, Susan A. *Taking Trade to the Streets: The Lost History of Public Efforts to Shape Globalization.* Ann Arbor: University of Michigan Press, 2001. Examines the efforts undertaken in the public sphere, by both critics and mass movements, to shape public policy. Focuses on the interrelationship of trade policy with regulation in general.

Butler, Michael A. *Cautious Visionary: Cordell Hull and Trade Reform, 1933-1937.* Kent, Ohio: Kent State University Press, 1998. Examines one of the leading figures in Great Depression diplomacy, holding that Hull was responsible for the movement of the United States toward free trade over the latter part of the twentieth century.

Eckes, Alfred E., and Thomas W. Zeiler. *Globalization and the American Century.* New York: Cambridge University Press, 2003. Discusses the twentieth century, particularly as it relates to trade. Argues that technology and trade combined to allow American dominance. Combines a discussion of diplomacy with that of trade.

Engdahl, William. *Century of War: Anglo-American Oil Politics and the New World Order.* Ann Arbor, Mich.: Pluto Press, 2004. Examines the variety of companies that are involved in the international oil trade and their effect on world politics. Argues that the oil companies have played a shaping role in the world.

Gibson, Martha Liebler. *Conflict Amid Consensus in American Trade Policy.* Washington, D.C.: Georgetown University Press, 2000. Examines the effect of domestic politics on trade policy. Argues that a games-theory approach best explains how trade policy has developed. Focuses on the changes occurring during the 1990's.

Katznelson, Ira, and Martin Shefter, eds. *Shaped by War and Trade: International Influences on American Political Development.* Princeton, N.J.: Princeton University Press, 2002. Edited volume containing essays by many well-known scholars who survey how politics affects trade. Both domestic politics and international wars are examined as factors.

McCusker, John J., and Kenneth Morgan, eds. *The Early Modern Atlantic Economy.* New York: Cambridge University Press, 2000. Combines economic history with the growing field of Atlantic world history. Discusses the colonies, the international issues, and labor concerns, among many other issues.

Pearson, Charles S. *United States Trade Policy: A Work in Progress.* Hoboken, N.J.: J. Wiley, 2004. Focuses on the 1980's and beyond. Discusses the difference between actual trade policy and the various theories that exist. Includes coverage of the various ways policy is negotiated and issues affecting trade, such as labor practices.

Rothgeb, John M. *U.S. Trade Policy: Balancing Economic Dreams and Political Realities.* Washington, D.C.: CQ Press, 2001. Examines the political issues shaping trade policy. Discusses international issues, corporate pressures, and domestic concerns. Recaps the important historical developments in trade policy.

Satre, Lowell J. *Chocolate on Trial: Slavery, Politics, and the Ethics of Business.* Athens: Ohio University Press, 2005. Examines the Cadbury company and its use of cocoa on slave-labor plantations during the early twentieth century. Also looks at a libel trial that grew out of the slave labor and a critical editorial.

Siekmeier, James F. *Aid, Nationalism, and Inter-American Relations: Guatemala, Bolivia, and the United States, 1945-1961.* Lewiston, N.Y.: E. Mellen, 1999. Argues that U.S. trade policy toward Latin America was driven by economics, not Cold War ideology. Holds that the United States opposed nationalism there because it wanted to be able to control the local economies, not out of a desire to keep communism out.

GOVERNMENT REGULATION AND LAW

Freyer, Tony Allan. *Regulating Big Business: Antitrust in Great Britain and America, 1880-1990.* New York: Cambridge University Press, 1992. Examines the large corporations that grew up during the late nineteenth century and the two governments' reaction to them. Discusses the major legal cases and theoretical doctrines that developed.

Goldin, Claudia, and Gary D. Libecap, eds. *The Regulated Economy: A Historical Approach to Political Economy.* Chicago: University of Chicago Press, 1994. Examines the political starts of economic regulation. Discusses state and local levels as well as federal. Also considers interest groups and the influence of the market.

Hart, David M., ed. *The Emergence of Entrepreneurship Policy: Governance, Start-Up, and Growth in the U.S. Knowledge Economy.* New York: Cambridge University Press, 2003. Argues that government policy can help increase entrepreneurship. Suggests that government and business should work together, rather than opposing one another.

Hartmann, Thom. *Unequal Protection: The Rise of Corporate Dominance and the Theft of Human Rights.* Emmaus, Pa.: Rodale, 2004. Examines the power of corporations and the damages that this ascendancy has inflicted. Discusses the growth of corporate might and how corporations have stifled attempts to decrease their strength.

Himmelberg, Robert F. *The Rise of Big Business and the Beginnings of Antitrust and Railroad Regulation, 1870-1900.* New York: Garland, 1994. Looks at the rise of regulation during the late nineteenth century. Provides a number of more in-depth studies that discuss specific instances involving large railroads and their regulatory environment.

_____, ed. *The Monopoly Issue and Antitrust, 1900-1917.* New York: Garland, 1994. Examines the Progressive approach toward monopolies. Discusses various court cases and the responses of businesses toward trust busting. Besides discussing national trends, the work also provides case studies of several lesser-known industries.

Hovenkamp, Herbert. *Enterprise and American Law, 1836-1937.* Cambridge, Mass.: Harvard University Press, 1991. Examines how the legal system treated businesses in the century before the New Deal's constitutional revolution of 1937. Discusses the effects of various writings on the legal system's views toward business and suggests that a general belief in free enterprise led to freedom for the businesses.

Shaffer, Butler D. *In Restraint of Trade: The Business Campaign Against Competition, 1918-1938.* Lewisburg, Pa.: Bucknell University Press, 1997. Argues that businesses decided to push for cooperation after World War I, desiring self-regulation. Also holds that many government leaders, including Herbert Hoover, wanted managed cooperation and discusses the effect of these views on the New Deal.

Soule, Edward. *Morality and Markets: The Ethics of Government Regulation.* Lanham, Md.: Rowman & Littlefield, 2003. Discusses whether (and when) government regulation is moral and thus should be imposed. Uses classical philosophy, such as that of John Locke, to analyze this area.

Labor

Buhle, Paul. *Taking Care of Business: Samuel Gompers, George Meany, Lane Kirkland, and the Tragedy of American Labor.* New York: Monthly Review, 1999. Examines three presidents of the American Federation of Labor (and later the AFL-CIO), arguing that they moved away from the interests of the working class. Argues that the well-being of white men was protected, while others' concerns were defeated.

Hattam, Victoria Charlotte. *Labor Visions and State Power: The Origins of Business Unionism in the United States.* Princeton, N.J.: Princeton University Press, 1993. Looks at the start of unionism and why labor played a limited part in politics. Discusses various unions and their stance toward electoral issues.

Lichtenstein, Nelson. *State of the Union: A Century of American Labor.* Princeton, N.J.: Princeton University Press, 2002. Examines the twentieth century history of American unions, arguing that many workers are worse off now than they were in 1900. Discusses the reasons for the decline in union power.

McCartin, Joseph A. *Labor's Great War: The Struggle for Industrial Democracy and the Origins of Modern American Labor Relations, 1912-1921.* Chapel Hill: University of North Carolina Press, 1997. Looks at labor relations and issues just before, during, and just after World War I. Although unions did not immediately keep many of the modest gains that they made in the war, McCartin argues that New Deal legislation and attitudes came out of the period.

Montgomery, David. *The Fall of the House of Labor: The Workplace, the State, and American Labor Activism, 1865-1925.* New York: Cambridge University Press, 1987. Discusses labor relations from the point of view of the worker. Argues that management and owners triumphed against workers in this period.

Puette, William. *Through Jaundiced Eyes: How the Media View Organized Labor.* Ithaca, N.Y.: ILR Press, 1992. Argues that the negative view of labor in the media has weakened unions. Suggests that the media link labor to crime unfairly and prefer negative stories about unions to positive or fair ones.

Voss, Kim. *The Making of American Exceptionalism: The Knights of Labor and Class Formation in the Nine-*

teenth Century. Ithaca, N.Y.: Cornell University Press, 1993. Holds that the fall of the Knights of Labor doomed American labor to a different path from that followed by labor in Europe.

Zinn, Howard, Robin Kelley, and Dana Frank. *Three Strikes: Miners, Musicians, Salesgirls, and the Fighting Spirit of Labor's Last Century*. Boston: Beacon Press, 2001. Three different strikes from the early twentieth century are described, and the collective stories inform about concepts of labor, unionism, business, and gender.

THE MILITARY

Caldicott, Helen. *The New Nuclear Danger: George W. Bush's Military-Industrial Complex*. New York: New Press, 2004. Discusses the influence of large corporations on U.S. defense spending. Argues that Bush is heavily relying on nuclear weapons in his defense policies.

Coulter, Matthew Ware. *The Senate Munitions Inquiry of the 1930's: Beyond the Merchants of Death*. Westport, Conn.: Greenwood Press, 1997. Examines the Nye Committee of the 1930's and its relationship to the Neutrality Acts and the United States' isolationism of the period. Holds that the committee performed far better than most accounts have suggested and that it analyzed well the early military-industrial complex.

Franklin, Roger. *The Defender: The Story of General Dynamics*. New York: Harper & Row, 1986. Provides a history of General Dynamics, one of the larger defense contractors. Discusses its rise and difficulties, and focuses on the military side. Also outlines the leading figures in the company.

Gottlieb, Sanford. *Defense Addiction: Can America Kick the Habit?* Boulder, Colo.: Westview Press, 1997. Examines the massive defense industry and discusses how those companies compete for federal dollars. Analyzes the dependence of this industry on federal funds and the consequences of that dependence.

Himmelberg, Robert F., ed. *Government-Business Cooperation, 1945-1964: Corporatism in the Post-war Era*. New York: Garland, 1994. Studies the twenty years after World War II and argues that there was a high level of corporatism in the period. Surveys, among other things, the military-industrial complex (and its critics), deficit spending, and fair trade.

Markusen, Ann, Peter Hall, Scott Campbell, and Sabina Deitrick. *The Rise of the Gunbelt: The Military Remapping of Industrial America*. New York: Oxford University Press, 1991. Discusses how the rise of the military-industrial complex has shaped the population patterns of the United States. Examines the rise of significant defense contractors as well.

Markusen, Ann, and Sean S. Costigan, eds. *Arming the Future: A Defense Industry for the Twenty-first Century*. New York: Council on Foreign Relations Press, 1999. This examines the contractions in the defense industry that occurred during the 1990's, along with the government policies that developed then. Discusses the successes and failures of those policies and predictions for the future.

Ndiaye, Pap A. *Nylon and Bombs: DuPont and the March of Modern America*. Baltimore: Johns Hopkins University Press, 2007. Studies the lives of engineers in DuPont to better understand that industry and that profession. Focuses on the production of nylon and plutonium in this arms effort.

Weir, Gary E. *Forged in War: The Naval-Industrial Complex and American Submarine Construction, 1940-1961*. Washington, D.C.: Naval Historical Center, 1993. Examines the growth of the submarine industry during and after World War II. Argues that many different factors went into the growth of this industry.

RACE, CLASS, GENDER, AND CULTURE

Clark, Terry Nichols, and Seymour Martin Lipset, eds. *The Breakdown of Class Politics: A Debate on Post-industrial Stratification*. Baltimore: Johns Hopkins University Press, 2001. Argues that social classes are becoming less prominent and less important in the postindustrial era.

Drachman, Virginia G. *Enterprising Women: Two Hundred Fifty Years of American Business*. Chapel Hill: University of North Carolina Press, 2002. Examines many successful businesswomen all throughout the existence of the United States. Mixes well-known figures with the relatively obscure.

Green, Venus. *Race on the Line: Gender, Labor, and Technology in the Bell System, 1880-1980*. Durham, N.C.: Duke University Press, 2001. Examines the role of telephone operators and their changing jobs throughout this century. Shows how technology, race, and society interacted in this workplace.

Hornstein, Jeffrey M. *A Nation of Realtors: A Cultural History of the Twentieth-Century American Middle Class*. Durham, N.C.: Duke University Press, 2005. Outlines the effect of a little-noted business—the real estate business—on the American middle class. Holds that real estate agents caused people to think of themselves as being middle class.

Hunter, Tera. *To 'Joy My Freedom: Southern Black Women's Lives and Labors After the Civil War.* Cambridge, Mass.: Harvard University Press, 1997. Examines working black women inside and outside formal businesses in the period after the Civil War. Looks more at laborers than business.

Johnson, Robert D. *The Radical Middle Class: Populist Democracy and the Question of Capitalism in Progressive Era Portland, Oregon.* Princeton, N.J.: Princeton University Press, 2003. Uses Portland as a case study in the role of the lower middle class. Argues that this group powered Progressivism and that Progressivism was democratic.

Landry, Bart. *Black Working Wives: Pioneers of the American Family Revolution.* Berkeley: University of California Press, 2000. Discusses how black women of the middle class worked and created the first two-income households. Notes how these women escaped the cult of domesticity while white middle class women were trapped in it.

Nelson, Dana D. *National Manhood: Capitalist Citizenship and the Imagined Fraternity of White Men.* Durham, N.C.: Duke University Press, 1998. Argues that the nation came to consider itself as a nation of white men. Suggests that nationalism and business were tied together and were used to limit power to white men.

Strom, Sharon Hartman. *Beyond the Typewriter: Gender, Class, and the Origins of Modern American Office Work, 1900-1930.* Urbana: University of Illinois Press, 1992. Examines how secretarial work came to be viewed as a female occupation in this period and the social and economic forces behind this change. Also looks at how men maintained their control of the workplace.

Woody, Bette. *Black Women in the Workplace: Impacts of Structural Change in the Economy.* New York: Greenwood Press, 1992. Discusses how changes in the United States have affected black women. Argues that the rising service economy has affected this group dramatically.

Scott A. Merriman

Notable Persons in American Business History

Names marked with asterisks are subjects of full essays in the main text.

Allen, Paul (1953-   )

Cofounder of Microsoft Corporation

An early interest in technology led Allen and his childhood friend Bill Gates to create the BASIC programming language while he was still in high school. Allen and Gates used royalties from early licenses of BASIC to found Microsoft Corporation in 1975. As executive vice president, Allen played a key role in the development of Microsoft's earliest successful software products, including MS-DOS, Windows, and Word for Windows. Allen was diagnosed with Hodgkin's disease in 1982 and left the company the following year, but he retained a substantial stake in Microsoft. After undergoing successful radiation treatment, he used his Microsoft fortune to invest in other industries. He purchased the Portland Trailblazers basketball team and the Seattle Seahawks football team; created a film production company, Vulcan Productions; and invested substantially in Dreamworks SKG. In 2003, he announced the creation of the Allen Institute for Brain Science, which he endowed with $100 million. In the years following Allen's departure from the company, Microsoft earned enormous market shares for its Windows operating system, its Internet browser Internet Explorer, and a variety of computer network-related software. *Forbes* magazine ranked Bill Gates as the world's third richest person in 2008. Allen was not far behind, at number forty-one.

Amos, Wally (1936-   )

Founder of Famous Amos cookie company

The Famous Amos cookie company grew out of Wally Amos's lifelong fascination with chocolate chip cookies. A veteran of the U.S. Air Force and the first African American to serve as an agent for the William Morris talent agency, Amos found himself unemployed in Los Angeles in 1967 with a growing family to support. He returned to his childhood obsession and began baking cookies for friends, who suggested he sell them. With a $25,000 loan, he opened a small shop in Hollywood. With a high-quality product and savvy marketing he turned the Famous Amos brand into a multimillion-dollar enterprise during the 1980's. When profits ebbed, he

licensed the brand to a series of investors and was eventually pushed out of the company. Amos then created the Uncle Noname (later renamed Uncle Wally's Muffin Company) brand of cookies and muffins before returning to Famous Amos in 1998 after Keebler purchased the company rights. Amos's trademark panama hat and cotton shirt were included in the Smithsonian's Collection of Business Americana in 1980, and President Ronald Reagan named Amos as one of the earliest recipients of the Awards for Entrepreneurial Excellence in 1986.

Aoki, Rocky (1940-2008)

Founder of Benihana restaurants

The Aoki family opened its first Benihana restaurant amid the rubble of Tokyo after War II. Rocky Aoki, a celebrated Olympic wrestler in 1960, moved to New York to attend college on an athletic scholarship. In 1964, he and his wife opened their first Benihana restaurant in the United States. After a sluggish start, the Manhattan restaurant flourished, thanks to good reviews and frequent celebrity patrons. Aoki's vigorous self-promotion and the novelty of the theatrical *teppanyaki* table cooking style made Benihana one of the most successful restaurant chains in the world. Franchises soon cropped up across North America, Great Britain, and Southeast Asia. In 1995, Aoki sold the company to publicly traded Benihana, Inc., a family trust, but remained the principal shareholder and chief executive until 1998. A family battle for control of the company by Aoki's heirs and a series of health problems marked the next decade of the restaurant, though profits continued to soar. Aoki is credited with making Japanese cuisine and culture more accessible in the United States as well as popularizing theme restaurants.

Arnold, Thurman Wesley (1891-1969)

Politician and prominent antitrust lawyer

A graduate of Princeton University and Harvard Law School, Arnold fought in France during World War I and returned to his birthplace, Laramie, Wyoming, where he served as mayor. Following stints as the dean of West Virginia University's law school and a professorship at Yale, he was appointed assistant attorney general in President Franklin D. Roosevelt's cabinet in 1939 and was placed in charge of the antitrust division. There, he made his name as a hard-nosed trust-buster with vigorous action against the building industry, the American Medical Association, and tobacco industries, among others, emphasizing the rights of consumers over profits. At the outbreak of World War II, the Roosevelt administration reined in their antitrust efforts and Arnold left the Justice Department for a short-lived career as a federal circuit court judge in Washington, D.C., and later an attorney specializing in civil liberties cases. His aggressive approach to the enforcement of antitrust legislation created friction within the Roosevelt administration but also helped shape the application of several of Roosevelt's New Deal programs designed to pull the nation out of the Depression.

Ash, Mary Kay (1918-2001)

Founder of Mary Kay Cosmetics
Ash learned the art of direct marketing as a part-time student working her way through medical school. Her success with Stanley Home Products in 1939 led her to pursue sales full time. Her employer's approach to selling, through home parties among friends and neighbors, suited Ash well and gave her a model that she would later perfect. After achieving a substantial sales record with Stanley, she joined World Gift in 1952 and eventually rose to the level of national sales director. However, after the company promoted a less-qualified male colleague above her in 1963, she left World Gift and began to prepare her own business plan. With five thousand dollars in savings and the help of her husband and a group of friends, she launched Beauty by Mary Kay, which manufactured and sold skin-care lotion. Over the next two decades, Ash turned her small start-up company, renamed Mary Kay Cosmetics in 1965, into an international publicly traded company with annual sales nearing $1 billion. Ash fueled her success by empowering her saleswomen, called "consultants," and by providing them with such incentives as pink Cadillacs, jewelry, and expensive vacations.

Astor, John Jacob* (1763-1848)

Entrepreneur, real estate developer, and pioneer of international marketing whose American Fur Company and related ventures earned him one of the largest private fortunes in U.S. history.

Bailey, Thomas (1939-   )

Financier and founder of Janus Capital Group
After earning his master's degree in business administration at Western Ontario University in 1962, Bailey joined the brokerage firm Boettcher & Company in Aspen, Colorado. In 1968, he found investors who contributed twenty-five thousand dollars each for a mutual fund investment that he managed in his spare time. A year later, his profits allowed him to leave Boettcher and found the Janus Fund. His aggressive approach to investing saw fund profits regularly outperform Standard and Poor's 500 over the next decade. During the 1980's, Bailey increased his staff of managers and analysts and created several new funds, some of which saw as much as 51 percent returns. In 1996, the aggregate value of Bailey's funds reached $30 billion. With profits mounting, Bailey resigned as chief executive officer in 2002. Two years later, he gave up his position as chairman in the wake of Janus's investigation by the Security and Exchange Commission for manipulating fund investments for the benefit of short-term investors. The Janus Capital Group settled the matter for $100 million and remained one of the largest equity management firms in the United States. In late 2008, *Forbes* ranked Bailey at 322 on its list of the four hundred richest Americans.

Bell, Alexander Graham* (1847-1922)

Scottish American inventor and founder of the Bell Telephone Company, which later became American Telephone and Telegraph (AT&T).

Bezos, Jeff (1964-   )

Founder of Amazon.com
During the mid-1980's, Bezos began building a promising career in the corporate world, first with a small financial trading start-up, and later as senior vice president at the online trading company D. E. Shaw & Company. In 1994, he struck out on his own, choosing books as the most promising foundation for an online store. Initially operating under the name Abracadabra, Bezos launched his first Web site in 1995. Success was nearly immediate. He took the company public two years later, and over the next decade he fine-tuned Amazon with the addition of products ranging from music and DVDs to kitchenware, consumer electronics, and clothing. Bezos soon opened Amazon international sites in Canada, Great Britain, Germany, France, and

China. Fueled by low prices and fast delivery, Amazon weathered the dot-com bubble bust in 2000 by creating partnerships with Borders Books, Toys 'R Us, and other companies, while always emphasizing the quality of customer experience. In 2007, Amazon's sales tipped $2.8 billion, and *Forbes* magazine ranked Bezos eighty-second on its list of the world's richest people.

Bloomberg, Michael R. (1942-   )
Media entrepreneur and mayor of New York City
A graduate of Harvard Business School in 1966, Bloomberg spent his early career with equity trader Salomon Brothers, Inc., in which he became a general partner and led the company's shift to computer-based financial services. In 1981, he left the company, cashed out his stock, and founded Innovative Market Systems (IMS) to sell subscriptions to real-time securities information through desktop computer terminals. In 1986, he rechristened the company Bloomberg L. P. Over the next decade, he built it into one of the largest financial news and media organizations in the world with a presence in print, radio, and television marketplaces. In 2001, Bloomberg won a surprise victory in New York City's mayoral race, and he was reelected four years later. Meanwhile, Bloomberg L. P. remained a significant rival to older, more established financial news firms such as Dow Jones and Reuters, and made its founder one of the richest men in the world. Bloomberg used much of his fortune to fund city projects in New York, particularly in the wake of the terrorist attacks of September 11, 2001. In 2008, he undertook to overturn a term-limits law so he could run for a third term as mayor.

Boeing, William Edward (1881-1956)
Pioneer of military and commercial aviation
The only son of a wealthy timber and mining family in the Midwest, Boeing moved to Seattle, Washington, in 1902 to establish his own timber company. His interests in the next decade turned to the burgeoning aircraft industry. In 1916, he founded his first aviation company and won a contract to build Curtiss seaplanes for use in World War I. However, the Armistice of November, 1981, brought an end to the contract before production began and forced his Pacific Aero Products company to make furniture and other items to stay in business. Boeing's fortunes improved 1920, when he won a government contract to build two hundred Thomas-Morse MB-3 fighter planes. In 1927, Boeing Air Transport began shuttling mail and passengers between San Francisco and Chicago. During the 1930's, Boeing introduced numerous innovations for lightweight, fixed-wing aircraft that would help his company get lucrative contracts for military aircraft during World War II. Boeing made two vital contributions to the war effort credited with helping win the war: the B-17 Flying Fortress and the B-29 Superfortress. In successive decades, Boeing Aircraft made major contributions to aviation technology and the expanding commercial aircraft industry and remained the largest commercial aircraft manufacturer in the world during the early twenty-first century.

Borden, Gail (1801-1874)
Inventor and pioneer of food preservation
Borden played a central role in the development of Texas before it became a U.S. state during the 1840's. An accomplished surveyor, he planned the cities of Galveston and Houston and helped write independent Texas's constitution in 1836. He also cofounded Texas's first permanent newspaper, the *Telegraph and Texas Land Register,* and was twice appointed collector of customs by Texas president Sam Houston. During the 1840's, Borden began research on food preservation and developed a meat biscuit made of condensed beef broth and flour. In 1856, he founded the New York Condensed Milk Company, later called Borden, Inc. The U.S. Civil War (1861-1865) increased demand for canned and preserved foods, and Borden secured several patents during the 1860's, branching out to include condensed fruit and fruit juice, concentrated tea, coffee, and cocoa. During his final years, he made substantial philanthropic contributions to the state of Texas by building schools and churches. A century after Borden's 1874 death, Borden, Inc. remained one of the largest producers of dairy and pasta products in the United States and also produced such popular nonfood items as Elmer's glue and Krazy Glue.

Bradham, Caleb (1867-1934)
Pharmacist and inventor of the formula for Pepsi cola
Bradham intended to pursue a career as a doctor but left school when his father declared bankruptcy during the 1890's. Following a short stint as a school-

teacher, he opened a drugstore in New Bern, North Carolina. There, he invented a recipe for what became known as Brad's Drink in 1898 and sold it at his drugstore's soda fountain. He incorporated the Pepsi-Cola Company in 1902 and rented a nearby building to manufacture the soft drink. Over the next two decades, he built his company into a national brand by employing a vigorous marketing campaign. He also created new job opportunities at his bottling companies throughout the South and invested much of his profits in community campaigns and scholarship program at the University of North Carolina's school of pharmacy. By 1910, he had sold the rights to Pepsi franchises in twenty-four states. The outbreak of World War I, and the subsequent rationing of sugar, brought a steep decline in sales of Pepsi, and Bradham was forced to file for bankruptcy in 1923, after which he returned to work in his drugstore in New Bern.

Brin, Sergey (1973-   )

Computer scientist and cofounder of Google
Born in Moscow, Russia, and raised in Maryland, Brin studied computer science and mathematics at the University of Maryland. While pursuing his doctorate at Stanford, he met Larry Page, with whom he wrote a paper on the principles of Internet search engines. In 1996, he and Page collaborated on the development of an early Internet search engine called BackRub. By 1998, they had decided to postpone their academic work in order to launch Google from a friend's garage as a privately held corporation. In 2004, their company went public. Afterward, it continued to grow rapidly through the steady introduction of new technology and strategic partnerships. Serving as Google's president of technology, Brin has amassed a net worth approaching an estimated $20 billion. In 2008, he announced he was investing $5 million in Space Adventures, a Virginia-based company that arranges civilian flights into space on Russian Soyuz spacecraft.

Buffett, Warren* (1930-   )

Chairman and chief executive officer of Berkshire Hathaway whose knack for picking winning stocks has made him one of the richest men in the world.

Bush, George H. W. (1924-   )

Business executive and forty-first president of the United States
After serving as a naval aviator during World War II, Bush studied economics at Yale University and took a job at Dresser Industries as an oil field supply salesperson in Odessa, Texas. In 1953, he started his own company, Zapata Petroleum Corporation, an oil and gas drilling firm. After amassing a sizable fortune, he moved his headquarters to Houston, where he won a U.S. congressional seat in 1966 and rose quickly within the Republican Party. A succession of posts, including ambassador to the United Nations, director of the Central Intelligence Agency, and vice president under Ronald Reagan, culminated in his election as the president of the United States in 1988. As president, he presided over a record budget deficit and a savings and loan collapse. He also proposed the North American Free Trade Agreement, which would ultimately fall to his Democrat successor, President Bill Clinton, to see enacted.

Carnegie, Andrew* (1835-1919)

Scottish American industrialist and steel magnate who devoted his vast fortune to philanthropic endeavors during his later years.

Carrier, Willis Haviland (1876-1950)

Inventor of air conditioning
Carrier is credited with inventing modern air conditioning technology. After studying engineering at Cornell University, he took a job with a heating and exhaust systems manufacturer in 1901. While working for that company, he created a heat and humidity control system for a New York printing plant that led to his first "air conditioning" patent in 1906. He would go on to secure more than eight more patents. In 1911, he published the "Rational Psychometric Formula," which established the burgeoning air conditioning industry as a legitimate engineering discipline. During World War II, he created a device to simulate freezing conditions for American aircraft to test their capabilities at high altitude. After he died in 1950, the Carrier Company developed into a global corporation with 45,000 employees and annual sales of more than $15 billion.

Carver, George Washington* (1861?-1943)

African American agricultural chemist, inventor, and educator who made seminal contributions to the American agricultural industry.

Case, Steve (1958-   )

Cofounder of America Online (AOL)

After growing up in Honolulu, Hawaii, Case graduated from Williams College in Massachusetts before embarking on a long career as a corporate executive. He got his start with Procter and Gamble and Pizza Hut, Inc. before crossing paths with Bill von Meister, owner of Control Video Corporation, an early online game downloading service. Case helped found Quantum Computer Services in 1985 and later became its chief executive officer (1991). During that same year, he changed the company's name to America Online and helped build its subscriber base, which reached 1 million members in 1994. In 2003, Case resigned from America Online, following the turbulent aftermath of its $106 billion merger with media giant Time-Warner. He remained a board member for Time-Warner until 2005.

Casey, James E. (1888-1983)

Founder of United Parcel Service

Born in Nevada, Casey founded the American Messenger Service in Seattle, Washington, in 1907. He and his business partner employed family members and friends to make deliveries—during the early years, mainly parcels from department stores and food deliveries from local restaurants—on foot and by bicycle. In 1919, Casey began expanding the business outside Seattle and changed his company's name to United Parcel Service. He credited the success of the company under his leadership to employee ownership of the business. For the technical innovations adopted during his tenure, and for his emphasis on labor over profits, Casey was inducted to the Labor Hall of Fame in 2002. The modest company he founded on one hundred dollars in borrowed capital eventually became one of the largest international corporations in the world, shipping more than 6 million packages annually to more than two hundred countries and territories.

Chavez, César* (1927-1993)

Hispanic American labor activist who created the first union to represent the labor interests of agricultural workers in California.

Chavez-Thompson, Linda (1947-   )

Labor leader

The daughter of Texas sharecroppers, Chavez-Thompson got her start as a labor organizer with the Laborer's International Union of North America before serving with several other local organizations, including the Texas AFL-CIO. In 1993, she was elected to the executive council of the AFL-CIO, becoming the first Hispanic woman to reach that level. Over the next two years, she headed efforts to raise the minimum wage and to reform immigration law. In 1995, she was elected by voice vote for the position of executive vice president of the AFL-CIO, a new position created especially for her. After retiring from the organization in 2007, she continued to serve as vice chairperson of the Democratic National Committee, a position she had held since 1997.

Chrysler, Walter P. (1875-1940)

Founder of Chrysler Corporation

A machinist and railroad mechanic during the early years of his working life, Chrysler maintained an abiding interest in the emerging automobile industry at the turn of the twentieth century. In 1911, he took a job with the Buick Motor Company in Flint, Michigan, as head of production. He resigned in 1916 but was lured back with the promise of complete control of Buick. He remained as head of the company until 1919, when he again resigned and sold his shares—making him one of the wealthiest men in America at the time. In 1925, he founded his namesake company out of the ashes of the Maxwell Motor Company. Under his leadership, Chrysler Corporation acquired the Plymouth, DeSoto, and Dodge brands. In 1928, he directed the building of the Chrysler Building in New York City, and was named that year as *Time* magazine's Man of the Year. He retired from the Chrysler Corporation in 1936 and devoted his final years to property development in Virginia.

Cohen, Ben (1951-   )

Cofounder of Ben & Jerry's ice cream

Cohen met his future business partner, Jerry Greenfield, when both were junior high school students in Long Island, New York. However, several years would pass before they began collaborating on what would become their popular ice cream brand. Cohen first entered the ice cream trade in high school as a neighborhood ice cream truck driver. After dropping out of Colgate University, he held a series of odd jobs before opening the Ben & Jerry's Homemade Ice Cream Parlor in Burlington, Vermont, in 1978. The company soon earned a reputation for both its commitment to social responsibility and its unusual flavors of ice cream, many of which capitalized on pop cultural references. Cohen began donating a percentage of pretax profits to numerous nonprofit organizations and established a foundation for charitable giving.

Coxe, Tench (1755-1824)
Political economist
Born in Philadelphia, Coxe was initially a British loyalist when American Revolutionary War began. He served in the British Army under General Howe, but after his capture, imprisonment, and release, he embraced the revolutionary cause. He was a strong advocate of industrialization as a means of national prosperity and pushed for the imposition of stronger tariffs to protect American manufacturers during the early years of American independence. He coauthored "Report on Manufactures" with Alexander Hamilton, under whom he was later assistant secretary of the treasury during the administrations of presidents Washington and Jefferson. Coxe published widely on economic and political matters; however, by the early nineteenth century, his aggressive land acquisitions in North Carolina and Tennessee nearly brought him to financial ruin. He is regarded as one of the progenitors of the American cotton industry for his aggressive support of that industry in the South.

Croly, Herbert (1869-1930)
Journalist and political theorist
Born in New York and educated at Harvard University, Croly spent thirteen years as editor of the *Architectural Record* before signing on as the first editor of *The New Republic* in 1914. Five years earlier, he had published *The Promise of American Life*, in which he presented a liberal, progressive political agenda, including more governmental spending on education and support for social programs, that some claim later influenced the policies of President Woodrow Wilson and the crafting of President Franklin D. Roosevelt's New Deal. Croly's role at *The New Republic* put him in touch with the leading writers of the day in the United States and Europe, and the publi-

cation's editorial board threw its considerable weight behind the Progressive movement. Croly remained at the magazine until his death in 1930.

Curtis, Cyrus H. K. (1850-1933)
Publisher and businessman
Curtis began in the publishing business with the *Young America* weekly paper in Portland, Maine. After similar small ventures in Boston and Philadelphia, he founded the Curtis Publishing Company in 1891. One of his earliest successes began as a one-page column written by his wife, Louisa Knapp, whose "Women at Home" column later became the *Ladies' Home Journal*, which achieved print runs of nearly 5 million by the turn of the twentieth century. In 1897, Curtis purchased the ailing *Saturday Evening Post* and built it into one of the early twentieth century's best-selling magazines, with more than 6 million copies in circulation by 1962. His success in magazine publishing led him to invest in the newspaper trade in his later years. He purchased the *New York Evening Post* in 1923 and the *Philadelphia Enquirer* in 1930, but profits plummeted and he eventually sold his newspaper interests.

Davis, James J. (1873-1947)
Steelworker and Republican politician
Born in Wales, Davis emigrated to the United States in 1881 and settled with his family in Pittsburgh, Pennsylvania. There, he was apprenticed as a steel puddler's assistant, earning the nickname Puddler Jim that followed him through most of his public life. In 1898, he began a long career in public life as a city clerk in Indiana. In 1921, he was appointed secretary of labor by President Warren G. Harding and retained that position under presidents Calvin Coolidge and Herbert Hoover. As a cabinet officer, he created the U.S. Border Patrol and persuaded U.S. Steel to eliminate the twelve-hour workday. He resigned his cabinet post in 1930 after being elected to the U.S. Senate from Pennsylvania. In the Senate, he cosponsored the Davis-Bacon Act, which required workers on federal contracts to be paid prevailing private-sector wages and benefits.

Dayton, George (1857-1938)
Founder of the Dayton Department Store chain
After amassing a fortune in real estate and as head of the Bank of Worthington in Minnesota, Dayton founded his Dry Goods Store—later renamed

Dayton's Department Store—in 1902. Combining a successful business life with a strong commitment to community service, he created the Dayton Foundation, dedicated to social welfare projects, and became a member of the Community Fund, a precursor to the United Way. Upon his death in 1938, Dayton bequeathed a successful department store chain to his sons, who would found the Target chain of discount retail stores in 1962.

Debs, Eugene V.* (1855-1926)

Labor leader, union activist, and five-time Socialist Party nominee for the U.S. presidency.

Deere, John (1804-1886)

Founder of John Deere & Company

Born in Rutland, Vermont, Deere was apprenticed to a blacksmith in 1821 and opened his own business four years later. When he faced bankruptcy in 1836, he sold the business and moved to Indiana. There he made a plow with polished steel that worked more efficiently in tough prairie soil. Word of the plow's success spread rapidly, and three years later Deere was producing as many as one hundred plows per year. In 1848, Deere relocated to Moline, Illinois, on the Mississippi River—a location that allowed him to take advantage of more efficient transport of goods. By 1868, he was largely retired from the day-to-day operations of his company, which he entrusted to his sons. In the decades that followed, Deere would become the largest agricultural machinery company in the world.

Dell, Michael (1965-   )

Founder of Dell Computers

Dell showed early promise as a business mogul. After making a small fortune selling stamps at the age of twelve, he turned to selling subscriptions for the *Houston Post* newspaper. He got his first computer, an Apple II, at the age of fifteen and promptly took it apart and reassembled it. While attending the University of Texas, he founded the PC's Limited computer company out of his campus dorm room in 1984. Early success and a loan from family members allowed him to leave school at the age of nineteen and develop the company full time. Despite product setbacks during the 1990's, Dell built the company—renamed Dell, Inc. in 2003—into an international corporation and one of the most successful computer manufacturers in the world.

Deming, W. Edwards* (1900-1993)

Statistician and theorist who developed an innovative approach to track and improve efficiency in manufacturing after World War II.

Disney, Walt* (1901-1966)

Pioneer in animated film and in television production, and creator of the Disney media and theme park empire.

Dodge, William Earl (1805-1883)

Businessman, politician, and founding member of the Young Men's Christian Association (YMCA)

Dodge was born in Hartford, Connecticut, the son of the founder of the New York Peace Society. He would devote much of his life to social and humanitarian causes, but his early life was devoted to business. He founded the mining firm Phelps, Dodge and Company with his father-in-law in 1833. After the Civil War (1861-1865), he acquired vast timber interests in his namesake Dodge County, Georgia, where he was instrumental in building the Macon and Brunswick Railroad. In 1869 he toured present-day Oklahoma as part of the government-sponsored Board of Indian Commissioners and later lobbied unsuccessfully for a cabinet-level department for Indian affairs. He met several representatives from Native American tribes and sought the prosecution of U.S. Cavalry commanders following the massacre of Blackfeet Indians in Montana in 1870. Dodge served in the U.S. House of Representatives for New York's Eighth District from 1866 to 1867 and helped found the Young Men's Christian Association.

Doheny, Edward L. (1856-1935)

Oil tycoon

The son of Irish immigrants, Doheny was born in Fond du Lac, Wisconsin. At the age of seventeen he joined the U.S. Geological Survey and surveyed Indian land in Kansas. After stints as a prospector in South Dakota's Black Hills and in Arizona and New Mexico, Doheny met Albert Fall, the future secretary of the interior, and Charles Canfield, his future business partner, in 1883. In subsequent years, Doheny's fortunes declined. In 1891, he moved to Los Angeles, California, where Canfield was doing a lucrative trade in the burgeoning real estate market. There, Doheny drilled the first productive oil well in Southern California and built a fortune with which he would later buy up vast tracts of oil land in Mexico. In 1922, he and Fall were implicated in the Teapot Dome Scandal, in which he and another oil man, Harry Sinclair, were accused of bribing Fall to secure oil fields in California and Wyoming without competitive bidding. Doheny was later acquitted. In later years, Doheny gave generously to the state of California, contributing funds to the University of Southern California and donating large tracts of land to the state.

Dow, Herbert Henry (1866-1930)
Founder of Dow Chemical Company
Born in Canada, Dow grew up in Connecticut and Ohio. He attended what later became Case Western Reserve University and taught chemistry briefly following his graduation. As a student, he had conducted research on the chemical extraction of bromine, which served a variety of industrial and consumer uses at the time. He formed his first company in 1889 but quickly went bankrupt. In 1891, he invented a new process to extract bromine through electrolysis. Five years later, he founded Dow Chemical to research additional uses for the process. During World War I, 90 percent of the Dow Chemical Company's production was linked to the war effort. In subsequent years, Dow began research on consumer applications of magnesium. At the time of his death in 1930, he held more than ninety patents. The company he founded remained a leading provider of consumer and industrial chemicals, with revenues of more than $50 billion annually during the early twenty-first century.

Du Pont, Eleuthère Irénée (1771-1834)
Patriarch of the Du Pont family
Born in Paris, Du Pont moved with his wife and children to Rhode Island in 1799 in the wake of violence following the French Revolution. In 1802, he built the Eleutherian Mills, his family home and business on Brandywine Creek, where he manufactured gunpowder, principally for the U.S. government. Over the next several decades, he supplied gunpowder for the Mexican and Crimean Wars. During the U.S. Civil War (1861-1865), the company sold 4 million barrels of gunpowder. The mill was closed following World War I and turned into an industrial history museum. The Eleutherian Mills and Hagley Museum was named a National Historical Landmark in 1966.

Du Pont de Neumours, Pierre Samuel (1739-1817)
French economist
The father of Du Pont family patriarch Eleuthère Irénée Du Pont, Pierre Samuel had distant connections through his mother to nobility in King Louis XV's France. He appeared frequently at the French court and drew widespread attention among French economists during the 1760's with his book *Physiocracy*, in which he argued for low tariffs and free trade agreements with foreign nations. He supported the French Revolution in 1789 but physically defended King Louis XVI and Marie Antoinette from violence, thereby earning a death sentence that was later revoked. He fled with his family to the United States in 1799. There he became an informal adviser to President Thomas Jefferson, who he advised to buy the Louisiana Territory from Napoleon Bonaparte.

Durant, William Crapo (1861-1947)
Automobile pioneer
Durant came to the automobile industry via his success as a manufacturer of horse-drawn carriages in Flint, Michigan. By 1890, the Durant-Dort Carriage Company had become the largest manufacturer of carriages in the country, producing nearly one-half million cars each year. In 1904, Durant became general manager of the Buick Motor Company. Four years later, he incorporated General Motors (GM) and acquired several other brand automobiles, including Oldsmobile and Cadillac. He was forced out of GM in 1910 when investors assumed control of the corporation and partnered with Louis Chevrolet to found a new automobile company. Nevertheless, Durant's earlier success allowed him to purchase a controlling interest in GM in 1916. He left the company for good in 1920 after GM was purchased by the DuPont family. He founded the Durant Motor Company in 1921, but the stock market crash of 1929 brought an end to his business life and fortune. Among Durant's innovations as an automobile pioneer was the creation of a holding company that controlled and manufactured multiple company brands.

Eastman, George (1854-1932)
Founder of Eastman Kodak and inventor of rolled photographic film
Eastman's early interest in photography led to his invention of the dry photographic plate in 1877—a

product that shifted photographic technology from unwieldy glass plates to more manageable and efficient paper rolls that ultimately led to the development of motion-picture film. He manufactured the film for his Eastman Dry Plate Company. In 1888 Eastman patented a camera to be used with the new roll film and trademarked the name Kodak. He renamed his company Eastman Kodak in 1892 and introduced a second camera, the Brownie, that sold for only one dollar in 1900. The Brownie became a best seller and helped popularize photography among the masses. Eastman later focused more particularly on the film market as competition among still-camera makers increased. In 1925, he gave up control of the daily operations of the Eastman Kodak Company to devote more time to philanthropic projects. During the early twenty-first century, Eastman Kodak remained the world's largest manufacturer of still and motion-picture film, but by then the bulk of its operations were concerned with digital photography and digital printing.

Edison, Thomas Alva* (1847-1931)

Inventor whose creation of incandescent light bulbs led to the founding of the company that became General Electric.

Fargo, William George (1818-1881)

Cofounder of American Express

Fargo was born in Pompey, New York. By the age of thirteen, he had left school to begin working as a mail carrier. He worked as a mercantile clerk for numerous grocery stores until he landed employment as a freight agent for the Auburn & Syracuse Railway in 1841. In 1844, he partnered with Henry Wells to form Wells & Company, the first express freight enterprise to operate west of Buffalo, New York. In 1850, Fargo joined the newly consolidated American Express Company, and the following year created Wells, Fargo & Company, a transcontinental express service that connected New York and San Francisco by way of the Isthmus of Panama. The company capitalized on California's gold rush and established several banks in towns along the Pacific coast. Fargo served as mayor of Buffalo from 1862 to 1866, after which he continued with American Express as president until his death in 1881.

Firestone, Harvey (1868-1938)

Industrialist and founder of the Firestone tire company

Firestone sealed his future career when he stumbled upon the idea of putting rubber tires on the wheels of horse-drawn carriages to improve their handling and increase the comfort of passengers. After graduating from high school, he worked at the Detroit office of a carriage manufacturer. At the age of thirty-one, he moved to Chicago and founded the Firestone Tire & Rubber Company to provide tires for the emerging "horseless carriage" market. In 1904, he struck an alliance with Henry Ford to supply tires for Ford automobiles. Two years later, his company reached $1 million in sales. By 1926, Firestone needed a cheaper supply of rubber to make tires, so he invested in rubber plantations covering nearly 1 million acres in Liberia, West Africa. In subsequent years, he continued to innovate, producing the first pneumatic tires as well as additional brands for use on other transport and farm equipment. Company sales broke the $100 million mark at the time of Firestone's death in 1938.

Fisk, James (1834-1872)

Stock broker and financier

In 1859, sixteen-year-old Fisk left home to join a traveling circus before settling into a series of peddling and dry goods sales jobs. During the Civil War (1861-1865), he secured textile contracts with the Union government and amassed a fortune that he soon squandered. In 1864, he moved to New York and became a stockbroker, a position that put him in company with some of the wealthiest industrialists of the late nineteenth century, including Cornelius Vanderbilt, against whom Fisk aided his employer Daniel Drew to seize control of the Erie Railroad. Fisk's shady attempts to corner the market on gold were blamed for the stock market's Black Friday crash in 1869. Personal and financial recklessness followed Fish until his death in 1872 at the hands of a jealous rival for the attentions of a former showgirl. Shunned by polite society for his sexual indiscretions and unscrupulous business dealings, Fisk nonetheless became something of a hero among New York's working classes, particularly employees of the Erie Railroad.

Fitch, John (1743-1798)

Steamboat pioneer

Fitch was born in Connecticut and apprenticed to a clockmaker. During the Revolutionary War, he fought briefly with the Continental Army but left to run a munitions factory in New Jersey. After a short stint as a land surveyor, he began working on plans for a steam engine and successfully launched a prototype steamship in 1787. Additional models followed, but his failure to secure a broad patent on the engine led to disputes with fellow inventor James Rumsey, and Fitch lost much-needed investment capital. Although he successfully operated several river steamships in Delaware, Pennsylvania, and New Jersey, he failed to demonstrate conclusively the benefits of steam power. That achievement would fall to Robert Fulton, who built his first steamship after Fitch's death in 1798 and later became known as the founder of steam navigation.

Ford, Henry* (1863-1947)

Pioneering automobile maker and industrialist whose development of the assembly line revolutionized the efficiency with which goods were produced.

Franklin, Benjamin* (1706-1790)

Early statesman who also distinguished himself as a scientist, inventor, and businessman.

Frick, Henry Clay (1849-1919)

Industrialist who helped found U.S. Steel

Born in West Overton, Pennsylvania, Frick left his university early to form a partnership with friends to extract coke from coal. With assistance from family friend Andrew Mellon, Frick later bought out the partnership and acquired several coal mines as well as several competitors. By the time he was thirty, Frick was the world's largest producer of coke. Coke is a vital component in the manufacture of steel, and Frick later formed a partnership with steel magnate Andrew Carnegie. In 1889, he became chairman of the Carnegie Company and in 1892 the acting head of the newly named Carnegie Steel Company. Frick ruled the Carnegie steel mills tightly. When workers at the Homestead Works in Pennsylvania decided to strike in 1892, he used three hundred tough strikebreakers to disband the workers. Sixteen people died and dozens more were injured in the ensuing violence. After the strike, Frick was shot and stabbed in his office but survived the attack. He retired from Carnegie Steel in 1899 but later played a central role in the formation of U.S. Steel. During his life, Frick amassed a vast collection of art, which he bequeathed to the city of New York upon his death.

Friedman, Milton (1912-2006)

Nobel laureate in economics

Born in Brooklyn, New York, to Hungarian immigrants, Friedman studied mathematics at Rutgers and did his graduate work in statistics at the University of Chicago. He and his wife—fellow economist Rose Director—came of age economically during President Franklin D. Roosevelt's New Deal era. Supportive of efforts such as the Works Progress Administration, Friedman was nonetheless critical of the price-control approach of the National Recovery Administration and other New Deal agencies. During the 1940's, he worked with the Division of War Research at Columbia University assisting with weapons design and military testing. In 1946, Friedman began a thirty-year tenure as professor of economics at the University of Chicago, where he was responsible for assembling a tight-knit community of theorists who were later dubbed the Chicago School of Economics. In 1976, he become one of several Chicago economists to win a Nobel Prize. His award was made for "for his achievements in the fields of consumption analysis, monetary history and theory, and for his demonstration of the complexity of stabilization policy." He later served as an economic adviser during Ronald Reagan's two terms as president.

Fulton, Robert (1765-1815)

Steamboat inventor and engineer

Born in Pennsylvania, Fulton was apprenticed as a painter in England before pursuing his childhood interest in steam engines. In 1797, Fulton moved to Paris, where he designed the first practical submarine for Napoleon Bonaparte in 1800-1801. He and three mechanics successfully descended to a depth of twenty-five feet. He also built his first experimental steamship, but it sank during a trial run on the Seine River. His improved second model in 1803 was a success. After returning to the United States, Fulton partnered with his father-in-law, France Robert Livingston—the U.S. ambassador—to establish the first commercial steamboat, the *North River Steamboat* (later renamed the *Clermont*), which operated between New York City and Albany. Fulton was neither the first to invent a practical steamboat nor the first to operate a regular steamboat route; however, he has nevertheless been credited with establishing the first commercially practical steamboat.

Gallatin, Abraham (1761-1849)

Longest-serving U.S. secretary of the treasury
Gallatin emigrated to the United States from Switzerland during the 1780's and settled in Pennsylvania. He began as a tea merchant and later established a glass factory. In 1788, he entered local politics as a delegate to Pennsylvania's state constitutional convention, which proposed amendments to the new U.S. Constitution, and later served as a state senator. A strong advocate of states' rights and a weak federal government, Gallatin made important contributions to federal fiscal policy and helped secure a charter for the Bank of Pennsylvania. In 1793, he was elected to the U.S. Senate but was later dismissed over a dispute about the constitutional citizenship requirement. His intervention in the Whiskey Rebellion in Pennsylvania in 1794 earned him election to the U.S. House of Representatives, in which he served from 1795 to 1801 and where he further demonstrated his proficiency in federal fiscal matters. He helped found the House Ways and Means Committee and became a ranking member of the Democratic-Republican Party. In 1801, newly elected President Thomas Jefferson appointed Gallatin secretary of the Treasury—a post he held until 1814. In that office, he worked tirelessly to reduce the public debt. In his final years, Gallatin held diplomatic posts in France and Great Britain.

Gannett, Frank Ernest (1876-1957)

Founder of the Gannett Media Company
Gannett was born in New York and graduated from Cornell University. He purchased his first newspaper, the *Elmira Gazette*, at the age of thirty and built a national media company that encompassed twenty-two newspapers as well as regional radio and television stations. Technological advances adopted in Gannett's newsrooms included the teletypesetter—a device used to transmit and typeset news wire copy—and shortwave radio to speed transmission of news reports. An active Unitarian Church member and Republican, Gannett came to oppose President Franklin D. Roosevelt's New Deal policies and made an unsuccessful bid for the presidency in 1940. The

company that Gannett built would expand throughout the United States after he died in 1957 and eventually own the national daily *USA Today*.

Garner, John Nance* (1868-1967)

Vice president of the United States who helped reform banking practices and shape economic policy under President Franklin D. Roosevelt.

Garvey, Marcus* (1887-1940)

Jamaican American civil rights activist and leader of the Universal Negro Improvement Association, which promoted entrepreneurship and commercial development for African Americans.

Gary, Elbert Henry (1846-1927)

Founder of U.S. Steel Corporation
Gary graduated from the Union College of Law in Indiana in 1868 and began practicing corporate law in Chicago in 1871. He served as mayor of Wheaton, Illinois, and spent two terms as a judge in DuPage County from 1884 to 1892. While he was a judge, Gary grew interested in the steel industry. With the support of J. P. Morgan and others, he became president of the Federal Steel Corporation in 1898. In 1901, he founded U.S. Steel, the world's first billion-dollar corporation. In 1920, he became a target of Theodore Roosevelt's antitrust campaign but later won a U.S. Supreme Court case against the government and served as chairman of the board of U.S. Steel until his death in 1927. The city of Gary, Indiana, founded in 1906 as the home of U.S. Steel's corporate headquarters, was named in Gary's honor.

Gates, Bill* (1955-   )

Founder and chief executive officer of Microsoft Corporation, whose success as a software developer and executive made him one of the richest men in the world.

Geneen, Harold (1910-1997)

President of International Telephone and Telegraph (ITT) and founder of modern international conglomerates
Born in Hampshire, England, Geneen emigrated to the United States as a child. He studied accounting at New York University and rose to senior vice president for Raytheon (1956-1959) before assuming control of ITT. Over nearly two decades, Geneen built the modest-sized company into a multina-

tional conglomerate with close ties to the federal government and its intelligence community. The growth of ITT was fueled by Geneen's purchase of a variety of other businesses in eighty countries, including rental car agencies, commercial and residential real estate, and hotels. When Geneen left ITT, the company employed 375,000 people and had more than $16 billion in annual revenue. Geneen's aggressive business tactics made him a symbol of corporate greed and arrogance. During the 1970's, allegations emerged that Geneen had made political contributions to the Republican Party in return for a favorable judgment in an antitrust case. The charges were never proven. The company was also suspected of funneling hundreds of thousands of dollars to Chile in an effort to overthrow the country's Marxist president, Salvador Allende, who had nationalized a local ITT subsidiary and was later overthrown in a military coup. The company admitted in 1976 that it might have made legal political contributions, but not for violent purposes.

Gerber, Daniel Frank, Jr. (1898-1974)
Founder of Gerber Baby Food

The Gerber brand of baby food owes its existence largely to the Fremont Canning Company, created in 1901 by Daniel Gerber's father to sell canned fruit and vegetables. By 1926, Gerber himself had become assistant general manager. At the suggestion of his wife, Gerber began research in 1927 on how to manufacture and package baby food. After he launched the Gerber brand a year later, a clever marketing campaign in *Good Housekeeping* magazine helped company sales rise to more than $300,000 during its first year. More than anything else, the Gerber Baby Food advertising campaign extended the company's market share as more competitors entered the baby food industry. Gerber presided over the company until 1971. During his tenure, the company also developed a line of baby toys, earned a listing on the New York Stock Exchange, and opened a subsidiary in Mexico. At the time of Gerber's death in 1974, the company was the largest producer of baby food in the world, with annual sales of $278 million.

Getty, J. Paul* (1892-1976)
Oil tycoon and art collector who made Getty Oil Company one of the largest oil production ventures of the early twentieth century.

Gimbel, Bernard (1885-1966)
Retail department store magnate

After graduating from college in 1907, Gimbel began working in one of his father's stores in Philadelphia. The next year, he was appointed vice president of the store. In 1910, he took a risk by trying to penetrate the New York retail market, pitting Gimbels against such powerhouses as Macy's and Saks and using aggressive marketing tactics, such as bargain-basement promotions, to make Gimbels competitive. He took Gimbels public in 1922 and raised enough capital within a year to buy out the neighborhood rival Saks & Company. Gimbel was a master of publicity. His clever use of advertising slogans, retail promotions, and even a featured spot in the 1947 classic film *Miracle on 34th Street* fueled the company's success. Gimbel steered the company successfully through both the Depression era and World War II. Until he died in 1966, he aggressively expanded the chain through suburban shopping mall outlets. The Gimbels chain finally closed for business in 1986.

Gompers, Samuel* (1850-1924)
Labor leader who became first president of the American Federation of Labor.

Goodyear, Charles (1800-1860)
Inventor of vulcanized rubber

Born in New Haven, Connecticut, Goodyear worked at his father's hardware store until the business failed in 1830. His subsequent experiments with India rubber—at that time not much in use because of its instability in extreme heat and cold—led to the process of vulcanization, by which rubber could be stabilized to endure the extremes of temperature without melting or cracking. In 1836, Goodyear experimented with a nitric acid treatment to cure the rubber and in 1844 acquired his first patent. His discovery would revolutionize the industrial use of rubber, from factory machinery to the emerging automobile industry, but he saw little financial reward because of persistent infringements on his patents. He died a poor man in 1860. Nearly forty years later, Frank Seiberling named his Goodyear Tire and Rubber Company in Goodyear's honor.

Gordy, Berry, Jr. (1929-   )

Record producer and founder of the Motown record label

The seventh of eight children in a middle-class African American family in Detroit, Gordy dropped out of high school to become a professional boxer. He enjoyed some success as a featherweight before being drafted into the U.S. Army during the Korean War. After his discharge in 1953, he opened the 3-D Record Mart to indulge his love of jazz music, but the store eventually went bankrupt. He then served a short stint as an assembly-line worker at a Lincoln-Mercury plant but left in 1957 to pursue a career as a songwriter. His first big success was with the song "Reet Petite," recorded by Jackie Wilson in 1957. That same year, he discovered Smokey Robinson and the Miracles. In 1959, he founded Motown Records. In the decade the followed, he signed several of the most influential artists of the era, including the Supremes, Marvin Gaye, the Temptations, the Four Tops, Stevie Wonder, and the Jackson Five. By the late 1970's, Gordy still had a successful stable of artists but musical trends were changing, so he sold his interest in Motown to MCA in 1988. He was inducted into the Rock and Roll Hall of Fame in 1990.

Gould, Jay* (1836-1892)

Financier who rose from poverty to become one of the most prominent—and most vilified—of the nineteenth century "robber barons."

Grant, William Thomas (1876-1972)

Founder of the W. T. Grant Company retail chain

Grant was born in Pennsylvania but raised in Massachusetts. He began his prolific business career at the age of seven as a flower seed salesman. At thirty, he opened his first retail store, W. T. Grant Company, a general merchandise "five-and-dime" store, in Lynne, Massachusetts. The combination of merchandise variety and low prices fueled rapid expansion of the retail chain to Connecticut and New York City by 1917. Grant took the company public in 1928 and achieved $100 million in sales by 1936. He had stores in forty-four states by 1940. Aside from his business interests, Grant also founded the W. T. Grant Foundation to serve the educational and development needs of children and young adults. He retired from business in 1966 and died six years later at the age of ninety-six. A victim of changing retail trends, his retail empire filed for bankruptcy in 1975.

Greenspan, Alan* (1926-   )

Chairman of the Federal Reserve Board (1987-2006) whose tenure during the 1990's coincided with a period of unprecedented economic growth.

Guggenheim, Daniel (1856-1930)

Industrialist and philanthropist

The eldest son of mining and smelting magnate Meyer Guggenheim, Daniel Guggenheim was born in Philadelphia, where his father settled after emigrating from Switzerland in 1847. Daniel would play a vital role in extending the family's mining interests and presiding over his father's multinational business interests. Following the family's acquisition of the American Mining and Smelting Company in 1901, he headed the trust until 1919. During those years, he extended operations throughout North and South America and Africa. In later years, he and his wife established two foundations to direct philanthropic and educational projects.

Guggenheim, Meyer (1828-1905)

Swiss American industrialist and patriarch of the influential Guggenheim family

After emigrating to the United States from Switzerland in 1847, Guggenheim began selling general merchandise in the coal belt of Pennsylvania. He manufactured stove polish, lye, and coffee before opening a wholesale business trading in household goods and later in imported machine-made lace. Guggenheim made his principal fortune in the mining and smelting trade, first in Colorado's silver mines and later throughout North and South America and in Africa. Guggenheim purchased the American Smelting and Refining Company in 1901, making the family a fortune and putting them in control of most of the world's industrial metal processing. Guggenheim's eldest son, Daniel, oversaw much of the expansion of the family's business interests following his death in 1905.

Hall, Joyce C. (1891-1982)

Founder of the Hallmark Greeting Card Company

Raised in poverty in rural Nebraska, Hall sold perfume door-to-door as a child to help support his family. At eighteen, he moved to Kansas City and founded a mail-order postcard business. He opened a card and stationery shop in 1914 with an older brother. When the shop burned down a year later, the Hall brothers began manufacturing their own cards. In 1928, the Hall Card Company built a new head office and employed the name Hallmark on the backs of its greeting card line. From its earliest years, the company took pains to protect its employees and could later boast that it survived the Great Depression without laying off any workers. In subsequent years, Joyce Hall added new products and innovations, including decorative gift wrap and vertical greeting card displays. In 1940, the company's celebrated advertising slogan, "When you care to send the very best," began airing on radio stations, and Hall licensed images, from Walt Disney characters to the paintings of British statesman Winston S. Churchill, to decorate his cards. The company formally adopted the Hallmark name in 1954 and made its first foray into television with the Hallmark Hall of Fame specials. Hall presided over the company until 1966 and spent his final years devoted to civic duties, including building Kansas City's downtown Crown Center, a mixed business and shopping complex surrounding the company's headquarters.

Hamilton, Alexander* (1755-1804)

First U.S. secretary of the treasury, whose advocacy of a strong capitalist economy established the principles upon which American business has operated ever since.

Harriman, Edward H. (1848-1909)

Railroad executive

The son of a clergyman and a New Jersey socialite, Harriman began work on Wall Street as a message boy at the age of fourteen. Moving up the ranks, he became a broker with a seat on the exchange in 1870. Afterward, he purchased interests in the railway industry. By 1881, he had acquired his first railroad line in upstate New York. During the 1890's he purchased the Union Pacific railroad and helped resurrect the ailing line. A captain of industry and with considerable financial resources, Harriman decided in 1899 to conduct a scientific expedition to Alaska aboard the steamship *George W. Elder.* Among the scientists and crew attending the expedition was the naturalist John Muir. Upon his return, Harriman continued to fund his team of researchers to analyze data collected during the expedition, and he added several more railroads to his empire.

Hearst, William Randolph (1863-1951)

Newspaper magnate

Born in San Francisco, Hearst inherited vast mining interests and attended Harvard University before acquiring control of the *San Francisco Herald Examiner* from his father in 1887. Hearst increased the paper's circulation by gearing editorial content to civic issues and local government corruption. He made substantial additions to his publishing empire after relocating to New York, where he acquired the *New York Journal* in 1895. At its height, Hearst's empire controlled thirty newspapers across the United States and pioneered a brand of news reporting dubbed "yellow journalism" that prized sensationalism above objectivity and fact. Hearst also published several magazines, including *Cosmopolitan* and *Harper's Bazaar,* and acquired the Universal News and International News Services news wires. The market collapse in 1929 hit Hearst's media empire hard, and in subsequent years he was forced to sell off many of his holdings. Throughout his career, Hearst used his media empire to support political ambitions. He served two terms as a New York congressman (1903-1907). He also made unsuccessful bids for mayor of New York City, governor of New York, and the U.S. Senate, and sought the Democratic presidential nomination in 1904.

Hefner, Hugh (1926-   )

Founder and publisher of Playboy magazine

Hefner was born in Chicago and served in the U.S. Army after graduation from college. Upon his discharge, he attended the Chicago Art Institute and then held editorial posts at several magazines, including *Esquire*. In 1953, he launched *Playboy* magazine from his kitchen table. Film star Marilyn Monroe appeared on the cover of the first issue, which was an instant success. Hefner built *Playboy* into a commercial empire by promoting what he called the "playboy lifestyle" in his magazine and in his personal life. Married twice, he has had an impressive list of mistresses—many of them his magazine's nude models. Once presiding over a media conglomerate that included the magazine, television and cable programs, a string of nightclubs, and the celebrated Playboy Mansion in Los Angeles, Hefner scaled back his operations in the early twenty-first century, giving up daily control to his daughter Christie.

Heinz, Henry John (1844-1919)

Founder of H. J. Heinz Company

The son of German immigrants, Heinz was born in Pittsburgh, Pennsylvania, and got an early start in business by peddling his mother's vegetable produce door-to-door. The H. J. Heinz Company he would later make famous began as a side project Heinz started as a teenager to manufacture and bottle horseradish. He joined his father's brick-making company and eventually purchased an interest in it before deciding to focus on the manufacturing of vegetable preserves in 1869. He expanded operations by creating the partnership Heinz, Noble and Company, but a shortfall in profits caused the venture to fail in 1875. Heinz raised capital from family members to launch a new company, which became the H. J. Heinz Company in 1888; he incorporated it in 1905. Heinz was known for his benevolence toward employees. His factory workers were provided health care, vocational training, and educational opportunities. He staunchly supported the Pure Food and Drug Act of 1906 and instituted several measures to ensure sanitary conditions in his factories.

Helmsley, Leona (1920-2007)

Real estate mogul

The daughter of Jewish immigrants from Poland, Helmsley began her rise in business as a vice president at a New York real estate firm. After becoming a millionaire in her own right, she married real estate investor Harry Helmsley in 1972. Together, the Helmsleys built a vast real estate empire built initially on the conversion of Manhattan apartments to condominiums and later on luxury hotels in New York and Florida. The Helmsleys also managed the Empire State Building. A demanding employer, Helmsley earned her nickname "Queen of Mean" following a dispute with a contractor who was renovating Helmsley's private home in Connecticut that later led to a public and bitter tax evasion case in 1988. Her husband was judged unfit to stand trial for health reasons, but Helmsley herself was convicted. She served eighteen months in prison. After her husband died in 1997, many of the Helmsley hotels were sold. Helmsley spent her final years in seclusion in a luxury penthouse atop the Park Lane Hotel.

Hershey, Milton (1857-1945)

Founder of the Hershey Chocolate Company

Born in Derry Church, Pennsylvania, Hershey dropped out of grade school and when he was apprenticed to a printer, but he soon began a four-year apprenticeship to a candy maker. His initial attempts to strike out on his own met with failure in New York and Chicago, so he returned to Pennsylvania in 1883 and opened a caramel shop, which showed initial promise. Seeing German chocolate manufacturing equipment at the 1893 World's Columbian Exhibition in Chicago altered his views about candy manufacturing. In 1900, he sold his caramel company and began working on a formula for his own brand of milk chocolate. In 1905, he built what would later become the largest chocolate manufacturing plant in the world and turned the Hershey brand of milk chocolate into a household name. He used much of his fortune for philanthropic efforts. He created the town of Hershey for the employees of his factory, complete with housing, public schools, recreational facilities, and tourist attractions that would make his namesake town a popular tourist destination long after his death. He also founded an orphanage and the M. S. Hershey Foundation in 1935 to provide educational opportunities for local residents.

Hill, James Jerome (1838-1916)

Canadian American railroad executive

Born in Ontario, Canada, Hill moved to St. Paul, Minnesota, as a teenager. There, he began a long career as a shipping agent specializing in the transport of railway fuel. By 1878, he had raised enough capital to purchase controlling interest in the St. Paul and Pacific Railroad, which he extended north to the Canadian border and west to Washington State. The Great Northern Railway, as it was renamed in 1890, was the first transcontinental line built without public money. Hill's company was one of the only railway lines to survive the economic Panic of 1893. In 1901, Hill set his sights on the Northern Pacific line, which pitted him against the Union Pacific railway owned by Edward H. Harriman and backed financially by William Rockefeller. The stock purchasing war that ensued threw Wall Street into turmoil until both sides both sides called a truce. Hill and Morgan subsequently formed the Northern Securities Company to consolidate their railways, but Theodore Roosevelt's accession as president following William McKinley's assassination in 1901 led to the company's dissolution for antitrust violations. Hill continued to prosper with the acquisition of the Colorado and Southern Railroad and the Spokane, Portland and Seattle Railway, and had amassed a fortune of more than $50 million at the time of his death in 1916.

Hoffa, Jimmy* (1913-1975?)

Labor union leader who was president of the powerful International Brotherhood of Teamsters from 1959 to 1971.

Hopkins, Mark (1813-1878)

Cofounder of the Central Pacific Railroad
Born in New York, Hopkins relocated with his family to St. Clair, Michigan, during his childhood. He left school in 1828 to begin work as a clerk. He attended law school briefly in 1837 and subsequently worked as a bookkeeper and business manager for James Rowland and Company before moving west. He arrived in San Francisco in 1849 and opened a dry goods store in Sacramento the following year. In 1861, he and Collis Huntington, Leland Stanford, and Charles Crocker collaborated to found the Central Pacific Railroad, the western portion of the first transcontinental railway. Its portion ran from California to Utah. The Big Four, as Hopkins and his associates were called, financed the project, which was planned in 1862 and completed seven years later. Hopkins died in 1878 aboard a Central Pacific rail car in Yuma, Arizona.

Howe, Elias (1819-1867)

Inventor of the lockstitch sewing machine
Born in Massachusetts, Howe was apprenticed to a textile factory at the age of sixteen and later worked for the master mechanic Ari Davis, through whom he developed an interest in solving the riddle of creating a sewing machine. Efforts had been made worldwide to create a practical machine for decades before Howe began his research. He was awarded the first U.S. patent for the lockstitch machine he built in 1846. That year, he traveled to Great Britain to promote his new invention but returned to find that other inventors—most notably, Isaac Singer—had incorporated his lockstitch design into improved models. After a long legal battle, Howe successfully defended his patent in 1854 and was paid royalties for two years.

Hughes, Howard* (1905-1976)

Aviator, businessman, and film producer who founded Hughes Aircraft and became one of America's wealthiest men.

Hunt, Haroldson Lafayette (1889-1976)

Oil tycoon
The son of an Illinois farmer, Hunt left home at the age of sixteen and crossed the United States, while working as a lumberjack, farmhand, cowboy, and holder of other odd jobs. With an inheritance of six thousand dollars in 1911, he purchased a cotton plantation in Arkansas. By 1920, he owned some 15,000 acres in Arkansas and Louisiana. When the cotton market foundered during World War I, Hunt began speculating in oil near El Dorado, Arkansas, working as a land broker selling farmland to oil prospectors for a handsome profit. He later began drilling his own wells and struck oil. By 1924, he was operating forty-four oil-rich wells and was acquiring other oil-producing land in Oklahoma and Texas. In 1930, he acquired land in eastern Texas that would become in its day the richest cache of oil in the United States. He founded the Hunt Oil Company in 1936 to develop the land and became the largest producer of oil for the Allies during World War II, as well one of the largest providers of natural gas. During the 1950's, Hunt began to diversify his holdings, adding a variety of products, including cosmetics and pecan plantations, to his oil empire, which made him one of the wealthiest Americans at the time of his death.

Iacocca, Lee* (1924-   )

Auto industry executive who spearheaded innovations in the financing, design, and marketing of automobiles.

Insull, Samuel (1859-1938)

Anglo-American investor who pioneered the concept of holding companies
Insull emigrated to the United States from England in 1881 and served as secretary to Thomas Edison for more than a decade before moving to New York and cofounding Edison General Electric, the forerunner to the corporate giant General Electric. In 1892, he moved to Chicago and acquired an electricity plant serving five thousand customers. There he devised a plan to provide electricity—at the time a costly luxury—at variable rates based on usage

times, thereby expanding the market. Over the next two decades, he built an empire of public utilities and invested heavily in the local power infrastructure, creating the Commonwealth Edison Company, a holding company that later included numerous additional public utilities as well as railway and streetcar lines. Insull's holding company was heavily leveraged, and when the Great Depression struck, his 600,000 investors lost everything. His spectacular failure would ultimately lead to the passage of the Public Utility Holding Company Act of 1935.

Jobs, Steve (1955-   )
Cofounder of Apple Computers

Born in San Francisco, Jobs grew up in nearby Mountain View, which became a regional powerhouse for electronics research and engineering. Following his graduation from high school, he attended Reed College in Portland, Oregon, for a year but returned to California, where he and his friend Steve Wozniak collaborated on the production of a personal computer. In 1976, they founded Apple Computers, which made both of them a fortune when the company went public in 1980. A turbulent relationship with the company's chief executive officer saw Jobs depart from active participation in Apple in 1985, but he would later return and oversee innovative marketing strategies and product lines, as well as a partnership with former rival Bill Gates's Microsoft that would make Apple one of the most distinctive and successful computer companies in the world.

Johnson, Robert L. (1946-   )
Founder of Black Entertainment Television (BET)

The ninth of ten children, Johnson was born in Hickory, Mississippi, but grew up in Freeport, Illinois. He studied at the University of Illinois and Princeton University, where he graduated with a degree in international affairs. He began his career in media with positions at the Corporation for Public Broadcasting, the National Urban League, and the National Cable Television Association before launching his own cable channel, Black Entertainment Television, devoted to African American audiences. He built a loyal following by airing hip-hop videos and college sports programming not available on other stations. In 1991, BET became the first African American-owned company to be listed on the New York Stock Exchange. Johnson took the company private in 1999 and extended his media services to include pay-per-view events and several print publications. In 2001, he sold BET to Viacom for $3 billion to become the first African American billionaire. Afterward, he founded the RLJ Companies.

Johnson, Robert Wood (1845-1910)
Founder of Johnson & Johnson

Born in Carbondale, Pennsylvania, Johnson became an apprentice to a New York apothecary at the age of sixteen. He later partnered with George Seabury to form Seabury & Johnson, which conducted research on the production of aseptic surgical supplies. Both were interested in the research of Joseph Lister, an English surgeon and pioneer in the use of carbolic acid to sterilize surgical instruments and clean wounds. The partnership lasted until 1880, after which Johnson joined with two of his brothers to form Johnson & Johnson. In 1887, he met pharmacist Fred Kilmer, who joined the company and established its first research laboratory. Through Kilmer's research, the company introduced many of its most innovative products, including sterile bandages and dressings, and first-aid kits.

Kaiser, Henry J.* (1882-1967)
Entrepreneur who founded numerous successful business ventures, including the large health maintenance organization that became known as Kaiser Permanente.

Knight, Phil (1938-   )
Cofounder of Nike, Inc.

Knight was born in Portland, Oregon, and studied journalism at the University of Oregon, where he distinguished himself as a middle-distance runner under celebrated track coach Bill Bowerman. After a year in the U.S. Army, he began graduate studies in business at Stanford University, where he graduated in 1962. Knight visited a Japanese athletic shoe manufacturing plant making Tiger-brand running shoes and secured a distribution deal for the United States. On his return, he partnered with Bowerman and began selling shoes out of his car at track meets throughout the Pacific Northwest. By 1969, he was earning enough to give up his job as an accountant and focus full time on his company Blue Ribbon Sports, which he later renamed Nike. Knight's emphasis on creative, sports celebrity-driven marketing built the fledgling company into a multibillion-dollar operation and the most successful athletic apparel manufacturer in the world, and made Knight one of the wealthiest men in the United States. Among the athletes with whom the Nike brand has been inextricably linked are basketball star Michael Jordan and golfer Tiger Woods.

Kroc, Ray (1902-1984)\

Founder of McDonald's Corporation

For several years, Ray Kroc sold multimixer machines to drug store soda fountains and restaurants before meeting Don and Mac MacDonald, brothers who had opened a small hamburger stand in San Bernardino, California, in 1940. Convinced that the restaurant's assembly-line methods and stripped-down menu would succeed as a franchise, Kroc obtained the rights to sell franchises and built the small family operation into the world's most successful fast food chain. He opened his first store in Des Plaines, Illinois, in 1955. Ten years later, Kroc opened his seven-hundredth franchise and made the company the first fast food chain to go public. In the process, he became a millionaire. Kroc demanded scrupulous attention to the methods and measures of food preparation at his restaurants, writing an official manual on the subject that later became the basis for Hamburger U, McDonald's training college in Elk Grove, Illinois. At the time of Kroc's death in 1984, McDonald's was the largest provider of meals in the United States.

Kroger, Bernard H. (1860-1938)

Founder of the Kroger supermarket chain

Kroger opened his first grocery store, the Great Western Tea Company, in 1883, and from these modest beginnings built a supermarket empire that during the 1920's included more than five thousand stores and survived into the twenty-first century as one of the leading grocery chains in the United States. In 1901, Kroger introduced the first in-store bakery. The following year, he incorporated the company and adopted the name Kroger Grocery and Baking Company. He also pioneered the concept of a combination store, selling meat and groceries under the same roof for the first time in 1904. In 1928, Kroger retired from the business and sold his shares for $28 million.

Lay, Kenneth (1942-2006)

Chief executive officer of Enron Corporation

Born into a Missouri family of modest means, Lay studied economics at the University of Missouri and received a doctorate in economics from the University of Houston in 1970. After serving as a naval officer at the Pentagon and an aide to a federal energy regulator, he joined the private sector, specializing in natural gas. He was named chief executive officer of Houston Natural Gas in 1984 and engineered its merger with Omaha-based Internorth, a partnership that was renamed Enron in 1985. Lay became one of the highest-paid chief executives during his tenure at Enron, but when the company filed for bankruptcy in 2001—after Lay had cashed out more than $300 million in stocks—the U.S. Senate Commerce Committee began an investigation. Some twenty thousand employees lost their jobs and pensions, while shareholders lost billions of dollars in investments. In 2004, Lay was indicted by a grand jury on eleven counts of securities and wire fraud and making false or misleading statements to investigators. He was convicted in May, 2006, but died of a heart attack before his sentencing hearing.

Lewis, John L.* (1880-1969)

Labor organizer who led the United Mine Workers and later became the first president of the Congress of Industrial Organizations.

Lowell, Francis Cabot (1775-1817)

Industrialist who founded the first American textile mill

Lowell was the son of the noted Massachusetts lawyer and delegate to the Continental Congress John Lowell. After graduating from Harvard College in 1793, the younger Lowell entered the merchant trade and traveled to London, where he viewed plans for a power loom in a Lancashire textiles mill in 1810. Three years later, he founded the Boston Manufacturing Company—the young nation's first textile mill, which turned raw cotton into finished cloth—and funded it by selling public shares in the mill. The practice soon became the enduring method of establishing corporations in the United States. Lowell also pioneered what became known as the Lowell System, by which mills established housing and other services for their employees, effectively creating a new town. Three years after Lowell's death, the Boston Manufacturing Company moved its mill in Waltham to a new location, still known as Lowell, Massachusetts.

McConnell, David (1858-1937)
Founder of Avon Products

The son of Irish immigrants, McConnell was born in Oswego, New York, where he attended high school and hoped to become a math teacher. However, he moved to Chicago in 1880 to sell books door-to-door for the Union Publishing Company. After settling in Atlanta, Georgia, where he was placed in charge of the company's southern division, McConnell got the idea of selling perfumes the same way he was selling books—from door to door. In 1886, he founded the California Perfume Company and began manufacturing perfume, which he sold alongside his books until the volume of his sales and the need for a full-time factory forced him to abandon books-selling. The following year, he employed twelve women he called "Avon Ladies" to sell his eighteen different fragrances. McConnell incorporated the company in 1916. It adopted the name Avon Products, Inc. in 1939, by which time it owned several subsidiary companies in the United States and Canada.

McCormick, Cyrus (1809-1884)
Inventor of the first horse-drawn reaper

McCormick was born in Virginia's Shenandoah Valley, where his father worked for years to develop a horse-drawn reaper before abandoning the project. Cyrus took up the project and built a working model by 1831. He received a patent three years later. By 1847, demand for the new machine had outstripped McCormick's ability to produce them. He relocated to Chicago and built a manufacturing plant. Sales remained brisk, largely because of the benefit of easy transport by railway lines. McCormick received numerous honors for his invention, which initiated an unprecedented shift of labor from rural to urban areas. After a prolonged illness, McCormick died in 1884, two years before labor strikes at his Chicago factories led to the Haymarket Riot in 1886.

Macy, Rowland H. (1822-1877)
Founder of R. H. Macy and Company

Born on New England's Nantucket Island, Macy joined the crew of a whaling ship at the age of fifteen. After brief stints in printing and gold speculating, he started a small chain of dry goods stores in 1843, beginning in Haverhill, Massachusetts. That chain ultimately failed, but he began again in 1858, when he built a new Macy's dry goods store in New York City. There, he pioneered retail methods that would define the way future department stores would operate. For example, he introduced such concepts as the one-price system, in which products were sold at the same prices to all customers. He relied heavily on newspaper advertising to distinguish the Macy brand from his competitors, and he also introduced the first in-store Santa Claus. Macy was also the first retailer to promote a woman to an executive-level position.

Mellon, Andrew (1855-1937)
Banker and industrialist

Mellon was born in Pittsburgh, Pennsylvania, the son of a successful banker whose firm he joined when he was nineteen. After taking over his father's business, he began investing heavily in industry. His business interests included oil, steel, shipbuilding, and the manufacture of aluminum, industrial abrasives, and coke. His facility as a financier made him one of the wealthiest people in the United States, alongside other business magnates such as John D. Rockefeller and Andrew Carnegie. In 1921, Mellon was named secretary of the treasury by President Warren G. Harding, and he served in that capacity under Presidents Calvin Coolidge and Herbert Hoover. As treasury secretary, he set out an agenda—later becoming known as the Mellon Plan—of low taxes on businesses, debt reduction, and a balanced budget. His influence began to wane during the Great Depression as his probusiness policies came under attack. In 1932, Mellon left the Treasury Department and was named ambassador to Great Britain. In his retirement years, he devoted himself to philanthropic efforts, including a vast collection of art he later donated to the National Gallery of Art, which was built on the Mall in Washington, D.C., with his $10 million donation.

Mergenthaler, Ottmar (1854-1899)
Inventor of linotype composing machine

Mergenthaler was born in Germany and apprenticed to a watchmaker. In 1872, he emigrated to Baltimore, Maryland, where he worked in a machine shop of which he eventually became a partner. At the age of thirty-two, he created a prototype of his first linotype composing machine, in which type could be set and cast in one step by entering letters on a keyboard similar to a typewriter. His invention revolutionized the printing and publishing industries and earned him the nickname Second Gutenberg, after the inventor of movable type. First used by the *New York Tribune* in 1886, linotype remained the predominant system of setting type until the 1970's, when electronic typesetting began to replace it.

Morgan, J. P.* (1837-1913)

Pioneer of investment banking who created one of the largest private fortunes in American history and oversaw the merger that created U.S. Steel.

Morris, Robert (1734-1806)

Anglo-American financier and politician

Born in Liverpool, England, Robert Morris emigrated with his family to Maryland at the age of thirteen. Two years after becoming an apprentice to a Philadelphia shipping and banking firm owned by Charles Willing at the age of sixteen, he became a partner in the company. Willing, Morris and Company formed in 1757 and prospered until 1779. Initially opposed to the Declaration of Independence, Morris eventually signed it and played a key role in funding and arming the Continental Army. His extensive shipping network also proved valuable for intelligence gathering during the Revolutionary War. Morris later served as a U.S. senator and was appointed first secretary of the treasury but ultimately deferred to Alexander Hamilton. During the 1790's, he lost much of his fortune in land speculating and served more than three years in prison for debt. He was released in 1801 after the passage of bankruptcy laws. A lavish mansion he had started building in Philadelphia was later abandoned and earned the name Morris's Folly, and he died a broken man. Despite his failings, he is widely credited with helping shape the country's financial systems.

Nader, Ralph (1934-   )

Consumer rights advocate

Born to Lebanese immigrants in Connecticut, Nader graduated from Princeton University in 1955 and Harvard Law School three years later. In 1964, he joined the staff of Assistant Secretary of Labor Daniel Patrick Moynihan. His interest in consumer safety issues began at Harvard, but he first targeted the au-

tomobile industry in the pages of *The Nation* in 1959. His best-known work, *Unsafe at Any Speed*, was published in 1965. It focused on General Motors, and its notoriously accident-prone Corvair model. Nader's research helped lead to passage of the National Traffic and Motor Vehicle Safety Act in 1966, which placed greater responsibility for automobile safety on manufacturers. During the 1970's, Nader organized fellow activists to investigate other consumer-related issues and publishing results in numerous books. He also founded the nongovernment organization Public Citizen in 1971 to coordinate his research efforts. During the 1980's, he became a leader in the antinuclear movement, advocating for the elimination of nuclear energy in favor of alternative sources such as wind, solar, and geothermal. He also made several bids for the presidency of the United States.

Nooyi, Indra K.* (1955-   )

Indian American chief executive officer of Pepsico who sealed her corporate position by heading Pepsi's multi-billion-dollar acquisition of Quaker Oats Company.

Norris, Frank (1870-1902)

Novelist who wrote on business themes

Born in Chicago, Norris moved to San Francisco as a teenager. He attended the University of California at Berkeley and Harvard University, and spent two years in Paris, France, studying painting. There, he was influenced by the naturalist writings of Émile Zola. He also worked as a journalist in South Africa and San Francisco and served as a correspondent for *McClure's* magazine in Cuba during the Spanish-American War. His most celebrated works of fiction are the first two volumes of his planned "Trilogy of Wheat." The first and most famous volume, *The Octopus* (1901), chronicles the impact of railroads on rural farmers. Norris died 1902, and the second volume of his trilogy, *The Pitt*, about price fixing in the wheat market, was published posthumously the following year. The final volume, *The Wolf*, was never written.

Page, Larry (1973-   )

Cofounder of Google

The son of two computer programmers, Page was born in Lansing, Michigan, and earned his bachelor's degree in engineering at the University of Michigan. While considering his doctoral thesis subject at Stanford University, he was encouraged to pursue a mathematical study of the World Wide Web. His research led him to evaluate how Internet search engines identified and ranked Web sites. In 1998, Page partnered with fellow student Sergey Brin to launch the search engine Google. Page served as chief executive officer of the new company until 2001 and afterward as head of products. In 2004, Page and Brin took the company public and quickly became among the richest people in the world. Under Page's leadership, Google has introduced numerous products, including Google Earth and Google Docs, that have increased the company's market share and generated billions in revenue. The company has become so synonymous with its revolutionary search engine that the word "Google" has entered the English language as a colloquial verb.

Paley, William S. (1901-1990)
Chief executive of the Columbia Broadcasting System (CBS)

Paley was born in Chicago to Jewish immigrants from the Ukraine who later relocated to Philadelphia. In 1927, his father, who ran a cigar shop, purchased the Columbia Phonographic Broadcasting System, a radio network of sixteen stations that he intended to use to advertise his cigars. Paley operated the radio network, and his father's cigar sales skyrocketed. Over the ensuing decade, the network expanded to 114 affiliates. During his half century at CBS, Paley oversaw the radio network's expansion from a struggling regional radio network to a global media empire by building one of the most respected news organizations of its day. Paley helped shape the policies that still govern the way network radio and television operate. In 1946, he hired Frank Stanton to head the programming department—a move that saw the introduction of numerous beloved series and news programming, including the long-running television news program *60 minutes.*

Pemberton, John Stith (1831-1888)
Druggist who invented Coca-Cola

Pemberton was born in Georgia and attended medical school in Macon, where he graduated at the age of nineteen. From an early age, he expressed an interest in what would later be called nontraditional medicine, including herbal remedies and steam baths. During the U.S. Civil War (1861-1865), he served as a lieutenant colonel in a Georgia cavalry regiment. Afterward, he worked as a druggist in Columbus and built a laboratory in which he manufactured health remedies, photographic chemicals, and cosmetics. After relocating to Atlanta in 1870, he began research on a coca nut-based beverage to alleviate headaches and calm the nerves. His first product, French Wine Coca, proved popular throughout the Southeast but contained wine, which could not be sold in Atlanta, which had introduced prohibition in 1863. Pemberton then created a second, nonalcoholic elixir, which he dubbed Coca Cola after its principal ingredients—coca leaves and kola nuts. In 1887, he decided to give up his work as a druggist and promote his new drink. He incorporated the Coca Cola Company in March, 1888, but died five months later.

Penn, William* (1644-1718)
Founder of Pennsylvania whose vast land holdings and administration of the laws and economy of the colony made him an important early business leader.

Penney, James Cash (1875-1971)
Founder of J. C. Penney Company

Penney was born in Missouri, the seventh of twelve children. His father was a farmer and Baptist minister. After graduating from high school in 1893, he took a job as a salesman at a local dry goods store. Five years later, he began work at a small retail chain of Golden Rule stores, one of whose franchises he later purchased in Wyoming. When the owners dissolved the partnership in 1907, he purchased the entire chain and began to expand. In 1913, he incorporated Golden Rule as the J. C. Penney Company. He relinquished control of the company in 1917 but remained chairman of its board until 1946. By 1929, the J. C. Penney Company was operating 1,400 stores nationwide. Poor health and financial ruin plagued Penney in subsequent years. He devoted his final years to philanthropy through the J. C. Penney foundation, which he established in 1954.

Perkins, Frances (1880-1965)
Social activist and first woman U.S. secretary of labor

Born into an affluent Massachusetts family, Perkins graduated from Mount Holyoke College in 1902 and completed a master's degree in sociology in 1910. She relocated to Chicago and became involved with Hull House, founded by Jane Addams and Ellen Gates Starr in 1889 to provide social and educational opportunities for working-class youths. A witness to the Triangle Shirtwaist Factory fire in New York City the following year, Perkins was affected by the tragedy and began to campaign for better working conditions. In 1919, she accepted an offer by New York governor Al Smith to join the state's Industrial Commission, of which she became chairperson in 1926. When Franklin D. Roosevelt became governor in 1929, he appointed her industrial commissioner for the city. Under her tenure, she lowered the workweek to forty-eight hours for women and lobbied for a minimum wage and unemployment insurance. When Roosevelt was elected president in 1932, he appointed Perkins his secretary of labor, making her the first woman to serve in a cabinet-level position. Perkins remained a cabinet member through the duration of Roosevelt's administration and played a vital role in shaping his New Deal policies.

Perot, H. Ross (1930-   )
Businessman
Born in Texarkana, Texas, Perot graduated from the U.S. Naval Academy in 1953 and served four years aboard naval vessels. In 1957, he became a salesman in the data processing department of International Business Machines (IBM). Five years later, he founded his own company, the data processing firm Electronic Data Services. He took the company public in 1968 and later sold it for more than $2 billion to General Motors, on whose board of directors he served until 1986. Two years later, he founded the information technology firm Perot Systems. A strong advocate of protectionist trade policies and a balanced budget, he made a bid for the U.S. presidency in the 1992 election as an independent candidate. Polls indicated that he enjoyed substantial support among voters, but he finished a distant third. He ran again in 1996 on the Reform Party ticket and based his platform on opposing the North American Free Trade Agreement but failed to generate substantial support. His falling out with the Reform Party led him essentially to abandon politics until 2004, when he formally endorsed George W. Bush for president. In 2008, Perot launched a blog devoted to the national economy and to resurrecting many of the concerns about fiscal responsibility that highlighted his political career.

Post, C. W. (1854-1914)
Breakfast cereal manufacturer and pioneer of packaged foods
Post was born in Illinois, where he attended Illinois Industrial College (later the University of Illinois) briefly before opening a short-lived general store in Independence, Kansas. He manufactured farm equipment following his return to Springfield and later became a property developer in Texas. Two nervous breakdowns led him to the sanitarium of John Harvey Kellogg in Battle Creek, Michigan, in 1890. There, he ate a vegetarian grain-rich diet of foods created by Kellogg. In the months following his discharge, Post ran a rival clinic called La Vita Inn and published the book *I Am Well!*, in which he promoted his ideas on mental and physical health. In 1895, he began manufacturing Postum, a grain-based breakfast drink designed as a substitute for coffee. His Grape-Nuts cereal appeared the following year, and his liberal use of advertising rapidly fueled sales. In 1902, after reaping a fortune from his Postum Ltd. Company, Post turned control over to his managers.

Randolph, A. Philip* (1889-1979)
African American civil rights and labor leader who organized the Brotherhood of Sleeping Car Porters, the first African American union to reach a labor agreement with white employers.

Rockefeller, John D.* (1839-1937)
Industrialist and founder of Standard Oil who became the first American billionaire and ranked as the world's richest man at the time of his death.

Roosevelt, Franklin D. (1882-1945)
Thirty-second president of the United States
Roosevelt began his political career in the New York State Senate in 1911. Two years later, President Woodrow Wilson appointed him assistant secretary of the Navy. Roosevelt resigned in 1920 and was nominated for vice president on the Democratic ticket, headed by James Cox, who was soundly defeated by Warren G. Harding. In 1928, Roosevelt was elected governor of New York, and he served until 1933, when he became president of the United States. His greatest legacy was his New Deal, through which he sought to put the unemployed back to work, bring economic recovery, and restore confidence to the banking industry during the Great De-

pression. Under his leadership, Congress granted broad regulatory powers to the Federal Trade Commission. Roosevelt also created the Civilian Conservation Corp and the Works Progress Administration, which found employment for the jobless. Other programs instituted under his leadership included the Federal Deposit Insurance Corporation (1933), the Tennessee Valley Authority (1933), and the Securities and Exchange Commission (1934) to regulate Wall Street. Roosevelt also signed into law the Social Security Act in 1935.

Roosevelt, Theodore (1858-1919)

Twenty-sixth president of the United States
Roosevelt rose from the vice presidency to the presidency in 1901 following the assassination of President William McKinley. A staunch Republican, he came to embrace the ideals of the Progressive Party, particularly its insistence on greater regulation of the influential American business classes. He expressed his intentions of busting the trusts in an address before Congress in 1901. The following year, Roosevelt directed the Justice Department to begin investigating the business practices of some of the country's largest companies. The first target was the Northern Securities Company, created by financier J. P. Morgan and railroad tycoon Andrew Hill. Found guilty of violating the Sherman Antitrust Act, that company was dismantled in 1904. Roosevelt would later bring forty-four lawsuits against major companies, earning him the nickname Trust-Buster. He also spearheaded legislation to provide better government oversight, including the Pure Food and Drugs Act and the Meat Inspection Act of 1906. Also that year, the Hepburn Act was passed, which standardized railway rates and accounting practices for interstate commerce. Other contributions included the successful establishment of a Department of Commerce and the Bureau of Corporations, both tasked with ensuring the regulation of big business.

Rosenwald, Julius (1862-1932)

Clothier and part owner of Sears, Roebuck and Company
Born into a family of Illinois clothiers, Rosenwald was joined a cousin to manufacture men's clothing in 1885. One of his clients was Richard Sears, who purchased clothing for sale in the Sears, Roebuck and Company catalog. Ten years later, Rosenwald

joined Sears as a partner and later as vice president. Under his tenure, the company's annual sales soared to $50 million. He helped take the company public in 1906 and became president two years later. Rosenwald invested more than $20 million of his personal wealth following World War I to save the company from bankruptcy. Sears eventually regained its financial footing, and Rosenwald would remain with the company until his death in 1932. In addition to his contributions to Sears, Rosenwald was a devoted philanthropist. He joined the board of Booker T. Washington's Tuskegee Institute in 1912 and contributed substantially to its endowment. He also built and funded more than five thousand Rosenwald schools for the rural southern poor. He was recognized in 1927 by the Harmon Foundation for his contributions to the education of African American youth.

Sinclair, Upton (1878-1968)

Pulitzer Prize-winning novelist and Socialist
Sinclair was born in Baltimore, Maryland. An early love of literature set put him on the course to a career in writing. His keen interest in social justice influenced his early years and converted him to socialism. He entered New York City College at the age of fourteen, and by seventeen was supporting himself and funding his studies by publishing stories in newspapers and magazines. In 1904, he was commissioned by the editor of a socialist journal to write a book about immigrant workers in Chicago's meatpacking plants. He spent seven weeks researching, then published *The Jungle* in 1905 in serialization in the journal *Appeal to Reason*. The following year, President Theodore Roosevelt ordered an investigation of the Chicago plants. Legislation to improve conditions in the plants followed. The Pure Food and Drugs Act and the Meat Inspection Act were passed in 1906. In later years, Sinclair became active in the Socialist Party. He ran unsuccessfully for a congressional seat from New Jersey and later for governor of California on the Democratic ticket. His 1942 novel *The Dragon's Teeth*, about the rise of Nazism, earned him a Pulitzer Prize for fiction.

Slater, Samuel (1768-1835)

Pioneer of the American Industrial Revolution
Born in England, Slater was apprenticed at the age of fourteen to the owner of one of Derbyshire's first cotton mills. After eight years of service, he emi-

grated to the United States in 1790 to earn his fortune in the young country's burgeoning textile sector. There, he used his knowledge of the building and operating of textile machines to succeed where others failed. In 1793, he built the first water-powered textile mill in Pawtucket, Rhode Island. He and his brother built the city of Slatersville, in present-day North Smithfield, on the banks of the Branch River. There, he constructed the Slater Mill, as well as housing for workers, a company store, and housing for the mill's managers. In 1807, the Slatersville Mill was the largest industrial building of its day, and Slater's mill village model influenced other industrialists throughout the state.

Sloan, Alfred P. (1875-1966)
Inventor of the modern corporation

Born in Connecticut, Sloan was educated at the Massachusetts Institute of Technology, where he received a degree in electrical engineering. Afterward, he acquired a ball-bearing manufacturing company, which he revived and ran successfully for nearly two decades before selling it to General Motors (GM). He joined the GM management team following the sale and served five years before approaching the company with a radical alteration to its operations. Sloan theorized that breaking GM into smaller divisions would improve its efficiency. He later became chairman of GM and then president of the company in 1923. Under his leadership, GM finally surpassed the Ford Motor Company in market share by 1931, largely through the adoption of Sloan's innovative business models—many of which have now become commonplace for corporations but at the time were revolutionary. He also established the philanthropic Alfred P. Sloan Foundation in 1934. At the time of Sloan's death, GM was the largest industrial corporation in the world.

Smith, Frederick W. (1944-   )
Founder of Federal Express (FedEx)

Smith was born to well-to-do parents in Memphis, Tennessee. His father founded the Dixie Greyhound Bus Line but died when Smith was four. As a student at Yale University, Smith conceived the idea of an overnight delivery service. He joined the Marine Corps after graduation and served in the Vietnam War. In Vietnam, he observed the challenges of logistical supply shipments and later applied what

he learned to his business model. In 1970, after his discharge, he acquired an aircraft maintenance company. A year later, he invested $4 million of his personal wealth and more than $90 million in venture capital to found Federal Express. After two years of steep losses, the company began to turn a profit. Over the next three decades, it became a leading global provider of express shipments. In 1997, Smith acquired the Caliber System and its trucking subsidiary RPS, adding ground service to the Fed Ex portfolio and making further gains on its principal competitor, the United Parcel Service. Smith amassed a vast personal fortune on the success of FedEx, which has consistently embraced new technology—particularly the rise of Internet commerce—to find new avenues for business expansion.

Stanford, Leland* (1824-1893)
Politician and industrialist who helped found the first transcontinental railroad.

Stewart, Martha* (1941-   )
Entrepreneur and founder of Martha Stewart Living Omnimedia, one of the world's most recognized brands in home decor, entertainment, and cuisine.

Strauss, Levi (1829-1902)
First manufacturer of denim jeans

Strauss emigrated to the United States from Bavaria in 1847, first settling in New York to work with his half brothers at a dry goods store. He later moved west to seek his fortune during the California gold rush. He established the Levi Strauss Company, a dry goods store on Battery Street in San Francisco. In 1873, he formed a partnership with Jacob Davis, a Nevada tailor, to secure a patent for the manufacture of heavy trousers with copper rivets to strengthen stress points at the pockets. The blue denim fabric for the jeans was purchased at the Amoskeag Mill in New Hampshire, and the Levi's blue jean brand was born. In his later years, Strauss developed several additional business interests in the insurance and banking sectors, while contributing generously to educational and civic organizations. His blue jeans brand has remained one of the most successful clothing products in the world and has become emblematic of American lifestyle.

Swift, Gustavus F. (1839-1903)
Founder of the Swift meatpacking empire in Chicago

Born in Massachusetts, Swift became a partner in the butcher company Hathaway and Swift in 1872. The company relocated to Chicago to take advantage of access to the city's rail yards for transporting cattle. In 1878, Swift left the partnership and joined his brother to form Swift Brothers and Company. That same year, he also tapped inventor Andrew Chase to create a refrigerated rail car to transport fresh meat across the country. By 1881, refrigerated cars were in wide use, revolutionizing the meat distribution industry. Swift also used conveyor belts to move meat among departments in his butcher plant, a method that auto manufacturer Henry Ford said inspired his adoption of an assembly line in his manufacturing plants. Swift also pioneered the use of all parts of the cattle processed in his plants for secondary products.

Trump, Donald* (1946-   )
Real estate developer who made his fortune in commercial and residential real estate in Manhattan during the 1980's.

Tupper, Earl S. (1907-1983)
Inventor of Tupperware

Born into a poor New Hampshire farming family, Tupper spent his early youth helping on the farm and selling its produce door-to-door. Meanwhile, he filled notebooks with his ideas for elaborate inventions—from a dagger-shaped comb to a fish-powered boat. He started a landscaping company under the name Tupper Tree Doctors, but it folded in 1936 during the Great Depression. He took a job at a DuPont-owned plastics factory but left after a year. He formed the Earl S. Tupper Company in 1938 and, working under subcontract to DuPont, secured several defense contracts during World War II to produce parts for gas masks as well as navy signal lamps. After the war, Tupper developed a process of purifying polyethylene slag, a by-product of oil refining, to create flexible plastic products. He also invented an air-tight lid patterned on those used for paint cans. In 1948, he adopted the home sales model used successfully by Stanley Home Products. With sales partner Brownie Wise, he introduced the world to the Tupperware "parties." Tupper sold the company to the Rexall Drug Com-

pany in 1958 for $16 million and later moved to Costa Rica.

Underwood, John T. (1857-1937)
Founder of Underwood Typewriter Company

Born in London, Underwood emigrated to the United States in 1873 and founded the Underwood Typewriter Company, which produced typewriter ribbons. When Remington, his company's principal buyer, decided to produce its own ribbons, Underwood decided to manufacture his own brand of typewriters. He purchased the patent for a new front-stroke model—an innovative model that allowed operators to see the letters as they were typed. Underwood later opened a factory in Hartford, Connecticut, and by 1915 was the largest of its kind in the world, produced five hundred machines each day.

Vanderbilt, Cornelius* (1794-1877)
Industrialist who made his fortune in freight transportation, shipping lines, and railroads.

Walker, Madam C. J.* (1867-1919)
Entrepreneur who became the first African American millionaire, with a cosmetics empire targeting African American women.

Walton, Sam (1918-1992)
Entrepreneur and founder of Wal-Mart and Sam's Club retail chains

Born in Oklahoma, Walton was raised in Missouri, where his family relocated in 1921. He distinguished himself academically and athletically in high school and studied economics at the University of Missouri. After graduation, he accepted a job at J. C. Penney Company as a management trainee but left in 1942 to serve in World War II. After his military discharge in 1945, he bought a Ben Franklin store in Arkansas and implemented policies that would drive his later success, particularly the principle of maintaining well-stocked inventory at low prices. In 1962, he opened the first Wal-Mart store in Arkansas. Over the next three decades, he built the Wal-Mart chain into the world's most successful retail operation. From 1985 until his death, he was the richest man in the United States. In 1998, *Time* magazine named him one of the twentieth century's most influential people for his innovations in the retail sector.

Ward, Montgomery (1843-1913)

Pioneer of mail-order business

Ward got his start in business as a young traveling salesman of general merchandise in the American Midwest. During the 1860's, he worked for the dry good firm Field, Palmer & Leiter, which later became Marshall Fields, and later for Wills, Greg & Company. During his travels across rural Illinois, he conceived a direct mail method for providing goods more efficiently and at a lower cost to shops in smaller towns. In 1872, he founded Montgomery Ward & Company with only two other employees and capital of only $1,600. His first mail-order catalog listed more than 150 products. In following years, the company prospered and inspired other businesses to follow the mail-order business model; the most notable of these was the Sears, Roebuck Company.

Washington, Booker T.* (1856-1915)

African American educator and founder of the Tuskegee Institute, which fostered economic independence among African Americans by teaching practical manual trades.

Washington, George* (1732-1799)

First president of the United States, architect of much of the nation's political and economic infrastructure, and a major landowner and businessman in his own right.

Watson, Thomas J., Sr. (1874-1956)

President of International Business Machines (IBM)

The son of the owner of a small New York lumber business, Watson worked brief stints as a teacher and bookkeeper before turning to sales. After repeatedly failing to establish himself as a salesman, he joined National Cash Register, at that time a leading manufacturing company specializing in the sale of mechanical cash registers for retail stores. As a salesman in the company's Buffalo, New York, branch, Watson soon proved the extent of his talents and joined the head office in 1899, at the age of twenty-five. However, his scheme to corner the market on used cash registers ultimately led to his indictment in an antitrust suit in 1913. The following year, he became general manager of the Computing Tabulating Recording Company (CTR), which he renamed International Business Machines. During World War II, he secured contracts for data process-ing support of the United States armed forces and the Soviet Union and began development of early analog computers. He stepped down as head of IBM in 1949 and handed control over to his son, Thomas Watson, Jr. By the time of his death in 1956, IBM was the largest American producer of tabulating machines, with an estimated 90 percent market share.

Welch, Jack (1935-   )

Chairman and chief executive officer of General Electric

Welch studied chemical engineering at the University of Massachusetts at Amherst before completing his master's and doctoral degrees in engineering at the University of Illinois in 1960. He joined General Electric that year as a junior engineer. By 1972, he was a vice president, and in 1981 he became General Electric's youngest chief executive officer. His long-running tenure was marked by drastic reductions in employees and management restructuring toward eliminating bureaucracy—earning Welch the nickname Neutron Jack. Meanwhile, General Electric increased its annual revenues from $26.8 billion to $130 billion. The company's market value also sky-rocketed from $14 billion prior to Welch's tenure to more than $400 billion in 2004, making it the most valuable company in the world. In 1999, *Fortune* magazine named him manager of the century. When Welch left General Electric in 2001, he received an unprecedented $8-million-per-year retirement package.

Wells, Henry (1805-1878)

Cofounder of American Express and Wells, Fargo & Company

Born in Vermont, Wells was apprenticed to a tanner and shoemaker in his youth. In 1836, he became a freight agent for goods transported on the Erie Canal. He held subsequent positions with other express freight companies before joining Livingston, Wells & Company, at which he worked with William George Fargo. A year later, the two men formed the Wells and Company's Western Express, running express freight as far west as Michigan. In 1850, Wells joined the American Express Company, formed by the consolidation of several regional freight agencies, and served as its president until 1868. Wells had also formed a partnership with Fargo, under the name Wells, Fargo and Company, to provide express banking services to California during the gold rush.

He retired from the company in 1867 and left American Express the following year. In retirement, he founded Wells College in Aurora, New York, one of the first women's colleges in the United States.

Westinghouse, George (1846-1914)
Pioneer in electrical engineering

Westinghouse made his early mark as an industrialist in the railroad industry. After his invention of the rotary steam engine at the age of nineteen, he created several technological innovations for the railroads, including a "car replacer," which helped guide derailed cars back onto railway tracks; a "reversible frog," used to move trains between railway lines; and a compressed air brake system for railway cars, which he patented in 1872. He subsequently founded the Westinghouse Air Brake Company to market his inventions. In the years following Thomas Edison's experiments with a direct-current (DC) delivery system for electricity, Westinghouse began conducting his own experiments with alternating-current (AC) systems in the belief that AC held the best hope for electrical power systems in the United States. His work sparked a feud with Edison that became known as the War of the Currents. In the end, AC prevailed and Westinghouse turned his attention to steam engines and later to the emerging automobile industry. He gave up control of his business interests in 1907 and withdrew from business in 1914 as his health began to decline.

Whitman, Margaret "Meg" (1956-   )
Chief executive officer of eBay

Born in Long Island, New York, Whitman studied economics at Princeton University before earning a master's degree from Harvard Business School in 1979. She held senior positions with Procter and Gamble, the Walt Disney Company, and other companies before joining eBay as president and chief executive officer in 1998. At that time, the fledgling Internet start-up had about thirty employees. Whitman's aggressive branding effort and scrupulous attention to the needs of the company's online users helped move the company from a quirky online collectibles site into a global marketplace and the world's leading Internet-only business, successfully outmaneuvering such online auction rivals as Yahoo! and Amazon.com. By the time she left the company, eBay had more than 9,000 employees and 100 million users worldwide, and she herself had amassed an estimated personal net worth of $1.4 billion. In 2008, she served as a member of Republican presidential candidate Mitt Romney's national finance team. After his withdrawal from the campaign, she advised Republican presidential nominee John McCain.

Winfrey, Oprah (1954-   )
Media mogul

Born in rural Mississippi to a single mother, Winfrey was raised by extended family members in Wisconsin and Tennessee. She excelled in high school and studied communications at Tennessee State University, after beginning work as a news reader at a local radio station while still in high school. During the 1970's, she became the first African American female news presenter for Nashville's WLAC-TV. After stints in Baltimore as a news presenter and talk show cohost, she relocated to Chicago to host the struggling talk show *AM Chicago* in 1984. After she led the program to first place in local ratings in only a few months, the program was renamed the *Oprah Winfrey Show.* In 1986, the show went national in syndication. In addition to hosting the world's most successful talk show, Winfrey also earned an Oscar nomination for her supporting role in the film *The Color Purple* in 1985 and produced and starred in 1998's *Beloved*, adapted from the Toni Morrison novel. Winfrey heads Harpo Productions, which produces film and television programs, and introduced *O, The Oprah Magazine* in 2002. She also cofounded the cable television channel Oxygen in 1998. Her show became syndicated worldwide, and she presides over a media organization that made her, for a time, one of the few African American billionaires. She is widely considered one of the most influential people in the world for her contributions to media and through philanthropic efforts through her Oprah's Angels Network and a leadership academy for young women in South Africa.

Wozniak, Steve (1950-   )
Computer engineer and cofounder of Apple, Inc.

Wozniak met his future partner Steve Jobs in 1970 while working at Hewlett Packard. He and Jobs conceived of a personal computer company that six years later would become Apple Computers. Wozniak himself designed the company's first two computer models—the Apple I and Apple II systems—and assembled the first prototypes for local hobbyists. The company went public in 1980, making Wozniak a millionaire. He continued with Apple as head of research and development, writing most of the early software for the company. In 1981, a plane crash left him with minor but lingering injuries, and he left the company to return to the University of California to complete the degree he had abandoned in 1975. He formally ended his full-time employment at Apple in 1987 but remained an employee and shareholder. He was inducted into the National Inventors Hall of Fame in 2000 for his contributions to the creation of the personal computer, which he and Jobs are credited with inventing. After leaving Apple, he founded Wheels of Zeus, which produced global positioning system (GPS) technology, and he cofounded Acquicor Technology, a holding company for technology-related firms. He has also taught primary school and remains active in numerous educational and philanthropic community programs.

Wrigley, William, Jr. (1861-1932)

Industrialist and chewing gum magnate

Born in Philadelphia, Wrigley left school at the age of thirteen and began selling soap door-to-door for his father's company. In 1891, he started his own soap company in Chicago, where he settled with his wife and began offering a free chewing gum with every purchase. The marketing campaign proved so successful that he abandoned soap and began manufacturing his own brand of chewing gum under the name Wrigley's Spearmint Gum, later adding the Juicy Fruit brand. A master of marketing, Wrigley was the first to put gum displays near cash registers in restaurants. In addition to his business interests, Wrigley invested in the Chicago Cubs baseball franchise, whose Wrigley Field was named in his honor in 1926. He also invested heavily in the development of Catalina Island, off the coast of California, which he purchased in 1919.

Yang, Jerry (1968-   )

Cofounder of Yahoo!

At the age of ten Yang emigrated with his family from Taiwan to San Jose, California. He studied electrical engineering at nearby Stanford University, where he met David Filo and cofounded an online directory called "Jerry's Guide to the World Wide Web" in 1994. The following year, he and Filo incorporated Yahoo! and began building their company as a portal to other Web sites. In succeeding years, the company branched out to offer search engine, advertising, news, and e-mail services, making Yahoo! one of the most visited Web sites on the Internet. After several years of consistent growth and the establishment of Yahoo! as a reliable Internet brand, Yang began talks with Microsoft, Inc. in 2008 for a potential buyout, but negotiations fell through and Yang turned instead to an advertising partnership with rival Google, Inc. In November, 2008, Yang announced his intention to step down as Yahoo!'s chief executive officer when a replacement could be found. Yang, who drew only one dollar in annual salary from the company, compiled an estimated net worth of more than $2 billion.

Philip Bader

Notable American Companies and Corporations

Names marked with asterisks are subjects of essays in the main text.

Abbott Laboratories

Pharmaceuticals and health care company, founded in 1888

Wallace Abbott, a physician and drugstore owner, discovered a novel plant-alkaloid-based delivery system for medicine that improved its effectiveness. On the basis of his discovery, he founded the Abbott Alkaloidal Company in 1888. As the popularity of his methods increased, Abbott incorporated the company and expanded his sales force. In 1904, the company was renamed Abbott Laboratories and began researching synthetic medicines. Abbott's first synthetic drug, an antiseptic called Chlorazene, was used widely during World War I. Abbott's research-based approach and aggressive acquisitions led to numerous breakthroughs in subsequent decades. For example, the company introduced the sedative Nembutal (pentobarbital) in 1930 and the anesthetic Pentothal (thiopental sodium) in 1936. After the discovery of penicillin in 1924, Abbott became first manufacturer of the drug in the United States. In 1946, Abbott became the first company to devote a research lab to radiopharmaceuticals. This work made it a world leader in the diagnosis of thyroid disorders. In 2008, the company operated in 130 countries and its annual revenues exceeded $25 billion.

Aflac

Supplementary health and life insurance company, founded in 1955

After brothers John, Paul, and Bill Amos founded Aflac as American Family Life Assurance of Columbus in 1955, they sold insurance policies door-to-door for three years. In 1958, they introduced a supplemental cancer insurance policy that covered expenses not included in traditional comprehensive insurance policies. Aflac also began marketing products to groups and companies. In 1973, the company incorporated, and it expanded operations to Japan the following year. During the 1980's, Aflac diversified its holdings by purchasing a variety of media organizations that bolstered its annual revenues. A growing market share in Japan, collaborative policies with other American service providers, and supplemental coverage for Alzheimer's disease and other ailments helped Aflac reach $4 billion in assets by 1992. During the late 1990's, Aflac increased its brand recognition with the introduction of the Aflac duck in a humorous television advertising campaign that employed celebrities such as Yogi Berra and Chevy Chase. *Fortune* magazine has frequently listed Aflac among America's Most Admired Companies and its One Hundred Best Companies to Work for in America.

AIG

Multinational insurance company, founded in 1919

Now based in New York City, AIG, or the American International Group, was founded in Shanghai, China, in 1919 by Cornelius Vander Starr. It was the first foreign insurance company to sell its services to the Chinese. Its success in Asia led to its expansion into European and Latin American markets. Starr's successor, Hank Greenberg, took the company public in the United States in 1969. By the early twenty-first century, AIG employed more than 100,000 people in 130 different countries and had more than $110 billion in annual revenues. The company is a major underwriter of commercial and industrial insurance in the United States. It also offers a variety of financial services, mutual funds, and other investment products. AIG owns the International Lease Financing Organization, the largest aircraft leasing company in the world, and sponsors the Manchester United soccer team in England's Premier League. At the beginning of 2008, AIG ranked as the eighteenth-largest publicly held company in the world. Toward the end of that year, however, the company suffered a massive liquidity crisis at the same time other major financial institutions were threatened with collapse and had to rely on a huge government bailout to stay afloat.

Alcoa

Aluminum producer, founded in 1888

In 1888, Charles Martin Hall founded the Pittsburgh Reduction Company after he helped discover a process for smelting aluminum—a lightweight metal found in abundance in the United

States but one that had previously been difficult to extract profitably. After opening his first aluminum-processing plant in 1891, Hall rapidly expanded his operations. In 1910, he renamed his company the Aluminum Company of America, which was later shortened to Alcoa. The company researched new production methods of and applications for aluminum. Orville and Wilbur Wright used aluminum parts manufactured by Hall in the plane they flew at Kitty Hawk, North Carolina, in 1903, and aluminum became an integral part of the burgeoning aircraft and automobile industry. The outbreak of World War II led to new innovations by Alcoa as the United States armed itself, and the company had a virtual lock on American aluminum production until the 1950's. Alcoa extended its operations to Australia, eastern Europe, and Asia in subsequent decades. In the early twenty-first century, it ranked as the world's third-largest producer of aluminum, with more than 100,000 employees in forty-four countries and large market shares in the aerospace, defense, construction, transportation, and packaging industries.

Allergan

International eye care and pharmaceuticals company, founded in 1948

Allergan began as a small ophthalmological supplies store founded by Garvin Herbert, Sr., above his Los Angeles drugstore in 1948. Herbert released his first product, an antihistamine eye drop, two years later. During the 1960's, Allergan invested in the emerging contact lens market by marketing a hydrating solution for hard lenses, and it continued to earn a large market share with the advent of soft lenses during the 1980's. As the company's sales slumped during the 1990's, Allergan shifted its focus to specialty pharmaceutical products. In 1991, it purchased Oculinum—at that time, the only producer of the botulinum A toxin sold under the name Botox. An antiwrinkle agent and a treatment for ailments such as migraines and muscular and neurological disorders, Botox became the company's best-selling product. Meanwhile, Allergan also entered the breast-implant market under the Natrelle brand name and developed the gastrointestinal surgical procedure Lap Band to treat obesity.

Allstate Corporation

Largest publicly held personal insurer, founded in 1931

Allstate originated as a direct-mail automobile insurer. Its founder, Carl Odell, pitched the idea of direct-mail insurance sales to the president and chief executive officer of Sears, Roebuck, and Company in 1930. The following year, the Sears catalog began selling insurance policies under the name Allstate Insurance Company. Four years later, Allstate opened its first sales office in a Sears store in Chicago. The post-World War II economic boom brought rapid growth to the company. In 1952, the company introduced its first personal injury policy. Fire, personal theft, and homeowner's insurance services were added by 1957. Diversification and expansion of insurance and financial services marked the company's operations during the 1960's and 1970's. After Hurricane Andrew ravaged South Florida and parts of the Gulf Coast in 1992, Allstate made costly payouts in claims settlements that led in 1995 to its separating from Sears, which had owned an 80 percent stake in the company. Nevertheless, it finished the decade strong, holding nearly 12 percent of home and automobile insurance policies in the United States. In 2008, it ranked as the second-largest property and casualty insurer—as measured by premiums—in the United States.

Altria Group

Tobacco and food services company, founded in 1847

Altria traces its roots to a small tobacco shop opened in London, England, by a man named Philip Morris in 1847. Philip Morris & Company was incorporated in New York in 1902. It quickly became the largest producer and manufacturer of tobacco products in the United States. In 1919, a group of American investors purchased the company and reincorporated it in Virginia. The reorganized company introduced the Marlboro brand of cigarettes in 1924. During the 1950's, the company created an international division and purchased holdings in Australia and across Europe. Initially focused on tobacco manufacturing, it diversified its holdings between 1988 and 2003, when it officially changed its name to Altria. It purchased Kraft Foods, Nabisco, and the Miller Brewing Company. Altria produces dozens of brands of cigarettes in the United States, Europe, and Asia, and its Marlboro brand—popularized by the successful Marlboro man marketing campaign started during the 1950's—has been the world's best-selling cigarette brand since 1972.

Amazon.com

Online bookstore and retailer, founded in 1994

Founded by Jeff Bezos in 1994, Amazon became one of the earliest electronic commerce sites when it went online the following year to sell books on the Internet under the name Cadabra.com. That name was soon abandoned for Amazon.com, and the company enjoyed early success during the midst of the dot-com boom that ended in 2001. Its slow but steady growth helped the company survive while other technology-based, fast-growth companies failed. At the end of 2002, Amazon had its first profitable quarter. Afterward, it continued to improve its net profits by introducing additional products and creating international sites. Bezos added music CDs, DVDs, clothing, consumer electronics, cookware, and consumer electronics, among other goods, and introduced an innovative shipping strategy that allowed consumers to get free shipping on all products in exchange for monthly membership fees. Amazon has also created partnerships with companies such as Borders and Target to operate their retail Web sites. In 1999, *Time* magazine featured Bezos on its cover in recognition of his success in popularizing online commerce. Headquartered in Seattle, Washington, Amazon joined Standard & Poor's 500 index in 2005 and operates its online megastores in the United States, the United Kingdom, Germany, France, and China.

America Online (AOL)

Global Internet and media services company, founded in 1991

America Online began as a small game downloading company during the early 1980's that catered to Atari 2600 computer console owners. Among the company's early online innovations were a graphical chat room (1986), an interactive fiction series (1988), and the first large-scale multiplayer role-playing game (1991). The company adopted the name America Online in 1991 and built a "walled garden" on the Internet, which offered subscribers an organized online community and e-mail services through its proprietary software. In contrast to other providers such as Prodigy and Compuserve, AOL targeted consumers unfamiliar

with computers and built a subscriber base of more than 30 million with regional offices around the world. By the late 1990's, AOL began allowing open access to the Internet, but the number of subscribers fell as more Internet provider options became available. The company merged with Time Warner in 2001, but AOL subsequently dropped to just more than 10 million subscribers and the value of its stock dropped more than $200 billion. In 2005, Google purchased a 5 percent share in AOL after speculation of further buyouts and joint ventures, and AOL has since shifted its focus toward content diversity and advertising-driven operations.

American Express

Global financial services company, founded in 1850

American Express was created by the merger of three express mail services owned by Henry Wells, William George Fargo, and John Butterfield. The company originally focused on express mail and package delivery. In 1891, American Express began selling money orders for international travelers. This service would later help thousands of American travelers who were trapped in Europe at the outset of World War I. In 1958, American Express began issuing its first charge cards. The company later evolved a tier system with cards that targeted specific market segments. It issued its first Gold Card in 1966 and its first Platinum Card in 1984. As these cards were charge cards, they required their holders to pay their balances in full each month. The Optima card, introduced in 1987, became the first American Express credit card, allowing clients the option of paying all or part of their balances. American Express has also marketed a series of cards designed specifically for small-business owners and corporations. During the 1980's, the company added a full selection of financial services to its portfolio, including investment products and asset management. By the early twenty-first century, the company was one of the largest credit, financial, and travel service providers in the world.

American Sugar Refining Company

Sugar manufacturer, founded in 1891

William and Frederick Havemeyer of England opened their first sugar refinery in New York in 1807. Less than a decade later, their refinery was producing nearly 9 million tons of sugar annually.

In 1828, the Havemeyers' sons took over production and purchased several local refineries to consolidate control of the sugar market. The company adopted the name American Sugar Refining Company in 1891 and, at the time, produced an estimated 1,200 tons of refined sugar each day. Investment in new technology and the inability of smaller companies to compete allowed the company to secure nearly 100 percent of the sugar market across the United States. The company later survived numerous attempts by the U.S. Supreme Court and the U.S. Congress to curb its control of the sugar market. In 1900, the company adopted the name Domino Sugar. Federal litigation attempted to break up the company in 1910, but a ruling in 1921 stated that the company's control of the sugar market did not constitute a monopoly. Domino thrived during the Great Depression and the economic boom of the post-World War II years, but the creation and popularity of artificial sweeteners and health concerns about excess consumption of refined sugar caused its profits to decline by the 1980's. At that time, Tate & Lyle purchased the company. Tate & Lyle has continued to operate the company as a subsidiary focused on research and development of new applications of artificial sweeteners in products as diverse as cake frosting, sports drinks, and salad oil.

American Telephone and Telegraph Corporation (AT&T)

Telecommunications company, founded in 1983
American Telephone and Telegraph Corporation (AT&T) is the largest provider of telecommunications services, including local and long-distance calling, data services, and wireless technology, in the United States. It was founded in 1983 as the Southwestern Bell Corporation—one of the original Baby Bells—following an antitrust suit against AT&T Corporation, but its roots lay in the birth of telecommunications services in the United States during the late nineteenth century. In 1995, Southwestern changed its name to SBC Communications and acquired several regional carriers, including Pacific Telesis and Ameritech. SBC entered the Dow Jones Industrial Index in 1999. After its purchase of AT&T Corporation in 2005, the company focused primarily on extending its wireless and broadband Internet market share.

American Tobacco Company

Tobacco manufacturer, founded in 1890
Founded in 1890, the American Tobacco Company became one of the original twelve companies on the Dow Jones Industrial Average in 1896 and controlled most of the tobacco production in the United States until antitrust litigation split the company into several smaller ones in 1911. The dissolution created R. J. Reynolds and Lorillard, and allowed the American Tobacco Company to continue its operations on a smaller scale. During the 1970's, American Tobacco began to acquire several nontobacco products. In 1986, the company changed its name to American Brands, with American Tobacco continuing as a subsidiary until the 1990's, after which the company sold its tobacco holdings to competitors.

Anheuser-Busch Companies

Brewing company, founded in 1852
Originally founded as a small brewery in St. Louis, Missouri, Anheuser-Busch became the largest brewery and distributor in the United States and one of the largest in the world based on revenues. Eberhard Anheuser purchased the brewery in 1860. His son-in-law, Adolphus Busch, became a partner in 1869 and took control of the company after Anheuser's death in 1880. Among the company's numerous industry innovations were pasteurization and bottling. The company introduced its signature beer, Budweiser, in 1876, and by 1951, it was the largest beer maker in the United States. An international subsidiary began operations in 1981. Anheuser-Busch also produces the Busch, Michelob, and Natural Light brands of beer, as well as colas and malt liquor beverages. Anheuser-Busch announced in 2008 a merger with European beverage giant Inbev. Annual revenues for Anheuser-Busch reached nearly $17 billion. Revenues after the Inbev merge are expected to surpass $36 billion, making the company the largest brewer and distributor in the world.

Apple*

Computer and consumer electronics company, founded in 1976, which markets the Apple line of personal computers, the popular iPod digital media player, and other electronic devices.

Archer Daniels Midland (ADM)

Agribusiness and food manufacturer, founded in 1902

An agricultural conglomerate specializing in processed grains and seed oils, Archer Daniels Midland operates nearly three hundred plants worldwide. Founded in 1902 by George Archer and John Daniels as a linseed processor, the company acquired the rival Midland Linseed Oil Company in 1923, also the year it was incorporated. ADM showed steady growth in the decades that followed as it diversified operations into areas such as processed ingredients for foods, nutritional products, animal feedstocks, beverage production, and biofuels such as ethanol. The company drew criticism in 2001 for its sale of wheat to Cuba, following passage of a U.S. law permitting the sale of food and medicine to the otherwise trade-embargoed nation. ADM has also been criticized for benefiting from substantial government subsidies on agricultural products. Capitalizing on a growing interest in alternative fuels, ADM announced in 2008 a partnership with Bayer CropScience and Daimler AG to explore the potential of the jatropha plant as a new biofuel source. ADM employs more than 27,000 people worldwide and had about $44 billion in revenues in 2007.

Armour and Company

Slaughterhouse and meatpacking company, founded in 1867

Philip and Herman Armour founded their namesake company in 1867 in Chicago. By 1880, they had transformed Chicago into the hub of all slaughtering and meatpacking operations in the United States. The Armour brothers built an empire on meat and animal-related products, with business interests in the production of everything from glue to hair brushes to pharmaceuticals. The company took a staunchly antiunion stance. Working conditions were grim, wages were low, and accidents were frequent. Novelist and labor activist Upton Sinclair drew on his experiences in Chicago to explore labor conditions among immigrant populations, particularly in the meatpacking industry. During the 1920's, the Armour family sold its stake in the company amid slumping revenues. The company closed its Chicago slaughterhouse in 1959, but prospects improved on the strength of its Dial brand of soap, introduced in 1948. Made in part from animal by-products, the soap became a best seller during the 1950's. Over the next several decades, the company changed ownership as divisions were spun off or made public. It adopted the name Dial Corporation in 1991 and was purchased by Germany-based Henkel KGaA in 2004. Its popular Armour brand of potted and processed meats was sold to Pinnacle Foods Group in 2006.

Avon Products

Direct-marketing cosmetics company, founded in 1886

Avon grew out of a marketing ploy by David McConnell, a door-to-door book salesperson, who found that his sales increased when he included a free bottle of perfume with each order. Soon, the perfume became more popular than the books, and the California Perfume Company was born in 1886. By 1928, the company—incorporated in New York with offices in Quebec—achieved $2 million in sales. The company adopted the Avon Products name in 1939. During the 1950's, the company introduced its successful "Avon calling" advertising campaign, as its direct-marketing campaign—fueled by cadres of Avon saleswomen—brought annual revenues above $55 million. Avon continued to prosper, with $3 billion in sales in 1979 and about 1 million direct-sales agents. The company's largest emerging markets are in China and Russia, where products are largely sold in retail stores rather than door-to-door or via catalogs. In 2005, Avon opened a $100 million research and development complex in New York. Its products largely target female consumers, but a line of products for men promoted through its M catalog and product line have begun earning larger market shares. Annual revenues exceeded $9 billion in 2007.

Bank of America

Commercial bank, founded in 1998

Bank of America is the largest U.S. commercial bank in terms of deposits and market capitalization. The company has its roots in the Bank of Italy founded by Amadeo Giannini in 1904. Giannini purchased the Bank of America, Los Angeles, and adopted part of the name in 1929. He attempted to make it a nationwide bank under his holding company, Transamerica Corporation, but the insurance and banking aspect were separated in the 1950's. Banking regulations prevented the bank's expansion beyond California until 1980. BankAmerica Corporation was created in the 1960's to own Bank of America and its subsidiaries. In the 1980's and 1990's, the company made a number of acquisitions, some more successful than others. In 1998, Bank of America was acquired by North Carolina's NationsBank, although the acquisition was structured as a merger. At the time, it was the largest banking merger in history. During the financial crisis that struck the mortgage and financial markets in 2008, Bank of America acquired Merrill Lynch, making it the world's largest financial services company.

Barnes & Noble

Specialty book retailer, founded in 1917

The partnership of William Barnes and Clifford Noble began with the opening of their first bookstore in New York City in 1917, but its roots extend back to William's father, Charles Barnes, who founded a book printing company in 1873. Leonardo Riggio purchased the company in 1971 and began a decades-long expansion, first into the discount book trade—through the acquisition of the B. Dalton bookstore chain—and later into larger retail locations and online book sales. The company publishes inexpensive reprints, special classics collections, and formerly out-of-print titles. The company's other book-related subsidiaries include Scribner's bookstores, Sterling Publishing's how-to imprint, and SparkNotes, an educational publisher. Barnes & Noble is the largest retail book company in the United States, with more than $5 billion in annual revenues.

Bell Labs*

Research laboratory for Alcatel-Lucent Company—originally created in 1925 as part of the Bell Telephone Company—which has produced a wide range of technological discoveries, from radio astronomy and the C programming language to the transistor and the laser.

Benihana

Chain of Japanese food restaurants, founded in 1964

An alternate in wrestling for the 1960 Olympic Games, Rocky Aoki would make a larger mark in the restaurant industry with the opening of his first Benihana restaurant in 1964 in New York City. The

restaurant's *teppanyaki*-style service featured an iron griddle around which guests sat to eat. Mixing Japanese cuisine with theatrical presentation, Aoki's restaurant eventually caught on, becoming a pop culture phenomenon during the late 1960's and 1970's. The company went public in 1982, though Aoki continued to operate some stores independently. In 1995, all Benihana restaurants were merged into Benihana, Inc. Aoki died in 2008, but the company continues to operate in twenty-five states, the District of Columbia, and throughout Central and South America.

Berkshire Hathaway

Holding and insurance company, founded in 1955

Berkshire Hathaway was founded in 1955 by a merger between the Berkshire Fine Spinning Associates (originally founded in 1839) and the Hathaway Manufacturing Company, which dated to 1888. Until 1960, the company operated fifteen manufacturing plants. In the wake of several plant closures, Warren Buffett purchased a controlling interest in the company in 1962 and expanded the focus from manufacturing to insurance by acquiring the National Indemnity Company and the Government Employees Insurance Company (GEICO). The last of the company's textile operations ended in 1985 as Buffett began using insurance operations to generate capital for investments. The company has earned a reputation for stability under Buffett's management. Its Class A stocks have never been split and remain the highest-priced stocks on the New York Stock Exchange.

Best Buy

Consumer electronics company, founded in 1983

Richard Shultze entered into a partnership in 1966 to sell automobile and home stereo equipment at a store called Sound of Music in St. Paul, Minnesota. He bought out his partners and introduced additional home appliances in 1982. A year later, he changed the company's name to Best Buy. By 1987, the company had gone public and earned a listing on the New York Stock Exchange. Its earnings broke the $1 billion mark by 1992. The company acquired several subsidiaries, including the Canada-based Future Shop chain in 2001 and the twenty-four-hour computer support service Geek Squad in 2002. Best Buy opened its first store in China in 2007 and had expanded to Mexico in 2008. A *Fortune* 100 company and the leading consumer electronics retailer in the United States, Best Buy has annual revenues of more than $30 billion.

Blockbuster

Video disc and video game rental company, founded in 1985

Founded by David Cook in 1985, Blockbuster capitalized on the boom in film rentals during the 1980's at a time when most rental companies were small-scale businesses. Cook opened his first store in Dallas, Texas, using computer software to track inventory. By 1987, Cook had left the company, and a new team of investors spearheaded a move to expand nationally. In 1994, Blockbuster reached a merger agreement with entertainment giant Viacom, and three years later brokered a revenue-sharing agreement with major film studios. However, by the late 1990's, the company faced new forms of competition from the success of video on demand and the rise of Internet competitors such as Netflix. Blockbuster introduced game rentals in 2002 and an online subscription and mail-order service similar to Netflix in 2004. In the wake of flagging profits, the company purchased Movielink, a video-on-demand service, in 2007. The company operates more than 7,800 outlets worldwide, with annual revenues of more than $5 billion.

Boeing Company

Aerospace, commercial aircraft, and defense contractor, founded in 1916

The Boeing Company was founded in 1916 as Pacific Aero Products Company. It introduced its first aircraft, the B&W seaplane, that same year. Boeing's innovative 247 model was built in 1933. The revolutionary design was the first to introduce several technologies, including cantilevered wings and retractable landing gear that would later become standard on passenger aircraft. Five years later, Boeing released the 307 Stratoliner, the first passenger plane to feature a pressurized cabin. Boeing continued to deliver innovative aircraft, first to the military during and after World War II, and later to the commercial sector. In 1958, Boeing introduced the 707 model, the United States' first commercial jet airliner. The 747 model debuted in 1970 and transformed long-distance passenger air travel by improving range and capacity. Boeing contributed

heavily to the Apollo space program during the 1960's and remains a leading defense contractor. The company's annual revenues top $66 billion; it ranks first among global manufacturers in revenue as well as orders and deliveries.

Bristol-Myers Squibb

Pharmaceuticals company, founded in 1989

Bristol-Myers was founded in 1887 when William Bristol and John Myers purchased the ailing Clinton Pharmaceutical Company. Bristol-Myers had early success with a mineral salt concoction called Sal Hepatica and Ipana toothpaste, the first toothpaste to include a disinfectant. During World War II, the company mass-produced penicillin for the U.S. Armed Forces. Over the next several decades, the company acquired several subsidiaries until, in 1989, Bristol-Myers merged with the Squibb Company, founded in 1858, which had first specialized in penicillin production and in 1975 introduced a breakthrough drug, Capoten (captopril), for the treatment of high blood pressure. The merger made Bristol-Myers Squibb one of the leading global pharmaceutical research and development firms. The company has revenues of nearly $20 billion annually and employs more than 40,000 worldwide.

Cable News Network*

International cable television news network, founded in 1980, which helped revolutionize television news broadcasting.

Campbell Soup Company

Soup and processed food manufacturer, founded in 1869

The Campbell Soup Company was founded in 1869 by fruit merchant Joseph Campbell and ice-box manufacturer Abraham Anderson as the Anderson Campbell Preserve Company. The partnership dissolved in 1877, and Campbell focused the company's attention on the manufacture of condiments and a beefsteak tomato soup, which became one of the company's most successful products. The company introduced condensed soup in 1897. With the help of illustrator Grace Wiederseim Drayton, the company maintained a successful marketing campaign that featured the Campbell kids for nearly twenty years. The company's soups became an integral part of American culture, even becoming the subject of a pop art painting by Andy Warhol. Camp-bell Soup's main products and its Pepperidge Farms and V8 brands are sold in 120 countries, and the company maintains annual revenues of more than $7 billion.

Chevron Corporation
Global energy company, founded in 1879
Chevron has its roots in the Pacific Coast Oil Com-pany, which discovered oil in the Pico Valley in Los Angeles in 1879. The company was first known as Standard Oil of California, formed after the breakup of John D. Rockefeller's Standard Oil. In 1933, the company was granted a concession to ex-plore for oil in Saudi Arabia, where it discovered the world's largest oil field in Gawahar. The company maintained operations in Saudi Arabia until 1988, when the Saudi government acquired full owner-ship. In 1984, Standard Oil of California merged with Gulf Oil. The name Chevron was adopted following the merger. In 2001, Chevron acquired Texaco and its subsidiaries in Europe and South America. With active operations in 180 countries, Chevron employs an estimated 60,000 workers and ranks as one of the world's six largest oil companies with total assets of more than $148 billion.

Chrysler LLC
Michigan-based automobile manufacturer,
founded in 1925
Walter Percy Chrysler reorganized Maxwell Motor Company in 1925 to form the Chrysler Corpora-tion. The company began producing and selling a Chrysler car that sold 19,960 units during its first year. By 1928, Chrysler had added Plymouths, DeSotos, and Dodges to its line, targeting low-, me-dium-, and high-income purchasers, respectively, and becoming the second-largest automaker in the world, behind General Motors. Chrysler dropped to third in the 1950's, when it was overtaken by Ford. In 1979, on the verge of bankruptcy, it appealed to the U.S. government for emergency funds, which it re-ceived. In 1998, Daimler-Benz bought Chrysler and formed DaimlerChrysler. In August, 2007, the Chrysler group was sold to Cerberus Capital Man-agement, and it was renamed Chrysler LLC. In 2008, Chrysler, suffering from a precipitous drop in sales due to a change in consumer preferences and a credit crisis, again appealed to the U.S. government for emergency loans to stave off bankruptcy. In De-cember, President George W. Bush announced that $17.4 billion in emergency loans would be made available to keep Chrysler, as well as General Motors and Ford, out of bankruptcy; however, the loans were provided on condition that the automakers make major concessions and organizational changes by March 31, 2009, to demonstrate that they could re-turn to profitability.

Circuit City
Consumer electronics retailer, founded in 1984
The Circuit City chain of retail consumer electron-ics stores grew out of Samuel Wurtzel's Virginia-based Wards Company electronics stores. Wurtzel adopted the Circuit City name in 1984 and began a rapid expansion across the United States, Canada, and Puerto Rico. During the 1990's and early 2000's, the company operated 650 superstores across the United States and Puerto Rico, as well as 850 retail outlets across Canada. In November, 2008, the company announced it would close 155 stores and eliminate up to 17 percent of its workforce due to flagging sales and a failure to compete with other discount consumer electronics retailers. Later in the month, it filed for bankruptcy protection. In January, 2009, the company announced it was going out of business.

Citigroup
Financial services company, founded in 1998
Citigroup was formed by the merger of Citicorp and the Travelers Group in 1998, but its history stretches back to the City Bank of New York, first chartered in 1812. Following several mergers and acquisitions over the course of more than a century, the com-pany was renamed Citibank in 1976. By 1984, Citibank had become the largest commercial bank in the United States and the largest provider of credit and charge cards worldwide, with operations in 90 countries. Following the merger with Travelers Group, Citigroup acquired the world's largest finan-cial services network with operations in 107 coun-tries and 12,000 offices worldwide. In the wake of the subprime mortgage crisis in 2008, in which the company sustained dramatic losses, Citigroup be-came the recipient of a substantial government bail-out. It continues to employ more than 300,000 peo-ple worldwide and retains more than $2 trillion in assets.

Coca-Cola Company*

Founded in 1886, the leading manufacturer, distributor, and marketer of nonalcoholic beverages in the world.

Colgate-Palmolive Company

Household, health care, and personal products company founded in 1806

The Colgate-Palmolive Company has its roots in early nineteenth century New York, when William Colgate—a soap and candle maker by trade—opened a factory under the William Colgate Company name to manufacture and market starch, soap, and candles. The company introduced individually wrapped scented soaps in 1841 and toothpaste in 1873. Meanwhile, the B. J. Johnson Company in Milwaukee, Wisconsin, had developed a soap made of palm and olive oils in 1898 that would eventually become the world's best-selling soap. In 1928, the Palmolive-Peet company purchased Colgate. The company became Colgate-Palmolive in 1953. The company introduced its Fab brand of laundry detergent in 1947 and its Palmolive dishwashing liquid in 1966, one of its most successful products. In 1968, Colgate-Palmolive reformulated its toothpaste brands to include fluoride. The company's other holdings include Soft Soap and Mennen, as well as the Hills brand of pet products. Colgate-Palmolive operates in more than 70 countries and employs more than 36,000 workers.

CompuServe

Commercial online service, founded in 1969

Founded in 1969 by Jeffrey Wilkins as an in-house computer processing service provider for Golden United Life Insurance Company, CompuServe was an early innovator of Internet technology. It became the first company to offer electronic mail services for personal computer users in 1979. The following year, the company offered the first real-time online chat service. During the 1980's, CompuServe expanded to markets in Japan and Europe to provide networking solutions to corporate clients. CompuServe expanded rapidly during the 1990's, providing a personalized portal to the World Wide Web. Increased competition during the 1990's made revenues decline. In 1998, with a subscriber base of more than 2 million users, CompuServe became a wholly owned subsidiary of rival Internet provider America Online.

Dell

Computer hardware and technology company, founded in 1984

In 1984 while he was a student at the University of Texas, Michael Dell founded a computer company he called PC's Limited. He hoped to market IBM-compatible personal computers made from stock components directly to consumers, and his gamble paid off. Sales during his company's first year topped $73 million. In 1988, the company changed its name to Dell and began expanding into the international market. In 1996, Dell began selling computers through its company Web site. Four years later, it surpassed Compaq as the largest seller of personal computers in the United States. Two years later, Dell moved into the television, handheld computer, network server, and storage markets. The company's Internet sales during the late 1990's helped fuel the expansion of electronic commerce, but a loss of market share in the 2000's to companies such as Apple and Hewlett-Packard inspired a shift away from the company's pioneering direct-sales approach. Dell improved its sales later in the decade by selling its products in discount retailers such as Wal-Mart. Dell currently ranks thirty-fourth in the *Fortune* 500 with more than $60 billion in revenues.

Dow Chemical Company

Chemical company, founded in 1902

The first products offered by Dow Chemical, founded in 1902, were bleach and potassium bromide. In its first two decades, the company rapidly diversified its production with the introduction of various agricultural chemicals, dyes, and magnesium metals. Dow built its first magnesium extraction plant in 1941, becoming the first company to produce magnesium from seawater. Profits soared during World War II with the manufacture of lightweight magnesium aircraft parts. The company expanded to Canada in 1942 and Japan ten years later. The company's sales topped $1 billion in 1964, largely on its growing plastics production. During the Vietnam War, Dow was the sole provider of napalm for the United States military. It also produced the defoliant dioxin, named Agent Orange, in plants in New Zealand and the United States. Aggressive acquisitions and joint ventures during the 1990's saw the company expand its international operations. Dow operates in 175 countries and has annual revenues of more than $53 billion. It is the second-largest chemical manufacturer by revenue in the world behind BASF.

DuPont

Chemical company, founded in 1802

DuPont was founded in 1802 as a gunpowder mill by Eleuthère Irénée Du Pont and remained the major American supplier of gunpowder throughout the nineteenth century. DuPont acquired several smaller chemical companies but was forced to divest some of its holdings following antitrust litigation. In 1914, the company acquired substantial shares of General Motors, and Pierre S. Du Pont helped make General Motors one of the leading automobile manufacturers in the world. In 1957, DuPont was forced to give up its holdings in General Motors under the Clayton Antitrust Act. DuPont researchers discovered neoprene in 1928 and nylon in 1935. In subsequent years, researchers also developed Teflon (polytetrafluoroethylene). In 1943, DuPont built the Hanford plutonium plant used in the Manhattan Project. During the 1960's, the company's continued research into synthetic materials produced Kevlar, a main component in body armor for law enforcement and the military. DuPont acquired the Conoco petroleum company in 1981. It divested Conoco in 1999 and announced that it would pursue research into plant-based synthetic materials instead of petroleum-based products. The company employs an estimated 60,000 workers worldwide and ranks second among global chemical companies by market capitalization.

eBay*

Online auction, founded in 1995, that allows users to buy and sell goods on the Internet.

Edison International

Public utility holding company, founded in 1886

Edison International got its start in the population boom that hit Los Angeles during the late nineteenth and early twentieth centuries. In 1909, Southern California Edison acquired several early electric companies in California to extend its generation and distribution facilities. The company more than doubled its capacity in 1917 with the acquisition of H. E. Huntington's Pacific Light & Power Company and the Mount Whitney Power & Electric Company. The oil embargo of the 1970's led the

company to make investments in alternative energy sources during the 1980's, including the construction of a wind turbine installation near Palm Springs, California. Deregulation during the 1990's opened California markets to outside competition, and a rise in energy demand in 2001 precipitated a statewide energy crisis in California that left the company under the threat of bankruptcy. Edison recovered in subsequent years to stand at number 205 on *Fortune* magazine's top five hundred companies, with more than $13 billion in revenues.

Elizabeth Arden

Cosmetics manufacturer and retailer, founded in 1909

Born Florence Nightingale Graham in Toronto, Canada, Elizabeth Arden reinvented herself with a new name and career in New York City, where she opened the first of her many cosmetic salons in 1910. Arden introduced several innovations in the cosmetics industry. Among her earliest products were the facial cream called Venetian Cream Amoretta and the facial lotion called Arden Skin Tonic. By 1929, Arden had opened salons in several countries, and her products became synonymous with glamour and exclusivity. Her celebrity clients included British royalty, American first ladies, and some of the biggest film stars in Hollywood. Following Arden's death in 1966, the company was purchased first by the Eli Lilly Company in 1970 and then by Unilever in 1990. Under the ownership of Unilever, the company was part of a portfolio that became the second-largest cosmetics and perfume company in the world. When sales flagged, French Fragrances purchased the Elizabeth Arden brand in 2001.

Enron Corporation

Energy company, founded in 1932

Before its bankruptcy in 2001, Enron was a leading energy company with claimed revenues of more than $100 billion. The company traced its roots to the Northern Natural Gas Company, founded in Omaha, Nebraska, in 1932. Following a company reorganization in 1979, the company became a holding of Internorth and later adopted the name Enron. The company's headquarters were relocated to Houston, Texas, under Kenneth Lay's tenure as chief executive officer. Enron operated a coast-to-coast network of lucrative gas pipelines and managed electricity distribution to the Pacific Southwest. From 1996 to 2001, the company was named *Fortune* magazine's Most Innovative Company. The first signs of financial misdealings were reported in August, 2001. Enron had excluded much of its debt on its financial statements and overvalued many of its legitimate holdings. Following its bankruptcy, the company adopted the name Enron Creditors Recovery Corporation and functions as a holding company to liquidate any remaining company assets.

ExxonMobil Corporation
Global energy company, founded in 1999
In 1904, the U.S. Supreme Court ordered the breakup of John D. Rockefeller's Standard Oil into thirty-four separate companies, two of which were Jersey Standard and Sacony (or Standard Oil Company of New York). Through a series of mergers and acquisitions, Jersey Standard became Exxon in 1972, and Sacony began operating under the name Mobil Oil in 1966. The companies merged in 1999. The oil giant operates a vast portfolio of global operations that include the exploration, refining, and sale of gasoline and petroleum-based products. Based in Irving, Texas, ExxonMobil produces more than 4 million barrels of oil per day and has the equivalent of 75 billion barrels in reserves. The company—and all of its competitors—faced increased criticism beginning in 2005 about the steady rise of gasoline prices and its billions in annual profits. ExxonMobil still has legal action pending over the devastating Exxon *Valdez* oil tanker spill that flooded Alaska's Prince William Sound with 11 million gallons of oil. Punitive damages remain pending, but ExxonMobil's profits have never been higher. It ranks first in the world in net income, with more than $40 billion in profits in 2007.

Famous Amos
Cookie manufacturer, founded in 1975
Wally Amos pioneered the boutique bakery business with the Famous Amos Chocolate Chip Cookie Company. An aggressive advertising campaign and Amos's skill at self-promotion turned his small Sunset Strip cookie shop in Hollywood, California, into an international phenomenon. By the mid-1980's, sales had flagged and the company endured several changes of ownership. Keebler purchased the Fa-

mous Amos brand in 1998 and continues to market the cookies in retail grocery stores and vending machines. Amos left the company during the early 1990's and was prohibited from using the Famous Amos name. He founded what would become the Uncle Wally's Muffin Company in 1994 and marketed fat-free muffins to retail and club grocery chains. Amos re-established connections to the Famous Amos brand when Keebler invited him back to help promote the product following their purchase of the company. Famous Amos cookies remain a brisk seller for the Kellogg Company, which purchased Keebler in 2001.

FedEx Corporation*
International logistics and package delivery company, founded in 1971, which revolutionized the overnight shipping industry.

Ford Motor Company*
Automobile manufacturer founded in Dearborn, Michigan, in 1903, which ranks as the world's third-largest automaker in global vehicle sales.

Freddie Mac
Credit services company, founded in 1970
The Federal Home Loan Mortgage Company, more commonly known as Freddie Mac, was created in 1970 by a charter from the U.S. Congress to end the monopoly of the secondary mortgage market by the Federal National Mortgage Association. Freddie Mac is a government-backed corporation that acquires mortgages on the secondary market and sells them to a group of investors. The company earns its profits by charging a fee for its guarantee that the principal and interest on the loans will be paid regardless of whether the borrower satisfies the terms of the loan. The purchase of secondary loans allows lending institutions to free up capital for primary and first-time home mortgages. Freddie Mac prospered through the 1990's and the early 2000's. *Fortune* magazine ranked it twentieth in its list of the top two thousand public corporations in 2007, but a decline in the home mortgage market in 2008, spurred on by the proliferation of subprime home loans threatened company assets. On September 8, 2008, it was placed under the conservatorship of the Federal Housing Finance Agency.

Fuller Brush Company*

Brush and home care products manufacturer, founded in 1906, which pioneered direct, or door-to-door, marketing.

Genentech*

Biotechnology company, founded in 1976, which is widely considered as the foundation of the biotechnology industry.

General Electric*

Multinational technology and services provider, founded in 1878 by Thomas Alva Edison, which ranks as the world's third-largest company based on market capitalization.

General Mills

Processed food manufacturer, founded in 1866

General Mills traces its roots to a large mill opened by Cadwallader Washburn in 1866 and officially adopted the name of General Mills in 1928 after the merger of several regional mills. The merger made General Mills the largest flour miller in the world, with milling operations in sixteen states. James Ford Bell led the company through the Great Depression, a period of slow but steady growth for General Mills. The company's mechanical division spurred expansion with the development of its Betty Crocker appliance brand during the 1940's. General Mills made substantial contributions to the war effort during the 1940's and the burgeoning space race during the 1960's through its development of specialty packaged foods. In 1970, General Mills acquired the Red Lobster restaurant chain. Its restaurant division later introduced the Olive Garden chain before divesting its restaurant holdings in 1995. General Mills holdings include more than one hundred popular brands, such as Pillsbury, Häagen-Dazs, Green Giant, Wheaties, and Cheerios. A *Fortune* 500 company, General Mills employs nearly 30,000 workers worldwide with annual revenues of more than $13 billion.

General Motors*

Major American automobile manufacturer and frequent leader in annual global vehicle sales that was founded in 1908.

Georgia-Pacific

Pulp and paper manufacturer, founded in 1927

Owen Roberts Cheatham founded Georgia-Pacific as the Georgia Hardwood Lumber Company in 1927. During the next two decades, the company acquired numerous sawmills and lumber facilities across the United States. In 1957, Georgia-Pacific entered the pulp trade with acquisitions in Oregon and built a diverse product line that made it one of the world's leading manufacturers and distributors of tissue, pulp, packaging, paper, building products, and related chemicals. Among its popular consumer goods brands are Quilted Northern tissue paper, Brawny paper towels, and the Dixie brand of disposable plates and cups. The company sold four of its uncoated-paper mills to Canadian paper company Domtar in 2001. Four years later, Georgia-Pacific was acquired by Witchita, Kansas-based Koch Industries, a private corporation, at a cost of $21 billion. Georgia-Pacific employs 55,000 people worldwide at more than three hundred locations in North America, South America, and Europe.

Goodyear Tire & Rubber Company

Tire manufacturer, founded in 1898

Named after Charles Goodyear, the inventor of vulcanized rubber, Goodyear Tire & Rubber Company was founded by Frank Sieberling in 1898. The company's first factory opened in 1898 in Akron, Ohio, where it produced tires for bicycles and horse-drawn carriages. Beginning in 1901, Goodyear partnered with Henry Ford to supply tires for the burgeoning automobile industry. The first of the company's famous Goodyear blimps appeared in 1925 and became one of the most recognizable marketing tools in the world. Goodyear expanded operations internationally during the 1930's and acquired rival manufacturer Kelly-Springfield in 1935. The company built Corsair fighter planes for the United States military during World War II. By 1984, company sales exceeded $10 billion. Restructuring during the 1990's saw massive layoffs, but the company remains a leading supplier of tires for automobiles, trucks, race cars, and heavy machinery, with nearly $20 billion in annual revenue.

Great Atlantic and Pacific Tea Company (A&P)*

Company originally founded in 1870 as a tea importer and retailer that established itself as the premier discount grocery chain of the early twentieth century and remains a leading U.S. supermarket.

H. J. Heinz Company

Processed foods manufacturer, founded in 1869
German immigrant Henry John Heinz founded his namesake company in 1869 as a condiment delivery service in Pittsburgh, Pennsylvania, under the name Anchor Pickle and Vinegar Works. Its first product was grated horseradish. Following his bankruptcy in 1875, Heinz reorganized the company and introduced what would become its trademark product, tomato ketchup. In 1892, he introduced the slogan 57 Varieties, which would become the company's signature marketing slogan. In 1905, the company opened its first overseas factory in England, where it soon began producing its Heinz Baked Beanz brand, which remains a best-selling brand throughout Great Britain. The company went public in 1946. During the next two decades, it acquired several subsidiaries, including Starkist Foods, Ore-Ida Foods, and Weight Watchers International. During the 1990's, the company acquired the Budget Gourmet line of frozen packaged meals and divested itself of its Weight Watcher holdings. The company has more than $10 billion in annual revenues and sells its products in more than fifty countries, with an estimated 650 million bottles of its iconic tomato ketchup sold worldwide every year.

Halliburton

Energy services provider, founded in 1919
Founded in 1919, Halliburton is a leading American oil exploration and drilling company with operations in nearly seventy countries. Aggressive expansion during the 1920's and 1930's led to the company's opening operations in Mexico, South America, and Asia. During the Gulf War in 1991, Halliburton subsidiaries provided logistical support to the United States military in the oil fields of Iraq. In the 1990's, Halliburton began operations in Russia and became the first foreign country to set up operations in mainland China. The company has been the subject of numerous controversies, from charges of no-bid contracts in Iraq to allegations of having a spotty environmental record. Despite legal challenges, the company continues to employ an estimated 55,000 employees worldwide and has annual revenues of more than $15 billion.

Hallmark Cards

Greeting card and gift company, founded in 1910
Hallmark is a privately owned greeting card company based in Kansas City, Missouri. Founded in 1910 by eighteen-year-old Joyce Hall, the company began as a small family operation that by 1915 specialized in Valentine's Day and Christmas cards. In 1928, Hall and his brother Rollie adopted the name Hallmark (the company would formally adopt that name in 1958) and began producing greeting card lines for a variety of holidays and occasions. Sponsorship for a National Broadcasting Company (NBC) telecast in 1951 led to a recurring series of made-for-television films under the series name Hallmark Hall of Fame. In 2001, Hallmark launched its own cable channel. The company employs about 18,000 workers worldwide and earns annual revenues of more than $4 billion.

Hewlett-Packard

Computer technology manufacturer, founded in 1939
Hewlett-Packard was founded by two Stanford University graduate students, William Hewlett and David Packard. Between 1940 and 1990, the company focused on the production of electrical testing equipment and large-scale computer hardware. The company's first computer, which it called a desktop calculator, was created in 1968. The company later rejected a proposal by company employee Steve Wozniak, who offered them a first look at the Apple I personal computer he designed while working for Hewlett-Packard. The company introduced a line of inkjet computer printers during the 1980's and continued to expand its computer line during the 1990's. In 1999, Hewlett-Packard divested of all noncomputer holdings by spinning off the Agilent Company, which carried on its production of semiconductors and scientific instruments. In 2002, Hewlett-Packard merged with former rival Compaq. The company acquired Electronic Data Services in 2008. Headquartered in Palo Alto, California, Hewlett-Packard is the largest worldwide seller of personal computers with revenues of more than $118 billion.

Home Depot

Home improvement products retailer, founded in 1978

Home Depot was founded in 1978 outside Atlanta, Georgia, as a one-stop retailer for construction and home improvement products. The combination of inexpensive tools and construction materials, as well as the introduction of home improvement educational programs, helped invigorate an industry that was previously dominated by professional contractors. The company went public in 1981 and began rapid expansion that saw the opening of its one hundredth store in 1989. Home Depot entered the Canadian market in 1994 with the acquisition of the Aikenhead retail chain. The company expanded to Mexico in 2001 with the purchase of Total HOME, and to China in 2006 with the acquisition of the Home Way, a twelve-store retail chain. Home Depot remains the largest home improvement retail chain in the United States and the country's second-largest retailer overall, behind Wal-Mart.

Home Shopping Network*

Television-based shopping network that pioneered technological advances to target at-home shoppers, founded in 1982.

Hughes Aircraft Company

Aerospace and defense services company, founded in 1932

Hughes Aircraft was founded in 1932 by Howard Hughes, Jr., as an offshoot of the Hughes Tool Company. Its first aircraft, the H-1 Racer, was built in 1935 and brought the company its first public notice. Hughes built the ill-fated H-4, or Spruce Goose, a prototype all-wood transport aircraft, which never proved viable and later became a tourist attraction in Long Beach, California. The years during and following World War II saw the company's fortunes rise as a major airline component manufacturer and defense contractor. In 1948, Hughes opened its Aerospace Group, which focused on advanced avionics and air-to-air missile guidance systems, and which remained the basis for aircraft missile systems until the 1980's. Other subsidiaries included helicopter manufacturer Kellett Aircraft and the Hughes Space and Communications Company, which developed the first geosynchronous communications satellite in 1963 and the lunar probe Surveyor I and the Pioneer Venus probe in 1978. In 1985, Hughes Aircraft was acquired by General Motors, which sold off most of its subsidiaries to the Raytheon Corporation in 1997.

Intel Corporation

Manufacturer of semiconductors and computer microprocessors, founded in 1968

Intel Corporation was founded in 1968 as Integrated Electronics, a manufacturer of semiconductors. In the 1970's, it became a manufacturer of computer memory storage devices. Competition from foreign and American companies led Intel to focus primarily on the manufacture of microprocessors and related hardware for the growing personal computer market during the 1980's and 1990's. Its products included network cards, graphic memory cards, and the x86 series of microprocessors, which became the standard chipset for the majority of personal computers. Among its more successful product lines is the Pentium brand of microprocessors. A longtime rival, and then partner, of Microsoft, Intel began a collaboration with Apple in 2006, which saw the introduction of its x86 processor in Apple's line of personal computers. Later product lines have focused on flash memory devices, computer motherboard chipsets, and wireless technology. The company employs more than 80,000 employees worldwide and exceeds $38 billion in annual revenues.

International Business Machines (IBM)*

Multinational computer technology company founded in 1924 that produces computer hardware, software, and business solutions.

International Paper

Pulp and paper manufacturer, founded in 1898

The largest paper and pulp manufacturer in the world, International Paper was founded in 1898 by the merger of seventeen independent paper mills. Rapid expansion during the early 1900's soon made the company a leading supplier of newsprint in the United States and a major exporter of paper to South America and Europe. Until the 2000's, the company controlled millions of acres of timber land in Canada. In 1951, the company established a research laboratory in Mobile, Alabama, and began to diversify its manufacturing. International Paper acquired several international manufacturers beginning during the 1980's, including Germany's Zanders Feinpapiere and France's Aussedat Rey. In addition to its extensive line of paper and pulp products, the company is also the leading supplier of paper cups and plastic lids for major U.S. fast-food chains. With headquarters in Memphis, Tennessee, International Paper employs more than 50,000 workers worldwide and has more than $22 billion in annual revenue.

J. C. Penney
Department store chain and catalog vendor, founded in 1902

Founded by James Cash Penney in 1902, J. C. Penney began as a discount retail chain operating as the Golden Rule chain of shops. It incorporated under the name of J. C. Penney in 1913, after which it began aggressive expansion. By 1941, the company operated 1,600 stores. During the 1960's, J. C. Penney began offering mail-order catalog sales. It acquired the Thrift Drug Store chain in 1969. When Sears, Roebuck ended its catalog sales in 1993, J. C. Penney became the largest catalog retailer in the United States. In 1998, the company began Internet sales. Although flagging store sales led to the closure of dozens of retail locations after 2001, Internet sales began to rise, exceeding $1 billion in sales by 2005. The company has relied heavily on the marketing of exclusive fashion brands to help compete with discount retailers such as Wal-Mart and Target. Among these private brands are the Sephora perfume line, St. John's Bay, and the American Living brand, designed by Ralph Lauren.

Johnson & Johnson
Global pharmaceutical and medical supply company, founded in 1887

Founded by Robert Wood Johnson and his brothers, Johnson & Johnson was founded on the research of Joseph Lister, a pioneer of antiseptic surgery. Robert Wood Johnson manufactured the first sterile surgical dressings in 1885 and incorporated the company, along with three brothers, in New Brunswick, New Jersey, in 1887. During the early 1900's, the company introduced several innovative personal healthcare products, including dental floss, Band-Aid brand adhesive strips, and female sanitary napkins. The company introduced the first U.S. prescription birth control pill in 1931. Johnson & Johnson became a publicly traded company in 1944 and expanded into Mexico, South America, Europe, Asia, and Africa, with a growing emphasis

on pharmaceutical research and manufacturing. The company's best-known products include the Tylenol brand of medications, Johnson's baby powder and oils, the Neutrogena skin care line, and Acuvue contact lenses. The company acquired Pfizer's consumer healthcare division in 2006. Johnson & Johnson controls some 250 subsidiaries whose products are sold in 175 countries.

Johnson Publishing Company
International media and cosmetics company, founded in 1942

Founded in 1942 by John H. Johnson as the Negro Digest Publishing Company, after the name of its first publication, *Negro Digest*, the firm later became the Johnson Publishing Company and released additional publications targeting the African American community. *Ebony* magazine was created in 1945 and *Jet* magazine appeared in 1951. Under Johnson's leadership, the company maintained interests in the insurance industry, where Johnson got his start in business, and later branched out into the fashion, cosmetics, and book publishing sectors.

JPMorgan Chase & Company
Financial services company, founded in 2000

JPMorgan Chase & Company was formed in 2000 with the merger of J. P. Morgan Company and the Chase Manhattan Corporation, two of the oldest financial institutions in the United States. The company built its more than $2 trillion in assets through aggressive acquisitions in successive years, including the incorporation of Bank One and Bear Stearns companies to the company's growing list of subsidiaries. J. P. Morgan's company history stretches back to nineteenth century industrialist J. P. Morgan, while Chase Manhattan was first formed by merger in 1955. The company manages one of the largest capitalized hedge funds in the world, controlling an estimated $34 billion in assets. During the financial crisis of 2008, the company purchased the ailing Washington Mutual, previously one of the largest holders of consumer mortgages.

Kellogg Company
Packaged food company, founded in 1906

The Battle Creek Toasted Corn Flake Company was founded in 1906 by Will Kellogg, brother of John Harvey Kellogg, who operated a natural foods and health sanatorium. The company's toasted corn flake breakfast cereal was invented by the Kellogg brothers in 1894 and soon became a staple breakfast food. The company adopted its current name in 1922. Despite amassing a vast fortune, Kellogg remained committed to philanthropy and to the welfare of his employees. He ran his factories on a thirty-hour workweek until the 1940's and created the W. K. Kellogg Foundation in 1934 with an endowment in Kellogg Company stock of $66 million. The Kellogg Company continues to manufacture many of the most popular breakfast and snack foods. It acquired the Keebler brand in 2001, as well as several other breakfast and snack food companies, including the Cheez-It, Morningstar Farms, and Famous Amos brands, and earns nearly $12 billion in annual revenues.

Levi Strauss and Company
Clothing manufacturer and retailer, founded in 1853

Levi Strauss and Company made its first pair of blue jeans, then called "waist overalls," in 1873. Bavaria-born Levi Strauss founded a dry goods store in San Francisco, California, and formed a partnership with Nevada tailor Jacob Davis to manufacture sturdy trousers that would withstand the rigors of the California mining camps. Strauss purchased the denim fabric from a mill in New Hampshire and Davis invented the company's trademark rivets designed to strengthen stress points on the jeans. In 1912, the company introduced its first nationally distributed product, Koveralls, a one-piece play suit for children. A rise in the price of cotton during the 1920's and the Great Depression of the 1930's slowed company sales and expansion. Lady Levi's were introduced in 1934, its first product designed for women. The 1960's saw the company's expansion into Asia and Europe, where the company opened its first official international stores in Spain in 1983. Endorsements by musicians and the company's sponsorship of the 1984 Summer Olympics helped strengthen Levi's already growing popularity as an emblem of American culture. The company remains one of the most successful clothing manufacturers in the world.

McDonald's*
Fast-food restaurant chain founded in 1954 that became the world leader in its field with more than $3 billion in annual net revenues.

Macy's
Department store chain, founded in 1858

Macy's was founded by Rowland Hussey Macy in 1858. Its flagship department store was built in New York City. The store was expanded during the 1920's and 1930's and designed in the Art Deco style. It has since become a National Historic Landmark. The company went public in 1922 and subsequently began expanding with semi-autonomous regional stores in the Midwest and on the Pacific Coast. Macy's acquired several smaller chains during the 1960's and 1970's. Following an unsuccessful bid to buy the Federated Department Stores in 1988, Macy's acquired Federated's Bullocks and I. Magnin divisions. In 1992, Macy's filed for bankruptcy, and new management restructured the company by divesting several underperforming divisions. Two years later, Macy's agreed to a merger with Federated, which later adopted the name Macy's for all of its department store chains. In 2005, Federated acquired the May department store chain and two years later adopted the name Macy Group and maintained the Macy's and Bloomingdales company names. Macy Group continues to operate more than eight hundred stores nationwide.

Marshall Field
Department store chain, founded in 1852

Marshall Field & Company traces its roots to a small dry goods store founded by Potter Palmer in Chicago in 1852. Palmer sold the company to twenty-one-year-old Marshall Field. Following the store's destruction in the Great Fire of 1871, Field began to rebuild at the corner of State Street. As business began to grow during the 1880's and 1890's, the store began to expand until it occupied nearly a full city block in downtown Chicago. The store's neoclassical design became a city landmark, and what began as a humble dry goods store became a luxury department store catering to the city's elite. Customer lounges provided out-of-town visitors the opportunity to book hotel rooms, send and receive cables and telegrams, and arrange further transportation. During the 1920's and 1930's, Marshall Field opened several additional branches in Chicago and throughout Illinois. Further acquisitions saw the company expand operations with several discount retailers. In 1982, Marshall Field was acquired by British-American Tobacco. It was later divested and purchased by the Dayton Hudson Corporation in 1990. Dayton Hudson adopted the Marshall Field name until its acquisition by Macy's in 2005.

Microsoft Corporation

Computer technology company, founded in 1975
Microsoft was founded by Bill Gates in 1975. Its initial focus was the development and sale of BASIC computer language interpreters for the Altair computer. Microsoft introduced its Microsoft Disk Operating System (MS-DOS) in 1985 and began its conquest of the personal computer software market. The company went public in 1986 and introduced the Microsoft Office Suite in 1989, through which it earned a majority market share over rival Novell's WordPerfect software. In 1995, Microsoft began to address the burgeoning World Wide Web by introducing its online Microsoft Network (MSN). Two years later, it introduced its Internet Explorer Web browser, which quickly outstripped its principal rival Netscape. The company integrated its business and personal computing applications with the release of its Windows XP operating system in 2001. Strategic licensing agreements with computer manufacturers helped Microsoft extend its market share and earn record profits. Its closely integrated software later led to several antitrust disputes in the United States and the European Union. Largely on the success of its operating system and office productivity suite, Microsoft maintains a virtual monopoly on personal computing software, earning more than $60 billion in annual revenues and making its founder, Bill Gates, one of the wealthiest men in the world.

Montgomery Ward*

Former department store chain and current online retailer founded in 1872 as one of the earliest mail-order businesses.

National Broadcasting Corporation (NBC)*

American broadcast television network founded in 1926 that operates as a division of General Electric and Vivendi.

New York Life Insurance Company

Mutual life insurance company, founded in 1845
Founded in 1845 as the Nautilus Insurance Company, it became the New York Life Insurance Company in 1849. Among the company's insurance in-

novations were the introduction of guaranteed cash values for policies and the payment of cash dividends to policyholders. It was also the first insurer to offer policies to women at the same rates as it charged men. New York Life also became the first insurer to issue policies to people with disabilities in 1896. The company introduced group insurance during the 1950's and began to diversify in the postwar period. During the 1980's, New York Life acquired the Mackay Shields Financial Corporation and began marketing mutual funds. In 1987, the company purchased Sanus Healthcare Systems, one of the largest health care companies in the United States. Additional diversification, including the introduction of New York Life Investment Management, helped the company increase revenues during the early 2000's. The company remains one of the largest life insurers and financial institutions in the world.

Nike

Sportswear and equipment maker, founded in 1964
Nike was founded in 1964 under the name Blue Ribbon Sports by University of Oregon track coach Bill Bowerman and one of his track stars, Phil Knight. It initially operated as a distributor for the Japanese brand of Tiger track shoes, and early sales were made out of the back of a car at regional track meets. The company began selling its own products in 1971 with the introduction of a football shoe, called Nike, which featured the trademark "swoosh" insignia. The company adopted the Nike name in 1978. Early innovations included the development of the waffle sole designed to better grip urethane track surfaces. Nike went public in 1980 and began to diversify its product line. The company's iconic advertising slogan Just Do It was introduced in 1988. Its sponsorship of athletes such as basketball star Michael Jordan and golf phenomenon Tiger Woods helped secure its growing reputation as the leading athletic shoe manufacturer in the world. Nike acquired Converse, which manufactures the popular Chuck Taylor brand, in 2003. The company also manufactures sportswear, athletic equipment, and accessories, and operates a chain of retail stores under the Niketown name. The company has more than $18 billion in annual revenue and remains one of the most recognized brands in the world.

Owens Corning

Manufacturer of glass and fiberglass products, founded in 1938

Owens Corning was founded in 1938 when the Corning Glass Works and Owens-Illinois formed a partnership to manufacture glass fiber. Owens Corning was spun off as in independent company three years later. The company's trademark Fiberglas earned more than $2 million in sales in its first year of operations. Owens Corning received lucrative contracts during World War II producing insulation and fireproof materials for aircraft and ships. The company expanded in the postwar years with the introduction of housing insulation and related products. The company went public in 1952. During the 1960's, Owens Corning manufactured glass-fiber-reinforced plastic, which the company marketed as a replacement for steel underground storage tanks because of its noncorrosive qualities. During the 1970's and 1980's, Owens Corning expanded its operations to Europe and the Middle East. In 1990, the company fought off a leveraged buyout but amassed enormous debt in the process. Owens Corning also faced litigation for its use of asbestos in its products. Resurgent sales marked its operations through the late 1990's, but Owens Corning was forced to file for bankruptcy in 2000. It emerged from bankruptcy six years later and continues to manufacture a variety of goods, including building supplies and composite materials used in the automotive and communications industries.

Pan American World Airways

International airline company, founded in 1927

Pan American was the leading international air carrier in the United States, from its founding in 1927 to its collapse in 1991. It began operations as a foreign airmail carrier. In 1928, Pan Am flew its maiden international passenger flight between Key West, Florida, and Havana, Cuba. Partnerships with existing South American airlines and the development of larger and better-equipped aircraft, including the Sikorsky clipper aircraft, allowed Pan Am to extend operations throughout the 1930's. It began transpacific passenger service in 1934 and transatlantic service in 1939. During World War II, many of the airline's aircraft were pressed into service in support of the military. A new crop of planes were acquired in the postwar years, including the new Boeing 377 and the DC-6. Pan Am continued acquiring the most sophisticated aircraft. It was one of the first airlines to fly the Boeing 747 in 1966 and adopted it for regularly scheduled flights in 1970. Having enjoyed an enduring reputation as the most experienced international air carrier, the company fell on difficult times beginning with the energy crisis in 1973. Pan Am's acquisition of National Airlines further imperilled its weakening financial health. Two terrorist attacks, first a hijacking in 1986 in Pakistan and then the downing of Pan Am flight 103 over Lockerbie, Scotland, further damaged the company's image. Pan Am filed for bankruptcy in 1991, and Delta Airlines purchased most of its assets. The company formally ceased operations in December, 1991.

Parker Brothers

Toy and game manufacturer, founded in 1888

Parker Brothers was founded by George S. Parker and his brothers in 1888. The company's earliest board games were based on significant current events. Klondike was inspired by the Alaskan gold rush, and War in Cuba was based on the Spanish-American War. The company enjoyed brisk profits as board games grew in popularity. In 1935, Parker Brothers released what would become its best known and most successful board game, Monopoly, which has been rendered in numerous international editions. In successive decades, the company introduced such future classic games as Risk and Clue. Parker Brothers remained a family-owned company until 1963, when it was purchased by General Mills. Later products included the first Nerf ball and electronic versions of classic Parker Brothers titles. The company became a division of Hasbro in 1991. In its 120-year history, Parker Brothers published more than 1,800 games, many of which remain in production.

PepsiCo

Beverage manufacturer and distributor, founded in 1903

Pepsi was invented by pharmacist Caleb Bradham in 1898. The combination of kola nut, vanilla, and rare oils was an instant hit. What was originally known as Brad's Drink was renamed Pepsi-Cola, and Bradham began looking for ways to market it. In 1902, he began manufacturing Pepsi on a larger scale in a back room of his pharmacy. The following year, he moved operations into a nearby warehouse. Bradham initially sold his product as syrup, then introduced bottled Pepsi in 1904. He also began to sell franchises that saw the expansion of Pepsi sales to twenty-four states by the end of 1910. Bradham's company went bankrupt during the Great Depression and was later purchased by candymaker Charles Guth, who reformulated the original formula. The company changed ownership again in the 1940's. It adopted the name PepsiCo following its merger with Frito Lay in 1965. In 1975, Pepsi introduced its Pepsi challenge in a push to compete with Coca-Cola that was dubbed the Cola wars. PepsiCo acquired several nonbeverage companies, including the fast-food chains KFC, Taco Bell, and Pizza Hut. It divested its restaurant holdings in 1997. The company also purchased Tropicana in 1998 and Quaker Oats in 2001. In 2005, Pepsi surpassed archrival Coca-Cola in market share for the first time. PepsiCo, which also manufactures Mountain Dew, distributes products worldwide and has annual revenues of more than $40 billion.

RadioShack

Retail electronics chain, founded in 1921
Radio Shack was founded in 1921 by Theodore and Milton Deutschmann as a retailer of Ham radio equipment. The company began mail-order sales during the 1940's and introduced its own product line of consumer electronics under the brand name Realist in 1954. Poor sales during the 1960's drove the company to the brink of bankruptcy, but the small retail chain was purchased by the Tandy Corporation, a leather goods retailer, in 1962. Radio Shack regained profitability throughout the 1970's, particularly with the introduction of the TRS80 computer, one of the first mass-produced personal computers, in 1978. Increased competition led the company to drop its line of computers during the early 1990's. Radio Shack continues to produce its own consumer electronics lines, including audio and video equipment, under the Presidian, Accurian, and Optimus brand names. Layoffs and restructuring marked much of the company's operations during the early 2000's, but the company continues to operate retail stores across the United States and in Europe and South America.

Sears, Roebuck and Company*

Department store chain founded in 1886 that began as a mail-order business and grew to become the largest U.S. retailer through the 1950's.

Standard Oil Company*

Oil exploration and refining firm founded in 1870 by John D. Rockefeller that became one of the world's first multinational corporations until its breakup by the Supreme Court in 1911.

Staples

Office supply superstore operator, founded in 1986
Founded by Thomas Stemberg in 1986, Staples has since become the world's leading retailer of office equipment and supplies. The company went public in 1989 and began aggressive expansion across North America, Europe, South America, and Asia during the 1990's. Following an unsuccessful bid to acquire rival Office Depot in 1997, Staples launched a successful Internet sales operation in 1998. Despite flagging sales during the early 2000's, the company continued to expand its foreign market share with stores in India in 2007 and the acquisition of the Dutch office supply giant Corporate Express the following year. Staples operates more than two thousand retail stores in twenty-seven countries, with annual revenues of $27 billion.

Starbucks Corporation

Retailer and roaster of specialty coffee, founded in 1971
The first Starbucks store opened in Seattle, Washington's Pike Place Market in 1971. It originally sold only coffee beans and brewing equipment. In 1983, the company began selling brewed coffee, espresso, and related beverages. In 1987, the company was purchased by entrepreneur Howard Schultz, who had created the Il Giornale coffee bar chain in 1985. He rebranded the Il Giornale chain as Starbucks and began a program of rapid expansion. By 1992, he had opened 165 stores and taken the company public. Starbucks opened its first store in Tokyo in 1996 and acquired the sixty-store United Kingdom-based Seattle Coffee Company in 1998. The following year, Starbucks acquired the music label Hear Music and began in-store music CD sales. Starbucks also created the film company Starbucks Entertainment in 2006. In the same year, Starbucks partnered with Apple to promote iTunes online music sales. At the height of its success, Starbucks was opening a new store every working day. Market saturation ultimately led to store closures and layoffs in early 2008, but the company continues to operate more than 15,000 locations worldwide, employing an estimated 270,000 workers.

State Farm Insurance

Insurance company, founded in 1922

State Farm Insurance was founded in 1922 by George Jacob Mecherle as a mutual automobile insurer wholly owned by its policyholders. By the 1930's, the company had expanded operations to Canada. State Farm became the leading automobile insurer in the United States in 1942—a position it has held ever since. The company added fire and casualty insurance in 1935 and homeowner's insurance in 1955. A struggling musician named Barry Manilow wrote the jingle for the company's new advertising slogan, Like a Good Neighbor, State Farm Is There, in 1971. The company added banking services in 1998 through its bank-certified agents, whereby customers could access financial services through their insurance agents, the Internet, through direct mail, or through a call center. State Farm ranks in the top fifty *Fortune* 500 companies with annual revenues of more than $61 billion and is one of the largest mutual property and casualty insurers in the world.

Target Corporation

Retail discount chain, founded in 1962

Target Corporation has its roots in the Dayton Dry Goods Company founded by George Dayton in Minneapolis in 1902. The first Target discount store opened in Minnesota in 1962. Dayton's experiment in discount retail sales performed poorly in its first five years, but sales steadily grew, and by 1967 Dayton had taken the chain public. Initial expansion focused primarily on midwestern states, but Target began operations on both coasts in 1982 with the acquisition of the popular discount chain FedMart. The company changed its name from the Dayton Hudson Corporation to Target Corporation in 2000. By 2005, the company operated nearly 1,400 stores and had topped $52 billion in annual sales. That same year, Target opened its first store in Bangalore, India, with plans for further expansion throughout India. The company operates three chains: Target stores, Target Greatland general merchandise superstores, and SuperTarget stores. It employs an estimated 366,000 employees and has annual revenues of more than $63 billion.

Texas Instruments

Computer technology and semiconductor company, founded in 1930

Texas Instruments traces its roots to the Geophysical Service, a seismic exploration company active in the petroleum industry and founded in 1930. The company became Texas Instruments in 1951, having spent more than a decade building electrical and guidance systems for the United States military. During the 1950's, Texas Instruments purchased a license to produce semiconductors and would later revolutionize the emerging electronics industry. Among its early innovations were the first silicon-based semiconductor and the first transistor radio, both in 1954. Further discoveries in microprocessor technology produced applications that would be vital to the emerging computer industry and a wide variety of consumer electronics, military and industrial engineering, and wireless technology. Today, the company's principal focus is semiconductors. It regularly ranks among the top ten semiconductor producers in the world. Texas Instruments also continues to produce its popular line of consumer and scientific calculators. The company has more than 30,000 employees and annual revenues of more than $13 billion.

3M

Adhesives and abrasives manufacturer, founded in 1902

3M was founded in 1902 as the Minnesota Mining and Manufacturing Company to mine stone to make grinding wheels. It struggled through its first decade to secure steady markets for its mining and industrial goods. In 1916, the company opened its first research and development laboratory and launched a stream of new products, including a variety of adhesive tapes and acoustic suppression materials. By the 1950's, 3M had expanded operations throughout North America, Europe, and Australia, and produced an increasingly diverse product line, from board games and traffic signals to the popular line of Post-It Notes, magnetic data storage devices, and one of the earliest digital audio recording devices. 3M operates sales offices in two hundred countries and has annual revenues of nearly $25 billion.

Time Warner

Media and entertainment company, founded in 1990

Time Warner was created when Time, Inc., purchased Warner Communications in 1990 for $14 billion. Time had built a magazine publishing empire through its flagship magazine, launched in 1921, and the introduction of several others, including *Fortune* in 1930, *Life* in 1936, and *Sports Illustrated* in 1956. In 1974, Time launched the Home Box Office (HBO) cable television network. Warner Communications traced its roots back to the Warner Bros. film studio founded in 1923 and renamed Warner Communications in 1971. Time Warner acquired the Turner Broadcasting System in 1996. The company consolidated its position as the leading media conglomerate with the acquisition of America Online in 2001. Time Warner is one of the world's largest media and entertainment conglomerates with holdings that include cable news and entertainment channels, publishing subsidiaries, comic book publishers, and major recording labels.

Tupperware*

Manufacturer of plastics products for homes, founded in 1938, which used an innovative marketing system.

Union Pacific Railroad

Railroad network, founded in 1862

The Pacific Railroad Act of 1862, signed into law by President Abraham Lincoln, gave the Union Pacific Railroad—one of two corporations named in the bill—the task of building the first transcontinental American railroad. The Union Pacific broke ground the following year and joined the Central Pacific at Promontory Summit in Utah to complete the cross-country line in 1869. Union Pacific continued to expand throughout successive decades, acquiring several subsidiary lines, but mounting debt and overextension sent the railroad into receivership in 1893. Portions of the line were purchased by Edward H. Harriman, who later acquired other segments and returned the company to profitability. During both world wars, the Union Pacific moved equipment and troops across the country, but following World War II, a boom in car sales and the development of an interstate highway system led to a drop in passenger train travel. The company discon-tinued passenger service in 1971 but remains a leading transportation company with tracks operating in twenty-three states.

United Airlines

International airline, founded in 1926

United Airlines, a subsidiary of UAL Corporation, regards pioneering airman Walter Varney as its founder. Boeing Air Transport purchased Varney's airmail service and adopted the name United Aircraft and Transport Company in 1929. The Air Mail Act of 1934 prohibited common ownership of air transport manufacturers and passenger airlines, and Boeing's company was broken into individual companies, one of which became United Airlines. In 1961, United merged with Capital Airlines to become the world's largest commercial passenger airline with a network offering countrywide service. United began international service in 1983 with the purchase of Pan American Airways. Labor disputes plagued the company during the 1980's and early 1990's. Two of the four flights hijacked on September 11, 2001, were United Airlines flights. That year, the company filed for Chapter 11 bankruptcy protection and sought financial backing from the private sector. United Airlines scaled back operations in 2008 because of a sharp rise in fuel costs, but it remains one of the largest airlines in the world, offering more than three thousand flights daily to destinations in more than two hundred countries.

United Parcel Service (UPS)

Package delivery service, founded in 1907

The United Parcel Service got its start in 1907 as the American Messenger Service, a neighborhood delivery service in Seattle, Washington. Employees worked out of a basement and made deliveries—including food from local restaurants—on foot or on bicycle. The company purchased its first delivery vehicle—a Model T Ford—in 1913. Before the creation of the U.S. Parcel Post, the company's largest client was the post office. In 1919, the renamed Merchants Parcel Post extended operations to Northern California. It opened offices in Los Angeles in 1922 and became the United Parcel Service. Also that year, the company began offering scheduled daily pickups. By the 1950's, the company moved beyond retail delivery service to offer direct service to public and private customers. The company made a short-lived attempt to provide air delivery service in

1929. In 1953, UPS resurrected its delivery service to the East and West coasts via cargo holds of regularly scheduled domestic flights. Dubbed Blue Label Air, the service offered second-day deliveries to all fifty states by 1978. Ten years later, UPS acquired its own air fleet and began next-day air service. The company operates more than 1,000 facilities in 120 countries and delivers more than 15 million packages daily. Strategic partnerships with companies such as Wal-Mart have allowed UPS to branch out into logistics services, making it a leader in global supply chain management. UPS, known as the Big Brown Machine, has nearly half a million employees and earned more than $49 billion in revenues in 2007.

United States Steel Corporation*

American steel producer, cofounded by J. P. Morgan in 1901, which later ranked as both the largest steel producer and the largest corporation in the world.

United Technologies Corporation

Multinational engineering and technology conglomerate, founded in 1929

United Technologies was founded in 1929 as the United Aircraft and Transport Corporation, through the merger of two Boeing aircraft and transport companies and several smaller companies. In the wake of the Air Mail Act of 1934, which prohibited joint ownership of aircraft manufacturers and passenger airlines, United Aircraft broke into three separate companies: United Aircraft, Boeing, and United Airlines. United Aircraft continued under this name until 1975 and focused principally on aerospace and defense-related engineering. Renamed United Technologies in 1975, the company entered a period of aggressive expansion. It acquired Otis Elevator and Carrier Refrigeration during the 1970's and branched out into commercial fire and security services in 2001. Other acquisitions include aircraft and rocket engine manufacturer Pratt & Whitney, Hamilton Sundstrand, and the commercial and military helicopter manufacturer Sikorsky Aircraft Corporation. A major defense contractor for the U.S. government, United Technologies produces the UH-60 Black Hawk helicopter as well as other military aircraft and missile systems.

Valero Energy Corporation

Oil refining company and retail gas supplier, founded in 1980

San Antonio, Texas-based Valero is a *Fortune* 100 company with more than $90 billion in annual revenues. The largest refining company in the United States, Valero ranks as one of the country's largest gasoline retailers, with more than 5,000 stations in the United States, Canada, and the Caribbean. Founded in 1980, the company developed out of the Coastal States Gas Corporation and focused on natural gas production. Valero purchased its first refinery in 1981 in Corpus Christi, Texas, and began refining three years later. In the next two decades, it acquired refineries in Louisiana, New Jersey, and California. With the acquisition of Connecticut-based Premcor in 2005, Valero became the largest U.S. oil refining company, with a total daily output of nearly 3.3 million barrels. Its fast growth has flattened, but revenues remain high.

Verizon Communications

Telecommunications company, founded in 2000

Verizon descends from the Bell Atlantic Corporation, one of the Baby Bell companies created in 1983 following a governmental antitrust case against American Telegraph and Telephone (AT&T). The company became Verizon in 2000 with the acquisition of GTE in one of the largest mergers in U.S. business history. Verizon built a nationwide network for its wireless telephone and broadband Internet technology. Although market share for its wireless services grew steadily, competition from AT&T as well as cable companies offering bundled Internet and home telephone services saw profits in household telephone services shrink. Verizon acquired MCI in 2006 and currently ranks as the second-largest telecommunications company in the United States, with nearly $100 billion in annual revenues.

Walgreen Company

Retail pharmacy, founded in 1901

Walgreen Company began as a neighborhood drugstore founded by Charles Walgreen, Sr., in Chicago in 1901. A combination of efficient service and savvy marketing quickly made the drugstore a success in Chicago's South Side, and the Walgreen Company opened four additional stores by 1915. The Great Depression did not seriously affect the company, which by that time had opened nearly six hundred stores in thirty-three states. The company became the first drugstore to advertise on the radio in 1931. Walgreen continued to expand during and after World War II, even opening a not-for-profit pharmacy in the Pentagon that earned a commendation from President Dwight D. Eisenhower. Expansion during the 1990's included an Internet- and satellite-based system linking all stores to track inventory and patient records. Walgreen opened its six thousandth store near New Orleans in 2007 and averages 425 new stores each year. In a bid to compete with rival CVS, Walgreen took steps in 2008 to enter the health care services market with Take Care centers at four hundred of its stores.

Wal-Mart*

International discount store chain, founded in 1962, which began as a small five-and-dime retailer and became the largest private employer in the world with annual revenues of nearly $400 billion.

Walt Disney Company

Media and entertainment company, founded in 1923

Founded in 1923 by Walt Disney and his brother Roy, the fledgling company was called the Disney Brothers Cartoon Studio and secured a contract for a series of live action and animated cartoons. The company became the Walt Disney Studio in 1926, and its progress over the next several decades was marked by innovations in animation and the creation of some of the most beloved characters in film and cartoon history. In addition to animated films, Disney branched out into live-action films with the creation of Touchstone Films in 1984 and the acquisition of Miramax in 1993. Michael Eisner took the helm in 1984 and presided over a period of rapid expansion. A failed hostile takeover attempt by Comcast in 2004 led to Eisner's ouster, but the company's diversification of services and a string of global hit films have created steady growth. Disney's eleven theme parks, network and cable channels, including ABC and ESPN, and its consistently popular theatrical releases have positioned the Walt Disney Company as one of the largest global corporations in the world.

Washington Mutual

Savings and loan association, founded in 1889

Washington Mutual was founded in 1889 as a building and loan company in the wake of a devastating fire that nearly destroyed the city of Seattle, Washington. Its amortized home loan, introduced in 1890, helped bolster Seattle's growing population and helped it rebuild after the fire. The company grew an impressive 68 percent through World War I. It financial strength allowed it to acquire other institutions that had lost stability with the advent of the Great Depression, beginning with the Continental Mutual Savings Bank in 1930. Washington Mutual was an early member of the first shared automated teller machine (ATM) network, called the Exchange, and helped introduce the first pay-by-phone program during the 1970's. In 1983, Washington Mutual became a capital stock savings bank and one of the largest financial services and consumer lending organizations in the United States. In 2008, Washington Mutual faced losses from a growing home mortgage crisis. In September, it failed and was merged into JPMorgan Chase.

Wells Fargo & Company

Financial services company, founded in 1852

Henry Wells and William George Fargo founded Wells Fargo during the midst of the gold rush in San Francisco, California, in 1852. They opened offices in mining camps and the new cities that sprouted up around the camps to purchase gold and provide banking services. During the 1860's, the company opened a stage coach line and began shipping express mail, goods, and financial transactions across the country. By the turn of the century, Wells Fargo had operations in six thousand locations and had built a reputation for quick, reliable services. Following the nationalization of all express transportation routes during World War I, Wells Fargo shifted focus to its banking services. Fueled by several mergers and acquisitions, it opened new branches across northern California during the 1960's and expanded statewide during the 1980's. Wells Fargo became the first major financial institution to offer Internet banking services in 1995. Norwest purchased the company in 1998 but kept the Wells Fargo name. The bank boasts nearly six thousand branches and 23 million customers.

Western Union*

Financial services and communications company, founded in 1851, which pioneered national and global communications through its telegraph services.

Whirlpool

Home appliance manufacturer, founded in 1911
Founded in 1911 as the Upton Machine Company by the Upton brothers, Whirlpool has become the largest producer of home appliances in the world. Its flagship product, a motor-driven wringer clothes washer, quickly became a best seller, and Upton machines were added to the Sears catalog under the brand name Allen in 1916. The company adopted the name Whirlpool in 1950 and sold its first top-loading washing machine that year. After acquiring RCA's line of cooking ranges, Whirlpool successfully marketed its RCA Whirlpool Miracle Kitchen in 1957 to television audiences across the United States. Annual revenues surpassed the $2 billion mark in 1978 as Whirlpool acquired several new companies in the United States and Europe. In 2006, the U.S. Justice Department approved Whirlpool's acquisition of the Maytag Corporation, making it the largest appliance maker in the world. The company markets its products under brand names including Whirlpool, Maytag, KitchenAid, and Amana in nearly every country in the world.

Whole Foods Market

Organic food retailer, founded in 1980
Founded in 1980 through a merger of Austin, Texas-based Safer Way Natural Foods and the Clarksville Natural Grocery, Whole Foods Market targeted a growing trend toward healthy and organically grown foods. The company nearly failed in 1981 when Austin was struck by a flood that destroyed the fledgling store's entire stock of products. With the help of investors and friends, the store reopened in less than a month. By 1988, Whole Foods had opened stores in Houston, Dallas, and New Orleans. It expanded to the West Coast in 1989. Expansion was stimulated by the company's acquisition of several other natural food chains across the United States. Whole Foods Market opened its first store in Canada in 2002, and two years later, it expanded to the United Kingdom with the purchase of the Fresh & Wild chain. The Federal Trade Commission filed a complaint against the company's acquisition of its principal rival Wild Oats Market in 2007, but the merger was ultimately approved. The company ranks consistently among the world's most socially conscious businesses, according to Harris International's annual corporate rankings, for its focus on organic foods and the measures it has taken toward environmentally sound practices.

Woolworth Company

Discount retail chain, founded in 1878
F. W. Woolworth's was one of the earliest five-and-dime stores, which sold goods at low, fixed prices that undercut larger competitors. The first store, opened in 1878 in Utica, New York, failed in its first year, but a second store in Pennsylvania thrived. Several new branches were opened by 1910. That year, owner Frank Woolworth initiated the construction of the Woolworth Building in New York City. Completed in 1913, it was the tallest building in the world until 1930 and served as the company's headquarters. Woolworth incorporated the company in 1911 and brought together several chains of stores, including friendly rivals, with which he had established collaborations. The company introduced lunch counters in many of its stores. One of them in Greensboro, North Carolina, became the site of a famous civil rights sit-in when a group of African Americans were refused service in 1960. The company expanded during the 1960's and 1970's, and Woolworth purchased Kinney Shoes and Foot Locker as independent subsidiaries. A failure to compete with larger discount chains and an increased focus on athletic goods led to a significant decline during the late 1980's. In 1997, Woolworth's closed its U.S. stores and adopted the name Venator. Two years later, the company left the Woolworth's Building and changed its name to Foot Locker.

Xerox Corporation

Global document management company, founded in 1906
Xerox began as a small photographic paper supplier called the Haloid Company in 1906. It licensed the new technology of electrophotography, developed by Chester Carlson, in 1947 and began a decade of research and development. The company changed its name to Haloid Xerox in 1958 and produced its first plain-paper copy machine, the Xerox 914, the following year. Xerox also created the first desktop photocopier in 1963 and the first laser printer in

1969. During the 1970's, the company founded a research and development center in Palo Alto, California, and developed several key computer components, such as the mouse and the graphical user interface (GUI). In 1973, the company produced a minicomputer called the Xerox Alto but saw no commercial sales potential. Apple bought the rights to the user interface and adapted it for use in its Apple Macintosh personal computer in 1984. During the 1990's, Xerox produced a number of digital office solutions incorporating photocopying and digital printing in a computer network environment and shifted its focus toward document management technology. The term "xerox" has become synonymous with the word "photocopy," and from its early roots as a paper supplier, the Xerox Corporation built a global document management firm with operations throughout North America, Europe, and Asia.

Yahoo!

Global Internet services company, founded in 1994

Jerry Yang and David Filo created the Yahoo! search engine while they were graduate school students in engineering at Stanford University. High traffic on the search engine led Yang and Filo to incorporate as Yahoo! in 1995, and the company expanded its services over the next four years to include Web mail, news, games, and other consumer services. The company was one of the few Internet start-ups to survive when the dot-com bubble burst in 2001. In the next few years, Yahoo! formed strategic partnerships with telecommunications companies to expand into broadband services and acquired several other search engines and Web technologies in the United States, Europe, and Asia. The growing popularity of its rival search engine Google and the advent of Google Mail, or G-Mail, curbed the growth of Yahoo! It had negotiated a potential merger with Microsoft for several years, but a friendly takeover bid in early 2008 was ultimately rejected. A second, unsolicited bid for purchase by Microsoft was also rejected later in the year, just as the company announced plans for a possible advertising collaboration with Google. Amid criticism from shareholders, Yang stepped down as chief executive officer in 2008.

Philip Bader

Federal Government Agencies and Commissions

Agencies marked with asterisks are subjects of full essays in the main text.

FEDERAL CABINET-LEVEL DEPARTMENTS

Agriculture (USDA)*

Established: 1862; became a cabinet-level department in 1889

With more than 100,000 employees and an annual budget of almost $100 billion, the U.S. Department of Agriculture is one of the largest cabinet offices in the federal government. It offers a wide range of research and subsidy programs that benefit both food-processing and agribusiness corporations. Although the department continues to assist small family farms, its greatest assistance is given to larger enterprises.

Commerce (DOC)*

Established: 1903 as Commerce and Labor; became Commerce in 1913

The U.S. Department of Commerce was originally established as the Department of Commerce and Labor, but within a decade of its creation, workers felt that their interests could not be adequately represented by the department because of its strong business focus. With a budget of less than $10 billion and a workforce of about 36,000 employees, the main focus of the modern Commerce Department is research and educational assistance. One of the department's subdivisions is the Patent and Trademark Office, which was originally part of the Department of State, although its functions were more consistent with those of the Commerce Department.

Defense (DOD)

Established: 1947

In both manpower and budget, the U.S. Department of Defense is easily the largest of all cabinet-level departments, as it oversees the U.S. Army, U.S. Navy and Marines, and U.S. Air Force. The department was created after World War II by combining the War (Army) and Navy Departments under a single unified command. The Air Force was later separated from the Army. Also included are a number of intelligence-gathering agencies. Obviously, with personnel numbering between 2 million and 3 million people, the department must purchase a great deal of services and material to perform its duties. These purchases offer a tremendous opportunity for a wide range of businesses.

Education (ED)*

Established: 1867; became cabinet-level department in 1979

The U.S. Department of Education became an agency in 1867 but underwent many changes before gaining cabinet-level status until 1979. It is the smallest of all cabinet-level departments, having only about 6,000 employees. Because most elementary and secondary schools and many colleges are the responsibility of state and local governments, the Department of Education is primarily involved in research. The chief business connection of the Education Department is in the demand it creates for books and other educational materials.

Energy (DOE)*

Established: 1977

The Organization of Petroleum Exporting Countries (OPEC) oil embargo of the 1970's brought widespread public attention to the fact that the United States was no longer self-sufficient in petroleum. The federal government responded by creating a new cabinet-level department to develop an energy policy. In addition to its research function, the U.S. Department of Energy provides regulation of the nuclear energy industry and controls the Strategic Petroleum Reserve. Its main business constituency is the oil industry.

Health and Human Services (HHS)

Established: 1953 as Health, Education, and Welfare; became Health and Human Services in 1980

The U.S. Department of Health and Human Services is principally the old Department of Health, Education, and Welfare minus the education function, which was transferred to the Department of Education in 1979. This department has a mandatory budget of almost $600 billion, part of which goes to entitlements, as one of its subdivisions is the

Centers for Medicare and Medicaid Services. Its discretionary budget of $70 billion is spent on oversight of health and human services functions, including the Head Start Program, which some think should be under the Education Department. Medical and health industries are its primary business constituencies.

Homeland Security (DHS)*
Established: 2002

In the wake of the terrorist attacks of September 11, 2001, the concern over national security and public safety led to the establishment of the U.S. Department of Homeland Security, a new omnibus department that placed a wide variety of intelligence functions under one roof. The belief was that the intelligence agencies had failed to protect the public because they were in various departments and therefore found it difficult to coordinate their actions. In addition to intelligence gathering, certain public safety functions were judged to be more effective if placed under a single department. Although no additional terrorist attacks occurred on American soil after 2001, it remains to be seen whether the establishment of this cabinet-level department actually provided enhanced security. The department has more than 200,000 employees and a budget of more than $45 billion. A wide variety of businesses that provide security materials and services are the principal business constituencies of this department.

Housing and Urban Development (HUD)*
Established: 1965

As originally envisioned by President Lyndon B. Johnson, the U.S. Department of Housing and Urban Development would have had a major role in restructuring all American cities. As enthusiasm for Johnson's Great Society faded, the urban-development function atrophied, and the department focused almost entirely on providing housing all across the United States. The mortgage lending, real estate, and construction industries are the principal constituencies of this department. As a result of the lack of supervision from a number of presidential administrations, this department has developed a reputation for widespread corruption and contributed to the mortgage crisis of the early twenty-first century.

Interior (DOI)*
Established: 1849

The U.S. Department of the Interior was created after the Mexican War, when it was recognized that the existing federal agencies were inadequate to control such a large block of territory as had been taken from Mexico in the war. At the same time, some functions, which had been scattered under the State, War, and Treasury Departments, were combined in this new department. Over the coming decades, other functions were deposited in the department, giving it the nickname of the "Department of Everything Else." Oversight of such a diverse agency has been difficult, resulting in a number of scandals that have involved the many constituencies dependent on this agency.

Justice (DOJ)*
Established: 1870

Although the attorney general was a cabinet officer in the administration of President George Washington, the U.S. Department of Justice was not created until almost eighty years later. Because the department has an obvious regulatory function, any business involved in interstate commerce can come within its purview if the enterprise engages in illegal activities. The department does not have any obvious business constituencies.

Labor (DOL)*
Established: 1884; became a cabinet-level department in 1913

The U.S. Department of Labor was created out of the old Department of Commerce and Labor in 1913 to give labor greater national recognition. With a budget of $60 billion and a workforce of fewer than 18,000 employees, the Department of Labor is one of the smaller cabinet-level departments. Its main constituency is labor unions, although it has a limited regulatory function over all businesses with employees.

State
Established: 1789

The U.S. Department of State is the main foreign-policy division of the federal government. Its business constituencies are those with extensive foreign connections. Through its embassies and consulates across the globe, the State Department has long been involved in fostering business interests throughout the world.

Transportation (DOT)*

Established: 1966

The U.S. Department of Transportation was created to follow some thirty different transportation-related agencies and programs scattered across the federal government. This omnibus department is heavily involved in all forms of travel, whether by air, water, or land. It has both regulatory and financial assistance programs that aid its business constituencies in the highway construction, aviation, maritime, and land shipping industries.

Treasury*

Established: 1789

The U.S. Department of the Treasury was one of the original cabinet departments established in 1789. In addition to raising revenue for the federal government, the Treasury Department has important economic functions in maintaining the solvency of the nation and the integrity of its currency. As such, it is vitally important to all business interests in the United States.

Veterans Affairs (VA)

Established: 1930 as Veterans Administration; became Veterans Affairs in 1988

The U.S. Department of Veterans Affairs was elevated to cabinet-level status in 1988 in an attempt to increase the recognition given to veterans in the federal system. There are no obvious business constituencies for this department, but this department obviously assists the entire business community by providing medical and other welfare benefits to veterans.

OTHER FEDERAL AGENCIES

Amtrak. *See* National Railroad Passenger Corporation

Broadcasting Board of Governors (BBG)

Established: 1994

The Broadcasting Board of Governors is an independent federal agency that supports American business in international trade. It was created to take over the functions of Voice of America and other related government international nonmilitary broadcasting ventures. The International Broadcasting Bureau, which is the administrative vehicle for this agency, supports the day-to-day functioning of Voice of America and Voice of Cuba Broadcasting.

Chemical Safety and Hazard Investigation Board, U.S. (CSB)

Established: 1998

The U.S. Chemical Safety and Hazard Investigation Board (also known as the Chemical Safety Board) is the federal agency charged with investigating chemical safety and hazard accidents at fixed industrial facilities. Although it does not investigate chemical accidents that occur in transportation, it does seek to find the root causes of accidents to better prevent them in the future.

Commodity Futures Trading Commission, U.S. (CFTC)

Established: 1974

The U.S. Commodity Futures Trading Commission replaced the Commodity Exchange Authority. It is in charge of a comprehensive regulatory system to fight against fraud, manipulation, and abusive practices that may be involved in the sale of commodity and financial futures and options. It seeks to foster transparent, competitive, and financially sound options and futures markets.

Consumer Product Safety Commission, U.S. (CPSC)

Established: 1972

The U.S. Consumer Product Safety Commission was created as an independent agency to help guard against "unreasonable risks" of injuries from consumer products. Any American industry that manufactures consumer products is potentially under regulation from this independent agency. This agency is perhaps best known for publicly announcing recalls of dangerous products as they become known. It maintains a hotline on which consumers may call to complain about the safety of products. The commission also maintains a list of important safety precautions that have to be included on consumer products, especially those used by children.

Environmental Protection Agency, U.S. (EPA)*

Established: 1970

The U.S. Environmental Protection Agency was created by President Richard M. Nixon to safeguard public health and protect the natural environment. Although the agency is not a cabinet-level department, the administrator of the agency typically is a member of the president's cabinet. With a budget of more than $7 billion and more than 17,000 employees, the agency regulates a wide range of manufacturing industries that might have an adverse effect on the environment.

Equal Employment Opportunity Commission, U.S. (EEOC)*
Established: 1964

The U.S. Equal Employment Opportunity Commission is devoted to ending workplace discrimination based on an individual's color, race, national origin, sex, religion, age, or disability. In principle, any business with more than a few employees is subject to regulation by this commission. As a practical matter, the commission has a very restricted budget and uses a very narrow definition of discrimination, so that many regard the commission as not very effective in achieving its goal.

Export-Import Bank of the United States (Ex-Im Bank)*
Established: 1934

Established by executive order in 1934, the Export-Import Bank of the United States became an independent federal agency in 1945. Its purpose is to provide credit for purchases that would not take place if the bank did not provide credit. It does not compete with private lenders because it deals only with transactions that could not be financed in any other way. It is critically important to those American businesses that are involved in exporting and importing goods.

Farm Credit Administration (FCA)*
Established: 1933

The Farm Credit Administration regulates the banks, cooperatives, and associations in the Farm Credit System. These are borrower-owned financial institutions that provide credit to farmers, ranchers, and rural utility cooperatives and that enable participants to obtain lower interest rates than those available from regional and national banks. The administration was established in 1933 and newly authorized by the Farm Credit Act of 1971, as amended.

Federal Communications Commission (FCC)*
Established: 1934

The Federal Communications Commission regulates all interstate telecommunications, whether by wire, satellite, cable, or radio, as well as all international communications that start or end in the United States. The commission is best known for its regulation of radio and television broadcasting, the industries most closely connected with this agency.

Federal Deposit Insurance Corporation (FDIC)*
Established: 1933

The Federal Deposit Insurance Corporation is generally seen as the most widely accepted New Deal reform of the presidency of Franklin D. Roosevelt. Liberals and conservatives agree that this agency has been successful in preventing runs on commercial banks in the United States. No depositor has lost any money in an insured account up to the limit of liability since the FDIC was created, and it has been a great boon to the banking industry.

Federal Emergency Management Agency (FEMA)*
Established: 1979

The Federal Emergency Management Agency, a branch of the Department of Homeland Security, was originally created in 1979 to coordinate responses to natural or human-caused disasters that were more than could be handled by state and local authorities. In most cases, a state governor must declare a state of emergency before the agency can go to work. If a disaster occurs on federal property, the agency can begin relief efforts immediately.

Federal Housing Finance Board (FHFB)
Established: 1989

The Federal Housing Finance Board is a financing agency created to replace the Federal Home Loan Bank Board that failed during the savings and loan crisis of the late 1980's. Although it is an independent agency of the federal government, it does not receive any direct taxpayer funds and is financed entirely by fees assessed on Federal Home Bank Loans. Its business constituency is any institution making home loans.

Federal Maritime Commission, U.S. (FMC)
Established: 1961

The Federal Maritime Commission is responsible for regulating oceanic transportation of foreign commerce. An independent federal agency, it regulates shipping lines, cruise ships, and other passenger ship lines, making sure that they have sufficient resources to pay compensation for personal injuries, and monitors international agencies in an attempt to protect American shipping from unfair competition.

Federal Mediation and Conciliation Service (FMCS)
Established: 1947
The Federal Mediation and Conciliation Service is an independent federal agency created to mediate labor disputes and other contract issues between corporations and workers within the United States.

Federal Mine Safety and Health Review Commission (FMSHRC)
Established: 1977
The Federal Mine Safety and Health Review Commission is an independent quasi-judicial agency of the federal government that adjudicates complaints filed against mine owners regarding the safety and health of workers. Regulations adjudicated by this commission are passed by the federal Mine Safety and Health Administration (MSHA) in the Department of Labor. The commission's principal business constituencies are mine owners and the members of the labor unions for mine workers.

Federal Reserve System (the Fed)*
Established: 1913
The Federal Reserve System was established in 1913 to act as a central banking system in the United States. Although some elements of a central banking system existed before 1913, the first full-fledged banking system was created in that year as a quasi-public entity. The members of the Federal Reserve System, the Federal Open Market Committee, and the twelve regional Federal Reserve banks act as fiscal agents for the United States Treasury. Publicly, the Federal Reserve System's Board of Governors sets the federal discount rate, or the interest rate on which the federal government lends money to its member banks all across the country. Raising the interest rate slows economic growth and prevents inflation, and lowering the rate stimulates economic growth and helps avoid business slowdowns and deflation. The tools of the Federal Reserve System are more effective in retarding inflation than they are in avoiding deflation.

Federal Retirement Thrift Investment Board (FRTIB)
Established: 1986
The Federal Retirement Thrift Investment Board is a small federal agency with only about 100 employees. It allows federal employees to supplement their retirement plans with tax-exempt savings.

Federal Trade Commission (FTC)*
Established: 1914
The Federal Trade Commission is an independent federal agency, designed to eliminate anticompetitive practices of monopolies and promote fair trade practices, that was created at the request of President Woodrow Wilson. Many of its functions have been taken over by other law-enforcement agencies, but it remains an important agency to its business constituency.

Food and Drug Administration (FDA)*
Established: 1906
The Food and Drug Administration is responsible for promoting the safety of food, drugs, dietary supplements, vaccines, biological medical products, blood products, medical devices, cosmetics, veterinary products, and radiation-emitting devices throughout the United States. It is housed in the U.S. Department of Health and Human Services. Any business producing or selling products within the purview of this administration is subject to regulation.

International Trade Commission, U.S. (ITC)
Established: 1916
The U.S. International Trade Commission began as the U.S. Tariff Commission and was renamed in 1974. It is a staff agency for the executive and legislative branches of the United States government. As an independent, nonpartisan, quasi-judicial agency, it seeks to determine the impact of imports on American industries and can take certain actions against unfair trade practices from abroad, such as dumping and patent, trademark, and copyright infringement.

Merit Systems Protection Board (MSPB)
Established: 1978
The Merit Systems Protection Board is a small independent agency that handles disputes between em-

ployees and the agencies of the federal government for which they work.

National Credit Union Administration (NCUA)
Established: 1934
The National Credit Union Administration began as the Bureau of Federal Credit Unions and was renamed when it became an independent federal agency in 1970. It charters, licenses, and regulates federal credit unions within the United States. Federal credit unions are its principal constituency.

National Labor Relations Board (NLRB)*
Established: 1935
The National Labor Relations Board is an independent regulatory agency that supervises relationships among labor unions and employers. It holds elections to determine if the employees of a particular company wish to join a union. As such, any business with employees is potentially subject to its jurisdiction.

National Mediation Board (NMB)
Established: 1934
The National Mediation Board was created to govern labor-management relations in the railroad and airline industries. It has functions similar to those of the National Labor Relations Board.

National Railroad Passenger Corporation (Amtrak)*
Established: 1971
The National Railroad Passenger Corporation is an intercity passenger railroad service best known as Amtrak. It was created to promote passenger rail service between cities in the United States and does not have jurisdiction over commuter rail service lines or the Northeast Corridor rail service, which are supervised by the U.S. Department of Transportation.

National Science Foundation (NSF)*
Established: 1950
The National Science Foundation supports non-medical research and education in the areas of science and engineering. Its principal constituencies are American colleges and universities, which receive approximately 20 percent of all federal basic research funding. The agency has about 1,700 employees and a budget of more than $6 billion.

National Transportation Safety Board (NTSB)
Established: 1967
The National Transportation Safety Board has the prime responsibility for investigating all major transportation disasters, whether on air, land, or water, but it does not investigate military or intelligence department accidents.

Nuclear Regulatory Commission (NRC)
Established: 1974
The Nuclear Regulatory Commission regulates all aspects of the peaceful uses of nuclear energy, including nuclear power plants and other research facilities that use nuclear materials.

Occupational Health and Safety Review Commission (OSHRC)
Established: 1971
The Occupational Health and Safety Review Commission is the principal independent federal agency that reviews the enforcement-action priorities and cases under the Occupational Safety and Health Act. The commission is a quasi-judicial arm of the Occupational Safety and Health Administration of the U.S. Department of Labor. Virtually any business is subject to its jurisdiction.

Overseas Private Investment Corporation (OPIC)
Established: 1971
The Overseas Private Investment Corporation assists businesses in investing overseas and promotes economic development in emerging markets. The agency receives no taxpayer money and charges market-based fees. It has accumulated as much as $4 billion in profits while assisting American corporations operating overseas.

Pension Benefit Guaranty Corporation (PBGC)
Established: 1974
The Pension Benefit Guaranty Corporation is funded entirely by fees from participating businesses and was established to promote voluntary, private, defined pension plans.

Postal Service, U.S. (USPS)*
Established: 1775
The U.S. Postal Service is the successor to the U.S. Post Office Department, which was a cabinet-level

department in the federal government. Congress decided that the Post Office Department was no longer important enough to be a cabinet-level agency and that the department was too inefficient. Congress decided to operate the Postal Service more like a private business and created a government corporation to take over the responsibility for delivering the mail in the United States.

Railroad Retirement Board (RRB)
Established: 1930's
The Railroad Retirement Board is an independent agency created during the 1930's to provide a social insurance program and retirement benefits to American railroad workers, who do not pay into Social Security or gain Social Security benefits.

Securities and Exchange Commission (SEC)*
Established: 1934
The Securities and Exchange Commission is the main independent regulatory agency of the U.S. government for enforcing the federal securities law and regulating the stock market and related securities industries. Created during the Great Depression, the commission enforces a series of securities regulations including the Sarbanes-Oxley Act of 2002.

Small Business Administration (SBA)*
Established: 1953
The Small Business Administration is an independent regulatory agency that assists small businesses. It also assists individual homeowners and small businesses to recover from economic and natural disasters.

Social Security Administration (SSA)
Established: 1935
The Social Security Board was created in 1935, and became part of the Federal Security Agency in 1939. It 1946 it was abolished and replaced by the Social Security Administration. It is an independent agency that administers Social Security programs, with a budget of $657 billion in fiscal year 2008.

Tennessee Valley Authority (TVA)*
Established: 1933
The Tennessee Valley Authority, a government corporation started during the Great Depression, was created to develop hydroelectric power in the Tennessee River Valley. In addition to hydroelectric power, the TVA also promoted the development of electric power from other sources and manages various enterprises, such as fertilizer plants, which use the power it generates. The TVA also has an environmental division and seeks to promote tourism in the southeastern United States and in areas under its jurisdiction.

Richard L. Wilson

Federal Laws

Laws marked with asterisks are subjects of full essays in the main text.

Age Discrimination in Employment Act (1967)

Forbade employers of twenty or more workers to fire or refuse to hire an individual forty to sixty-five years of age because of age, unless age was a bona fide qualification, and banned employment agencies from refusing to refer a job applicant because of age and from indulging in other discriminatory practices. The act was amended in 1978 to allow an employer to require workers to retire involuntarily at age seventy.

Agricultural Marketing Act (1929)

In response to falling crop prices, the act created the Federal Farm Board (FFB), with a revolving fund of $500 million. The FFB's two major duties were promoting the effective merchandising of agricultural commodities in interstate and foreign commerce and making agriculture economically equivalent to other industries. The FFB bought, sold, and stored agricultural surpluses, and lent money to farm cooperatives to strengthen them. However, the federal purchases served mostly to encourage farmers to raise larger crops to generate larger profits. In the end, the failing FFB had to sell its holdings at a loss of $200 million.

Agriculture Adjustment Act (1933)

Intended to provide emergency assistance to farmers during the Depression years as well as to support prices and provide assistance with farm mortgages, the act authorized the secretary of agriculture to fix marketing quotas for major farm products, to take surplus production off the market, and to offer producers of staple crops payments in return for voluntarily reducing the acreage devoted to raising such crops. The act created the Commodity Credit Corporation to undertake price-support activities for certain agricultural commodities. It also granted loans to farmers who agreed to sign production-control agreements. Certain production-control features of the act were later declared unconstitutional.

Airline Deregulation Act (1978)

Removed government control from commercial aviation and exposed the passenger airline industry to market forces. Since 1938, the Civil Aeronautics Board (CAB) had regulated all domestic air transport as a public utility, setting fares, routes, and schedules. The regulation gradually resulted in inefficiency and higher costs. The Federal Aviation Administration was directed to develop safety standards for commuter airlines, transfer remaining regulatory authority in the CAB to the U.S. Department of Transportation, and dissolve the board in 1985. The effects of deregulation included increased air travel due to generally lower airfares, the greater use of major airports by airline companies, and the transfer of shorter routes from major carriers to smaller, regional airline companies.

Americans with Disabilities Act (1990)

Modeled after the Civil Rights Act of 1964, the Rehabilitation Act of 1973, and the Education for All Handicapped Children Act of 1975, this act prohibited discrimination on the basis of disability in the areas of private employment, state and local governments, public accommodations, commercial facilities, transportation, and telecommunications. Qualified individuals with disabilities were protected in job application procedures, hiring, firing, advancement, compensation, job training, and other terms, conditions, and privileges of employment. An employer was required to make a reasonable accommodation to the known disability of a qualified applicant or employee if it would not impose an undue hardship on the operation of the business.

Antidumping Act (1974)

Prevented the sale of goods at a lower price than the sales price in the country in which the goods were made. The act allowed extra duties to be imposed on imported products if the U.S. Treasury found that they were sold at less than fair value, thereby harming domestic manufacturers of similar goods.

Architectural Barriers Act (1968)

Required that all new federal buildings and facilities constructed or altered with federal funds since 1968 be accessible to and usable by individuals with disabilities. The act also mandated that modifications be made to existing buildings and facilities to ensure that individuals with disabilities have equal access to any program or opportunity provided to employees or visitors. It recommended that the following officials work together to develop accessibility standards for their respective agencies: the administrator of general services and the secretaries of housing and urban development, defense, and health, education, and welfare. To ensure compliance with the standards, the act established the Architectural and Transportation Barriers Compliance Board (ATBCB) in accordance with section 502 of the Rehabilitation Act of 1973. The act also made it unlawful to design and construct covered buildings and facilities that did not meet the minimum design requirements of the Uniform Federal Accessibility Standards (UFAS), published in the Federal Register on August 7, 1984.

Ashurst-Sumners Act (1935)

Forbade shipping of prison-made goods into states that prohibited convict labor. The act also required that prison-made goods shipped into states that allowed convict labor have labels identifying the place of manufacture. The act was amended in 1979.

Bank Holding Company Act (1956)

Created in response to banks forming holding companies that owned both banking and nonbanking businesses, the act established standards for the formation of bank holding companies, which were defined as companies that controlled two or more banks. It limited the holding companies to such activities as banking, managing banks, and providing services to affiliated banks. The act prohibited holding companies from acquiring voting securities of certain companies that were not banks and prohibited bank holding companies in one state from acquiring banks in other states. It was amended in 1966, 1970, 1994, and 1998.

Bank Secrecy Act (1970)

Also known as the Currency and Foreign Transactions Reporting Act, Anti-Money Laundering Law

Required banks to keep records of their customers' transactions and report any daily financial dealings involving more than $10,000 to the U.S. Department of the Treasury, because these dealings might involve money laundering, tax evasion, or other criminal activities.

Banking Act (1935)

Amended the Glass-Steagall Act of 1933, the Federal Reserve Act of 1913, and other banking regulations to make these laws more specific. The act increased the maximum liability per depositor from $2,500 to $5,000 and authorized the Federal Deposit Insurance Corporation to assist in merging failing banks into ongoing banks or to engage in purchase and assumption transactions. The act renamed the Federal Reserve Board as the Board of Governors of the Federal Reserve system. The board was given authority to regulate the discount rates of the district banks, to vary required reserve ratios within prescribed limits, to impose credit controls, and to set margin requirements on the purchase of stocks and bonds. The act renamed the Federal Reserve's policy-making group as the Federal Open Market Committee and moved it to Washington, D.C. It also extended Regulation Q ceilings on interest rates to nonmember banks and prohibited nonmember banks from paying interest on demand deposits.

Bankruptcy Reform Act (1978)

The first complete overhaul of bankruptcy in seventy-five years, the act restructured old laws to permit a company to return to fiscal soundness. The act enabled business creditors, in certain instances, to file their own reorganization plans for a company and allowed them to keep more property after bankruptcy than they could under state laws. It also allowed small businesses to pay off their debts gradually under a procedure similar to a reorganization.

Bituminous Coal Act (1937)

Regulated the sale and distribution of bituminous coal in interstate commerce to eliminate unfair competition. The act also included rights of collective bargaining and price regulation.

Bland-Allison Act (1878)

Created in response to the five-year depression following the Panic of 1873, the act was meant to solve the liquidity problems brought on by the gold standard by providing for freer coinage of silver. The U.S. Treasury was required to buy $2-4 million worth of silver bullion monthly at market prices, and the silver was to be used to make coins at the ratio of 16:1 silver to gold. In reality the U.S. Treasury bought less than $2 million worth of silver and never circulated the silver dollars. The act was repealed by the Sherman Silver Purchase Act of 1890.

Budget Reconciliation Act
(Deficit Reduction Act; 1993)

Raised taxes retroactively so that the United States could sustain its economic growth and balance the budget by 1998. The act increased taxes only for the top 2 percent of taxpayers. It was credited as the major cause of the deficit reduction and eventual surpluses during the 1990's.

Chinese Exclusion Act (1882)

Prohibited Chinese laborers and mining workers from entering the United States for ten years, and excluded Chinese immigrants from U.S. citizenship. Repealed by the Magnuson Act of 1943, which permitted an annual quota of 105 Chinese immigrants.

Civil Rights Act* (1964)

Outlawed segregation in American schools and public places.

Clayton Antitrust Act* (1914)

Strengthened antitrust laws while protecting labor unions from its restrictions.

Clean Air Act (1990)

Aimed at reducing smog and air pollution that existed anywhere in the United States, was leaving the United States and headed for Mexico and Canada, or was entering the United States from those two countries. Through the Environmental Protection Agency, the U.S. government provided research, studies, engineering, and money to support clean air programs in the states. States with heavy air pollution were required to use oxygenated gasoline.

Coinage Act (1873)

Also known as the Crime of '73

Revised coinage laws, embraced the gold standard, and demonetized silver. After 1874, because the market value of silver was higher than the price paid by the U.S. Treasury, very little silver had come to the U.S. Mint. The act was a contributing factor in the subsequent depression and later was labeled the Crime of '73.

Commodity Exchange Act (1936)

Replaced the Grain Futures Act of 1922, established the Commodity Exchange Commission to regulate trading in the contract markets, and authorized the commission to prevent fraud and manipulation in commodities and set limitations in trading for the purpose of preventing excessive speculation. The act was the basis for the creation of the Commodity Futures Trading Commission in 1974 and the National Futures Association in 1982.

Communications Act (1934)

Combined and reorganized existing provisions of laws concerning radio and telephone service (the Radio Act of 1927 and the Mann-Elkins Act of 1919). The act replaced the Federal Radio Commission with the Federal Communications Commission (FCC) and transferred regulation of interstate telephone service from the Interstate Commerce Commission to the FCC. It was amended by the Telecommunications Act of 1996.

Comprehensive Employment and Training Act (1975)

One of the five major domestic programs called block grants, the act invested $55 billion in helping place disadvantaged, long-term unemployed or inefficiently employed people in jobs with a future. It was replaced by the Job Training Partnership Act of 1983.

Consumer Credit Protection Act (Truth-in-Lending Act; 1968)

The first major attempt to protect consumers from predatory credit practices, the act applied to loans made for personal, family, and household purposes. It required lenders to disclose the annual percentage rate and the total finance charge on a loan and to provide consumers with standardized information regarding terms of credit for the purpose of comparing the cost of borrowing among different lenders.

Consumer Product Safety Act (1972)

The first attempt to protect consumers from dangerous products, the act controlled the processing, manufacturing, and distribution of products that may cause unreasonable risk of personal injury. The act established the Consumer Safety Commission to develop safety standards, pursue recalls for dangerous products, and ban dangerous products with no feasible alternative.

Copeland Act (Copeland Anti-Kickback Act; 1934)

Made it illegal for employers or their agents to extract a payment as a condition of continued employment and prohibited them from using force, threats, or other means to secure the return of any part of a worker's wages as a condition of retaining the job.

Copyright Revision Act (1976)

A significant revision of the copyright laws of 1909, this act extended the length of copyright protection to the duration of the creator's life plus seventy years. It set standards for fair use and reproduction of copyrighted material and created a new system of compulsory licensing for cable television and jukeboxes. The act preempted state laws governing copyrighted materials that come within the scope of the act. It was amended in 1980 to include computer software and by the Copyright Extension Term Act of 1998.

Gold Standard Act (Currency Act; 1900)

Established gold as the sole legal-tender coinage, putting a halt to bimetallism. The act set the value of the U.S. dollar at $20.67 per troy ounce of gold. The U.S. Treasury was required to maintain a minimum gold reserve of $150 million and was authorized to issue bonds to protect the minimum when necessary.

Davis-Bacon Act (1931)

Protected local labor wage standards and fringe benefits on government contracts. The act required that wages be based on rates usually paid for the service in a particular geographic area. It applied to all contracts of more than $2,000 and was amended in 1935, 1940, and 1964.

Depository Institutions Deregulation and Monetary Control Act (1980)

Abolished the power of the Board of Governors of the Federal Reserve system to set the interest rates on savings accounts. The act allowed credit unions and savings and loans institutions to offer checking accounts, allowed banks to merge, and gave the Federal Reserve greater control over nonmember banks.

Electronic Fund Transfer Act (Regulation E; 1978)

Primarily a consumer protection measure, the act required financial institutions to inform new customers of the terms and conditions of electronic fund transfer services, and the type and availability of services and service charges. The act also required these institutions to disclose consumers' rights to receive documentation of transfers and to have errors corrected, their liabilities for unauthorized transfers, preauthorized transfer procedures, and the institutions' liabilities if they fail to make or stop transfers.

Embargo Acts* (1806-1813)

Created in response to British and French abuses of United States shipping during the Napoleonic Wars, the act was designed to prove U.S. neutrality by stopping trading with either country, causing a devastating economic downturn in the United States while having no noticeable effect on either of the belligerents.

Emergency Home Finance Act (1970)

Created the Federal Home Mortgage Corporation (Freddie Mac) under the Federal Home Loan Bank System to provide a secondary market for conventional loans as well as for Federal Housing Administration and Veterans Administration mortgages. The act extended from twenty to thirty years the period allowed for associations to accumulate the reserves required by the Federal Savings and Loans Insurance Corporation.

Emergency Price Controls Act (1942)

Created in response to inflationary pressures resulting from the transformation of a peacetime economy to wartime economy, the act established the Office of Price Administration to set up a universal, nationwide price regulatory system. Price controls also applied to apartment rentals in residential areas. However, items were bought and sold without the price controls in the black market.

Employment Retirement Income Security Act (1974)

Enforced by the Employee Benefits Security Administration in the U.S. Department of Labor, the act protected retirement benefits, especially for spouses, for the first time. Participants were provided with information about their benefit plans (features, funding, minimum standards for participation, vesting benefit accrual, and so on) and the right to sue for benefits and breaches of financial duty. Payment of certain benefits was also guaranteed through the Pension Benefit Guaranty Corporation.

Energy Independence and Security Act (CLEAN Energy Act; 2007)

Focused on measures of energy efficiency and energy savings, development of alternative energy, and automobile fuels.

Energy Policy Act (1992)

Administered by the U.S. Department of Energy, the act aimed at reducing dependence on imported petroleum; achieving energy efficiency for commercial buildings, utilities, and equipment; and developing alternative fuels, renewable energy technologies, and electric vehicles.

Energy Policy Act (2005)

Created in response to the growing energy problem, the act provided tax incentives and loan guarantees to develop various kinds of energy. It also amended the Uniform Time Act of 1966 for daylight saving time.

Energy Tax Act (1978)

Imposed excise taxes on gas guzzlers, changed excise taxes on motor fuels, eliminated excise taxes on re-refined lubricating oil, gave tax credits for energy saving in the home, and gave additional investment credits to encourage business energy conservation.

Equal Credit Opportunity Act (1975)

Required that credit be made available to individuals without regard to marital status or sex. The act applied to banks, financial companies, department stores, credit card issuers, and providers of business and consumer loans. Credit applicants were to be notified of the action taken on their applications within thirty days of applying for credit and were to be informed of the reason if credit was denied. The act was oriented more toward upholding civil rights than consumer protection.

Equal Pay Act (1963)

This act, which amended the Fair Labor Standards Act of 1938, aimed at abolishing wage differentials based on sex. It required that men and women doing the same work be paid equal wages, and it prohibited lowering pay for men to equalize rates. It acted as a wage equalizer between men and women for equal jobs and had the potential of acting as a price floor on the salaries of men or women for particular jobs.

Fair and Accurate Credit Transactions Act (2003)

Aimed at protecting consumers against identity theft by providing them with free reporting of their credit history. The act allowed consumers to receive one report yearly from each of the three major credit bureaus (Experian, Equifax, and Trans-Union).

Fair Credit Reporting Act (1970)

Passed as an amendment to the Consumer Credit Protection Act of 1968 to protect consumers against the dissemination of inaccurate information that might reduce their chances of obtaining credit, insurance, or employment. The act gave consumers access to their credit files at any credit bureau, required the deletion of obsolete information, and provided for the correction of inaccurate data. It presented consumers with detailed descriptions of their rights and stated that their complaints had to be filed within sixty days and resolved within ninety days after filing.

Fair Labor Standards Act (Federal Wage-Hour Act; 1938)

Established a national minimum wage, guaranteed time and a half for work beyond forty hours a week, and regulated employment of those less than eighteen years of age. Administered by the U.S. Department of Labor, the act applied to employees engaged in interstate commerce and employed by an enterprise engaged in commerce or in the production of goods for commerce unless the employer can claim an exemption from coverage. A 2007 amendment was designed to result in a minimum wage of $7.25 by the summer of 2009.

Family Entertainment and Copyright Act (2005)

Criminalized the use of recording equipment to make copies of films in motion picture theaters and prohibited making a commercially distributed film available on a computer network accessible to the public.

Federal Coal Mine Safety Act (1952)

Administered by the Bureau of Mines of the U.S. Department of the Interior, the act set hazard standards and provided for enforcement of safety regulations. It was extended to all underground mines in 1966.

Federal Corrupt Practices Act (1910)

Required for the first time the public disclosure of financial spending by single-state political parties and election committees in House general elections. An amendment to the act in 1911 applied this requirement to primary elections and Senate candidates and also for the first time required financial disclosure by candidates. An amendment in 1925 extended the requirement to multistate political parties and election committees. The act was repealed by the Federal Election Campaign Act of 1971.

Federal Credit Union Act (1934)

Created the Bureau of Federal Credit Unions to charter and oversee nonprofit, member-owned unions, where credit was to be made available and thrift promoted. The act has been amended periodically to keep it up to date.

Federal Hazardous Substances Act (1960)

Authorized the secretary of the Department of Health, Education, and Welfare to require warning labels for hazardous household substances (toxic, corrosive, irritant, and radioactive substances, among others). It was amended by the Child Protection Act of 1966 and the Child Protection and Toy Safety Act of 1969.

Federal Reserve Act (Glass-Owen Act; 1913)

Established a system of twelve federal banks called the Federal Reserve system to manage the nation's money supply. The Federal Reserve system was designed to act as the last-resort lender to banks, regulate the money supply, determine the legal reserves of member banks, oversee the U.S. Mint, effect transfer of funds, facilitate the payment system, provide for monetary policy, and control inflation and interest rates.

Financial Institutions Rescue, Recovery and Enforcement Act (1989)

Abolished the Federal Savings and Loan Insurance Corporation and placed deposit insurance for savings and loans under the Federal Deposit Insurance Corporation. The act also abolished the Federal Home Loan Bank Board and placed the regulation of thrifts under the Office of Thrift Supervision within the U.S. Department of the Treasury. It established the Federal Housing Finance Board as the regulator and supervisor of the twelve district Federal Home Loan Banks and established housing programs through funding from the Federal Home Loan Banks to member institutions for long-term, low- and moderate-income, owner-occupied and affordable rental housing. It also provided funds to help with the liquidation of failing savings and loans institutions. Surviving savings and loans institutions were made subject to higher deposit insurance premiums and tighter financial standards. The act created the Resolution Trust Corporation to help with closing or merging problematic savings and loans.

Flammable Fabrics Act (1953)

Banned the sale of certain items of clothing and household furnishings that present an unreasonable risk of significant property damage, personal injury, or death due to fire. The act provided flammability requirements for children's sleepwear up to size fourteen.

Food, Drug, and Cosmetics Act (Title XXI; 1938)

Created in response to the death of more than one hundred patients due to a sulfanilamide medication, the act replaced the Pure Food and Drug Act of 1906. The act stipulated that the Food and Drug Administration would oversee the safety of foods, drugs, and cosmetics. It has been amended many times.

Freedom of Information Act (1966)

Declared that, with certain exceptions, the public had the right to information collected and kept by federal government agencies. The act made these records more accessible to public scrutiny by preventing the agencies from withholding the information. It was amended in 1974 and 1976.

Fur Products Labeling Act (1951)

Required fur garments be labeled with the names of the animals killed. The act did not apply to garments made with a relatively small quantity or value of fur, defined by the Federal Trade Commission as anything worth $150 or less.

G.I. Bill* (Servicemen's Readjustment Act; 1944)

Provided subsidized education for soldiers who served in the armed forces in World War II.

Glass-Steagall Act (Banking Act; 1933)

Enacted after the Great Depression and widespread bank failures, the act divided the banking industry into two by separating commercial banking from investment banking, prohibited paying interest on demand deposits, established Regulation Q to set maximum interest rates on interest-bearing deposits, and established the Federal Deposit Insurance Corporation (FDIC). It prohibited commercial banks from underwriting corporate securities for fear of bank failures and prohibited investment banks from accepting deposits. The act also prohibited banks from sponsoring or distributing mutual fund shares. The primary goals of the FDIC were providing deposit insurance to bank customers and preventing individual bank failures from spreading to other banks.

Gold Purchase Act (1974)

Ended the ban on the private possession of gold imposed by the Gold Reserve Act of 1934. Created in response to the Great Depression, the 1934 act nationalized all gold by ordering the Federal Reserve banks to turn over their gold supply to the U.S. Treasury and devalued the gold dollar so that it would be worth no more than 60 percent of its existing weight.

Gold Reserve Act (1934)

Created in response to the effects of the Great Depression, the act authorized the president of the United States to devalue the dollar in terms of gold from 50 to 60 percent, authorized the U.S. Treasury to acquire all gold held by the Federal Reserve banks in return for gold certificates, and abolished coinage of gold and the redemption of money in gold.

Hart-Scott-Rodino Act (HSR Act; 1976)

An amendment to antitrust laws, this act required companies to notify the Federal Trade Commission and the assistant attorney general in the U.S. Department of Justice of their plans to buy more than $1.5 million worth or 15 percent of a company.

Highway Beautification Act (1985)

Passed as the result of the lack of participation in the Bonus Act of 1958, the act was the first to attempt to control billboards along highways. States were required to remove nonconforming signs along highways after a five-year period but had to pay their owners just compensation for removal costs. States that failed to do so were subject to losing 10 percent of their federal highway funds.

Homeowners' Loan Act (1933)

Established the Homeowners' Loan Corporation with $200 million from the Reconstruction Finance Corporation and authorized it to release up to $2 billion in tax-exempt bonds in exchange for mortgages. The act was credited as the force behind the rise of homeownership during the 1990's.

Homestead Act* (1862)

Gave federal land to farmers who would live on the land for a number of years and improve it, producing a very significant political and economic impact.

Immigration Reform and Control Act (Simpson-Mazzoli Act; 1986)

Granted amnesty to undocumented immigrants who had entered the United States before January 1, 1982, and had resided there continuously. Based on the theory that low prospects for employment would reduce illegal immigration, it criminalized the act of knowingly hiring or recruiting undocumented aliens.

Income Tax Law (1861)

The act, part of the Revenue Act of 1861, for the first time imposed a tax on personal income to help pay for the war effort in the U.S. Civil War. It was declared unconstitutional in 1895.

Independent Treasury Act (1840)

Created in response to the damage done by the destruction of the Second Bank of the United States under the administration of Andrew Jackson, the act aimed at setting up a treasury isolated from all other banks. After Jackson transferred government funds from the central bank to state banks, the funds were used as a basis for speculation. The subsequent drain on these banks led to their collapse in the Panic of 1837. The act was repealed in 1841.

Internal Revenue Code* (1953)

Reorganized and expanded the Internal Revenue Code of 1939, which was made up of previously existing U.S. tax statutes.

Federal-Aid Highway Act of 1956 (National Interstate and Defense Highways Act; 1956)

Primarily intended to build highways for national defense, the act created the largest domestic public works project in the history of the United States. Some $25 billion generated through new taxes on fuels, automobiles, and tires was used to construct 40,000 miles of interstate highways over a ten-year period. The money was handled in a highway trust fund that paid 90 percent of construction costs, while the remaining 10 percent was paid by the states. A result of the act was the direct subsidization of the suburban road infrastructure.

Interstate Commerce Act (1887)

Created in response to the abuse of economic power by the railroad industry, the act established the Interstate Commerce Commission (ICC) to regulate the practices, rates, and rules of railroads, and later of trucks engaged in interstate shipping. The ICC was abolished in 1995, and its remaining functions were transferred to the Surface Transportation Board.

Interstate Land Sales Full Disclosure Act (1968)

Required all large land sales promoters to furnish prospective buyers with a detailed and accurate report on the land and to spell out buyers' rights in the transactions.

Investment Advisers Act (1940)

Regulated investment advisers to protect the public from false presentation and dishonest investment tactics by identifying specific unlawful activities. The act required investment advisers to register with the Securities and Exchange Commission.

Job Training Partnership Act (1982)

Provided summer work for high-school students and training programs for low-income workers, Native Americans, migrant and seasonal workers, and veterans. The act turned over the management of training programs to the private sector and lessened the involvement of local governments. It was repealed by the Workforce Investment Act of 1998.

Kerr-Smith Tobacco Control Act (1934)

Imposed processing taxes on the tobacco industry, financed a quota system for growers, and provided penalties for marketing beyond individual quotas. The act was amended in 1935.

Landrum-Griffin Act (Labor-Management Reporting and Disclosure Act; 1959)

Designed to rid unions of corruption and to ensure democracy within unions by stipulating one person, one vote. The act contained procedures for union elections. It gave states authority over labor disputes, required workers to work on or handle goods made and shipped by nonunion labor, outlawed specific types of picketing, barred convicted felons from holding office within five years of their release from prison, and barred Communists from holding office.

Lanham Trademark Act (1947)

Governed trademarks and other symbols for identifying goods sold in interstate commerce. The act allowed a manufacturer to protect its brand or trademark by having it recorded on a government register in the U.S. Patent Office.

Lend-Lease Act* (1941)

Authorized the president of the United States to give material aid to the Allies during World War II, thereby helping to create massive new production for American industry and employment for labor.

Married Women's Property Rights Law (1848)

Gave married women some limited property rights for the first time. Before the law, women who married relinquished their right to control their property to their husbands and did not have the right to acquire any property.

Medicare and Medicaid* (1965)

Titles XVIII and XIX, respectively, of the Social Security Act of 1965. These amendments stipulated that Medicare would provide health insurance coverage to people age sixty-five and above, or who met other special criteria, and that Medicaid would provide medical and health-related services for people with limited income and resources.

Metric Conversion Act (1975)

Created the U.S. Metric Board for planning, coordination, and public education regarding implementation of the metric system. Under the act, the metric system was to gradually replace the U.S. customary system of weights and measures for trade and commerce, and federal agencies were directed to begin conversion. The Metric Board was abolished in 1982, and the act was amended in 1988, 1996, and 2004.

Monetary Control Act (1980)

Required that all banks and institutions that accepted deposits from the public make periodic reports to the Federal Reserve system. The act required the federal government to charge banks for services that it had provided free in the past, including check clearing, wire transfer of funds, and the use of automated clearinghouse facilities.

Morrill Land-Grant Act (1862)

Also known as the Land Grant College Act

Gave an eligible state 30,000 acres of federal land for each member of Congress the state had as of the 1860 census. The act stipulated that the land, or the proceeds from its sale, was to be used toward establishing and funding agricultural and industrial colleges. The federal government granted a total of 17.4 million acres, which, when sold, yielded a total endowment of $7.55 million.

Motor Vehicle Air Pollution Control Act (1965)

This amendment to the Clean Air Act of 1963 set the first federal vehicle emissions standards, beginning with the 1968 models. These standards were based on 1963 emissions levels and required reductions of 72 percent in hydrocarbons, 56 percent in carbon monoxide, and 100 percent in crankcase hydrocarbons.

National Bank Act (1863)

Designed to raise money for the federal government during the U.S. Civil War, the act established a system of federally chartered banks and the Office of the Comptroller of the Currency as a national security holding body. The act was meant to entice banks to buy federal bonds and to tax state bonds out of existence. It was replaced by the National Bank Act of 1964.

National Bankruptcy Act (1898)

Established the conditions and procedures for an institution or business to declare bankruptcy. The act was amended several times and was superseded by the Bankruptcy Reform Act of 1978.

National Housing Act (1934)

Created in response to bank foreclosures on homes during the Great Depression, the act established the Federal Savings and Loans Insurance Corporation to insure savings accounts at member savings associations up to $5,000. The act also established the Federal Housing Administration to insure home mortgages, low-income housing project loans, and home improvement loans made by private lenders.

National Industrial Recovery Act (1933)

Established the National Recovery Administration to stabilize the economy and the National Resources Planning Board to assist in planning the economy by providing recommendations and information. The act resulted in the imposition of pricing and production standards for all sorts of goods and services and was declared unconstitutional in 1935.

National Labor Relations Act (Wagner Act; 1935)

Created the National Labor Relations Board to investigate and decide on charges of unfair labor practices and to supervise elections in which workers could decide if they wanted to be represented by a union. The act protected the rights of most workers in the private sector but did not apply to those covered by the Railroad Labor Act, agricultural employees, domestic employees, supervisors, independent contractors, and some close relatives of individual employers. The act was unenforceable during its first few years because Congress did not have the authority to regulate interstate commerce. It was declared constitutional in 1937 and amended in 1947.

National Origins Act (1924)

Part of the Immigration Act of 1924, the act limited the number of immigrants who could be admitted from any country to 2 percent of the number of people from that country who were already living in the United States in 1890. Although the act prohibited East Asians and Asian Indians from immigrating and effectively curtailed immigration from southern and eastern Europe, it did not set limits on immigration from Latin America.

Natural Gas Policy Act (1978)

Authorized the Federal Energy Regulatory Commission to regulate intrastate and interstate natural gas production. The act set wellhead price ceilings and established rules for allocating the costs of certain types of high-cost gas to industrial customers. It allowed interstate pipeline companies to sell or transport gas on behalf of an intrastate pipeline company without prior approval.

Neutrality Act* (1794)

Forbade U.S. citizens from participating in military action against any country with which the United States was not at war.

Noise Control Act (Noise Pollution and Abatement Act; 1972)

Established noise standards for items made in the United States that produced excessive sound. The act authorized the Environmental Protection Agency (EPA) to administer programs on noise pollution, enforce noise pollution standards, and provide information about noise pollution litigation. It also authorized the EPA to work with the Federal Aviation Agency in creating noise control standards for aircraft.

Norris-LaGuardia Act (1932)

Gave employees the right to form unions without employer interference and prohibited the federal courts from issuing injunctions to prevent nonviolent labor disputes. It also prohibited so-called yellow-dog contracts, under which, as a condition of employment, workers agreed that they would not join a labor union.

North American Free Trade Agreement* (1994)

Eliminated the majority of tariffs on products traded among the United States, Mexico, and Canada, and gradually phased out other tariffs over a fifteen-year period.

Occupational Safety and Health Act* (1970)

Created the National Institute for Occupational Safety and Health and the Occupational Safety and Health Administration (OSHA), which assumed responsibility for developing and enforcing workplace safety and health regulations.

Pacific Railway Act (1862)

Granted the Union Pacific Railroad and the Central Pacific Railroad extensive land in the western United States and issued 6 percent, thirty-year U.S. government bonds for them for their construction of the transcontinental railroad. By 1971, the railroad companies had received more than 175 million acres of public land.

Pacific Telegraph Act (1866)

To facilitate commercial, postal, and military communication among the states, the act consolidated all the telegraph companies with Western Union and continued financing the construction of a transcontinental telegraph line.

Pregnancy Discrimination Act (1978)

This amendment to the sex discrimination section of the Civil Rights Act of 1964 required employers to provide the same benefits to pregnant women as they do for others with medical conditions. It applied to all areas of employment: hiring, pregnancy and maternity leave, health insurance, and fringe benefits.

Prescription Drug User Fee Act (1992)

Authorized the Food and Drug Administration (FDA) to collect fees from drug manufacturers when they submit a new drug approval application for use in the drug approval activities at the Center for Drug Evaluation and Research or the Center for Biologics Evaluation and Research. To continue collecting the fees, the act required the FDA to meet certain performance benchmarks in the review process.

Privacy Act (1974)

Designed to protect citizens from invasion of privacy by the federal government, the act allowed individuals to inspect information about themselves contained in federal agency files and to challenge, correct, or amend the material. It prohibited an agency from selling an individual's name or address for mailing list use, established a privacy protection study commission to provide Congress and the president information about problems related to privacy in the public and private sectors, and made it illegal for any federal, state, or local agency to deny an individual any benefit provided by law because of refusal to disclose his or her Social Security number to the agency. The act exempted the Central Intelligence Agency, the U.S. Census Bureau, congressional investigations, and federal law enforcement and statistical agencies. It was amended by the Computer Matching and Privacy Protection Act of 1988.

Pure Food and Drug Act (1906)

Initially concerned with the correct labeling of products, the act outlawed unsafe and, later, safe but inefficacious products. It was replaced by the more comprehensive Food, Drug, and Cosmetics Act of 1938.

Racketeer Influenced and Corrupt Organizations Act* (1970)

Provided for extended penalties for criminal acts performed as part of an ongoing criminal organization.

Railroad Retirement Act (1935)

Administered by the Railroad Retirement Board, the act set up railroad pension payments for retired employees and their families.

Railway Labor Act (1926)

Provided for mediation of labor disputes between railway companies and the unions that represented their employees. The act authorized the National Railroad Adjustment Board, established by the parties, to resolve disputes, and established the National Mediation Board to resolve disputes that the Adjustment Board could not. It also promoted voluntary arbitration to resolve any disputes that remained after going through both boards. The 1934 amendment to the act prohibited so-called yellow-dog contracts that forced workers to agree, as a condition of employment, that they would not join a labor union. The 1936 amendment extended the act to cover airline employees.

Real Estate Settlement Procedures Act (1974)

Created in response to kickback practices in the real estate settlement process, the act, which became effective in 1975, provided comprehensive guidelines for loan closing costs and settlement practices. It stipulated that the consumers receive specific disclosures at the time of application for a mortgage, before closing, and at and after settlement. It also prohibited kickbacks and referral fees on federally related mortgage loans. It was amended in 1976.

Reconstruction Finance Corporation Act (1932)

Established the Reconstruction Finance Corporation with a $2 billion fund to provide aid to state and local governments, and to make loans to banks, railroads, farm mortgage associations, and other businesses. The agency became bogged down in bureaucracy and failed to disburse many of its funds or to reverse the increase in unemployment. In 1933, President Franklin D. Roosevelt streamlined the agency's bureaucracy, increased its funding, and used it to help restore business prosperity.

Sarbanes-Oxley Act (Public Company Accounting Reform and Investor Act, Sox, and Sarbox; 2002)

Created in response to the accounting scandals at companies such as Enron, Tyco International, and WorldCom, which cost investors billions of dollars, the act established the Public Company Accounting Oversight Board and authorized it to oversee, regulate, inspect, and discipline accounting firms in their roles as auditors of public companies. The act also established new or enhanced standards for public company boards, management, and public accounting firms.

Sherman Antitrust Act* (1890)

Addressed single-firm conduct by providing a remedy against monopolies acquired or maintained through prohibited conduct. With regard to multiple-firm conduct, the act prohibited contracts restraining interstate trade or commerce.

Sherman Silver Purchase Act (1890)

Created in response to the growing complaints of farmers who were in debt because of droughts, the act was designed to boost the economy. The act required the U.S. government to buy 4.5 million ounces of silver bullion every month in addition to the $2-4 million worth of silver required by the Bland-Allison Act of 1878. It also stipulated that the U.S. Treasury make purchases with notes that could be redeemed for either silver or gold. When investors turned in their silver U.S. Treasury notes for gold dollars, the government's gold reserves were in danger of depletion. The act was repealed after the Panic of 1893.

Smith-Hughes National Vocational Education Act (1917)

Provided for basic vocational education by making federal grants to states to encourage training in agriculture, trade, and industry.

Social Security Act (Old-Age Pension Act; 1935)

The act, which originally created a retirement and benefits program for the primary worker, was amended to establish a national social program providing old age and survivor benefits; public assistance to the aged, the blind, and needy children; unemployment insurance; and disability benefits.

Staggers Rail Act (1980)

This act, the first designed to abolish railroad regulations from as far back as 1887, authorized the railway companies to set rail service rates and enter into long-term agreements with their customers. It made it easier for railroads to eliminate unprofitable routes.

Standard Container Act (1928)

Set standard sizes for baskets and containers for fruits and vegetables.

Surface Mining Control and Reclamation Act (1977)

Established the Office of Surface Mining within the U.S. Department of the Interior to regulate active coal mines and to reclaim abandoned mines.

Synthetic Liquid Fuels Act (1944)

Established the Bureau of Mines and provided it with $30 million to develop technologies for producing synthetic fuel from coal over a five-year period. The program was abolished after forty years of futile work and $8 billion in spending.

Taft-Hartley Act* (Labor-Management Relations Act; 1947)

Restricted the activities and power of labor unions and authorized states to pass right-to-work laws, making union membership an option rather than a requirement for employment.

Tariff of Abominations* (1828)

Aimed at protecting industry in the northern United States from competing European goods, the act increased the prices of European products by creating a tariff on these goods.

Tax Equity and Fiscal Responsibility Act (1982)

Designed to increase government revenues and intended to curtail perceived abuses and unintended benefits in the tax system, the act increased excise taxes on selected products and services (including tobacco and telephone service) and ensured better compliance with existing tax laws.

Toxic Substances Control Act (1976)

Required chemical manufacturers to give the Environmental Protection Agency (EPA) at least three months' notice before beginning commercial production of a new chemical or before marketing an existing chemical for a new use. It allowed manufacturers to proceed with their plans if no risks could be identified. The act focused primarily on polychlorinated biphenyl (PBC) products; later amendments applied to asbestos, lead, and radon.

Trade Expansion Act (1962)

Permitted the president to negotiate additional tariff reductions, eliminate or reduce tariffs on items of the European Common Market, reduce tariffs on the basis of reciprocal trade agreements, and grant technical and financial assistance to employers whose business is adversely affected by tariff reduction.

Underwood Tariff Act* (1913)

Reduced import tariff levels and created the federal income tax. The law was initially designed to lower tariffs, but its long-term significance was the manner in which it offset the loss of tariff revenue by creating the federal income tax on individuals.

Walsh-Healey Public Contracts Act (1936)

Set basic labor standards for work on government contracts exceeding $10,000 in value. Under the provisions of the act, administered by the U.S. Department of Labor, employees were to be paid at least the prevailing wage rate and paid time-and-a-half for work in excess of eight hours a day, or forty hours a week, whichever was greater. The act also set standards for child and convict labor and for safe working conditions.

Welfare and Pension Plans Disclosure Act (1958)

Covered all nongovernmental welfare and pension plans affecting more than twenty-five employees. The act required administrators to file annual reports to the secretary of labor describing annual financial statements.

Whiskey Tax* (Whiskey Act; 1791)

Created to pay down the states' debt from the Revolutionary War that the federal government had assumed, the act was imposed to advance and secure the power of the new government.

Anh Tran

Notable Court Decisions

All rulings are by the U.S. Supreme Court, except where otherwise noted.

Adair v. United States (1908)
Limited the extent to which the federal government could protect the rights of workers.

Adkins v. Children's Hospital (1923)
Struck down a minimum-wage law in a prime example of the Court's commitment to the freedom of contract doctrine and laissez-faire principles.

AFSCME v. Woodward (1969)
Eighth Circuit Court of Appeals case dealing with whether public employees had a right to join a labor union. The court held that they did and that employees could not be fired for joining a labor union.

Allgeyer v. Louisiana (1897)
Used the freedom of contract doctrine to overturn a state law as unconstitutional.

Atherton v. Federal Deposit Insurance Corp. (1997)
Held that federal law, if it set up only a general standard of gross negligence, did not eliminate state laws that set a higher standard but only those laws with a lower standard. Federal common law was held to not apply in this case because Congress found it inapplicable when setting up the law and federal interests must be threatened before state laws are trumped in the absence of specific federal law.

Auten v. United States National Bank (1899)
Held that a bank was not responsible when an official in another bank used normal banking practices to steal, an act that would not have been detected without extraordinary monitoring efforts.

Automobile Workers v. Johnson Controls (1991)
Held that companies cannot use sex-based qualifications in a workplace to protect a fetus unless those qualifications are part of a bona fide occupational requirement. Mere possible protection of the fetus is not enough.

Bailey v. Drexel Furniture Co. (1922)
Held that Congress could not use its taxing power to impose regulations on production, which were powers reserved to the states by the Tenth Amendment.

Bank of the United States v. Deveaux (1809)
Dealt with whether a corporation (the Bank of the United States) could sue in federal court under diversity of citizenship jurisdiction. The Court held that a corporation was a citizen for the purpose of diversity jurisdiction, but the location of its citizenship depended on the citizenship of its shareholders.

Barnett Bank of Marion County v. Nelson (1996)
Held that banks were to be able to sell insurance despite a local law prohibiting banks from doing so. A federal law had specifically allowed banks to sell insurance, and the Court held that this law preempted the state ban.

Beasley v. Food Fair (1974)
Held that the federal National Labor Relations Act trumped state law in the area of supervisors. Even though federal law was applied, the company was still allowed to fire the supervisors.

Briggs v. Spaulding (1891)
Dealt with the level of supervision needed by a board of directors of a company. It held that directors were responsible for exercising a normal level of care, but that directors did not ensure the performance of those below them. It also held that unforeseeable risks and dangers that directors had no chance to see because of circumstances were not the fault of the directors.

Berman v. Parker (1954)
Dealt with the exact meaning of the Fifth Amendment's takings (eminent domain) clause. The Court held that private property could be taken for a public purpose, not just for public use, under the takings clause of the Fifth Amendment.

Boys Market, Inc. v. Retail Clerks' Local 770 (1970)
Held that courts could issue injunctions against sit-down strikes, despite federal anti-injunction laws.

Notable Court Decisions   1045

Carter v. Carter Coal Co. (1936)

Overturned a 1935 coal act that set up local boards to regulate coal prices and to help workers negotiate wages and hours. The Court held that only the states had the right to regulate coal mining.

Champion v. Ames (1903)

Upheld a federal statute that prohibited the transportation of lottery tickets in interstate commerce, thereby defining commerce broadly and authorizing the development of a federal police power.

Charles River Bridge v. Warren Bridge (1837)

Held that only clear and explicit terms of contracts were legally binding. The Court's narrow interpretation of the charter granted to the Charles River Bridge Company increased the power of state legislatures to regulate private corporations.

Chicago, Burlington, and Quincy Railroad Co. v. Chicago (1897)

Held that the due process clause of the Fourteenth Amendment applied to the states and that, therefore, a state needed to compensate a railroad adequately when it seized the railroad's assets.

Chicago, Milwaukee, and St. Paul Railroad Co. v. Minnesota (1890)

Held that the courts had the power to review utility rates and incorporated part of the due process clause of the Fourteenth Amendment and applied it to the states.

City Ladue v. Gilleo (1994)

Held that a city could not ban all yard and window signs, as this would violate the First Amendment.

Clement National Bank v. Vermont (1913)

Held that states could tax deposits in banks and that this taxation did not violate federal law, which prohibited discrimination against interstate banks. The ruling also stipulated that banks could also be ordered or allowed to collect the taxes.

Colorado National Bank v. Bedford (1940)

Held that a state tax on the use of safety deposit boxes was allowable and that the banks could collect the taxes.

Cooke v. United States (1875)

Held that when the federal government is a party to a commercial transaction, it incurs all the responsibilities of a private person in the same circumstances.

Daly's Lessee v. James (1823)

Held that the terms of a will need to be carefully followed and that failure to act within the time limits specified by the will makes the actions improper.

Dartmouth College v. Woodward (1819)

In a ruling deciding that a state charter of a private institution was protected by the contracts clause of the U.S. Constitution, the Court enhanced protection of corporate property and contracts in general.

Davis v. Elmira Savings Bank (1896)

Held that federal law trumped state law when a bank became insolvent, thereby changing how banks were regulated.

DeLaval Steam Turbine Co. v. United States (1931)

Dealt with government contracts that were canceled on the eve of World War I. It held that the government must pay the value of the contract, not the value plus whatever profit was to be made. Eminent domain allowed the government to cancel the contracts.

Dolan v. City of Tigard (1994)

Held that the government may not attach conditions to building permits that result in the taking of private property without just compensation, in violation of the Fifth Amendment.

Duplex Printing Co. v. Deering (1921)

Held that injunctions against organized labor were still allowed, in spite of clear language seeming to say the opposite in the Clayton Act of 1914. The Court held that "illegal" activities on the part of the union removed it from the protection of the Clayton Act.

Erie Railroad v. Tompkins (1938)

Held that federal courts cannot create a common law, or judge-made law, when dealing with diversity cases (in which the parties are from different states). Thus, in cases that arise under state law and are argued in federal court because the plaintiffs are of two different states, the court follows the law of the state that has jurisdiction rather than a law created by the federal court.

Farmers' and Mechanics' National Bank v. Dearing (1875)

Held that state laws about interest, but not those about usury, could still apply to banks chartered nationally. Thus, federal law did not wholly exempt banks from state laws.

Federal Crop Insurance Corp. v. Merrill (1947)

Held that the published regulations were binding, regardless of whether the insurance agent was verbally informed of conditions violating those regulations. In short, if the agent exceeded the authority granted in making a contract, the government did not have to honor it.

Federal Deposit Insurance Corp. v. Meyer (1994)

Held that the Federal Deposit Insurance Corporation could be sued and was not covered by sovereign immunity. However, actions could not be implied, especially when suits for direct actions are available.

First National Bank v. City of Hartford (1927)

Held that state laws cannot tax shares of national banks at a higher rate than the rate at which they tax local bank shares. The purpose of the legislation in question was held to be irrelevant.

First National Bank v. Lanier (1870)

Upheld a policy of preventing one bank from loaning its shares to another bank. This policy was put in place by the National Banking Act and helped banks be solvent.

First National Bank v. Missouri (1924)

Held that nationally chartered banks were still subject to state banking laws, as long as those laws did not conflict with specific federal laws. Specifically, it held that controls on branches were valid state laws.

First National Bank v. National Exchange Bank (1875)

Held that banks were generally not allowed to buy and sell stocks, but they could buy stocks in a general commercial transaction in the hope of reselling them and losing less than they would have earlier in the transaction.

First National Bank of Logan v. Walker Bank and Trust Co. (1966)

Held that state law governing how and when bank branches could be established is also binding on nationally chartered banks. In this area, state-chartered and federally chartered banks were judged to be equal.

Fletcher v. Peck (1810)

Enhanced protection for businesses from legislative interference for vested rights in private property through a broad interpretation of the contracts clause. Also held a state law to be unconstitutional.

Franklin National Bank v. New York (1954)

Held that regulations banning banks from using the term "savings" in their name were unconstitutional. The decision stated that as savings was a part of banking business, banks could use that term in their names and advertising.

Garcia v. San Antonio Metropolitan Transit Authority (1985)

Using the commerce clause, removed almost all limitations on Congress's power to regulate the states and held that the Fair Labor Standards Act could be imposed on municipalities.

Gibbons v. Ogden (1824)

Supported the federal license of a steamboat operator over a state monopoly license holder, thus expanding federal control through the commerce clause.

Gold Clause Cases (1935)

Upheld the right of Congress to set monetary policy even if it appeared that contracts calling for payment in gold would be negated by devalued money repayment.

Griggs v. Duke Power Co. (1971)

Interpreted Title VII of the 1964 Civil Rights Act to mean that if employment practices and tests have an adverse effect on minorities or women, employers are required to show that the tests and practices are necessary for the job.

Hadacheck v. Sebastian (1915)

Held that the state could, by virtue of its police power, declare something to be a nuisance and could ban a business previously held to be acceptable. It also held that the state could ban a business in one part of the city and not another and not run afoul of the equal protection clause of the Fourteenth Amendment.

Hague v. Congress of Industrial Organizations (1939)

Struck down an ordinance that prohibited meeting without a permit and distributing literature. That ordinance had been used against the Congress of Industrial Organizations, an umbrella labor organization. The individual members' rights, including freedom of speech and assembly, not those of the organization, were held to have been violated.

Hammer v. Dagenhart (1918)

While striking down federal restrictions on child labor, held that Congress could regulate only interstate commerce, not the manufacturing of goods destined for such commerce.

Hawaii Housing Authority v. Midkiff (1984)

Dealt with when a court could issue a stay and when it could recall that stay of its original order. The ruling gives relatively broad authority, particularly when that authority maintains the status quo during an appeal.

Heart of Atlanta Motel Inc. v. United States (1964)

Dealt with the 1964 Civil Rights Act, which declared that there should be equal accommodations in motels, restaurants, and other public places regardless of race and which also barred discrimination on the basis of race in employment. The Court upheld the public accommodations sections of the 1964 act and enjoined an Atlanta motel from refusing to serve African Americans.

Helvering v. Davis (1937)

Affirmed the constitutionality of the Social Security Act of 1935, adding a tax for business to pay.

Hoffman Plastic Compounds v. National Labor Relations Board (2002)

Held that illegal immigrants are not entitled to the protections of the National Labor Relations Board. Companies can still be penalized for the National Labor Relations Board violations, but the undocumented workers cannot be awarded back pay or any other benefits.

Holden v. Hardy (1898)

Recognized that a state, under its police power, could place some restrictions on freedom of contract.

Home Building and Loan Association v. Blaisdell (1934)

Dealt with a Great Depression-era law that increased the amount of time a person had to repay a loan. The companies argued that this law impaired a contract, which states are not allowed to do, but the Court held that this was allowable as states need to protect the people and the general welfare, rather than businesses.

Hunt v. Washington State Apple Advertising Commission (1977)

Struck down a North Carolina law requiring the use of only national apple grades, rather than also allowing state apple grades that exceed the national standards. This move gave local growers advantages and gained the consumer little, and so was struck down by the court as discriminatory.

In re Debs (1895)

Dealt with an injunction issued against Eugene V. Debs, leader of the American Railway Union, who led a strike against the Pullman Palace Car Company. The injunction ordered Debs to cease the strike, and when he refused, he was imprisoned. The Court upheld the injunction, issued theoretically because the U.S. mail was on the same trains as the Pullman cars that Debs's union refused to handle.

Investment Co. Institute v. Camp (1971)

Upheld a law banning a bank from being involved in the investment fund industry, even though the involvement had been approved by a government official.

Jenkins v. Collard (1892)

Dealt with the legal force of a public proclamation and held that courts had to listen to the proclamations of the president as well as pay attention to the acts signed. This increased regulations, or possible regulations, over corporations.

Johnson v. M'Intosh (1823)

Held that Native Americans could sell their land to only the federal government and that Native Americans did not have traditional ownership rights to the land, as they did not view land rights in the same way as Europeans did.

Johnson v. Santa Clara County (1987)

Upheld a county's adoption of a sex-based affirmative action program to remedy past policies that had resulted in the concentration of women in lower-paying jobs. No quotas were used, but sex was taken into account when two applicants ranked close to each other applied for the same job.

Katzenbach v. McClung (1964)

Upheld regulations ordering an end to racial discrimination in restaurants. Although the restaurant involved was small and privately owned, it served interstate travelers and obtained foodstuffs out of state. Therefore, the Court held that the commerce clause prohibited the restaurant from discriminating against minorities.

Kelo v. City of New London (2005)

Held that a state could take private land through the eminent domain power, even where that land was taken for a private company's use, as long as the private development benefited the general public and as long as the state had not specifically banned such a seizing.

Keystone Bituminous Coal Association v. DeBenedictis (1987)

Held that a regulation limiting coal mining and forcing coal mines to leave a certain amount of coal under a structure was legal. The Court held that the regulation did not destroy the mineral value of the land and so was not a taking (use of eminent domain), which would have been illegal without compensation under the Fifth Amendment.

Kidd v. Pearson (1888)

Created a distinction between manufacturing and commerce that survived many years but was later invalidated.

Lauf v. E. G. Shinner (1938)

Held that courts were allowed to issue injunctions against unfair unions and employers, but they must limit those injunctions to only illegal activities and must first make findings of fact.

Legal Tender Cases (1870, 1871)

Clearly established the right of the U.S. government to pay its debts in paper money.

Leisy v. Hardin (1890)

Held that the federal government, not the states, had the right to regulate alcohol placed into interstate commerce and that an individual state could not ban the sale of alcohol in one state when the item was manufactured in another. This ruling was made moot by the passage of the Eighteenth Amendment.

Lewis v. BT Investment Managers (1980)

Held that a law banning all out-of-state chartered banks from owning investment companies and another law allowing local banks to own investment companies were not legal, as they served to burden interstate commerce, which is unconstitutional.

Linmark Associates Inc. v. Willingboro (1977)

Held that an ordinance banning "for sale" signs within a town was unconstitutional as it was a content-related ban, which is generally prohibited, and that even though it affected commercial speech, commercial speech still had some First Amendment rights.

Lochner v. New York (1905)

Most famous case in which the Court used the doctrine of substantive due process to overturn a statute regulating labor conditions.

Loewe v. Lawlor (1908)

Also known as Danbury Hatters' case, held that a boycott against a manufacturer of hats, initiated in an attempt to force unionization, was an illegal restraint of trade.

Loretto v. Teleprompter Manhattan CATV Corp. (1982)

Held that when land is permanently occupied by the government, it is a taking (under eminent domain), regardless of the importance of the function achieved.

Lucas v. South Carolina Coastal Council (1992)

Held that when land-use and environmental regulations deprive property owners of the total value of their land, the owners have a takings clause claim unless the use is harmful or noxious.

McCray v. United States (1904)

Established that the federal tax power could be used to regulate commerce.

McCulloch v. Maryland (1819)

Ruled that Maryland could not tax the Bank of the United States and established the basic outlines of the relationship between the federal government and the states.

Maine v. Taylor (1986)

Narrow interpretation of the Constitution's commerce clause allowing a local regulation that affected commerce because it served a worthwhile local need that could not be served any other way.

Merchants Bank v. State Bank (1870)

Ruled that corporations were liable for the actions of their employees, even if the actions were not specifically authorized, when the actions taken were fairly similar to normal and authorized actions taken in the past. This ruling gave banks the power to certify checks.

Meritor Savings Bank v. Vinson (1986)

By deciding that sexual harassment is a form of gender discrimination, cleared the way for employees, usually women, to sue employers for sexual harassment under Title VII of the 1964 Civil Rights Act.

Meyer v. Holley (2003)

Ruled that the owner of a brokerage, absent a showing of responsibility or error, is not liable for the actions of one of the brokerage's employees. However, if that employee can be shown to have violated the Fair Housing Act, that broker would be liable and the brokerage itself might be liable.

Milk Wagon Drivers Union v. Meadowmoor Dairies; American Federation of Labor v. Swing (1941)

These two cases, decided the same day, were ruled on quite differently because of their notable differences. In the first case, acts of violence accompanied the picketing by milk wagon drivers, and the Court ruled that state courts could issue injunctions to stop picketing when violence occurs. In the case involving the American Federation of Labor, no violence occurred, and a picket line had been established, even though there was not a strike (or a union) at the affected company, and the Court disallowed the injunction against this strike.

Miller v. King (1912)

Held that national banks were not allowed to act as holders of land, but that they could perform usual and necessary acts in order to collect on debts.

Minnesota Rate Cases (1913)

Ruled that the Interstate Commerce Commission could regulate intrastate railroad rates that discriminated against interstate rates.

Morehead v. New York ex rel. Tipaldo (1936)

Unpopular decision that overturned 1930's minimum-wage legislation.

Mulford v. Smith (1939)

Used a broad interpretation of the commerce clause to uphold the constitutionality of the Agricultural Adjustment Act of 1938.

National Bank v. Commonwealth (1869)

Held that states were allowed to tax national banks and to collect the tax from the bank rather than individual shareholders as long as the tax imposed was not higher than it would be on a state bank similarly chartered.

National Labor Relations Board v. Building and Construction Trades Council of Delaware (1978)

This decision by the Third Circuit Court of Appeals held that unions cannot picket companies where union elections either have not been held or are not scheduled to be held.

National Labor Relations Board v. Fansteel Metallurgical Corp. (1939)

Held that the sit-down strike was generally not supported by the National Labor Relations Act and therefore was illegal.

National Labor Relations Board v. Jones & Laughlin Steel Corp. (1937)

In upholding the National Labor Relations Act, departed from its precedents of prohibiting governmental interference with freedom of contract and also allowed the government the right to regulate business elements, including manufacturing and some employment conditions.

National Labor Relations Board v. Yeshiva University (1980)

Held that professors at a private university are managerial employees and so are not eligible for unionization under the National Labor Relations Act.

National League of Cities v. Usery (1976)

Resurrected and expanded the concept of state sovereignty under the Tenth Amendment when it held that Congress had no authority to require state and local governments to pay their workers minimum wages.

NationsBank of North Carolina v. Variable Annuity Life Insurance Co. (1995)

Held that banks were able to sell life insurance annuities, increasing the range of services banks can perform (a move opposed by life insurance companies).

Nebbia v. New York (1934)

Reversing several Court precedents, held that the Fourteenth Amendment did not prohibit the states from regulating most aspects of any business open to the public.

Nectow v. City of Cambridge (1928)

Held that a city must prove that the general health and safety of an area was promoted by a zoning change to have that change become effective. In other words, it held that cities must prove an advantage from proposed zoning rather than just enacting it.

Nollan v. California Coastal Commission (1987)

Expanded a property owner's rights in eminent domain cases by requiring that the state show a substantial connection between the harm asserted by the state and its regulation. It held that the state cannot force a landowner to lose rights without compensation in the absence of that substantial connection.

Northeast Bancorp v. Board of Governors (1985)

Held that a state may partially lift a ban on out-of-state bank holding companies acquiring branches in the home state without totally lifting the ban.

Northern Securities Co. v. United States (1904)

Found that a large holding company was an unlawful combination within the meaning of the Sherman Antitrust Act of 1890.

Ogden v. Saunders (1827)

Established bankruptcy as an area in which both states and the federal government can exercise jurisdiction. Also held that the states could act within their own borders in areas in which the federal government has not acted but cannot act in ways affecting citizens of other states.

Osborn v. Bank of the United States (1824)

Continuation of the case of *McCulloch v. Maryland* upholding the right of the United States to establish a bank. General legal procedures and suits were allowed with an eye toward enabling the bank to stay operational. States were again held not to be able to tax the Bank of the United States.

Oulton v. German Savings and Loan Society (1872)

Held that the method by which savings depositors were repaid was not the controlling fact determining whether an enterprise was a bank, but rather whether the bank aimed to make a profit and pay that money to its shareholders.

Palazzolo v. Rhode Island (2001)

Held that even if a regulation has somewhat decreased the value of land held, it is not a total taking if the parcel still has significant value and that allegations that different parts of a parcel should be considered separately must be made early in the proceeding.

Penn Central Transportation Co. v. New York City (1978)

Established several important principles governing the takings (eminent domain) impact of regulations. It generally ruled in favor of city regulations, limiting what would be considered a taking.

Pennsylvania Coal Co. v. Mahon (1922)

Held that a state cannot ban coal mining without that ban being a taking (an exercise of the government's right of eminent domain), if the ban on coal mining removes significant value of the land.

Raymond Motor Transportation v. Rice (1978)

Held that a state ban on tractor-trailers longer than a certain length constituted a restriction on interstate commerce and that there was no proof that these regulations helped safety. For these two reasons, it overturned the law.

Santa Clara County v. Southern Pacific Railroad (1886)

Ruled that corporations were "persons" within the meaning of the Fourteenth Amendment. This allowed corporations to sue and seek protections.

Schechter Poultry Corp. v. United States (1935)

One of three Supreme Court cases voiding vague delegations of power to executive branch agencies, this decision ruled against the constitutionality of the National Industrial Recovery Act of 1933.

Securities Industry Association v. Board of Governors of the Federal Reserve System (1984)

Ruled that because the law permits banks to buy closely related companies, a bank is allowed to acquire a securities company when that company is limited to buying and selling of securities. Buying and selling of securities was held to be closely related, while the offering of investment advice in securities was judged not to be as related.

Shelley v. Kraemer (1948)

Held that private covenants placed into deeds could not be enforced if those covenants were racially discriminatory. If the court enforced one of these provisions, it would create discrimination, and the court's action would be "state action," which is banned under the Fourteenth Amendment.

Shreveport Rate Cases (1914)

Railroad cases that strengthened the powers of the Interstate Commerce Commission.

Slaughterhouse Cases (1873)

Largely eliminated the Fourteenth Amendment's due process clause as a protection of individuals from actions of the state in which they resided.

Standard Oil Co. v. United States (1911)

Upholding a lower court's decree to break up the Standard Oil Company, this ruling concluded that the Sherman Antitrust Act of 1890 forbade only unreasonable combinations or agreements in restraint of trade.

Steele v. Louisville & Nashville Railroad Co. (1944)

Held that a union agreement that did not represent some workers because of their race could not be enforced because the federal act allowing such contracts required that all people under them be treated without discrimination.

Stone v. Mississippi (1880)

A government lottery was allowed to operate one year and then outlawed the next. Those running the lottery claimed that the revocation was illegal as it violated the charter they had been granted, which allowed the lottery. This ruling held that states could revoke previous acts and charters by their own legislatures as long as that revocation was based on the police power to protect the public's health, welfare, and morals.

Sure-Tan v. National Labor Relations Board (1984)

Held that the National Labor Relations Act applied to illegal aliens as well and that they could not be targeted for union activities, regardless of their immigration status. This limited the power of businesses to discharge workers for union activities. However, how much back pay they might receive was affected.

Swift v. Tyson (1842)

Held that federal courts could independently judge principles of general commercial law, even if their decisions were inconsistent with those of state courts. Under the ruling, a bill of exchange between parties from different states that could have been voided by a state court was held to be valid and payable under the rules of interstate commerce.

Swift and Company v. United States (1905)

Adopted the stream of commerce doctrine and held that antitrust laws could be constitutionally applied to stockyard transactions.

Teresa Harris v. Forklift Systems (1993)

Ruled that conduct that is sexual harassment does not have to rise to the level of creating serious damage to a psyche in order for a person to sue under Title VII. Instead, all a person has to do is prove a hostile or abusive work environment.

Thornhill v. Alabama (1940)

Overturned a labor leader's conviction for peaceful picketing. The Court also declared the underlying statute to be invalid. The statute in question dealt only with picketing against companies and was held to interfere with the freedom of speech.

Tiffany v. National Bank of Missouri (1874)

Held that when state banks were limited to a certain rate of interest, but people in general were allowed to charge more, national banks were allowed to charge more than the state banks.

Trafficante v. Metropolitan Life Insurance (1972)

Held that all people affected by racial discrimination in housing can sue, not just those who are denied housing by the discrimination but also those who are already in the housing area and lose the benefits of racial diversity.

Truax v. Corrigan (1921)

Struck down a state law protecting strikers against injunctions.

United States v. Butler (1936)

Struck down the regulatory features of the Agricultural Adjustment Act of 1933 as inconsistent with the Tenth Amendment, but it also interpreted the general welfare clause as giving Congress the power to spend public money for public purposes.

United States v. Darby Lumber Co. (1941)

Using a broad interpretation of the commerce clause, upheld a federal law mandating minimum wages and maximum hours for employees producing goods for interstate commerce.

United States v. Dewitt (1870)

Ruling about the constitutionality of a federal revenue act that made it illegal to sell a certain type of illuminating oil that held control over the possession and sale of any item within the states is not a power held by Congress.

United States v. E. C. Knight (1895)

First Supreme Court ruling on the Sherman Antitrust Act of 1890; it found the framers of the act had not intended it to apply to manufacturing processes.

United States v. Lopez (1995)

Held that the government may not pass laws regulating things not directly affecting interstate commerce. It was the first ruling in nearly sixty years that limited Congress's interstate commerce power.

United States v. Paradise (1987)

Upheld a plan by the Alabama Department of Public Safety to reserve half of the appointments for African Americans because the Alabama Department of Public Safety in the past had systematically excluded African Americans from the department and had not, in spite of hiring African Americans for several years, promoted a significant number of them to higher positions.

United States v. Phillipsburg National Bank and Trust Co. (1970)

Dealt with the merger of two banks, holding that the relevant geographical area to be considered when looking at the merger's effect on competitiveness was the local area in which the banks operated. It also held that the type of banking (in this case, commercial rather than savings) conducted by the banks needed to be considered.

United States v. Starrett City Associates (1988)

Held that an apartment's practice of holding certain apartments for one race and other apartments for another was discriminatory as it violated the Fourteenth Amendment.

United States v. United Mine Workers (1947)

Case involving miners being ordered back to work after the president seized the coal mines that held the 1932 Norris-LaGuardia Act, which prohibited the federal courts from issuing injunctions, did not apply when the government was in effect the employer.

United States Trust v. New Jersey (1977)

Upheld a state law breaking part of a public bond contract and held that such breaking of contracts is allowed when the breaking serves a "an important public purpose." Thus, contracts are allowed to be broken under some circumstances.

United Steelworkers v. Weber (1979)

Held that it was okay for a company to use race as a factor in selecting trainees for a program in order to reverse past discrimination.

Veazie Bank v. Fenno (1869)

Held that a tax of a certain percentage on banks' notes was not a direct tax on a state agency, although Veazie Bank was chartered by Maine. This ruling upheld Congress's right to tax bank notes issued by a state-chartered bank.

Village of Belle Terre v. Boraas (1974)

Ruled that an ordinance defining what a family was in order to set limits on single-family housing was constitutional as it did not discriminate against any group protected under federal law.

Village of Euclid v. Ambler Realty Co. (1926)

Upheld a zoning ordinance, holding that the ordinance was not arbitrary, but was reasonable and did not destroy value, and thus was constitutional. This allowed zoning practices to continue.

Wabash, St. Louis, and Pacific Railway Co. v. Illinois (1886)

Struck down a state law regulating railroad pricing policies, encouraging Congress to enact national standards. This decision brought about the creation of the Interstate Commerce Commission and increased regulation of railroad corporations.

Ward v. Rock Against Racism (1989)

Held that regulations on noise could be adopted as long as they were aimed at the time, place, and manner of the noise and were neutral as to content.

West Coast Hotel v. Parrish (1937)

Allowed states great discretion in regulating working conditions and protecting the rights of workers in a decision in which the Court abandoned its longstanding freedom of contract doctrine.

Wickard v. Filburn (1942)

Broadened the definition of interstate commerce to justify regulations established to support New Deal legislation.

Wolff Packing Co. v. Court of Industrial Relations (1923)

Taking a broad view of economic freedom, placed the majority of businesses outside the reach of state regulations.

Wyman v. Wallace (1906)

Awarded federal courts general jurisdiction over a case dealing with a national bank, its liabilities, and its stockholders.

Youngstown Sheet and Tube Co. v. Sawyer (1952)

Disallowed the president's right to invoke emergency powers to seize and operate private businesses without prior congressional approval.

Scott A. Merriman

Time Line of Notable Events

Unless otherwise stated, all court rulings are U.S. Supreme Court decisions.

Date	Event
1492-1504	Christopher Columbus's explorations open Western Hemisphere to European settlement, trade, and development.
1607	First permanent British colonies are established in Virginia.
1609-1610	English navigator Henry Hudson explores Atlantic seaboard, Hudson River, and Hudson's Bay in search of new trade routes.
1619	First African slaves are imported to Jamestown, Virginia.
1620	(Dec. 26) *Mayflower* pilgrims arrive at Plymouth Rock in Massachusetts.
1626	(May) Dutch begin colonizing Manhattan Island.
1628	Massachusetts Bay Company is chartered as joint-stock company to finance Pilgrims bound for New England.
1639	First American printing press operates in Cambridge, Massachusetts, which along with Boston will become center of American publishing.
1651 and 1660	English parliament enacts Navigation Acts, which restrict use of non-English ships in trade with American colonies.
1664	(Aug. 29) England annexes New Netherlands, which it will rename New York.
1673	Louis Jolliet and Jacques Marquette explore Upper Mississippi River.
1681-1682	Robert Cavelier, Sieur de La Salle explores Lower Mississippi River.
1681	(Mar. 4) England's King Charles II of England grants William Penn a charter to found colony of Pennsylvania.
1690	First American papermaking plant opens in Germantown, Pennsylvania.
	Benjamin Harris publishes first American newspaper, *Publick Occurrences, Both Forreign and Domestick*, in Boston.
c. 1732	New Jersey stagecoach line is colonies' first public transport system.
1741	American magazine industry begins with Andrew Bradford's *American Magazine*, followed shortly by Benjamin Franklin's *General Magazine*.
1742	Benjamin Franklin's *General Magazine* carries first magazine advertisements in colonies.
1744	Benjamin Franklin publishes first mail-order catalog, offering scientific and academic materials.
1754	(May 24) French and Indian War begins.

Date	Event
1763	British parliament grants Crown trade monopoly in British North America.
	(Feb. 10) Treaty of Paris ends French and Indian War.
1765	(Nov. 1) Britain's Stamp Act imposes taxes on American printed publications and documents; it will be repealed on March 18, 1766.
1767	(June 29) British parliament passes Townshend Act, which adds import duties on certain American imports.
1770	(Mar. 5) British parliament partially repeals Townshend Act.
1773	(May 10) Britain's Tea Act gives East India Company monopoly over exports of tea to North American colonies.
	(Dec. 16) Colonists board British ships and dump their tea cargoes into Boston Harbor in tax protest that will be remembered as "Boston Tea Party."
1774	British parliament passes Coercive Acts to restore order in Massachusetts after Boston Tea Party and other anti-British acts; new restrictions include closing Boston's port.
1775	U.S. Post Office begins.
	Daniel Boone and others build Wilderness Road.
	(Apr. 18, 1775-Sept. 3, 1783) North American colonies fight for independence from Great Britain.
1776	(July 4) Among principles articulated in Declaration of Independence is call for free trade.
1780	(Mar. 1) Pennsylvania is first state to abolish slavery.
1781	(Mar. 1) Former colonies adopt Articles of Confederation.
1783	(Sept. 3) Treaty of Paris ends Revolutionary War.
1784, 1785, and 1787	Northwest Ordinances establish principles for governing and developing Northwest Territory.
1784	Economic downturn caused by low production and insufficient money supply creates national depression.
	Alexander Hamilton establishes Bank of New York.
	(Sept. 22) Russia begins to colonize Alaska.
1785	First public toll road, in Virginia, opens.
	First American toll bridge corporation is formed in Boston.
	Continental Congress adopts decimal coinage system.
1786	(Jan. 16) Massachusetts farmers, led by Daniel Shays, mount armed rebellion against taxes.
	(Sept. 11) Representatives from five states convene in Annapolis to discuss problems of Articles of Confederation.

Date	Event
1789	U.S. Constitution is ratified; Congress creates Departments of State and Treasury.
	(Sept. 11) Alexander Hamilton becomes first secretary of the treasury.
1790	Congress enacts first federal copyright law.
	Congress enacts first patent law, which will soon be replaced.
1791	(Feb.) Federal government charters First Bank of the United States as a private institution.
	(Mar. 3) Whiskey Act imposes first federal excise tax, to pay state debts from Revolutionary War.
	(Dec.) Bill of Rights is ratified.
1792	(Apr. 2) U.S. Mint is established.
	(May 17) New York Stock Exchange opens.
1794	Congress extends excise tax of 1791's Whiskey Act to carriages, snuff, sugar, and salt.
	First large urban American hotel opens in New York City.
	(Mar. 14) Eli Whitney patents cotton gin.
	(June 4) Neutrality Act prohibits American nationals from becoming involved in foreign military forces.
1801	(Mar.) Treaty of Madrid returns Louisiana Territory from Spain to France.
1802	By this date, all federal excise taxes, except that for salt, are repealed.
	(Mar. 16) Congress creates U.S. Army Corps of Engineers to help develop national infrastructure, particularly harbors and waterways.
1803	(Dec. 20) United States completes purchase of Louisiana Territory from France.
1804	(May 14) Meriwether Lewis and William Clark begin exploratory expedition through Louisiana Territory.
1805-1806	Zebulon Montgomery Pike leads exploratory expeditions into West.
1806	Congress passes series of Embargo Acts to retaliate against British and French abuses of American shipping during Napoleonic Wars.
	(Sept. 23) Lewis and Clark complete their exploratory expedition.
1807	(Mar. 2) Congress outlaws importation of African slaves.
	(Aug. 17) Robert Fulton's steamboat *Clermont* makes first run from New York City to Albany.
1808	Collapse of foreign trade caused by embargo precipitates national depression.
	(Apr. 6) John Jacob Astor founds American Fur Company.
1809	Non-Intercourse Act bans trade with France and Great Britain.
	Bank of the United States v. Deveaux holds that bank depositors in Pennsylvania may sue in federal court to recover deposits from state of Georgia.

Date	Event
1810	(Mar. 16) *Fletcher v. Peck* holds a state law to be unconstitutional.
1811	Charter of First Bank of the United States is not renewed.
1811-1818	Cumberland Road is built with federal funding.
1812	(June 18) War of 1812 begins.
1813	Congressional attempts to create national income tax are abandoned.
1814	(Dec. 24, 1814) War of 1812 ends.
1816	Second Bank of the United States is chartered.
	First gas utility company in United States is established in Baltimore; other cities will soon follow.
	(Apr.) Second Bank of the United States is chartered.
1817	William Underwood introduces hermetic canning of food to United States.
1819	Collapse of American credit markets brings on national panic.
	Dartmouth College v. Woodward holds that state charters of private institutions are protected by Constitution's contracts clause.
	(Feb. 22) Spain cedes Florida to United States.
	(Mar. 5) *McCulloch v. Maryland* holds that Maryland cannot tax Bank of the United States, thereby establishing basic principle of federal government's relationship with states.
	(May 22-June 20) *Savannah* is first steamship to cross Atlantic Ocean.
1820	First portion of Erie Canal opens to traffic.
	(Feb. 20) Congress adopts Missouri Compromise, maintaining balance between free and slave states and prohibiting slavery in western part of Louisiana Territory.
	(Apr. 24) Congress passes Land Act laying basis for transferring former Indian lands to individual U.S. citizens.
1821	(Sept. 28) Mexico declares its independence from Spain.
1823	First steamboat reaches Minneapolis and St. Paul.
	Daly's Lessee v. James holds that terms of wills must be carefully followed.
	Johnson v. M'Intosh holds that Native Americans may sell their land only to federal government, as they do not have traditional ownership rights to the land.
	(Dec. 2) President James Monroe articulates doctrine of European nonintervention in Western Hemispheric affairs.
1824	*Osborn v. Bank of the United States* upholds right of United States to establish a bank.
	Henry Clay's American system is instituted.

Date	Event
1824 *(cont.)*	(Mar. 2) *Gibbons v. Ogden* supports federal license of steamboat operator over that of a state monopoly license holder.
1825	(Oct. 25) Completion of Erie Canal connects Lake Erie with Albany, New York.
1826	(Feb. 26) Samuel Colt patents revolver.
1827	Baltimore and Ohio Railroad corporation is formed.
	Ogden v. Saunders permits both states and federal government to have jurisdiction in bankruptcy cases.
1828	(May 19) Tariff of Abominations protects industries in northern states from European competition.
1830	(Jan. 7) Baltimore and Ohio, first long-distance railroad in United States, opens.
	(May 28) Congress passes Indian Removal Act to force members of several eastern Native American tribes to migrate west.
1831	First clipper ship is built in Baltimore.
	Congress extends copyright protection to musical compositions.
	(Summer) Cyrus McCormick invents reaper.
1832	South Carolina legislature votes to veto federal Tariff of Abominations of 1828 on principle that every state has sovereign power to overrule federal laws.
	Railroads begin carrying U.S. mails in eastern states.
	(July 10) Second Bank of the United States becomes national political issue when President Andrew Jackson vetoes its rechartering.
	(Nov. 26) Streetcar service begins in New York City.
1833	Congress passes Compromise Tariff Act to mitigate economic hardships in southern states caused by Tariff of Abominations of 1828.
	Benjamin Davis founds *New York Sun.*
1834	(Oct. 14) Henry Blair patents seed planter.
1835	George Gordon Bennett founds *New York Morning Herald.*
1836	Sugarcane cultivation begins in Hawaii.
	New federal Patent Act tightens requirements for patentable inventions.
	Charter of Second Bank of the United States expires and is not renewed, but bank will continue to do business until 1839.
	(Mar. 2) American settlers declare Texas independent of Mexico.
1837	Loss of faith in American banking system starts six-year depression.
	Charles River Bridge v. Warren Bridge holds that only clear and explicit contract terms are legally binding.

Date	Event
1838	(Apr.) Regular transatlantic steam passenger service begins between Boston and England.
1840	Independent Treasury Act is passed to fix damage done to Second Bank of United States under Andrew Jackson's administration.
1841	Volney Palmer sets up first American advertising agency in Philadelphia.
	Horace Greeley founds *New York Tribune*.
1842	*Swift v. Tyson* holds that federal courts can independently judge principles of general commercial law.
	New York Curb Market, which will later become American Stock Exchange (AMEX), is founded.
	(Sept. 2) In *Commonwealth v. Hunt*, Massachusetts court articulates first legal basis for American workers to organize and strike.
1843	(Sept. 2) James Wilson founds *The Economist*, a London-based weekly financial news magazine.
1844	(May 24) Samuel Morse sends first telegraph message
	(June 15) Charles Goodyear patents rubber vulcanization process.
1845	(Dec. 29) United States annexes Texas.
1845-1854	Ireland's potato famine increases Irish emigration to United States.
1846	(June 14) Mexican War begins.
	(June 15) United States acquires Oregon Territory.
	(Sept. 10) Elias Howe patents sewing machine.
1847	(July 1) United States issues first postage stamps.
	(July 24) Mormons begin settlement of Utah.
1848	Federal Married Women's Property Rights Law gives married women limited property rights for first time.
	(Jan. 24) Discovery of gold in Northern California begins gold rush.
	(Feb. 2) Treaty of Guadalupe Hidalgo ends Mexican War.
	(July 19-20) First American women's rights convention is held at Seneca Falls, New York.
1849	Congress creates Department of the Interior.
1850	First U.S. petroleum refinery is built in Pittsburgh, Pennsylvania.
1851	First American cheese factory is established in Rome, New York.
	Western Union telegraph company is founded as New York and Mississippi Valley Printing Telegraph Company.
	(Mar. 13) Chicago Board of Trade becomes first American exchange on which derivatives contracts are traded.
	(Sept. 18) *New York Times* is founded.

Date	Event
1853	(Dec. 31) United States signs treaty to buy Gadsden Purchase territory from Mexico.
1854	United States signs Canadian-American Reciprocity Treaty to increase trade with British Canada.
	(Mar. 31) Commodore Matthew Perry negotiates treaty opening Japan to American trade.
1855	Allan J. Pinkerton founds first major American private detective agency in Chicago.
	(Jan. 28) Completion of Panama railroad reduces travel time between East and West Coasts of United States.
1856	Congress extends copyright protection to dramatic works.
	American greeting card industry begins.
	(Apr. 21) First bridge across Mississippi River links Davenport, Iowa, and Rock Island, Illinois.
1857	First attempt to lay transatlantic cable linking Great Britain and United States fails.
	(Mar. 23) Elisha Graves Otis installs first passenger elevator in New York department store.
	(Aug. 24) Bank failures begin panic in financial markets and national economic downturn.
1858	(Aug. 16) First transatlantic telegraph message is sent, but cable will soon fail.
	(Oct. 9) Overland Mail stagecoaches link San Francisco and St. Louis.
1859	Predecessor of Great Atlantic and Pacific Tea Company (A&P) is founded.
	(Aug. 27) Commercial oil drilling at Titusville, Pennsylvania, demonstrates that petroleum industry can be basis of national industry.
1860	(Apr. 3) Pony Express begins providing transcontinental mail service.
	(Oct. 26) South Carolina is first of eleven southern states to secede from Union.
1861	(Mar. 9) Confederate Congress authorizes printing of paper currency, launching inflationary trend.
	(Apr. 12) Civil War begins.
	(Aug. 5) Congress passes first federal income tax law as part of Revenue Act of 1861; law will be declared unconstitutional in 1895.
	(Oct. 24) First transcontinental telegraph line is completed.
	(Oct. 26) Pony Express is disbanded.
1862	California passes Anti-Coolie Act, which establishes special tax on Chinese workers.
	Federal Morrill Land-Grant Act gives states large tracts of federal land to help create and fund agricultural and industrial colleges.
	Federal Pacific Railway Act grants Union Pacific and Central Pacific Railroads extensive land in western United States.
	Congress creates Department of Agriculture.

Date	Event
1862 *(cont.)*	Major enlargement of Erie Canal is completed.
	(May 20) President Abraham Lincoln signs Homestead Act, which will give about 30 percent of western federal lands to settlers.
	(July 1) Congress passes comprehensive Internal Revenue Act.
1863	U.S. Post Office standardizes rates, based on weight.
	(Apr.) Confederate government imposes sweeping taxes.
1863-1864	(Feb. 25, 1863-June 3, 1864) National Bank Acts raise money for Union government during Civil War by organizing network of government-chartered National Banks.
1864	Eureka Iron Works of Wyandotte, Michigan, becomes first American producer of Bessemer steel.
1865	Congress extends copyright protection to photographs; over next five years protection will be extended to paintings, drawings, sculptures, and models and designs in fine arts.
	Chicago Union Stock Yards open; they will eventually became world's largest livestock-receiving center.
	Congress creates Department of Housing and Urban Development.
	(Apr. 9) Civil War ends, and Reconstruction begins in defeated southern states.
	(Apr. 14) U.S. Secret Service is established to combat counterfeiting.
	(Dec.) Ratification of Thirteenth Amendment to U.S. Constitution abolishes slavery.
1866	Congress passes Pacific Telegraph Act to facilitate commercial, postal, and military communication by consolidating all telegraph companies.
	United States ends Canadian-American Reciprocity Treaty.
	National Labor Union is founded.
	(July 27) First successful transatlantic cable is completed.
1867	Foundation of National Grange of Patrons of Husbandry launches Granger movement.
	(Mar. 2) President Andrew Johnson signs law creating Department of Education, an agency without cabinet status; the following year it will be renamed Office of Education and attached to the Department of the Interior.
	(Mar. 30) Russia sells Alaska to United States.
	(July 1) Canada becomes dominion with British Empire.
1868	Horatio Alger publishes *Ragged Dick: Or, Street Life in New York with the Bootblacks*, first in a long series of rags-to-riches stories for juvenile readers.
	(June 23) Christopher Latham Sholes patents first practical typewriter.

Date	Event
1869	*National Bank v. Commonwealth* allows states to tax national banks.
	Veazie Bank v. Fenno holds that taxes of a certain percentage on bank notes are not direct taxes on state agencies.
	(May 10) Transcontinental railroad is completed.
	(Sept. 24) Financiers' failed attempt to corner market on New York Gold Exchange causes panic that will be remembered as "Black Friday."
	(Nov. 25) Knights of Labor is founded.
1870	Revised Patent Act requires applicants to provide written descriptions of their inventions.
	First National Bank v. Lanier upholds law preventing one bank from loaning its shares to another bank.
	Merchants Bank v. State Bank holds corporations liable for actions of employees.
	United States v. Dewitt holds that Congress has no power over possession and sale of items within states.
	Legal Tender Cases establishes right of U.S. government to pay its debts in paper money.
	John D. Rockefeller creates Standard Oil Company of Ohio.
	(July 1) U.S. Department of Justice begins operating.
1871	J. P. Morgan establishes private banking company that will later become the powerful J. P. Morgan and Company.
1872	U.S. Post Office is elevated to cabinet-level department.
	U.S. congressmen are revealed to have taken bribes from construction company in Crédit Mobilier scandal.
	Oulton v. German Savings and Loan Society holds that method by which savings depositors are repaid does not determine if an enterprise is a bank.
	Montgomery Ward department stores are founded.
	National Labor Union collapses.
1873	*Slaughterhouse Cases* largely eliminate Fourteenth Amendment's due process clause as protection of individuals from actions of states in which they reside.
	Treaty of Washington increases U.S.-Canadian trade.
	Coinage Act revises coinage laws and makes U.S. Mint part of the Treasury Department.
	(Mar. 3) Congress passes Comstock Law, which bans use of U.S. mail to advertise, publish, or sell sexually suggestive material.
	(Sept. 18) Economic instability aggravated by growing railroad speculation begins six-year depression.

Date	Event
1874	Mark Twain and Charles Dudley Warner publish *The Gilded Age*, a novel about political and business corruption that gives its name to late nineteenth century era of American history.
	Tiffany v. National Bank of Missouri allows national banks to charge more interest on loans than state banks.
	(July) Discovery of gold in Black Hills of Dakota Territory begins major gold rush.
	(Nov. 24) Joseph Glidden patents barbed wire.
1875	United States signs Treaty of the Meter, an international agreement to use metric units in international matters, especially business.
	Cooke v. United States holds that when federal government is party to commercial transactions, it incurs all responsibilities of private parties in similar circumstances.
	Farmers' and Mechanics' National Bank v. Dearing holds that federal law does not wholly exempt national banks from state laws.
	First National Bank v. National Exchange Bank limits right of banks to buy and sell stocks.
	Andrew Carnegie starts steel plant in Pennsylvania.
1876	Thomas Alva Edison establishes industrial research lab in Menlo Park, New Jersey.
	(Feb. 2) National League forms as first major league baseball league.
	(May 10) Philadelphia hosts Centennial Exposition, which celebrates American industrial progress and international trade.
	(June 25) Alexander Graham Bell demonstrates telephone at Philadelphia's Centennial Exposition.
1877	Desert Land Act permits would-be farmers to buy federal land at low prices in return for bringing it under irrigation.
	Washington Post is founded.
	(July 16) Railroad workers throughout central and eastern states begin strike to protest wage cuts and poor working conditions.
	(Dec. 24) Thomas Alva Edison patents cylinder phonograph.
1878	American Bar Association (ABA) is established.
	Federal Bland-Allison Act provides for freer coinage of silver to relieve liquidity problems caused by gold standard; it will be superseded by Sherman Silver Purchase Act of 1890.
1879	(Oct. 21) Thomas Alva Edison demonstrates incandescent lights.
1881	Samuel Gompers helps form Federation of Organized Trades and Labor Unions of the United States and Canada, which will disband and reform as American Federation of Labor in 1886.
	First college-level business school is established at University of Pennsylvania.
	James Bonsack's high-speed cigarette-rolling machine revolutionizes American tobacco industry.

Date	Event
1882	Chinese Exclusion Act bans Chinese workers from entering United States for ten years and excludes all Chinese immigrants from becoming U.S. citizens; it will be repealed by Magnuson Act of 1943.
	United States is divided into four time zones.
	American Association forms to challenge baseball's National League; it will later be renamed American League.
1883	Construction on world's first skyscraper begins in Chicago.
	(May 24) Brooklyn Bridge opens to traffic.
1884	Congress creates Bureau of Labor within Department of Interior.
	National Cattle Growers Association is established.
1886	*Santa Clara County v. Southern Pacific Railroad* holds that corporations have same legal rights as "persons."
	Wabash, St. Louis, and Pacific Railway Co. v. Illinois strikes down state law regulating railroad pricing policies, while encouraging Congress to enact national standards.
	Sears, Roebuck and Company is founded as mail-order retailer.
	Ottmar Mergenthaler's invention of Linotype begins typesetting revolution in printing industry.
	(May 4) Striking workers clash with Chicago police in Haymarket Riot.
	(Dec. 8) American Federation of Labor (AFL) is organized with Samuel Gompers as president.
1887	Congress passes Interstate Commerce Act to correct abuses of economic power by railroad industry and to establish Interstate Commerce Commission.
1888	George Eastman introduces first Kodak camera.
	Adams Gum Company begins first successful American vending machine operation.
	Kidd v. Pearson creates distinction between manufacturing and commerce.
1889	U.S. Department of Agriculture is raised to cabinet level.
	(Apr. 22) Opening of federal land in Oklahoma to homesteaders creates massive land rush.
	(July 8) *Wall Street Journal* begins publication.
1890	Federal Sherman Silver Purchase Act requires federal government to buy more silver bullion.
	Chicago, Milwaukee, and St. Paul Railroad Co. v. Minnesota holds that courts have power to review utility rates.
	Leisy v. Hardin holds that federal government, not states, may regulate alcohol placed into interstate commerce.
	Milwaukee department store is first American retailer to use trading stamps to promote sales.

Date	Event
1890 *(cont.)*	(Jan. 22) United Mine Workers of America is founded.
	(July 2) President Benjamin Harrison signs Sherman Antitrust Act into law to protect consumers from monopolistic business practices.
1891	*Briggs v. Spaulding* holds that company directors are responsible for exercising only a normal level of care over company business.
	American Express issues first travelers' checks.
	U.S. Post Office inaugurates rural free delivery (RFD).
1892	*Jenkins v. Collard* increases government power to regulate corporations.
	Edison General Electric and Thomas-Huston merge to form General Electric company.
	International Longshoremen's Association is founded.
	(Jan. 1) Ellis Island opens as immigrant reception center in New York Harbor.
	(Jan. 29) Asa G. Candler founds Coca-Cola Company.
	(July) Union steelworkers strike against Homestead Steel Works Company.
1893	American Railway Union is formed with Eugene V. Debs as president.
	(Feb.) Failures of Reading Railroad and National Cordage Company trigger stock market collapse that begins national panic.
	(May 1-Oct. 30) Chicago World's Fair celebrates technological advances of nineteenth century.
	(Aug.) American Bimetallic League holds national convention in Chicago.
1894	William Hope Harvey publishes *Coin's Financial School.*
	Kellogg's Corn Flakes launches dry cereal industry.
	(Jan. 7) Thomas Alva Edison copyrights first motion picture.
	(Mar. 26-May 1) Unemployed people in "Coxey's Army" stage first mass protest march on Washington, D.C., to lobby for federally supported public works program.
	(May-July) Pullman workers strike against railroads.
	(June 28) Congress votes to make first Monday in September a federal holiday—Labor Day.
1895	*In re Debs* upholds injunction against labor leader Eugene V. Debs.
	United States v. E. C. Knight finds that framers of Sherman Antitrust Act of 1890 did not intend for act to apply to manufacturing processes.
	(Jan. 24) Hawaiian monarchy is overthrown and replaced by republic controlled by Americans.
	(Sept. 18) Booker T. Washington delivers Atlanta Compromise speech proposing racial accommodation that would relegate African Americans to inferior position.

Date	Event
1896	Orison Swett Marden publishes *How to Succeed: Or, Stepping-Stones to Fame and Fortune.*
	Davis v. Elmira Savings Bank holds that federal law takes precedence over state law when banks became insolvent.
	Herman Hollerith founds Tabulating Machine Company, which will become International Business Machines (IBM) in 1924.
	Sperry & Hutchinson (S&H) Green Stamps Company opens.
	(May 6) *Plessy v. Ferguson* ruling establishes "separate-but-equal" principle in racial segregation of public transportation.
	(May 26) Dow Jones Industrial Average makes its first appearance.
	(July 9) William Jennings Bryan delivers "Cross of Gold" speech at Democratic National Convention, advocating free silver policy.
	(Aug. 17) Discovery of gold strike in Canada's Yukon Territory begins American rush to Klondike.
	(Nov. 16) First American hydroelectric plant opens at Niagara Falls.
1897	*Allgeyer v. Louisiana* uses freedom of contract doctrine to overturn a state law.
	Chicago, Burlington, and Quincy Railroad Co. v. Chicago holds that Fourteenth Amendment's due process clause applies to states.
	American automotive industry begins with Pope Manufacturing Company in Hartford, Connecticut.
	(July 24) Congress passes Dingley Tariff Act, instituting new protective tariff policies.
1898	Federal National Bankruptcy Act establishes conditions and procedures for institutions and businesses to declare bankruptcy; act will be superseded by Bankruptcy Reform Act of 1978.
	Holden v. Hardy recognizes that states have police powers to place some restrictions on freedom of contract.
	Pepsi-Cola company is founded.
	University of Chicago business school opens.
	(Feb. 1) Travelers Insurance Company issues first automobile insurance policy.
	(Apr. 25-Aug. 12) United States fights Spain in Spanish-American War.
	(Aug. 12) United States annexes Hawaii.
1900	Gold Standard Act (Currency Act) makes gold sole legal-tender coinage in United States, thereby ending bimetallism.
	Socialist labor leader Eugene V. Debs mounts first of his five unsuccessful runs for the U.S. presidency.
	John D. Rockefeller ranks as first American billionaire.
	Booker T. Washington organizes National Negro Business League.

Date	Event
1900 *(cont.)*	International Ladies' Garment Workers' Union is founded.
	(Mar.) Kodak Brownie camera makes photography more widely affordable.
1901	Frank Norris's novel *The Octopus* explores abuses of monopolistic railroads.
	(Jan. 10) Oil discovery at Spindletop launches Texas oil boom.
	(Feb. 25) J. P. Morgan organizes United States Steel, which quickly becomes world's largest corporation.
	(Dec. 12) Guglielmo Marconi demonstrates first transatlantic telegraph signal sent by radio.
1902	First major fast-food chain, Horn & Hardart Automat, opens in Philadelphia.
	(Mar. 4) American Automobile Association is founded.
	(May 12-Oct. 23) Pennsylvania coal miners strike for safer conditions, better pay, and recognition of their union.
1903	*Champion v. Ames* upholds federal statute prohibiting transportation of lottery tickets in interstate commerce.
	American and National Leagues join to form what will later become known as Major League Baseball.
	(Feb. 14) Congress creates Department of Commerce and Labor, incorporating Bureau of Labor from Department of Interior.
	(June 17) Ford Motor Company is founded.
	(Aug.) Team Drivers International Union and Teamsters National Union unite to form International Brotherhood of Teamsters.
	(fall) Gillette markets first razor with disposable blades.
	(Oct.) Pittsburgh Pirates of National League and Boston Pilgrims of American League pennant meet in baseball's first World Series.
	(Nov. 6) U.S. government recognizes independence of Panama, with which it will enter into treaty to build Panama Canal.
	(Dec. 17) Orville and Wilbur Wright fly first powered airplane at Kitty Hawk, North Carolina.
1904	*McCray v. United States* holds that federal tax powers can be used to regulate commerce.
	Northern Securities Co. v. United States upholds federal government's power to break up industrial monopolies under Sherman Antitrust Act.
	National Child Labor Committee is established.
	Ida Tarbell's *The History of the Standard Oil Company* tarnishes reputations of Standard Oil and John D. Rockefeller.
	National Federation of Advertising Clubs of America forms to police truth in advertising.

Date	Event
1905	First gas station opens in St. Louis, Missouri.
	U.S. Forest Service is created within Department of Agriculture.
	Lochner v. New York uses doctrine of substantive due process to overturn a statute regulating labor conditions.
	Swift and Company v. United States uses stream of commerce doctrine to hold that antitrust laws can be constitutionally applied to stockyard transactions.
	Chicago-based clothing retailer Spiegel mails its first catalog.
	(June) Industrial Workers of the World (IWW) is founded.
1906	Federal Pure Food and Drug Act outlaws unsafe products; it will be replaced by more comprehensive Food, Drug, and Cosmetics Act of 1938.
	Wyman v. Wallace gives federal courts general jurisdiction over national bank cases.
	Food and Drug Administration is created within U.S. Department of Agriculture.
	Protection of presidents is added to duties of U.S. Secret Service.
	(Jan. 1) Fuller Brush Company is founded.
	(Feb. 28) Upton Sinclair publishes *The Jungle*, a novel exposing conditions in meatpacking industry.
1907	(Aug. 28) United Parcel Service (UPS) is founded in Seattle, Washington, as American Messenger Company.
	(Oct.) Stock market crash and bank failures trigger new panic in financial markets.
1908	Chicago enacts first American law requiring pasteurization of milk.
	Adair v. United States limits extent to which the government can protect worker rights.
	Loewe v. Lawlor forbids labor unions from organizing boycotts against specific companies.
	Ford Motor Company begins two decades of producing Model T motorcars.
	(Sept. 16) William Crapo Durant founds General Motors.
1909	Congress passed comprehensive copyright statute that incorporates all earlier amendments and extends protection to motion pictures.
1910	Metro-Goldwyn-Mayer motion-picture company begins as Loew's.
	National Collegiate Athletic Association (NCAA) is formed.
	(Mar. 23) Arthur J. Morris founds first Morris Plan bank.
1911	*Standard Oil Co. v. United States* upholds lower court decree to break up Standard Oil Company.
	Federal government orders Standard Oil Company to divest itself of its thirty-three largest companies.
	(Jan.) U.S. Post Office begins operating postal savings banks.
	(Mar. 25) Fire in New York's Triangle Shirtwaist Company kills 146 workers.

Date	Event
1912	Massachusetts enacts first American minimum-wage law.
	Miller v. King holds that national banks cannot act as holders of land.
	Children's Bureau is first federal agency regulating child labor.
	Leon L. Bean founds mail-order business in Freeport, Maine.
1913	*Clement National Bank v. Vermont* holds that states may tax deposits in banks.
	Minnesota Rate Cases holds that Interstate Commerce Commission can regulate certain intrastate railroad rates.
	Ford Motor Company begins using moving assembly lines.
	(Jan. 1) U.S. Post Office begins parcel post delivery of packages.
	(Feb. 3) Ratification of Sixteenth Amendment to U.S. Constitution authorizes imposition of federal income tax.
	(Mar. 14) U.S. Department of Commerce and Labor is divided into Department of Commerce and Department of Labor.
	(Oct. 3) President Woodrow Wilson signs into law Underwood Tariff Act, which is designed to lower tariffs.
	(Dec. 23) Federal Reserve Act establishes Federal Reserve system to manage national money supply; act will be amended in 1935 by Federal Banking Act.
1914	Harrison Act regulates production and distribution of certain narcotic substances.
	Shreveport Rate Cases strengthen powers of Interstate Commerce Commission.
	(Feb. 13) American Society of Composers, Authors, and Publishers (ASCAP) is founded.
	(July) New York Stock Exchange closes during beginning of World War I.
	(Aug.) World War I begins in Europe.
	(Aug. 15) Panama Canal opens to shipping.
	(Sept. 26) Congress creates Federal Trade Commission to combat monopolistic practices in business and to promote fair trade practices.
	(Oct. 15) Federal Clayton Antitrust Act goes into effect, strengthening antitrust laws while protecting labor unions from its restrictions.
1915	African Americans begin Great Migration from South to northern cities.
	Fox motion-picture company is founded.
	(Mar. 16) Federal Trade Commission begins operating.
1916	New York City enacts first comprehensive urban zoning plan.
	Federal Tariff Commission is created to collect information on tariff rates for U.S. president and Congress; it will be renamed International Trade Commission in 1974.
	First accreditation agency for business schools is established.

Date	Event
1916 *(cont.)*	Paramount motion-picture company is founded.
	(Mar. 16) Jamaican immigrant Marcus Garvey arrives in New York and begins to build Universal Negro Improvement Association.
	(Aug.) Junior Achievement begins as Boys' and Girls' Bureau.
	(Sept. 1) Child Labor Act (Keating-Owen Act) regulates interstate transportation of products made by children.
1917	Smith-Hughes National Vocational Education Act promotes training in agricultural education.
	National Hockey League is formed in Canada.
	Union Carbide forms to manufacture petroleum products.
	Knights of Labor is disbanded.
	(Apr. 6) United States enters World War I.
	(Sept.) *Forbes* magazine is launched.
1918	Congress enacts minimum-wage law for female workers in District of Columbia.
	First regularly scheduled airmail service, between New York and Washington, D.C., begins.
	(June 3) *Hammer v. Dagenhart* overturns Child Labor Act of 1916.
	(Nov. 11) Armistice ends World War I.
1919	General Electric and American Telegraph and Telephone launch Radio Corporation of America (RCA).
	Home radios go on the market.
	National Restaurant Association is established.
	(June 23) Marcus Garvey's Universal Negro Improvement Association launches Black Star Line—the first black-owned and operated shipping line.
	(Dec.) Charles Ponzi launches fraudulent pyramid investment scheme in Boston.
1920	Sinclair Lewis's novel *Main Street: The Story of Carol Kennicott* puts concept of "Main Street" into language as symbol of American middle-class values.
	John L. Lewis begins four decades of service as president of the United Mine Workers of America.
	(Jan. 17) Prohibition era begins.
	(Aug.-Sept.) American Professional Football Association, which will later become National Football League, is formed.
1921	*Duplex Printing Co. v. Deering* permits injunctions against organized labor.
	Truax v. Corrigan strikes down state law protecting strikers against injunctions.
	First drive-in restaurant chain, the Pig Stand, opens in Dallas, Texas.
	White Castle, the first fast-food hamburger chain, opens in Wichita, Kansas.

Date	Event
1921 *(cont.)*	*Barron's*, a weekly financial magazine for investors, is founded.
	West Virginia becomes first state to impose sale tax.
1921-1924	High federal government officials take bribes in Teapot Dome scandal.
1922	Narcotic Drugs Import and Export Act increases federal regulation of narcotic substances.
	Bailey v. Drexel Furniture Co. holds that Congress cannot use its taxing power to impose regulations on production.
	Pennsylvania Coal Co. v. Mahon rules against a state ban on coal mining.
	Sinclair Lewis's novel *Babbitt* portrays American businessmen as shallow and spiritually empty.
	Federal Baseball Club v. the National League exempts professional baseball from antitrust laws.
	(Feb.) *Reader's Digest* begins publication.
1923	First American drive-in eatery opens in Dallas, Texas.
	Adkins v. Children's Hospital strikes down minimum-wage laws.
	Wolff Packing Co. v. Court of Industrial Relations places most businesses outside reach of state regulation.
	Warner Bros. motion-picture company is founded.
1924	Immigration Act sets quotes for immigrants based on percentages of nationalities already in United States.
	First National Bank v. Missouri holds that nationally chartered banks are subject to state banking laws that do not conflict with federal laws.
	(Mar. 21) Massachusetts Investors Trust is first mutual fund.
1925	Congress authorizes Army Corps of Engineers to develop hydroelectric power stations.
	Bell Telephone Laboratories (Bell Labs) is founded as telecommunications research and development company.
	Burma Shave advertisements begin four decades of lining American highways.
	Sears, Roebuck opens its first department store in Chicago.
	(June 25) Brotherhood of Sleeping Car Porters is founded under the leadership of A. Philip Randolph.
1926	First cigarette vending machines appear.
	Federal Railway Labor Act provides for mediation of labor disputes between railway companies and unions representing their employees.
	Village of Euclid v. Ambler Realty Co. upholds a zoning ordinance.
	Sears, Roebuck issues metal charge cards.
	(Nov. 15) National Broadcasting Company (NBC) is launched.

Date	Event
1927	*First National Bank v. City of Hartford* holds that states cannot tax shares of national banks at rates higher than those at which they tax local banks.
	Bell Laboratories demonstrates television broadcasting.
	(May 26) Ford Motor Company builds its last Model T motorcar.
1928	Standard Container Act sets standard sizes for baskets and containers for fruits and vegetables.
	RKO motion-picture company is founded.
	Jazz Singer begins era of sound motion pictures.
1929	Agricultural Marketing Act creates Federal Farm Board to promote merchandising of agricultural products in interstate and foreign commerce and help make agriculture economically viable.
	(Oct.) *Wall Street Journal* launches Pacific coast edition.
	(Oct. 24) Stock market crash begins dramatic decline in financial sector and launches Great Depression.
1930	Congress creates Veterans Administration.
	National Mediation Board is created to govern labor-management relations in railroad and airline industries.
	Colonel Harland Sanders launches Kentucky Fried Chicken restaurants, which will later be renamed KFC.
	(Feb.) Henry Luce founds *Fortune* magazine.
1931	Federal Davis-Bacon Act protects local labor wage standards and fringe benefits on government contracts.
	DeLaval Steam Turbine Co. v. United States rules that companies are entitled to compensation for value of contracts only at dates of cancellation.
	Sears, Roebuck establishes Allstate Insurance Company.
	Nevada becomes first state to permit casino gambling.
	(July) Columbia Broadcasting System's New York City station begins first regularly scheduled television broadcasting; a Los Angeles station will begin in December.
1931-1938	Dust Bowl drought conditions devastate farmlands in South and Midwest.
1932	Norris-LaGuardia Act gives employees right to form unions without employer interference.
	Federal Reconstruction Finance Corporation Act establishes Reconstruction Finance Corporation.
	Congress of Industrial Organizations (CIO) is founded.
	American Federation of Labor and Congress of Industrial Organizations merge to form AFL-CIO.

Date	Event
1932 *(cont.)*	Phrase "trickle-down theory" is used during election campaign to describe President Herbert Hoover's economic policies.
1933	Agriculture Adjustment Act provides emergency assistance to farmers during Depression years, supports farm prices, and provides assistance with farm mortgages.
	Glass-Steagall Act (Banking Act) reorganizes banking industry.
	Federal Homeowners' Loan Act establishes Homeowners' Loan Corporation.
	National Industrial Recovery Act establishes National Recovery Administration to stabilize economy and National Resources Planning Board to assist in planning economy.
	Congress creates Farm Credit Administration to oversee financial institutions that extend credit to farmers.
	Congress creates Federal Deposit Insurance Corporation to protect deposits in banks.
	(Mar. 4) President Franklin D. Roosevelt's inauguration begins New Deal programs.
	(May 18) Congress creates Tennessee Valley Authority to develop hydroelectric power in Tennessee River Valley.
	(June 6) First drive-in movie theater opens in Camden, New Jersey.
	(Dec. 5) Prohibition ends.
1934	Reciprocal Trade Agreements Act gives president power to reduce tariffs on foreign trade, and United States begins signing bilateral trade agreements with many nations.
	Copeland Act makes it illegal for employers and their agents to make employees pay to keep their jobs.
	Federal Credit Union Act creates Bureau of Federal Credit Unions to charter and oversee nonprofit, member-owned unions.
	Gold Reserve Act authorizes U.S. president to devalue dollar against gold, authorizes U.S. Treasury to acquire gold held by Federal Reserve banks, and abolishes gold coinage and redemption of U.S. currency in gold.
	Kerr-Smith Tobacco Control Act imposes processing taxes on tobacco industry.
	National Housing Act establishes Federal Savings and Loans Insurance Corporation and Federal Housing Administration.
	Bureau of Federal Credit Unions is created to oversee credit unions throughout United States; it will later be renamed National Credit Union Administration.
	Home Building and Loan Association v. Blaisdell upholds state law limiting farm and home foreclosures.
	Nebbia v. New York holds that Fourteenth Amendment does not prohibit states from regulating most aspects of businesses open to public.
	By executive order, Franklin D. Roosevelt creates Export-Import Bank of United States.
	Federal Communications Act consolidates laws pertaining to radio and telephone service, creates Federal Communications Commission, and transfers regulation of interstate.

Date	Event
1934 *(cont.)*	(June 6) Securities and Exchange Commission is established to help maintain structural integrity of national capital markets.
1935	Rural Electrification Act extends electricity to many areas for first time.
	Kodak begins marketing color film.
	Ashurst-Sumners Act forbids shipping of prison-made goods into states that prohibit convict labor.
	Schechter Poultry Corp. v. United States rules National Industrial Recovery Act unconstitutional.
	Federal Railroad Retirement Act sets up railroad pension payments for retired employees and their families.
	Gold Clause Cases upholds right of Congress to set monetary policy.
	Schechter Poultry Corp. v. United States rules against constitutionality of National Industrial Recovery Act of 1933.
	Federal Banking Act amends earlier banking laws to increase maximum liabilities of depositors and to authorize Federal Deposit Insurance Corporation to assist failing banks to merge with strong banks.
	(July 5) National Labor Relations Act (Wagner Act) creates National Labor Relations Board to arbiter management-labor disputes and combat unfair labor practices.
	(Aug. 14) Franklin D. Roosevelt signs Social Security Act, which creates federally managed retirement and benefits program for workers.
	(Dec. 17) DC-3 aircraft makes its maiden flight.
1936	Federal Commodity Exchange Act replaces Grain Futures Act of 1922, establishing Commodity Exchange Commission to regulate trading in commodity-contract markets.
	Federal Walsh-Healey Public Contracts Act sets basic labor standards for work on government contracts.
	Completion of Boulder Dam (later renamed Hoover Dam) creates Lake Mead.
	United States v. Butler strikes down regulatory features of Agricultural Adjustment Act of 1933.
	Carter v. Carter Coal Co. overturns federal law setting up local boards to regulate coal prices and help workers negotiate wages and hours.
	Morehead v. New York ex rel. Tipaldo overturns minimum-wage legislation.
	(Dec.) Fort Knox opens as the primary storage facility for federal government gold supply.
	(Dec. 30) General Motors employees begin six-week sit-down strike.
1937	Bituminous Coal Act imposes new regulations on sale and distribution of bituminous coal in interstate commerce.
	Napoleon Hill publishes *Think and Grow Rich.*
	Housing Act finances slum clearance and building of public housing.
	Franklin D. Roosevelt introduces tree-planting campaign to alleviate Dust Bowl conditions.

Date	Event
1937 *(cont.)*	*Helvering v. Davis* affirms constitutionality of Social Security Act of 1935.
	National Labor Relations Board v. Jones & Laughlin Steel upholds National Labor Relations Act.
	West Coast Hotel v. Parrish permits states broad discretion in regulating working conditions.
	(May 7) *Hindenburg* crash in Lakehurst, New Jersey, ends brief era of airship transportation.
	(Sept.) Sharp economic downturn causes nine-month recession within Great Depression.
1938	Civil Aeronautics Board begins regulating all domestic air transportation as public utility; it sets fares, routes, and schedules.
	Fair Labor Standards Act establishes national minimum wage, guarantees overtime pay, regulates employment of workers under eighteen, and prohibits child labor.
	Mexican government nationalizes petroleum industry.
	Federal Food, Drug, and Cosmetics Act supersedes Pure Food and Drug Act of 1906, authorizing Food and Drug Administration to exercise oversight over more foods, drugs, and cosmetics.
	Erie Railroad v. Tompkins repudiates doctrine of national common law.
	Lauf v. E. G. Shinner overrules lower court's antiunion injunction.
	(Oct. 31) New York Stock Exchange creates investor protection program.
1939	DuPont begins marketing synthetic nylon.
	Hague v. Congress of Industrial Organizations upholds right of labor organizations to hold peaceful meetings and distribute literature.
	Mulford v. Smith upholds constitutionality of Agricultural Adjustment Act of 1938.
	National Labor Relations Board v. Fansteel Metallurgical rules sit-down strike illegal.
	Broadcast Music Incorporated (BMI) is founded.
	Federal government oversees Food Stamp Plan.
	Earl S. Tupper Company begins marketing Tupperware.
	John Steinbeck's novel *The Grapes of Wrath* exposes agribusiness exploitation of Dust Bowl refugees.
	(Sept. 1) World War II begins in Europe.
1940	Investment Advisers Act regulates investment advisers.
	Colorado National Bank v. Bedford allows state tax on safety-deposit-box use.
	Thornhill v. Alabama overturns labor leader's conviction for peaceful picketing.
	First Dairy Queen opens in Joliet, Illinois.
	Radio Corporation of America (RCA) demonstrates color television to members of Federal Communications Commission board.

Date	Event
1941	*United States v. Darby Lumber Co.* upholds federal law mandating minimum wages and maximum hours.
	Milk Wagon Drivers Union v. Meadowmoor Dairies and *American Federation of Labor v. Swing* allow state courts to stop picketing when violence erupts but not otherwise.
	Standard & Poor's financial services company is founded.
	(Mar. 11) Franklin D. Roosevelt signs Lend-Lease Act to provide war material to Allied nations fighting in World War II.
	(Apr. 20) U.S. president Franklin D. Roosevelt and Canadian prime minister William Lyon Mackenzie King sign Hyde Park Declaration, an agreement for cooperative war production.
	(June 25) Franklin D. Roosevelt's Executive Order 8802 outlaws racial discrimination in defense industry and establishes Committee on Fair Employment Practices.
	(July) First television commercial is broadcast in the United States.
	(Dec.) American entry into World War II ends Great Depression.
	(Dec. 7) Japan's surprise attack on Pearl Harbor draws United States into World War II.
1942	Congress passes Emergency Price Controls Act to counter inflationary pressures resulting from transformation of peacetime economy to wartime conditions and to establish Office of Price Administration.
	Wickard v. Filburn broadens definition of interstate commerce.
	(Jan.) United States and Mexico launch bracero program to bring Mexican farmworkers into the United States; program will be renewed every two years until 1964.
1943	Magnuson Act repeals Chinese Exclusion Act of 1882 and permits small quota of Chinese immigrants.
1944	Federal Synthetic Liquid Fuels Act establishes Bureau of Mines.
	Steele v. Louisville & Nashville Railroad Co. establishes doctrine of fair representation.
	(June 24) Franklin D. Roosevelt signs Servicemen's Readjustment Act, better known as G.I. Bill, which subsidizes education for veterans of World War II for ten years.
	(July 1-22) United States participates in international convention that drafts Bretton Woods Agreement, establishing International Monetary Fund and International Bank for Reconstruction and Development.
1945	(Aug. 16) Japanese surrender ends World War II.
	(Aug. 21) Lend-Lease Act expires.
	(Autumn) Passenger car production resumes after World War II.
1946	Southland convenience stores adopt name 7-Eleven.
	Congress creates Atomic Energy Commission to provide for civilian control of nuclear energy.
	(Nov. 12) First drive-through American bank opens in Chicago.

Date	Event
1946-1947	United States oversees postwar Japanese trade.
1947	Lanham Trademark Act governs trademarks and other symbols used to identify goods in interstate commerce.
	New Department of Defense combines War and Navy Departments.
	Federal Mediation and Conciliation Service to mediate labor disputes.
	Federal Crop Insurance Corp. v. Merrill holds that government need not honor contracts when agents exceed authority granted in those contracts.
	United States v. United Mine Workers finds that 1932 Norris-LaGuardia Act does not apply when government is, in effect, employer.
	(Feb. 21) Edwin Land introduces instant Polaroid cameras.
	(June 23) Taft-Hartley Act (Labor-Management Relations Act) amends National Labor Relations Act of 1935 by limiting power of labor unions.
	(July 12) United States launches Marshall Plan to help Europe recover from World War II.
	(Dec. 23) Invention of transistors revolutionizes electronics industries.
1948	*Shelley v. Kraemer* invalidates racially based restrictive covenants on property sales.
	(Jan. 1) United States signs General Agreement on Tariffs and Trade (GATT).
1949	Founding of People's Republic of China virtually ends Chinese trade with United States.
	Arthur Miller's play *Death of a Salesman* portrays man discarded by American business.
	(Aug. 3) Basketball Association of America and National Basketball League merge to form National Basketball Association (NBA).
1950	National Science Foundation is created to promote science and engineering in United States.
	Association of New York restaurants begin issuing Diners Club charge cards.
	(June 25) North Korea's invasion of South Korea begins Korean War.
1951	Fur Products Labeling Act requires fur garments be labeled with names of animals killed.
	Tupperware switches marketing from retail stories to direct sales in private homes.
	CBS broadcasts world's first color program.
1952	Federal Coal Mine Safety Act sets hazard standards and provides for enforcement of safety regulations; act will be extended to all underground mines in 1966.
	Veterans' Adjustment Act provides new compensations to returning Korean War veterans.
	New Patent Act overhauls U.S. patent system.
	Youngstown Sheet and Tube Co. v. Sawyer disallows president's right to invoke emergency powers to seize and operate private businesses without congressional approval.
	Holiday Inn motel chain begins.
	(Apr.-June) U.S. government seizes steel mills whose workers threaten to strike.

Date	Event
1953	Flammable Fabrics Act bans sales of clothing and household furnishings that present serious risks of causing property damage or injuries.
	Congress reorganizes and expands Internal Revenue Code of 1939, which was made up of previously existing U.S. tax statutes.
	Congress creates Department of Health, Education, and Welfare.
	Small Business Administration is established as independent regulatory agency to assist small businesses.
	J. Paul Getty forms Getty Oil Corporation.
	Francis Crick and James D. Watson's discovery of structure of deoxyribonucleic acid (DNA) makes possible genetic engineering.
	(July 27) Negotiated cease-fire ends fighting in Korean War.
	(Nov. 9) U.S. Supreme Court affirms 1922 ruling that Major League Baseball is exempt from antitrust laws because it is a sport, not a business.
1954	*Berman v. Parker* holds that government can take private property for public purposes under Fifth Amendment's takings clause.
	Franklin National Bank v. New York rules regulations banning banks from using "savings" in their name are unconstitutional.
	Burger King Corporation is established in Miami, Florida.
	(July 10) President Dwight D. Eisenhower signs into law Food for Peace program, which is designed to help American farmers sell surplus food abroad.
	(July 21) United States supports partition of Vietnam.
c. 1954-1968	Civil Rights movement helps bring African Americans more deeply into national economy.
1955	Henry Bloch and his brothers incorporate their tax-preparation service as H&R Block.
	Term "agribusiness" is coined.
	(Apr. 15) Ray Kroc opens first McDonald's franchise restaurant.
	(July 18) Disneyland opens to the public in Anaheim, California.
1956	Bank Holding Company Act establishes standards for formation of bank holding companies.
	Federal-Aid Highway Act creates largest domestic public works project in national history to build highways for national defense.
	Carl N. Karcher opens first Carl's Jr. restaurants in Southern California.
	Sociologist William Allan Whyte's *The Organization Man* explores dehumanizing and conformist nature of work in corporations.
1957	First American commercial nuclear power plant begins operating in Shippingport, Pennsylvania.
	(Mar. 25) Treaty of Rome creates European Common Market.
	(Oct. 4) Soviet Union puts first artificial satellite in orbit.

Date	Event
1958	Congress passes Welfare and Pension Plans Disclosure Act to cover large nongovernmental welfare and pension plans.
	Pizza Hut, the first national pizza chain, begins in Wichita, Kansas.
	American Express begins issuing first general-purpose credit cards; Bank of America begins issuing BankAmericards.
	(Feb. 1) United States puts its first satellite in orbit.
1959	Landrum-Griffin Act (Labor-Management Reporting and Disclosure Act) combats labor union corruption.
	Opening of St. Lawrence Seaway increases shipping from the Great Lakes to the Atlantic Ocean.
	(July 29) Eisenhower signs legislation creating National Aeronautics and Space Administration (NASA).
1960	Federal Hazardous Substances Act authorizes secretary of Health, Education, and Welfare to require warning labels for hazardous household substances; act will be amended by Child Protection and Toy Safety Act of 1969.
	Tyco International begins operations.
	(Sept.) Iran, Iraq, Saudi Arabia, Kuwait, and Venezuela form Organization of Petroleum Exporting Countries (OPEC).
1961	Congress creates U.S. Federal Maritime Commission to regulate oceanic transportation of foreign commerce.
	(Jan. 17) Dwight D. Eisenhower warns of power of military-industrial complex in farewell address to nation.
	(Mar. 6) President John F. Kennedy's Executive Order 10925 requires firms doing business federal government not to discriminate in employment.
	(Apr. 12) Soviet Union puts first astronaut into space.
	(May 5) United States first its first astronaut in space in suborbital flight.
	(Nov. 3) U.S. Agency for International Development (AID) is established.
1962	Trade Expansion Act permits U.S. president to negotiate tariff reductions with European Common Market nations.
	Rachel Carson publishes *Silent Spring*, alerting public to dangers of pesticides and other environmental hazards.
	NASA creates Technology Utilization Program to disseminate space technology information.
	Glen Bell opens first Taco Bell in Downey, California.
	César Chávez founds National Farm Workers Association, which will become United Farm Workers of America in 1966.
	(Mar. 1) First Kmart store opens in Garden City, Michigan.
	(July 2) Sam Walton opens first Wal-Mart store.

Date	Event
1963	Equal Pay Act amends Fair Labor Standards Act of 1938, abolishing wage differentials based on sex.
	Jessica Mitford's *The American Way of Death* exposes abuses in American funeral industry.
	(June 22) John F. Kennedy's Executive Order 11114 empowers federal agencies to terminate contracts with companies not complying with affirmative action order.
	(July 26) United States puts first geosynchronous satellite into orbit.
	(Nov.) New Hampshire voters approve first state-run lottery since nineteenth century; other states soon follow suit.
1964	International Business Machines introduces first mass-produced mainframe computer.
	Congress creates U.S. Equal Employment Opportunity Commission.
	Heart of Atlanta Motel Inc. v. United States upholds public accommodations sections of the 1964 Civil Rights Act.
	Katzenbach v. McClung upholds regulations outlawing racial discrimination in restaurants.
	(Jan. 11) Office of U.S. Surgeon General issues first official warning of health hazards of smoking.
	(July 2) President Lyndon B. Johnson signs Civil Rights Act, which outlaws segregation in schools, public places, and public accommodations.
	(Dec.) Bracero program ends.
1965	Mexico launches *maquiladora* program to build manufacturing plants, mostly along northern border.
	President Lyndon B. Johnson signs federal Medicare and Medicaid programs into law.
	Motor Vehicle Air Pollution Control Act amends federal Clean Air Act of 1963 by setting first federal vehicle emissions standards.
	United States begins sending combat troops to Vietnam.
	United Farm Workers of America begins five-year strike against grape growers.
	Predecessor of Subway sandwich shops opens in Bridgeport, Connecticut.
	Ralph Nader publishes *Unsafe at Any Speed: The Designed-In Dangers of the American Automobile*.
	(Jan.) Canada and United States sign Automotive Products Trade Agreement.
	(Sept. 24) Johnson's Executive Order 11246 extends affirmative action to recruitment, screening, and selection of new employees.
1966	Federal Uniform Time Act regulates dates of daylight saving time among states.
	Federal Coal Mine Safety Act of 1952 is extended to all underground mines.
	Child Protection Act amends Federal Hazardous Substances Act of 1960.
	Veterans Readjustment Benefits Act extends G.I. Bill benefits to noncombat veterans.
	First National Bank of Logan v. Walker Bank and Trust Co. limits expansion of national banks.

Date	Event
1966 *(cont.)*	(Apr. 25) U.S. Post Office stops accepting deposits to postal savings banks.
	(Oct. 15) Department of Transportation is created.
1967	Age Discrimination in Employment Act limits ability of large employers to refuse to hire older workers because of age.
	National Transportation Safety Board is created to investigate major civilian transportation accidents.
	Consortium of California banks begin issuing Master Charge cards, which will be renamed MasterCards in 1979.
	(Oct. 13) Johnson's Executive Order 11375 extends affirmative action to cover sex discrimination.
	(Dec.) Civil rights leaders launch multiracial Poor People's Campaign to protest poverty and economic injustice.
1968	Architectural Barriers Act requires new federal buildings and facilities built or altered with federal funds to be accessible to persons with disabilities.
	Consumer Credit Protection Act, also known as Truth-in-Lending Act, is federal government's first major attempt to protect consumers from predatory credit practices.
	Federal Interstate Land Sales Full Disclosure Act requires large land sale promoters to furnish prospective buyers with detailed reports on the land and to explain buyers' rights.
	National Bureau of Standards recommends that United States make metric system its predominant system of weights and measures by 1981.
	Fair Housing Act prohibits discrimination in sale, purchase, and leasing of properties used for housing.
1969	Child Protection and Toy Safety Act amends Federal Hazardous Substances Act of 1960.
	In *AFSCME v. Woodward*, a federal appeals court holds that employees cannot be fired for joining labor unions.
	(July 20) First manned landing on moon.
	(Nov.) Dave Thomas opens first Wendy's hamburger restaurant in Columbus, Ohio.
1970's	Junk bond industry arises.
1970	Bank Secrecy Act requires banks to keep records of customer transactions and report daily financial dealings involving more than $10,000 to Treasury Department.
	Emergency Home Finance Act creates Federal Home Mortgage Corporation (Freddie Mac) to provide secondary market for conventional loans and Federal Housing Administration and Veterans Administration mortgages.
	Federal Fair Credit Reporting Act amends Consumer Credit Protection Act of 1968 by protecting consumers against inaccurate information.
	Bureau of Federal Credit Unions is renamed National Credit Union Administration.

Date	Event
1970 *(cont.)*	*Boys Market, Inc. v. Retail Clerks' Local 770* permits courts to issue injunctions against sit-down strikes.
	(Oct. 15) Racketeer Influenced and Corrupt Organizations Act (RICO) provides for extended penalties for crimes performed by criminal organizations.
	(Dec. 2) U.S. Environmental Protection Agency, created to safeguard public health and protect natural environment, begins operating.
	(Dec. 29) Occupational Safety and Health Act creates National Institute for Occupational Safety and Health and Occupational Safety and Health Administration (OSHA).
1971	Congress creates Overseas Private Investment Corporation to assist American businesses investing in other counties and promote economic development of emerging markets.
	U.S. Post Office becomes U.S. Postal Service and ceases to be U.S. cabinet department.
	Griggs v. Duke Power Co. rules that hiring and promotion policies with "racially disparate impact" must be clearly job related to be lawful.
	Investment Co. Institute v. Camp upholds law banning banks from involvement in investment fund industry.
	Federal Express (FedEx) is founded.
	First videocassette recorders (VCRs) for home use go on the market.
	(Feb. 8) NASDAQ begins operations as the first computerized stock exchange.
	(Mar. 24) Congress kills funding to develop U.S. supersonic jetliner.
	(May 1) National Railroad Passenger Corporation, better known as Amtrak, begins offering passenger rail service.
1972	Noise Control Act establishes standards for products made in United States that produce excessive noise.
	Congress creates U.S. Consumer Product Safety Commission to help protect against injuries from consumer products.
	Trafficante v. Metropolitan Life Insurance holds that all people affected by racial discrimination in housing can sue.
	(Feb. 21-27) President Richard Nixon visits China.
	(Apr. 1) First player strike in Major League Baseball begins.
	(June 14) Congress votes to ban DDT.
1973	Drug Enforcement Administration (DEA) is created by combining federal agencies already involved in combating illegal drugs.
	(Oct. 17) Arab states put embargo on oil exports to United States and Western European nations; Americans quickly face gas shortages.

Date	Event
1974	Antidumping Act forbids sale of goods at prices lower than those within countries where goods are made.
	Congress creates Commodity Futures Trading Commission.
	Gold Purchase Act ends federal ban on private possession of gold imposed by Gold Reserve Act of 1934.
	Education Amendments Act asks schools to prepare students for adoption of metric system.
	Real Estate Settlement Procedures Act provides comprehensive guidelines for loan closing costs and settlement practices.
	Congress creates Commodity Trading Futures Trading Commission to oversee operations of commodity markets.
	Federal Tariff Commission is renamed U.S. International Trade Commission.
	Nuclear Regulatory Commission is established to regulate all aspects of peaceful uses of nuclear energy.
	Beasley v. Food Fair holds that National Labor Relations Act has priority over state law.
	Village of Belle Terre v. Boraas holds that ordinance defining "family" to set limits on single-family housing is constitutional.
	Employee Retirement Income Security Act (ERISA) creates first comprehensive federal program to regulate private pension funds.
	(Mar. 17) Arab oil embargo ends.
1975	Comprehensive Employment and Training Act invests $55 billion in helping to find jobs for disadvantaged, long-term unemployed, and inefficiently employed persons.
	Equal Credit Opportunity Act makes credit available to individuals without regard to marital status or sex.
	Federal Metric Conversion Act creates U.S. Metric Board to plan, coordinate, and educate public on planned switch to metric system.
	National Transportation Safety Board is made independent federal agency.
	(Apr. 5) Billionaire industrialist Howard Hughes dies.
	(Apr. 30) United States ends its involvement in Vietnam War; President Gerald R. Ford soon imposes U.S. trade embargo on Vietnam.
	(July 17) Joint mission ends competitive space race between United States and Soviet Union.
1976	Copyright Revision Act extends copyright protection to duration of creators' lives plus seventy years; act will be amended in 1980 to include computer software and in 1998 by Copyright Extension Term Act of 1998.
	Hart-Scott-Rodino Act amends antitrust laws by requiring companies to notify Federal Trade Commission and assistant U.S. attorney general when they plan to buy heavily into other companies.

Date	Event
1976 *(cont.)*	Federal Toxic Substances Control Act requires chemical companies to give Environmental Protection Agency advance notice of new chemical products.
	National League of Cities v. Usery holds Congress has no authority to require state and local governments to pay workers minimum wages.
	(Apr. 1) Steve Wozniak and Steve Jobs found Apple Computers.
	(Apr. 7) Biotechnology corporation Genentech is founded.
1977	Federal Surface Mining Control and Reclamation Act establishes Office of Surface Mining within U.S. Department of Interior to regulate active coal mines and to reclaim abandoned mines.
	Congress creates Department of Energy.
	Federal Mine Safety and Health Review Commission is created to adjudicate complaints filed against mine owners.
	Hunt v. Washington State Apple Advertising Commission rules that one state may not require grading system for apples that discriminates against a state whose apples are graded differently.
	Linmark Associates Inc. v. Willingboro holds that banning "for sale" signs within a town is unconstitutional.
	United States Trust v. New Jersey invalidates state law abrogating public bond covenant on use of revenues.
	BankAmericard licensees band together to form Visa.
	(May 31) Construction of Alaska Pipeline is completed.
1978	Congress amends Federal Age Discrimination in Employment Act (1967) to permit employers to require workers to retire involuntarily at seventy.
	Airline Deregulation Act reduces government controls over airline industry.
	Bankruptcy Reform Act restructures old laws to permit companies to return to fiscal soundness.
	Electronic Fund Transfer Act requires financial institutions to inform new customers of terms and conditions of electronic fund transfer services.
	Energy Tax Act imposes excise taxes on motor fuels.
	Bankruptcy Reform Act supersedes National Bankruptcy Act of 1898.
	Natural Gas Policy Act authorizes Federal Energy Regulatory Commission to govern intrastate and interstate natural gas production.
	Pregnancy Discrimination Act amends sex discrimination section of Civil Rights Act of 1964 by requiring employers to provide pregnant women with same benefits received by other employees.
	Merit Systems Protection Board is created to handle disputes between employees and federal agencies for which they work.

Date	Event

1978 *(cont.)* *Penn Central Transportation Co. v. New York City* establishes important principles governing takings clause.

Raymond Motor Transportation v. Rice invalidates state restriction on length of tractor-trailers.

New Jersey permits casino gambling in Atlantic City.

(Jan.) Overthrow of Iran's shah begins revolution that cuts off Iranian oil exports and begins world energy crisis.

(Feb. 28) Brotherhood of Sleeping Car Porters merges with Brotherhood of Railway and Airline Clerks.

1979 Video rental industry begins in Los Angeles.

Union membership peaks in United States at more than 21 million, while percentage of total workers in unions continues to decline.

Congress approves loan package to save Chrysler Corporation from bankruptcy.

United Steelworkers v. Weber permits companies to consider race in trainee selection to reverse past discrimination.

Inc. magazine for small-business owners begins.

Amalgamated Meat Cutters Union and Retail Clerks International Union merge to form United Food and Commercial Workers International Union (UFCW), which will continue to absorb other unions.

(Mar. 28) Three Mile Island nuclear power plant experiences worst U.S. nuclear accident, shaking public confidence in nuclear power industry.

(Apr. 1) President Jimmy Carter signs bill creating Federal Emergency Management Agency to coordinate responses to major natural and human-caused disasters.

(July) China and United States sign Bilateral Trade Agreement.

(Oct. 17) Carter signs bill making Education a cabinet-level federal department.

1980 Depository Institutions Deregulation and Monetary Control Act ends power of Board of Governors of the Federal Reserve system to set interest rates of savings accounts.

Federal Monetary Control Act requires all banks and institutions accepting public deposits to make periodic reports to Federal Reserve system.

U.S. Department of Health, Education, and Welfare becomes Department of Health and Human Services.

Congress's passing of Depository Institutions Deregulation and Monetary Control Act begins era of federal deregulation.

National Labor Relations Board v. Yeshiva University holds that private university professors are managerial employees and therefore not eligible for unionization.

Satellite Program Network begins as business and financial news channel that will become Consumer News and Business Network (CNBC) in 1989.

Diamond v. Chakrabarty upholds right of companies to patent genetically engineered life-forms.

Date	Event
1980 *(cont.)*	*Chiarella v. United States* clarifies reach of Securities Act of 1933.
	(Jan. 1) Federal Revenue Act of 1978 goes into effect, authorizing 401(k) retirement plans.
	(May 7) U.S. Department of Education officially opens.
	(June 1) Cable News Network (CNN) begins broadcasting.
	(Oct. 14) Carter signs Staggers Rail Act, which deregulates railroad industry.
	(Dec.) Iraq's invasion of Iran exacerbates world energy crisis.
1981	Michael Bloomberg founds Innovative Market Systems to disseminate business news.
	International Business Machines begins making personal computers.
	Congress enacts Indian Gaming Regulatory Act, legalizing casino gambling on Native American reservations
	(Jan. 28) President Ronald Reagan issues executive order ending federal price and allocation controls to alleviate energy crisis.
	(Aug. 3) Air traffic controllers begin nationwide strike that will lead to their losing more than eleven thousand jobs and decertification of their union.
1982	Congress creates National Futures Association.
	In joint venture with General Motors, Toyota establishes its first manufacturing facility in United States.
	Job Training Partnership Act provides summer jobs for students and training programs for low-income workers, Native Americans, migrant and seasonal workers, and veterans; act will be repealed by Workforce Investment Act of 1998.
	Reagan disbands U.S. Metric Board.
	Congress passes Tax Equity and Fiscal Responsibility Act to increase government revenues and curtail abuses in federal tax system.
	Loretto v. Teleprompter Manhattan CATV Corp. holds that when land is permanently occupied by government, it constitutes a taking under eminent domain.
	Phillips markets first compact discs (CDs).
	(July) Home Shopping Network begins broadcasting on cable television.
	(Sept. 15) *USA Today* begins publication.
	(Sept. 21) National Football League players begin eight-week strike that truncates season.
1983	Internet begins operating.
	Federal Orphan Drug Act requires drug companies to develop drugs for illnesses afflicting fewer than 200,000 persons.

Date	Event
1984	*Sure-Tan v. National Labor Relations Board* holds that National Labor Relations Act also applies to illegal aliens.
	Apple introduces Macintosh computer.
	NCAA v. Board of Regents of the University of Oklahoma et al. holds that National Collegiate Athletic Association must allow member schools to negotiate their own television contracts.
1985	Civil Aeronautics Board is dissolved, as regulatory authority over airlines passes to Department of Transportation.
	Montgomery G.I. Bill provides educational stipends to military veterans who have contributed payments during their service time.
	Highway Beautification Act adds federal controls to commercial billboards along highways.
	Enron Corporation begins operations as Texas natural gas supplier.
	Garcia v. San Antonio Metropolitan Transit Authority removes most limitations on Congress's power to regulate states.
	Northeast Bancorp v. Board of Governors holds that states may partially lift bans on out-of-state bank holding companies.
	Sears, Roebuck introduces Discover credit card.
	Three New England states establish first interstate lottery.
1986	Immigration Reform and Control Act grants amnesty to undocumented immigrants who have resided continuously in United States since before January 1, 1982.
	Congress substantially revises Internal Revenue Code.
	Federal Retirement Thrift Investment Board is created to help federal employees supplement their retirement plans with tax-exempt savings.
	Maine v. Taylor upholds Maine's ban on importation of live bait fish.
	Meritor Savings Bank v. Vinson clears way for employees to sue employers for sexual harassment.
1987	*Johnson v. Santa Clara County* upholds county's adoption of sex-based affirmative action program to remedy past gender discrimination.
	Keystone Bituminous Coal Association v. DeBenedictis allows regulation limiting coal mining.
	Nollan v. California Coastal Commission expands property owner rights in eminent domain cases.
	United States v. Paradise upholds Alabama state plan to reserve appointments for African Americans because of past discrimination.
	Alan Greenspan begins two decades as chair of Board of Governors of Federal Reserve system.
	Tom Wolfe's novel *Bonfire of the Vanities* satirizes New York investment bankers.
	(Oct. 19) American stock markets fall in crash that will be remembered as "Black Monday."
1988	Veterans Administration becomes Veterans Affairs.

Date	Event
1989	Financial Institutions Rescue, Recovery and Enforcement Act abolishes Federal Savings and Loan Insurance Corporation and places deposit insurance for savings and loans under Federal Deposit Insurance Corporation.
	United States and Canada sign bilateral free trade agreement.
	Stephen R. Covey's business-advice book *The Seven Habits of Highly Effective People* is huge best seller.
	Congress creates Federal Housing Finance Board to replace failed Federal Home Loan Bank Board.
	Ward v. Rock Against Racism upholds restrictions on noise levels that are neutral to content.
1990	Americans with Disabilities Act prohibits discrimination on basis of disability in private employment, state and local governments, public accommodations, commercial facilities, transportation, and telecommunications.
	Congress passes Clean Air Act to reduce air pollution throughout United States.
	Innovative Market Systems becomes Bloomberg's Business News Services.
1991	President George H. W. Bush signs executive order directing federal agencies and departments to convert to metric system.
	Automobile Workers v. Johnson Controls limits right of companies to use sex-based qualifications in workplace.
	(Jan. 16-Feb. 28) U.S.-led coalition drives Iraqi forces from Kuwait in Gulf War.
1992	Congress passes Energy Policy Act to reduce dependence on imported oil, improve energy efficiency in buildings and utilities, and develop alternative fuels and renewable energy.
	(Feb. 7) Treaty of Maastricht creates European Union (EU).
1993	Budget Reconciliation Act raises taxes retroactively to help sustain national economic growth and to balance federal budget by 1998.
	Major Soccer League is formed.
	Teresa Harris v. Forklift Systems expands protection of employees against workplace sexual harassment.
1994	Congress creates Broadcasting Board of Governors to take over functions of Voice of America and other nonmilitary government broadcasting ventures.
	City Ladue v. Gilleo holds that city of Ladue cannot ban all yard and window signs.
	Federal Deposit Insurance Corp. v. Meyer rules that FDIC may be sued.
	(Jan. 1) North American Free Trade Agreement (NAFTA), which begins eliminating tariffs on products traded among United States, Mexico, and Canada, goes into effect.
	(Feb.) United States lifts its trade embargo on Vietnam.
	(Aug.) Major League Baseball players begin strike that will lead to cancellation of parts of two seasons.

Date	Event
1995	Interstate Commerce Commission is abolished, and its remaining functions are transferred to new Surface Transportation Board.
	NationsBank of North Carolina v. Variable Annuity Life holds that banks may sell life insurance annuities.
	United States v. Lopez holds that Congress may not pass laws regulating things not directly affecting interstate commerce.
	(Jan. 1) World Trade Organization is founded.
	(Sept. 3) Online auction site eBay is launched.
1996	Telecommunications Act amends Federal Communications Act of 1934.
	Barnett Bank of Marion County v. Nelson holds that banks can sell insurance regardless of local prohibitions.
1997	*Atherton v. Federal Deposit Insurance Corp.* allows states to impose stricter rules for banks than those imposed by federal statutes.
	Montgomery Ward files for bankruptcy.
1997-1998	Sudden drop in value of currencies of several Asian nations leads to significant economic contraction that has global impact.
1998	Federal Workforce Investment Act repeals Job Training Partnership Act of 1982.
	Congress creates Chemical Safety and Hazard Investigation Board to investigate safety conditions at industrial facilities.
	NASDAQ buys American Stock Exchange.
	MP3 players go on market.
	(Sept.) Internet search engine and information organizer Google is founded.
	(Nov.) National Basketball Association owners begin player lockout that will lead to cancellation of first half of professional basketball season.
1999	Netflix begins renting films through mail.
	Martha Stewart Living Omnimedia goes public on New York Stock Exchange.
2000	U.S. Postal Act makes Postal Service only quasi-governmental entity under purview of Occupational Safety and Health Administration.
	United States cedes Panama Canal to Panama.
	(Jan. 1) Federal Motor Carrier Safety Administration is created to reduce accidents involving trucks and buses.
	(Mar. 10) NASDAQ rises to all-time high of 5048.62, on March 10, 2000, on dot-com bubble; by October, 2002, that figure will drop 78 percent.

Date	Event
2001	Homestake Mine in South Dakota's Black Hills closes after having yielded more than 40 million ounces of gold since its opening in 1876.
	India-born Indra K. Nooyi becomes president and chief financial officer of PepsiCo, of which she will later become chief executive officer and chair of the board.
	(July 1) President George W. Bush signs Economic Growth and Tax Relief Reconciliation Act, which gives large tax breaks to business owners and members of upper class.
	(Sept. 11) Middle Eastern terrorists hijack American jetliners and fly them into New York City's World Trade Center and Pentagon.
	(Oct.) Apple introduces iPod and iTunes Music Store.
	(Dec. 2) Enron Corporation files for bankruptcy.
2002	Federal Sarbanes-Oxley Act establishes Public Company Accounting Oversight Board to oversee accounting firms in their roles as auditors of public companies.
	Congress creates Department of Homeland Security to coordinate antiterrorist work of domestic law-enforcement agencies.
	Corporate fraud case nearly destroys Tyco International.
	Hoffman Plastic Compounds v. National Labor Relations holds that illegal immigrants are not entitled to all protections of National Labor Relations Act.
	(July 21) Telecommunications giant WorldCom files for bankruptcy.
	(Oct.) NASDAQ falls to only 22 percent of its peak value of March 10, 2000, as dot-com bubble bursts.
2003	Fair and Accurate Credit Transactions Act protects consumers against identity theft.
	Federal Bureau of Alcohol, Tobacco, and Firearms is split: Alcohol and Tobacco Tax and Trade Bureau remains with Treasury Department, and Bureau of Alcohol, Tobacco, Firearms, and Explosives is placed under Department of Justice.
	AMEX Membership Corporation buys American Stock Exchange back from NASDAQ.
	(Mar. 19) Securities and Exchange Commission halts trading of HealthSouth stock after learning of company's grossly inflated earnings reports.
	(Mar. 19) United States occupies Iraq.
	(Oct.) HealthSouth founder Richard Scrushy is indicted on eighty-five counts of financial fraud; in 2007, he will be sentenced to federal prison.
	(Nov.) Transatlantic flights of supersonic Concorde are discontinued.
2004	United States, Costa Rica, El Salvador, Guatemala, Honduras, and Nicaragua sign Central American Free Trade Agreement (CAFTA).
	United States and Chile sign bilateral free trade agreement; similar agreements with Peru and Colombia will soon follow.
	Media mogul Martha Stewart is sentenced to prison for involvement in insider trading scandal.

Date	Event

2004 *(cont.)* FedEx purchases Kinko's chain of photocopy shops.

Kmart discount chain purchases Sears, Roebuck.

(Jan. 8) Real estate mogul Donald Trump begins hosting television's *The Apprentice*, challenging young contestants to perform business-related tasks.

(Apr. 19) Google becomes publicly traded company on NASDAQ.

(Oct.) Player strike leads to cancellation of entire 2004-2005 National Hockey League season.

(Nov. 30) Pipeline and Hazardous Materials Safety Administration is created.

2005 Energy Policy Act provides tax incentives and loan guarantees to develop alternative forms of energy; act also amends Uniform Time Act of 1966 by extending number of daylight savings time days.

Federal Family Entertainment and Copyright Act criminalizes use of recording equipment to copy films in motion-picture theaters and prohibits making copies of commercially distributed films.

Kelo v. City of New London holds that states can exercise eminent domain power to take land for private uses, provided public benefits result.

Bankruptcy Abuse Prevention and Consumer Protection Act addresses individual bankruptcies.

(Aug. 29) Hurricane Katrina devastates southeastern Louisiana, southern Mississippi, and southern Alabama.

2006 About 15 million American workers are in unions; about half of them are in private employment, where they represent 8 percent of all salaried workers.

Fortune magazine names Indra K. Nooyi, the head of PepsiCo, the most powerful businesswoman in the world.

(Jan.) Western Union delivers its last telegraph message.

2007 Energy Independence and Security Act (Clean Energy Act) promotes energy efficiency and development of alternative forms of energy.

Rupert Murdoch purchases *Wall Street Journal.*

(Apr. 4) New York Stock Exchange merges with pan-European stock exchange Euronext.

(Aug.) Collapse of Minneapolis bridge over Mississippi River raises concerns about nation's aging bridges.

2008 Consumer Product Safety Improvement Act strengthens safety requirements on consumer products.

Post 9/11 Veterans Assistance Act substantially increases tuition and housing assistance to military veterans.

Lehman Brothers files for bankruptcy.

Forbes magazine names Warren Buffett the richest person in the world.

Date	Event
2008 *(cont.)*	Top U.S. trading partners are Canada (17.9 percent), China (11.2 percent), and Mexico (10.7 percent).

(Jan.) NYSE Euronext buys American Stock Exchange.

(Mar. 16) Federal Reserve arranges sale of investment banking firm Bear Stearns to JPMorgan Chase to prevent its collapse.

(July) Mortgage-lending bank Countrywide is taken over by Bank of America to avoid collapse.

(July 26) Congress passes Foreclosure Prevention Act to provide relief to homeowners threatened with foreclosure.

(Sept. 7) Federal government takes control of Federal National Mortgage Association (Fannie Mae) and Federal Home Loan Mortgage Corporation (Freddie Mac), giving each a $100 billion line of credit.

(Sept. 16) U.S. Treasury agrees to lend huge insurance company American International Group (AIG) $85 billion, in return for 80 percent ownership interest.

(Sept. 25) Federal Deposit Insurance Corporation presides over forced merger of failing Washington Mutual (WaMu) into JPMorgan Chase.

(Oct.) Chrysler, Ford, and General Motors, in serious financial straits, request $50 billion in loans from the federal government, but their request is refused.

(Oct.) Problems in subprime mortgage industry and financial markets reach critical level that causes major lending institutions to collapse and stock markets to drop precipitously; U.S. government intervenes to bail out financial institutions.

(Dec.) President George W. Bush announced that $13.4 billion in emergency loans would be made available to keep Chrysler, General Motors, and Ford out of bankruptcy, with an additional $4 billion to be available in February. However, the automakers were given the loans on condition that they make major concessions and organizational changes by March 31, 2009, to demonstrate that they could return to profitability.

2009	(Feb. 17) President Barack Obama signed into law the American Recovery and Reinvestment Act, a $787 billion recovery package that included funds for renewable energy, infrastructure, education, and health care, as well as about $282 billion in tax relief for individuals and businesses.

(Feb. 18) President Barack Obama announced a $275 billion housing relief plan. About $200 billion was aimed at helping people with little equity in their homes refinance their loans through government-controlled mortgage giants Fannie Mae and Freddie Mac. Another $75 billion was meant to encourage lenders to modify loan terms for people at risk of foreclosure or in foreclosure. On the same day, General Motors and Chrysler, citing adverse economic conditions that further depressed sales of vehicles, asked for an additional $14 billion in aid, while presenting restructuring plans designed to return their companies to profitability.

R. Kent Rasmussen

INDEXES

Categorized List of Entries

LIST OF CATEGORIES

ADVERTISING

Advertising industry, 2-6
Christmas marketing, 141-142
Online marketing, 614-615
Truth-in-advertising codes,
    877

AGRICULTURE

Agribusiness, 15
Agriculture, 15-19
Agriculture, U.S. Department of,
    20-22
Bracero program, 101-102
Carver, George Washington, 124
Cereal crops, 127-128
Chávez, César, 129
Chemical industries, 130-132
Colonial economic systems,
    162-167
Commodity markets, 173-175
Cotton gin, 196

Cotton industry, 197-198
Dairy industry, 215-217
DDT banning, 223
Dust Bowl, 244-245
Farm Credit Administration,
    280
Farm labor, 281-284
Farm protests, 285
Farm subsidies, 286-287
Food for Peace, 318
Food Stamp Plan, 323
Forestry industry, 327-330
Genetic engineering, 356
Granger movement, 369-370
Horses, 399
Indentured labor, 426
Irrigated farming, 473
Plantation agriculture,
    660-661
Pork industry, 667
Poultry industry, 673-675

Rice industry, 733-734
Sharecropping, 757-758
Sugar industry, 806-807
Tobacco industry, 854-857
United Farm Workers of America,
    883

ANIMAL HUSBANDRY AND FISHING

Agribusiness, 15
Agriculture, U.S. Department of,
    20-22
Dairy industry, 215-217
Farm Credit Administration,
    280
Fishing industry, 314
Genetic engineering, 356
Horses, 399
Pork industry, 667
Poultry industry, 673-675
Whaling industry, 924-925

Personages Index

Subject Index